Ross and Jerry

COMPENDIUM OF SEASHELLS

BOOKS BY R. TUCKER ABBOTT

Seashells of the World (Golden Guide, 1962)
American Seashells (Van Nostrand Reinhold, 1954 and 1976)
Seashells of North America (Golden Press, 1968)
Kingdom of the Seashell (Crown Publ. Co., 1972)
The Shell (with Hugh and Margarite Stix) (Harry Abrams, Co., 1968)
How to Know the American Marine Shells (New World Library, 1961)
Standard Catalog of Shells (with R. J. L. Wagner) (American Malacologists, Inc., 1978)
Caribbean Seashells (with G. L. Warmke) (Dover Pub., 1976)

BOOKS BY S. PETER DANCE

Shell Collecting: An Illustrated History (Faber & Faber, 1966)
Rare Shells (Faber & Faber, 1969)
Seashells (Hamlyn, 1971)
The Shell Collector's Guide (David & Charles, Newton Abbott, 1976)
The Collector's Encyclopedia of Shells (McGraw-Hill, 1974)
Shells and Shell Collecting (Hamlyn, 1972)
Art of Natural History (Overlook Press, 1978)
Seashells. Bivalves of the British and Northern European Seas (with J. Moller Christensen) (Penguin Books, 1980)

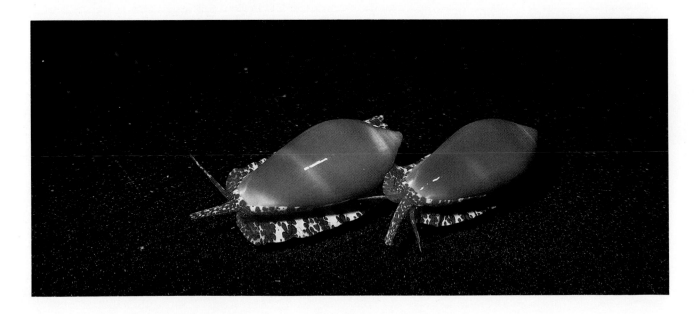

Compendium
of Seashells

A Color Guide to More than 4,200 of the World's Marine Shells

by
R. Tucker Abbott and S. Peter Dance

E.P. DUTTON, INC. / *New York*

First published in 1982 in the United States by E. P. Dutton, Inc., 2 Park Avenue, New York, N.Y. 10016

Library of Congress Catalog Card Number: 81-67757

Printed and bound by Dai Nippon Printing Co., Ltd., Tokyo.

ISBN: 0-525-93269-0

Published simultaneously in Canada by Clarke, Irwin & Company Limited, Toronto and Vancouver

10 9 8 7 6 5 4 3 2 1

First Edition

Title page: A living gastropod snail, the Orange Marginella (*Marginella carnea* Storer, 1837), from the West Indies. *(Photo: Robert Lipe)*

This book is
dedicated to our wives—
Cecelia Abbott and Una Dance

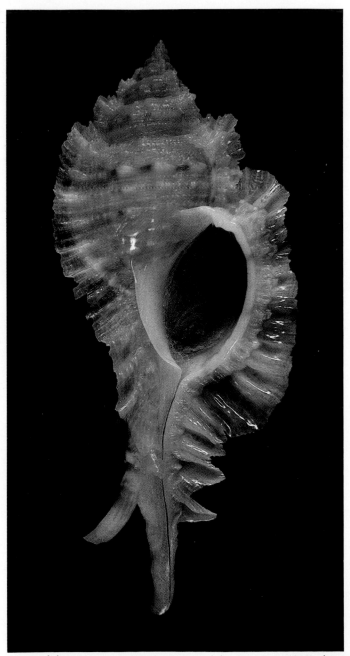

Annandale's Murex *Naquetia annandalei* (Preston, 1910), from Southeast Asia.

CONTENTS

A Gastropod: Glory-of-the-Atlantic Cone (*Conus granulatus* Linnaeus, 1758), from the Caribbean Sea.

PREFACE

Shell collecting as a hobby has had a remarkable resurgence in the last few years. To a considerable extent this has been brought about by an increasing interest in ocean life and a deep concern for anything to do with our fragile natural environment. More particularly, however, it is due to the availability of a host of remarkable, long-lost or newly discovered species of mollusks now being obtained by various methods, such as netting and diving, from exotic parts of the globe.

Although science has not kept pace with these recent discoveries, amateur collectors are well aware that a new Golden Age of conchology has dawned. This situation underlines the need for good shell identification guides. Some excellent regional shell books compiled by professional conchologists are available for some areas, such as New Zealand, Hawaii, and North America, but no book has given a useful and reliable overview of most of the world's better known marine shells.

About 30,000 species of marine mollusks are known. Thousands are less than half an inch in size, even in the adult stage; many hundreds are confined to the great depths of the oceans. Our book concentrates on all the others. Their inclusion here is based on several factors: attractiveness, desirability, rarity, and availability. Included are most species belonging to popular groups, such as the cones, volutes, cowries, murexes, scallops, and thorny oysters. At the same time we have not overlooked periwinkles, oysters, limpets, and other less attractive groups. We have attempted to strike a balance between the popular and the less popular.

Intended primarily for the amateur shell collector, our book also serves the scientific community. It contains photographs of several hundreds of type specimens from museums and private collections, those unique specimens to which scientists *must* refer when the exact identity of a species must be established. As such specimens are seldom allowed to leave the institutions in which they are housed, the publication of their portraits herein may save someone considerable time and traveling expense.

The photographs and the brief accompanying texts provide a quick guide to those marine species the amateur conchologist is most likely to encounter while doing fieldwork, exchanging, or purchasing from commercial sources. The combined classification and bibliography, arranged by families and by geographical regions, will guide him to more sophisticated monographs and textbooks.

R. TUCKER ABBOTT
S. PETER DANCE

Snowflake Marginella (*Marginella guttata* Dillwyn, 1817), from Florida and the West Indies. (*Photo: Pat Armes*)

INTRODUCTION

SEASHELLS

Hard external coverings are typical of several very different kinds of marine animals, including barnacles, crabs, sea urchins, and mollusks. The coverings of all these animals may be described as shelly, but only those associated with mollusks are correctly known as seashells. Essentially, a seashell is the solid and usually inflexible outer covering of a soft-bodied, fleshy animal. It is to a mollusk what the skeleton is to a mammal: a means of support and protection for the otherwise unsupported and vulnerable soft body parts. Some mollusks, such as land slugs and sea slugs, do not have a shell, but it is the most characteristic feature of the great majority of them.

Shell-bearing or not, all mollusks belong to one of the major groups of the animal kingdom: the Mollusca. Second in size only to the Arthropoda (which includes insects, crustaceans, etc.), the phylum Mollusca includes cockles, mussels, oysters, conchs, land snails, sea slugs, nautiluses, and many more. There may be as many as 60,000 living species, many of them found in land or freshwater habitats, but most of them living in the world's seas.

Kinds of Shells

In order to understand and organize such a large number of species, it has been necessary to follow the age-old system of classifying the phylum into various categories, or groups. Our book is arranged in the standard systematic order. The more primitive, or more simply constructed, families are dealt with first, and the more advanced or more highly evolved ones follow in a regular, widely accepted sequence. It is worth remembering that without good classification, good biological or economic work in zoology is scarcely possible. The taxonomy, or classification, of a group, however, depends on the concept of a species. After all, shells are not like stamps and coins; they are living organisms subject to the laws of nature.

Species

Ever since Charles Darwin challenged the notion that a species is something specially created and not subject to change or evolution, specialists have been arguing about the nature and definition of a species. The argument is far from being resolved. At present it is widely accepted that there is more than one kind of "species," each kind requiring its own definition. The only one that need concern us here is the biological species, or "biospecies." A biospecies consists of individuals that look alike and are potentially capable of interbreeding to produce further examples of their own kind. Should a population become geographically isolated from the main stock of individuals comprising the biospecies it may, in time, evolve its own distinct morphological features. Eventually members of that isolated population may differ so markedly from the parent stock that they are no longer capable of interbreeding with it. At this point the isolated population has become a different species. Before that stage is reached, however, the observable differences in the external appearance of its members, if sufficiently striking, may warrant its being accorded subspecific rank and its own scientific name. A number of subspecies, indicated by a three-part scientific name, are to be found in this book.

As in garden flowers, domestic breeds of animals, and even in human beings, there are numerous color and shape variations. Some are caused by simple genetic differences (red, white, or yellow flowers); others are caused by lack of adequate food, overcrowding, or adverse environmental conditions. These differences are not permanent, but are sometimes so distinctive that it is practical to give forms displaying them a scientific name. Form names (e.g., *rubra* for a red shell; *imbricata* for a scaly shell) are used in conchology as "handles" for odd specimens that do not represent different species or subspecies.

CLASSIFICATION

To comprehend such a varied assemblage of life forms, the phylum Mollusca is divided and subdivided into manageable groups. Most authorities now place living mollusks in seven classes: Aplacophora, Polyplacophora (the chitons), Monoplacophora, Gastropoda (the univalve snails), Bivalvia (the clams), Scaphopoda (the tusk shells), and Cephalopoda (the squids). Of these the Gastropoda and the Bivalvia account for the great majority of living mollusks. Some of the salient features of each class are outlined below.

Gastropoda (snails, whelks, slugs, limpets, cowries, etc.): mollusks usually with tentacles and eyes, a broad foot, and a visceral hump, the latter being commonly contained within a shell that may be coiled. Within the mouth of these univalves there may be many or few teeth, arranged in rows on a ribbonlike structure (the *radula*). A characteristic feature of many gastropods is the *operculum,* a horny or calcareous structure attached to the foot. The operculum seals, or partially seals, the aperture when the animal withdraws into its shell, or is used to help the animal obtain a purchase during locomotion. It is estimated that there are about 20,000 living species of marine gastropods.

Bivalvia (cockles, mussels, oysters, razor shells, etc.): laterally compressed mollusks contained within a two-piece (or *bivalved*) shell, the valves being hinged, and joined, as a rule, by an elastic ligament. One or two adductor muscles open and close the valves. Most bivalves have a large foot, a pair of siphons, and a fleshy, shell-forming mantle lining each valve. There may be 10,000 living species of bivalves in the world's seas.

Scaphopoda (tusk shells, or tooth shells): bilaterally symmetrical mollusks with a tusklike shell, open at each end, the anterior end being the larger. The posterior end commonly protrudes above the sand in which tusk shells live. There is a large foot and a radula, but head, eyes, and gills are lacking. About 350 living species, all marine, are known.

A Bivalvia: Living Bay Scallop (*Argopecten concentricus* Say, 1822),
from the Eastern United States. (*Photo: D. M. Opreska*)

Aplacophora (solenogasters): wormlike, mostly very small mollusks covered with calcareous spicules. Exclusively marine, they feed on bottom-dwelling animals, such as coelenterates, or on organic debris, and have been recorded from great depths. About 250 species have been described.

Polyplacophora (chitons, or coat-of-mail shells): elongate-oval mollusks with a broad or narrow foot and a flattened visceral hump over which is situated an articulated, eight-piece shell, the outside edges of which are embedded in and surrounded by a flexible "girdle." About 650 species are known, mostly found clinging to in-shore rocks, though a few deep-water species have been recorded.

Monoplacophora (segmented limpets, or gastroverms): limpetlike mollusks with internal segmentation and a thin, almost circular, caplike shell. About 10 species of these "living fossils" are known, all from deep water. Of abiding interest to zoologists, the shells of these primitive creatures are not featured in this book because they are so small and rare.

Cephalopoda (nautiluses, cuttlefish, octopuses, squids): equipped with large eyes, a powerful beak, and sucker-studded tentacles, a cephalopod seems to have little in common with other mollusks, although the possession of a radula and, occasionally, a shell indicates that it may be more closely related to them than outward appearances and habits suggest. There may be as many as 1,000 different species of cephalopods living in the world's seas.

Each of these classes is further subdivided into progressively smaller categories, the ultimate category being the species (or subspecies). To show the relationship of these

A Cephalopod: A cut section of the Chambered Nautilus (*Nautilus pompilius* Linnaeus, 1758), from the Philippines.

categories, the classification of the Great Scallop is set out below. The authorities for the names and the dates those names were first proposed in print have been added.

In the *Systema* Linnaeus described a majority of the animal species then known to Europeans and gave each animal a two-part name. It was then that the Great Scallop received the scientific name *Ostrea maximus*. The first part of the name, *Ostrea,* is the genus (or generic) name. The second part, *maximus,* is the specific (or trivial name), rooted in Latin and intended to be universally understood and accepted (for reasons that made more sense in 1758 than they do now).

All the species Linnaeus placed in his genus *Ostrea* he considered to be closely related. As his knowledge of mollusks was superficial and was based almost entirely on shell characters (often only on crude pictures of shells in old books), later workers have been compelled to make many alterations and additions to his treatment of the Mollusca. It was obvious to the Danish naturalist O. F. Müller, for instance, that the Linnaean genus *Ostrea* contained species totally unrelated to each other. He removed *Ostrea maximus* and some other scallop species from the genus *Ostrea* (which genus is now used exclusively for oysters) and placed them in a new genus of his own invention,

Pecten. Switching species from one genus to another goes on all of the time because our knowledge of mollusks, indeed of all animals, is changing constantly. When a change from the original genus occurs, the author's name and date are put into parentheses: for example, *Pecten maximus* (L., 1758).

The classification of the Great Scallop (*Pecten maximus*)

Phylum	Mollusca	Cuvier, 1797
Class	Bivalvia	Linnaeus, 1758
Subclass	Pteriomorpha	Beurlen, 1944
Order	Pterioida	Newell, 1965
Suborder	Pteriina	Newell, 1965
Superfamily	Pectinacea	Rafinesque, 1815
Family	Pectinidae	Rafinesque, 1815
Subfamily	Pectininae	Rafinesque, 1815
Genus	*Pecten*	Müller, 1776
Subgenus	*Pecten*	Müller, 1776
Species	*maximus*	Linnaeus, 1758

The genus name is always capitalized (for example, *Pecten*), while the species, or trivial name, and any subspecies name, is not (for example, *maximus*). The name of the describer, or author, follows (for example, Linnaeus—abbreviated in this book in the interest of space to L.). Then follows the year in which the species was described. Thus, "L., 1758" or "Reeve, 1847," gives us a bibliographic indication to the describer and the date of the description. It is customary to print the name of the genus and species in italics (for example, *Pecten maximus*), but not the higher categories.

Zoological Taxonomy

From the discussion on classification it is evident that the naming of animals is a science in itself. Ever since the birth of language animals have been given common (or vernacular) names, but it was not until the eighteenth century that a logical system of zoological nomenclature was proposed. The official starting point for the scientific naming of animals is 1758, the year in which the Swedish naturalist Carl Linnaeus published the tenth edition of his *Systema Naturae*.

Because several scientific (Latinized) names may have been applied to the same species by different research workers, the international rules require that the earliest name be used. The later names are known as *synonyms* and should not be used. Rarely, an earlier name is discovered in an obscure and overlooked publication. If that over-looked name has not been used for the last fifty years, the International Commission can officially reject the earlier name, thus saving a well-known name from being discarded.

Sometimes the same name is proposed for two different species. For example, in 1819 Lamarck might have described a *Conus albus* as a European fossil. Later, in 1910, and not knowing about Lamarck's use of the name, Mr. Smith may have described a

Conus albus, a totally different species from, say, Australia. Smith's *C. albus* is a *homonym,* and if it is a valid species, must be given a new name.

The term *of authors* sometimes appears in the synonymy (e.g., *Conus magus* of authors). This means the shell has been called *magus* in the past by various authors, but that this is not the true *magus* Linnaeus, 1758.

The code of rules drawn up for the guidance of zoological taxonomists is available, in a book titled *International Code of Zoological Nomenclature* (1964), from the International Trust for Zoological Nomenclature, c/o British Museum (Natural History), Cromwell Road, London, SW7. A full treatment of zoological taxonomy is the subject of R. E. Blackwelder's *Taxonomy* (1967), John Wiley & Sons, Inc., New York, N.Y.

Type Specimens

One of the novel features of this book is the large number of type specimens used to illustrate species. As the expression *type specimen* will be meaningless to some readers, a few words of explanation are called for.

When a supposedly new species is described it is reasonable to assume that specimens of it exist, or have existed, somewhere. It cannot always be assumed that the original describer has seen or handled specimens himself; he may have described the species on the basis of earlier published figures of specimens representing it. Specimens upon which the original description and/or illustrations are known to be based are called *type specimens,* or simply *types.*

There are several different categories of type specimens, the most important being the following:

Holotype: the single specimen, designated in the original description as the primary or "name-bearing" specimen. If the new species was based on a single specimen, it is automatically the holotype.

Paratype: any specimen from the original type series other than the holotype.

Syntype: one of a series of two or more specimens upon which the original description was based and in which a holotype was not selected.

Lectotype: a specimen from the syntype series, designated subsequent to the original description as the primary or "name-bearing" specimen; it is equivalent in status to the holotype.

HABITATS OF MOLLUSKS

Mollusks are adapted to live almost anywhere except in barren, lifeless zones where food is non-existent or inaccessible. Thus, sandy areas are havens for mollusks with long siphons and bodies adapted for burrowing, such as a majority of bivalves, many gastropods, and most tusk shells.

A mixture of sand and mud will provide an even better habitat for burrowers because it is more food-laden. Here is the ideal environment for *Nassarius* and many miters, numerous bivalve groups, and particularly those with delicately constructed shells. Mangrove swamps provide an even richer environment, consisting mostly of sticky mud.

Mollusks with stronger shells are often able to withstand the very rough conditions associated with open rocky shores. On the exposed surfaces of rocks and cliffs may be found limpets, top-shells, and chitons in abundance. Many less sturdy mollusks find homes in crevices or under rocks. Some bivalves, such as the piddocks *(Pholas)*, bore holes in solid rock, imprisoning themselves for life, secure against any predator, except, of course, a shell collector with rock-breaking equipment.

Where coral flourishes mollusks may flourish too. Soft corals and seafans provide homes for a wide assortment of species including many of the most colorful. As many species again may be found among dead coral rubble, under coral blocks, and in coral sand.

Many mollusks, including larval forms of sedentary shells, spend part of their lives drifting about in the upper levels of the sea. Some are pelagic all their lives. Here, for instance, is the entire world of those butterflies of the ocean, the pteropods. Here, too, the purple snails *(Janthina)*, drift about attached to their egg rafts. If they do not drift onto a beach, they will spend their entire lives out at sea.

At the other extreme many mollusks eke out a precarious existence on the ocean floor at great depths. The quiet, cold, lightless environment usually ensures that mollusks will produce thin, white shells. Recent explorations near the Galapagos Islands, however, have revealed populations of large, robust bivalves thriving about one and a half miles below the surface. Warm, bacteria-laden water gushing up from fissures in the ocean floor has created unusually favorable conditions for marine life in what would have been an otherwise sterile environment. Evidently mollusks are capable of exploiting almost any ecological niche as long as there is an adequate food supply and not too high a level of predation.

SHELL FEATURES AND IDENTIFICATION

A shell is composed of one, two or eight pieces. It may be thick or thin, opaque or translucent, colorful or colorless, smooth or variously ornamented with spines, scales, ridges, furrows, pits, and other relief or incised features. Its overall shape is what makes it so obviously a shell and gives us our first clue to its identity.

For many of us a typical shell is formed of one piece and is coiled. Essentially that describes most gastropod shells, their normal form being an elongated cone spirally twisted around an imaginary axis, the spiral usually following a clockwise course from apex to aperture. The illustrations in this book show that every conceivable variation on the spiral has been exploited by gastropods. Fundamentally, however, a gastropod shell is an expanding tube having an anterior and a posterior end (the direction of the contained animal's forward locomotion dictates which end is the anterior—almost invariably the apertural end).

The successive turns of the shell are called *whorls,* the largest being the last formed. The largest whorl contains the bulk of the animal and is called the *body whorl.* The *aperture* is the hole or space at the anterior end of the body whorl, the edge of the aperture being called the *lip* (or peristome). When the lip is thickened it usually indicates that the shell has reached maturity. In some families, such as Muricidae and Cassidae, the lip is thickened at fairly regular intervals, the successive thickenings being known as *varices* (singular *varix).*

The *outer lip* is that part of the lip farthest away from the shell's imaginary axis. On the opposite side is the *inner lip* (or, in place of it, the *parietal wall).* Winding around the imaginary axis is the *columella,* which may be encircled by folds or plicae. The colu-

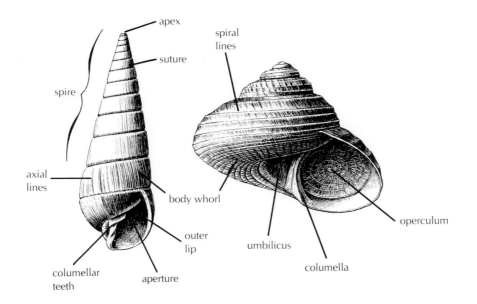

apex

suture

spire

spiral
lines

axial
lines

body whorl

outer
lip

operculum

umbilicus

columella

columellar
teeth

aperture

Drawing of parts of gastropod

mella may be greatly extended forward to form a *siphonal canal,* as can be easily seen in the genus *Murex.* The hole bounded by the columella is known as the *umbilicus.* It varies in width and apparent depth from species to species and genus to genus, but many gastropods do not have one at all. It is still a constant enough feature within a single species, however, to be important in identification.

In some genera, such as *Bursa,* there is a small *posterior canal* at the upper end of the aperture. In the slit shells *(Pleurotomaria)* there is a broad band encircling the whorls and confluent with the prominent slit in the outer lip characteristic of members of this genus. The band, resulting from shelly matter being deposited on the site of the slit as the mollusk grows, has been christened the *selenizone,* an allusion to the crescent-moon shape of the successive depositions.

Shells belonging to the family Turridae have a slit or groove in the upper half of the outer lip that is filled in as the shell enlarges. Its track, clearly visible on earlier whorls, is known as the *anal fasciole.* The lower part of the outer lip in *Strombus* shells has a shallow embayment resembling the depression left when a potter's finger is pressed into the lip of a moist clay pot. This is the *stromboid notch.*

The meeting place of the whorls is the *suture,* which may be scarcely perceptible or marked by a fine line, a thickened crest, or a deep channel. Like the groove in a phonograph record the suture is continuous. A gastropod shell has only a single suture.

Among mollusks whose shells are not coiled the family Fissurellidae is noteworthy for the apical hole found in most of its members. A vertical slit at the edge of the shell is the hallmark of most species of *Emarginula,* while the expansive shell perforated with a row of holes is characteristic of the Haliotidae.

These shell features correspond to features in the mollusks' soft anatomy or have a function related to certain needs of the animals. The siphonal canal of a *Murex,* for instance, is for the reception of a siphon. The stromboid notch, strange though it may

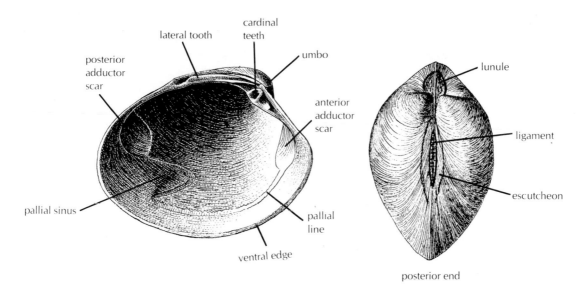

Drawing of parts of bivalve

seem, is to make it possible for the animal's right eyestalk to protrude (that part of the shell being adjacent to the right eyestalk when the animal is active).

Various superficial, but often very conspicuous, features ornament the surface of a gastropod shell. Always it has *axial* growth lines (these being parallel to the apertural lip). Sometimes it will have thick or thin axial *ribs,* small or large *nodes* or *nodules, scales* or *spines,* their arrangement being axial or *spiral* (in line with the direction of growth). Occasionally axial and spiral features combine to form a *reticulate* ornament. A *cancellate* or *decussate* ornament is similar, but the spiral and axial features cross at right angles to form a pattern of tiny squares.

The shell may also be ornamented with incised features, known variously as *lines, striae* or *furrows,* depending on their depth and width. Close examination may reveal that these incised features are actually rows of minute pits. Shells so ornamented are said to be *punctate.*

Because successive whorls largely overlap one another, the gastropod animal eventually resorbs or obliterates some of the ornamental features it has laid down previously. The bivalve animal, following a different growth pattern, rarely interferes with any part of its shell once it has been formed.

With few exceptions bivalves have two-piece shells, each piece being called a *valve.* The two valves, equal or unequal in shape and size, are joined together by a flexible, chitinous *ligament* and they close effectively because the upper, inner edge of each has a *hinge* embellished with interlocking teeth and pits. The small teeth immediately below the *umbones* (embryonic valves) are the *cardinals,* the longer ones on each side of them, the *laterals.*

Also visible on the inside of each valve are marks left by certain muscles. The adductor muscles (those that are used to pull the two valves together) leave prominent *adductor scars* in the valves. In some bivalves, such as oysters and scallops, there is only one adductor scar in each valve, but many more have two in each valve. Those with two

9

in each valve usually have a clearly visible pallial line connecting them, the muscular edge of the animal's mantle having been attached along it. In most bivalves the pallial line has a distinct embayment, known as the *pallial sinus,* indicating the former presence of siphons. The characteristics and disposition of all these internal features provide vital clues to the identification of bivalves and sometimes they have significance for their classification as well.

Often it is possible to identify a bivalve by its external characteristics alone, for these are many and varied. It is often necessary to distinguish one valve from the other, however, to be sure of an identification. With very few exceptions bivalves have an upper or *dorsal* margin (where the hinge is located) and a lower or *ventral* margin (usually where the valves open widest). The umbones (singular *umbo*) are situated on the dorsal margin and usually incline toward the anterior end of the shell.

Many bivalve shells have a *lunule* (a heart-shaped impression anterior to the umbones) visible in its entirety only when the closed valves are viewed end on. Sometimes the ligament is set in an elongate depression. This is the *escutcheon,* usually differing from the rest of the shell in ornament and color.

Peculiar to some bivalves are the so-called *ears,* lateral extensions on each side of the umbo, or on one side only, of each valve. A prominent feature of scallop shells is the anterior ear, which may be markedly longer than the posterior one. The anterior ear of the right valve may also be indented by a *byssal notch.* It is through this feature that a kind of all-purpose anchor made of fine threads protrudes. Known as a *byssus,* it enables the bivalve to secure itself to other objects. Sometimes the byssus takes the form of a *byssal plug* and this is fixed to other objects through a byssal hole, easily visible in jingle shells *(Anomia)* and always perforating the right (lower) valve.

Clearly, the correct identification of a species may depend on characteristics present in one valve, either the right or the left. It is necessary, therefore, to be able to distinguish one from the other. There are two simple ways of orienting the valves of most bivalves correctly. If the closed valves are placed so that the umbones are uppermost and the external ligament is between them and you, then the valve on your right is a right valve. The inside of the valves may also provide a clue. With the umbones uppermost, locate the pallial sinus, assuming one is present. If the indentation opens to the right, then it is a right valve.

As with gastropod shells, bivalve ornament may be raised above the shell surface or engraved into it. Both kinds of ornament are laid down either concentrically or radially. *Concentric* ornament always lies parallel to the margins of the valves and is frequently identical with a growth stage. It varies from exceedingly fine to conspicuous and may take the form of raised lines, threads, ribs and *folds,* or incised striae, grooves and punctations. *Radial* ornament (which tends to be similar to but stronger than concentric ornament) radiates outward toward the margins from the umbones.

Radial and concentric ornament are frequently present on the same shell, but one is usually stronger than the other and overrides it. If of equal strength the concentric ornament often takes the form of *beads, pustules, tubercles,* or *scales.* In a few species the ornament on the right valve differs from that on the left, as may be seen clearly in various scallops.

The shells of gastropods and bivalves may have a horny covering over the outer surface. Known correctly as the *periostracum* (and incorrectly as the epidermis), it may be thin and translucent, thick and fibrous, or may even appear to be hairy. It is seldom colorful, but in the gastropod genus *Latirus* it is iridescent. Occasionally the periostracum is helpful in identification but more often it is a hindrance.

Chitons have eight-piece shells, each piece being called a valve. The end valves are known as the *head valve* and *tail valve*, respectively, the other six being the *median* or *intermediate valves*. Encircling them and keeping them in place is a band of muscular tissue, the *girdle*, which is smooth or variously ornamented with *scales*, *spicules*, or *spines*.

The valves themselves may be ornamented but seldom in high relief and are never spiny. Specialists use several technical terms to denote parts of chiton valves, but they need not concern us here.

Tusk shells are altogether simpler in their construction than most other molluscan shells. The large opening is the *anterior orifice*, the smaller is the *posterior orifice*. Some species have a small *terminal pipe* projecting beyond the edge of the posterior orifice, which may or may not have a slot, a notch, or a slit in its edge.

The concave side of the shell is the *dorsal face*, the convex side is the *ventral face*. The ornament of tusk shells is of the simplest, longitudinal ribs being the most obvious and most important surface features. The identification of all but the best known tusk shells is a job for experts.

Most shells have at least a trace of color and some have a great deal of it. Often the color forms a distinctive pattern and is laid down by the mantle independently of the ornamental surface features. The colors laid down on a shell and the patterns they make undoubtedly provide important diagnostic features, and most of the descriptions of shells given in books give as much prominence to color and pattern as to ornament.

At the same time we can be easily led to believe that color and pattern are reliable features for identification purposes. Sometimes they are, but sometimes they are not. Certainly they are difficult to describe and just as certainly they are impossible to ignore, as the pictures in this book amply demonstrate.

SHELL CONDITION

In recent times, collectors and shell dealers have agreed on international shell-grading standards. In most instances specimens in "gem" condition are more desirable. Other factors, such as the accuracy and details of the collecting information (locality, habitat, date, etc.), are also important.

Gem. A perfect specimen, fully adult, normally colored, and without any visible breaks or flaws. Gastropods must have a perfect spire, with intact nuclear whorls, no broken spines, an outer lip without chips. Bivalves must have matching valves. Gastropods that are accompanied by their proper operculum and have the periostracum properly preserved intact are sometimes referred to as *super-gem*. No excessive oiling. Well cleaned inside and out.

Fine. An adult shell with only minor flaws or with not more than one shallow growth mark. Must have original color and gloss. A cone or volute lip may have one small chip or some roughness; a *Murex* or *Spondylus*, for instance, may have one or two minor spine breaks. No repairs, such as filed lips, mended knobs, or filled sponge holes. Well cleaned inside and out.

Good. A reasonably acceptable shell with few defects, such as growth marks, broken spines, a worn spire, or lip chips. Specimen may be subadult, but must display all the characteristics of the species. Well cleaned inside and quite well cleaned outside.

Poor. Worn or faded, with obvious breaks, loss of spines, eroded spire, or other loss of characters because of weathering or rough handling under adverse conditions. Referred to as "commercial grade" or "beach specimen" by some specimen dealers.

Juv. Juvenile or immature specimen. May be gem in the case of a half-grown specimen in a species that does not form a curled or flaring lip in the adult, such as *Cypraea* or *Strombus*.

W/O. With operculum (in gem quality the operculum must have come from the very specimen at hand).

Full Data. Detailed geographical origin, habitat, exact date of collecting, and original collector.

Basic Data. Localized geographical data as supplied by field dealers (Zamboanga, Philippines; or off Anping, Taiwan; Tampa Bay, Florida), year of collecting; original collector or dealer.

CONSERVATION

Studies have shown that no real menace to molluscan populations is caused by the collecting of specimens to satisfy the needs of museums, students and shell collectors. Pollution and massive disturbance of the habitats are the main causes of the decline of some shell beds, although commercial dredging for scallops and clams is known to reduce the numbers of shells temporarily.

Nonetheless, informed shell collectors are well aware of the need for restraint in collecting specimens. The influential national society, the American Malacological Union (A.M.U.), has endorsed the following guidelines for its members' field studies and collecting activities:

1. Observation and photography of mollusks in their natural habitats can yield important biological information and is often a more rewarding activity than the collecting of living animals. The A.M.U. encourages such observational research by both amateur and professional malacologists.

2. Living specimens should be collected only in those minimal numbers necessary to satisfy the requirements of the study. Dead shells often make valuable specimens, and their collection does not further endanger the population. The A.M.U. encourages the collection of dead shells, especially in cases where soft parts are not required for anatomical or physiological research.

3. Because detailed, properly documented material is needed to establish the ranges and habitats of all molluscan species and to ensure the success of efforts to conserve these animals, the A.M.U. urges all collectors to carefully label all specimens, photographs, and field notes with the precise locality, the exact date, and the full name of the observer and collector. It further recommends that arrangements be made for the deposition of such documentation and specimens in permanent museum reference collections. These may then be studied by other malacologists when the original studies are completed.

4. The results of field studies should be shared as widely as possible by means of educational exhibits, published papers, letters, seminars, and lectures.

5. The laws concerning collecting and trespass are to be known and obeyed by all.

Fieldworkers will obtain all necessary licenses and permits from official agencies and landowners before engaging in collecting or other activities.

The Hawaiian Malacological Society has issued a sheller's creed to be followed by collectors in tropical waters:

1. *Leave the live coral heads alone!* That's not where the shells live. Look in rubble, under the slabs, in the sand, and among the loose chunks.
2. *Put rock and coral back in place*, the way you found them, even in deep water. Things live under them. Continued exposure will kill them.
3. *Be alert for shell eggs and protect them.* They have a slim chance of survival, at best. Don't take the shell that is guarding them. Avoid disturbing breeding groups.
4. *Collect only what you really need.* Take time to examine your finds. Imperfect and immature shells are of no use to you. Leave them to grow and to breed.

GEOGRAPHICAL RANGES

In our brief treatment of each species we have given the areas where various species live. Space does not permit a detailed outline of the geographical range of each species. That information may be obtained in specialized faunal books or scientific monographs. The term *Indo-Pacific,* frequently used in this book, refers to the tropical marine province of the Indian and Western Pacific oceans. Many species have a range from the eastern shores of Africa and the Red Sea to the Central Pacific and northward to southern Japan.

On the other hand many species have limited ranges. As an example, *Aulica imperialis* is known only from the Sulu Sea in the southern Philippines. The Dragon Head Cowrie *(Cypraea caputdraconis)* has only been found on Easter Island in eastern Polynesia. It should also be remembered that some widespread species may have a specialized habitat, and, if the type of habitat occurs only rarely throughout the species range, the distribution of that shell will be scattered and sporadic.

Some marine species have been accidentally introduced to other parts of the world. Their present distribution may not conform to their normal range. The Atlantic Slipper Shell *(Crepidula fornicata)*, originally an eastern United States species, is now abundant in northwest Europe. A few Japanese gastropods have established themselves in British Columbia and Washington.

MEASUREMENTS

Our measurements are given in English inches and in centimeters (with approximate equivalents). Our sizes represent the maximum length or diameter of an average adult specimen. Naturally, younger or immature specimens will be smaller than our stated size. Similarly, occasional specimens will exceed our stated dimensions. The known maximum sizes of many hundreds of species are recorded in Wagner and Abbott's *Standard Catalog of Shells.*

OBTAINING SHELLS

There are three major ways of acquiring shells for your collection: personal collecting, trading and purchasing. Some people prefer to limit their collections to what they have personally collected. Field notes and labels giving the exact date and place of collection add to the value of the specimens, for some day they may be added to the scientific collections of a research museum.

A detailed account of collecting and cleaning shells may be found in *How to Know and Study Shells*, a symposium of the American Malacological Union, as well as in dozens of shell books for beginners. In simplest terms, live mollusks may be cleaned of the soft parts by boiling them in water for about ten minutes, and then pulling the meat out with a bent pin or probe. Save the operculum of the gastropods. If you wish to preserve the animal, use seventy percent alcohol, not formaldehyde, as the latter is acidic and affects the calcareous shell.

A great deal of satisfaction may be obtained by corresponding and exchanging shells with collectors overseas. Their names may be obtained from shell magazines and shell club newsletters. A list of shell clubs appears in Tom Rice's *A Sheller's Directory of Clubs, Books, Periodicals and Dealers* (P.O. Box 33, Port Gamble, Washington 98364 USA). When exchanging, always try to send the very best specimens and supply good locality data.

Although a few shell shops carry specimen shells, most of today's sales of rare and unusual shells are through the mail-order business. Prices vary from one dealer to another, but in general perfect specimens bring higher prices than imperfect ones. A list of mail-order dealers may be found in Tom Rice's directory.

CARE OF SHELLS

Although shells are quite durable and have a great advantage over some other natural objects favored by collectors, they do require protection from dirt, excessive moisture, and direct sunlight.

Depending on the size of his pocketbook and the nature of his specimens a collector may arrange his collection in various ways. A few large specimens may be decoratively placed about a room or placed on shelving in a glass-fronted cabinet. A large collection containing several hundred species and bearing data labels is best housed in cabinets with sliding drawers. Many collectors place choice specimens in plastic boxes with a felt or cloth bottom. Plastic foam padding should be avoided because it will eventually break down and stick to the specimens. Cabinets made of oak should also be avoided because an acid fume will affect the surface of shells.

A certain amount of "face-lifting" of freshly collected specimens may be accomplished by soaking them in a fifty percent solution of bleach, later rinsing in warm water, and applying a very light touch of mineral oil. Do not treat shells with muriatic acid. This gives the shell surface an unnatural greasy appearance, and under a microscope one can see the resulting myriads of tiny pits.

In some countries where cool, humid conditions prevail, a bacterial blight (sometimes known as "Byne's disease") may attack glossy shells. The surface becomes chalky white and has a faint odor of vinegar. Badly damaged shells should be thrown away. Lightly affected shells should be soaked for a day in strong alcohol, then dried. Keep your collection in as dry and airy a place as possible.

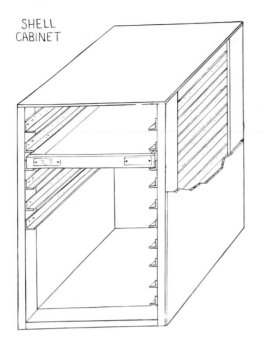

SHELL
CABINET

Drawing of cabinet and catalog samples

PERSONAL CATALOG NUMBER	STANDARD CATALOG NUMBER	IDENTIFICATION (Genus, species and author)	LOCALITY DATA

DATE OF COLLECTING	COLLECTOR OR SOURCE	NUMBER OF SPECIMENS	PRICE PAID OR VALUE	DATE CATALOGED	HABITAT; REMARKS

CATALOGING YOUR COLLECTION

A well-organized and fully documented collection of shells serves as a useful reference and identification tool. Its growth, permanency and value are enhanced by proper arrangement and curatorial care. Furthermore, such a collection adds to our scientific knowledge and may someday be a major contribution to a natural history museum or teaching institution. A catalog is most essential, and its most important purpose is to prevent the loss or mixing of locality data. If every specimen of each species from one locality (called a *lot*) bears the same number on the label and in the catalog entry, it can be returned to its proper tray in case of accidental spilling or mishandling. For example, if you collect several specimens of a periwinkle from a tide pool in Rockport, Maine, on May 13, 1977, this information should be entered in the catalog, and each shell should be given the same catalog number.

It is not necessary to have an identification of the species in order to catalog your specimens, for the real purpose is to associate a number with the more important information, such as *locality data, date of collecting, name of collector* and *habitat.* If the species name is written in pencil, it may be corrected or changed at a later date, although such updating is usually done only on the label.

Specimens should be numbered with black India ink with a fine-tipped pen. Shells too small to number may be placed in plastic boxes or in small glass or plastic vials, the latter either sealed with a snap lid or a plug of cotton. In each container place a small slip of heavy paper bearing the same number as that on the label and in the catalog entry.

Ringed Top-shell, *Calliostoma annulatum* (Lightfoot, 1786), from kelp beds off the Californian coast.

ACKNOWLEDGMENTS

Our debt to others for allowing us to photograph their shells and for information of various kinds is a large one. In particular we should like to express our gratitude to members of the staff of the Division of Mollusks at the U.S. Natural History Museum, Smithsonian Institution, Washington, D.C., including Joseph Rosewater, Harald Rehder, Richard "Joe" Houbrick (Cerithiidae), and Clyde Roper (Cephalopoda); Kenneth J. Boss, Curator of Mollusks, and Ruth D. Turner, Museum of Comparative Zoology at Harvard University; George M. Davis and Robert Robertson of the Department of Malacology, Academy of Natural Sciences of Philadelphia; William K. Emerson and William E. Old, Jr., of The American Museum of Natural History, New York; staff members of the British Museum (Natural History); Graham Oliver and Peter Morgan of the Zoology Department, National Museum of Wales, Cardiff, Wales; David Heppell of the Natural History Department, Royal Scottish Museum, Edinburgh, Scotland. The unstinting help given us by these professionals and the generous way they allowed us access to the collections in their care has made this book possible.

Without the help of numerous private collectors, however, we should have been unable to illustrate many shells which have come on to the market only in recent years. Undoubtedly, too, the better quality specimens of many species are only to be found in private hands and we have been privileged to photograph many of these. We are especially thankful for the help and encouragement given to us by the owners of some of the finest shell collections in the United States and the United Kingdom.

We have received help from the following people and wish to thank them.

From the United States: Cecelia W. Abbott, of Melbourne, Florida (editing, typing manuscript); Mr. and Mrs. Stewart F. Armington, Jr., of Sarasota, Florida (rare shells); Helene Avellanet of Venice, Florida *(Latiaxis)*; Alice Barlow of Tenafly, New Jersey (photographs); John Bernard of Brooksville, Florida *(Cypraea)*; Jerome M. Bijur of Naples, Florida (Caribbean shells); William Bledsoe of Los Angeles, California (rare shells); Walter and Peggy Carpenter of Burke, Virginia (cones and rare shells); Phillip W. Clover of Glen Ellen, California (Marginellidae); Jim and Bobbi Cordy of Merritt Island, Florida; Roberta Cranmer of Louisville, Kentucky (Conidae); Lowell and Dorothy DeVasure of Tekamah, Nebraska (Conidae); Albert E. and Beverly Deynzer of Sanibel, Florida (Mitridae); Joseph A. Ellul of Palm Bay, Florida (photographs); Betty Witt Evans (typing manuscript); Gene D. Everson of Ft. Lauderdale, Florida; Rachel N. Germon of Gaithersburg, Maryland (Muricidae and typing manuscript); Richard Goldberg of Flushing, New York (photographs of *Murex* and *Conus*); Jerry M. Harasewych of Wilmington, Delaware (photographs); Charles and Violet Hertweck of Venice, Florida (Pectinidae); Bob and Dottie Janowsky of Brooklyn, New York (rare shells); Johnnie Johnson of the Brevard County (Florida) Museum; Mrs. Jo Kotaro of St. Petersburg, Florida *(Haliotis)*; Dr. Harry Lee of Jacksonville, Florida (photographs of *Strombus* and Volutidae); Hal Lewis of Philadelphia, Pennsylvania (photographs of Cymatiidae); Robert and Betty Lipe of St. Petersburg, Florida (Marginellidae and photographs); Joe Little of Melbourne Beach, Florida; Gary Magnote of Pompano Beach, Florida; Sandi McGhee of Coral Springs, Florida (photographs); Richard E. Petit of North Myrtle Beach, South Carolina (Cancellariidae); Bernard and Phyllis Pipher of Tekamah, Nebraska (Conidae); George and Dorothy Raeihle of Babylon, New York (photographs); Tom Rice of Port Gamble, Washington (chitons); Cheryl T. Richardson of Marathon, Florida *(Conus)*; Graham Saunders of England and McLean, Virginia (rare shells); Gloria Scarboro of Indian Harbor Beach, Florida (Florida shells); Robert J. L. and Fran Wagner of Marathon, Florida (rare shells); Jerry Walls of Hightstown, New Jersey (photographs); Carl C. Withrow of St. Petersburg, Florida (Galapagos shells).

From the United Kingdom, we have been helped by Michael Dixon of Kent (Naticidae); Walter Karo of London (Volutidae); Tom and Celia Pain of London (Muricidae and Buccinidae). From Japan we have benefited from the services of Dr. Takashi Okutani (photographs of types).

THE UNIVALVES
CLASS GASTROPODA

ORDER ARCHAEOGASTROPODA
SUPERFAMILY PLEUROTOMARIACEA
SLIT SHELLS
FAMILY PLEUROTOMARIIDAE

The large, primitive slit shells are limited to deep water, and most are quite rare in collections. There are 16 living species, all having a horny, circular operculum. The slit in the last whorl allows waste water to escape from the mantle chamber.

African Slit Shell (5") 12 cm
Pleurotomaria africana Tomlin, 1948. South Africa. Deep water; dredged. Moderately rare. *P. teramachii* Kuroda, 1955, is a Japanese subspecies, resembling it closely.

Hirasé's Slit Shell (4") 10 cm
Pleurotomaria hirasei Pilsbry, 1903. Off Japan; deep water. Uncommon. Rarely has albino shell. Best known species.

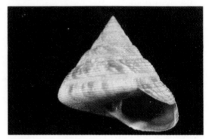

Beyrich's Slit Shell (4") 10 cm
Pleurotomaria beyrichii Hilgendorff, 1877. Off China and Japan; deep water; rare. Slit short; surface rough.

Rumphius's Slit Shell (8") 20 cm
Pleurotomaria rumphii Schepman, 1879. Off Taiwan and Japan; Indonesia. Deep water; uncommon. Umbilicus large and deep; slit very long.

Salmiana Slit Shell (4") 10 cm
Pleurotomaria salmiana Rolle, 1899. Off central Japan; deep water. Rare. *P. schmalzi* Shikama is a more pointed form.

Atlantic Slit Shell (3") 7 cm
Pleurotomaria atlantica Rios and Matthews, 1968. Off Brazil; deep water, 200 meters; rare. Slit narrow and short.

Pyramus Slit Shell (2") 5 cm
Pleurotomaria pyramus (F. M. Bayer, 1967). Off Guadeloupe, Lesser Antilles; 648 meters; rare. Spire low; slit short; fragile. Holotype illustrated.

Dawn Slit Shell (3.5") 8.5 cm
Pleurotomaria diluculum (Okutani, 1979). Off central Japan; deep water; rare. Umbilicus narrow; slit short. Holotype specimen illustrated.

Quoy's Slit Shell (2") 5 cm
Pleurotomaria quoyana Fischer & Bernardi, 1856. Gulf of Mexico—West Indies; deep water; rare. Slit short.

Jewel Slit Shell (1.7") 4 cm
Pleurotomaria gemma (F. M. Bayer, 1965). Off Barbados, Lesser Antilles; 300 meters; rare. Finely beaded. Slit short.

Lovely Slit Shell (3") 7 cm
Pleurotomaria amabilis (F. M. Bayer, 1963). Off West Florida and Lower Florida Keys; deep water; uncommon. Slit narrow and short.

Adanson's Slit Shell (7") 17 cm
Pleurotomaria adansoniana Crosse & Fischer, 1861. Bermuda; West Indies—Brazil. Deep water; uncommon. Umbilicus deep; slit very long.

King Midas's Slit Shell (3.5") 9 cm
Pleurotomaria midas (F. M. Bayer, 1965). Off central Bahama Islands; deep water; rare. Holotype illustrated.

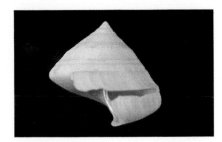

Lucayan Slit Shell (1") 2.5 cm
Pleurotomaria lucaya (F. M. Bayer, 1965). Off Grand Bahama Island; deep water; rare. Holotype illustrated.

ABALONES or ORMERS
FAMILY HALIOTIDAE

The abalones, sea ears or ormers have low flattish, spiral shells with an iridescent interior and with small holes for exhaling water. Adults lack an operculum. There are about 70 living species, most living on rocks in shallow water. The foot is edible and marketed in many countries.

Threaded Abalone (5") 13 cm
Haliotis assimilis Dall, 1878. S. Calif.—Baja Calif. Shallow water; common. 4 or 5 holes open. Syn.: *aulaea* Bartsch.

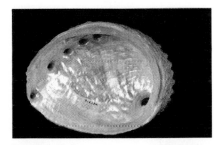

Threaded Abalone (5") 13 cm
Haliotis assimilis Dall, 1878. Interior view. Some consider this a southern subspecies of *H. kamtschatkana*. Exterior weakly threaded.

Green Abalone (8") 20 cm
Haliotis fulgens Philippi, 1845. S. Calif.—Baja Calif. Offshore to 10 meters; common. 5 or 6 holes open. Syn.: *splendens* Reeve; *revea* Bartsch.

Black Abalone (6") 15 cm
Haliotis cracherodii Leach, 1814. Oregon—Baja Calif. Intertidal; abundant. 5-8 holes open. Freaks lack holes. Surface smooth.

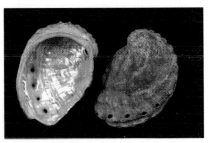

Japanese Abalone (4") 10 cm
Haliotis kamtschatkana Jonas, 1845. N. Calif.—Alaska; Japan. Intertidal to 5 meters; common. 4 or 5 holes open.

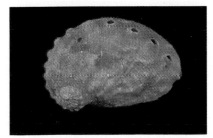

Pourtales's Abalone (1") 2.5 cm
Haliotis pourtalesii Dall, 1881. S. E. United States to Brazil. On rocks, offshore, 130 to 400 meters. Rare. Interior pearly white.

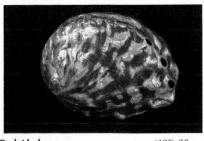

Red Abalone (12") 30 cm
Haliotis rufescens Swainson, 1822. Exterior view of polished shell. Meat of foot is marketed in Calif. Shell is used in jewelry.

Red Abalone (12") 30 cm
Haliotis rufescens Swainson, 1822. Oregon—Baja Calif. Intertidal to 150 meters on rocks; common. Exterior surface rough. 3 or 4 holes open.

Northern Green Abalone (5″) 12 cm
Haliotis walallensis Stearns, 1899. Brit. Columbia—S. Calif. Uncommon; 1-20 meters. 5 or 6 holes open. Exterior with spiral threads. Holotype illustrated.

White Abalone (10″) 25 cm
Haliotis sorenseni Bartsch, 1940. S. Calif.—Baja Calif. Offshore to 40 meters; common. 3-5 rimmed holes. Interior pearly white, with border of red.

Pink Abalone (6″) 15 cm
Haliotis corrugata Wood, 1828. S. Calif.—Baja Calif. Intertidal to 30 meters; abundant. 3 or 4 tubular holes open. Interior brilliant iridescent.

Rosy Abalone (2″) 5 cm
Haliotis rosacea Reeve, 1846. West Africa. Intertidal to 2 meters; common. Exterior with fine decussated sculpture. Columella flat, wide. Syn.: *decussata* Philippi.

Lamellose Ormer (3″) 8 cm
Haliotis tuberculata subspecies *lamellosa* Lamarck, 1822. Mediterranean and Adriatic Seas. Subtidal; common. Exterior rough. Many synonyms.

Tuberculate Ormer (3″) 8 cm
Haliotis tuberculata L., 1758. Channel Is. to Canaries; Mediterranean. Intertidal to 5 meters; common. About 6-8 holes open. Spirally threaded.

Virgin Abalone (2.5″) 7 cm
Haliotis virginea Gmelin, 1791. New Zealand. Subtidal on rocks; uncommon. Animal black with white foot.

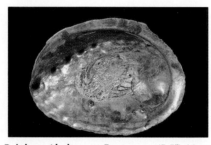

Rainbow Abalone or **Paua** (5.5″) 14 cm
Haliotis iris Martyn, 1784. New Zealand. Subtidal on rocks; common. Exterior dull, rough. Animal black. *H. iris* Gmelin is the same.

Austral Abalone (3″) 8 cm
Haliotis australis Gmelin, 1791. New Zealand. Subtidal on rocks; moderately common. Strongly corrugated. Foot is orange.

Brazier's Abalone (1.2″) 3 cm
Haliotis brazieri Angas, 1869. S. E. Australia. Subtidal on rocks; uncommon. Sometimes blood-red or with green zigzags.

Emma's Abalone (4″) 10 cm
Haliotis emmae Reeve, 1846. South Australia—Tasmania. Subtidal on rocks; moderately common. 6 open holes.

Staircase Abalone (2.5″) 7 cm
Haliotis scalaris Leach, 1814. South and West Australia. Subtidal on rocks; uncommon. Syn.: *tricostalis* Menke; *rubicundus* Gray.

Ruber Abalone (6″) 16 cm
Haliotis ruber Leach, 1814. Southern Australia—Tasmania. Subtidal; abundant. Syn.: *naevosa* Martyn; *improbulum* Iredale.

Roe's Abalone (4.5″) 12 cm
Haliotis roei Gray, 1826. Western Australia—Victoria. Offshore; commercially abundant. About 7 holes open.

Reddish-rayed Abalone (2″) 5 cm
Haliotis coccoradiata Reeve, 1846. S. E. Australia. Intertidal; common. 6 or 7 holes open.

Scaly Australian Abalone (2.5″) 6 cm
Haliotis squamata Reeve, 1846. Western Australia. Subtidal on rocks; common. 7 or 8 holes open.

Canaliculate Abalone (1.5″) 4 cm
Haliotis parva L., 1758. South Africa. Intertidal, uncommon. 6 holes open. Syn.: *canaliculata* Lamarck; *carinata* Swainson.

Quekett's Abalone (1.5″) 3.5 cm
Haliotis queketti E. A. Smith, 1910. Natal, South Africa. Subtidal on rocks; rare. 7 holes open, with high rims.

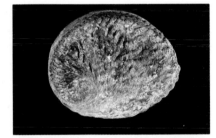

Midas's Abalone or Perlemoen (7″) 17 cm
Haliotis midae L., 1758. Table Bay—Natal, South Africa. Subtidal on rocks; moderately common. Commercially fished.

Blood-spotted Abalone (3″) 7 cm
Haliotis spadicea Donovan, 1808. Table Bay to Natal, South Africa. Intertidal on rocks; common. Syn.: *sanguinea* Hanley.

Japanese Abalone (2.5″) 6 cm
Haliotis aquatilis Reeve, 1846. Japan—Korea. Intertidal to 20 m. on rocks; common. Alias *japonica* Reeve; *supertexta* Lischke; *exigua* Dunker.

Giant Abalone (8″) 20 cm
Haliotis gigantea Gmelin, 1791. Japan—Korea. Subtidal on rocks to 20 m.; common. Commercially fished.

Disk Abalone (6″) 15 cm
Haliotis discus Reeve, 1846. Japan, Korea, N. China. On rock, subtidal to 20 m. Very common; commercial seafood.

Donkey's Ear Abalone (2.5″) 6 cm
Haliotis asinina L., 1758. S. W. Pacific. Subtidal, shallow water; abundant. Color variable. Foot large.

Close-sculptured Abalone (2.5") 6 cm
Haliotis crebrisculpta Sowerby, 1914. Japan—N. Australia. Intertidal on rocks; moderately common. Syntype illustrated.

Variously Colored Abalone (3") 8 cm
Haliotis diversicolor Reeve, 1846. S.W. Pacific. Subtidal on rocks; common. Color variable. Syn.: *gruneri* Philippi; *tayloriana* Reeve.

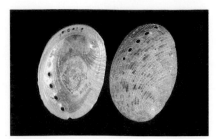

Glistening Abalone (2") 5 cm
Haliotis glabra Gmelin, 1791. Philippines—N. Australia. Intertidal on rocks; common. Syn.: *picta* Röding, 1798.

Jacna Abalone (0.5") 1.2 cm
Haliotis jacnensis Reeve, 1846. Philippines. Subtidal on rocks; uncommon. Coarse spiral ribs. *H. jacnaensis* is a misspelling.

Oval Abalone (1.5") 4 cm
Haliotis ovina Gmelin, 1791. Southern Japan—N. Australia. Intertidal on rocks; common. Interior silvery. Syn.: *latilabris* Philippi.

Planate Abalone (1.7") 4 cm
Haliotis planata Sowerby, 1883. S. W. Pacific. Intertidal on rocks; uncommon. Spire usually flat, eroded. 5 holes open.

Most Beautiful Abalone (1") 2.5 cm
Haliotis pulcherrima Gmelin, 1791. Eastern Polynesia. Offshore, shallow water. Locally common.

Variable Abalone (3") 7 cm
Haliotis varia L., 1758. Indo-Pacific. Subtidal on rocks. Widespread and common. Variable coloration. Syn.: *semistriata* Reeve.

Elegant Abalone (3") 7 cm
Haliotis elegans Philippi, 1874. Western Australia. Offshore, on rocks. Uncommon to rare.

Smooth Australian Abalone (6") 15 cm
Haliotis laevigata Donovan, 1808. South Australia. Offshore shallow water. Common. Syn.: *albicans* Q. & G.; *excisa* Gray.

Whirling Abalone (2.5") 6 cm
Haliotis cyclobates Péron, 1816. South Australia and Victoria. On rocks and shells, subtidal to 30 m; common. Syn.: *excavata* Lamarck.

Conical Pore Abalone (8") 20 cm
Haliotis conicopora Péron, 1816. Southern Australian rocky coasts. Subtidal; common. Top flat. Syn.: *cunninghami* Gray and *granti* Pritchard and Gatliff.

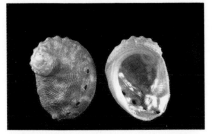

Dall's Abalone (2″) 5 cm

Haliotis dalli Henderson, 1915. Galapagos; West Colombia. 20 to 80 m; uncommon to rare.

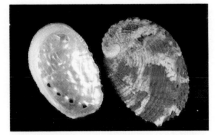

Dohrn's Abalone (2″) 5 cm

Haliotis dohrniana Dunker, 1863. New Hebrides to Indonesia. Rocks in shallow water; uncommon.

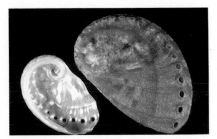

Semiplicate Abalone (2.5″) 6 cm

Haliotis semiplicata Menke, 1843. Western Australia. Shallow water; uncommon. 6 or 7 holes open.

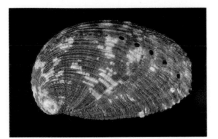

Squamose Abalone (2″) 5 cm

Haliotis squamosa Gray, 1826. Western Australia. Subtidal rocks; common.

Lord Howe Abalone (1.5″) 3.5 cm

Haliotis howensis Iredale, 1929. Eastern Australia; Lord Howe Island; uncommon to rare.

Mimic Abalone (1.5″) 3.5 cm

Haliotis ethologus Iredale, 1927. N. E. Australia. Subtidal; uncommon.

Honey Abalone (1.5″) 3.5 cm

Haliotis melculus Iredale, 1927. Queensland, Australia. Offshore; uncommon.

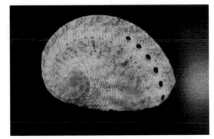

Shield Abalone (1.5″) 3.5 cm

Haliotis ancile Reeve, 1846. Gulf of Suez, N.W. Indian Ocean. Subtidal; uncommon.

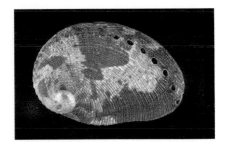

Splendid Abalone (3″) 5 cm

Haliotis speciosa Reeve, 1846. South Africa. Subtidal rocks; common.

Many-holed Abalone (2.5″) 7 cm

Haliotis multiperforata Reeve, 1846. Indian Ocean. Intertidal rocks; uncommon.

Lovely Abalone (2.5″) 6 cm

Haliotis venusta Adams & Reeve, 1850. South China Sea. Intertidal rocks; locally uncommon.

Hargraves's Abalone (3″) 7 cm

Haliotis hargravesi Cox, 1869. Eastern Australia. Subtidal rocks; uncommon.

KEYHOLE LIMPETS
SUPERFAMILY
FISSURELLACEA

These primitive limpets have two feathery gills. They live on rocks below the low-tide mark in most parts of the world. A few are deep-sea dwellers. Most have a natural hole at the top (Fissurellidae), but some have only a slit or weak indentation at the front end. In some, the mantle covers the shell. All are vegetarians, and they shed their floating eggs in the water. None has an operculum.

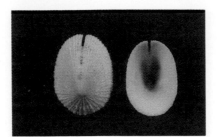

Striated Emarginula   (0.5″) 1.2 cm
Emarginula striatula Quoy & Gaimard, 1834. New Zealand. Subtidal on stones. Moderately common. Sculpture delicate.

Crass Emarginula   (1″) 2.5 cm
Emarginula crassa J. Sowerby, 1812. N. W. Europe, West Indies. Offshore, on rocky bottom; uncommon. Edges thickened. Interior glossy white.

Dagger Emarginula   (0.5″) 1.2 cm
Emarginula sicula Gray, 1825. W. Europe—Mediterranean; Florida—West Indies. Offshore, 4-150 meters, uncommon.

Compressed Emarginula   (0.5″) 1.2 cm
Emarginula tuberculosa Libassi, 1859. Off Azores; Georgia—Brazil. Offshore to 225 meters; uncommon. Syn.: *compressa* Jeffreys; *guernei* Dautzenberg & Fischer.

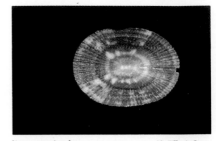

Slit Emarginula   (0.7″) 1.8 cm
Emarginula fissurata Holten, 1802. Philippines. Intertidal, under rocks; uncommon. Syn.: *rubra* Lamarck.

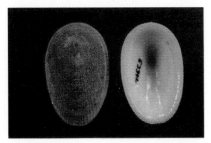

Elegant Tugalia   (0.7″) 1.8 cm
Tugalia elegans Gray, 1843. New Zealand—eastern Australia. Intertidal, on rocks; common. Animal orange. Syn.: *parmophoidea* Q. & G.

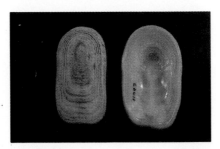

Short Shield Limpet   (2″) 5 cm
Scutus antipodes Montfort, 1810. New Zealand. Intertidal, rocks; common. Front truncated. Syn.: *ambiguus* Dillwyn; *breviculus* Blainville.

Hoof Shield Limpet   (2″) 5 cm
Scutus unguis (L., 1758). Indo-Pacific. Intertidal; common. Surface partially corrugated. Syn.: *corrugatus* Reeve.

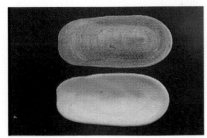

Duck Shield Limpet   (2″) 5 cm
Scutus anatinus (Donovan, 1820). Australia. Intertidal on rocks; common. Animal black. Syn.: *elongatus* Blainville; *australis* Lamarck.

Eight-rayed Emarginula   (1″) 2.5 cm
Hemitoma octoradiata (Gmelin, 1791). Florida—Brazil. Subtidal on rocks; common. Notch weak in front. Animal blue and red.

Emarginate Emarginula   (1″) 2.5 cm
Hemitoma emarginata (Blainville, 1825). Florida—Caribbean. Subtidal on rocks; uncommon. Form *ostheimerae* Abbott, 1958, is illustrated here.

Three-ribbed Emarginula (0.4") 1 cm
Hemitoma tricarinata (Born, 1778). Indo-Pacific. Subtidal on rocks; locally common. Interior green.

Remarkable Limpet (0.7") 1.8 cm
Clypidina notata (L., 1758). Indian Ocean. Intertidal; locally common. Exterior eroded.

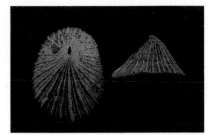

Hooded Puncturella (1") 2.5 cm
Puncturella cucullata (Gould, 1846). Alaska—off Mexico. Subtidal to 35 meters; common. Interior glossy white.

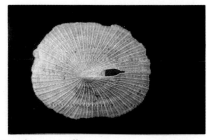

Broad Puncturella (1.5") 4 cm
Puncturella expansa (Dall, 1896). Baja Calif.—Panama; Galapagos. Offshore, deep water. Rare. Holotype illustrated.

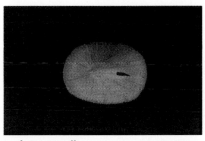

Hawk Puncturella (1") 2.5 cm
Puncturella asturiana (Fischer, 1882). No. Carolina—West Indies; off Spain. Offshore, deep water; rare.

Rough Keyhole Limpet (2") 5 cm
Diodora aspera (Rathke, 1833). Alaska—W. Mexico. Intertidal to 9 meters, on stones and kelp weed; common. Syn.: *murina* Arnold.

Greek Keyhole Limpet (1") 2.5 cm
Diodora graeca (L., 1758). W. Europe; Mediterranean. Intertidal; on rocks; common. Syn.: *apertura* Montagu.

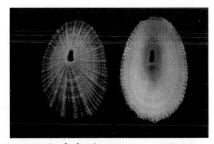

Cayenne Keyhole Limpet (1.5") 3.5 cm
Diodora cayenensis (Lamarck, 1822). Maryland—Brazil; Bermuda. Intertidal to 5 meters, on rocks; common. Syn.: *alternata* Say.

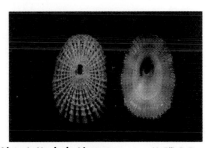

Lister's Keyhole Limpet (1.5") 3.5 cm
Diodora listeri (Orbigny, 1842). Florida—Brazil; Bermuda. Intertidal on rocks, common.

Dwarf Keyhole Limpet (0.6") 1.5 cm
Diodora minuta (Lamarck, 1822). S.E. Florida—Brazil. Subtidal on rocks, 1-25 meters; uncommon.

Say's Keyhole Limpet (0.7") 1.8 cm
Diodora sayi (Dall, 1899). S.E. Florida—Brazil. Offshore from 6-110 meters. Ribs equal in size.

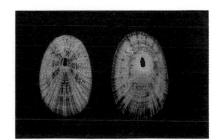

Dyson's Keyhole Limpet (0.7") 1.8 cm
Diodora dysoni (Reeve, 1850). Florida—Brazil; Bermuda. Subtidal on rocks; moderately common. Orifice black inside.

Green Keyhole Limpet (1") 2.5 cm
Diodora viridula (Lamarck, 1822). Lower Florida Keys—Caribbean. Intertidal on rocks; common in Lesser Antilles. Interior bluish gray.

Tanner's Keyhole Limpet (2") 5 cm
Diodora tanneri Verrill, 1883. Eastern U.S.—West Indies. Offshore in deep water; uncommon.

Patagonian Keyhole Limpet (1.2") 3 cm
Diodora patagonica Orbigny, 1847. Trinidad—Argentina. Subtidal on rocks; common.

Unequal Keyhole Limpet (1") 2.5 cm
Diodora inaequalis (Sowerby, 1835). Baja Calif.—Panama; Galapagos. Subtidal on rocks; uncommon.

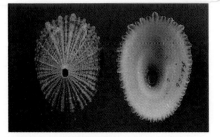

Jukes's Keyhole Limpet (1.5") 4 cm
Diodora jukesii (Reeve, 1849). Southern Australia. Subtidal on rocks; common. 19-23 riblets.

Rüppel's Keyhole Limpet (1") 2.5 cm
Diodora ruepellii (Sowerby, 1834). Red Sea—Cape of Good Hope. Intertidal on rocks; common. Syn.: *elevata* Dunker; *australis* Krauss.

Cup Keyhole Limpet (1") 2 cm
Diodora calyculata (Sowerby, 1823). Knysna—Natal, South Africa. Intertidal, rocks; common. Septum behind inside of hole.

Elizabeth's Keyhole Limpet (1.8") 4.5 cm
Diodora elizabethae (E. A. Smith, 1901). Still Bay—Natal, South Africa. Subtidal on rocks. Moderately common.

Cancellate Fleshy Limpet (1") 2.5 cm
Lucapina suffusa (Reeve, 1850). So. Florida—Brazil; Bermuda. Subtidal on rocks; common. Hole blackish. Syn.: *cancellata* Sowerby.

File Fleshy Limpet (0.3") 7 mm
Lucapinella limatula (Reeve, 1850). No. Carolina—Brazil. Subtidal to 30 meters; common. Mantle covers shell.

Hard-edged Fleshy Limpet (1") 2.5 cm
Lucapinella callomarginata (Dall, 1871) Calif.—Nicaragua. Under intertidal rocks; uncommon. Feeds on sponges.

Great Keyhole Limpet (4") 10 cm
Megathura crenulata (Sowerby, 1825). Central Calif.—Baja Calif. Subtidal on rocks; common. Black-brown mantle covers shell.

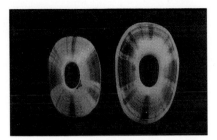

Two-spotted Keyhole Limpet (0.7") 1.8 cm
Megatebennus bimaculatus (Dall, 1871). Alaska—Baja Calif. Under stones at low tide; common. Yellow or red animal covers shell.

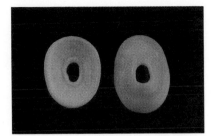

South African Keyhole Limpet (0.6") 1.5 cm
Megatebennus africanus Tomlin, 1926. Still Bay—Natal, South Africa. Intertidal on rocks; common. Surface pitted.

Double-edge Keyhole Limpet (1.5") 4 cm
Fissurellidea aperta (Sowerby, 1825). Table Bay—Natal, South Africa. Intertidal under rocks; common. Edge of shell is double.

Tasmanian Slot Limpet (1") 2.5 cm
Foralepas tasmaniae (Sowerby, 1866). Southern Australia; Tasmania. Subtidal reefs to 30 meters; common. Syn.: *tasmanica* and *roseoradiata* T.-Woods.

Oblong Slot Limpet (1") 2.5 cm
Amblychilepas oblonga (Menke, 1843). Southern Australia. Subtidal to 12 meters; common.

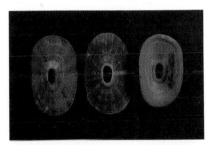

Shield Slot Limpet (0.7") 1.8 cm
Amblychilepas scutella (Gmelin, 1791). South Africa. Intertidal on rocks; common. Ends turned up.

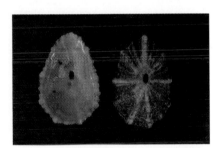

Narrow-end Keyhole Limpet (1") 2.5 cm
Fissurella angusta (Gmelin, 1791). Florida Keys—West Indies. Intertidal rocks; common. End narrowing.

Barbados Keyhole Limpet (1") 2.5 cm
Fissurella barbadensis (Gmelin, 1791). So. Florida—Brazil; Bermuda. Intertidal, oceanic rocks; abundant in West Indies.

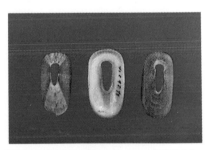

Dilated Slot Limpet (0.5") 1.2 cm
Macroschisma dilatatum (A. Adams, 1851). South Japan. Subtidal to 150 meters; common.

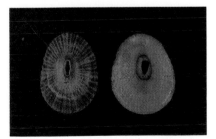

Wobbly Keyhole Limpet (1") 2.5 cm
Fissurella fascicularis Lamarck, 1822. S. E. Florida—West Indies. In potholes in intertidal zone. Locally common. Ends turned up.

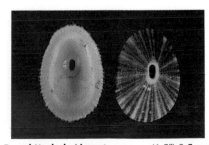

Rayed Keyhole Limpet (1.5") 3.5 cm
Fissurella nimbosa (L., 1758). Puerto Rico—Brazil. Intertidal rocks; common. Keyhole not black-lined.

Rosy Keyhole Limpet (1") 2.5 cm
Fissurella rosea (Gmelin, 1791). S. E. Florida—Brazil. On rocks; uncommon. Callus around hole has pinkish line. Syn.: *radiata* Lamarck.

Knobby Keyhole Limpet   (1.2″) 3 cm
Fissurella nodosa (Born, 1778). West Indies. Intertidal shore rocks; abundant. Interior pure-white. Syn.: *rudis* Röding.

Cloudy Keyhole Limpet   (1″) 2.5 cm
Fissurella nubecula (L., 1758). W. Europe—Mediterranean; Cape Verde Is. Subtidal on rocks; common.

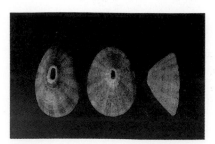

Volcano Keyhole Limpet   (1″) 2.5 cm
Fissurella volcano Reeve, 1849. Calif.—Baja Calif. Intertidal rocks; common. Foot yellow; mantle with red stripes.

Green Panama Keyhole Limpet   (2″) 5 cm
Fissurella virescens Sowerby, 1835. Gulf of Calif.—Peru; Galapagos Is. Intertidal rocks; common.

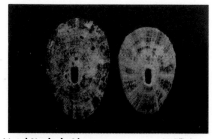

Natal Keyhole Limpet   (1.5″) 3 cm
Fissurella natalensis Krauss, 1848. South Africa—Mozambique. Intertidal rocks; common.

Black Keyhole Limpet   (4″) 10 cm
Fissurella nigra Lesson, 1830. Peru—Chile. Intertidal rocks; common. Interior white. Syn.: *latemarginata* Sowerby, *grandis* Sowerby.

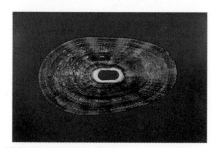

Rising Sun Keyhole Limpet   (2.5″) 6 cm
Fissurella oriens Sowerby, 1835. Chile to Magellan Straits. Subtidal rocks to 15 meters; common.

Grand Keyhole Limpet   (4″) 10 cm
Fissurella maxima Sowerby, 1835. Peru—Chile. Subtidal rocky reefs; common. Interior white, with purple margin.

Thick Keyhole Limpet   (3″) 8 cm
Fissurella crassa Lamarck, 1822. Peru—Chile. On intertidal rocks; common. Syn.: *clupeiformis* Sowerby.

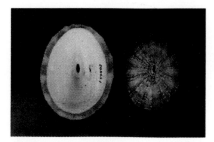

Costate Keyhole Limpet   (2.6″) 7 cm
Fissurella costata Lesson, 1830. Peru—Chile. On intertidal rocks among red algae. Common. Syn.: *rudis* Deshayes; *chilensis* Sowerby.

Painted Keyhole Limpet   (4″) 10 cm
Fissurella picta (Gmelin, 1791). Ecuador—Magellan Straits. Intertidal rocks; common. Interior white. Syn.: *darwini* Reeve, 1845.

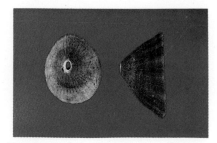

Peruvian Keyhole Limpet   (1″) 2.5 cm
Fissurella peruviana Lamarck, 1822. Peru—Chile. On intertidal rocks; common. Interior white with red margin.

SUPERFAMILY PATELLACEA
TRUE LIMPETS
FAMILY PATELLIDAE

Limpetlike, flat to conical snails, without a hole at the apex of the shell. The family Patellidae contains shore-rock dwellers, such as *Patella*, *Cellana* and *Nacella*. Gill cordon encircles inner mantle edge. Family Acmaeidae has one gill plume at front end. All are vegetarians. Many wander about the rocks at night, but return to their original site at dawn. Many species.

Common European Limpet (2.5") 6 cm
Patella vulgata L., 1758. Norway to Spain. Intertidal on rocks; abundant. Very variable. Many synonyms.

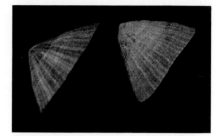

Common European Limpet (2.5") 6 cm
Patella vulgata L., 1758. Side views of a low-spired form (left) and a high-spired form (right). Edible.

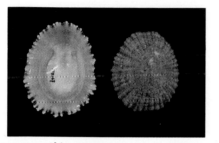

European China Limpet (2") 5 cm
Patella aspera Röding, 1798. British Isles and France. Intertidal on rocks; common. Ribs sharper than *vulgata*. Syn.: *aspera* Lamarck.

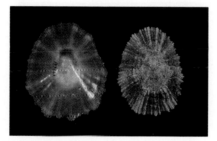

Rayed Mediterranean Limpet (2") 5 cm
Patella caerulea L., 1758. Mediterranean to Azores. Intertidal; abundant. Interior with 7-9 bluish rays. Syn.: *tarentina* Lamarck.

Ribbed Mediterranean Limpet (2.5") 6 cm
Patella ferruginea Gmelin, 1791. Mediterranean. Intertidal rocks; common. Margin corrugated. Syn.: *lamarckii* Payraudeau.

Safian Limpet (3") 7 cm
Patella safiana Lamarck, 1819. Algeria to West Africa. Intertidal on rocks, common. Internal scar elongate. Syn.: *kraussii* Dunker.

Giant Mexican Limpet (14") 35 cm
Patella mexicana Broderip & Sowerby, 1829. Gulf of Calif. to Peru. Subtidal on rocks; common. Syn.: *gigantea* Lesson; *maxima* Orbigny.

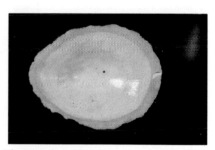

Giant Mexican Limpet (14") 35 cm
Patella mexicana Broderip & Sowerby. Internal view. Usual length about (6") 15 cm. Largest known limpet.

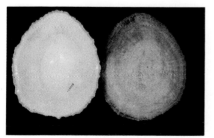

Kermadec Limpet (6") 15 cm
Patella kermadecensis Pilsbry, 1894. Kermadec Is., off New Zealand. Subtidal; locally common. Syn.: *pilsbryi* Brazier.

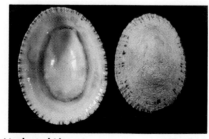

Neglected Limpet (4") 10 cm
Patella laticostata Blainville, 1825. S. W. Australia. Intertidal rocks; common. Syn.: *neglecta* Gray.

Chapman's Limpet (0.7") 1.8 cm
Patella chapmani Tenison-Woods, 1876. Southern Australia; Tasmania. Intertidal rocks; common. Syn.: *octoradiata* Hutton; *alba* T.-Woods.

Star-shaped Limpet   (1″) 2.5 cm
Patella flexuosa Quoy & Gaimard, 1834.
Malaya to Polynesia. Intertidal on coral
stones; common. Syn.: *stellaeformis*
Reeve, *paumotensis* Gould.

Spoon Limpet   (2.5″) 6 cm
Patella cochlear Born, 1778. Port Nolloth—
Natal, South Africa. Intertidal rocks; abun-
dant.

South African Variable Limpet   (1.5″) 4 cm
Patella concolor Krauss, 1848. Port Elizabeth—Natal, South Africa. Intertidal
shore; common. Syn.: *variabilis* Krauss
(not Röding).

South African Variable Limpet   (1.5″) 4 cm
Patella concolor Krauss, 1848. South Africa.
Color form *polygramma* Tomlin, 1931, illus-
trated here.

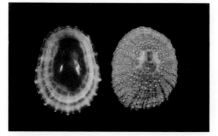

Granular Limpet   (2.5″) 6 cm
Patella granularis L., 1758. All South Africa.
Shore rocks; abundant. Syn.: *morbida*
Reeve; *natalensis* Krauss.

Long-ribbed Limpet   (2.5″) 6 cm
Patella longicosta Lamarck, 1819. Cape to
Natal, South Africa. Shore rocks; common.
Syn.: *decemcostata* E. A. Smith.

Cinnabar Limpet   (2″) 5 cm
Patella miniata Born, 1778. Port Nolloth—
Natal, South Africa. Intertidal shore; com-
mon. Bleaches to bright pink. Syn.: *pulchra*
Lightfoot.

South African Eye Limpet   (4″) 10 cm
Patella oculus Born, 1778. West South Africa. Flattish; 5 prongs at back end. Interior
brown. Syn.: *scutellaris* Lamarck. Common.

Tabular Limpet   (5″) 13 cm
Patella tabularis Krauss, 1848. South Africa.
Shore rocks; common. Largest limpet in
Africa. Syn.: *patriarcha* Pilsbry.

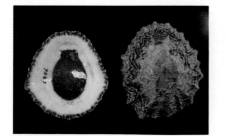

Sandpaper Limpet   (3″) 7 cm
Patella granatina L., 1758. Port Nolloth—
False Bay, South Africa. Shore rocks; cold
water; common. Thin-shelled.

Barbara Limpet   (3″) 8 cm
Patella barbara L., 1758. All South Africa.
Intertidal rocks; common. Variable in
height and color. Syn.: *spinifera* Lamarck.

Blue-rayed Limpet   (1″) 2.5 cm
Helcion pellucidus (L., 1758). Norway—
Portugal. Offshore to 8 meters on brown
seaweeds; common. Syn.: *laevis* Pennant.

Common Turtle Limpet (3") 7 cm
Cellana testudinaria (L., 1758). Malaya—S. W. Pacific. Subtidal on blackish rocks; abundant. Syn.: *insignis* Dunker; *rumphii* Blainville.

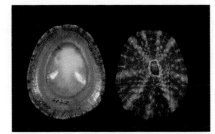

Indo-Pacific Limpet (1") 2.5 cm
Cellana radiata (Born, 1778). East Africa—eastern Polynesia—Japan. Variable in color. Margin finely toothed. Syn.: *rota* Gmelin.

Denticulate Limpet (2.5") 6 cm
Cellana denticulata (Martyn, 1784). No. New Zealand. Rocky shores; abundant. Syn.: *imbricata* Reeve; *reevei* Hutton.

Striped Limpet (2.5") 6 cm
Cellana strigilis (Hombron & Jacquinot, 1841). So. New Zealand. Rocky shores; abundant. Several subspecies; *redimiculum* Reeve illus. here.

Common New Zealand Limpet (1.5") 4 cm
Cellana radians (Gmelin, 1791). No. New Zealand. Intertidal rocks. Common.

Bonin Island Limpet (3") 7 cm
Cellana mazatlandica (Sowerby, 1839). Intertidal rocks; abundant. Syn.: *boninensis* Pilsbry; *nigrisquamata* Reeve.

Japanese Grata Limpet (1.5") 4 cm
Cellana grata (Gould, 1859). Japan and Korea. Rocky shores; abundant. Syn.: *stearnsii* Pilsbry; *eucosmius* Pilsbry, 1895, not 1891.

Hawaiian Limpet; Opihi (1.5") 3 cm
Cellana exarata (Reeve, 1854). Hawaiian Islands. Intertidal rocks; locally common. Eaten in Hawaii.

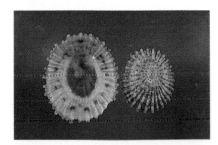

Ariel Limpet (2") 5 cm
Cellana tramoserica (Holten, 1802). Southern and east Australia; Tasmania. Intertidal rock shores; abundant. Syn.: *ariel* Iredale; *sontica* Iredale.

Patagonian Copper Limpet (2") 5 cm
Nacella deaurata (Gmelin, 1791). Patagonia; Falkland Is. Intertidal to offshore on seaweed; common. Syn.: *aenea* Martyn. In subgenus *Patinigera*.

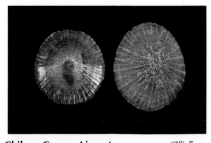

Chilean Copper Limpet (2") 5 cm
Nacella clypeater (Lesson, 1831). Chile. Subtidal on seaweeds; common. Thin-shelled.

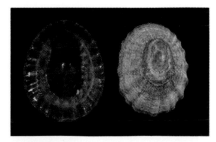

Magellanic Copper Limpet (2") 5 cm
Nacella magellanica (Gmelin, 1791). Straits of Magellan; Falkland Is. Intertidal to offshore on seaweeds; abundant. Syn.: *metallica* Roch. & Mab.

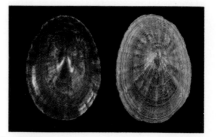

South Polar Limpet (2") 5 cm
Nacella concinna (Strebel, 1908). Islands around Antarctica. Intertidal to 100 meters; on large seaweeds; common. Syn.: *polaris* Homb. & Jacq. (not Röding).

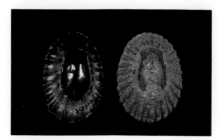

Tierra del Fuego Limpet (2") 5 cm
Nacella fuegiensis (Reeve, 1855). Tierra del Fuego; Falkland Is., So. Georgia Is. Subtidal, common. Thin-shelled.

TRUE LIMPETS
FAMILY ACMAEIDAE

Many dozens of species occur in great numbers on rocks throughout the world, especially on the Pacific coast of North America. The muscle scar on the inner side is horseshoe-shaped and open in front. One gill present. The shape of the shell will sometimes vary depending upon the type of habitat. Most live on intertidal rocks, but often are found on other snail shells and on seaweeds. The foot is edible. There is no operculum.

Half-white Limpet (1") 2.5 cm
Scurria mesoleuca (Menke, 1851). West Mexico—Ecuador. Intertidal on rocks; common. Syn.: *diaphana* Reeve; *vespertina* Reeve.

Zebra Limpet (2") 5 cm
Scurria zebrina (Lesson, 1831). Chile. Intertidal rocks; common. 12 radiating ribs. Syn.: *concepcionensis* Lesson.

Green Chilean Limpet (2.5") 6 cm
Scurria viridula (Lamarck, 1819). Peru and Chile. On chitons and subtidal rocks; common. Syn.: *petrei* Orbigny.

Schrenck's Limpet (1") 2.5 cm
Notoacmea schrenckii (Lischke, 1868). Japan, Korea, north China. Intertidal on rocks; abundant.

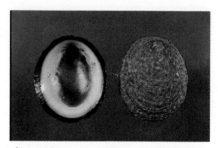

Felt-cap Limpet (1") 2.5 cm
Notoacmea pileopsis (Quoy & Gaimard, 1834). New Zealand. Intertidal on rocks; common. Syn.: *cellanoides* Oliver; *sturnus* Homb. & Jacquinot.

Atlantic Plate Limpet (1") 2.5 cm
Collisella testudinalis (Müller, 1776). Arctic Seas—New York; Alaska—Oregon. Intertidal rock pools; common. Rarely elongate (on eelgrass).

Black-ribbed Limpet (0.6") 1.5 cm
Collisella leucopleura (Gmelin, 1791). Florida Keys—West Indies. Subtidal on rocks or underside of whelks; common. Syn.: *jamaicensis* Gmelin.

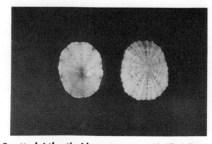

Spotted Atlantic Limpet (0.6") 1.5 cm
Collisella antillarum (Sowerby, 1831). Florida Keys (rare)—West Indies (common). Intertidal shore rocks. Elongate, pink form (on turtle grass).

Abrolhos Island Limpet (0.8") 2 cm
Collisella abrolhosensis (Petuch, 1979). Off east coast of Brazil. On subtidal rocks; locally common. Paratypes illustrated.

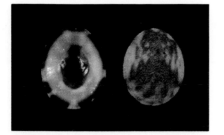

California File Limpet (1″) 2.5 cm
Collisella limatula (Carpenter, 1864). Puget Sound, Wash.—Baja Calif. Intertidal rocks; common. Radial rows of minute beads. Interior edge solid brown band.

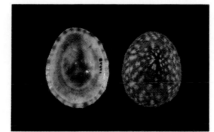

California Shield Limpet (1″) 2.5 cm
Collisella pelta (Rathke, 1833). Alaska—Baja Calif. Intertidal rocks; abundant. 25 weak riblets. Interior edge checkered in black & cream.

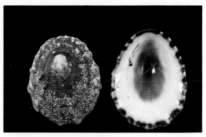

California Finger Limpet (1.5″) 3 cm
Collisella digitalis (Rathke, 1833). Alaska—West Mexico. Wave-dashed rocks; abundant. 15-25 coarse ribs. Syn.: *textilis* Gould.

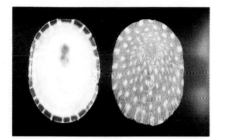

Dall's Limpet (1.5″) 3 cm
Collisella dalliana (Pilsbry, 1891). Gulf of California. On rocks at mid-tide zone. Uncommon.

California Rough Limpet (1.5″) 4 cm
Collisella scabra (Gould, 1846). Southern Oregon—Baja Calif. Upper tide level on flat rocks; abundant. Interior center coarse and dull.

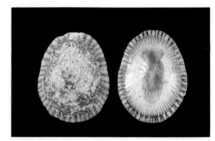

Antillean Limpet (1″) 2.5 cm
Collisella antillarum (Sowerby, 1831). West Indies (rarely Florida Keys). Intertidal rocks; common. Syn.: *candeana* Orbigny.

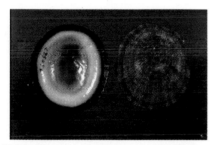

Striate Limpet (1.5″) 4 cm
Collisella striata (Quoy & Gaimard, 1834). East Indies; Philippines. Intertidal on rocks. Syn.: *borneensis* Reeve.

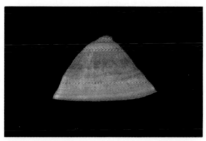

White-cap Limpet (1″) 2.5 cm
Acmaea mitra Rathke, 1833. Alaska—Baja Calif. Subtidal on rocks; common. Sometimes covered with knobby growths.

Giant Owl Limpet (3.5″) 9 cm
Lottia gigantea (Sowerby, 1834). Calif.—Baja Calif. On rocks near high-tide line; very common. Usually solid brown-gray, rarely maculated (as shown here).

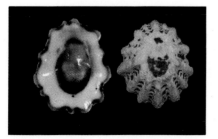

High-ribbed Limpet (1″) 2.5 cm
Patelloida alticostata (Angas, 1865). Southern Australia; Tasmania. Intertidal rocks; abundant. Feeds on sea lettuce, *Ulva*.

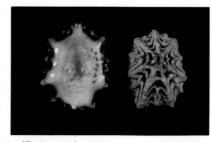

Pacific Sugar Limpet (1.5″) 4 cm
Patelloida saccharina (L., 1758). South Western Pacific—Melanesia. Intertidal rocks; abundant. Syn.: *stellaris* Quoy & Gaimard.

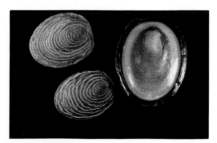

Blue-ringed Limpet (0.8″) 2 cm
Atalacmea fragilis (Sowerby, 1823). New Zealand. Under smooth rocks, intertidal; moderately common. Used in shellcraft.

TOP-SHELLS
FAMILY TROCHIDAE

This is a very large worldwide family with numerous genera and hundreds of species. Most are top-shaped, have an iridescent interior and a round, many-whorled, horny operculum. They occur from tidal rock pools to the deepest portions of the oceans. Most feed on seaweeds but many eat bryozoans and sponges.

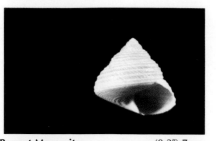

Puppet Margarite   (0.3") 7 mm
Margarites pupillus (Gould, 1849). Alaska—Calif. Subtidal rocks to 30 m; common. Umbilicus minute.

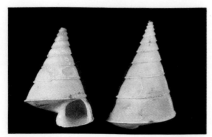

Tower of Babel Top   (2") 5 cm
Basilissa babelica Dall, 1907. Off eastern coast of Japan; deep water. Rare. Shell on left is the holotype.

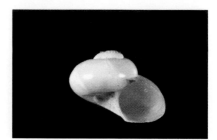

Glistening Margarite   (0.6") 1.5 cm
Bathymophila nitens (Dall, 1881). Off Baja Calif., deep water, 900 m. Rare. Holotype specimen.

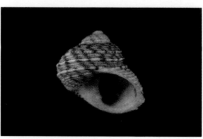

Four-keeled Margarite   (0.5") 1.2 cm
Euchelus quadricarinatus (Holten, 1802). Indo-Pacific. Under subtidal rocks; common. Syn.: *tricarinatus* Lamarck.

Roughened Margarite   (0.7") 1.8 cm
Euchelus aspersus (Philippi, 1846). So. Australia—Tasmania. Reefs below low tide to 300 m; common. Syn.: *baccatus* Menke.

Blackish Margarite   (0.6") 1.5 cm
Euchelus atratus (Gmelin, 1791). Indo-Pacific. Intertidal, under rocks; common. Syn.: *canaliculatus* Lamarck.

Imbricate Margarite   (1.2") 3 cm
Granata imbricata (Lamarck, 1816). So. Australia; on rocky reefs, subtidal. Common.

Mysticus Margarite   (0.3") 7 mm
Hybochelus mysticus (Pilsbry, 1889). S. W. Pacific. Subtidal, under rocks. Moderately common.

Subangular Margarite   (0.5") 1.2 cm
Minolia subangulata Kuroda and Habe, 1952. Japan. Sandy bottom, 50-200 m; common. Syn.: *angulata* Yokoyama.

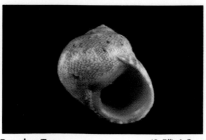

Paradox Top   (0.5") 1.2 cm
Chrysostoma paradoxum (Born, 1778). Indo-Pacific. Intertidal rocks; abundant. Shell thick, surface smooth.

West Indian Top   (3") 7 cm
Cittarium pica (L., 1758). Caribbean. Subtidal rocks near open ocean; common. Horny operculum greenish black. *Livona* is a synonym. Used in soups.

Changing Margarite (1.5") 4 cm
Bathybembix aeola (Watson, 1879). Japan and off east China. Deep water; uncommon.

Baird's Margarite (1.5") 4 cm
Bathybembix bairdii (Dall, 1889). Alaska—Chile. Deep water; 10 to 1200 m. Uncommon.

Humboldt's Margarite
(1.5") 4 cm
Bathybembix humboldti Rehder, 1971. Off Chile. Deep water. Rare.

Silvery Margarite (1.5") 4 cm
Bathybembix argenteonitens (Lischke, 1872). Japan and east China. Sandy bottom, 50-400 m; common.

Crump's Margarite (1.2") 3 cm
Bathybembix crumpii (Pilsbry, 1893). South half of Japan. Sandy bottom, 50-400 m. Uncommon.

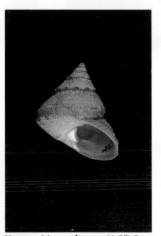

Korean Margarite (1.2") 3 cm
Turcica coreensis Pease, 1860. Japan; Korea, east China. Sandy bottom; 50-300 m. Uncommon.

Giant Imperial Margarite (2")
5 cm Lischkeia imperialis (Dall, 1881). Off Florida and Caribbean. Deep water, 60-360 m. Rare. Syn.: *deichmannae* Bayer.

Smooth Silver Margarite
(2") 5 cm
Bathybembix convexiusculus (Yokoyama, 1920). Japan. Deep water; uncommon.

Shinagawen Top (1.5") 4 cm
Calliostoma shinagawensis Tokunaga, 1902. Japan; east China. Deep water. Moderately common.

Japan Jewel Top (0.7") 1.8 cm
Cantharidus japonicus (A. Adams, 1853). Southern Japan. Subtidal to 20 m; on seaweeds; common. Syn.: *hilaris* Lischke.

Rambur's Jewel Top (0.3") 7 mm
Prothalotia ramburi (Crosse, 1864). South Australia. Intertidal on weeds. Common.

Dusky Jewel Top (0.3") 7 mm
Cantharidus infuscatus (Gould, 1861). Japan; offshore on gravel; 5-30 m. Common.

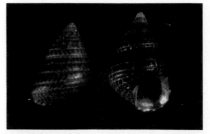

Beautiful Jewel Top   (0.6″) 1.5 cm
Prothalotia pulcherrima (Wood, 1828). South Australia. Intertidal weeds; common. Syn.: *preissii* Menke; *puella* Philippi; *mariae* Tenison-Woods.

Otto's Spiny Margarite   (0.6″) 1.5 cm
Calliotropis ottoi (Philippi, 1844). Nova Scotia to No. Carolina. Offshore; 100-200 m; common. Syn.: *regalis* Verrill, holotype illustrated.

Albatross Margarite   (0.7″) 1.8 cm
Calliotropis diomediae (Verrill, 1880). Off Massachusetts. Deep water, 3,000 m. Rare.

CALLIOSTOMA TOPS
Genus *Calliostoma*

These beautiful top-shells are common around the world, and because of their curious shapes have been placed in various subgenera or related genera, such as *Maurea*, *Tristichotrochus* and *Ziziphinus*. There are several hundred species. Operculum horny and circular.

European Painted Top   (1″) 2.5 cm
Calliostoma zizyphinus (L., 1758). West Europe—Azores. Intertidal; on rocks; common. Syn.: *conuloide* Lamarck.

Gualteri's Top   (0.6″) 1.5 cm
Calliostoma gualterianum (Philippi, 1848). Mediterranean. Intertidal on weeds among rocks; common.

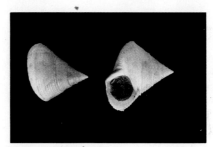

European Granular Top   (1.2″) 3 cm
Calliostoma granulatum (Born, 1778). Mediterranean to Canary Is. Offshore, 26-240 m. Common. Syn.: *papillosum* da Costa; *fragilis* Pulteney.

Ringed Top   (1.2″) 3 cm
Calliostoma annulatum (Lightfoot, 1786). Alaska to So. California. Offshore, 1-20 m. Common. Nucleus pink.

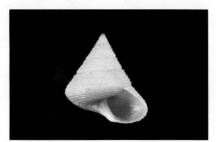

Variable Top   (1″) 2.5 cm
Calliostoma variegatum Carpenter, 1864. Alaska to So. California. Offshore, 30-800 m; Uncommon.

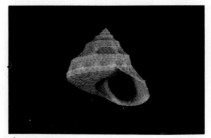

Palmer's Top   (1″) 2.5 cm
Calliostoma palmeri Dall, 1871. Gulf of California. Intertidal to 45 m; uncommon.

Glorious Top   (1″) 2.5 cm
Calliostoma gloriosum Dall, 1871. So. California. Subtidal to 50 m, in kelp weeds. Common. Nucleus white.

Channeled Top   (1.5″) 3.5 cm
Calliostoma canaliculata (Lightfoot, 1786). Offshore on floating kelp weeds; common. Syn.: *doliarium* Holten.

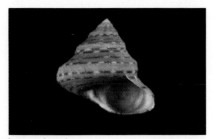

Three-colored Top (0.7") 1.8 cm
Calliostoma tricolor Gabb, 1865. So. Calif. to Baja California. Offshore, 16-70 m; common. Sometimes axially streaked.

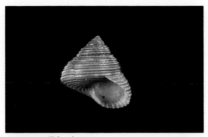

Western Ribbed Top (1") 2.5 cm
Calliostoma ligatum (Gould, 1849). Alaska to So. California. Intertidal to subtidal on rocks; common. Syn.: *costatum* Martyn.

Western Gem Top (0.7") 1.8 cm
Calliostoma gemmulatum Carpenter, 1864. California and Gulf of Calif. Intertidal, on rocks and wharf pilings; common. Syn.: *formosum* Carpenter.

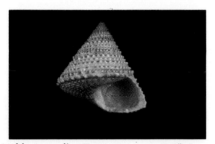

Noble Australian Top (0.8") 2 cm
Calliostoma nobilis (Philippi, 1848). West and No. Australia. Offshore to 50 m; uncommon. Syn.: *rubiginosus* Valenciennes.

Australian Necklace Top (0.5") 1.2 cm
Calliostoma monile (Reeve, 1863). West Australia. Subtidal to 20 m; moderately common. Usually on blue sponges.

Hedley's Top (1") 2.5 cm
Calliostoma hedleyi Pritchard and Gatliff, 1902. So. Australia and Tasmania. Subtidal to 14 m. Moderately common.

Keeled Australian Top (1.5") 4 cm
Calliostoma ciliare (Menke, 1843). West Australia. Offshore; uncommon.

Jujube Top (1") 2.5 cm
Calliostoma jujubinum (Gmelin, 1791). No. Carolina to Brazil. Under rocks, offshore from 1 to 30 m; common locally. Syn.: *tampaense* Conrad.

Adele's Top (0.7") 1.8 cm
Calliostoma adelae Schwengel, 1951. Southeast Florida. In shallow water grass beds, 2 to 7 m. Locally common.

Sculptured Top (0.7") 1.8 cm
Calliostoma euglyptum (A. Adams, 1854). No. Carolina to east Mexico. Subtidal to 64 m, among rocks; moderately common.

Baird's Top (1.3") 3 cm
Calliostoma bairdii Verrill and Smith, 1880. Massachusetts to Florida. Offshore 80 to 500 m. Uncommon. Holotype illustrated.

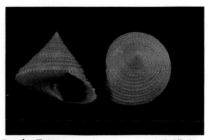

Psyche Top (0.8") 2 cm
Calliostoma bairdii psyche Dall, 1889. No. Carolina to Key West, Florida. Offshore, 60 to 260 m. Moderately common.

Rosewater's Top   (1.3") 3 cm
Calliostoma bairdii rosewateri Clench and Turner, 1960. Lesser Antilles to Colombia. Deep water, 300 to 400 m. Rare. Paratypes illustrated.

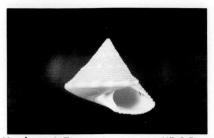

Henderson's Top   (1") 2.5 cm
Calliostoma bairdii hendersoni Dall, 1927. Florida Keys, 3 to 20 m. Among rubble. Uncommon. Holotype illustrated.

Dawn Top   (2") 5 cm
Calliostoma aurora Dall, 1888. Off the Lesser Antilles from 280 to 1,140 m. Rare. Holotype illustrated.

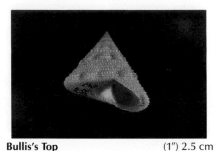

Bullis's Top   (1") 2.5 cm
Calliostoma bullisi Clench and Turner, 1960. Off eastern Brazil in 70 m. Rare. Paratype illustrated.

Hassler's Top   (1.2") 3 cm
Calliostoma hassler Clench and Aguayo, 1939. East coast of Brazil. Offshore in 70 m; uncommon to rare. Holotype illustrated.

Panama Rainbow Top   (0.2") 5 mm
Calliostoma iridium Dall, 1896. Gulf of Panama in 360 to 460 m; uncommon. Paratype illustrated.

Von Ihering's Top   (1.5") 3.5 cm
Calliostoma militare von Ihering, 1907. Argentina. Dredged just offshore. Rare. Syn.: *amazonica* Finlay; *iheringi* Dall, holotype illus.

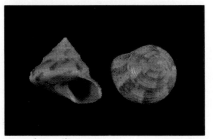

Spotted Brazilian Top   (0.8") 2 cm
Calliostoma adspersum (Philippi, 1851). So. Brazil. Subtidal; uncommon. Syn.: *depictum* Dall.

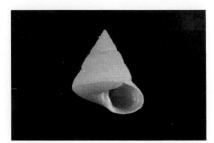

Carcelles's Top   (0.7") 1.8 cm
Calliostoma carcellesi Clench and Aguayo, 1940. Argentina. Offshore in 60 m. Rare. Holotype illustrated.

Bigelow's Top   (1") 2.5 cm
Calliostoma bigelowi Clench and Aguayo, 1938. Cuba, offshore from 300 to 460 m. Rare collector's item. Holotype illus.

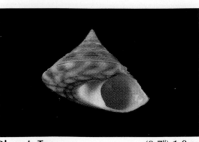

Olsson's Top   (0.7") 1.8 cm
Calliostoma olssoni Bayer, 1971. Off St. Vincent, West Indies. 230 m. Very rare. Holotype illustrated.

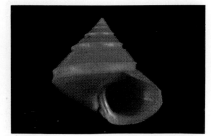

Atlantis Top   (1.5") 3.5 cm
Calliostoma atlantis Clench and Aguayo, 1940. Off Pinar del Rio, Cuba, in 660 m. Known only from this holotype specimen.

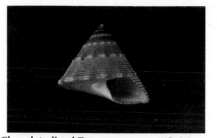

Chocolate-lined Top (1") 2.5 cm
Calliostoma javanicum (Gmelin, 1791). So. Florida Keys and West Indies. On reefs, 1 to 35 m. Uncommon. Syn.: *zonamestum* A. Adams.

Springer's Top (1.4") 3 cm
Calliostoma springeri Clench and Turner, 1960. Gulf of Mexico, off Mississippi in 520 m. Rare. Wide umbilicus. Holotype illustrated.

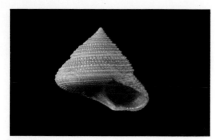

Say's Top (1.5") 3.5 cm
Calliostoma sayanum Dall, 1889. No. Carolina to So. Florida. Offshore, 130 to 400 m. Uncommon. Holotype illustrated.

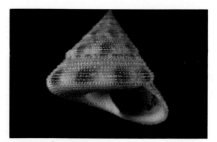

Oregon Atlantic Top (0.8") 2 cm
Calliostoma oregon Clench and Turner, 1960. Gulf of Mexico in 232 to 380 m. Uncommon. Holotype illustrated.

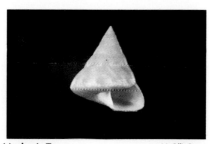

Marion's Top (1.2") 3 cm
Calliostoma marionae Dall, 1906. Off Florida to Mexico. Offshore from 46 to 180 m. Uncommon. Holotype illustrated.

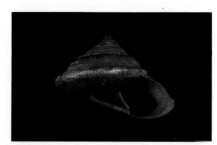

Tejedor Top (1") 2.5 cm
Calliostoma tejedori Aguayo, 1949. Off north Cuba. Known only from this holotype. Nuclear whorls reticulated.

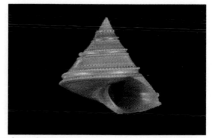

Schroeder's Top (1.3") 3 cm
Calliostoma schroederi Clench and Aguayo, 1938. Bahamas and Cuba, in 320 to 460 m. Paratype illustrated.

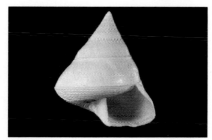

Chilean Top (1.5") 3.5 cm
Calliostoma chilena Rehder, 1971. Off Valparaiso, Chile, in 200 m. Rare. Holotype illustrated.

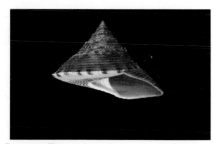

Formosa Top (2.4") 5.5 cm
Calliostoma formosense E. A. Smith, 1907. Japan to Taiwan. Deep water to 300 m. Common.

Nephelo Top (1") 2.5 cm
Calliostoma nepheloide Dall, 1913. West Mexico to Panama. Offshore from 146 to 256 m. Uncommon.

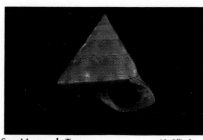

Sea Monarch Top (1.6") 4 cm
Calliostoma haliarchus (Melvill, 1889). Japan. Sandy bottom, 50 to 200 m. Fairly common.

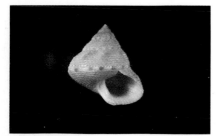

Dall's Unicum Top (0.9") 2.2 cm
Calliostoma unicum (Dunker, 1860). Japan, Korea, China. Intertidal gravels to 150 m. This is form *affinis* Dall (holotype illus.). Uncommon.

Soyo's Top   (0.5″) 1.2 cm
Calliostoma soyoae Ikebe, 1942. So. Japan; sandy bottom, 10-80 m; uncommon.

Panama Spiny Margarite   (1.3″) 3 cm
Turcica panamensis Olsson, 1971. Gulf of Panama. Offshore, 55 to 84 m. Rare.

Prickly Japanese Top   (0.9″) 2.2 cm
Calliostoma aculeatum (Sowerby, 1912). So. Japan; sandy bottom, 20-200 m; common. Syn.: *spinigera* Yokoyama.

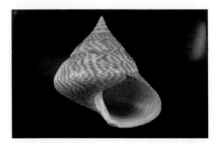

Tiger Maurea   (2.4″) 6 cm
Maurea tigris (Martyn, 1784). New Zealand. Subtidal among boulders. Uncommon. Syn.: *tigris* Gmelin.

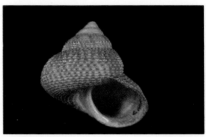

Punctate Maurea   (1.5″) 4 cm
Maurea punctulata (Martyn, 1784). New Zealand. Intertidal to offshore among boulders. Uncommon.

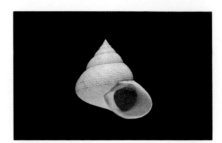

Multibeaded Maurea   (1.5″) 4 cm
Maurea multigemmata (Powell, 1952). Southern New Zealand. Offshore; rare.

Black's Maurea   (2.5″) 6 cm
Maurea blacki (Powell, 1950). Southern New Zealand. Shallow water; uncommon.

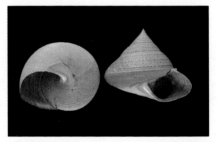

Pellucid Maurea   (2″) 5 cm
Maurea pellucida (Valenciennes, 1846). Northern New Zealand. Subtidal, rocky bottom. Not uncommon. Has several forms.

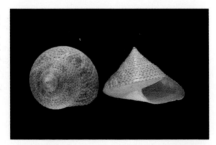

Select Maurea   (2″) 5 cm
Maurea selecta (Dillwyn, 1817). Northern and Central New Zealand. Sandy ocean beaches. Moderately common.

Superb Gaza   (1.2″) 3 cm
Gaza superba (Dall, 1881). Northern Gulf of Mexico and West Indies. Deep water, over 100 m. Locally common. Rare in collections.

Rathbun's Gaza   (1.2″) 3 cm
Gaza rathbuni Dall, 1890. Galapagos Islands. 717 to 915 m. Rare. Holotype illustrated.

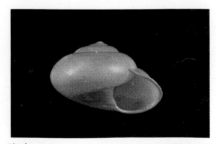

Fischer's Gaza   (1″) 2.5 cm
Gaza fischeri Dall, 1889. Off Cuba and the Lesser Antilles. Deep water to 846 m. Rare. Holotype illustrated.

Banded Bankivia (0.6") 1.5 cm
Bankivia fasciata (Menke, 1830). Western to S. E. Australia; Tasmania. Abundant on weeds in shallow waters. Smooth; variable colors.

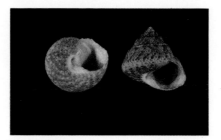

Whitish Gibbula (0.8") 2 cm
Gibbula albida (Gmelin, 1791). Mediterranean. Subtidal among rocks; common. Base with 6 to 8 threads. Syn.: *bornii* Cantraine.

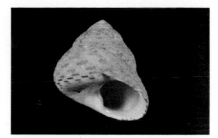

Turbinate Monodont (1.2") 3 cm
Monodonta turbinata (Born, 1778). Portugal and Mediterranean. Intertidal among rocks; common. Syn.: *tessellata* Born, not Gmelin.

Lined Monodont (1") 2.5 cm
Monodonta lineata (da Costa, 1778). Gt. Britain to Portugal. Intertidal among rocks; common. Syn.: *crassa* Montagu.

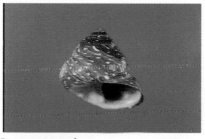

Punctate Monodont (0.8") 2 cm
Monodonta punctulata (Lamarck, 1822). West Africa. Intertidal among rocks and weeds; common. No umbilicus. Syn.: *osilin* Deshayes.

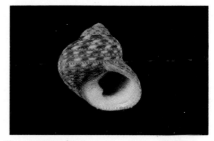

Dama Monodont (0.8") 2 cm
Monodonta dama (Philippi, 1848). Red Sea; Arabia. Subtidal on rocks; common. Curved groove on lower inner lip.

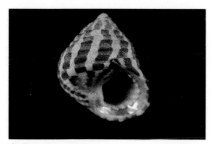

Obtuse Monodont (1.2") 3 cm
Austrocochlea obtusa (Dillwyn, 1817). Northern half of Australia. Intertidal rocks; common.

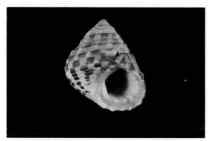

Constricted Monodont (1.2") 3 cm
Austrocochlea constricta (Lamarck, 1822). South Australia; Tasmania. Intertidal rocks; common. 5 or 6 spiral ribs.

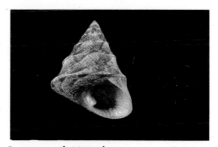

Green-mouth Monodont (1") 2.5 cm
Thalotia chlorostoma (Menke, 1843). South and Western Australia. Subtidal to 39 m; common. Some forms have rounded whorls.

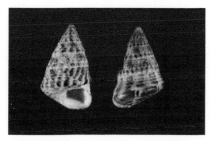

Striate Jujubine (0.5") 1.2 cm
Jujubinus striatus (L., 1758). Azores to Mediterranean. Intertidal among rocks; common.

Black Monodont (1") 2.5 cm
Diloma nigerrima (Gmelin, 1791). New Zealand, cold water. Intertidal on black rocks; common. Syn.: *digna* Finlay.

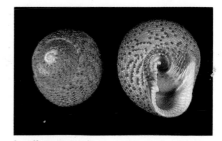

Flagellate Monodont (1") 2.5 cm
Clanculus flagellatus (Philippi, 1848). South Australia; Tasmania. Intertidal; common.

Speckled Monodont   (1″) 2.5 cm
Diloma concamerata (Wood, 1828). South-ern Australia; Tasmania. Abundant on in-tertidal reefs. Syn.: *striolatus* Q. & G.

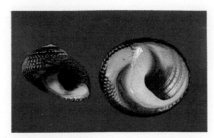

Scorched Monodont   (1″) 2.5 cm
Melagraphia aethiops (Gmelin, 1791). New Zealand. Intertidal rocks; abundant.

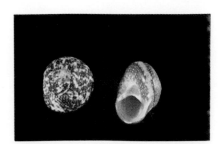

Smooth Atlantic Tegula   (0.7″) 1.8 cm
Tegula fasciata (Born, 1778). South Florida to Brazil. Subtidal under rocks; common. Umbilicate. Syn.: *maculostriata* C. B. Ad-ams.

Silver-mouthed Monodont   (2.5″) 6 cm
Chlorostoma argyrostomum (Gmelin, 1791). Japan. Intertidal among rocks; abun-dant. Green callus over base.

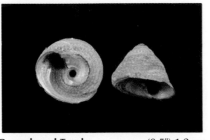

Green-based Tegula   (0.5″) 1.2 cm
Tegula excavata (Lamarck, 1822). Florida Keys and West Indies. Subtidal under rocks; abundant locally.

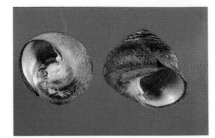

California Black Tegula   (1.2″) 3 cm
Tegula funebralis (A. Adams, 1855). West Canada to Baja California. Intertidal on rocks; common.

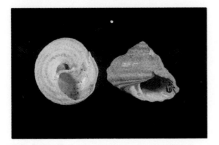

Gilded Tegula   (1″) 2.5 cm
Tegula aureotincta Forbes, 1850. Southern California to W. Mexico. Intertidal on rocks; moderately common.

Serpent-tongue Tegula   (1.6″) 4 cm
Tegula pellisserpentis (Wood, 1828). El Sal-vador to W. Colombia. Intertidal on boul-ders; moderately common.

Rugose Monodont   (1.5″) 3.5 cm
Chlorostoma rugosum (A. Adams, 1853). Throughout Gulf of California. On rocks, upper intertidal zone; common.

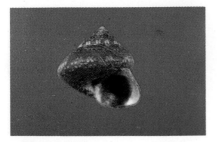

Umbilical Gibbula   (0.6″) 1.5 cm
Gibbula umbilicalis (da Costa, 1778). N. W. Europe and Mediterranean. Intertidal on rocks; moderately common.

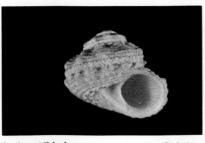

Sloping Gibbula   (1″) 2.4 cm
Gibbula declivis (Forskal, 1775). Red Sea and Arabia. Subtidal under rocks, com-mon. Syn.: *aegyptiaca* Lamarck.

Divaricate Gibbula   (1″) 2.4 cm
Gibbula divaricata (L., 1758). Mediterra-nean and Adriatic. Intertidal rocks, moder-ately common. Shell thick.

Kotschy's Gibbula (1.2") 3 cm
Gibbula kotschyi (Philippi, 1847). N. W. Indian Ocean. Subtidal to 2 m among small boulders; uncommon.

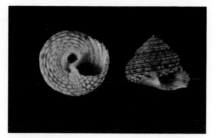

Beauty Gibbula (0.8") 2 cm
Monilea callifera (Lamarck, 1822). Indo-Pacific. Intertidal, under rocks; common. Syn.: *callosus* Wood.

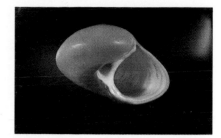

Norris Shell (1.5") 4 cm
Norrisia norrisi (Sowerby, 1838). Central California to W. Mexico. Among kelp weed beds; moderately common.

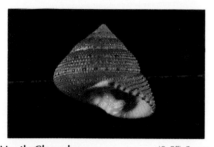

Mantle Clanculus (0.8") 2 cm
Clanculus pharaonius (L., 1758). Indian Ocean. Intertidal under rocks; locally common.

Purplish Clanculus (0.7") 1.8 cm
Clanculus puniceus (Philippi, 1846). East Africa. Intertidal to 2 m, under rocks; locally common.

Rare Clanculus (0.5") 1.2 cm
Clanculus rarus (Dufo, 1840). Indian Ocean. Subtidal, under rocks; uncommon. Syn.: *flosculus* Fischer.

Beautiful Clanculus (0.6") 1.5 cm
Clanculus margaritarius (Philippi, 1847). Indo-Pacific. Subtidal, under rocks; uncommon.

Secret Clanculus (0.6") 1.5 cm
Clanculus clanguloides (Wood, 1828). S. W. Pacific and northern Australia. Subtidal among weeds and rocks; moderately common.

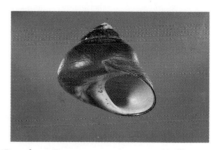

Rosy-base Top (1.5") 4 cm
Oxystele sinensis (Gmelin, 1791). South Africa. Intertidal pools along rocky shores; common. Syn.: *merula* Lamarck.

Guam Button Top (0.5") 1.2 cm
Umbonium guamensis (Quoy & Gaimard, 1834). S. W. Pacific. Subtidal to 2 m in sand; moderately common. Syn.: *montrouzieri* Souverbie.

Common Button Top (0.4") 1 cm
Umbonium vestiarum (L., 1758). Indo-West Pacific. Sandy mud bottoms, subtidal to 4 m; locally abundant.

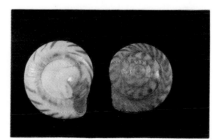

Zealandic Button Top (0.6") 1.5 cm
Umbonium zelandicum A. Adams, 1854. New Zealand. Subtidal to 6 m on sandy mud; common. Syn.: *anguliferus* Philippi.

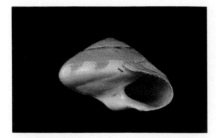

Giant Button Top (1″) 2.5 cm
Umbonium giganteum (Lesson, 1831). Japan. Fine sand bottom, 5 to 30 m; common.

Red Stomatella (0.6″) 1.5 cm
Stomatolina rubra (Lamarck, 1822). Japan to S. W. Pacific. Gravel bottoms, subtidal to 20 m; common. Syn.: *angulata* A. Adams. In family Stomatellidae.

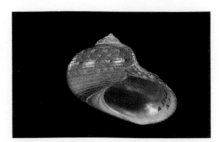

Papery Stomatella (1.2″) 3 cm
Pseudostomatella papyracea (Gmelin, 1791). S. W. Pacific. Subtidal to 6 m on gravel bottoms; moderately common. In family Stomatellidae.

Colored Stomatella (0.8″) 2 cm
Pseudostomatella decolorata (Gould, 1848). Central Pacific to Philippines. Sand and rock bottoms, 1 to 10 m; uncommon.

Elegant Stomatella (1″) 2.5 cm
Pseudostomatella elegans (Gray, 1847). S. W. Pacific. Subtidal among boulders and weeds; uncommon.

Variable Stomatella (0.4″) 1 cm
Stomatella (Gena) varia (A. Adams, 1850). Japan to S. W. Pacific. Subtidal to 20 m; common. Syn.: *dilecta* Gould; *lutea* A. Adams. *Gena* is a subgenus.

Flattened Stomatella (0.6″) 1.5 cm
Stomatella (Gena) planulata Lamarck, 1816. Southwest Pacific. Intertidal to 10 m. among rocks; common.

Strigose Stomatella (1″) 2.5 cm
Stomatella (Gena) impertusa (Burrows, 1815). S. W. Pacific; Australia. Subtidal on gravel; uncommon. Syn.: *strigosa* A. Adams.

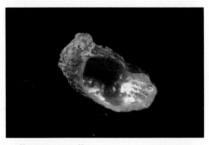

Swollen Stomatella (1.5″) 3 cm
Stomatia phymotis Helbling, 1779. Japan to S. W. Pacific. Subtidal on rocky bottoms; moderately common. Syn.: *australis* A. Adams.

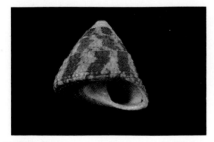

Radiate Top (1.5″) 4 cm
Trochus radiatus (Gmelin, 1791). Indo-Pacific. Subtidal on coral reefs; common. Syn.: *fultoni* Melvill (from Pakistan).

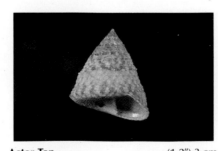

Actor Top (1.2″) 3 cm
Trochus histrio Reeve, 1848. Central Pacific to S. E. Asia. Subtidal on rocks; common. Syn.: *calcaratus* Souverbie.

Yellow-mouth Top (1.5″) 3.5 cm
Trochus ochroleucus Gmelin, 1791. Indian Ocean. Subtidal on reefs; common.

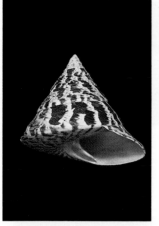

Commercial Trochus (5") 13 cm
Trochus niloticus L., 1767. Indo-Pacific. Reefs to 20 m; abundant. Syn.: *maximus* Philippi. Used for making buttons.

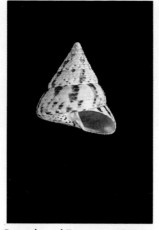

Cone-shaped Top (3") 7 cm
Trochus conus (Gmelin, 1791). Indo-Pacific. Near reefs to 5 m; common. Base rounded.

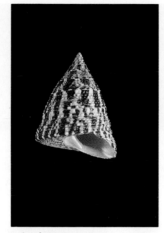

Striped Top (2.5") 6 cm
Trochus virgatus Gmelin, 1791. Indo-Pacific. Reef flats; moderately common.

Fenestrate Top (1.5") 4 cm
Tectus fenestratus (Gmelin, 1791). Central and S. W. Pacific. Reef flats, intertidal; moderately common.

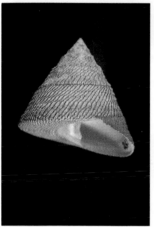

Lined Top (2.2") 6 cm
Trochus hanleyanus Reeve, 1842. Warm reef waters of Australia; uncommon. Syn.: *lineatus* Lamarck (not da Costa, 1778).

Maculated Top (2") 5 cm
Trochus maculatus L., 1758. Indo-Pacific. Reef flats, shallow water; common. Variable. Syn.: *verrucosus* Gmelin; *granosus* Lamarck.

Pyramid Top (3") 7 cm
Tectus pyramis (Born, 1778). Indo-Pacific. Shallow reefs; locally abundant. Syn.: *obeliscus* Gmelin; *acutus* Lamarck.

Noded Pyramid Top (3") 7 cm
Tectus pyramis form *noduliferus* Lamarck, 1822. S. W. Pacific and Indian Ocean; uncommon.

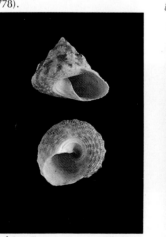

Red Sea Top (2") 5 cm
Trochus erythraeus Brocchi, 1821. Red Sea; N. W. Indian Ocean. Subtidal to 3 m, on rocks and weeds; common locally.

Green Jewel Top (1.5") 4 cm
Phasianotrochus eximius (Perry, 1811). South coasts of Australia. Subtidal to 3 m, among weeds; common.

TURBAN SHELLS
FAMILY TURBINIDAE

This is a large family of top-shaped snails, usually with thick shells, an iridescent interior, and usually with a shelly operculum that seals the aperture. Several hundred species are known, most from tropical seas. *Angaria* belongs to the Trochidae. Most species are vegetarians, feeding on marine algae.

Jourdan's Turban (8") 21 cm
Turbo jourdani Kiener, 1839. Southern Australia. Just offshore along rocky coast; not uncommon. Syn.: *verconis* Iredale.

Magnificent Turban   (3") 7 cm
Turbo magnificus Jonas, 1844. South Ecuador to Chile. Offshore to 25 m; uncommon.

Tapestry Turban   (2.5") 6 cm
Turbo petholatus L., 1758. Central and Western Pacific. Shallow reefs; common. Operculum green, called "cat's eye."

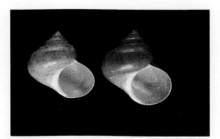

Reeve's Turban   (2.5") 6 cm
Turbo reevei Philippi, 1847. Philippines; Indonesia. Shallow reefs; common. Operculum white to brown-stained.

Miniature Turban   (1.5") 3.5 cm
Turbo parvulus Philippi, 1848. Western Pacific. Shallow water reefs; uncommon.

Great Green Turban   (8") 20 cm
Turbo marmoratus L., 1758. Indo-Pacific, west of Fiji. Rubble bottom 4 to 20 m, locally abundant. Syn.: *regenfussii* Deshayes.

Horned Turban   (3") 7 cm
Turbo cornutus Lightfoot, 1786. Japan; East China. Offshore on sand, 2 to 10 m; abundant. Used as food. Syn.: *cornutus* Gmelin.

Silver-mouth Turban   (3") 7 cm
Turbo argyrostoma L., 1758. Indo-Pacific. Reefs, intertidal to 3 m.; common. Syn.: *carduus* Fischer.

Silver-mouth Turban   (3") 7 cm
Turbo argyrostoma L., 1758. One of the long-spined variations of this common Indo-Pacific turban.

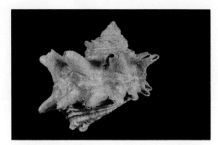

Lajonkaire's Turban   (3") 7 cm
Turbo lajonkairii Deshayes, 1839. Indian Ocean, especially Cocos-Keeling Atoll. Extreme variation of *argyrostoma*.

Rough Turban   (2.5") 6 cm
Turbo setosus Gmelin, 1791. Central and S. W. Pacific. Edge of outer reefs; abundant. Operculum finely granulate in the center.

Brown Pacific Turban   (2") 5 cm
Turbo bruneus (Röding, 1798). Indo-Pacific. Shallow reefs; abundant. Syn.: *ticaonicus* Reeve.

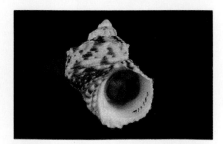

Gold-mouth Turban   (2.4") 6 cm
Turbo chrysostomus L., 1758. Indo-Pacific. Subtidal near reefs; common.

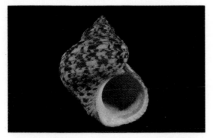

Corded Turban (3″) 7.5 cm
Turbo sparverius Gmelin, 1791. S. W. Pacific. Near reefs in 1 to 5 m; uncommon. Operculum purple-brown in center.

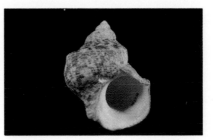

Crass Turban (3″) 8 cm
Turbo crassus Wood, 1829. Central to S. W. Pacific. Near reefs in 1 to 5 m; common. Operculum pustulose, brown in center.

Beautiful Turban (3″) 8 cm
Turbo intercostalis Menke, 1843. West and S. W. Australia. Subtidal, shallow reefs; common. Operculum with coarse pustules. Syn.: *pulcher* Reeve (not Dillwyn).

Gruner's Turban (1.5″) 3.5 cm
Turbo gruneri Philippi, 1846. Southern Australia; Tasmania. Offshore to 160 m; common. Syn.: *circularis* Reeve.

Channeled Turban (3″) 7 cm
Turbo canaliculatus Hermann, 1781. S. E. Florida to Brazil. Offshore near reefs to 10 m; uncommon. Operculum smooth, white.

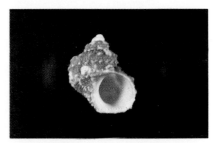

Chestnut Turban (1.5″) 3.5 cm
Turbo castanea Gmelin, 1791. S. E. United States to Brazil. Subtidal to 30 m on sand; common. Rarely red, white, lavender.

Filose Turban (0.7″) 1.8 cm
Turbo cailletii Fischer and Bernardi, 1856. S. E. Florida and Caribbean. Near coral reefs, 4 to 40 m; rare. Syn.: *filosus* Kiener. Rarely yellow.

South African Turban (3″) 7 cm
Turbo sarmaticus L., 1758. South Africa. Subtidal on rocky shores; abundant. Polished specimen.

South African Turban (3″) 7 cm
Turbo sarmaticus L., 1758. Specimen in natural condition with periostracal covering. Operculum crudely pustulose.

Natal Turban (1.5″) 4 cm
Turbo natalensis Krauss, 1848. South Africa. Subtidal to 4 m on rocks; moderately common.

Crown Turban (2.4″) 6 cm
Turbo cidaris Gmelin, 1791. False Bay to Port Alfred, South Africa. Shore rocks; common. Banded form.

Crown Turban (2.4″) 6 cm
Turbo cidaris Gmelin, 1791. South Africa. Mottled form. Operculum granulate, with a central pit.

Stony Turban (2") 4.5 cm
Turbo saxosus Wood, 1828. Nicaragua to Peru. Subtidal to 5 m among rocks; common. Syn.: *venustus* Philippi.

Wavy Turban (2.5") 6 cm
Turbo fluctuosus Wood, 1828. W. Mexico to Peru. Intertidal among rocks; common. Syn.: *fluctuatus* Reeve.

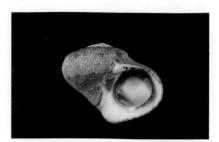

Smooth Moon Turban (1.2") 3.5 cm
Lunella cinerea (Born, 1778). Indo-Pacific. Intertidal among shore rocks; abundant. Syn.: *porphyrites* Gmelin; *picta* Röding.

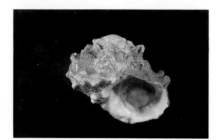

Granulated Moon Turban (1.2") 3.5 cm
Lunella granulata (Gmelin, 1791). Indian Ocean. Intertidal on shore rocks to 3 m; locally common.

Coronate Moon Turban (1.2") 3.5 cm
Lunella coronata (Gmelin, 1791). Japan and Korea. Intertidal among rocks and gravel. Syn.: *coreensis* Récluz.

Emerald Moon Turban (2.7") 7 cm
Lunella smaragdus (Gmelin, 1791). New Zealand. Intertidal rocky shores; common. Operculum green.

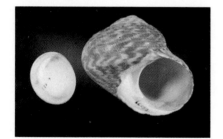

Lightning Moon Turban (2.4") 6 cm
Subninella undulata (Lightfoot, 1786). South Australia. On reefs, low-tide mark to 30 m; common.

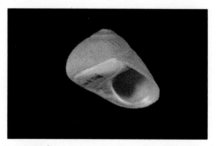

Snare Turban (1") 2.5 cm
Homalopoma transenna (Watson, 1879). Off Japan, in 840 m; rare. Surface cut into little diamonds. Operculum whitish.

Péron's Liotia (0.6") 1.5 cm
Liotina peronii (Kiener, 1839). Indo-Pacific. Subtidal under dead coral; uncommon. Operculum with shelly granules. Syn.: *hermanni* Pilsbry.

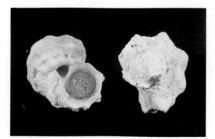

Miss Cooke's Liotia (0.7") 1.8 cm
Macrarene cookeana (Dall, 1918). Baja California. Offshore, 10 to 183 m; on gravel bottom; uncommon. Syn.: *coronadensis* Stohler.

Californian Liotia (0.6") 1.5 cm
Macrarene californica (Dall, 1908). Off Cedros Is. to Gulf of California; uncommon. Holotype illus. Syn.: *pacis* Dall.

Captain Cook's Turban (3.5") 9 cm
Cookia sulcata (Gmelin, 1791). New Zealand. Intertidal among rocks; common. Shelly operculum with 2 ribs.

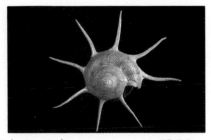

Yoka Star Turban (3") 7.5 cm
Guildfordia yoka Jousseaume, 1888. Off Japan in 100 to 500 m; moderately common.

Triumphant Star Turban (2") 5 cm
Guildfordia triumphans (Philippi, 1841). Off Japan in 50 to 100 m; common. Syn.: *guildfordiae* Reeve.

Kurz's Star Turban (1.5") 3.5 cm
Guildfordia kurzi Petuch, 1980. Philippines. Deep water, 50 to 100 m. Probably a dwarf form of *triumphans*. Uncommon.

Aculeate Star Turban (1.6") 4 cm
Guildfordia aculeata Kosuge, 1979. Central Philippines. Deep water in about 200 m; uncommon.

Sunburst Star Turban (3.5") 9 cm
Astraea heliotropium (Martyn, 1784). New Zealand. Offshore in deep water; uncommon. Syn.: *imperialis* Gmelin.

Sunburst Star Turban (3.5") 9 cm
Astraea heliotropium (Martyn, 1784). Underside view. Species discovered during Captain Cook's voyages to New Zealand.

Bartsch's Bolma (2") 5 cm
Bolma bartschi Dall, 1913. Off Moluccas, Indonesia. 410 m; rare. Holotype specimen illustrated.

Modest Bolma (2.2") 5.5 cm
Bolma modesta (Reeve, 1843). Japan; China; Taiwan. In gravel, 20 to 100 m; common. In subgenus *Harisazaea* Habe.

Jacqueline Bolma (1") 2.5 cm
Bolma jacquelineae (Marche-Marchad, 1957). Off Sierra Leone, West Africa; uncommon.

Bridled Bolma (3") 7 cm
Bolma aureola (Hedley, 1907). N. E. Australia. Offshore in 40 m; uncommon.

Sandpaper Bolma (1.5") 3.5 cm
Bolma guttata (A. Adams, 1863), subspecies *millegranosa* (Kuroda & Habe, 1958). Japan. Offshore in 20 to 50 m; uncommon. In subgenus *Galeoastraea* K. & H.

Abyssal Bolma (1.5") 3.5 cm
Pseudastralium abyssorum (Schepman, 1908). Indonesia. Deep water in 500 m; uncommon.

Peach Bolma   (1") 2.5 cm
Pseudastralium persica (Dall, 1907). Off Kagashima, Japan. In deep water; rare. Holotype illustrated.

Little Star Bolma   (0.5") 1.2 cm
Bolma asteriola (Dall, 1925). Sea of Japan. In deep water; rare. Holotype illustrated.

Busch's Star-shell   (2") 5 cm
Astraea buschii (Philippi, 1844). Nicaragua to Peru. Intertidal rocky zone; common.

Half-ribbed Star-shell   (1") 2.5 cm
Astraea semicostata (P. Fischer, 1875). Southeast Asia. Intertidal under rocks; locally common.

Long-spined Star-shell   (2") 5 cm
Astraea phoebia Röding, 1798. Florida to Brazil; Bermuda. Shallow grassy flats; common. Syn.: *longispina* Lamarck.

Carved Star-shell   (2.5") 6 cm
Astraea caelata (Gmelin, 1791). Florida and the West Indies. Subtidal on rocks to 10 m; common. Operculum finely pustulose.

Green Star-shell   (2") 5 cm
Astraea tuber (L., 1767). Florida and the West Indies. Subtidal on rocks to 10 m; common. Operculum with curved ridge.

American Star-shell   (1.5") 3.5 cm
Astraea tecta subspecies *americana* (Gmelin, 1791). Southeast Florida. Grassy flats and rocks; locally abundant.

Imbricate Star-shell   (2") 5 cm
Astraea tecta (Lightfoot, 1786). Lesser Antilles. On rocks, 1 to 20 m; uncommon. Syn.: *imbricata* Gmelin. Rare in Florida.

Turban Star-shell   (6") 1.5 cm
Astraea turbanica (Dall, 1910). Baja California. Kelp beds; uncommon. Syn.: *petrothauma* Berry; *rupicollina* Stohler.

Red Western Turban   (3") 7 cm
Astraea gibberosa (Dillwyn, 1817). Western Canada to Baja California. Subtidal rocks; common. Operculum white, smooth.

Wavy Turban   (3") 7 cm
Astraea undosa (Wood, 1828). California to W. Mexico. Subtidal rocks; common. Operculum with 3 prickly ridges.

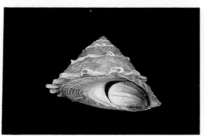

Blood-spotted Turban   (2.5″) 6 cm
Astraea olivacea (Wood, 1828). West Mexico. Subtidal on rocks; common. Umbilicus red.

Japanese Star-shell   (3″) 8 cm
Astraea japonica (Dunker, 1844). Japan and Korea. Subtidal to 20 m; common. In subgenus *Pomaulax* Gray.

Taylor's Star-shell   (3″) 7.5 cm
Bolma tayloriana (E. A. Smith, 1880). Japan. Deep water between 200 and 300 m; uncommon to rare.

Girgyllus Star-shell   (2″) 5 cm
Bolma girgyllus (Reeve, 1861) Philippines; Taiwan. Deep water; rare.

Rotary Star-shell   (1.5″) 4 cm
Astraea rotularia (Lamarck, 1822). West and N. W. Australia. Subtidal rocks; common. Operculum brownish green.

Kesteven's Star-shell   (1″) 2.5 cm
Astraea kesteveni (Iredale, 1924). S. E. Australia. Subtidal on rocks; common. Syn.: *fimbriatus* Lamarck, not Borson.

Pacific Star-shell   (1″) 2.5 cm
Astraea haematraga (Menke, 1829). S. W. Pacific to Japan. Intertidal rocks to 20 m; common.

Common Delphinula   (3″) 7 cm
Angaria delphinus (L., 1758). Indo-Pacific. Sublittoral rocks; abundant. Has many forms. This genus belongs in Trochidae.

Imperial Delphinula   (3″) 7 cm
Angaria delphinus form *melanacantha* (Reeve, 1842). Philippines. Offshore. Uncommon. Spines grow longer in quiet waters. Syn.: *imperialis* Reeve.

Tyria Delphinula   (3″) 7 cm
Angaria delphinus form *tyria* (Reeve, 1842). S. W. Pacific and Australia. Operculum is chitinous.

Kiener's Delphinula   (2″) 5 cm
Angaria sphaerula (Kiener, 1839). Philippines. Offshore in quiet waters; moderately common. Variable in spine growth.

Victor Dan's Delphinula   (2″) 5 cm
Angaria vicdani Kosuge, 1980. Southern Philippines. Offshore in deep water. Uncommon.

PHEASANT SHELLS
FAMILY PHASIANELLIDAE

The pheasant shells are very colorful externally, but the interiors are porcelaneous, not pearly as in the turbans. The operculum is chalky white and glossy. *Phasianella* species from Australia are large. The genera *Hiloa*, *Tricolia* and *Gabrielona* are less than a quarter-inch in size.

Variegated Pheasant   (0.6″) 1.5 cm
Phasianella variegata Lamarck, 1822. Western Pacific and Indian Ocean. Subtidal among seaweeds; locally common. Many synonyms.

Australian Pheasant   (2″) 5 cm
Phasianella australis (Gmelin, 1791). Southern Australia and Tasmania; common. Color extremely variable. Operculum white.

Tessellate Pheasant   (0.2″) 5 mm
Tricolia tessellata (Potiez & Michaud, 1838). Southern half of Caribbean. Shallow water grass beds; common.

Mediterranean Pheasant   (0.4″) 1 cm
Tricolia speciosa (Mühlfeld, 1824). Adriatic and Mediterranean Seas. Subtidal; on weeds; common.

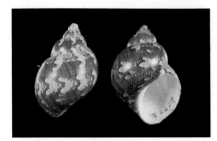

Swollen Pheasant   (1.5″) 4 cm
Phasianella ventricosa Swainson, 1822. Southern Australia and Tasmania; common. Variable in color. Syn.: *zebra* Reeve; *perdix* Wood.

THE NERITES
FAMILY NERITIDAE

The nerites are mainly shore dwellers and live either on rocks or mangrove trees. A few, like *Septaria*, live in freshwater. The shelly operculum has a short projection. There are about 50 species, mostly found in the tropics. The related family Neritopsidae has only one living genus, *Neritopsis*.

Radula Nerite   (1″) 1.5 cm
Neritopsis radula (L., 1758). Indo-Pacific. Shallow water near reefs; uncommon. Columella has square U-shaped notch. Operculum white, very thick.

Bleeding Tooth   (1.2″) 3 cm
Nerita peloronta (L., 1758). South Florida, West Indies and Bermuda. Shore rocks; abundant. Operculum dark red.

Tessellate Nerite   (0.7″) 1.8 cm
Nerita tessellata Gmelin, 1791. Florida to Brazil; Bermuda. Shore rocks; abundant. Operculum bluish or yellowish gray.

Four-toothed Nerite   (0.7″) 1.8 cm
Nerita versicolor Gmelin, 1791. South Florida and West Indies; Bermuda. Shore rocks; abundant. Operculum gray, pimpled.

Antillean Nerite   (1″) 2.5 cm
Nerita fulgurans Gmelin, 1791. Southeast U.S. to Brazil; Bermuda. Rocks and sand near freshwater seepage; uncommon.

Polished Nerite (1″) 2.5 cm
Nerita polita L., 1758. Indo-Pacific. Intertidal on rocks near sand; abundant. Smooth. Variable colors.

Rumpf's Nerite (0.7″) 1.8 cm
Nerita polita form *rumphii* Recluz, 1841. Spirally striate; smaller, frequently banded.

Ancient Nerite (1″) 2.5 cm
Nerita polita subspecies *antiquata* Récluz, 1841. Northern half of Australia. Intertidal; common. Syn.: *australis* Wood, not Gmelin.

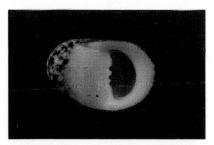

Maximum Nerite (1.3″) 3 cm
Nerita maxima Gmelin, 1791. Central Pacific; uncommon. Teeth squarish, yellow. Surface finely incised.

Waved Nerite (0.7″) 1.8 cm
Nerita undata L., 1758. Indo-Pacific. Intertidal rocks; abundant. Variable in color. Syn.: *striata* Burrow; *undulata* Gmelin.

Black African Nerite (0.7″) 1.8 cm
Nerita atra Gmelin, 1791. Western Africa. Intertidal rocks; common. Syn.: *senegalensis* Gmelin.

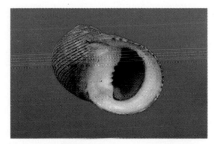

Black Australian Nerite (0.7″) 1.8 cm
Nerita aterrima Gmelin, 1791. South Australia; New Zealand. Intertidal; common. Syn.: *nigerrima* Gmelin; *atramentosa* Reeve.

Chameleon Nerite (1″) 2.5 cm
Nerita chamaeleon L., 1758. Indo-Pacific. Intertidal rocks; common. Operculum dark-green, pustulose.

Snake-skin Nerite (1″) 2.5 cm
Nerita exuvia L., 1758. Southwest Pacific. Intertidal rocks; common. Near mangroves.

Costate Nerite (1.2″) 3 cm
Nerita costata Gmelin, 1791. Indo-Pacific. Intertidal rocks; common.

Ascension Nerite (1.2″) 3 cm
Nerita ascensionis Gmelin, 1791. Ascension Island; Eastern Brazil. Syn.: *deturpensis* and *trinidadensis* Vermeij.

Reticulate Nerite (0.7″) 1.8 cm
Nerita signata Macleay in Lamarck, 1822. Indo-Pacific. Intertidal reefs; common. Syn.: *reticulata* Karsten (non-binomial).

Plicate Nerite (1") 2.5 cm
Nerita plicata L., 1758. Indo-Pacific. Intertidal rocks; abundant. Rarely speckled.

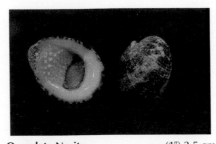

Ox-palate Nerite (1") 2.5 cm
Nerita albicilla L., 1758. Indo-Pacific. Intertidal inshore rocks; abundant. Syn.: *ustulata* Sowerby.

Flat-spired Nerite (1.2") 3 cm
Nerita planospira Anton, 1839. Indo-Pacific. Intertidal, near mangroves; locally common in Southwest Pacific.

Textile Nerite (1.5") 4 cm
Nerita textilis Gmelin, 1791. Indian Ocean. Higher shore rocks; locally common. Syn.: *plexa* Dillwyn.

Ornate Nerite (1.5") 4 cm
Nerita scabricosta Lamarck, 1822. W. Mexico to Ecuador. Intertidal rocks; common. Syn.: *ornata* Sowerby; *fuscata* Menke.

Funiculate Nerite (1") 2.5 cm
Nerita funiculata Menke, 1851. W. Mexico to Peru; Galapagos. Intertidal rocks; common. Syn.: *bernhardi* Récluz.

Zigzag Nerite (0.5") 1.2 cm
Neritina communis (Quoy & Gaimard, 1832). S. W. Pacific. Among mangroves; abundant. Syn.: *ziczac* of authors.

Turreted Nerite (0.7") 1.8 cm
Neritina turrita (Gmelin, 1791). S. W. Pacific. Intertidal, near mangroves; common.

Violet Nerite (1") 2.5 cm
Neritina violacea (Gmelin, 1791). S. W. Pacific. Intertidal, near mangroves; common.

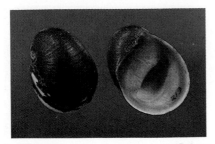

Dusky Nerite (1.2") 3 cm
Neritina pulligera L., 1767. S. W. Pacific. Intertidal, near mangroves; common.

Olive Nerite (0.5") 1.2 cm
Neritina reclivata (Say, 1822). S. E. United States and West Indies. Intertidal, brackish mud flats; abundant. Syn.: *sphaera* Pilsbry.

Virgin Nerite (0.4") 1 cm
Neritina virginea (L., 1758). Florida to Brazil; Bermuda. Intertidal, brackish mud and grass flats; abundant.

Dotted Nerite (0.7") 1.8 cm
Neritina puncticulata Lamarck, 1822. West Indies. Rocky bottoms near rivers; locally common.

Dubious Nerite (1") 2.5 cm
Neritodryas dubia (Gmelin, 1791). S. W. Pacific. Intertidal, brackish; common.

Weakly cut Nerite (1") 2.5 cm
Neritodryas subsulcata (Sowerby, 1836). S. W. Pacific; Philippines. Intertidal in mangroves; common.

Horny Nerite (1") 2.5 cm
Neritodryas cornea (L., 1758). S. W. Pacific. Intertidal, on mangroves; abundant.

Painted Panama Nerite (0.5") 1.2 cm
Theodoxus luteofasciatus (Miller, 1879). Gulf of California to Peru. Mangrove mud flats; abundant. Syn.: *picta* Reeve (not Eichwald).

Guamanian Nerite (0.4") 1 cm
Theodoxus oualaniensis (Lesson, 1831). Indo-Pacific. Intertidal grass flats; very common. Syn.: *guamensis* Lesson.

Coronate Nerite (0.4") 1 cm
Theodoxus coronatus (Leach, 1815). S. W. Pacific. On weeds, entrance to small rivers; abundant. Syn.: *longispina* Récluz.

Crown Nerite (0.4") 1 cm
Theodoxus corona (L., 1758). S. W. Pacific. On weeds in brackish ditches; abundant. Syn.: *brevispina* Lam.; *spinosa* Wood.

Zebra Nerite (0.7") 1.8 cm
Puperita pupa (L., 1758). S. E. Florida, West Indies and Bermuda. Rocky tide pools; abundant. Syn.: *tristis* Orbigny.

Dark Zebra Nerite (0.7") 1.8 cm
Puperita pupa form *tristis* (Orbigny, 1842.) Mostly in West Indies. Rocky pools. Common.

Emerald Nerite (0.3") 7 mm
Smaragdia viridis (L., 1758). S. E. Florida, West Indies, Bermuda. On eelgrass; common. Similar *S. rangiana* (Récluz, 1841) is from Indo-Pacific. .

Pitchy Nerite (1") 2.5 cm
Nerita picea Récluz, 1841. S. W. Pacific (uncommon); Hawaii (common). Intertidal rocks.

Widest Nerite (1.2") 3 cm
Clypeolum latissimum (Broderip, 1833). W. Mexico to Ecuador. Mouths of small rivers; common. Syn.: *cassiculum* Sowerby.

Eared Nerite (1.2") 3 cm
Clypeolum auriculatum (Lamarck, 1816). S. W. Pacific; S. E. Asia. Freshwater; mouths of small rivers on rocks; common. Syn.: *subulata* Récluz.

Granose Nerite (1.2") 3 cm
Clypeolum granosum (Sowerby, 1825). Endemic to Hawaii. Freshwater; rocks at mouths of small rivers and upstream; common.

Bourbon Nerite (1") 2.5 cm
Septaria borbonica (Bory, 1803). S. W. Pacific (large islands); S. E. Asia. Freshwater; on smooth rocks in rivers; common. Operculum internal.

Janella Nerite (1") 2.5 cm
Septaria janelli (Récluz, 1841). S.W. Pacific; Indonesia. Freshwater, on stones in small rivers; uncommon.

ORDER CAENOGASTROPODA

This is the largest division of the gastropods, differing from the previous primitive group in having lost, through evolution, the right gill, right auricle of the heart and right kidney. The radula is reduced to only seven or fewer rows of teeth. None produces pearly shells. The order contains such snails as the periwinkles, conchs, cowries and cones.

DEEPSEA AUGERS
FAMILY ABYSSOCHRYSIDAE

This is a rare, relict family of strange little shells seldom treated in popular books. The animal is blind and has its copulatory organ on the mantle edge. The operculum is soft and horny. The two known species of this family live on mud at very great depths in the ocean.

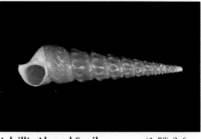

Melvill's Abyssal Snail (1.5") 3.6 cm
Abyssochrysos melvilli (Schepman, 1909). S. W. Pacific and S. E. Africa. Deep water, 491 to 1,479 m; rare. Syn.: *tomlini* Barnard.

Melanioides Abyssal Snail (1.6") 4 cm
Abyssochrysos melanioides Tomlin, 1927. Off South Africa, 1,456 to 2,712 m; rare.

THE PERIWINKLES
FAMILY LITTORINIDAE

The true periwinkles are a well-known family living in the littoral region of most parts of the world. There are about 30 species, some living on rocky coasts, others preferring mangroves. The sexes are separate. Females either give birth to live young, shed eggs into the water, or lay jelly masses. The operculum has few whorls and is horny.

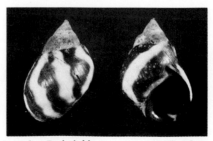

Peruvian Periwinkle (0.5") 1.2 cm
Littorina peruviana (Lamarck, 1822). Ecuador to Chile. Intertidal on rocks; common.

Common Periwinkle (1") 2.5 cm
Littorina littorea (L., 1758). Western Europe; N. E. North America. Intertidal on rocks; abundant. Used as food.

Marsh Periwinkle (1") 2.5 cm
Littorina irrorata (Say, 1822). New York to central Florida to Texas. Shell heavy. On marsh sedges; abundant.

Ziczac Periwinkle (0.7") 1.8 cm
Littorina ziczac (Gmelin, 1791). S. E. Florida; West Indies; Bermuda. Intertidal rocks; abundant.

Angulate Periwinkle (1") 2.5 cm
Littorina scabra angulifera (Lamarck, 1822). S. E. United States to Brazil; Bermuda. Mangrove areas; common.

Scabra Periwinkle (1") 2.5 cm
Littorina scabra scabra (L., 1758). Indo-Pacific. Among mangroves; abundant.

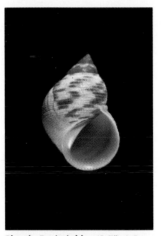

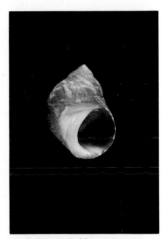

Cloudy Periwinkle (0.7") 1.8 cm
Littorina nebulosa (Lamarck, 1822). S. E. United States to Brazil. Intertidal; common. Columella mauve.

Undulate Periwinkle
(0.7") 1.8 cm
Littorina undulata Gray, 1839. Indo-Pacific. Intertidal rocks; abundant.

Banded Periwinkle (1.2") 3 cm
Littorina fasciata Gray, 1839. W. Mexico to Ecuador. Intertidal rocks; common.

Eroded Periwinkle (0.7") 1.8 cm
Littorina keenae Rosewater, 1978. Pacific Canada to W. Mexico. Intertidal rocks; abundant. Syn.: *planaxis* Philippi.

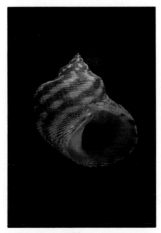

Zebra Periwinkle (1.3") 3.2 cm
Littorina zebra Donovan, 1825. Costa Rica to W. Colombia. Intertidal rocks; common. Syn.: *pulchra* Sowerby.

Modest Periwinkle (0.6") 1.5 cm
Littorina modesta Philippi, 1846. W. Mexico to Ecuador. Intertidal rocks; common. Syn.: *conspersa* Philippi.

Scarlet Periwinkle (1") 2.5 cm
Littorina coccinea (Gmelin, 1791). Central and S. W. Pacific. Intertidal rocks; abundant. Syn.: *obesa* Sowerby.

Dotted Periwinkle (0.7") 1.8 cm
Littorina pintado (Wood, 1828). Indo-Pacific. Intertidal rocks; abundant.

Common Prickly-winkle (0.5")
1.2 cm *Nodilittorina tuberculata*
(Menke, 1828). Southern Florida; Bermuda. Intertidal rocks;
common. Syn.: *trochiformis*
Dillwyn.

Beaded Periwinkle (1") 2.4 cm
Tectarius muricatus (L., 1758).
Southern Florida, West Indies,
Bermuda. Upper intertidal
rocks; abundant.

Pagoda Prickly-winkle (2") 5 cm
Tectarius pagodus (L., 1758). S.
W. Pacific. High intertidal
rocks; common. Syn.: *major*
Swainson.

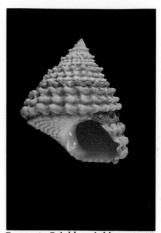

Coronate Prickly-winkle (1.5")
4 cm *Tectarius coronatus* Valenciennes, 1832. Philippines and
Celebes. Intertidal rocks; locally common. Syn.: *rugosus*
Wood.

Papillate Prickly-winkle (1.2")
3 cm *Tectarius tectumpersicum*
(L., 1758). S. W. Pacific. Intertidal rocks; common. Syn.: *papillosus* Lamarck.

Hailstorm Prickly-winkle (1.5")
4 cm *Tectarius grandinatus*
(Gmelin, 1791). S. E. Polynesia.
Intertidal rocks; common.
Syn.: *bullatus* Martyn.

Rustic Prickly-winkle
                      (1.5") 4 cm
Tectarius rusticus (Philippi,
1846). N. W. Australia. Rocks at
high-tide line; uncommon.

RISSO SNAILS and VITRINELLIDAE

SUPERFAMILY RISSOACEA

This large group of several families of tiny snails includes the
Caecidae, Rissoinidae, and Vitrinellidae. Most species are
less than 5 mm and require a
hand lens or microscope for
proper identification. Many are
freshwater, a few parasitic.
Operculum is always horny.

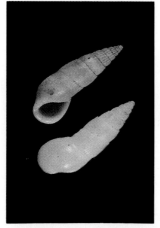

Spiral Risso (0.6") 1.5 cm
Rissoina spirata (Sowerby,
1824). Central Pacific. Shallow
water in sand; uncommon.

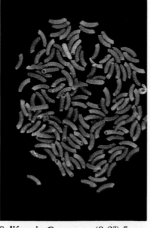

California Caecum (0.2") 5 mm
Caecum californicum Dall,
1885. California to W. Mexico.
Sand, shallow water; common.
30-40 rings.

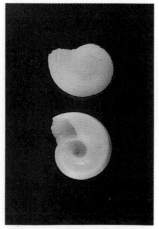

Beau's Vitrinella (0.3") 7 mm
Cyclostremiscus beaui (Fischer,
1857). S. E. United States to Brazil. Sand, shallow water; uncommon. 6 spiral threads on
top.

TURRITELLAS FAMILY TURRITELLIDAE

A worldwide, abundant group
of sandy mud snails found offshore. Operculum chitinous,
many whorls, sometimes with
bristles on the edge. Several
hundred species known,
mostly tropical. No siphonal canal. Also see the Augers, Terebridae.

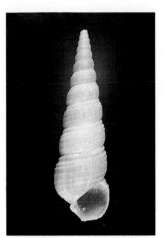

Mesal Turritella (2") 5 cm
Mesalia brevialis (Lamarck, 1822). W. and N. Africa. Shallow water, in sand; common. Syn.: *mesal* Deshayes.

Opal Turritella (1") 2.5 cm
Mesalia opalina (Adams & Reeve, 1850). West Africa. Offshore in sand; uncommon. Minutely striate.

Variegate Turritella (3") 8 cm
Turritella variegata (L., 1758). West Indies. Subtidal, sandy mud bays; locally common.

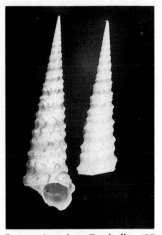

Eastern American Turritella (2") 5 cm *Turritella exoleta* (L., 1758). S. E. United States to Brazil. Offshore, 1 to 99 m, sand; common. Rarely purplish.

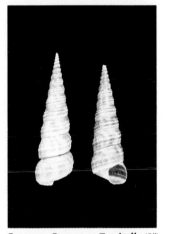

Common European Turritella (2") 5 cm *Turritella communis* Risso, 1826. Western Europe. In sand, 6 to 200 m; common. Syn.: *linnaei* Deshayes.

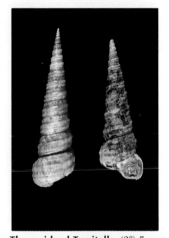

Three-ridged Turritella (2") 5 cm *Archimediella triplicata* (Brocchi, 1814). Mediterranean; Canary Is.; W. Africa. Offshore, 18 to 36 m; common.

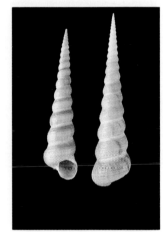

Screw Turritella (6") 16 cm
Turritella terebra (L., 1758). S. W. Pacific. Subtidal, sandy mud; abundant.

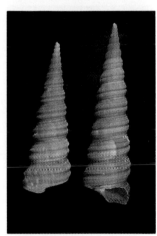

Pointed Turritella (2") 5 cm
Turritella fastigiata Adams & Reeve, 1850. East Indies. Subtidal mud flats; common.

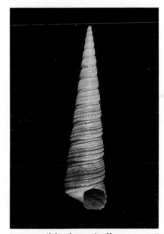

Strong-ribbed Turritella (1") 2.5 cm *Turritella fortilirata* Sowerby, 1914. Japan, cool water. Offshore, sand; moderately common.

Rosy Turritella (2.3") 6 cm
Maoricolpus rosea (Quoy & Gaimard, 1834). New Zealand. Intertidal, mud; common. Syn.: *manukauensis* Powell.

Striped Turritella (1.5") 4 cm
Zeacolpus vittatus (Hutton, 1873). New Zealand. Offshore, sand; uncommon.

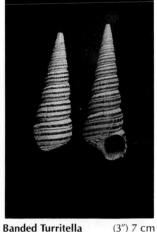

Banded Turritella (3") 7 cm
Turritella cingulata Sowerby, 1825. Chile. Subtidal; common. Syn.: *tricarinata* King.

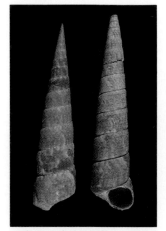

Angle-mouth Turritella (4")
10 cm *Turritella gonostoma* Valenciennes, 1832. W. Mexico to Ecuador. Subtidal; common. Syn.: "*goniostoma.*"

White-mouthed Turritella (4")
10 cm *Turritella leucostoma* Valenciennes, 1832. Baja California to Panama. 1 to 40 m, mud; common. Syn.: *tigrina* Kiener.

Duplicate Turritella (5") 12 cm
Turritella duplicata (L., 1758). S. E. Asia; Indian Ocean. Subtidal, sand; common. Syn.: *acutangula* L.

Master Turritella (5") 12 cm
Turritella anactor Berry, 1957. W. Mexico. Offshore; uncommon. Paratype specimen illustrated.

Ligar Turritella (4") 10 cm
Turritella ligar Deshayes, 1843. W. Africa. Offshore to 20 m; uncommon. Syn.: *flammulata* Kiener.

Carinate Turritella (3") 7 cm
Turritella carinifera Lamarck, 1822. South Africa. Offshore to 240 m; common.

Bloody Turritella (4") 10 cm
Turritella sanguinea Reeve, 1849. South Africa. Offshore to 110 m; common.

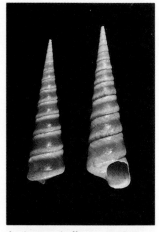

Sloping Turritella (3.5") 9 cm
Turritella declivis Adams & Reeve, 1850. South Africa. Offshore to 178 meters; uncommon. Syn.: *excavata* Sowerby.

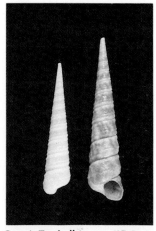

Gunn's Turritella (2") 5 cm
Turritella gunnii Reeve, 1849. Tasmania; South Australia. Subtidal; uncommon.

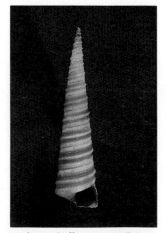

Kowie Turritella (2") 5 cm
Turritella kowiensis Sowerby, 1900. South Africa. Subtidal to 51 m; uncommon.

Knocker's Turritella (2.5") 6 cm
Protoma knockeri Baird, 1870. West Africa. Intertidal to offshore; moderately common.

Projecting Turritella (3") 7.5 cm
Turritella torulosa Kiener, 1843. West Africa. Shallow water, sandy mud; common.

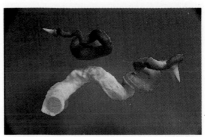

West Indian Worm-shell (4") 10 cm
Vermicularia spirata (Philippi, 1836). S. E. Florida; West Indies; Bermuda. In sponges, shallow water. Family Turritellidae.

WORM-SHELLS
FAMILY VERMETIDAE

Long, slender, usually coiling shells resembling "worm tubes" and growing in clumps or attached singly to rocks and shells. Operculum, when present, many-whorled and horny. Contains *Vermetus, Dendropoma (Spiroglyphus)* and *Serpuloides.*

Variable Worm-shell (6") 15 cm
Petaloconchus varians (Orbigny, 1841). Florida to Brazil; Bermuda. Forms reefs in shallow water. Types of *nigricans* Dall illustrated.

Irregular Worm-shell (2") 5 cm
Dendropoma irregularis (Orbigny, 1842). S. E. Florida to Brazil. Bermuda. Attached to rocks; common.

Slit Worm-shell (1.5") 4 cm
Siliquaria squamata Blainville, 1827. S. E. United States to Brazil; Bermuda; common. In family Siliquariidae.

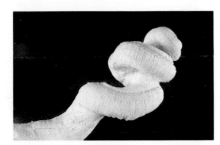

Ponderous Worm-shell (8") 19 cm
Siliquaria ponderosa (Mörch, 1860). S. W. Pacific. Shallow water; uncommon.

SUNDIALS
FAMILY ARCHITECTONICIDAE

The sundial shells are flat and with a large umbilicus. The operculum is horny, sometimes button-shaped. Most species are tropical in shallow to deep water. A few, like *Pseudomalaxis,* are microscopic.

Giant Sundial (2.5") 6 cm
Architectonica maxima (Philippi, 1849). Indo-Pacific. Sandy bottom, 10 to 50 m; common.

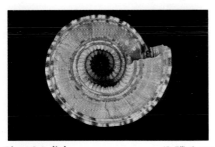

Giant Sundial (2.5") 6 cm
Architectonica maxima (Philippi, 1849). Underside view. The wide, deep umbilicus accommodates the beehive-shaped operculum.

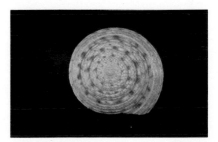

American Sundial (2") 5 cm
Architectonica nobilis Röding, 1758. S. E. United States to Brazil; W. Mexico to Peru. Shallow water; locally common. Syn.: *granulata* Lamarck.

Clear Sundial (2") 5 cm
Architectonica perspectiva (L., 1758). Indo-Pacific. Shallow water, sand; common to abundant.

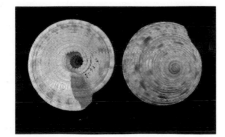

Smooth Sundial (1.5") 4 cm
Architectonica laevigata (Lamarck, 1816). Indian Ocean. Shallow water, sand; uncommon.

Sharp-edged Sundial   (1.2") 3 cm
Acutitectonica acutissima (Sowerby, 1914). Japan to northern Australia in 50 to 200 m; uncommon.

Straw Sundial   (1.4") 3.5 cm
Heliacus stramineus (Gmelin, 1791). Indo-Pacific. Shallow water; uncommon.

Noble Sundial   (0.3") 7 mm
Pseudomalaxis nobilis Verrill, 1885. S. E. United States; West Indies. Deep water to 140 m; rare.

PLANAXIS SNAILS
FAMILY PLANAXIDAE

Resembling *Littorina* periwinkles. Shell very thick, often spirally grooved. Siphonal notch present. Operculum corneous. Some species bear living young in the oviduct. All are tropical and live near shore.

Sulcate Planaxis   (0.7") 1.8 cm
Planaxis sulcatus (Born, 1778). Indo-Pacific. Subtidal among rocks; abundant.

Black Atlantic Planaxis   (0.5") 1.2 cm
Planaxis nucleus (Bruguière, 1789). S. E. Florida; West Indies; Bermuda. Littoral on rocks; abundant.

Dwarf Atlantic Planaxis   (0.3") 7 mm
Planaxis lineatus (da Costa, 1778). S. E. Florida to Brazil. Littoral, coral gravel; abundant.

Dwarf Pacific Planaxis   (0.3") 7 mm
Planaxis labiosa A. Adams, 1853. Central and S. W. Pacific. Midtidal line among coral gravel; abundant. Syn.: *fasciatus* Pease.

Hinea Planaxis   (0.7") 1.8 cm
Hinea brasiliana (Lamarck, 1822). S. W. Pacific; New Zealand. Intertidal, rocks; locally common. Syn.: *mollis* Sowerby.

Black-brown Planaxis   (0.6") 1.5 cm
Planaxis nigra Quoy & Gaimard, 1834. Indo-Pacific. Intertidal rocks; common. Syn.: *hanleyi* E. A. Smith; *abbreviatus* Pease.

Decollate Planaxis   (1.2") 3 cm
Quoyia decollata Quoy & Gaimard, 1834. S. W. Pacific. Intertidal rocks; locally common. Syn.: *michaudi* Crosse & Fischer.

MODULUS SHELLS
FAMILY MODULIDAE

Small, tropical snails living in shallow water. The top-shaped shell has a small tooth at the base of the columella. Operculum corneous, many-whorled. About 8 species known.

Atlantic Modulus   (0.5") 1.2 cm
Modulus modulus (L., 1758). S. E. United
States to Brazil; Bermuda. Shallow water
among sea grass; abundant.

Angled Modulus   (0.5") 1.2 cm
Modulus carchedonius (Lamarck, 1822).
Caribbean. Shallow water; uncommon.
Syn.: *angulata* C. B. Adams.

Little Chain Modulus   (0.5") 1.2 cm
Modulus catenulatus (Philippi, 1849). Gulf
of California to Ecuador. Intertidal grassy
flats; common.

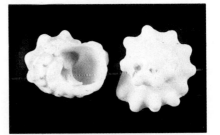

Waxy Modulus   (0.6") 1.5 cm
Modulus cerodes (A. Adams, 1851). Gulf of
California to Panama. Mud flats; common.

Tectum Modulus   (1.2") 3 cm
Modulus tectum (Gmelin, 1791). Indo-Pacific. Among weeds in shallow water; locally
common.

Glowing Modulus   (0.7") 1.8 cm
Modulus candidus Petit, 1853. Central and
S. W. Pacific. Shallow water; uncommon.
No black line on columella.

Little Disk Modulus   (0.6") 1.5 cm
Modulus disculus (Philippi, 1846). Gulf of
California to Panama. Intertidal grassy mud
flats; common.

HORN SNAILS
FAMILY POTAMIDIDAE

Slender, dull-colored shells usually living
in tropical muddy or brackish water areas.
Occur in large colonies. Operculum horny,
thin, circular and many-whorled.

False Caribbean Cerith   (0.3") 5 mm
Batillaria minima (Gmelin, 1791). Southern
Florida to Brazil; Bermuda. Mud flats;
abundant. Variable striping.

Zoned Cerith   (1.2") 3 cm
Batillaria zonalis (Bruguière, 1792). Japan;
S. W. Pacific. Mud flats; abundant. Intro-
duced to western United States.

Many-formed Cerith   (1") 2.5 cm
Batillaria multiformis (Lischke, 1869). Japan. Intertidal, gravel and mud bottoms;
abundant.

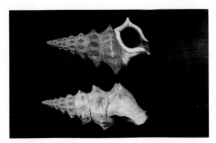

Rhino Cerith   (1.4") 3.5 cm
Rhinocoryne humboldti (Valenciennes,
1832). W. Mexico to Chile. Estuaries to 27
m; abundant. Syn.: *pacificum* Sowerby.

Ebony Swamp Cerith (4″) 10 cm
Pyrazus ebeninus (Bruguière,
1792). Eastern Australia. Mud
flats, intertidal. Locally abundant.

Sulcate Swamp Cerith (2″) 5 cm
Terebralia sulcata (Bruguière,
1792). Indo-West Pacific. Intertidal, estuary mud flats; abundant.

Mud Creeper (4″) 10 cm
Terebralia palustris (L., 1767).
Indo-Pacific. Mangrove mud
flats; abundant.

Australian Mud Creeper (4″)
10 cm *Terebralia palustris* subspecies *ceramica* (Link, 1807).
Western Australia. Mangrove
mud flats; common.

Telescope Snail (4″) 10 cm
Telescopium telescopium (L.,
1758). Indo-Pacific. Mangrove
mud flats; abundant.

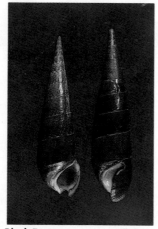

Black Faunus (2″) 5 cm
Faunus ater (Born, 1778). Philippines; East Indies. Freshwater
snail in family Thiaridae. Abundant.

THE CERITHS
FAMILY CERITHIIDAE

The ceriths are a major family of
mainly shallow-water dwellers,
most distributed in the tropics.
They live in large colonies feeding on mud detritus and de-
cayed algae. Some genera are
very small, such as *Bittium*, but
most *Cerithium* are about an
inch in size. Operculum horny
and with only a few whorls
(paucispiral).

Giant Knobbed Cerith
(5″) 13 cm
Cerithium nodulosum (Bruguière, 1792). Indo-Pacific.
Reef flats, shallow water; abundant.

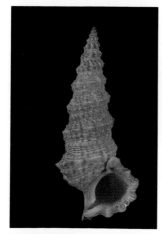

Red Sea Cerith (4″) 10 cm
Cerithium erythraeonense Lamarck, 1822. Red Sea. Shallow
water; locally common.

European Cerith (3″) 7.5 cm
Cerithium vulgatum Bruguière,
1792. Mediterranean; West Africa. Subtidal rock areas; abundant.

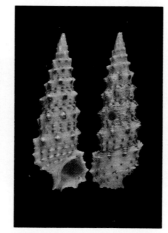

Lifu Cerith (1.5″) 4 cm
Cerithium lifuensis Melvill &
Standen, 1895. Central Pacific.
Subtidal grass flats; locally
common.

Strong Cerith (2″) 5 cm
Cerithium munitum Sowerby,
1855. S. W. Pacific. Subtidal,
grass and sand flats; uncommon.

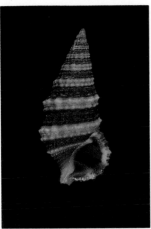

Zoned Cerith   (1.2") 3 cm
Clypeomorus zonatus (Wood, 1828). S. W. Pacific. Subtidal, sand; uncommon. Syn.: *lemniscatum* Q. & G.; *problema* Iredale.

Sutured Cerith   (1.5") 3.5 cm
Cerithium suturale Philippi, 1849. S. W. Pacific. Subtidal, grass and sand; uncommon.

Thin-lined Cerith   (1") 2.5 cm
Cerithium tenuifilosum Sowerby, 1866. Indo-Pacific. Shallow water near coral reefs; common.

White-studded Cerith
(1") 2.5 cm
Cerithium dialeucum Philippi, 1849. Indian Ocean. Shallow water; locally common.

Yellow Cerith   (2") 5 cm
Cerithium citrinum Sowerby, 1855. N. E. Australia; Melanesia. Subtidal; uncommon.

New Holland Cerith (1.5") 4 cm
Cerithium novaehollandiae Sowerby, 1855. Northern Australia. Shallow water; locally common.

Uneven Cerith   (1") 2.5 cm
Cerithium salebrosum Sowerby, 1855. Polynesia. Shallow sand and grass flats; common.

Column Cerith   (1.5") 4 cm
Cerithium columna Sowerby, 1834. Tropical Pacific. Subtidal, sand; common. Syn.: *fusiforme* Sowerby; *proditum* Bayle.

Rüppell's Cerith   (1.5") 4 cm
Cerithium ruppellii Philippi, 1849. Red Sea. Shallow water; locally common.

Channeled Cerith   (0.7") 1.8 cm
Cerithium alveolus Hombron & Jaquinot, 1854. Indo-Pacific. Weedy sand shallows; common. Syn.: *piperitum* Sowerby.

Stocky Cerith   (1") 2.5 cm
Cerithium litteratum (Born, 1778). S. E. Florida to Brazil. Subtidal; common. Syn.: *semiferrugineum* Lamarck.

Ivory Cerith   (0.8") 2 cm
Cerithium eburneum Bruguière, 1792. S. E. Florida and West Indies. Subtidal, sand; common. Syn.: *algicola* C. B. Adams (pointed beads).

Dwarf Atlantic Cerith (0.4") 1 cm
Cerithium lutosum Menke, 1828. S. E. United States; West Indies; Bermuda. Intertidal; abundant.

Florida Cerith (1.3") 3 cm
Cerithium atratum (Born, 1778). S. E. United States to Brazil. Subtidal, in weeds; common. Syn.: *floridanum* Mörch.

Fly-specked Cerith (1") 2.5 cm
Cerithium muscarum Say, 1832. Southern Florida; West Indies. Shallow semi-brackish waters; abundant.

Guinea Cerith (1.2") 3 cm
Cerithium guinaicum Philippi, 1849. Florida; Caribbean; West Africa. Subtidal; uncommon. Syn.: *auricoma* Schwengel.

Common Vertagus (2") 5 cm
Rhinoclavis vertagus (L., 1758). Indo-Pacific. Intertidal to 13 m on sand; abundant. Yellow or white.

Banded Vertagus (3") 8 cm
Rhinoclavis fasciata (Bruguière, 1792). Indo-Pacific. Subtidal to 18 m; abundant. Syn.: *procerum* Kiener; *pharos* Hinds.

Rough Vertagus (2") 5 cm
Rhinoclavis aspera (L., 1758). Indo-Pacific. Subtidal to 28 m; common. White or banded.

Obelisk Vertagus (2") 5 cm
Rhinoclavis sinensis (Gmelin, 1791). Indo-Pacific. Intertidal to 23 m; abundant. Syn.: *obeliscus* Bruguière.

Articulate Vertagus (1.8") 4.5 cm
Rhinoclavis articulata (Adams & Reeve, 1850). Indo-Pacific. Subtidal to 91 m; somewhat common.

Koch's Vertagus (1.5") 3.5 cm
Rhinoclavis kochi (Philippi, 1848). Indo-Pacific. Sand bottom, 2-62 m; uncommon. Syn.: *recurvum* Sowerby.

Brettingham's Vertagus (2") 5 cm
Rhinoclavis brettinghami Cernohorsky, 1974. N.W. Australia. Intertidal; common. Syn.: *pulchrum* Sowerby.

Bituberculate Vertagus (2") 5 cm
Rhinoclavis bituberculata (Sowerby, 1855). N. Australia; New Guinea. Intertidal; common. Syn.: *semigranosum* Lamarck.

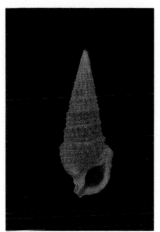

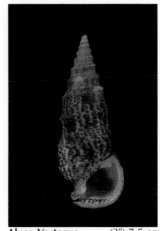

Gem Vertagus   (1.5″) 4 cm
Rhinoclavis gemmata (Hinds, 1844). Gulf of California to Ecuador. Subtidal to 130 m; common. Syn.: *tenuisculptum* Sowerby.

Long-snouted Vertagus (2″) 5 cm
Rhinoclavis longicaudata (Adams & Reeve, 1850). S. E. Asia; Fiji. Uncommon. Syn.: *attenuatum* Philippi.

Aluco Vertagus   (3″) 7.5 cm
Pseudovertagus aluco (L., 1758). S. W. Pacific. Intertidal to 9 m, sand; common. Smoothish to knobbed.

Noble Vertagus   (5″) 12 cm
Pseudovertagus nobilis (Reeve, 1855). Central East Africa and S. W. Pacific. 18 to 88 m; sand; rare.

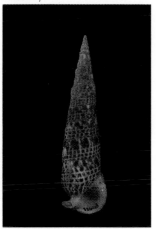

Amulet Vertagus   (3″) 7.5 cm
Pseudovertagus phylarchus (Iredale, 1929). Philippines to Australia. Offshore, 5-30 m; uncommon.

Club Vertagus   (5″) 13 cm
Pseudovertagus clava (Gmelin, 1791). Lower Polynesia to Australia; S. E. Africa. Subtidal to 40 m; common.

Morus Cerith   (0.5″) 1.2 cm
Clypeomorus concisus (Hombron & Jacquinot, 1854). Indo-Pacific. Shallow water; abundant. Syn.: *morus* Lamarck.

Necklace Cerith   (0.5″) 1.2 cm
Clypeomorus moniliferus (Kiener, 1841). Indo-Pacific. Shallow water; common.

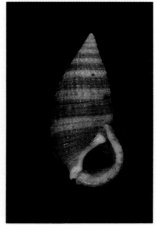

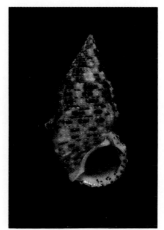

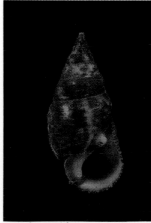

Short Cerith   (0.6″) 1.5 cm
Clypeomorus brevis (Quoy & Gaimard, 1834). Indo-Pacific. Shallow water; common. Syn.: *patiens* Bayle.

Chemnitz Cerith   (1.5″) 3.5 cm
Clypeomorus chemnitziana (Pilsbry, 1901). S. W. Pacific. Shallow water reef flats; uncommon.

Stony Cerith   (1.2″) 3 cm
Clypeomorus petrosus (Wood, 1828). S. W. Pacific. Shallow water reefs; common.

Swarthy Cerith   (1.6″) 4 cm
Cerithium adustum Kiener, 1841. W. Mexico to Ecuador. In sand among intertidal rocks; common.

Bent Cerith (0.5") 1.2 cm
Clypeomorus aduncus (Gould, 1849). Philippines. Shallow water; rare.

Gourmya Cerith (2") 5 cm
Gourmya gourmyi (Crosse, 1861). New Caledonia and New Hebrides. Offshore, shallow water; locally common.

Ribbon Cerith (2") 5 cm
Clavocerithium taeniatum (Quoy & Gaimard, 1834). New Guinea. Offshore, 2-20 m; locally common.

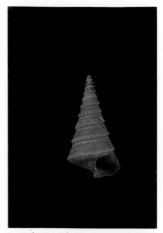

Pagoda Cerith (1") 2.5 cm
Trochocerithium tectiforme (Watson, 1884). Japan. Deep water; uncommon.

Bell Clapper (8") 20 cm
Campanile symbolicum Iredale, 1917. Western Australia. Offshore to 10 m. Locally uncommon.

Carinate False Cerith
(1.5") 3.5 cm
Fastigiella carinata Reeve, 1848. Bahamas and northern Cuba. Shallow water; rare.

WENTLETRAPS
FAMILY EPITONIIDAE

The wentletraps are popular collector's items because of their intricate ribbing. The 200 or so known species live in all seas from shallow to very deep water. The operculum is corneous, thin, and with a few whorls. Some feed on sea anemones. The Epitoniidae, Janthinidae and Architectonicidae belong to a recently accepted order, Heterogastropoda.

Precious Wentletrap (2.5") 6 cm
Epitonium scalare (L., 1758). Japan to S. W. Pacific. Subtidal to 29 m; locally common. Syn.: *pretiosum* Lamarck.

Lamellose Wentletrap
(1") 2.5 cm
Epitonium lamellosum (Lamarck, 1822). Southern Florida; Caribbean; Europe. Subtidal to 66 m; common.

Western Atlantic Wentletrap
(1") 2.5 cm
Epitonium occidentale (Nyst, 1871). S. E. Florida to Brazil. 1 to 120 m; fairly common.

Imperial Wentletrap (1") 2.5 cm
Epitonium imperiale (Sowerby, 1844). S. W. Pacific. Subtidal, sand; uncommon.

Guinea Wentletrap (2") 5 cm
Amaea guineensis (Bouchet & Tellier, 1978.) West Africa. Offshore; uncommon.

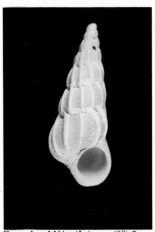

Greenland Wentletrap (2″) 5 cm
Epitonium greenlandicum (Perry, 1811). Circumpolar in north. 30 to 260 m; common. Syn.: *loveni* A. Adams.

Mitchell's Wentletrap (2″) 5 cm
Amaea mitchelli (Dall, 1896). Texas to eastern Panama. Offshore, shallow water; uncommon.

Blaine's Wentletrap
(1.5″) 3.5 cm
Epitonium blainei Clench & Turner, 1953. Southern Florida. Offshore to 44 m; rare. Holotype specimen.

Dall's Wentletrap (1.5″) 4 cm
Cirsotrema dalli Rehder, 1945. S. E. United States to Brazil. 36 to 150 m; uncommon. Holotype specimen.

Ferminia Wentletrap (1.5″) 4 cm
Amaea ferminiana (Dall, 1908). W. Mexico to W. Colombia. Offshore; rare. Similar *retifera* (Dall, 1889) is from Caribbean.

Few-ribbed Wentletrap
(1″) 2.5 cm
Cirsotrema rariforme (Lamarck, 1822). Indian Ocean. Subtidal under rocks; uncommon.

Abbreviated Wentletrap
(1″) 2.5 cm
Cirsotrema abbreviatum (Sowerby, 1874). East Indies. Shallow water; uncommon. Slender form of *varicosum?*

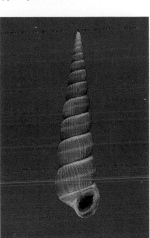

Acuminate Wentletrap
(1.5″) 4 cm
Epitonium acuminatum (Sowerby, 1844). Japan to Australia. Shallow water; uncommon.

Annulate Wentletrap (1.5″) 4 cm
Epitonium annulatum Kuroda & Ito, 1961. Japan; deep water; uncommon.

Gaze Wentletrap (1.5″) 3.5 cm
Amaea gazeoides (Kuroda & Habe, 1950). Southern Japan. Offshore; rare.

Varicose Wentletrap (2″) 5 cm
Cirsotrema varicosum (Lamarck, 1822). Japan; S. W. Pacific. Offshore; uncommon.

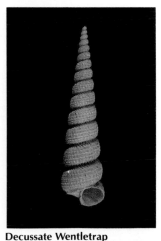

Decussate Wentletrap
(1″) 2.5 cm
Amaea decussata (Lamarck, 1804). Indo-Pacific. Offshore to 30 m; uncommon.

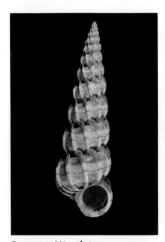

Common Wentletrap
          (1.2″) 3 cm
Epitonium clathrum (L., 1758).
Western Europe; Mediterranean. Intertidal; common.

Zelebor Wentletrap   (1″) 2.5 cm
Cirsotrema zelebori (Dunker, 1866). New Zealand. Offshore to 30 m; uncommon.

Magellanic Wentletrap
          (1.2″) 3 cm
Epitonium magellanicum (Philippi, 1845). Argentina and Chile. 55 to 100 m; common.

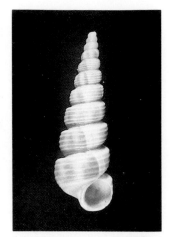

Spiral Wentletrap   (1.5″) 4 cm
Eglisia spirata (Sowerby, 1825).
Western Africa; West Indies.
Offshore to 200 m; uncommon.

Gould's Wentletrap   (1″) 2.5 cm
Alora gouldi (A. Adams, 1857).
W. Mexico to Panama. Offshore; rare.

Noble Wentletrap   (1.5″) 4 cm
Sthenorytis pernobilis (Fischer & Bernardi, 1857). S. E. United States; Caribbean. 100 to 1,600 m; rare.

PURPLE SEA SNAILS
FAMILY JANTHINIDAE

The fragile, purple sea snails live pelagic lives afloat on the open, tropical seas, buoyed up by mucus-covered bubbles. Often cast ashore after storms. They feed on other floating sea creatures. Some species are worldwide. All *Janthina* are purple; *Recluzia* with a yellow float and a brown shell. They are blind.

Common Janthina   (1.5″) 4 cm
Janthina janthina (L., 1758).
Worldwide, tropical seas. Common.

Elongate Janthina   (1″) 2.5 cm
Janthina globosa Swainson, 1822. Caribbean; western Pacific. Pelagic; common. Syn.: *prolongata* Blainville.

Dwarf Janthina   (0.2″) 5 mm
Janthina exigua Lamarck, 1816.
Worldwide, warm seas. Pelagic; uncommon.

Pallid Janthina   (1″) 2.5 cm
Janthina pallida (Thompson, 1840). Worldwide, warm seas. Pelagic; uncommon. Globular shape.

Recluzia Snail   (1″) 2.5 cm
Recluzia lutea (Bennett, 1840).
Caribbean; Indo-Pacific. Pelagic; rare. Syn.: *palmeri* Dall (holotype illustrated).

Helicoid Vanikoro (1") 2.5 cm
Vanikoro helicoidea (Guillou, 1842). Indo-Pacific. Shallow water; common. Syn.: *semiplicata* Pease. In family Vanikoroidae.

Cancellate Vanikoro (1") 2.5 cm
Vanikoro cancellata (Lamarck, 1822). Central and S. W. Pacific. Subtidal; moderately common.

Ligate Vanikoro (1.2") 3 cm
Vanikoro ligata (Récluz, 1844). S. W. Pacific. Subtidal on rocks; moderately common.

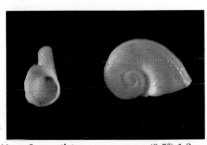

Irue Separatista (0.5") 1.2 cm
Separatista blainvilliana Petit, 1851. S. W. Pacific. Subtidal; rare.

Helicoid Separatista (0.5") 1.2 cm
Lippistes helicoides (Gmelin, 1791). S. W. Pacific. Subtidal; rare.

Horn Separatista (0.5") 1.2 cm
Lippistes cornu (Gmelin, 1791). South Africa. Offshore to 60 m; rare.

Two-keeled Hairy-shell (1.5") 4 cm
Trichotropis bicarinata (Sowerby, 1825). Arctic Seas. Offshore to 10 m; locally common. In family Trichotropidae.

Cancellate Hairy-shell (1") 2.5 cm
Trichotropis cancellata (Hinds, 1843). Bering Sea to Oregon. Offshore to 20 m; common.

Gray Hairy-shell (1") 2.5 cm
Trichotropis insignis Middendorff, 1849. Alaska to northern Japan. Offshore to 50 m; uncommon.

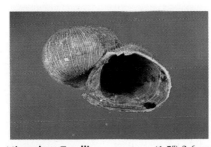

One-ribbed Hairy-shell (0.6") 1.5 cm
Iphinoe unicarinata (Broderip & Sowerby, 1829). Japan and Korea. 85 to 250 m; uncommon.

Miraculous Torellia (1.5") 3.6 cm
Torellia mirabilis E. A. Smith, 1907. Antarctic Seas. Offshore; locally uncommon.

HOOF-SHELLS
FAMILIES HIPPONICIDAE and CAPULIDAE

The shells of hoof (Hipponicidae) and cap (Capulidae) shells resemble limpets, but the animals are prosobranchs with one set of gills and 7 rows of teeth. The shells usually have an outer rough "skin" or periostracum. Eggs are brooded under the female's shell.

Trigonal Hoof-shell   (0.7") 1.8 cm
Pilosabia trigona (Gmelin, 1791). S. W. Pacific; Japan. Subtidal, on rocks and shells; common. Syn.: *barbatus* Sowerby.

Orange Hoof-shell   (0.5") 1.2 cm
Pilosabia subrufa (Lamarck, 1819). Caribbean; Eastern Pacific; Indo-Pacific. Syn.: *tumens* Carpenter.

Fool's Cap   (2") 5 cm
Capulus ungaricus (L., 1767). Iceland to Mediterranean. Offshore; on rocks; locally common.

California Cap   (1.5") 3.8 cm
Capulus californicus Dall, 1900. California to W. Mexico. Offshore, usually attached to *Pecten* shells; rare.

Deepsea Cap   (1") 2.5 cm
Malluvium lissus (E. A. Smith, 1894). S. W. Pacific. Deep water; on sea urchin spines; rare.

SLIPPER SHELLS
FAMILY CREPIDULIDAE

The slipper shells and cup-and-saucer shells have either an internal shelf or a small cup to protect the soft organs of the snail. *Crepidula* usually live one on top of the other. There is no operculum.

Atlantic Slipper   (1.5") 3.5 cm
Crepidula fornicata (L., 1758). Eastern United States; northwestern Europe. Subtidal on rocks and shells; abundant.

Spotted Slipper   (1.2") 3 cm
Crepidula maculosa Conrad, 1846. S. E. United States; Bahamas. Subtidal; on other shells; common.

Costate Slipper   (2") 5 cm
Crepidula costata Sowerby, 1824. New Zealand. Subtidal on mussels and rocks; abundant.

Dilated Slipper   (2.5") 6 cm
Crepidula dilatata Lamarck, 1822. Chile, Peru and Argentina. Subtidal on rocks; common.

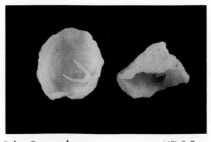

False Cup-and-saucer   (1") 2.5 cm
Cheilea equestris (L., 1758). Florida to Brazil; W. Mexico to Chile; Indo-Pacific. Offshore on rocks; uncommon.

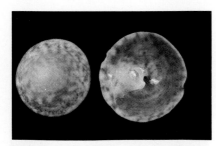

Conic Cup-and-saucer   (1") 2.5 cm
Calyptraea conica Broderip, 1834. W. Mexico to Ecuador. Offshore to 37 m; common.

Cape Cup-and-saucer (1.3") 3 cm
Calyptraea capensis Tomlin, 1931. South Africa. Offshore on rocks; uncommon. Form of *chinensis?*

Chinese Cup-and-saucer (0.6") 1.5 cm
Calyptraea chinensis (L., 1758). Europe. Subtidal on rocks; common.

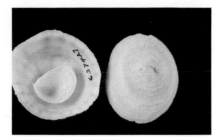

West Indian Cup-and-saucer (1") 2.5 cm
Crucibulum auricula (Gmelin, 1791). S. E. United States to Brazil. Subtidal to 60 m; uncommon.

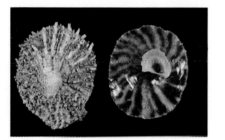

Spiny Cup-and-saucer (1") 2.5 cm
Crucibulum spinosum (Sowerby, 1824). Southern California to Chile. Subtidal to 60 m; common on rocks and shells.

Shield Cup-and-saucer (2") 5 cm
Crucibulum scutellatum (Wood, 1828). W. Mexico to Ecuador. Subtidal on shells and rocks; common. Syn.: *imbricata* Sowerby.

Trochita Shell (3") 7 cm
Trochita trochiformis (Born, 1778). Ecuador to Peru. Offshore; moderately common.

CARRIER-SHELLS
FAMILY XENOPHORIDAE

Most carrier-shells cement sea-floor debris to their shells, often obliterating surface features. Basically trochoidal in shape they are usually dull, coarsely ornamented and fragile. Corneous operculum assists animal in *Strombus*-like movements. Found in tropical and warm seas.

Atlantic Carrier-shell (2") 5 cm
Xenophora conchyliophora (Born, 1780). North Carolina to West Indies, Brazil; Bermuda. Shallow water; moderately common. Syn.: *onustus* Reeve.

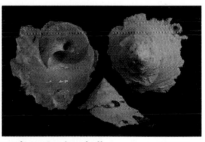

Longley's Carrier-shell (5") 13 cm
Tugurium longleyi (Bartsch, 1931). North Carolina to Barbados. Dredged, 70-450 fms; uncommon. Strong, curved growth lines on base.

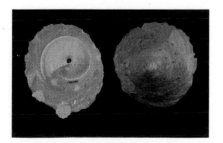

Caribbean Carrier-shell (2.5") 6 cm
Tugurium caribaeum (Petit, 1856). Brazil, South Carolina to West Indies. Dredged, 75-300 fms; moderately common. Small umbilicus.

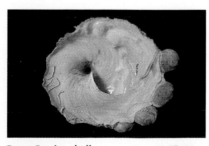

Great Carrier-shell (4.5") 11 cm
Tugurium giganteum (Schepman, 1909). Japan; Indonesia; South Africa. On mud, deep water; uncommon. Ventral view.

Great Carrier-shell (4.5") 11 cm
Tugurium giganteum (Schepman, 1909). Top view; few attachments at periphery of whorls.

Mediterranean Carrier-shell (1.5") 4 cm
Xenophora crispa (Koenig, 1831). Mediterranean and adjacent eastern Atlantic. Deep water; rare. Syn.: *mediterranea* Tiberi.

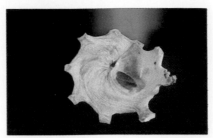

Digitate Carrier-shell (3") 7.5 cm
Xenophora digitata von Marten, 1878. West Africa. Offshore, mud, 5 to 30 m; locally common.

Torrida Carrier-shell (1.4") 3.5 cm
Xenophora torrida Kuroda & Ito, 1961. Japan and Ryukyu Islands. 20 to 80 m; uncommon. *X. turrida* is a misspelling.

Indian Carrier-shell (3") 7.5 cm
Tugurium indicum (Gmelin, 1791). Indo-W. Pacific. Shallow water; uncommon. Attachments only on early whorls. Syn.: *helvacea* Philippi; *wagneri* Philippi.

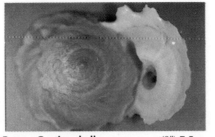

Barren Carrier-shell (3") 7.5 cm
Tugurium exutum (Reeve, 1843). Indo-W. Pacific. Shallow water; uncommon. Rarely attaches more than sand grains at apex.

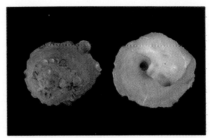

Fragment Carrier-shell (3") 7.5 cm
Xenophora calculifera (Reeve, 1843). Indo-W. Pacific. Shallow water; uncommon. Syn.: *sinensis* Philippi.

Solar Carrier-shell (1") 2.5 cm
Xenophora solarioides (Reeve, 1845). Indo-Pacific. Shallow water; uncommon. Among smallest in genus.

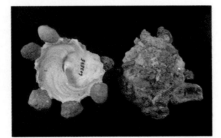

Australian Carrier-shell (2.5") 6 cm
Xenophora neozelanica form *peroniana* Iredale, 1929. Southern Australia. Offshore, to 150 m; uncommon. *X. tatei* Cossmann is a fossil.

Japan Carrier-shell (2") 5 cm
Xenophora japonica Kuroda & Habe, 1971. Japan, Taiwan, Philippines. Shelly and gravelly places, 50 to 300 m; uncommon.

Thin Carrier-shell (2") 5 cm
Xenophora tenuis Fulton, 1934. South of Honshu, Japan. Dredged, 50 to 80 fms; uncommon.

Rough Carrier-shell (2") 5 cm
Xenophora corrugata (Reeve, 1843). Indo-W. Pacific. Moderately deep water; moderately common. Umbilicus sometimes present.

Sunburst Carrier-shell (3.5") 7.5 cm
Stellaria solaris (L., 1767). Indo-Pacific. Offshore to considerable depths; common. No attachments at any stage of growth.

Pallid Carrier-shell (2.5") 6.5 cm
Xenophora pallidula (Reeve, 1842). Indo-W. Pacific; South Africa. Offshore to deep water; common. Wide variety of attached objects.

OSTRICH-FOOT SHELLS
FAMILY STRUTHIOLARIIDAE

Small family of medium-size gastropods noted for the thickened outer lip of their shells, supposedly resembling an ostrich foot. The large aperture has a short siphonal canal. Elongate foot has small corneous operculum used in locomotion. Species, mostly from New Zealand, are sand dwellers.

Large Ostrich-foot (2.5") 6.5 cm
Struthiolaria papulosa (Martyn, 1784). New Zealand. In sand, littoral and shallow water offshore; common.

Remarkable Ostrich-foot (1.5") 3.5 cm
Perissodonta mirabilis E. A. Smith, 1907. South Georgia and Kerguelen Islands. Deep water; rare.

PELICAN'S-FOOT SHELLS
FAMILY APORRHAIDAE

Small to medium-size gastropods with shells distinguished by pointed processes on outer lip from which they get their popular name. Animal has flattened footsole and a small operculum and makes lunging movements like *Strombus*. The minute egg cases are soft walled and are deposited in sand.

American Pelican's-foot (2") 5 cm
Aporrhais occidentalis Beck, 1836. Arctic Canada to North Carolina. Offshore to 350 fms; common. Syn.: *mainensis* Johnson (holotype on right); *labradorensis* Johnson.

Common Pelican's-foot (2") 5 cm
Aporrhais pespelecani (L., 1758). From Lofoten Islands to Mediterranean. Offshore to 140 m; common. Syn.: *michaudi* Locard; *sarsi* Kobelt.

MacAndrew's Pelican's-foot (1.3") 3.5 cm
Aporrhais serresianus macandreae Jeffreys, 1867. Norway to Mediterranean. Deep water; uncommon. Syn.: *pescarbonis* Forbes & Hanley.

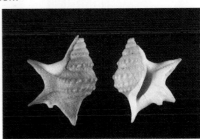

Senegal Pelican's-foot (1") 2.5 cm
Aporrhais senegalensis Gray, 1838. West Africa. Offshore, 60 to 80 fms; uncommon. Smallest member of genus.

African Pelican's-foot (2") 5 cm
Aporrhais pesgallinae Barnard, 1963. Southwest Africa, Angola. In sand, moderately deep water; uncommon.

TRUE CONCHS
FAMILY STROMBIDAE

Includes several genera differing widely among themselves in shell features, but closely allied anatomically. Most shells have a "stromboid notch" near anterior end. Animals herbivorous and make leaping movements using strong, horny, curved operculum. Eggs laid in long gelatinous strands.

Pink Conch (8") 20 cm
Strombus gigas L., 1758. Southeast Florida; Bermuda; West Indies. On sand, littoral and offshore; common. Syn.: *verrilli* McGinty. At left is young shell.

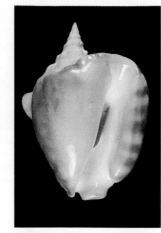

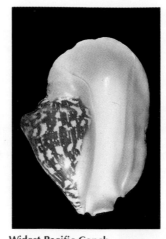

Three-knobbed Conch
(4″) 10 cm
Strombus tricornis Lightfoot,
1786. Red Sea and Gulf of Aden.
Shallow water; common.

Thersite Stromb (5.5″) 14 cm
Strombus thersites Swainson,
1823. S.W. Pacific. Offshore, 5
to 10 fms; rare. Syn.: *pondero-
sus* Philippi.

Widest Pacific Conch
(6″) 16 cm
Strombus latissimus L., 1758. S.
W. Pacific. 4 to 20 m; uncommon. Syn.: *picta* Röding.

Bull Conch (3.5″) 9 cm
Strombus taurus Reeve, 1857.
Marshall and Marianas Islands,
Pacific. Coral rubble or rock, to
15 fms; rare.

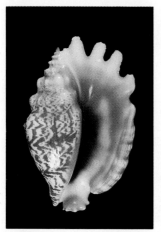

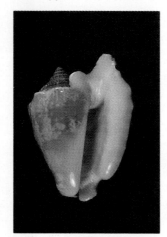

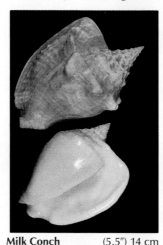

Laciniate Conch (4″) 10 cm
Strombus sinuatus Lightfoot,
1786. S. W. Pacific. Coral sand,
to 10 fms; uncommon. Syn.: *laciniatus* Dillwyn.

Hawk-wing Conch (3.5″) 9 cm
Strombus raninus Gmelin,
1791. S. E. Florida to Brazil.
Shallow water; common. Syn.:
bituberculatus Lamarck.

Milk Conch (5.5″) 14 cm
Strombus costatus Gmelin,
1791. Southern Florida; West
Indies; Brazil; Bermuda. Shallow water; common.

Rooster-tail Conch (5″) 12.5 cm
Strombus gallus L., 1758. S. E.
Florida; West Indies; Brazil;
Bermuda. Offshore to 10 m;
uncommon.

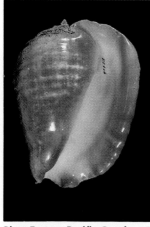

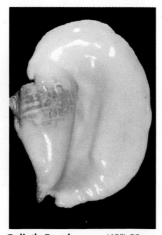

Giant Eastern Pacific Conch (7″)
18 cm *Strombus galeatus*
Swainson, 1823. Gulf of California to Ecuador. Shallow water;
uncommon.

Goliath Conch (13″) 33 cm
Strombus goliath Schröter,
1805. Brazil (endemic). On sand
offshore; uncommon. Largest
of all *Strombus*.

Kleckham's Conch (2″) 5 cm
Strombus kleckhamae Cerno-
horsky, 1971. New Britain and
New Guinea. 1 to 20 m; rare.

Kleckham's Conch (2″) 5 cm
Strombus kleckhamae Cernohorsky, 1971. Dorsal view. Spiral bands often present.

Peruvian Conch (5") 13 cm
Strombus peruvianus Swainson, 1823. West Mexico to northern Peru. Tide pools at about low-tide mark; common.

Florida Fighting Conch (3") 8 cm
Strombus alatus Gmelin, 1791. North Carolina to Florida and Texas. On sand and gravel, shallow water; common.

West Indian Fighting Conch (3") 8 cm
Strombus pugilis L., 1758. Southeast Florida; West Indies; Brazil. On sand and grass, to 5 fms; common.

Eastern Pacific Fighting Conch (3") 8 cm
Strombus gracilior Sowerby, 1825. Gulf of California to Peru. On sand and mud, to 45 m; common.

Dog Conch (2.5") 6.5 cm
Strombus canarium L., 1758. S. W. Pacific. Shallow water; common. Syn.: *isabella* Lamarck.

Little Bear Conch (1.7") 4.5 cm
Strombus urceus L., 1758. Western Pacific. Sand and mud, to 20 fms; common. Syn.: *incisus* Wood; *anatellus* Duclos.

Plicate Conch (1.5") 4 cm
Strombus labiatus (Röding, 1798). East Indian Ocean; western Pacific. Shallow water; common. Syn.: *plicatus* Lam.

Micro Conch (1") 2.5 cm
Strombus microurceus (Kira, 1959). Indonesia to southern Japan and Samoa. On sand and coral to 12 fms; uncommon.

Mutable Conch (1") 2.5 cm
Strombus mutabilis Swainson, 1821. Tropical Indo-Pacific. Coral sand, to 10 fms; common. Syn.: *floridus* Lamarck.

Maculated Conch (1") 2.5 cm
Strombus maculatus Sowerby, 1842. Central Pacific. Shallow water; common. Syn.: *depauperata* Dautz. & Bouge.

Elegant Conch (1.3") 3.2 cm
Strombus erythrinus erythrinus Dillwyn, 1817. Indo-Pacific. In sand offshore, to 30 fms; uncommon. Syn.: *elegans* Sowerby.

Rugose Conch (1.2") 3 cm
Strombus rugosus Sowerby, 1825. Fiji, Ellice, Samoan and Tonga Islands. Shallow water; uncommon. Columella white.

Fusiform Conch (1.5″) 3.8 cm
Strombus fusiformis Sowerby, 1842. Red Sea; western Indian Ocean. On coral sand to 35 fms; locally common.

Lavender-mouth Conch (0.8″) 2 cm *Strombus haemastoma* Sowerby, 1842. Western Indian Ocean, tropical Pacific. Uncommon. More slender than *S. helli.*

Hell's Conch (0.8″) 2 cm *Strombus helli* Kiener, 1843. Hawaiian Islands. On coral sand and rubble, 6 to 240 fms; uncommon.

Samar Conch (1.5″) 4 cm *Strombus dentatus* L., 1758. East Africa, tropical Pacific. On coral sand, to 50 fms; uncommon. Syn.: *samarensis* Reeve.

Fragile Conch (1.5″) 4 cm *Strombus fragilis* (Röding, 1798). Western and Central Pacific. On sand, 2 to 50 fms; uncommon.

Little Auger Conch (1.5″) 4 cm *Strombus terebellatus terebellatus* Sowerby, 1842. S. W. Pacific. Uncommon.

African Auger Conch (1.2″) 3 cm *Strombus terebellatus afrobellatus* Abbott, 1960. East Africa. Shallow water; uncommon.

Plicate Conch (2.3″) 6 cm *Strombus plicatus plicatus* (Röding, 1798). Red Sea. Uncommon. Has 4 subspecies.

Pigeon Conch (1.5″) 4 cm *Strombus plicatus columba* Lamarck, 1822. Western Indian Ocean. On coral sand, to 45 fms; common.

Sibbald's Conch (1.2″) 3 cm *Strombus plicatus sibbaldi* Sowerby, 1842. Gulf of Aden to Sri Lanka. Uncommon. Characteristically stunted.

Pretty Conch (1.2″) 3 cm *Strombus plicatus pulchellus* Reeve, 1851. Southern Japan to Micronesia and Melanesia. 8 to 50 fms; uncommon.

Dilate Conch (2″) 5 cm *Strombus dilatatus* Swainson, 1821. S. W. Pacific. On sand and mud, 4 to 40 fms; uncommon. Syn.: *orosminus* Duclos.

Marginate Conch (2″) 5 cm
Strombus marginatus L., 1758.
Southern India. Shallow water;
common.

Septimus Conch (1.5″) 4 cm
Strombus marginatus sub-
species *septimus* Duclos, 1844.
Philippines. Common.

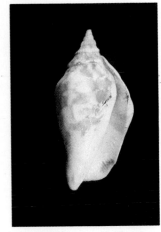

Tunic Conch (1.8″) 4.5 cm
*Strombus marginatus succinc-
tus* L., 1767. Madras to Sri
Lanka. Muddy sand, shallow
water; uncommon.

Solid Conch (1.8″) 4.5 cm
Strombus marginatus robustus
Sowerby, 1874. Japan to South
China Sea. On sand and mud,
to 25 fms; common.

Minute Conch (1″) 2.5 cm
Strombus minimus L., 1771.
South China Sea to Fiji. Sand or
mud, to 12 fms; common.
Chrome-yellow aperture.

Variable Conch (2″) 5 cm
Strombus variabilis Swainson,
1820. Northwest Pacific. Sandy
mud, to 25 fms; moderately
common.

Lip Conch (1″) 2.5 cm
Strombus labiosus Wood, 1828.
Indo-Pacific. Offshore to 50 m;
uncommon. With or without
apertural purple blotch.

Swan Conch (3″) 7.5 cm
Strombus epidromis L., 1758.
Philippines; Indonesia to New
Caledonia. Mud and sand, to 16
fms; uncommon.

Vittate Conch (3″) 7.5 cm
Strombus vittatus vittatus L.,
1758. South China Sea, southeast to Fiji. Offshore; uncommon. Syn.: *turritus* Lamarck.

Japanese Conch (2.2″) 5.5 cm
Strombus vittatus japonicus
Reeve, 1851. Japan. Offshore, 5
to 20 fms; common.

Campbell's Conch (2″) 5 cm
Strombus vittatus campbelli
Griffith & Pidgeon, 1834. North
Australia. Offshore to 12 fms;
common. Syn.: *sulcata* Wat-
son.

Lister's Conch (5″) 13 cm
Strombus listeri T. Gray, 1852.
Bay of Bengal; N. W. Indian
Ocean. Moderately deep wa-
ter; uncommon.

Old's Conch (4") 10 cm
Strombus oldi Emerson, 1965. Somali coast, East Africa. Offshore; rare. Has dark-brown stain in the aperture.

Silver Conch (3") 7.5 cm
Strombus lentiginosus L., 1758. Tropical Indo-Pacific. On coral sand, to 2 fms; common. Orange and cream aperture.

Butterfly Conch (2.3") 6 cm
Strombus pipus (Röding, 1798). Tropical Indo Pacific. On coral sand, 8 to 40 fms; uncommon. Syn.: *papilio* Dillwyn.

Granulated Conch (3") 7.5 cm
Strombus granulatus Swainson, 1822. Gulf of California to Ecuador. On rocks and sand offshore; common.

Bubonian Conch (4.5") 11 cm
Strombus latus Gmelin, 1791. Western Africa, Cape Verde Islands. Shallow water; common. Syn.: *bubonius* Lamarck.

Lineated Conch (1.5") 4 cm
Strombus fasciatus Born, 1778. Red Sea. In sand, shallow water; common. Syn.: *lineatus* Lamarck.

Diana Conch (2.3") 6 cm
Strombus aurisdianae L., 1758. Indo-W. Pacific. In weedy sand, shallow water; moderately common. Syn.: *chrysostomus* Kuroda.

Bubble Conch (2.3") 6 cm
Strombus bulla (Röding,1798). Indonesia to Samoa. On sand to 10 fms; uncommon. Syn.: *guttata* Kiener.

Vomer Conch (3") 7.5 cm
Strombus vomer vomer (Röding, 1798). S. W. Pacific. On sand, shallow water; uncommon. Syn.: *pacificus* Swainson.

Iredale's Conch (2.5") 6.5 cm
Strombus vomer iredalei Abbott, 1960. Northern Australia. Shallow water; uncommon. Syn.: *australis* Gray.

Strawberry Conch (2") 5 cm
Strombus luhuanus L., 1758. Western Pacific; east Australia; Japan. On sand, to 5 fms; common. Black columella.

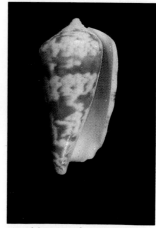

Mauritian Conch (2.2") 5.5 cm
Strombus decorus decorus (Röding, 1798). Indian Ocean. On sand, to 18 fms; common. Columella whitish. Syn.: *mauritianus* Lamarck.

Persian Conch (1.8") 4.5 cm *Strombus decorus persicus* Swainson, 1821. Arabian Sea and Persian Gulf. In sand, to 10 fms; common.

Hump-back Conch (2.2") 5.5 cm *Strombus gibberulus gibberulus* L., 1758. Indian Ocean. Intertidal to 10 fms; common. Largest of 3 subspecies.

Gibbose Conch (1.8") 4.5 cm *Strombus gibberulus gibbosus* (Röding, 1798). Tropical Pacific, excluding Hawaii. Intertidal to 10 fms; common.

White Hump-back Conch (1.8") 4.5 cm *Strombus gibberulus albus* Mörch, 1850. Red Sea and Gulf of Aden. Intertidal to 10 fms; moderately common.

Common Spider Conch (7") 18 cm *Lambis lambis* (L., 1758). Indo-Pacific. Shallow water; common. Females have longer "fingers" than males.

Orange Spider Conch (4.5") 11 cm *Lambis crocata crocata* (Link, 1807). Indo-W. Pacific. On reefs; moderately common. Syn.: *aurantia* Lamarck.

Pilsbry's Spider Conch (8") 20 cm *Lambis crocata pilsbryi* Abbott, 1961. Marquesas Islands (endemic). Uncommon.

Scorpio Conch (5") 13 cm *Lambis scorpius scorpius* (L., 1758). Western Pacific. Coral reef areas, shallow water; moderately common.

Lesser Scorpio Conch (5") 13 cm *Lambis scorpius indomaris* Abbott, 1961. Indian Ocean. Shallow water; uncommon. Syn.: *sinuatus* Perry.

False Scorpio Conch (5") 13 cm *Lambis robusta* (Swainson, 1821). Southeastern Polynesia. Rare. Syn.: *pseudoscorpio* Lamarck.

Violet Spider Conch (3.5") 9 cm *Lambis violacea* (Swainson, 1821). Western Indian Ocean. Moderately deep water; rare. Syn.: *multipes* Deshayes.

Milleped Spider Conch (4") 10 cm *Lambis millepeda* (L., 1758). S. W. Pacific. Shallow water; moderately common. Normally has 9 "fingers".

Elongate Spider Conch
(4.7") 12 cm
Lambis digitata (Perry, 1811).
Indo-Pacific. Shallow water;
uncommon. Syn.: *elongata*
Swainson.

Seba's Spider Conch (11") 28 cm
Lambis truncata subspecies *se-bae* (Kiener, 1843). Pacific; Red
Sea. Shallow water; common.
Spire of true *truncata* is flat.

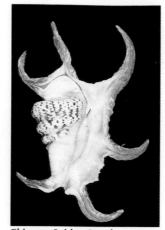

Chiragra Spider Conch (6")
15 cm *Lambis chiragra* (L., 1758).
Eastern Indian Ocean to Polynesia. Shallow water; common. Syn.: *rugosa* Sowerby.

Arthritic Spider Conch (6")
15 cm *Lambis chiragra* subspecies *arthritica* Röding,1798.
Eastern Africa. Coral reef areas.
Shallow water; common.

Cancellate Beak-shell
(1.2") 3 cm
Varicospira cancellata (Lamarck, 1822). Indo-Pacific. Offshore; uncommon. Posterior
canal covers 2 spire whorls.

Network Beak-shell (1") 2.5 cm
Varicospira crispata (Sowerby,
1842). Philippines. Deep water;
moderately rare. Posterior canal short and recurved.

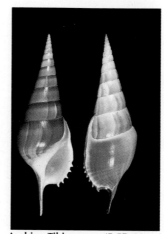

Arabian Tibia (5.5") 14 cm
Tibia insulaechorab Röding,
1798. Indian Ocean. Intertidal
to moderate depths; common.
Syn.: *curvirostris* Lamarck.

Shin-bone Tibia (9") 23 cm
Tibia fusus fusus (L., 1758).
Southwest Pacific, mainly Philippines. Moderately deep water; moderately common.

Dark-mouthed Tibia (6") 15 cm
Tibia fusus melanocheilus (A.
Adams, 1854). Philippines; Indonesia. Shallow water; uncommon. Syntypes illustrated.

Martin's Tibia (5.5") 14 cm
Tibia martinii (Marrat, 1877).
Philippines; Taiwan; Indonesia. Deep water; moderately
rare.

Delicate Tibia (3") 8 cm
Tibia delicatula (Nevill, 1881).
Arabian Sea. Deep water; moderately rare. Syn.: *nana* Ro-
magna-Manoja.

Powis's Tibia (2.2") 5.5 cm
Tibia powisi (Petit, 1842).
Southwest Pacific; Australia.
Dredged in moderately deep
water; uncommon.

Terebellum Conch (2.4") 6 cm
Terebellum terebellum (L., 1758). Indo-Pacific. Subtidal in sand; locally common. Patterns often zebralike or spotted.

FAMILIES LAMELLARIIDAE AND TRIVIIDAE

The Lamellariidae have a very thin shell covered by the mantle. No operculum. The Eratoidae and Triviidae contain the *Erato* and cowrielike *Trivia*, respectively. Most live in the tropics and feed upon spongelike, ascidian "sea potatoes." All live below the tidal level under rocks. No operculum.

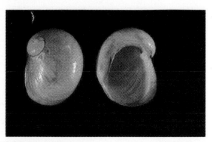

Black Lamellaria (1.2") 3 cm
Lamellaria niger (Blainville, 1825). Indo-Pacific. Subtidal, under rocks; uncommon. Shell internal in black soft parts.

Smooth Velutina (0.7") 1.8 cm
Velutina velutina (Müller, 1776). Arctic Seas. Offshore to 100 m; locally common in gravel.

Columbelle Erato (0.3") 7 mm
Erato columbella Menke, 1847. California to Panama. Subtidal to 100 m; near kelp weeds; common.

Four-spotted Trivia (0.2") 5 mm
Trivia quadripunctata (Gray, 1827). S. E. United States and West Indies. Subtidal under rocks; common.

Radians Trivia (0.7") 1.8 cm
Trivia radians (Lamarck, 1811). W. Mexico to Ecuador. Intertidal, under rocks; common. More ribs than *solandri*.

Solander's Trivia (0.6") 1.5 cm
Trivia solandri (Sowerby, 1832). Southern California to Peru. Intertidal, under rocks; common.

Coffee Bean Trivia (0.5") 1.2 cm
Trivia pedicula (L., 1758). S. E. United States to Brazil. Bermuda. Subtidal, under rocks; common.

Gaping Trivia (0.8") 2 cm
Trivia aperta (Swainson, 1822). South Africa. Offshore; common, especially in beach drift.

COWRIES
FAMILY CYPRAEIDAE

Among the most popular of all seashells, cowries number about 200 living species. The aperture is restricted and usually toothed, the surface glossy and smooth. All are from warm seas. They are omnivorous, lay circular egg masses and sit on them. Their mantles are often as colorful as their shells.

Marie's Cowrie (0.5") 1.2 cm
Cypraea mariae Schilder, 1927. Central Pacific; Philippines. On soft coral, shallow and deeper water; rare. Syn.: *annulata* Gray.

Chick-pea Cowrie (0.8") 2 cm
Cypraea cicercula L., 1758. Indo-Pacific. On live coral, shallow and deeper water; uncommon.

Lienard's Chick-pea Cowrie (0.5") 1.2 cm
Cypraea cicercula subspecies *lienardi* Jousseaume, 1874. S. W. Pacific. Granulated, unspotted.

Margarite Chick-pea Cowrie (0.5") 1.2 cm
Cypraea cicercula form *margarita* Dillwyn, 1817. S. W. Pacific. Shallow water; uncommon. Top smooth.

Maui Chick-pea Cowrie (0.7") 1.8 cm
Cypraea mauiensis Burgess, 1967. Hawaiian Islands. Offshore; uncommon.

Globular Cowrie (0.8") 2 cm
Cypraea globulus L., 1758. Indo-Pacific. On live coral, shallow water; uncommon. Dorsum quite smooth. Syn.: *affinis* Gmelin.

Checkerboard Cowrie (1.4") 3.5 cm
Cypraea tessellata Swainson, 1822. Hawaiian Islands. Under coral and in reef crevices, to 20 fms; uncommon.

Children's Cowrie (0.8") 2 cm
Cypraea childreni Gray, 1825. Indo-Pacific. Shallow water; rare.

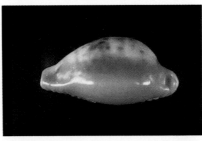

Surinam Cowrie (1.4") 3.5 cm
Cypraea surinamensis Perry, 1811. Southern Florida to Brazil. Offshore to 140 m; rare. Syn.: *bicallosa* Gray: *ingloria* Crosse.

Dillwyn's Cowrie (0.5") 1.2 cm
Cypraea dillwyni Schilder, 1922. Polynesia and Fiji Islands. On coral reefs, shallow and deeper water; uncommon.

Beck's Cowrie (0.5") 1.2 cm
Cypraea beckii Gaskoin, 1836. Philippines; Japan; Hawaii. Coral reefs, shallow and deeper water; rare.

MacAndrew's Cowrie (1") 2.3 cm
Cypraea macandrewi Sowerby, 1870. Northwest Indian Ocean; Red Sea. Subtidal, uncommon.

Dew-drop Cowrie (0.5") 1.2 cm
Cypraea irrorata Gray, 1828. Central Pacific. Coral reefs, shallow and deeper water; uncommon. Seldom collected living.

Grape Cowrie (0.8") 2 cm
Cypraea staphylaea L., 1758. Indo-Pacific. In and under coral blocks, shallow water; uncommon. Orange teeth across entire base.

Limacina Cowrie (1") 2.5 cm
Cypraea limacina Lamarck, 1810. Indo-W. Pacific. Under stones; moderately common. Nodules on dorsum.

Semiplota Cowrie (0.6") 1.5 cm
Cypraea semiplota Mighels, 1845. Hawaiian Islands. Offshore; uncommon (rare alive). Syn.: *polita* Roberts.

Nucleus Cowrie (1") 2.5 cm
Cypraea nucleus L., 1758. Indo-Pacific. Coral reefs, shallow water; uncommon. Form *gemmosa* Perry illustrated.

Granulated Cowrie (1.5") 4 cm
Cypraea granulata Pease, 1862. Hawaiian Islands; Marquesas. Coral reefs; moderately rare. Syn.: *honoluluensis* Melvill.

Lined-lip Cowrie (0.8") 2 cm
Cypraea labrolineata Gaskoin, 1849. Central to Western Pacific. Coral reefs; uncommon. Syn.: *helenae* Roberts; *maccullochi* Iredale.

Cernica Cowrie (1") 2.5 cm
Cypraea cernica Sowerby, 1870. Indo-Pacific. On coral and sand, moderately deep water; uncommon. Syn.: *tomlini* Schilder.

Contaminated Cowrie (0.5") 1.2 cm
Cypraea contaminata Sowerby, 1832. Indo-W. Pacific. Shallow water; moderately rare.

Gangrenous Cowrie (0.8") 2 cm
Cypraea gangranosa Dillwyn, 1817. Indian Ocean to New Guinea (mostly from Sri Lanka or Andaman Islands); uncommon.

Boivin's Cowrie (1.2") 3 cm
Cypraea boivinii Kiener, 1843. Japan; Philippines; Indonesia. Under rocks and coral slabs; moderately common.

Atlantic Yellow Cowrie (1") 2.5 cm
Cypraea spurca acicularis Gmelin, 1791. S. Florida; West Indies. Moderately common. Has white base. True *spurca* from Eastern Atlantic is yellow.

Albugine Cowrie (1") 2.5 cm
Cypraea albuginosa Gray, 1825. Gulf of California; W. Mexico; Panama to Ecuador. Under stones, shallow water; common.

Honey Cowrie (1″) 2.5 cm
Cypraea helvola L., 1758. Indo-Pacific. Coral areas; common. Syn.: *hawaiiensis* Melvill; *citrinicolor* Iredale.

King's Cowrie (0.7″) 1.8 cm
Cypraea kingae Rehder & Wilson, 1975. Off Pitcairn Island. Dredged, 25 to 70 fms; rare. Holotype illustrated at left.

Thomas's Cowrie (0.6″) 1.5 cm
Cypraea thomasi Crosse, 1865. Hawaii; Central Pacific. Offshore, rare. Syn.: *ostergaardi* Dall.

Serpent's-head Cowrie (1″) 2.5 cm
Cypraea caputserpentis L., 1758. Indo-Pacific. Coral reefs, shallow water; common. Syn.: *caputanguis* Philippi; *caputcolubri* Kenyon.

Father Englert's Cowrie (1″) 2.5 cm
Cypraea englerti Summers & Burgess, 1965. Easter Island. Intertidal; rare.

Dragon's-head Cowrie (1″) 2.5 cm
Cypraea caputdraconis Melvill, 1888. Easter Island (endemic). Locally common. Holotype illustrated.

Erosa Cowrie (1.5″) 4 cm
Cypraea erosa L., 1758. Indo-Pacific. Coral reefs, in shallow water; common. Syn.: *similis* Gmelin; *chlorizans* Melvill.

Twin-blotch Cowrie (1.2″) 3 cm
Cypraea nebrites Melvill, 1888. Red Sea to Gulf of Oman and Persian Gulf. Coral areas in shallow water; moderately common.

Porous Cowrie (0.8″) 2 cm
Cypraea poraria L., 1758. Indo-Pacific. Coral reefs, shallow water; common. Syn.: *kauaiensis* Melvill; *vibex* Kenyon.

Ocellate Cowrie (1″) 2.5 cm
Cypraea ocellata L., 1758. India; Sri Lanka, Gulf of Oman, Persian Gulf. Among muddy stones at low tide; moderately common.

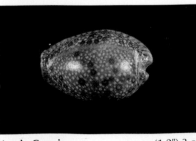

Margin Cowrie (1.2″) 3 cm
Cypraea marginalis Dillwyn, 1817. South Africa; western Indian Ocean; Gulf of Oman; uncommon.

Miliaris Cowrie (1.2″) 3 cm
Cypraea miliaris Gmelin, 1791. Western Pacific; northern Australia. Shallow water; common. Syn.: *magistra* Melvill.

Lamarck's Cowrie (1.5") 4 cm

Cypraea lamarckii Gray, 1825. Indian Ocean. Shallow, muddy water; moderately common. Syn.: *redimita* Melvill; *incurvata, beieri, sharoni, okutanii,* all Walles, 1980.

Thrush Cowrie (1.2") 3 cm

Cypraea turdus Lamarck, 1810. Western Indian Ocean; Red Sea. On dead coral or among muddy stones, to 10 fms; common.

Great Spotted Cowrie (2.3") 6 cm

Cypraea guttata Gmelin, 1791. S. W. Pacific; Japan. Coral reefs to moderate depths; rare. Syn.: *azumai* Schilder.

Gold-ringer Cowrie (1") 2.5 cm

Cypraea annulus L., 1758. Indo-Pacific. Coral reefs, shallow water; common. Syn.: *noumeensis* Marie; *camelorum* Rochebrune.

Walled Cowrie (0.8") 2 cm

Cypraea obvelata Lamarck, 1810. Eastern Polynesia. Coral reefs, in tide pools; common. Probably subspecies of *annulus.*

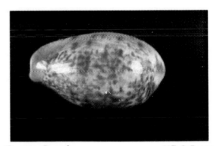

Money Cowrie (1") 2.5 cm

Cypraea moneta L., 1758. Indo-Pacific. One of the most variable cowries. Syn.: *icterina* Lamarck; *barthelemyi* Bernardi.

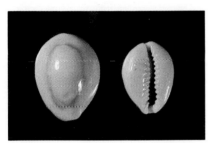

Agate Cowrie (1.4") 3.5 cm

Cypraea achatidea Sowerby, 1837. Eastern Mediterranean and West Africa. From 30 m to deep water; rare. Syn.: *oranica* Crosse.

Zoned Cowrie (1.2") 3 cm

Cypraea zonaria Gmelin, 1791. West Africa; Cape Verde Islands. On reefs, to 10 m; common. Syn.: *zonata* Lamarck.

Ornate Cowrie (1") 2.5 cm

Cypraea picta Gray, 1824. Cape Verde Islands. Among coral slabs, shallow water; uncommon. Syn.: *atava* Rochebrune.

Black-spotted Cowrie (1.2") 3 cm

Cypraea nigropunctata Gray, 1828. Galapagos; Ecuador; northern Peru. Shallow water; common. Syn.: *irina* Kiener.

Annette's Cowrie (1.5") 4 cm

Cypraea annettae Dall, 1909. Gulf of California, Baja California. Under stones, low tide; common. Syn.: *sowerbyi* Kiener.

Equinox Cowrie (1.6") 4 cm

Cypraea aequinoctialis Schilder, 1933. West Panama to Peru. Shallow water; uncommon to rare.

Chestnut Cowrie   (2.2″) 5.5 cm
Cypraea spadicea Swainson, 1823. California to central Baja California. Under rock ledges to 20 m; common.

Little Arabian Cowrie   (1.2″) 3 cm
Cypraea arabicula Lamarck, 1811. Baja California to Peru; Galapagos. Under rocks at low tide; common.

Wonder Cowrie   (3.5″) 9 cm
Cypraea armeniaca form *howelli* Iredale, 1931 (left); form *hesitata* Iredale, 1916 (right). Southeast Australia, offshore; uncommon.

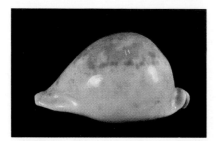

Armenian Cowrie   (3.5″) 9 cm
Cypraea armeniaca Verco, 1912. South and Southeast Australia. Deep-water form. Rare. Occasionally albino.

Shaw's Cape Cowrie   (1.5″) 4 cm
Cypraea fuscorubra Shaw, 1909. South Africa. Probably from deep water; uncommon. Syn.: *castanea* Higgins.

Dark-toothed Cowrie   (1.2″) 3 cm
Cypraea fuscodentata Gray, 1825. South Africa. Moderately deep water; uncommon (but rare live collected).

Toothless Cape Cowrie   (1″) 2.5 cm
Cypraea edentula Gray, 1825. South Africa. Probably from deep water; common (as a beached shell).

Yellow-toothed Cowrie   (1.2″) 3 cm
Cypraea xanthodon Sowerby, 1832. Northeastern Australia. Coral reefs, shallow water; uncommon. Teeth and base yellowish.

Pallid Cowrie   (1″) 2.5 cm
Cypraea pallida Gray, 1824. N. Indian Ocean to Borneo. Under muddy rocks, low tide; uncommon. Syn.: *insulicola* Schilder & Schilder.

Greenish Cowrie   (1.2″) 3 cm
Cypraea subviridis Reeve, 1835. N. Australia to Fiji. Coral areas, under rocks; uncommon. Syn.: *anceyi* Vayssière.

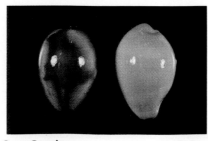

Onyx Cowrie   (1.5″) 4 cm
Cypraea onyx L., 1758. Indo-W. Pacific. Coral reefs and muddy areas; uncommon. (**right:** white form, *nymphae* Jay, 1850)

Dark Onyx Cowrie   (1.5″) 4 cm
Cypraea onyx form *adusta* Lamarck, 1810. Indo-Pacific. Moderately common color form.

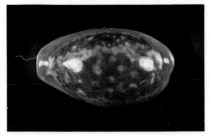

Petit's Cowrie (1") 2.5 cm

Cypraea petitiana Crosse, 1872. Off Dakar and Gambia. Trawled down to 40 m; moderately rare.

Hirase's Cowrie (2.3") 6 cm

Cypraea hirasei Roberts, 1913. East China Sea; Japan; Queensland. Trawled, to 100 fms; rare. Syn.: *queenslandica* Schilder.

Langford's Cowrie (2") 5 cm

Cypraea langfordi Kuroda, 1938. Japan to northern Australia. Dredged, 40 to 100 fms; rare. The form *moretonensis* Schilder is doubtfully distinct.

Teramachi's Cowrie (2.7") 7 cm

Cypraea teramachii Kuroda, 1938. Japan; South China Sea. Trawled in moderately deep water; rare.

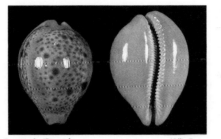

Porter's Cowrie (2") 5 cm

Cypraea porteri C. Cate, 1966. Philippines. Deep water; rare. *C. joycae* Clover is Taiwan subspecies.

Pear-shaped Cowrie (1") 2.5 cm

Cypraea pyriformis Gray, 1824. Malaysia; Philippines; western Australia. Shallow water; uncommon. Syn.: *smithi* Sowerby.

Beautiful Cowrie (1.5") 4 cm

Cypraea pulchella Swainson, 1823. Indo-Pacific. Dredged 15 to 70 fms; uncommon. Syn.: *pericalles* Melvill & Standen.

Barclay's Cowrie (1") 2.5 cm

Cypraea barclayi Reeve, 1857. Indian Ocean. Deep water. Known only from about a dozen specimens. 21 outer lip teeth, strong, orange. Syn.: *weaveri* Walles, 1980.

Walker's Cowrie (1") 2.5 cm

Cypraea walkeri Sowerby, 1832. Indian Ocean; S. W. Pacific. Coral reefs; uncommon. Syn.: *amabilis* Jousseaume; *merista* Iredale.

Breger's Cowrie (1") 2.5 cm

Cypraea bregeriana Crosse, 1868. Solomons to New Caledonia and Fiji. Coral reefs, shallow water; uncommon. Tiny white spots imbedded in the nacre.

Golden-mouth Cowrie (1.2") 3 cm

Cypraea ovum Gmelin, 1791. S. W. Pacific. Coral reefs; common. Yellowish teeth distinctive. Syn.: *cruenta* Gmelin; *olivacea* Lamarck.

Wandering Cowrie (1") 2.5 cm

Cypraea errones L., 1758. Western Pacific and eastern Indian Ocean. Coral reef areas; common. Syn.: *bimaculata* Gray; *coxi* Brazier.

Sowerby's Cowrie (1") 2.5 cm
Cypraea cylindrica form *sowerbyana* Schilder, 1932. Southwest Pacific. Shallow water; uncommon. Teeth much shorter.

Cylindrical Cowrie (1") 2.5 cm
Cypraea cylindrica Born, 1778. S. W. Pacific; Philippines. Shallow water; common. Syn.: *subcylindrica* Sowerby.

Four-spotted Cowrie (1") 2.5 cm
Cypraea quadrimaculata Gray, 1824. S. W. Pacific. Under stones and coral slabs; uncommon. Syn.: *nimbosa* Dillwyn.

Caurica Cowrie (1.5") 4 cm
Cypraea caurica L., 1758. Indo-Pacific. An extremely variable shallow-water species; common. Syn.: *obscura* Rossiter.

Compton's Cowrie (1") 2.5 cm
Cypraea comptonii Gray, 1847. South Australia; Tasmania. Intertidal; common. Syn.: *wilkinsi* Griffiths; *trenberthae* Trenberth.

Flea-bitten Cowrie (0.7") 1.8 cm
Cypraea pulicaria Reeve, 1846. Southwest Australia. Intertidal to 10 m; common.

Peppered Cowrie (1.3") 2 cm
Cypraea piperita Gray, 1825. Southern coast of Australia. Subtidal to 5 m; common. Syn.: *bicolor* Gaskoin.

Plump Cowrie (1.4") 3.5 cm
Cypraea angustata Gmelin, 1791. Southeast Australia; Tasmania. Under rocks, to 10 m; moderately common. Syn.: *emblema* Iredale; *molleri* Iredale.

Martin's Cowrie (0.7") 1.8 cm
Cypraea martini Schepman, 1907. Philippines to New Caledonia. Coral and rock seabeds; rare. Syn.: *superstes* Schilder.

Punctate Cowrie (0.8") 2 cm
Cypraea punctata L., 1771. Indo-Pacific. Coral reefs, shallow and deeper water; uncommon. Syn.: *peristicta* Iredale.

Asellus Cowrie (0.8") 2 cm
Cypraea asellus L., 1758. Indo-Pacific. Coral reefs, under stones and coral blocks; moderately common.

Saul's Cowrie (1") 2.5 cm
Cypraea saulae Gaskoin, 1843. Western Pacific. Coral reefs; moderately rare. Syn.: *nugata* Iredale; *siasiensis* C. Cate.

Clandestine Cowrie (0.8") 2 cm
Cypraea clandestina L., 1767. Indo-W. Pacific. Coral reefs, shallow water; moderately common. Syn.: *candida* Pease.

Sakurai's Cowrie (2") 5 cm
Cypraea sakuraii (Habe, 1970). Taiwan to Philippines. Deep water; uncommon.

Musume's Cowrie (1") 2.5 cm
Cypraea musumea (Kuroda & Habe, 1961). Japan. Offshore; uncommon.

Midway Cowrie (0.7") 1.8 cm
Cypraea midwayensis (Azuma & Kuroda, 1967). Midway Island. Deep water; rare. Like *C. hungerfordi* but smaller and teeth finer.

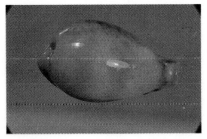

Katsua's Cowrie (0.7") 1.8 cm
Cypraea katsuae Kuroda, 1950. Southern Japan to Philippines. Offshore in deep water; rare.

Chinese Cowrie (1.5") 4 cm
Cypraea chinensis Gmelin, 1791. Central and western Pacific; Eastern Africa. Coral reefs, to 20 fms; uncommon.

Coloba Cowrie (1.5") 4 cm
Cypraea chinensis subspecies *coloba* Melvill, 1888. Northern Indian Ocean. Intertidal; locally common.

Lutea Cowrie (0.7") 1.8 cm
Cypraea lutea Gmelin, 1791. S. W. Pacific; N. Australia. Shallow reefs; uncommon.

Humphrey's Cowrie (0.7") 1.8 cm
Cypraea humphreysi Gray, 1825. Fiji; Solomons; Coral Sea. Under coral and among weed; uncommon. Syn.: *yaloka* Steadman & Cotton.

Zigzag Cowrie (0.8") 2 cm
Cypraea ziczac L., 1758. Indo-Pacific. In and under coral heads, shallow and deep water; uncommon. Syn.: *misella* Perry; *signata* Iredale.

Undulating Cowrie (0.8") 2 cm
Cypraea ziczac form *undata* Lamarck, 1810. A variation in which the base is reddish. Uncommon.

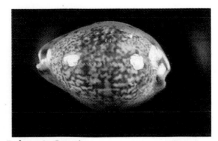

Roberts's Cowrie (1") 2.5 cm
Cypraea robertsi Hidalgo, 1906. Gulf of Calif. to Peru, Galapagos. Under rocks at low tide; common. Syn.: *punctulata* Gray.

Freckled Cowrie (1.2") 3 cm
Cypraea lentiginosa Gray, 1825. Persian Gulf; northern Arabian Sea. Among coral and stones, to about 10 fms; uncommon.

Fimbriate Cowrie (0.7") 1.8 cm
Cypraea fimbriata Gmelin, 1791. Indo-Pacific; South Africa. Shallow water; uncommon. Syn.: *waikikiensis* Schilder.

Cat Cowrie (0.7") 1.8 cm
Cypraea felina Gmelin, 1791. Indo-W. Pacific. Coral reefs, under stones; common. Syn.: *listeri* Gray; *melvilli* Hidalgo.

Hammond's Cowrie (0.6") 1.5 cm
Cypraea hammondae Iredale, 1939. Philippines to N. Australia. Subtidal; uncommon. This is form *raysummersi* Schilder, 1960.

Graceful Cowrie (1") 2.5 cm
Cypraea gracilis Gaskoin, 1849. Indo-Pacific. Coral reefs; moderately common. Syn.: *notata* Gill; *irescens* Sowerby.

Small-toothed Cowrie (0.3") 1 cm
Cypraea minoridens Melvill, 1901. Southwest Pacific; Japan to Samoa. Near coral, subtidal; uncommon.

Coxen's Cowrie (1") 2.5 cm
Cypraea coxeni Cox, 1873. New Guinea to Solomons. Shallow water; locally common. Syn.: *hesperina* Schilder & Summers.

Summers's Cowrie (0.7") 1.8 cm
Cypraea summersi Schilder, 1958. Fiji, Samoa and Tonga. Coral reefs in shallow water; uncommon. Brown smudges on anterior tip.

Rhinoceros Cowrie (1") 2.5 cm
Cypraea pallidula Gaskoin, 1849. Northern Australia to Japan and Samoa. Coral reef areas; uncommon. Syn.: *rhinoceros* Souverbie.

Kiener's Cowrie (0.7") 1.8 cm
Cypraea kieneri Hidalgo, 1906. Indo-Pacific. Shallow water; common. Syn.: *marcia* Iredale. Central teeth short.

Swallow Cowrie (0.7") 1.8 cm
Cypraea hirundo L., 1758. Indo-Pacific. Under coral slabs; moderately common. Syn.: *neglecta* Sowerby. Central teeth long.

Little Bear Cowrie (0.5") 1.2 cm
Cypraea ursellus Gmelin, 1791. Western Pacific. Under coral, shallow water; uncommon. Syn.: *coffea* Sowerby; *amoeba* Schilder & Schilder.

Red Sea Cowrie (1″) 2.5 cm
Cypraea erythraeensis Sowerby, 1837. Red Sea. Subtidal, under rocks; locally common.

Rashleigh's Cowrie (1″) 2.5 cm
Cypraea rashleighana Melvill, 1888. Hawaiian Islands to S. E. Asia. In branched coral offshore; uncommon. Syn.: *eunota* Taylor.

Teres Cowrie (1.5″) 4 cm
Cypraea teres Gmelin, 1791. Indo-Pacific. Coral reef areas mainly; common. Syn.: *tabescens* Dillwyn.

Stolid Cowrie (1″) 2.5 cm
Cypraea stolida L., 1758. Indo-W. Pacific. Under stones and in coral heads, shallow water; uncommon. Syn.: *crossei* Marie.

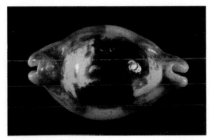

Rostrate Stolid Cowrie (1″) 2.5 cm
Cypraea stolida L., 1758. Several kinds of cowries in New Caledonia have ecologic black and rostrate forms.

Subteres Cowrie (1″) 2.5 cm
Cypraea subteres Weinkauff, 1881. Polynesia. Coral reefs; live-collected specimens rare. Large brown spots on right margin.

Goodall's Cowrie (0.8″) 2 cm
Cypraea goodallii Sowerby, 1832. Marianas to Society Is., central Pacific. Coral areas; moderately rare. Syn.: *fuscomaculata* Pease.

Sieve Cowrie (1″) 2.5 cm
Cypraea cribraria L., 1758. Indo-Pacific. Shallow reefs; uncommon. Syn.: *comma* Perry; *fallax* Smith; *melwardi* Iredale

Fine-sieve Cowrie (0.7″) 1.8 cm
Cypraea cribellum Gaskoin, 1849. Mauritius and Reunion. Subtidal; rare.

Esontropia Cowrie (1″) 2.5 cm
Cypraea esontropia Duclos, 1833. Mauritius. Under coral blocks; moderately common. Has larger dorsal spots than *C. gaskoini*.

Catholic Cowrie (0.8″) 2 cm
Cypraea catholicorum Schilder & Schilder, 1938. New Britain to New Caledonia. Coral reefs, usually beach collected; rare.

Gaskoin's Cowrie (1″) 2.5 cm
Cypraea gaskoini Reeve, 1846. Hawaiian Islands to Fiji. In coral, to 20 fms; uncommon. Syn.: *peasei* Sowerby.

Cuming's Cowrie (0.5") 1.2 cm
Cypraea cumingii Sowerby, 1832. Eastern Polynesia. Coral reefs, shallow water; rare. Syn.: *compta* Pease; *cleopatra* Schilder & Schilder.

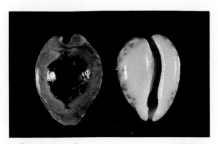

Teulère's Cowrie (2") 5 cm
Cypraea teulerei Cazanavelle, 1845. Red Sea to Gulf of Oman. Offshore; locally common. Syn.: *leucostoma* Gaskoin; *hidalgoi* Shaw.

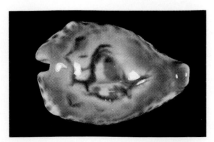

Fulton's Cowrie (2.5") 6.4 cm
Cypraea fultoni Sowerby, 1903. South Africa. From fish stomachs; rare. Possibly a deep-water species.

Mouse Cowrie (2") 5 cm
Cypraea mus L., 1758. Northern coast of Colombia to Gulf of Venezuela. On and under rocks offshore; uncommon.

Don Moore's Cowrie (2.2") 5.5 cm
Cypraea mus form *donmoorei* Petuch, 1979. Northern Venezuela. Offshore to 50 m; locally common.

Venusta Cowrie (3") 7.5 cm
Cypraea venusta Sowerby, 1846. Southwestern Australia. On sponges, 2 to 100 fms; moderately rare. Syn.: *thatcheri* Cox; *catei* Schilder.

Thatcher's Cowrie (3") 7.5 cm
Cypraea venusta form *thatcheri* Cox, 1869. Southwestern Australia. This is merely a blond color form.

Deceptive Cowrie (2.3") 6 cm
Cypraea decipiens E. A. Smith, 1880. Northwestern Australia. On sponges, 10 to 40 fms; locally common. Remarkably humped shell.

Perla Cowrie (2.3") 6 cm
Cypraea decipiens form *perlae* Lopez & Chiang, 1975. Northwestern Australia. Deep-water form; uncommon.

Friend's Cowrie (3") 7.5 cm
Cypraea friendii friendii Gray, 1831. Western Australia. On sponges, to 100 fms; uncommon. Syn.: *scottii* Broderip; *vercoi* Schilder.

Thersites Cowrie (2.7") 7 cm
Cypraea friendii form *thersites* Gaskoin, 1849. Southern Australia. On sponges, to 40 fms; uncommon.

Jean's Cowrie (2.7") 7 cm
Cypraea friendii form *jeaniana* Cate, 1968. Southwestern Australia. Uncommon.

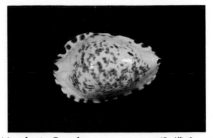

Marginate Cowrie (2.4") 6 cm
Cypraea marginata Gaskoin, 1849. Western and southern Australia. In coral with sponges, 12 to 250 m; rare. Syn.: *ketyana* Raybaudi.

Rossell's Cowrie (2") 5 cm
Cypraea rosselli (Cotton, 1948). Western Australia. On sponges, 3 to 40 fms, but occasionally beach collected; rare. Last 9 cowries in subgenus *Zoila*.

Atlantic Gray Cowrie (1.2") 3 cm
Cypraea cinerea Gmelin, 1791. S. E. United States to Brazil. Under rocks on reefs; moderately common.

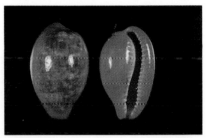

Pear Cowrie (1.8") 4.5 cm
Cypraea pyrum Gmelin, 1791. Mediterranean; Western Africa. Offshore to about 50 m; common. Syn.: *maculosa* Gmelin; *rufa* Lamarck.

Lurid Cowrie (1.8") 4.5 cm
Cypraea lurida L., 1758. Mediterranean; West Africa; Ascension Island. Shallow water; common. Syn.: *minima* Dunker.

Isabelle Cowrie (1.5") 4 cm
Cypraea isabella L., 1758. Indo-Pacific. Coral reefs; common. Animal has jet black mantle. Syn.: *controversa* Gray.

Mexican Cowrie (1.5") 4 cm
Cypraea isabella subspecies *isabellamexicana* Stearns, 1893. Gulf of California to Panama; Galapagos. Under stones; uncommon.

Lovely Cowrie (2") 5 cm
Cypraea pulchra Gray, 1824. Red Sea to Gulf of Oman and Persian Gulf. In branched coral, to about 7 fms; uncommon.

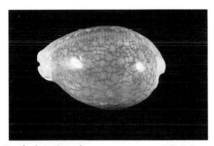

Broderip's Cowrie (3") 7.5 cm
Cypraea broderipi Sowerby, 1832. Madagascar to south of Durban. Usually from fish stomachs; rare.

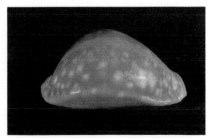

White-toothed Cowrie (3.2") 8.2 cm
Cypraea leucodon Broderip, 1828. Philippines (and ? Maldive Islands). Moderately deep water; rare. Syn.: *angioyna* Raybaudi.

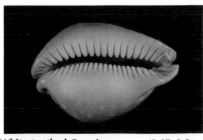

White-toothed Cowrie (3.2") 8.2 cm
Cypraea leucodon Broderip, 1828. Deepwater tangle nets set in the Philippines are now obtaining specimens frequently.

Cape Cowrie (1.2") 3 cm
Cypraea capensis Gray, 1828. S. Africa. Deep water; moderately common. Ridges extend around shell.

Golden Cowrie   (3.5″) 9 cm
Cypraea aurantium Gmelin, 1791. Philippines to Polynesia. In crevices and caves in coral reefs, 8 to 20 m; moderately rare.

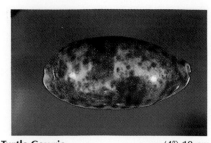

Turtle Cowrie   (4″) 10 cm
Cypraea testudinaria L., 1758. Indo-Pacific. Subtidal shores; uncommon. Syn.: *ingens* Schilder & Schilder.

Rat Cowrie   (3″) 7.5 cm
Cypraea stercoraria L., 1758. Western Africa; Cape Verde Islands. Under rocks in shallow water; common. Varies greatly in size.

Measled Cowrie   (3.3″) 8.5 cm
Cypraea zebra L., 1758. North Carolina to Yucatan; West Indies; Brazil. Intertidal to 140 m; moderately common. Syn.: *exanthema* L.

Atlantic Deer Cowrie   (4.5″) 11.5 cm
Cypraea cervus L., 1771. North Carolina to Cuba; Bermuda. Low tide to about 10 fms; moderately common. The largest cowrie, reaching (7″) 17 cm.

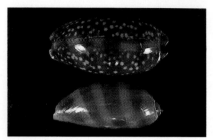

Panamanian Deer Cowrie   (3″) 7.5 cm
Cypraea cervinetta Kiener, 1843. Gulf of California to Peru. At low tide; common. Darker base than *cervus*. Syn.: *cervina* Lamarck.

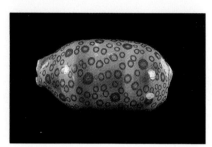

Eyed Cowrie   (3″) 7.5 cm
Cypraea argus L., 1758. Indian Ocean; Southwest Pacific. Coral reefs; uncommon. Syn.: *contrastriata* Perry.

Mole Cowrie   (2.5″) 6.5 cm
Cypraea talpa L., 1758. Indo-Pacific. Coral reefs; common. Syn.: *saturata* Dautzenberg; *imperialis* Schilder & Schilder.

Exusta Cowrie   (2.5″) 6.5 cm
Cypraea exusta Sowerby, 1832. Red Sea and Gulf of Aden. A rare species resembling *talpa* but teeth finer and aperture more curved.

Prince Cowrie   (3.5″) 9 cm
Cypraea valentia Perry, 1811. Northern Australia; New Britain; Philippines. Moderately deep water; rare. Syn.: *princeps* Gray (type illustrated).

Map Cowrie   (3″) 7.5 cm
Cypraea mappa L., 1758. Indo-Pacific. Coral reefs, under slabs, shallow water; uncommon. Base may be pink. Syn.: *alga* Perry.

Jester Cowrie   (1.7″) 4.5 cm
Cypraea scurra Gmelin, 1791. Indo-Pacific. In coral heads, shallow and moderately deep water; uncommon. Syn.: *retifera* Menke; *antelia* Iredale.

Eglantine Cowrie   (2.5″) 6.5 cm
Cypraea eglantina Duclos, 1833. Central Pacific; Philippines; northern Australia. Coral areas; common. Brown spot at apex. Syn.: *niger* Roberts (black form).

Gray's Cowrie   (2″) 5 cm
Cypraea grayana Schilder, 1930. Northwest Indian Ocean. Offshore, in 1 to 20 m; rarely on reefs; locally common.

Arabian Cowrie   (2.5″) 6.5 cm
Cypraea arabica L., 1758. Indo-Pacific. Coral reefs, shallow water; common. No brown spot at apex. Syn.: *intermedia* Gray; *brunnescens* C. Cate.

Reticulated Cowrie   (2.5″) 6.5 cm
Cypraea maculifera Schilder, 1932. Central Pacific. Coral reefs, shallow water; common. Dark blotch on base. Syn.: *reticulata* Martyn.

Histrio Cowrie   (2.5″) 6.5 cm
Cypraea histrio Gmelin, 1791. Indian Ocean. Under stones and coral slabs in tide pools; moderately common. Base all white.

Depressed Cowrie   (1.5″) 4 cm
Cypraea depressa Gray, 1824. Indo-Pacific. Coral reefs; locally common. Syn.: *intermedia* Redfield; *gillei* Jousseaume.

Humpback Cowrie   (3″) 7.5 cm
Cypraea mauritiana L., 1758. Indo-Pacific. Black rock shores, under rocks; common. Syn.: *regina* Gmelin; *adansonii* Blainville.

Tiger Cowrie   (3.5″) 9 cm
Cypraea tigris L., 1758. Indo-Pacific. Under coral rocks; common. Many color variations. Syn.: *schilderiana* C. Cate (large Hawaiian form).

Panther Cowrie   (2.5″) 6.5 cm
Cypraea pantherina Lightfoot, 1786. Red Sea and Gulf of Aden. Offshore, below 3 m; uncommon. Syn.: *vinosa* Gmelin; *tigrina* Lamarck.

Lynx Cowrie   (1.5″) 4 cm
Cypraea lynx L., 1758. Indo-Pacific. Coral reefs, shallow water; common. Syn.: *vanelli* L.; *caledonica* Crosse; *michaelis* Melvill.

Pacific Deer Cowrie   (2.5″) 6.5 cm
Cypraea vitellus L., 1758. Indo-Pacific; New Zealand. Under coral slabs and stones; common. Syn.: *sarcodes* Melvill.

Giraffe Cowrie   (2.3″) 6 cm
Cypraea camelopardalis Perry, 1811. Red Sea and Gulf of Aden. Offshore; uncommon. Columellar teeth stained black. Syn.: *melanostoma* Sowerby.

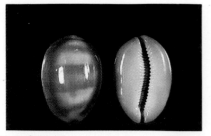

Ventral Cowrie   (2") 5 cm
Cypraea ventriculus Lamarck, 1810. Central Pacific. Coral reefs, shallow water; uncommon. Heavier and broader than *schilderorum*.

Carnelian Cowrie   (2.5") 6.5 cm
Cypraea carneola L., 1758. Indo-Pacific. Under coral slabs; common. Form *leviathan* Schilder & Schilder similar but larger.

Schilders' Cowrie   (1.7") 4.5 cm
Cypraea schilderorum Iredale, 1939. Central Pacific; Hawaiian Islands. Coral reefs, down to 10 fms; uncommon. Syn.: *arenosa* Gray.

Kurohara's Cowrie   (1.5") 4 cm
Cypraea schilderorum subspecies *kuroharai* Kuroda & Habe, 1961. Japan and China. Deep water; uncommon.

Square-toothed Cowrie   (1.5") 4 cm
Cypraea sulcidentata Gray, 1824. Hawaiian Islands (endemic). Associated with coral, to 20 fms; uncommon. Syn.: *xanthochrysa* Melvill.

Citrine Cowrie   (1") 2.5 cm
Cypraea citrina Gray, 1825. South Africa. Shallow water; common (but rare living). Like *helvola* but lacks dark dorsal spots.

Reeve's Cowrie   (1.4") 3.5 cm
Cypraea reevei Sowerby, 1832. S. W. and southern Australia. Intertidal rocky reefs; uncommon. Always looks immature.

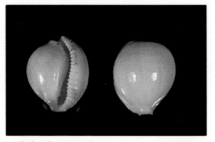

Cruikshank's Cowrie   (1") 2.5 cm
Cypraea cruikshanki Kilburn, 1972. South Africa. Deep water; rare. A very thin and light shell.

Pure White Cowrie   (1.5") 4 cm
Cypraea eburnea Barnes, 1824. Southern Pacific from New Guinea to Fiji. On coral reefs under stones; uncommon. A uniquely all-white cowrie.

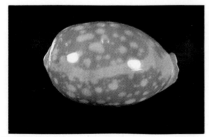

Cloudy Cowrie   (2.3") 6 cm
Cypraea nivosa Broderip, 1837. Northwestern Indian Ocean. Shallow water; uncommon now, but formerly rare. Syn.: *dama* Gray.

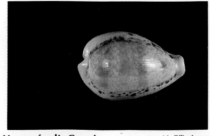

Hungerford's Cowrie   (1.5") 4 cm
Cypraea hungerfordi Sowerby, 1888. Japan. Trawled, 20 to 100 fms; uncommon. Form *coucomi* Schilder is from Queensland. Holotype *hungerfordi* illustrated.

Jenner's Cowrie   (1") 2.5 cm
Jenneria pustulata (Lightfoot, 1786). Gulf of California to Ecuador. Near masses of stony coral; moderately common.

EGG SHELLS
FAMILY OVULIDAE

The false, or allied, cowries are tropical in distribution and live in close association with colonial animals, such as soft corals, seafans and sponges. The soft mantle usually covers the egg- or spindle-shaped shell. There is no operculum. Most species occur in the Indo-Pacific.

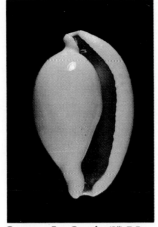

Common Egg Cowrie (3") 7.5 cm
Ovula ovum (L., 1758). Indo-Pacific. Shallow water reefs on black sponges; common. Syn.: *oviformis* Lamarck.

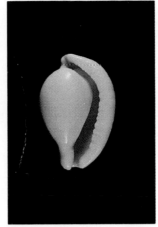

Pink-mouth Ovula (1.5") 4 cm
Ovula costellata (Lamarck, 1810). Indo-Pacific. Shallow water; uncommon. Syn.: *tortilis* Reeve; *angulosa* Lamarck.

Tinted Ovula (1") 2.5 cm
Margovula tinctilis C. Cate, 1973. East Asia. Offshore; uncommon.

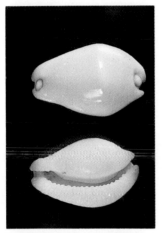

Umbilical Ovula (1.3") 3 cm
Calpurnus verrucosus (L., 1758). Indo-Pacific. Shallow reefs; locally common.

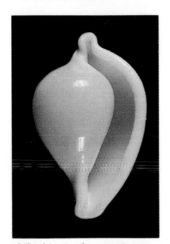

Ishibashi's Ovula (0.7") 1.8 cm
Prionovolva ishibashii (Kuroda, 1928). Southern Japan to Taiwan. Offshore; uncommon.

Chinese Ovula (0.7") 1.8 cm
Diminovula sinensis (Sowerby, 1874). Western Pacific; Japan. Offshore; uncommon.

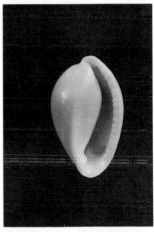

Fruit Ovula (0.6") 1.5 cm
Prionovula fruticum (Reeve, 1865). Western Pacific; Japan. Offshore 10 to 40 m; uncommon.

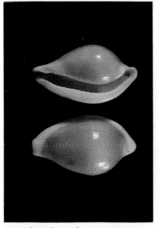

Dwarf Red Ovula (0.7") 1.8 cm
Pseudosimnia carnea (Poiret, 1789). Mediterranean; N.W. Africa; West Indies. Uncommon. May be yellow or violet.

Adriatic Ovula (1") 2.4 cm
Aperiovula adriatica (Sowerby, 1828). Mediterranean. Among corals; uncommon. Syn.: *virginea* Cantraine.

Gold-banded Cyphoma (1") 2.5 cm
Pseudocyphoma aureocinctum Dall, 1899. Off Florida in 1,200 m; rare.

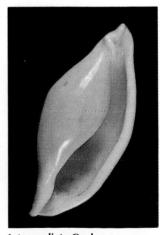

Intermediate Cyphoma (1.2") 3 cm
Pseudocyphoma intermedium (Sowerby, 1828). Florida to Brazil. Coral reefs; rare.

West Indian Simnia (0.5") 1.2 cm
Simnia acicularia (Lamarck, 1810). S.E. United States; West Indies; Bermuda. On seafans; locally common.

Rosy Ovula   (0.6") 1.5 cm
Primovula rhodia (A. Adams, 1855). Japan to Taiwan. Subtidal to 30 m on gorgonians; uncommon.

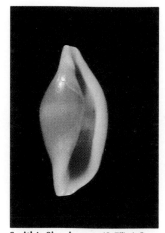

Smith's Simnia   (0.7") 1.8 cm
Subsimnia smithi (Bartsch, 1915). South Africa. Offshore on gorgonians; uncommon.

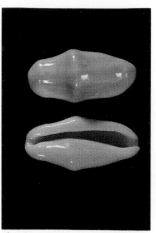

Flamingo Tongue   (1") 2.5 cm
Cyphoma gibbosum (L., 1758). S.E. United States to Brazil; Bermuda. On seawhip and seafan gorgonians; common.

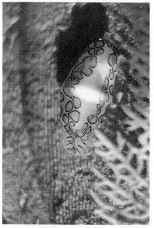

Flamingo Tongue   (1") 2.5 cm
Cyphoma gibbosum (L., 1758). The mantle, spotted like a giraffe, stretches over outer shell.

Emarginate Cyphoma
         (0.7") 1.8 cm
Cyphoma emarginatum (Sowerby, 1830). W. Mexico. On gorgonians; uncommon.

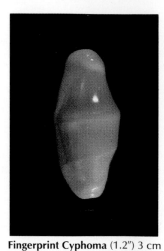

Fingerprint Cyphoma (1.2") 3 cm
Cyphoma signatum Pilsbry & McGinty, 1939. S.E. United States; West Indies. Rare. Mantle with black stripes.

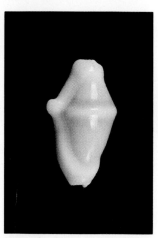

Macumba Cyphoma
         (0.8") 2.1 cm
Cyphoma macumba Petuch, 1979. Brazil. Near coral reefs; rare.

Shuttlecock Volva   (4.5") 12 cm
Volva volva (L., 1758). Indo-Pacific. Near coral reefs; locally common.

Long-snouted Volva
         (2.5") 6.5 cm
Phenacovolva longirostrata (Sowerby, 1828). Japan. Offshore; uncommon. Holotype

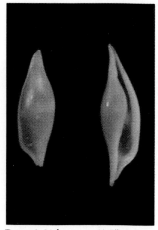

Dance's Volva   (1.5") 3.6 cm
Phenacovolva dancei Cate, 1973. Western Pacific. Offshore; rare. Right specimen is holotype.

Double-snouted Volva (1") 2 cm
Phenacovolva birostris (L., 1767). Japan to Philippines. On seafans; common. Syn.: *philippinarum* Sowerby.

HETEROPODS SUPERFAMILY ATLANTACEA

Small, pelagic gastropods usually with soft parts too large to be contained in the shell. Animals have large eyes and are active swimmers. Shells thin, translucent and variously shaped, disklike in the Atlantidae, cap-shaped in Carinariidae. Widely distributed in warm seas.

Tokio's Volva (1.7") 4.5 cm
Phenacovolva tokioi Cate, 1973. Southwestern Pacific. On gorgonians offshore; uncommon.

Rehder's Volva (1.5") 4 cm
Phenacovolva rehderi Cate, 1973. Kii, Japan. Dredged in deep water; uncommon. Holotype illus.

Angas's Volva (1.2") 3 cm
Phenacovolva angasi (Reeve, 1865). Japan to Northern Australia. Offshore, probably on gorgonians; uncommon.

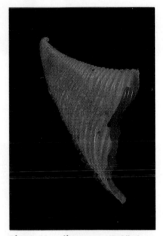

MOON SHELLS FAMILY NATICIDAE

Large worldwide family of small or moderate-size shells, globular or flattened in shape, smooth and glossy. Umbilicus open or closed, sometimes with an internal rib. Operculum thick and calcareous or thin and corneous. Carnivorous sand dwellers which lay eggs in a "collar" of sand and mucus.

Péron's Sea Butterfly (0.4") 1 cm
Atlanta peroni Lesueur, 1817. Pelagic in warm areas of Indo-Pacific and Atlantic waters; common.

Glassy Nautilus (3.2") 8 cm
Carinaria cristata (L., 1767). Pelagic in warm S.W. Pacific. Rare. Syn.: *vitrea* Gmelin; *japonica* Okutani.

Lamarck's Nautilus (3") 7.5 cm
Carinaria lamarcki Péron & Lesueur, 1810. Worldwide warm seas. Syn.: *fragilis* E. A. Smith; *challengeri* Bonnevie, 1920.

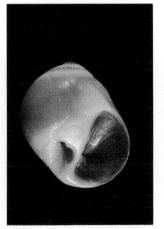

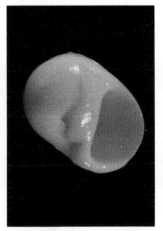

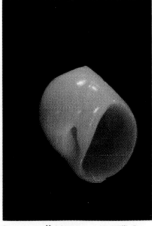

Wavy Moon (2") 5 cm
Globularia fluctuata (Sowerby, 1825). Philippines; North Borneo. Offshore; uncommon. Syn.: *imperforata* Jay.

Hackett's Moon (1") 2.5 cm
Polinices hacketti Marincovich, 1975. Galapagos Islands (endemic). In sand, offshore, 50 to 60 m; rare.

Powell's Moon (1") 2.5 cm
Polinices tawhitirahia Powell, 1964. New Zealand; Norfolk Island. Offshore, 30 to 40 m; rare.

Stone-wall Moon (0.75") 2 cm
Polinices putealis Garrard, 1961. New South Wales, Australia. Deep water; moderately rare.

Pear-shaped Moon   (1.5″) 4 cm
Polinices tumidus (Swainson, 1840). Indo-Pacific. Shallow offshore waters; common. Syn.: *pyriformis* Récluz.

Conical Moon   (1″) 2.5 cm
Polinices conicus (Lamarck, 1822). Australia; New Zealand (rare). Intertidal to offshore; moderately common. Syn.: *pyramis* Reeve.

Common Australian Moon   (1.5″) 4 cm
Polinices sordidus (Swainson, 1821). Australia. In sand, intertidal to shallow offshore waters; common. Syn.: *plumbea* Lamarck; *strangei* Reeve.

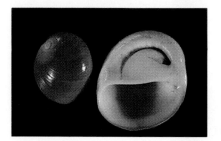

Egg-white Moon   (2″) 5 cm
Neverita albumen (L., 1758). Indo-Pacific. In clean sand to 70 m; uncommon. Very flattened shell.

Shark-eye Moon   (3″) 7.5 cm
Neverita duplicata (Say, 1822). Massachusetts to S.E. United States. Sand flats, shallow water; common. Syn.: *campeachiensis* Reeve.

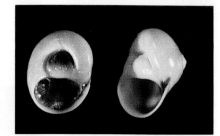

Ince's Moon   (1″) 2.5 cm
Neverita incei (Philippi, 1853). Australia. In sand, shallow water; uncommon. Syn.: *fibula* Reeve; *baconi* Reeve.

Josephine's Moon   (1.25″) 3 cm
Neverita josephinia Risso, 1826. Mediterranean; W. Europe. Offshore to 15 m; common. Syn.: *olla* Serres; *philippiana* Reeve.

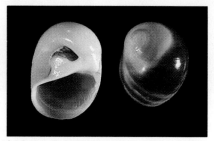

Elephant's-foot Moon   (1.5″) 4 cm
Neverita peselephanti (Link, 1807). Indo-Pacific. In sand to 10 m; moderately common. Syn.: *powisiana* Récluz; *columnaris* Récluz.

Sagami Bay Moon   (1.5″) 4 cm
Neverita sagamiensis (Pilsbry, 1904). Japan. In sand, offshore, 10 to 40 m; uncommon.

Adorned Moon   (1.25″) 3 cm
Neverita vestita Kuroda, 1961. Japan (endemic). In sand, offshore, to 50 m; uncommon.

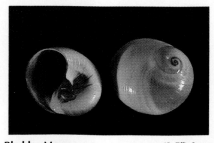

Bladder Moon   (2.5″) 6 cm
Polinices didyma (Röding, 1798). Western Pacific; Indian Ocean. Intertidal to 100 m; common. Syn.: *bicolor* Philippi; *vesicalis* Philippi.

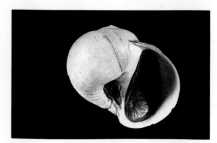

Drake's Moon   (2.5″) 6 cm
Neverita draconis (Dall, 1903). Alaska to northern Mexico. Offshore, 20 to 50 m; uncommon.

Two-banded Moon (1.6") 4 cm
Polinices bifasciatus (Griffith & Pidgeon, 1834). Gulf of California to Panama. Intertidal mud flats; common.

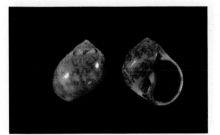

Guillemin's Moon (1") 2.5 cm
Euspira guillemini (Payraudeau, 1826). Mediterranean and north to Brittany. Offshore in shallow water; uncommon.

Common Northern Moon (3.5") 9 cm
Lunatia heros (Say, 1822.) Gulf of St. Lawrence to North Carolina. In sand, intertidal to offshore; common.

Lewis's Moon (4") 10 cm
Lunatia lewisi (Gould, 1847). British Columbia to Baja California. In sand, intertidal and offshore; common. Largest living naticid.

Poli's Necklace Shell (0.5") 1.2 cm
Euspira poliana (Chiaje, 1826). N.W. Europe; Mediterranean. In sand, intertidal and offshore; common. Syn.: *alderi* Forbes; *pulchella* Forbes.

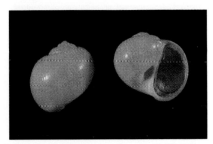

Yokoyama's Moon (0.5") 1.2 cm
Euspira yokoyamai Kuroda & Habe, 1961. Japan (endemic). Offshore, 70 to 100 m; uncommon. Syn.: *pallida* Yokoyama.

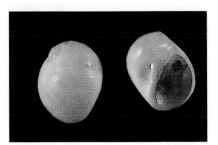

Umbilicate Moon (1") 2.5 cm
Sigaretotrema umbilicata (Quoy & Gaimard, 1833). South half of Australia. In sand, intertidal and offshore; uncommon. Syn.: *picta* Reeve.

Concave Ear Moon (1.3") 3 cm
Sinum concavum (Lamarck, 1822). West Africa. Trawled offshore in fairly deep water; uncommon.

Boat Ear Moon (2") 5 cm
Sinum cymba (Menke, 1828). Ecuador to Chile; Galapagos Islands. Shallow water; moderately common. Brown aperture.

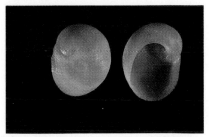

Baby's Ear Moon (1.5") 4 cm
Sinum perspectivum (Say, 1831). S.E. United States and West Indies; Bermuda. Shallow water, sand flats; common.

Spotted Ear Moon (1.2") 3 cm
Sinum maculatum (Say, 1831). North Carolina to Florida; Caribbean. In shallow water; uncommon. Syn.: *martinianum* Philippi probably.

Javanese Ear Moon (1.7") 4.5 cm
Sinum javanicum (Griffith & Pidgeon, 1834). Japan south to Indonesia. Offshore to 60 m; uncommon. Protoconch is purple-brown.

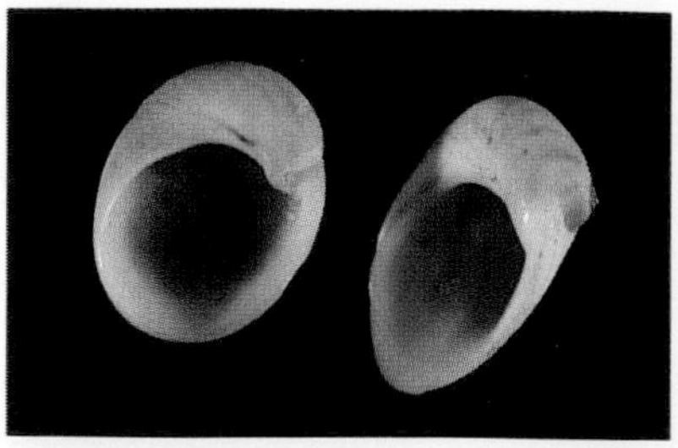

Neritelike Ear Shell (0.7") 1.8 cm
Sinum neritoideum (L., 1758). Bay of Bengal; Malaysia; Indonesia. Intertidal and offshore; moderately common.

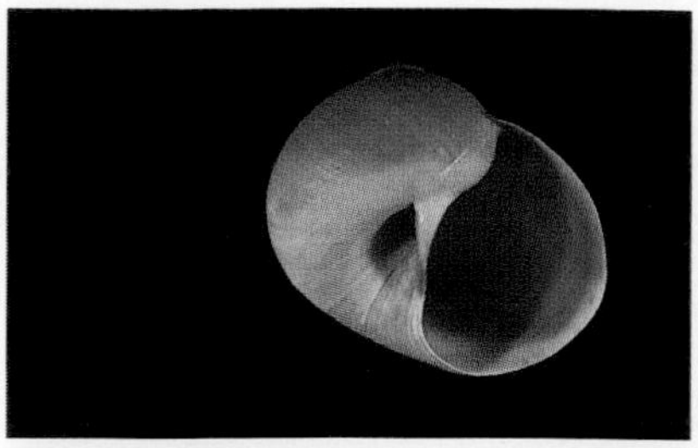

Oldroyd's Fragile Moon (3") 7 cm
Calinaticina oldroydii (Dall, 1897). Oregon to southern California. Sand bottom; 60 to 140 m; common.

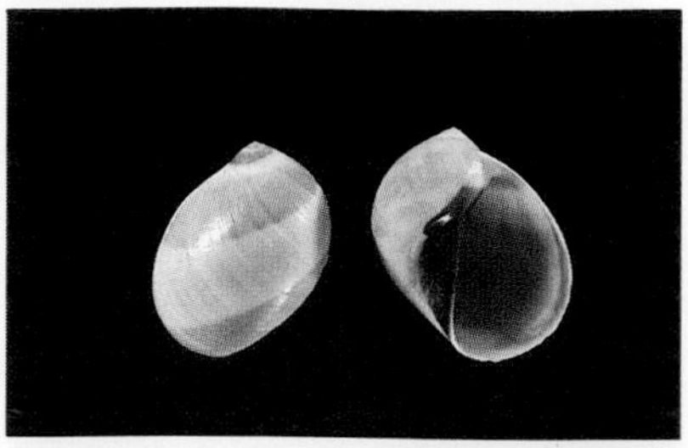

Black-mouth Moon (2") 5 cm
Polinices melanostomus (Gmelin, 1791). Indo-Pacific. Shallow water; common. Syn.: *opaca* Récluz; *succineoides* Reeve.

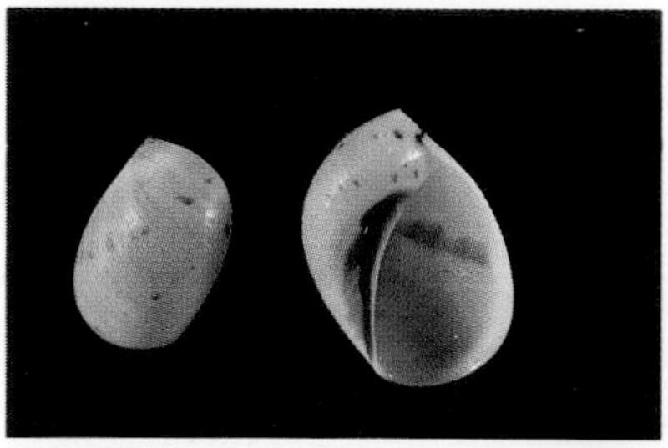

Seba's Moon (1.5") 3 cm
Polinices sebae (Récluz, 1844). Indo-Pacific. Shallow water; common. May be form of *mammata*.

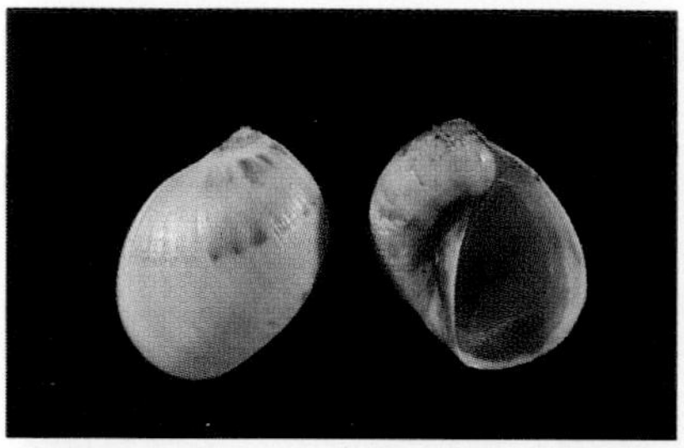

Mikawa Moon (2") 5 cm
Polinices mikawaensis Azuma, 1961. Western Pacific. Shallow water; uncommon.

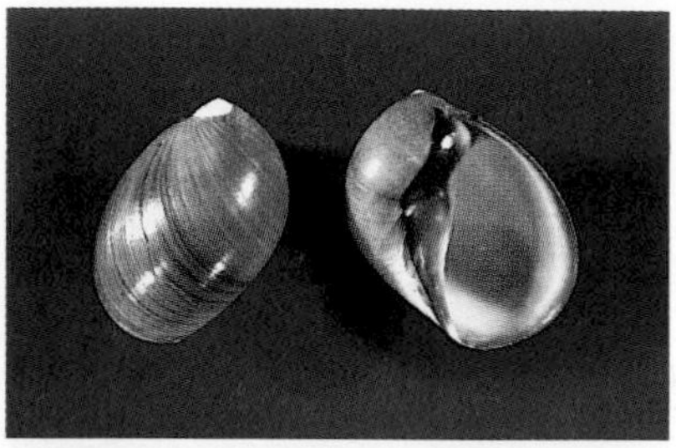

Maurus Moon (2") 5 cm
Polinices maurus (Lamarck, 1816). Indo-Pacific. Shallow sand flats; common. Syn.: *nuxcastanea* Hedley.

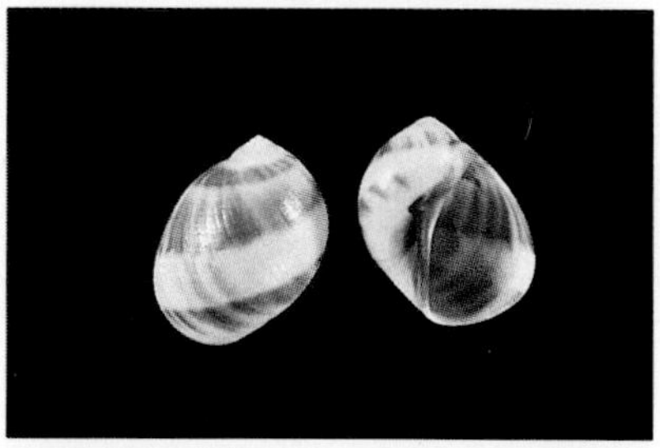

Breast-shaped Moon (1.5") 3 cm
Polinices mammatus (Röding, 1798). Western Pacific; Japan. In sand, offshore, 10 to 50 m; moderately common.

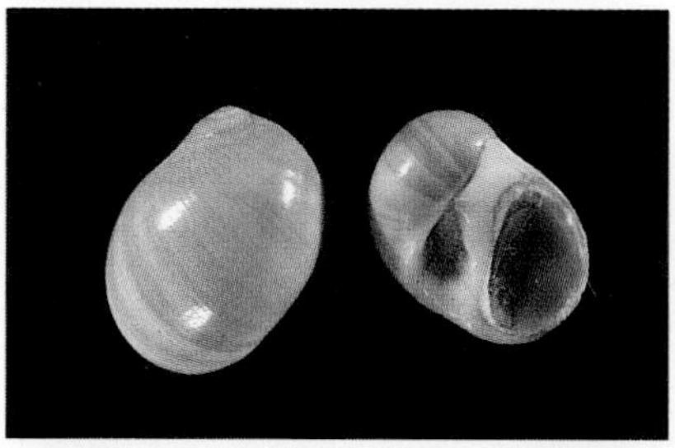

Brown Moon (1.5") 4 cm
Polinices hepaticus (Röding, 1798). Florida to Brazil. Shallow water, sand; uncommon. Syn.: *brunneus* Link.

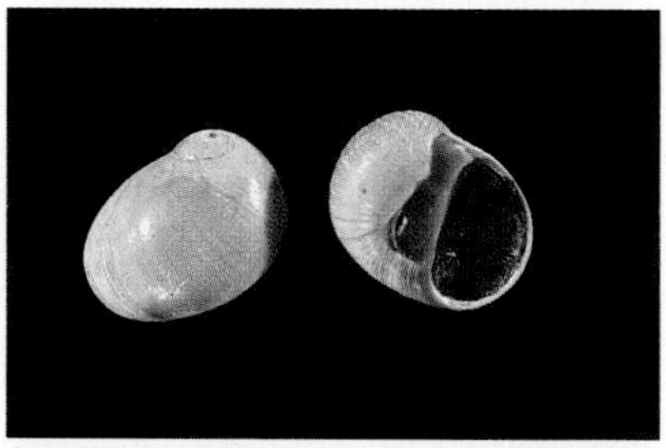

Swainson's Moon (1.2") 3 cm
Polinices melastomus (Swainson, 1821). Southwestern Pacific. Shallow water, sand. Uncommon. Syn.: *sanguinolenta* Deshayes.

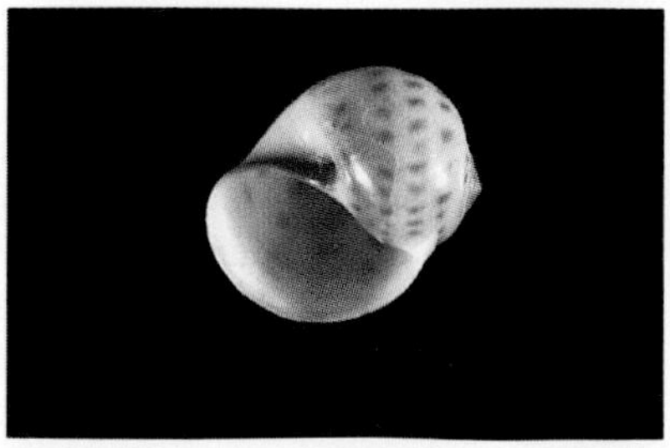

Senegal Moon (1") 2.5 cm
Polinices grossularius Marche-Marchad, 1957. N.W. Africa to Angola; Mediterranean. In sand offshore, 30 to 130 m; moderately rare.

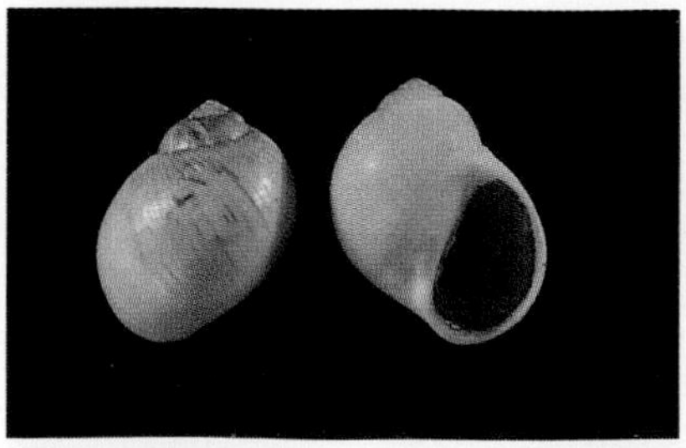

Plicispira Moon (1") 2.5 cm
Polinices plicispirus Kuroda, 1961. Japan. Offshore; uncommon.

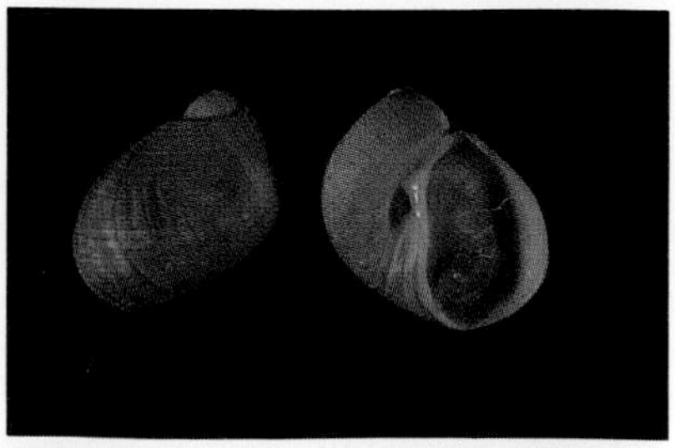

Papilla Moon (1") 2.5 cm
Eunaticina papilla (Gmelin, 1791). Melanesia to Indian Ocean. Shallow water in sand; uncommon.

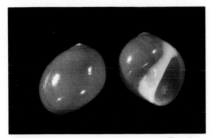

Golden Moon (1.7″) 4.5 cm
Polinices aurantius (Röding, 1798). Western and central Pacific. Clean sand to 20 m; moderately common. Syn.: *mellosum* Hedley; *straminea* Récluz.

Fleming's Moon (1.5″) 4 cm
Polinices flemingianus (Récluz, 1844). Japan to Australia and Fiji. Clean sand, intertidal and shallow water; moderately common. Syn.: *jukesii* Reeve.

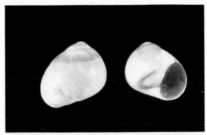

Récluz's Moon (2.5″) 6 cm
Polinices reclusiana (Deshayes, 1839). Northern California to W. Mexico. Intertidal and offshore; common. Syn.: *imperforata* Dall.

Spiral Moon (2″) 5 cm
Neverita helicoides (Gray, 1825). Baja California to Peru. Intertidal and offshore; moderately common. Syn.: *glauca* Lesson.

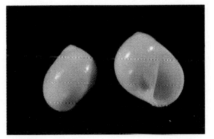

Caribbean Milk Moon (1″) 2.5 cm
Polinices lacteus (Guilding, 1834). S.E. United States to Brazil; Bermuda. Shallow water; common.

Panama Milk Moon (1.6″) 4 cm
Polinices panamaensis (Récluz, 1844). Panama to northern Peru. Offshore to 45 m; uncommon.

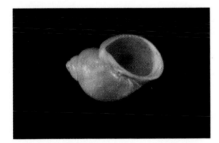

Purplish Alaskan Moon (0.7″) 1.8 cm
Amauropsis purpureus Dall, 1871. Alaska. Offshore; common. Holotype illustrated.

Iceland Moon (1″) 2.5 cm
Bulbus islandicus (Gmelin, 1791). Arctic seas south to Virginia; northern Europe. Offshore; moderately common. Syn.: *helicoides* Johnston.

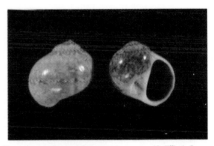

European Gray Moon (0.7″) 1.8 cm
Payraudeautia intricata (Donovan, 1804). Mediterranean; Europe; Azores. In sand in shallow water; moderately common. Syn.: *valenciennesi* Payraudeau.

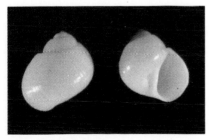

Carolina Moon (0.5″) 1.2 cm
Sigatica carolinensis (Dall, 1889). North Carolina south to Caribbean. In sand offshore to 180 m; uncommon.

European Necklace Shell (1.5″) 4 cm
Polinices catena (da Costa, 1778). N. W. Europe; Mediterranean. In sand, shallow water; common. Syn.: *monilifera* Lamarck; *ampullifera* Lamarck.

Dark-brown Necklace Shell (1″) 2.5 cm
Polinices fuscus (Blainville, 1825). N. W. Europe; Mediterranean. Offshore to 30 m; uncommon. Syn.: *sordida* Philippi.

Solid Moon (1") 2.5 cm
Natica fasciata (Röding, 1798). Southwest Pacific. Shallow water in sand. Syn.: *solida* Blainville.

Calf Moon (1.5") 4 cm
Natica vitellus (L., 1758). Western Pacific; Indian Ocean. Shallow water; common. Syn.: *rufa* Born; *spadicea* Gmelin; *helvacea* Lamarck.

Lined Moon (1.5") 4 cm
Natica lineata (Röding, 1798). Japan to Queensland; northern Indian Ocean. Sand or mud to 50 m; common. Red lines straight. Syn.: *lineata* Lamarck.

Starry Moon (1.5") 4 cm
Natica stellata Chenu, 1845. Western Pacific, possibly Indian Ocean. In sand to 20 m; moderately common. The *"vitellus"* of authors.

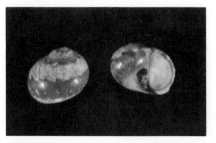

Traill's Moon (0.75") 2 cm
Natica traillii Reeve, 1855. Indian Ocean; Malaysia. Shallow water; uncommon. Syn.: possibly *buriasiensis* Récluz.

African Berry Moon (1") 2.5 cm
Natica acinonyx Marche-Marchad, 1957. Senegal and Gambia. Offshore, 20 to 220 m; rare.

Adanson's Moon (1") 2.5 cm
Natica adansoni Blainville, 1825. Western Africa. Fairly shallow water; uncommon. Syn.: *variabilis* Reeve.

Collared Moon (1") 2.5 cm
Natica collaria Lamarck, 1822. Western Africa. In sand, shallow water; moderately common. Syn.: *labrella* Lamarck; *gambiae* Récluz.

The Fanel Moon (1") 2.5 cm
Natica fanel (Röding, 1798). Western Africa. In sand, shallow water; moderately common. Syn.: *rocquignyi* Fischer-Piette.

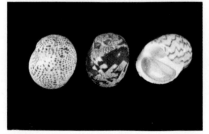

Lightning Moon (1.2") 3 cm
Natica fulminea (Gmelin, 1791). Western Africa. Shallow water; moderately common. Syn.: *cruentata* Gmelin; *punctata* Swainson.

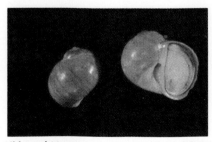

Ribboned Moon (0.5") 1.2 cm
Natica lemniscata Philippi, 1851. Japan and Okinawa. Fairly deep water; moderately rare.

Brown-lined Moon (1.5") 4 cm
Natica brunneolinea McLean, 1970. Galapagos Islands (endemic). Deep water; rare.

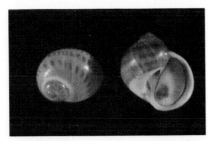

Moroccan Moon (0.7") 1.8 cm

Natica marochiensis (Gmelin, 1791). Florida; West Indies to Brazil; eastern Africa. Intertidal; moderately common. Syn.: *maroccana* Dillwyn.

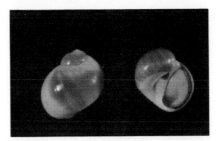

Gualtieri's Moon (0.75") 2 cm

Natica gualteriana Récluz, 1844. Indo-Pacific. Intertidal to fairly deep water; common. Syn.: *tessellata* Philippi; *antonii* Philippi.

Lavender Moon (3.8") 1 cm

Natica lavendula Woolacott, 1956. Northern Australia to Fiji. Clean sand, shallow water; uncommon. Syn.: possibly *pseustes* Watson.

Violet-mouthed Moon (1.5") 4 cm

Natica janthostomoides Kuroda & Habe, 1949. Japan (endemic). Muddy sand, 20 to 40 m; uncommon. One or two ribs on operculum.

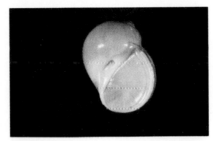

Nebulose Moon (0.6") 1.5 cm

Natica nebulosa Schepman, 1910. Indonesia. Offshore; rare. Holotype illustrated.

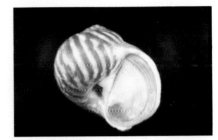

Broad-striped Moon (1") 2.3 cm

Natica inexpectans Olsson, 1971. Gulf of Panama. Offshore, 120 m; rare. Has broader stripes. Holotype illustrated.

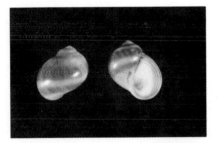

Scethra Moon (0.6") 1.5 cm

Natica scethra Dall, 1908. Mexico to northern Peru; Baja California. Deep water; moderately rare.

Single-banded Moon (1.2") 3 cm

Natica unifasciata Lamarck, 1822. Costa Rica to northern Peru. Intertidal and shallow offshore waters; common.

Colorful Atlantic Moon (2") 5 cm

Natica canrena (L., 1758). S. E. United States; Caribbean; Bermuda. Offshore to 60 m; common. Syn.: *verae* Rehder.

China Moon (1") 2.5 cm

Natica onca (Röding, 1798). Indo-Pacific. In sand, intertidal to shallow offshore waters; common. Syn.: *pavimentum* Röding; *chinensis* Lamarck.

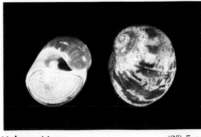

Hebrew Moon (2") 5 cm

Natica maculata (von Salis, 1793). Mediterranean; W. Europe. Sand and gravel to 100 m; moderately common. Syn.: *adspersa* Menke.

Seychelles Moon (0.7") 1.8 cm

Natica sertata Menke, 1843. Northern half of Australia; Indian Ocean. Intertidal to deep water; uncommon. Syn.: *colliei* Récluz.

Florida Moon   (1″) 2 cm
Natica floridana (Rehder, 1943). Southeastern Florida to Brazil. Offshore to 20 m; uncommon. Operculum with 4 ribs.

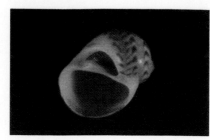

Cayenne Moon   (1″) 2.5 cm
Natica cayennensis Récluz, 1850. West Indies to Brazil. In sand in shallow water; moderately common. Syn.: *haysae* Nowell-Usticke.

Turton's Moon   (1.5″) 4 cm
Natica turtoni E. A. Smith, 1890. Western Africa; St. Helena. In sand to 50 m; moderately common.

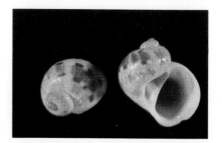

Four-banded Moon   (0.75″) 2 cm
Natica idiopoma Pilsbry & Lowe, 1932. Western Mexico to Panama; Galapagos Islands. Offshore to moderate depths; uncommon.

New Zealand Moon   (1″) 2.5 cm
Natica zelandica Quoy & Gaimard, 1832. New Zealand (endemic). Intertidal and shallow water offshore; moderately common.

Beautifully-banded Moon   (0.8″) 2 cm
Natica euzona (Récluz, 1844). Indo-Pacific. In sand, offshore to 60 m; uncommon. Syn.: *decora* Philippi; *cothurnata* Iredale.

Zebra Moon   (1″) 2.5 cm
Natica undulata (Röding, 1798). Japan; Philippines and possibly Indian Ocean. In sand to 40 m; uncommon. Syn.: *zebra* Lamarck.

Tabulated Moon   (0.75″) 2 cm
Natica tabularis Kuroda, 1961. Japan (endemic). In fine sand, 50 to 100 m; rare.

Arctic Moon   (1.2″) 3 cm
Natica clausa Broderip & Sowerby, 1829. Arctic seas of North America. Common. Syn.: *aleutica* Dall (holotype illustrated) and others.

Flamed Moon   (5.8″) 14 cm
Natica filosa Philippi, 1845. Mediterranean; W. Europe; N. W. Africa. Offshore, 10 to 20 m; uncommon. Syn.: *flammulata* Requien.

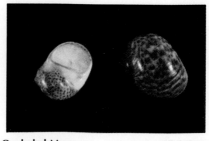

Occluded Moon   (1″) 2.5 cm
Natica tecta Anton, 1839. South Africa. Sand or mud, intertidal to 20 m; moderately common. Syn.: *imperforata* Gray; *genuanus* Reeve.

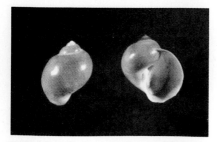

Mexican Moon   (1″) 2.5 cm
Natica lunaris Berry, 1964. Sonora to Nayarit, western Mexico. Offshore, 7 to 45 m; rare.

Sulcate Moon   (0.8") 2 cm
Stigmaulax sulcatus (Born, 1778). South-eastern Florida to Brazil. Shallow water; uncommon. Syn.: *cancellatus* Gmelin.

Broderip's Moon   (1") 2.5 cm
Stigmaulax broderipiana Récluz, 1844. W. Mexico to Peru. Offshore to 55 m; common. Syn.: *iostoma* Menke.

Spider Moon   (1") 2.5 cm
Natica arachnoidea (Gmelin, 1791). Indo-Pacific. Shallow water to 3 m; moderately common. Syn.: *raynoldiana* Récluz.

White-bottom Moon   (0.7") 1.8 cm
Natica lacteobasis Kuroda, 1961. Japan. Offshore; uncommon.

Violet Moon   (0.7") 1.8 cm
Natica violacea Sowerby, 1825. Indo-Pacific. Shallow water to 20 m; uncommon. Syn.: *rhodostoma* Philippi.

Canelo Moon   (1") 2.5 cm
Natica caneloensis Hertlein & Strong, 1955. W. Mexico to Ecuador. Shallow water, sand; uncommon.

Butterfly Moon   (1.2") 3 cm
Natica alapapilionis (Röding, 1798). Indo-Pacific. Shallow water, sand. Uncommon. Syn.: *zonaria* Lamarck; *plicifera* Philippi; *taeniata* Menke.

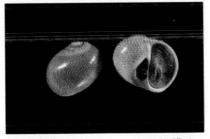

Fly-specked Moon   (1.5") 4 cm
Natica stercusmuscarum (Gmelin, 1791). Mediterranean; N. W. Africa. Offshore to 10 m; common. Syn.: *millepunctata* Lamarck.

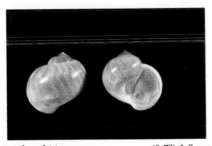

Bordered Moon   (0.7") 1.8 cm
Natica limbata Orbigny, 1840. Southern Brazil to Argentina. Muddy sand, 18 to 72 m; common. Syn.: *isabelleana* Orbigny.

Cheerful Moon   (1") 2.5 cm
Natica hilaris Sowerby, 1914. Japan to South Africa. Fine sandy bottom, 20 to 200 m; locally common. Syn.: *luculenta* Iredale.

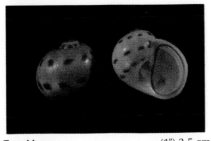

Tosa Moon   (1") 2.5 cm
Natica tosaensis Kuroda, 1961. Off Tosa, Japan. Dredged in deep water; uncommon.

Tiger Moon   (1") 2.5 cm
Natica tigrina (Röding, 1798). Eastern Asia. Offshore, 10 to 30 m; common. Syn.: *maculosa* Lamarck; *pellistigrina* Deshayes.

HELMET SHELLS
FAMILY CASSIDAE

Helmet shells live mostly in warm waters around the world. Shells of males may differ from those of females. Interspecific hybridization may take place and deep-water forms are particularly puzzling. Some species spawn towerlike egg masses and free-swimming larval stages. Food consists primarily of sea urchins. Operculum chitinous, small, elongate in *Cassis*, fan-shaped in *Phalium*.

Horned Helmet   (8.5″) 22 cm
Cassis cornuta (L., 1758). Indo-Pacific. Associated with coral reefs; common. 1 to 20 m.

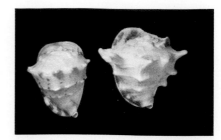

Horned Helmet   (8.5″) 22 cm
Cassis cornuta (L., 1758). Like several other helmet shells, the male of the species (left) is smaller than the female.

Horned Helmet   (3″) 7.5 cm
Cassis cornuta (L., 1758). Juvenile shells lack the 7 or 8 varices of adults. Shoulder knobs small, numerous.

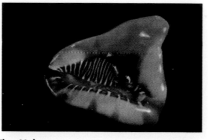

King Helmet   (6″) 15 cm
Cassis tuberosa (L., 1758). Brazil; Bermuda; North Carolina to Caribbean. Shallow water; common. 7 or 8 brown spots on each varix.

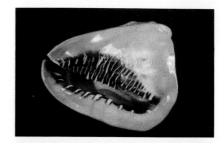

Emperor Helmet   (6.5″) 16.5 cm
Cassis madagascariensis Lamarck, 1822. Florida to Lesser Antilles; Bahamas. In sand, moderately shallow water; common.

Emperor Helmet   (6.5″) 16.5 cm
Cassis madagascariensis Lamarck, 1822. West Indian specimens were used to make large cameos.

Clench's Helmet   (12″) 30 cm
Cassis madagascariensis form *spinella* Clench, 1944. S. E. United States. 5 to 30 m; locally common. Largest *Cassis*.

Flame Helmet   (4.3″) 11 cm
Cassis flammea (L., 1758). Bermuda; Florida to Lesser Antilles. Shallow water; common. No brown between teeth.

Fimbriate Helmet   (3″) 7.5 cm
Cassis fimbriata Quoy & Gaimard, 1833. Western Australia to western Victoria. Intertidal to 200 m; common.

Dwarf Helmet   (1.5″) 4 cm
Cassis nana Tenison-Woods, 1879. Eastern Australia. On sand, 60 to 240 m; moderately common. Smallest living *Cassis*.

West African Helmet   (8″) 20 cm
Cassis tessellata (Gmelin, 1791). Southern West Africa. On sand to 60 m; uncommon. Syn.: *spinosa* Gronovius.

Reticulated Cowrie-helmet (2.5") 6.5 cm
Cypraecassis testiculus testiculus (L., 1758).
Southeastern Florida to Brazil. Shallow water; common. Form *crumena* Bruguière at right.

Senegal Cowrie-helmet (2.5") 6.5 cm
Cypraecassis testiculus senegalica (Gmelin, 1791). Western Africa and offshore islands. Shallow water; common.

Bullmouth Helmet (6") 15 cm
Cypraecassis rufa (L., 1758). Indo-Pacific (not India or Hawaii). Near coral reefs; common (rarer in center of range).

Bullmouth Helmet (6") 15 cm
Cypraecassis rufa (L., 1758). Shipped annually from eastern Africa to Italy for use in the manufacture of cameos.

Galapagos Cowrie-helmet (4.5") 11.5 cm
Cypraecassis tenuis (Wood, 1828). Baja California to Ecuador; Galapagos. Offshore, sometimes beached; uncommon.

Contracted Cowrie-helmet (2.5") 6.5 cm
Cypraecassis coarctata (Sowerby, 1825). Gulf of California to Peru. Intertidal and offshore; uncommon.

Gray Bonnet (3.5") 9 cm
Phalium glaucum (L., 1758). Indo-Pacific. Intertidal and offshore, on sand; common. 3 or 4 strong spines at base of outer lip.

Banded Bonnet (3.5") 9 cm
Phalium bandatum bandatum (Perry, 1811). Western Pacific, especially northern Australia. Shallow to deep water; common.

Furrowed Bonnet (3.5") 9 cm
Phalium bandatum exaratum (Reeve, 1848). Mascarene Islands, Indian Ocean. Offshore; rare. Deep spiral grooves.

Checkerboard Bonnet (2.5") 6.5 cm
Phalium areola (L., 1758). Eastern Africa to Melanesia and Samoa. Intertidal and offshore on sandy mud; common. Spots vary.

Striped Bonnet (3.5") 9 cm
Phalium flammiferum (Röding, 1798). Japan; Taiwan; eastern China. Offshore to 100 m; common. Syn.: *strigatum* Gmelin. Not *strigatum* Müller, 1776.

Decussate Bonnet (2.5") 6.5 cm
Phalium decussatum (L., 1758). Southeastern Asia; southern Japan. Offshore; common. Rarely striped.

Fimbriate Bonnet   (3″) 7.5 cm
Phalium fimbria (Gmelin, 1791). Indian Ocean and Indonesia. Offshore, occasionally beached; rare. Syn.: *plicaria* Lamarck.

Pilsbry's Bonnet   (2.5″) 6.5 cm
Phalium pilsbryi (Woodring & Olsson, 1957). Galapagos. Shallow water; rare. Resembles *P. wyvillei.*

Wyville's Bonnet   (4″) 10 cm
Phalium coronadoi wyvillei (Watson, 1886). Japan to Australia. Deep water; rare. Holotype illustrated.

(left) Chalky Bonnet   (2.5″) 6.5 cm
Phalium carnosum (Kuroda & Habe, 1961).
(right) Kuroda's Bonnet   (2.5″) 6.5 cm
Phalium kurodai Abbott, 1968. Both Japan. Deep water; rare.

Japanese Bonnet   (2.3″) 6 cm
Phalium bisulcatum (Schubert & Wagner, 1829). Indo-Pacific. Offshore to deep water; common. Syntypes illustrated.

Sophia's Bonnet   (3″) 7.5 cm
Phalium bisulcatum sophia (Brazier, 1872). Eastern Australia; Kermadec Islands. Offshore, 80 to 160 m; uncommon.

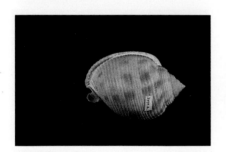

Japanese Bonnet   (2.3″) 6 cm
Phalium bisulcatum (Schubert & Wagner, 1829). One of the many synonyms is *japonica* Reeve (holotype illustrated).

Faurot's Bonnet   (2″) 5 cm
Phalium faurotis (Jousseaume, 1888). Western Indian Ocean. Offshore to deep water; uncommon. Apex purple.

Channeled Bonnet   (1.8″) 4.5 cm
Phalium canaliculatum (Bruguière, 1792). Bay of Bengal. Offshore; common. Has a subsutural channel.

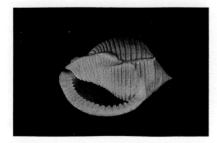

Hawaiian Bonnet   (2.2″) 5.5 cm
Phalium umbilicatum (Pease, 1860). Hawaiian Islands. Offshore to deep water; rare. Syn.: *fortisulcata* E. A. Smith. Paratype illustrated.

Narrow-mouthed Bonnet   (2.2″) 5.5 cm
Phalium microstoma (von Martens, 1903). Off Tanganyika to Somalia. Deep water; rare.

Smooth Bonnet   (2″) 5 cm
Phalium glabratum glabratum (Dunker, 1852). Philippines; Indonesia; New Guinea. Offshore to deep water; rare.

Bubble Bonnet (1.8") 4.5 cm
Phalium glabratum bulla (Habe, 1961). Southern Japan; southeast China; Hawaii. 50 to 200 m; moderately common.

Half-grained Bonnet (2") 5 cm
Phalium semigranosum (Lamarck, 1822). Southern Australia; Tasmania. On sand offshore to deep water; common.

Adcock's Bonnet (1.2") 3 cm
Phalium adcocki (Sowerby, 1896). Southern Australia. Offshore to 200 m; rare. Few specimens in private hands.

Saburon Bonnet (2") 5 cm
Phalium saburon (Bruguière, 1792). Mediterranean; Bay of Biscay to Ghana. Offshore; common. Syn.: *pomum* Schubert & Wagner.

South African Bonnet (2.5") 6.5 cm
Phalium craticulatum (Euthyme, 1885). Mozambique to South Africa. Deep water; uncommon. Syn.: *africana* Fulton.

Valdivia Bonnet (2") 5 cm
Phalium bituberculosum (von Martens, 1901). Eastern Africa. 100 to 1,079 m; rare. "Valdivia" dredged first known specimen.

Scotch Bonnet (3") 7.5 cm
Phalium granulatum granulatum (Born, 1778). S.E. United States to Brazil. Offshore; common. Some are smoothish.

Mediterranean Bonnet (3.5") 9 cm
Phalium granulatum subspecies *undulatum* (Gmelin, 1791). Mediterranean. Offshore; common. Syn.: *sulcosa* Bruguière.

Panamic Bonnet (2.3") 6 cm
Phalium granulatum subspecies *centiquadratum* (Valenciennes, 1832). W. Mexico to Peru; Galapagos. Offshore; common.

Pear Bonnet (2.5") 6.5 cm
Phalium pyrum pyrum (Lamarck, 1822). Southern Australia; Tasmania; New Zealand; South Africa. Offshore to deep water; common.

Roy Bell's Bonnet (4.5") 11.5 cm
Phalium pyrum royanum (Iredale, 1914). New South Wales; New Zealand; Kermadec Islands. Offshore, craypots; uncommon. Named after Roy Bell.

Few-wrinkled Bonnet (2") 5 cm
Phalium pauciruge (Menke, 1843). Southwestern Australia. 1 to 20 m; moderately common. Solid and heavy.

Thomson's Bonnet   (2.5") 6.5 cm
Phalium thomsoni (Brazier, 1875). South-
eastern Australia; northern New Zealand.
Deep water; uncommon.

Whitworth's Bonnet   (2.5") 6.5 cm
Phalium whitworthi Abbott, 1968. Western
Australia. Offshore, craypots; moderately
rare. Spiral cords strong.

Unadorned Bonnet   (2.2") 5.5 cm
Phalium inornatum (Pilsbry, 1895). Central
Japan to southern China Sea. Offshore to
30 m; moderately common.

Lipped Bonnet   (2.5") 6.4 cm
Phalium labiatum labiatum (Perry, 1811).
Victoria; southern Queensland; northern
New Zealand. Offshore to about 100 m;
common.

Iredale's Bonnet   (2.5") 6.5 cm
Phalium labiatum subspecies *iredalei*
(Bayer, 1935). South Africa. Offshore, often
beached; common. Remarkably variable.

Ihering's Bonnet   (2.5") 6.5 cm
Phalium labiatum subspecies *iheringi* (Carcelles, 1953). Northern Argentina; southern Brazil. Moderately deep water; uncommon.

Heavy Bonnet   (1.5") 4 cm
Casmaria ponderosa ponderosa (Gmelin,
1791). Indo-Pacific. In sand, shallow water;
common. Several named forms.

Atlantic Bonnet   (1") 2.5 cm
Casmaria ponderosa atlantica Clench, 1944.
Southeastern Florida; Caribbean. Offshore
to 50 m; rare.

Vibex Bonnet   (2") 5 cm
Casmaria erinaceus (L., 1758). Indo-Pacific.
Shallow water; locally common. Syn.: *vi-
bex* L.

Spiny Bonnet   (2.5") 6.5 cm
Galeodea echinophora (L., 1758). Mediterranean. Offshore to deep water; uncommon. Syn.: *tuberculosa* Schumacher.

Rugose Bonnet   (2.5") 6.5 cm
Galeodea rugosa (L., 1758). Mediterranean; western Europe. Offshore to deep
water; common. Syn.: *tyrrhena* Gmelin.

Royal Bonnet   (2") 5 cm
Sconsia striata (Lamarck, 1816). S.E. Florida
to off Texas to Brazil. Deep water; uncommon. Syn.: *grayi* A. Adams; *barbudensis*
Higgins & Marrat.

Nephele Bonnet   (1.5″) 3.78 cm
Sconsia nephele Bayer, 1971.
Off Grenada, Lesser Antilles. 18
m, rare. Holotype illustrated.

Alcock's False Tun   (2″) 5 cm
Oocorys alcocki (E. A. Smith,
1906). Bay of Bengal and Indonesia. Deep water; rare.

Alabaster False Tun   (2.3″) 6 cm
Galeoocorys leucodoma (Dall,
1907). Japan. Deep water; rare.

Atlantic Morum   (0.8″) 2 cm
Morum oniscus (L., 1767). S.E.
Florida to Brazil; Bermuda. Under coral slabs, low tide; common. Syn.: *purpureum* Röding.

Heavy Morum   (1.5″) 4 cm
Morum ponderosum (Hanley,
1858). Southwestern Pacific to
Pitcairn Island. On reefs; uncommon. Lectotype illustrated.

Dennison's Morum   (2″) 5 cm
Morum dennisoni (Reeve,
1842). Caribbean. Deep water,
150 to 260 m; rare.

Velero Morum   (1.5″) 4 cm
Morum veleroae Emerson,
1968. Off Cocos Island (Costa
Rica); Galapagos. Dredged, 50
to 100 m; rare.

Matthews's Morum   (1″) 2.5 cm
Morum matthewsi Emerson,
1967. Off Ceara, Brazil. From
fish stomachs, 30 m; rare.

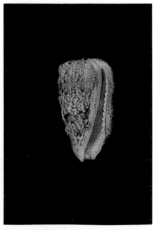

Kurz's Morum   (1″) 2.5 cm
Morum kurzi Petuch, 1979.
Central Philippines. 250 m;
rare. Type illustrated.

Noble Morum   (1.5″) 4 cm
Morum praeclarum Melvill,
1919. Western Indian Ocean.
Dredged, deep water; rare.
Holotype illustrated.

MacAndrew's Morum   (1.5″)
4 cm *Morum macandrewi* (Sowerby, 1889). East Asia. Offshore, to 100 m; uncommon.
Holotype illus.

Lumpy Morum   (0.6″) 1.5 cm
Morum tuberculosum (Reeve,
1842). Baja California to Peru.
Intertidal; uncommon. Type illustrated.

Giant Morum (2.5") 6.5 cm
Morum grande (A. Adams, 1855). Japan to Queensland, Australia. Trawled, deep water; moderately rare.

Cancellate Morum (1.8") 4.5 cm
Morum cancellatum (Sowerby, 1824). China Sea. Dredged, 50 to 150 m; uncommon.

Watson's Morum (1.5") 4 cm
Morum watsoni Dance & Emerson, 1967. Western Pacific. Rare. Syn.: *cithara* Watson. (Holotype illus.)

Bartsch's False Tun (4") 10 cm
Oocorys bartschi Rehder, 1943. Gulf of Mexico; southeast Florida. Deep water; uncommon. Holotype illus.

Lineated False Tun (2") 4 cm
Oocorys lineata (Schepman, 1909). Ceram Sea, Indonesia; eastern Asia. Deep water; rare.

Barbour's False Tun (2") 5 cm
Oocorys barbouri Clench & Aguayo, 1939. Off northern Cuba. Deep water; rare. Holotype illus.

Sulcate False Tun (2") 5 cm
Oocorys sulcata Fischer, 1883. Caribbean; N.W. Africa; Indian Ocean. Deep water; uncommon. Syn.: *indica* E. A. Smith.

Caribbean False Tun (1.5") 4 cm
Oocorys caribbaea Clench & Aguayo, 1939. North coast of Cuba. Deep water; rare. Holotype illus.

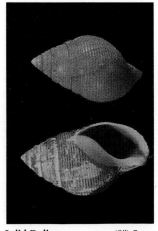

Solid Dalium (2") 5 cm
Dalium solidum Dall, 1889. Southern Caribbean; Surinam. 600 to 2,000 m; rare. Considerable size variation.

Pyriform False Tun (2") 5 cm
Eudolium pyriforme (Sowerby, 1914). Japan to S.E. Asia. Offshore; common.

FIG SHELLS
FAMILY FICIDAE

Small family of moderately large to small shells, characteristically fig- or pear-shaped and light in structure. Sand dwellers in warm-water areas, they lack an operculum. Animal's large foot has two flaps, one on each side of the anterior (siphonal) end. Shells of males may differ from those of females.

Swollen Fig Shell (3.5") 9 cm
Ficus ventricosa (Sowerby, 1825). Western Mexico to Peru. Offshore, sometimes beached; common.

Graceful Fig Shell (5") 13 cm
Ficus gracilis (Sowerby, 1825). Eastern Asia. Offshore to 100 m. Locally common. Syn.: *dussumieri* Chenu.

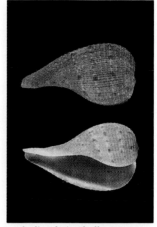

Underlined Fig Shell (4") 10 cm
Ficus subintermedia (Orbigny, 1852). Indo-Pacific. Offshore, in sandy mud; common.

True Fig Shell (3") 7.5 cm
Ficus variegata Röding, 1798. Eastern Asia; Japan. 1 to 20 m; uncommon. Linné's *ficus* is unidentifiable.

Carol's Fig Shell (2.5") 6 cm
Ficus carolae Clench, 1945. Gulf of Mexico from southeastern Florida to Mexico. Deep water; rare. Holotype illus.

Common Fig Shell (3.5") 9 cm
Ficus communis Röding, 1798. North Carolina to Gulf of Mexico. Offshore, often beached; common. Syn.: *papyratia* Say.

Threaded Fig Shell (3") 7.5 cm
Ficus filosa (Sowerby, 1892). Japan; China Sea, eastern Australia. Deep water; uncommon. Holotype illus.

Spotted Fig Shell (2") 5 cm
Ficus eospila (Péron-Lesueur, 1807). Western Australia. Offshore; common. Syn.: *tessellata* Kobelt.

Howell's Fig Shell (1.5") 4 cm
Ficus howelli Clench & Farfante, 1940. Cuba to Trinidad. Deep water; rare.

Atlantic Fig Shell (1.5") 4 cm
Ficus atlanticus Clench & Aguayo, 1940. Off Bahia, Brazil. Deep water; rare. *F. howelli*, may be male form.

Bengal Fig Shell (3") 7.5 cm
Ficus investigatoris E. A. Smith, 1906. Indian Ocean. Deep water; rare. Syn.: *sewelli* Prashad.

TUN SHELLS
FAMILY TONNIDAE

Tun shells are thinner and usually roomier than helmet shells. They are almost exclusively tropical, prefer deeper water, and feed mainly on fish, sea urchins and crustaceans. Their free-swimming larval life is lengthy and has helped some species to spread great distances. The identification of some tun shells is not easy and synonyms abound.

Grinning Tun (7") 18 cm
Malea ringens (Swainson, 1822). W. Mexico to Peru. Under rock ledges and on sand bars; common.

Pacific Grinning Tun
(2.5") 6.5 cm
Malea pomum (L., 1758). Indo-Pacific. Offshore; moderately common. Syn.: *labrosa* Gray.

Pacific Partridge Tun
(4.5") 11.5 cm
Ionna perdix (L., 1758). Indo-Pacific. Offshore, in sand. Moderately common.

Atlantic Partridge Tun
(3.5") 9 cm
Tonna maculosa (Dillwyn, 1817). S. E. Florida to Brazil. Offshore; moderately common.

Spotted Tun
(4") 10 cm
Tonna dolium (L., 1758). Indo-Pacific; New Zealand. Offshore; uncommon. Ribs vary in number.

Costate Tun
(3.5") 9 cm
Tonna allium (Dillwyn, 1817). Indo-W. Pacific. Offshore; moderately common. Syn.: *costatum* Menke.

Banded Tun
(4") 10 cm
Tonna sulcosa (Born, 1778). Indo-Pacific. Offshore; uncommon. Syn.: *fasciatum* Bruguière.

Channeled Tun
(4") 10 cm
Tonna cepa (Röding, 1798). Indo-Pacific. Intertidal; common. *T. canaliculata* L. may be this species.

Giant Tun
(6") 15 cm
Tonna galea (L., 1758). Caribbean; Atlantic; Mediterranean; Indo-Pacific. Offshore to 40 m; uncommon.

Black-mouthed Tun
(8") 20 cm
Tonna melanostoma (Jay, 1839). Central Pacific (Tonga) to New Zealand. Offshore; rare.

Gold-mouthed Tun (6.5") 16 cm
Tonna luteostoma (Küster, 1857). Western Pacific; New Zealand. Offshore to 200 m; uncommon.

Marginate Tun
(4") 10 cm
Tonna marginata (Philippi, 1845). Japan to Indonesia. Offshore; uncommon. Syn.: *reevei* Hanley (holotype illus.).

China Tun
(4.3") 11 cm
Tonna chinensis (Dillwyn, 1817). S. W. Pacific. Offshore; uncommon. Syn.: *magnificus* Sowerby (holotype illus.).

Noronha Tun (2.5") 6 cm
Malea pomum noronhensis
Kempf and Matthews, 1969. Islands off N.E. Brazil. Sand bottoms; uncommon.

Thompson's False Tun (2") 5 cm
Eudolium thompsoni McGinty,
1955. Florida Keys and Gulf of Mexico. Moderately deep water; uncommon.

TRITONS
FAMILY CYMATIIDAE

Predominantly dwellers of tropical and warm waters, tritons include some of the world's largest living gastropods. Shells mostly thick and solid, often covered by a bristly periostracum. Operculum thick, chitinous. Egg capsules attached to rocks. As veliger larvae may be free swimming for up to 3 months, the wide distribution of some species is at least partially explained.

Trumpet Triton (13") 33 cm
Charonia tritonis (L., 1758).
Indo-Pacific. Coral reefs in shallow water; moderately common.

Atlantic Trumpet Triton (10")
25 cm *Charonia variegata* (Lamarck, 1816). S.E. Florida; West Indies; Mediterranean. Moderately common. 1 to 15 meters.

Atlantic Trumpet Triton
Charonia variegata (Lamarck,
1816). Some specimens have heavy shoulder. May be orange. Syn.: *nobilis* Conrad.

Knobbed Triton (7") 18 cm
Charonia lampas (L., 1758).
Mediterranean and adjacent coasts. Shallow water; moderately common.

Red Triton (6") 15 cm
Charonia rubicunda (Perry,
1811). S. half of Australia; Kermadec Islands; New Zealand. Shallow water; uncommon.

Powell's Triton (6") 15 cm
Charonia rubicunda form *powelli* Cotton, 1957. South Australia. On intertidal reefs; uncommon.

Wide-mouth Triton (8") 20 cm
Charonia lampas capax Finlay,
1926. New Zealand. Rocky ground; uncommon. May be same as *C. l. rubicunda* Perry.

Saul's Triton (6") 15 cm
Charonia sauliae (Reeve, 1844).
Southern Japan. Offshore, 10 to 20 m; common.

Girdled Triton (2") 5 cm
Linatella cingulata (Lamarck,
1822). Western Atlantic; Indo-Pacific; South Africa. Offshore; uncommon.

Angular Triton (5") 13 cm
Cymatium femorale (L., 1758).
Southern Florida to Brazil. With
periostracum. Shallow water,
moderately common.

Angular Triton (5") 13 cm
Cymatium femorale (L., 1758).
Varies greatly in size and to a
lesser extent in color. Without
periostracum.

Tiger Triton (5") 13 cm
Cymatium tigrinum (Broderip,
1833). Gulf of California to Panama. Offshore to 20 m; moderately rare.

Black-spotted Triton (3.5") 9 cm
Cymatium lotorium (L., 1758).
Tropical Indo-Pacific. Coral
reefs, shallow water; uncommon.

Ranzani's Triton (6") 15 cm
Cymatium ranzanii (Bianconi,
1851). Mozambique; northern
Arabian Sea. Offshore; moderately rare.

Perry's Triton (4") 10 cm
Cymatium perryi Emerson &
Old, 1963. Sri Lanka; southern
India. Offshore; uncommon.
No brown spots on columella.

Common Hairy Triton (3")
7.5 cm *Cymatium pileare* (L.,
1758). Indo-Pacific; western
Atlantic. Shallow water; common. Many synonyms.

Common Hairy Triton (3")
7.5 cm *Cymatium pileare* (L.,
1758). Specimen with periostracum. In Atlantic, species ranges
from Bermuda to Brazil.

Aquatile Hairy Triton
(2.5") 6 cm
Cymatium pileare form *aquatile* (Reeve, 1844). Under coral
slabs in the Indo-Pacific region.

Intermediate Hairy Triton
(2.5") 6 cm
Cymatium pileare form *intermedium* (Pease, 1869). This Pacific form is moderately com-

Jeweled Triton (1.2") 3 cm
Cymatium gemmatum (Reeve,
1844). Indo-Pacific; West Indies. Under coral, on sand,
shallow water; uncommon.

Nicobar Hairy Triton (2") 5 cm
Cymatium nicobaricum (Röding, 1798). Indo-Pacific; West
Indies. Shallow water; common. Syn.: *L. chlorostomum*.

Thersites Hairy Triton (1.5″) 3.5 cm *Cymatium thersites* (Reeve, 1844). Indian Ocean. Shallow water; uncommon.

Dwarf Hairy Triton (1″) 2.5 cm *Cymatium vespaceum* (Lamarck, 1822). North Carolina; Bermuda to Brazil. Shallow water; uncommon.

Dwarf Hairy Triton (1″) 2.5 cm *Cymatium vespaceum* (Lamarck, 1822). A variable species, the form illustrated is *C. pharcidum* (Dall, 1889).

Krebs's Hairy Triton (2.5″) 6 cm *Cymatium krebsii* (Mörch, 1877). North Carolina to Florida; Caribbean. Offshore to 160 m; uncommon.

Coated Triton (2″) 5 cm *Cymatium amictum* Reeve, 1844, subspecies *amictoideum* Keen, 1971. W. Mexico to Panama. 30 to 100 m; uncommon.

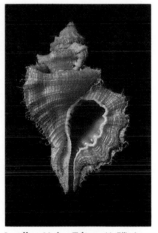

Swollen Hairy Triton (1.5″) 4 cm *Cymatium gibbosum* (Broderip, 1833). W. Mexico to Peru; Galapagos. Intertidal; moderately common.

Swollen Hairy Triton (1.5″) 4 cm *Cymatium gibbosum* (Broderip, 1833). Without periostracum.

Adair Hairy Triton (1″) 2.5 cm *C. gibbosum adairense* (Dall, 1910). W. Mexico (lower). Subsp. *klenei* Sby., 1889, from S. Africa (upper). Common.

Shouldered Triton (2.5″) 6.5 cm *Cymatium tabulatum* (Menke, 1843). Indo-Pacific; New Zealand. Shore rocks; common. Syn.: *exaratum* Reeve.

West African Hairy Triton (2″) 5 cm *Cymatium tranquebaricum* (Lamarck, 1816). Western Africa; Cape Verde Is. Uncommon.

Wide-lipped Triton (1.2″) 3 cm *Cymatium labiosum* (Wood, 1828). Indo-Pacific; West Indies. Shallow water; uncommon. Siphon long or short.

Wide-lipped Triton (1.2″) 3 cm *Cymatium labiosum* (Wood, 1828). Indo-Pacific; West Indies. Syn.: *rutilum* Menke; *loroisi* Petit.

Tinted Triton   (2.5″) 6 cm
Cymatium moritinctum (Reeve, 1844). Indo-Pacific. Shallow water; uncommon.

Blunted Triton   (2″) 5 cm
Cymatium retusum Lamarck, 1822. Indian Ocean; southeastern Asia. Shallow water; uncommon.

Tripus Triton   (2.5″) 6.5 cm
Cymatium tripus (Gmelin, 1791). Indian Ocean; southeastern Asia. Shallow coral waters; uncommon.

Bent-neck Triton   (2.4″) 6 cm
Cymatium caudatum (Gmelin, 1791). Indo-Pacific. On sand and coral, shallow water; uncommon.

Kii Triton   (2″) 5 cm
Cymatium kiiensis (Sowerby, 1915). Japan. Shelly bottoms, 50 to 150 m; common.

Parkinson's Triton (1.7″) 4.5 cm
Cymatium parkinsonianum (Perry, 1811). Victoria; Tasmania; New Zealand. Offshore; common.

Distorted Rock Triton (2″) 5 cm
Cymatium subdistortum (Lamarck, 1822). Southern Australia; Tasmania. Offshore, often beached; common.

Warted Sand Triton (0.8″) 2 cm
Cymatium verrucosum (Reeve, 1844). Southern Australia; Tasmania. Shallow water; common.

Lesueur's Sand Triton
     (0.8″) 2 cm
Cymatium lesueuri Iredale, 1929. Southern Australia; Tasmania. Shallow water; com-

Trigonal Hairy Triton   (2″) 5 cm
Cymatium trigonum (Gmelin, 1791). Western Africa; lower Caribbean. Shallow water; rare.

Pfeiffer's Hairy Triton   (3″)
7.5 cm *Cymatium pfeifferianum* (Reeve, 1844). Indo-Pacific. On sand and mud, shallow water; uncommon.

Lined Hairy Triton   (2″) 5 cm
Cymatium lineatum (Broderip, 1833). Galapagos Islands. Offshore; uncommon. Resembles *C. krebsii* superficially.

Thin-lined Triton (1.7″) 4.5 cm
Cymatium tenuiliratum (Lischke, 1873). Southern Japan. Offshore, 50 to 100 m; uncommon.

Short-neck Triton (2″) 5 cm
Cymatium muricinum (Röding, 1798). Indo-Pacific; S.E. United States; West Indies. Shallow water; common.

Long-neck Triton (3″) 7.5 cm
Cymatium gutturnium (Röding, 1798). Pacific. Offshore; uncommon. Syn.: *formosus* Perry; *clavator* Dillwyn.

Chinese Triton (3″) 7.5 cm
Cymatium sinense (Reeve, 1844). Western Pacific; Queensland. Moderately deep water; uncommon.

Rehder's Triton (3″) 7.5 cm
Cymatium testudinarium rehderi Verrill, 1950. Cuba to Lesser Antilles. Offshore to 400 m; rare.

Dog-head Triton (2″) 5 cm
Cymatium moritinctum subspecies *caribbaeum* Clench & Turner, 1957. S. Carolina to Brazil. Shallow water; uncommon.

Yellow-lip Triton (2.5″) 6.5 cm
Cymatium sarcostomum (Reeve, 1844). Indo-W. Pacific. Subtidal; uncommon.

Pear Triton (3″) 7.5 cm
Cymatium pyrum (L., 1758). Indo-Pacific. On coral and sand; uncommon. Syn.: *muricatum* Röding.

Robin Redbreast Triton (1.5″) 4 cm
Cymatium rubeculum (L., 1758). Tropical Indo-Pacific. Intertidal reefs; uncommon.

Black-striped Triton (2″) 5 cm
Cymatium hepaticum (Röding, 1798). Tropical Indo-Pacific. Under coral slabs; uncommon. Black stripes diagnostic.

Tall Triton (1.5″) 4 cm
Sassia semitorta (Kuroda & Habe, 1961). Japan. Dredged, 50 to 200 m; common.

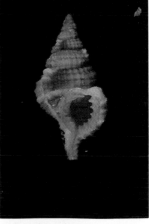

Hal Lewis's Triton (1″) 2.5 cm
Sassia lewisi Harasewych & Petuch, 1980. Yucatan, Mexico, to Barbados. Rare. Holotype illus.

Gaimard's Sand Triton
(0.8") 2 cm
Sassia gaimardi (Iredale, 1929). Southern Australia. Shallow water; uncommon.

Wandering Triton (5") 12.5 cm
Ranella olearium (L., 1758). Mediterranean; Africa; Australasia; Bermuda. Deep water; uncommon. Syn.: *gigantea* L.

Beaded Triton (4.5") 11.5 cm
Mayena gemmifera (Euthyme, 1889). South Africa, Mozambique. Offshore; uncommon.

Austral Triton (3.5") 9 cm
Mayena australasia (Perry, 1811). S. half of Australia; Tasmania; New Zealand. Rocky ground; common. Several subspecies.

Neapolitan Triton (4") 10 cm
Cymatium parthenopeum (von Salis, 1793). In nearly all tropical and warm seas. Offshore to 70 m; uncommon. Many synonyms.

Scabrous Triton (3") 7.5 cm
Priene scabrum (King, 1832). Peru to central Chile. 10 to 30 m; common.

Peruvian Triton (3") 7.5 cm
Priene rude (Broderip, 1833). Peru to central Chile. 10 to 18 m; common.

Spined Maple Leaf (1.7") 4.5 cm
Biplex aculeatum (Schepman, 1909.) Japan to W. Australia. Dredged, 200 m; uncommon. Syn.: *microstoma* Fulton.

Kookaburra Triton (1") 2.5 cm
Biplex jacundum (A. Adams, 1853). Indo-W. Pacific. In sand offshore; uncommon. Syn.: *pulchella* Forbes.

Maple Leaf Triton (2") 5 cm
Biplex perca (Perry, 1811). Western Pacific. Deep water; moderately common. Syn.: *pulchella* Sowerby.

Maple Leaf Triton (2") 5 cm
Biplex perca (Perry, 1811). Similar to *B. aculeatum* but has relatively larger aperture. Often very beaded.

Tadpole Triton (1") 2.5 cm
Gyrineum gyrinum (L., 1758). Tropical Pacific. Under coral slabs in shallow water; common. Syn.: *ranina* Lamarck.

Purple Gyre Triton (1") 2.5 cm
Gyrineum pusillum (Broderip, 1832). Tropical Pacific. On coral rubble or sandy mud; uncommon. Syn.: *facetum* Iredale.

Corded Gyre Triton (1.2") 3 cm
Gyrineum cuspidatum (Reeve, 1844). Indo-Pacific. Subtidal; uncommon. *G. bituberculare* (Lamarck, 1816) similar but siphonal canal longer.

Rosy Gyre Triton (1.2") 3 cm
Gyrineum roseum (Reeve, 1844). Tropical Pacific. Under coral below low-tide level; un common.

Tuberculate Gyre Triton
(1.2") 3 cm
Gyrineum natator (Röding, 1798). Indo-Pacific. Shallow water. Syn.: *tuberculata* Broderip.

Argus Triton (3") 7.5 cm
Argobuccinum pustulosum (Lightfoot, 1786). South Africa. Offshore, sometimes beached; common. Syn.: *argus* Gmelin.

Mediterranean Bark Triton
(3") 7.5 cm
Cabestana cutacea (L., 1767). Eastern Atlantic; Mediterranean; Cape Verde Islands. Moderate depths; uncommon.

Spengler's Triton (6") 15 cm
Cabestana spengleri (Perry, 1811). Southern Australia; Tasmania. Rock pools; common.

Ridged African Triton
(2.5") 6.5 cm
Cabestana dolarium (L., 1767). South Africa. Offshore to 460 m and beached; common.

Felippone's Triton (2") 5 cm
Cabestana felipponei (von Ihering, 1907). Espirito Santo (Brazil) to Uruguay. On muddy sand offshore; rare.

South African Triton (4") 10 cm
Cabestana africana (A. Adams, 1855). South Africa. Offshore to deep water; moderately common.

Lesser Girdled Triton (1.5") 4 cm
Gelagna succincta (L., 1771). Indo-Pacific. Offshore; uncommon. Syn.: *clandestina* Lamarck.

Swollen Triton (4") 10 cm
Argobuccinum tumidum (Dunker, 1862). New Zealand. Rocky bottom; common.

Magellanic Triton (2.5") 6.5 cm
Fusitriton magellanicus (Röding, 1798). Southern South America; New Zealand; S. Australia. Offshore; uncommon. Syn.: *cancellatus* L.

Oregon Triton (4.5") 11.5 cm
Fusitriton oregonense (Redfield, 1848). Bering Sea to California. Offshore; common.

Common Distorsio (2.7") 7 cm
Distorsio anus (L., 1758). Indo-Pacific. Under coral, shallow water; uncommon. Syn.: *rotunda* Perry.

Checkerboard Distorsio
(1.2") 4 cm
Distorsio burgessi Lewis, 1972. Hawaiian Islands (endemic). Offshore to 30 m; rare.

Decussate Distorsio (2") 5 cm
Distorsio decussata (Valenciennes, 1832). W. Mexico to Ecuador. Offshore to 85 m; uncommon. Syn.: *simillima* Sowerby.

Kurz's Distorsio (1.5") 3.5 cm
Distorsio kurzi Petuch & Harasewych, 1980. Central Philippines. Deep water; uncommon. Holotype illustrated.

Reticulate Distorsio (2.4") 6 cm
Distorsio reticulata Röding, 1798. Indo-Pacific. Offshore to moderate depths; uncommon. Syn.: *cancellinus* Lamarck.

Smith's Distorsio (2.5") 6 cm
Distorsio smithi (von Maltzan, 1884). Western Africa. Offshore, 20 to 25 m; uncommon.

Constricted Distorsio
(1.5") 4 cm
Distorsio constricta constricta (Broderip, 1833). Gulf of California to Ecuador. Offshore; uncommon.

McGinty's Distorsio (1.5") 4 cm
Distorsio constricta macgintyi Emerson & Puffer, 1953. North Carolina to Florida; Brazil. Dredged, 50 m; common.

Atlantic Distorsio (2.5") 6.5 cm
Distorsio clathrata (Lamarck, 1816). North Carolina to Texas; Caribbean; Brazil. Offshore to 130 m; common.

Bristly Distorsio (2.5") 6.5 cm
Distorsio perdistorta Fulton, 1938. Caribbean; Japan; Madagascar. Deep water; uncommon. Syn.: *horrida* K. & Habe.

FROG SHELLS
FAMILY BURSIDAE

Small family living in tropical or warm seas. Shells usually thick and heavy and have a deep canal at posterior end of aperture, the anterior canal being short. Operculum chitinous, oval, brown. Females may be larger than males. Most species live in or under coral and some eat marine worms. Egg capsules attached to rock or coral.

Giant Frog Shell (7") 18 cm
Bursa bubo (L., 1758). Indo-Pacific. Intertidal and offshore; common. Syn.: *gigantea* E. A. Smith; *lampas* of authors.

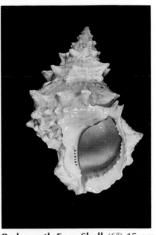

Ruddy Frog Shell (6") 15 cm
Bursa rubeta (Röding, 1798). Indo-Pacific. Intertidal and offshore; moderately common. Syn.: *tuberosum* Röding.

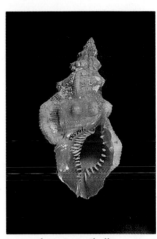

Red-mouth Frog Shell (6") 15 cm
Bursa lissostoma (E. A. Smith, 1914). Indo-Pacific. Intertidal and offshore to 50 m; moderately common. Syn.: *bufo* Röd.

Tall Frog Shell (3.5") 9 cm
Bursa condita (Gmelin, 1791). Southwestern Pacific. Offshore; uncommon. Syn.: *candisata* Dillwyn (and Lamarck).

Awati Frog Shell (2.7") 7 cm.
Bursa awatii Ray, 1949. India to Philippines. 180 to 550 m; rare. Syn.: *rehderi* Beu, 1978 (holotype illus.).

Dwarf Frog Shell (1.5") 4 cm
Bursa nana (Broderip & Sowerby, 1829). W. Mexico to Ecuador. Offshore to 40 m; common.

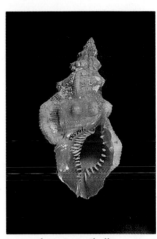

Fernandes's Frog Shell (3.5") 9 cm *Bursa fernandesi* (Beu, 1977). Mozambique. Trawled 110 to 175 m; rare. Holotype illustrated.

Blackened Frog Shell (3") 7.5 cm
Bursa nigrita Mulhaus & Blocker, 1979. Madagascar. Offshore; uncommon.

Granulate Frog Shell (2") 5 cm
Bursa granularis (Röding, 1798). Indo-Pacific; Caribbean. Shallow and deeper water; common. Syn.: *cubaniana* Orbigny.

Chestnut Frog Shell (2") 5 cm
Bursa bufo (Bruguière, 1792). Southeastern Florida to Brazil. Dredged 50 to 100 m. Syn.: *spadicea* Montfort.

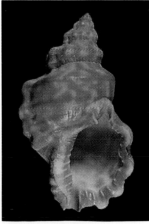

Pitted Frog Shell (2.5") 6.5 cm
Bursa scrobilator (L., 1758). Mediterranean; N.W. Africa. Offshore 15 to 40 m. *B. scrobiculator* is misspelling.

Noble Frog Shell   (2") 5 cm
Bursa margaritula (Deshayes, 1832). Indo-Pacific. Under coral, subtidal; uncommon. Syn.: *nobilis* Reeve.

Frilled Frog Shell   (3") 7.5 cm
Bursa crumena form *foliata* (Broderip, 1825). Indian Ocean. *B. c. crumena* (Lamarck, 1816) lacks red in aperture.

Common Frog Shell   (3") 7.5 cm
Bursa rana (L., 1758). Indo-Pacific. Offshore and beached; uncommon.

Elegant Frog Shell   (3") 7.5 cm
Bursa elegans (Sowerby, 1835). Indian Ocean. Shallow water; common.

Spiny Frog Shell   (2") 5 cm
Bursa echinata (Link, 1807). Indo-Pacific. Offshore; moderately uncommon. Syn.: *spinosa* Lamarck.

Swollen Bursa   (2") 5 cm
Bursa ventricosa (Broderip, 1833). Peru and Ecuador. Below tide level; moderately common.

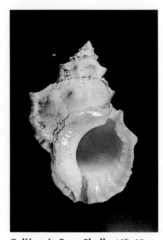

California Frog Shell   (4") 10 cm
Bursa californica (Hinds, 1843). California; W. Mexico. Among rocks offshore and beached; common.

Pacamon Frog Shell   (1.5") 4 cm
Bursa pacamoni Matthews & Coelho, 1971. S.E. Florida to Brazil. Offshore; rare.

Gaudy Frog Shell   (2") 5 cm
Bursa corrugata (Perry, 1811). S.E. Florida to Brazil; W. Mexico to Peru. Offshore; uncommon. Syn.: *caelata* Broderip.

Warty Frog Shell   (2.5") 6.5 cm
Bursa bufonia (Gmelin, 1791). Tropical Indo-Pacific. Under coral offshore; rare. Syn.: *leo* Shikama.

Wine-mouth Frog Shell   (1") 2 cm
Bursa rhodostoma (Sowerby, 1835). Tropical Indo-Pacific. On sand and coral offshore; uncommon.

St. Thomas Frog Shell   (.8") 2 cm
Bursa thomae (Orbigny, 1842). South Carolina to Brazil; Cape Verde Islands. Under rocks to 80 m; moderately common.

Finlay's Frog Shell (3") 7.5 cm
Bursa finlayi McGinty, 1962. S.E. Florida and West Indies. Uncommon.

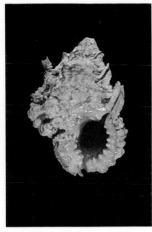

Udder Frog Shell (2.5") 6 cm
Bursa mammata Röding, 1798. Southwestern Pacific. Near coral reefs; uncommon. Syn.: *rosa* Perry.

Lamarck's Frog Shell (2") 5 cm
Bursa lamarcki (Deshayes, 1853). S.W. Pacific. Shallow reefs; uncommon.

Blood-stained Frog Shell (1.5") 4 cm
Bursa cruentata (Sowerby, 1841). Indo-Pacific. Near coral; moderately common.

Charming Frog Shell (1") 2.5 cm
Bursa venustula (Reeve, 1844). Indo-Pacific. Coral reefs; moderately common.

MUREX SHELLS
FAMILY MURICIDAE

This is a large and very diverse family, ranging from the beautiful, spiny Venus Comb Murex to the small, insignificant drupes and purpura rock shells. The genera in this family are very arbitrary and no two experts agree. The subfamily Thaidinae comprises the common rock-shells. Operculum corneous and brown.

Snipe's Bill Murex (5") 12.5 cm
Murex haustellum L., 1758. Indo-Pacific. 3 to 20 m; locally common. Typical form from southwestern Pacific.

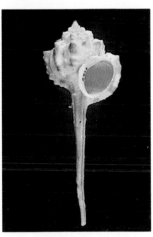

Baker's Snipe's Bill (4") 10 cm
Murex longicaudus F. C. Baker, 1891. Red Sea to Philippines. Syn.: *vicdani* Kosuge. Common.

Multiplicate Snipe's Bill (2.5") 6 cm
Murex multiplicatus Sowerby, 1895. Western Australia. Offshore; uncommon.

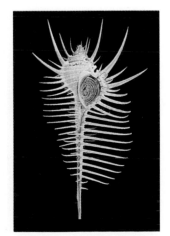

Venus Comb Murex (4") 10 cm
Murex pecten Lightfoot, 1786. Indo-Pacific. Common. Syn.: *ternispina* Lamarck; *triremis* Perry.

Troschel's Murex (6") 15 cm
Murex troscheli Lischke, 1868. Western Pacific. Common in Japan, 1 to 15 m.

Woodcock Murex (4") 10 cm
Murex scolopax Dillwyn, 1817. Indo-Pacific. Common. Lectotype illus. (Wales Museum). Syn.: *acanthostephes* Watson.

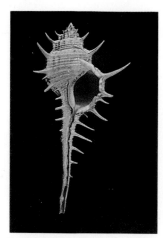

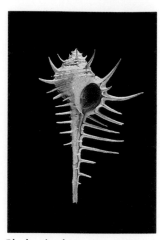

Rare-spined Murex   (4") 10 cm
Murex trapa Röding, 1798.
Southwestern Pacific. Common. Syn.: *rarispina* Lamarck.

Caltrop Murex   (3") 7 cm
Murex tribulus L., 1758. Indo-Pacific. Common.

Black-spined Murex (3") 7 cm
Murex nigrispinosus Reeve,
1845. Southwestern Pacific. 3 to
20 m; common.

Bent-spined Murex   (3") 7 cm
Murex aduncospinosus Sowerby, 1841. Southeastern Asia;
Philippines. Uncommon.

Carbonnier's Murex (2.5") 6 cm
Murex carbonnieri Jousseaume, 1881. Red Sea. Uncommon.

Erect-spined Murex   (3") 7.5 cm
Murex rectirostris Sowerby,
1841. East Asia. Offshore; common. Syn.: *sobrinus* A. Adams.

Brevispined Murex   (3") 7.5 cm
Murex brevispina Lamarck,
1822. Indo-Pacific. Common.

MacGillivray's Murex

                        (3") 7.5 cm
Murex macgillivrayi Dohrn,
1863. Northern Australia. Common. Form of *brevispina?*

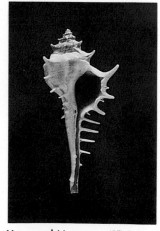

Heros Murex   (3") 7.5 cm
Murex heros Fulton, 1936. New
Guinea and Solomon Islands.
Offshore; uncommon.

Striking Murex   (3") 7.5 cm
Murex concinnus Reeve, 1845.
Indo-Pacific. Shallow water;
uncommon.

Mindanao Murex   (3.5") 9 cm.
Murex mindanoensis Sowerby,
1841. Philippine Islands. 20 to
100 m; uncommon. *M. mindanaoensis* is misspelling.

Harrowed Murex   (3") 7.5 cm
Murex occa Sowerby, 1834.
Southeastern Asia. Uncommon. May be form of *scolopax*.

Hirase's Murex (2.5") 6 cm
Murex hirasei Hirase, 1915. Japan to Taiwan. Offshore; uncommon.

Kii Murex (3.5") 9 cm
Murex kiiensis Kira, 1959. Indo-Pacific. Deep water; uncommon.

Tweed Murex (2.5") 6 cm
Murex tweedianus Macpherson, 1962. Eastern Australia. Common. Syn.: *espinosa* Macpherson.

Cabrit's Murex (2.5") 6 cm
Murex cabritii Bernardi, 1859. S.E. United States. Offshore; uncommon.

Tryon's Murex (2") 5 cm
Murex tryoni Hidalgo, 1880. Gulf of Mexico; Caribbean. 100 to 350 m; uncommon.

Rose Murex (1.5") 4 cm
Murex rubidus F. C. Baker, 1897. S.E. United States; Bahamas. Locally common. Shallow water.

Sallas's Murex (1.5") 4 cm
Murex sallasi Rehder & Abbott, 1951. Gulf of Mexico. 50 to 100 m. Rare. Holotype illustrated.

Belleglade Murex (1.5") 4 cm
Murex bellegladensis E. Vokes, 1963. Gulf of Mexico. Uncommon. Deep-water.

Don Moore's Murex (2") 5 cm
Murex cabritii subspecies *donmoorei* Bullis, 1964. Southern Caribbean. Deep water; locally common.

Goldmouth Murex (2") 5 cm
Murex chrysostoma Sowerby, 1834. Southern Caribbean to Brazil. Offshore; locally common.

Belle Murex (2") 5 cm
Murex chrysostoma form *bellus* Reeve, 1845. A bright form of the Goldmouth Murex. Uncommon.

Thompson's Murex (2") 5 cm
Siratus articulatus form *thompsoni* Bullis, 1964. Southern Caribbean; deep water; uncommon. Holotype illustrated.

Bent-beak Murex   (2.5″) 6 cm
Murex recurvirostris Broderip, 1833. W. Mexico to Ecuador. Shallow water; common.

Elena Murex   (2.5″) 6 cm
Murex elenensis Dall, 1909. W. Mexico to Ecuador. Shallow water; uncommon.

Messorius Murex   (2.5″) 6 cm
Murex messorius Sowerby, 1841. Lower Caribbean. Shallow water; common. Syn.: *woodringi* Clench.

Tricorn Murex   (2.5″) 6 cm
Murex elenensis form *tricornis* S.S. Berry, 1960. Gulf of California. Uncommon.

Near-elegant Murex (3″) 7.5 cm
Siratus perelegans E. Vokes, 1965. West Indies. Offshore to 50 m; uncommon. Syn.: *elegans* Sowerby.

Caillet's Murex   (3″) 7.5 cm
Siratus cailleti Petit, 1856. West Indies. Offshore to 50 m; uncommon. Syn.: *kugleri* Clench & Farfante.

Beauty Murex   (3″) 7.5 cm
Siratus formosus Sowerby, 1841. Caribbean. 20 to 100 m; uncommon. Siphon not crooked. Syn.: *aguayoi* C. & F.

Finlay's Murex   (3″) 7.5 cm
Siratus formosus Sowerby, form *finlayi* Clench, 1955. Caribbean. 100 to 300 m; uncommon.

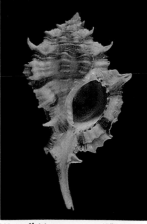

Antillean Murex   (3″) 7.5 cm
Siratus articulatus Reeve, 1845. Caribbean. 100 to 300 m; uncommon. *Murex antillarum* Hinds is unidentifiable.

Springer's Murex   (3″) 7.5 cm
Siratus springeri (Bullis, 1965). Lower Caribbean to Brazil. Deep water; uncommon.

Ciboney Murex   (3″) 7.5 cm
Siratus ciboney (Clench & Farfante, 1945). Caribbean; deep water; uncommon. Holotype illus.

Wagtail Murex   (3″) 7.5 cm
Siratus motacilla (Gmelin, 1791). Lesser Antilles; West Indies. Moderately common.

Beau's Murex (4") 10 cm
Siratus beauii (Fischer & Bernardi, 1857). Florida to Brazil. 200 to 400 m; locally uncommon. Syn.: *branchi* Clench.

Consuela's Murex (2.5") 6 cm
Siratus consuela A. H. Verrill, 1950. Eastern Caribbean. Uncommon. Syn.: *pulcher* A. Adams.

Senegal Murex (3") 7.5 cm
Siratus senegalensis (Gmelin, 1791). Brazil. Shallow water. Locally common.

Hen Murex (2.5") 6 cm
Siratus gallinago (Sowerby, 1903). Japan. Offshore; uncommon.

Ellis Cross's Murex (3") 7 cm
Siratus elliscrossi Fair, 1974. Japan; uncommon.

Lovely Murex (2") 5 cm
Siratus venustulus (Rehder & Wilson, 1975). Marquesas Islands, East Polynesia. 18 to 125 m; rare. Holotype illus.

Superb Murex (2.5") 6 cm
Siratus superbus (Sowerby, 1889). Eastern Asia. Offshore; common.

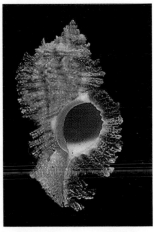

Laciniate Murex (2.5") 6 cm
Siratus laciniatus (Sowerby, 1841). Indo-Pacific. Shallow water; uncommon.

Barclay's Murex (2") 5 cm
Naquetia barclayi (Reeve, 1858). Indian Ocean. Offshore; rare.

Annandale's Murex (2.5") 6 cm
Naquetia annandalei (Preston, 1910). India to Philippines. Offshore; uncommon.

Trigonula Murex (2") 5 cm
Naquetia trigonulus (Lamarck, 1816). Southwestern Pacific. Uncommon.

Triquetra Murex (2") 5 cm
Naquetia triquetra (Born, 1778). Indian Ocean to Indonesia. Shallow water; uncommon.

Thin-bladed Murex   (4") 10 cm
Siratus tenuivaricosus (Dautzenberg, 1927). Brazil. Offshore; uncommon. Syn.: *carioca* E. Vokes.

Japanese Spike Murex
                    (4") 10 cm
Siratus pliciferoides (Kuroda, 1942). Japan; offshore to 200 m; common.

Alabaster Murex   (5") 12 cm
Siratus alabaster (Reeve, 1845). Japan to the Philippines. Deep water; locally common.

Stainforth's Murex   (2.5") 6 cm
Chicoreus stainforthi (Reeve, 1843). Northern Australia. Littoral to 3 m; locally common.

Apple Murex   (3") 7.5 cm
Phyllonotus pomum (Gmelin, 1791). S.E. United States to Brazil.1 to 20 m; common.

Globular Apple Murex   (2.5")
6 cm *Phyllonotus globosus* (Emmons, 1858). S. Caribbean. May be subspecies of *pomum*. Common.

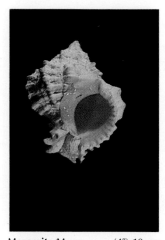

Margarita Murex   (4") 10 cm
Phyllonotus margaritensis (Abbott, 1958). Lower Caribbean. Uncommon. Rarely yellow-mouthed.

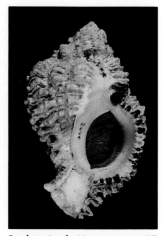

Oculate Apple Murex   (3")
7.5 cm *Phyllonotus pomum* form *oculatus* Reeve, 1845. Deep water Florida; West Indies. Locally uncommon.

Endive Murex   (4") 10 cm
Chicoreus cichoreum (Gmelin, 1791). Southwestern Pacific. Abundant. Syn.: *endivia* Lamarck.

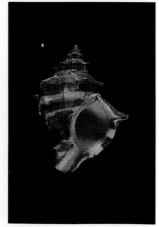

Trunculus Murex   (3") 7.5 cm
Hexaplex trunculus (L., 1758). Mediterranean. Shallow water; common.

Rosy-mouth Murex   (3") 7.5 cm
Hexaplex rosarium (Röding, 1798). Cape Verde Islands; West Africa; common. Syn.: *saxatilis* of authors.

Duplex Murex   (3.5") 9 cm
Hexaplex duplex (Röding, 1798). Western Africa. Common. Also once called *saxatilis* L.

Pink-mouth Murex   (4″) 10 cm
Phyllonotus erythrostomus
Swainson, 1831. W. Mexico to
Peru. Abundant. Syn.: *bicolor*
Valenciennes.

Regal Murex   (5″) 12 cm
Phyllonotus regius (Swainson,
1821). W. Mexico to Peru. Moderately common.

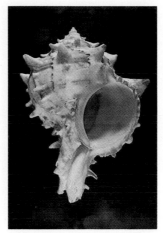

Cabbage Murex   (9″) 20 cm
Phyllonotus brassica (Lamarck,
1822). W. Mexico to Peru. Fairly
common.

Prince Murex   (5″) 13 cm
Hexaplex princeps (Broderip,
1833). W. Mexico to Peru. Moderately common.

Küster's Murex   (3″) 7.5 cm
Hexaplex kuesterianus (Tap-
parone-Canefri, 1875). Western
Africa. Uncommon.

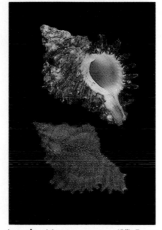

Angular Murex   (2″) 5 cm
Hexaplex angularis (Lamarck,
1822). Western Africa. Fairly
common in shallow water.

Varius Murex   (2″) 5 cm
Hexaplex varius (Sowerby,
1834). Western Africa. Fairly
common locally.

Thick-spined Murex (3″) 7.5 cm
Chicoreus megacerus (So-
werby, 1834). Western Africa.
Shallow water; uncommon.

Virgin Murex   (4″) 10 cm
Chicoreus virgineus (Röding,
1798). Red Sea. Shallow water.
Locally common. Syn.: *anguliferus* Lamarck.

Diver Murex   (2″) 5 cm
Chicoreus mergus E. Vokes,
1974. Caribbean (Barbados). 91
m; rare. Holotype illustrated.

West Indian Murex   (5″) 12 cm
Chicoreus brevifrons (Lamarck,
1822). West Indies to Brazil.
Fairly common; shallow water.

Giant Eastern Murex (6″) 15 cm
Hexaplex fulvescens (Sowerby,
1834). North Carolina to Texas.
Common offshore to intertidal.

Asian Murex (4″) 10 cm
Chicoreus asianus Kuroda, 1942. Japan and northern China. Common offshore. Syn.: *elongatus* Lamarck.

Martin's Murex (1″) 2.5 cm
Murexiella martini Shikama, 1977. Central Philippines. Deep water; uncommon.

Smelly Murex (3″) 7.5 cm
Chicoreus cnissodus (Euthyme, 1889). Japan to New Caledonia. Shallow reefs; uncommon. Syn.: *oligocanthus* Euthyme.

Spectral Murex (4″) 10 cm
Chicoreus spectrum (Reeve, 1846). West Indies to Brazil. Uncommon. Holotype illustrated.

Saul's Murex (4″) 10 cm
Chicoreus saulii (Sowerby, 1841). Southwestern Pacific. Offshore; uncommon. Columellar edge white.

Rose-branch Murex (4″) 10 cm
Chicoreus palmarosae (Lamarck, 1822). Sri Lanka to S.W. Pacific. Uncommon. Syn.: *foliatus* Perry.

Maurus Murex (3″) 7.5 cm
Chicoreus maurus (Broderip, 1833). Central Pacific. Uncommon. Syn.: *steeriae* Reeve (from Marquesas).

Mangrove Murex (2″) 5 cm
Chicoreus capucinus (Lamarck, 1816). Southwestern Pacific. Mangrove roots; common.

Firebrand Murex (3″) 7.5 cm
Chicoreus torrefactus (Sowerby, 1841). Indo-Pacific. Shallow water; common. Syn.: *affinis* Reeve.

Curly Murex (3″) 7.5 cm
Chicoreus microphyllus (Lamarck, 1816). Indo-Pacific. Shallow water; common. Syn.: *poirieri* Jousseaume.

Banks's Murex (3″) 7.5 cm
Chicoreus banksii (Sowerby, 1841). Indo-Pacific. Uncommon.

Denuded Murex (2″) 5 cm
Chicoreus denudatus (Perry, 1811). Eastern Australia. Common. Syn.: *palmiferus* Sowerby.

Reddish Murex (4") 10 cm
Chicoreus rubiginosus (Reeve, 1845). Southwestern Pacific. Locally common.

Penchinat's Murex (1.5") 4 cm
Chicoreus penchinati (Crosse, 1861). Japan to Taiwan. Offshore; uncommon.

Rossiter's Murex (1.5") 4 cm
Chicoreus rossiteri (Crosse, 1872). Southwestern Pacific. Shallow water; uncommon. *C. saltatrix* Kuroda, 1964, is subsp.

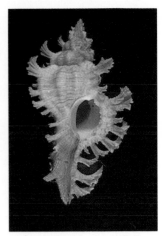

Pendant Murex (2") 5 cm
Chicoreus aculeatus (Lamarck, 1822). Japan to Philippines. Offshore; uncommon. Syn.: *artemis* Radwin & D'Attilio.

Cosman's Murex (2") 5 cm
Chicoreus cosmani Abbott and Finlay, 1979. Central Caribbean. Subtidal to 20 m; rare. Paratype illustrated.

Trivial Murex (2") 5 cm
Chicoreus trivialis (A. Adams, 1854). Japan to Australia. Uncommon.

Rubescent Murex (1.5") 4 cm
Chicoreus rubescens (Broderip, 1833). Southwestern Pacific. Shallow water. Uncommon.

Adusta Murex (2.5") 6 cm
Chicoreus brunneus (Link, 1807). S.W. Pacific. Abundant; sublittoral. Syn.: *adustus* Lamarck.

Lace Murex (3") 7.5 cm
Chicoreus dilectus (A. Adams, 1855). S.E. United States. Subtidal; common. Syn.: *arenarius* Clench & Farfante.

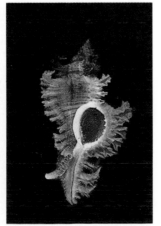

Saffron Murex (2") 5 cm
Chicoreus crocatus (Reeve, 1845). Philippines. 5 to 30 m; locally uncommon.

Bojador Murex (1.7") 4 cm
Murexiella bojadorensis Locard, 1897. West Africa. Offshore; uncommon.

Gubb's Murex (2.5") 6 cm
Chicoreus gubbi (Reeve, 1849). Western Africa. Shallow water; uncommon.

Thomas's Murex   (2″) 5 cm
Chicoreus thomasi (Crosse & Fischer, 1872). Marquesas Islands. Rare. Paratype illus.

Ramose Murex   (8″) 20 cm
Chicoreus ramosus (L., 1758). Indo-Pacific. Shallow reefs; very common.

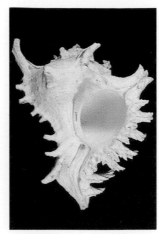

Radish Murex   (5″) 12 cm
Hexaplex radix (Gmelin, 1791). Panama to Ecuador. Shallow water; common.

Nigrite Murex   (6″) 15 cm
Hexaplex nigritus (Philippi, 1845). Gulf of California. Intertidal; common.

Deer Antler Murex   (2.5″) 6 cm
Chicoreus cervicornis (Lamarck, 1822). Northern Australia. Shallow water. Fairly common.

Monodon Murex   (4″) 10 cm
Chicoreus cornucervi (Röding, 1798). Northwestern Australia. Littoral. Uncommon. Syn.: *monodon* Sowerby.

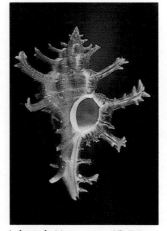

Axicornis Murex   (3″) 7.5 cm
Chicoreus axicornis (Lamarck, 1822). Japan to the Philippines. Offshore; uncommon. Syn.: *kawamurai* Shikama.

Damicornis Murex   (2″) 5 cm
Chicoreus damicornis (Hedley, 1903). Northern Australia. Common. Lower specimen is rare sinistral form.

Orchid Murex   (1.5″) 4 cm
Pterynotus orchidiformis (Shikama, 1973). Off Taiwan. Uncommon.

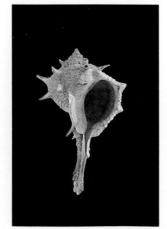

Purple Dye Murex   (3.5″) 9 cm
Bolinus brandaris (L., 1758). Mediterranean and N.W. Africa. Locally abundant.

Horned Murex   (6″) 15 cm
Bolinus cornutus (L., 1758). Western Africa; Cape Verde Islands. Offshore; common.

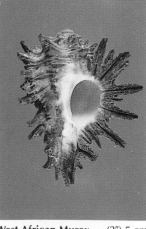

West African Murex   (2″) 5 cm
Homalocantha melanamathos (Gmelin, 1791). West Africa. Offshore; uncommon.

Lightbourn's Murex (1") 2.5 cm
Pterynotus lightbourni Harasewych & Jensen, 1979. Off Bermuda; 27 to 60 m; rare. Holotype illustrated.

Guest's Murex (1") 2.5 cm
Pterynotus guesti Harasewych & Jensen, 1979. Off Key West, Florida, in 275 m; rare. Holotype illustrated.

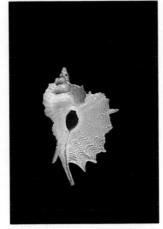

Radwin's Murex (1.2") 3 cm
Pterynotus radwini Harasewych & Jensen, 1979. Off Belize, Honduras, in 300 m; rare. Holotype illustrated.

Butterfly Murex (1.4") 3.5 cm
Pterynotus vespertilio (Kira, 1959). Japan. Offshore to 100 m; moderately common.

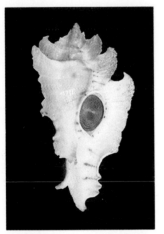

Pinniger Murex (2.5") 6 cm
Purpurellus pinniger (Broderip, 1833). W. Mexico to Ecuador. Deep water; rare. Syn.: *osseus* Reeve; *inezana* Durham, 1950.

Fluted Murex (2") 5 cm
Pterynotus laqueatus (Sowerby, 1841). Western Pacific. Offshore; rare.

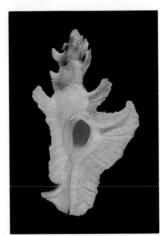

Club Murex (3") 7.5 cm
Pterynotus elongatus (Lightfoot, 1786). Indo-Pacific. Shallow reefs; uncommon. Rarely pink. Syn.: *clavus* Kiener.

Pinnacle Murex (2") 5 cm
Marchia bipinnatus (Reeve, 1845). Indo-Pacific. Rare. Sometimes placed in *Pterynotus*. Aperture violet.

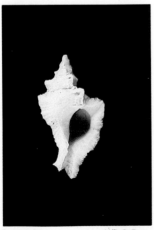

Better Murex (1") 2.5 cm
Pterochelus ariomus (Clench & Farfante, 1945). Off southeastern Florida in 100 m; rare.

Exquisite Murex (1") 2.5 cm
Subpterynotus exquisitus (Sowerby, 1904). Western Africa. Rare.

Bequaert's Murex (1.4") 3.5 cm
Pteropurpura bequaerti (Clench & Farfante, 1945). S.E. United States. Offshore; rare.

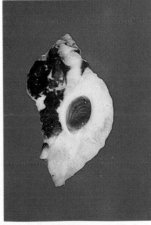

Decussate Murex (1.5") 4 cm
Jaton decussatus (Gmelin, 1791). Western Africa. Shallow water; uncommon.

Frill-wing Murex (2.5") 6 cm
Pteropurpura macroptera (Deshayes, 1839). Northern California. Offshore; common.

Esychus Murex (1.5") 3.5 cm
Pteropurpura esycha (Dall, 1925). Off Japan in 210 m; very rare. Holotype illustrated.

Adunca Murex (1.5") 3.5 cm
Pteropurpura adunca (Sowerby, 1834). Central Japan. Shallow water; common. Syn.: *eurypteron* Reeve.

Expansive Murex (1.5") 3.5 cm
Pteropurpura adunca form *expansa* Sowerby, 1860. Japan. Offshore; uncommon.

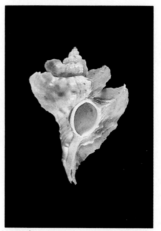

Weeping Murex (2") 5 cm
Pteropurpura plorator (Adams & Reeve, 1849). Southeastern Japan. Shallow water; common.

Centrifuge Murex (2.3") 6 cm
Pteropurpura centrifuga (Hinds, 1844). Gulf of California; Galapagos. Offshore. Uncommon. Syn.: *deroyana* Berry.

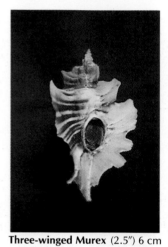

Three-winged Murex (2.5") 6 cm
Pteropurpura trialata (Sowerby, 1834). California and W. Mexico. Intertidal rocks; common.

Festive Murex (2") 5 cm
Pteropurpura festiva (Hinds, 1844). California and W. Mexico. Intertidal to 3 m; common.

Burnett's Murex (4") 10 cm
Ceratostoma burnetti (Adams & Reeve, 1849). Japan Sea; Korea; north China. Offshore to 10 m; locally common.

Fournier's Purpura (2.2") 6 cm
Ceratostoma fournieri (Crosse, 1861). North China; east Japan. Shallow water; common.

Nuttall's Purpura (2") 5 cm
Ceratostoma nuttalli (Conrad, 1837). California and W. Mexico. Littoral; common.

Dingy Purpura (2") 5 cm
Ceratostoma lugubre (Broderip, 1833). Costa Rica to Peru. Littoral; common. Syn.: *fontainei* Tryon.

New Zealand Murex (2.5″) 6 cm
Poirieria zelandicus (Quoy & Gaimard, 1833). New Zealand. Offshore; moderately common.

Paz's Murex (2″) 5 cm
Poirieria pazi (Crosse, 1869). Florida and Caribbean. 200 to 400 m; uncommon.

Orr's Muricop (1″) 2.5 cm
Muricopsis orri Cernohorsky, 1976. Thailand. Offshore; uncommon.

Nutting's Murex (1.5″) 4 cm
Poirieria nuttingi (Dall, 1896). Off Florida. 100 to 400 m; uncommon. Syn.: *oregonia* Bullis. Holotype illus.

Octagon Murex (2″) 5 cm
Murexsul octogonus (Quoy & Gaimard, 1833). New Zealand. Subtidal rocks; fairly common.

Hidalgo's Murex (1.5″) 4 cm
Murexiella hidalgoi (Crosse, 1869). S.E. United States and Caribbean. Deep water; uncommon.

McGinty's Murex (1″) 2.5 cm
Murexiella macgintyi (M. Smith, 1938). Caribbean to Brazil. Shallow water; locally uncommon.

Humilis Murex (1.5″) 3.5 cm
Murexiella humilis (Broderip, 1833). Gulf of California to Ecuador. Shallow water; uncommon. Syn.: *laurae* E. Vokes.

Girdled Dwarf Murex (0.8″) 2 cm
Murexiella balteatus (Sowerby, 1841). Indo-Pacific. Shallow water rocks; uncommon.

Burr Murex (1.3″) 3 cm
Murexiella lappa (Broderip, 1833). Gulf of Mexico to Ecuador. Shallow water; uncommon.

Gem Murex (1″) 2.5 cm
Maxwellia gemma (Sowerby, 1879). Central California to Baja California. Intertidal rubble to 60 m; common.

Santa Rosa Murex (1.5″) 4 cm
Murexiella santarosana (Dall, 1905). California to W. Mexico. Sublittoral; uncommon. Syn.: *fimbriatus* A. Adams.

Hexagonal Muricop (1.5″) 4 cm *Muricopsis oxytatus* (M. Smith, 1938). Florida and the West Indies. Syn.: *hexagonus* Lamarck, not Gmelin. Common.

Blainville's Muricop (1.2″) 3 cm *Muricopsis blainvillei* (Payraudeau, 1826). Mediterranean. Intertidal; common. Variable.

Mactan Dwarf Murex (0.7″) 1.8 cm *Favartia mactanensis* Fmerson & D'Attilio, 1979. Central Philippines. 30 m; uncommon.

Pitted Dwarf Murex (1″) 2.5 cm *Favartia cellulosa* (Conrad, 1846). S.E. United States to Brazil. Syn.: *nucea* Mörch. Very common; intertidal.

Dorothy's Dwarf Murex (.6″) 1.5 cm *Favartia dorothyae* Emerson & D'Attilio, 1979. Central Philippines. Offshore; 10 m; uncommon.

Pelepili Dwarf Murex (1″) 2.5 cm *Favartia pelepili* D'Attilio & Bertsch, 1980. Central Philippines. Offshore; uncommon.

Salmon Dwarf Murex (.7″) 1.8 cm *Favartia salmonea* (Melvill & Standen, 1899). Indo-Pacific. Shallow water; uncommon. Syn.: *pumilus* A. Adams.

Rugged Vitularia (3″) 7.5 cm *Vitularia salebrosa* (King & Broderip, 1832). W. Mexico to Panama; Galapagos. Rather common.

Thick-lipped Drill (1″) 2.5 cm *Eupleura caudata* (Say, 1822). New England to Florida. Shallow water on oyster banks; abundant.

Atlantic Oyster Drill (1″) 2.5 cm *Urosalpinx cinerea* (Say, 1822). Eastern Canada to N.E. Florida; Washington to California. On oyster banks; abundant.

Spindle Dwarf Triton (0.8″) 2 cm *Urosalpinx fusulus* (Brocchi, 1814). Mediterranean; western Europe. Offshore; uncommon.

Spotted Vitularia (2″) 5 cm *Vitularia miliaris* (Gmelin, 1791). S.W. Pacific. Coral reefs; locally common.

Poulson's Dwarf Triton
(1.5") 3.5 cm
Ocenebra poulsoni (Carpenter, 1864). California to Baja California. Littoral rocks; common.

Spineless Dwarf Triton (2") 5 cm
Ocenebra inermicosta E. Vokes, 1964. Western Africa. Intertidal; common. Syn.: *fasciata* Sowerby, not Gmelin.

Sting Winkle (1.2") 3 cm
Ocenebra erinacea (L., 1758). Northwestern Europe to northwestern Africa. Littoral; common.

Paiva's Dwarf Triton (1") 2.5 cm
Bedeva paivae (Crosse, 1864). Southern Australia; Tasmania. Shallow water; common. Syn.: *hanleyi* Angas.

File Dogwinkle (1.5") 3.5 cm
Nucella lima (Gmelin, 1791). Alaska to northern California. Littoral; common.

Emarginate Dogwinkle
(1") 2.5 cm
Nucella emarginata (Deshayes, 1839). Bering Sea to W. Mexico. Littoral rocks; abundant.

Frilled Dogwinkle (2.5") 6 cm
Nucella lamellosa (Gmelin, 1791). Bering Sea to California. Littoral; common. Very variable.

Atlantic Dogwinkle (2") 5 cm
Nucella lapillus (L., 1758). Eastern Canada to New York; Norway to Portugal. Rocky coasts; common. Very variable.

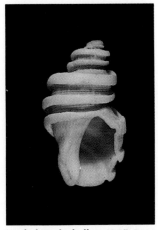

Corded Rock-shell (1.3") 3 cm
Trochia cingulata (L., 1758). South Africa. Lower littoral rock zone; common.

Orb Rock-shell (3.5") 9 cm
Neothais orbita (Gmelin, 1791). New Zealand; eastern Australia. Rocky shores; common.

Carinate Rock-shell (2") 5 cm
Cuma lacera (Born, 1778). Indian Ocean to S.E. Asia. Littoral; common. Syn.: *carinifera* Lamarck; *mutabilis* Link.

Biconic Rock-shell (1") 2.5 cm
Cronia biconica (Blainville, 1832). Indo-Pacific. Intertidal; moderately common.

Almond Rock-shell   (1″) 2.5 cm
Cronia amygdala (Kiener, 1836).
Northern Australia. Intertidal;
common.

Barnacle Rock-shell   (2.7″) 7 cm
Concholepas concholepas
(Bruguière, 1792). Peru and
Chile. Littoral; common. Syn.:
peruvianus Lamarck.

Wide-mouthed Purpura
                      (3″) 7.5 cm
Purpura patula (L., 1758). S.E.
Florida and the West Indies. In-
tertidal rock cliffs; common.

Columella Purpura   (2″) 5 cm
Purpura columellaris Lamarck,
1822. Southwestern Mexico to
Chile. Locally uncommon.

Drinking Cup Purpura
                      (3″) 7.5 cm
Purpura haustorium (Gmelin,
1791). New Zealand. Intertidal
rocks; common.

Persian Purpura   (2.5″) 6 cm
Purpura persica (L., 1758).
Southwestern Pacific to Japan.
Intertidal rocks; common.

Rudolph's Purpura   (2.5″) 6 cm
Purpura panama (Röding,
1798). East Indies. Littoral
rocks; common. Syn.: *ru-
dolphi* Lamarck.

Muricate Purpura   (2.5″) 6 cm
Neorapana muricata (Broderip,
1832). W. Mexico to Ecuador.
Intertidal; fairly common.

Eye-of-Judas Purpura
                      (2.5″) 6 cm
Purpura planospira Lamarck,
1822. W. Mexico to Peru; Galapagos. Uncommon. Syn.: *picta*
Perry (a suppressed name).

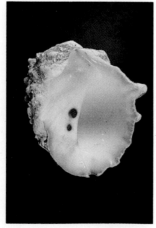

Nodose Purpura   (3″) 7.5 cm
Purpura nodosa (L., 1758). Brazil; western Africa. Littoral
rocks; locally common.

Tuberculate Purpura   (2″) 5 cm
Neorapana tuberculata (Sowerby, 1835). W. Mexico. Intertidal rocks; common.

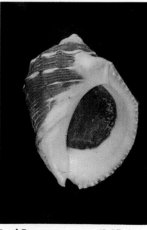

Toad Purpura   (2.5″) 6 cm
Thais bufo (Lamarck, 1822).
Indo-Pacific. Intertidal rocks;
common.

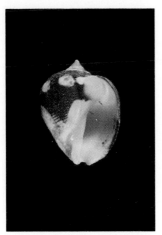

Gourd Rock-shell (2") 5 cm
Thais melones (Duclos, 1832).
W. Mexico to Peru; Galapagos.
Rocky shores; common.

Chocolata Rock-shell (2") 5 cm
Thais chocolata (Duclos, 1832).
Ecuador to Peru. Rocky shores;
common.

Hays's Rock-shell (3") 7.5 cm
Thais haemastoma form
canaliculata (Gray, 1839). N,W,
Gulf of Mexico. Oyster banks;
common. Syn.: *haysae* Clench.

Florida Rock-shell (2") 5 cm
Thais haemastoma subspecies
floridana (Conrad, 1037). S.E.
United States to Brazil. Intertidal muddy rocks; common.

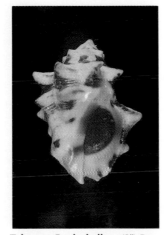

Two-row Rock-shell (2.5") 6 cm
Thais haemastoma subspecies
biserialis (Blainville, 1832). W.
Mexico to Chile. Littoral; common.

Tuberose Rock-shell (2") 5 cm
Thais tuberosa Röding, 1798.
S.W. and central Pacific. Coral
shores; common. Syn.: *pica*
Blainville.

Kiener's Rock-shell (1.5") 3.5 cm
Thais kieneri (Deshayes, 1844).
Japan to Australia. Littoral
rocks; common.

Chestnut Rock-shell
(1.5") 3.5 cm
Thais hippocastanum (L., 1758).
Southwestern Pacific. Rocky
shores; common.

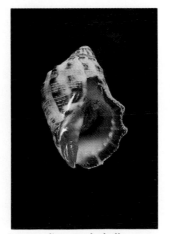

Aculeate Rock-shell (2") 5 cm
Thais aculeata Deshayes, 1844.
Southeastern Asia. Rocky
shores; common.

Intermediate Rock-shell
(1.5") 3.5 cm
Thais intermedia (Kiener, 1836).
Polynesia; southwestern Pacific. Reef edges; common.

Bituberculate Rock-shell
(1.5") 4 cm
Thais bitubercularis (Lamarck,
1822). Philippines to eastern Africa. Intertidal rocks; common.

Tissot's Rock-shell (0.6") 1.5 cm
Thais tissoti (Petit, 1852). Indian
Ocean; Andaman Sea. Interti-
dal; common.

Bicostal Rock-shell (2.4") 6 cm
Thais bicostalis Lamarck, 1816.
South Africa. Intertidal rocks;
common. Syn.: *capensis* Petit.

Speciosa Rock-shell (1.5") 4 cm
Thais speciosa (Valenciennes,
1832). W. Mexico to Peru. Intertidal rocks; common. Syn.: *triserialis* Blainville.

Kiosque Rock-shell (2") 5 cm
Thais kiosquiformis (Duclos,
1832). W. Mexico to Peru. Mangrove and oyster areas; common.

Blanford's Rock-shell
                    (0.8") 2 cm
Thais blanfordi (Melvill, 1893).
Northern Indian Ocean; Per-
sian Gulf. Intertidal; common.

Belligerent Rock-shell (3")
7.5 cm *Thais armigera* (Link,
1807). Southwestern Pacific.
Rock shores; common. Syn.:
armigera Lamarck.

Prickly Rock-shell (1.5") 4 cm
Thais echinata (Blainville,
1832). Southwestern Pacific.
Littoral; common. Rare umbilicate.

Mancinella Rock-shell (2") 5 cm
Thais mancinella (L., 1758).
Southwestern Pacific; Austra-
lia. Intertidal rocks; common.

Coronate Rock-shell (1.5") 4 cm
Thais coronata (Lamarck, 1816).
Senegal to Congo; Trinidad to
Brazil. Mangroves and rocks;
common.

Rustic Rock-shell (1.5") 4 cm
Thais rustica (Lamarck, 1822).
S.E. Florida to Brazil. Littoral;
common. Syn.: *undata* of
authors.

Rugose Rock-shell (1") 2.5 cm
Thais Rugosa (Born, 1778).
Southeastern Asia; India. Rock
and mud areas; common. Alias
sacellum (Gmelin, 1791).

Basket Drupe (1") 2.5 cm
Morula funiculus (Wood, 1828).
Southwestern Pacific. Littoral
rocks; common. Syn.: *triangu-
lata* Pease; *decussata* Reeve.

Grape Drupe (0.5") 1.2 cm
Morula uva (Röding, 1798).
Tropical W. Pacific. Intertidal
rocks; common. Syn.: *nodus*
Lamarck.

Monodon Thorn Drupe (1.5″) 4 cm *Acanthina monodon* (Pallas, 1774). Peru to Argentina. Rocky shores; common. Syn.: *calcar* Martyn; *unicornis* Bruguière.

Rough Thorn Drupe (1.5″) 4 cm *Acanthina monodon* form *imbricata* Lamarck, 1816. Chile; Falkland Islands. Common

Grand Purpura (2.5″) 6 cm *Neorapana grandis* (Sowerby, 1835). Galapagos Islands. Locally common.

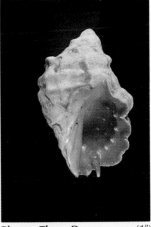

Gloomy Thorn Drupe (1″) 2.5 cm *Acanthina lugubris* (Sowerby, 1821). Southern California and western Mexico. Littoral rocks; abundant.

Spotted Thorn Drupe (1″) 2.5 cm *Acanthina punctulata* (Sowerby, 1825). Monterey, California, to Baja California. Upper intertidal zone; common.

Short-toothed Thorn Drupe (1″) 2.5 cm *Acanthina brevidentata* (Wood, 1828). W. Mexico to Peru. Littoral; common.

Checkered Thorn Drupe (1″) 2.5 cm *Acanthina paucilirata* (Stearns, 1871). San Pedro, California, to Baja California. Littoral; common.

Convoluted False Triton (1″) 2.5 cm *Phyllocoma convoluta* (Broderip, 1843). Southwestern Pacific. Offshore; rare.

Scaled False Triton (1.2″) 3 cm *Phyllocoma scalariformis* (Broderip, 1833). W. Mexico to Panama; Galapagos. Intertidal; uncommon.

Bezoar Rapa Whelk (3″) 7.5 cm *Rapana bezoar* (L., 1758). Japan to southeastern Asia. Offshore; moderately common.

Turnip-shaped Rapa (3.5″) 9 cm *Rapana rapiformis* (Born, 1778). Southeastern Asia and East Indies. Common. Syn.: *bulbosa* Lightfoot.

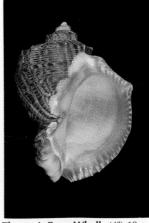

Thomas's Rapa Whelk (4″) 10 cm *Rapana venosa* (Valenciennes, 1846). Japan; China; introduced to Black Sea. Common. Syn.: *thomasiana* Crosse.

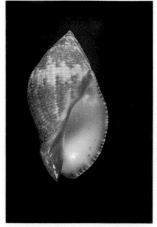

Wreath Jopas (2") 5 cm
Nassa serta (Bruguière, 1789).
Southwestern Pacific to Hawaii. Intertidal rocks; common.

Francolina Jopas (2") 5 cm
Nassa francolina (Bruguière, 1789). Indian Ocean. Common.
Smoothish.

Yellow Jopas (1") 2.5 cm
Pinaxia coronata A. Adams, 1851. Philippines to Japan. Shallow water. Japan form without stripes (*citrina* Kuroda).

Ribboned Jopas (1") 2.5 cm
Vexilla taeniata (Powis, 1835).
Central Pacific. Uncommon.

Vexillate Jopas (1") 2.5 cm
Vexilla vexillum (Gmelin, 1791).
Indo-Pacific. Shore rocks; uncommon. Syn.: *picta* Swainson.

Lined Jopas (1") 2.5 cm
Vexilla lineata (A. Adams, 1853).
Southwestern Pacific to Hawaii. Littoral; common. Syn.:
striatella Garrett.

Prickly Pacific Drupe
(1") 2.5 cm
Drupa ricinus (L., 1758). Indo-Pacific. Intertidal rocks; abundant.

Elegant Pacific Drupe (1")
2.5 cm *Drupa elegans* (Broderip & Sowerby, 1829). Central Polynesia. Intertidal rocks; uncommon.

Purple Pacific Drupe (1") 2.5 cm
Drupa morum Röding, 1798.
Indo-Pacific. Intertidal reefs; common. Syn.: *horrida* Lamarck.

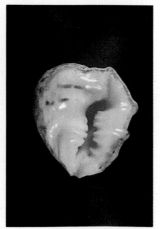

Iodine-mouth Drupe (1.2") 3 cm
Drupa morum subspecies
iodostoma (Lesson, 1840). Marquesas Islands; eastern Polynesia. Uncommon.

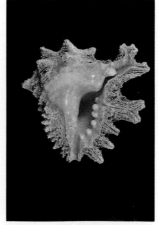

Digitate Pacific Drupe (1")
2.5 cm *Drupa grossularia* (Röding, 1798). S.W. Pacific to eastern Polynesia. Shallow water; common. Syn.: *digitata* Lamarck.

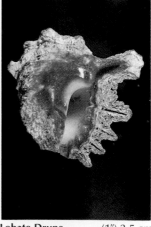

Lobate Drupe (1") 2.5 cm
Drupa lobata (Blainville, 1832).
Red Sea to western Australia.
Shallow water; locally common.

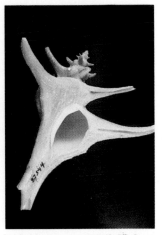

Strawberry Drupe (1.5") 4 cm *Drupa rubusidaeus* Röding, 1798. Indo-Pacific. Lower intertidal reefs; uncommon. Syn.: *fragum* Röding

Clathrate Drupe (1.5") 4 cm *Drupa clathrata* (Lamarck, 1816). S.W. Pacific. Intertidal. Widespread but uncommon. Syn.: *rubuscaesius* of authors.

Giant Forreria (5") 13 cm *Forreria belcheri* (Hinds, 1843). California to Baja California. Intertidal oyster bars; common.

Lee's Murex (3.5") 9 cm *Calcitrapessa leeana* (Dall, 1890). W. Mexico. 50 to 100 m; uncommon. Holotype illustrated.

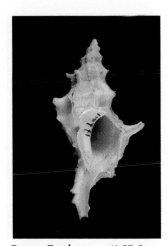

Cerros Trophon (3") 7.5 cm *Austrotrophon cerrosensis* form *pinnatus* (Dall, 1902). W. Mexico. 50 to 150 m; rare. Holotype.

Catalina Trophon (3") 7.5 cm *Austrotrophon cerrosensis* subspecies *catalinensis* Oldroyd, 1927. South third of California. Offshore; rare.

Gorgon Trophon (1.3") 3 cm *Boreotrophon gorgon* (Dall, 1913). Off Hondo, Japan. 300 m; rare. Holotype illustrated.

Thistle Trophon (1.3") 3 cm *Enixotrophon carduelis* (Watson, 1886). Off eastern Australia. 800 m; rare.

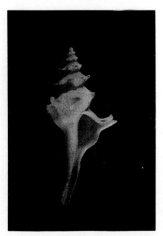

Prickly Trophon (1.3") 3 cm *Nipponotrophon echinus* (Dall, 1918). Sagami, Japan. Deep water; uncommon.

Clavate Trophon (1.3") 3 cm *Trophonopsis clavatus* (G. O. Sars, 1879). N.W. Europe; east Canada to off North Carolina. Deep water; uncommon.

Carinate Trophon (1.3") 3 cm *Trophonopsis vaginatus* (Cristofori & Jan, 1832). Mediterranean. Deep water. Syn.: *carinatus* Bivona.

Watson's Trophon (2.2") 6 cm *Trophonopsis acanthodes* (Watson, 1882). Off southeastern South America. Deep water; rare.

Alaska Trophon   (1.3″) 3 cm
Boreotrophon alaskanus (Dall, 1902). Japan and Alaska. Deep water; uncommon.

Dall's Trophon   (2″) 5 cm
Nodulotrophon dalli (Kobelt, 1878). Northern Pacific. Deep water; rare.

Laciniate Trophon   (2″) 5 cm
Stramonitrophon plicatus (Lightfoot, 1786). Southern South America. Offshore; common. Syn.: *laciniatus* Martyn.

Candelabrum Trophon
    (1.5″) 3.5 cm
Boreotrophon candelabrum (Reeve, 1848). Japan. Deep water; uncommon.

Gevers's Trophon   (4″) 10 cm
Trophon geversianus (Pallas, 1774). Southern South America. Offshore; common. Syn.: *magellanicus* Lamarck.

Gevers's Trophon   (4″) 10 cm
Trophon geversianus (Pallas, 1774). A very variable species with many intergrades.

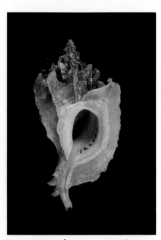

Northwest Pacific Trophon (1″) 2.5 cm *Boreotrophon pacificus* (Dall, 1902). Bering Sea to California. Offshore in south; intertidal in north. Common.

Stuart's Trophon   (1.5″) 4 cm
Boreotrophon stuarti (E. A. Smith, 1880). Alaska to California. Subtidal to 50 m; common. Holotype illustrated.

Truncate Trophon   (0.6″) 1.5 cm
Boreotrophon truncatus (Ström, 1768). Northwestern Europe; Greenland. Offshore in 4 to 140 m; common.

Triangular Trophon   (1.2″) 3 cm
Boreotrophon triangulatus (Carpenter, 1864). California. Offshore; moderately common.

Clathrate Trophon (0.6″) 1.5 cm
Boreotrophon clathratus (L., 1758). Arctic seas to W. Europe. Offshore; common. Syn.: *gunneri* Loven.

Sandpaper Trophon   (2″) 5 cm
Trophonopsis lasius (Dall, 1919). Bering Sea to off Baja California. 50 to 1,000 m; common.

Elongate Trophon   (1.5″) 4 cm *Trophon elongatus* Strebel, 1904. Magellan Straits; Falkland Islands. Offshore; uncommon.

Hoyle's Trophon   (1.2″) 3 cm *Trophon hoylei* Strebel, 1904. Falkland Islands. Offshore; uncommon.

Ambiguous Trophon   (1.5″) 4 cm *Zeatrophon ambiguus* (Philippi, 1844). New Zealand. Shallow water; common.

Broderip's Thistle Trophon
             (1″) 2.5 cm *Acanthotrophon carduus* (Broderip, 1833). W. Mexico to Peru. Subtidal; uncommon.

Panama Thistle Trophon   (1.5″) 4 cm *Austrotrophon panamensis* Olsson, 1971. Gulf of Panama. Deep water; rare. Holotype illustrated.

Beebe's Trophon   (1.5″) 3.5 cm *Trophon beebei* Hertlein & Strong, 1948. Gulf of California. 60 to 120 m; moderately common.

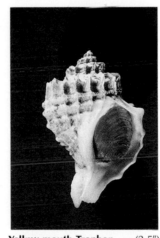

Yellow-mouth Trophon   (2.5″) 6 cm *Xanthochorus xanthostoma* (Broderip, 1833). Panama to Chile. Offshore; common. Syn.: *horridus* Brod.

Fimbriate False Latiaxis   (1.5″) 4 cm *Lataxiena fimbriata* (Hinds, 1844). N.W. Pacific; Japan. Shallow water; common. Syn.: *imbricatus* Smith.

Mawe's Latiaxis   (2″) 5 cm *Latiaxis mawae* (Griffith & Pidgeon, 1834). Japan. Offshore; locally common. Family Coralliophilidae.

Winding Latiaxis   (2″) 5 cm *Latiaxis tortilis* H. & A. Adams, 1863. South Africa. Offshore; uncommon.

Gyrate Latiaxis   (2″) 5 cm *Latiaxis gyratus* (Hinds, 1844). Southwestern Pacific. Offshore; uncommon. Also Japan.

Eugenia's Latiaxis   (2″) 5 cm *Latiaxis idoleum* Jonas, 1847. Japan. Offshore; uncommon. Syn.: *eugeniae* Bernardi.

Japanese Latiaxis (1") 2.5 cm
Latiaxis japonicus (Dunker, 1882). Japan. Offshore, 30 to 200 m; common.

Armored Latiaxis (1") 2.5 cm
Latiaxis armatus Sowerby, 1912. Japan. Offshore; common.

Purple-mouth Latiaxis
(1.5") 4 cm
Latiaxis purpuratus Chenu, 1859. Eastern Asia; Japan. Offshore; uncommon.

Carinate Latiaxis (1.5") 4 cm
Latiaxis purpuratus form *cariniferoides* Shikama, 1966. Japan. Offshore, 100 m; uncommon.

DeBurgh's Latiaxis (1.5") 4 cm
Latiaxis deburghiae (Reeve, 1857). Eastern Asia; southern Japan; 20 to 150 m; uncommon.

Lischke's Latiaxis (1.5") 4 cm
Latiaxis lischkeana (Dunker, 1882). Japan to off New Zealand. Deep water; common. Syn.: *australis* Laseron.

Dunker's Latiaxis (1.5") 4 cm
Latiaxis dunkeri Kuroda & Habe, 1961. Japan. Deep water; moderately common.

Kira's Latiaxis (1") 2.5 cm
Latiaxis kiranus Kuroda, 1959. Japan. Deep water; moderately common.

Takahashi's Latiaxis
(1.5") 3.5 cm
Latiaxis takahashii Kosuge, 1979. Cebu Island, Philippines. 100 m; uncommon.

Cristate Latiaxis (1") 2.5 cm
Latiaxis cristatus Kosuge, 1979. Cebu Island, Philippines. 100 m; uncommon.

Bushy Latiaxis (1.2") 3 cm
Latiaxis fruticosus Kosuge, 1979. Off Cebu Island, Philippines. 80 to 100 m; uncommon.

Prickly Latiaxis (1") 2.5 cm
Latiaxis echinatus Azuma, 1960. Off Tosa, Japan. 200 m; uncommon.

Santa Cruz Latiaxis
(1.5″) 3.5 cm
Latiaxis santacruzensis Emerson & D'Attilio, 1970. Galapagos Islands. 150 m; rare.

Julia's Latiaxis (0.8″) 2 cm
Latiaxis juliae Clench & Aguayo, 1939. Off Barbados, West Indies. 150 to 300 m; very rare.

Hinds's Latiaxis (1.5″) 3.5 cm
Latiaxis hindsi (Carpenter, 1857) W. Mexico to Panama; Galapagos. Offshore; uncommon.

Costate Latiaxis (1″) 2.5 cm
Latiaxis costatus (Blainville, 1832). W. Mexico to Panama. Intertidal rocks; fairly common.

Pilsbry's Latiaxis (1.5″) 3.5 cm
Latiaxis pilsbryi Hirase, 1908. Japan. Offshore; rare.

Winckworth's Latiaxis
(1.5″) 3.5 cm
Latiaxis winckworthi Fulton, 1930. Japan. Shallow water; moderately common.

Lamellose Coral-shell
(1″) 2.5 cm
Coralliophila meyendorffi (Calcara, 1845). Mediterranean. Common. Form *lamellosa* Phil., 1836.

Pyriform Coral-shell
(1.5″) 3.5 cm
Coralliophila pyriformis Kira, 1959. Japan. Offshore; uncommon.

Violet Coral-shell (1.5″) 3.5 cm
Coralliophila neritoidea (Lamarck, 1816). Indo-Pacific. Shallow reefs; common. Syn.: *violacea* Kiener.

Isshiki Coral-shell (1″) 2.5 cm
Coralliophila isshikiensis Shikama, 1971. Japan. Offshore; uncommon.

Fearnley's Coral-shell (2″) 5 cm
Coralliophila fearnleyi (Emerson & D'Attilio, 1965). Japan to Australia.

South Seas Coral-shell (1″)
2.5 cm *Coralliophila erosa* (Röding, 1798). Indo-Pacific. Subspecies *bulbiformis* Conrad, 1837, from Hawaii.

Spinose Latiaxis   (1″) 2.5 cm
Latiaxis pagodus form *spinosa* Hirase, 1908. Japan; common. At right: form *multi-spinosa* Shikama, 1966.

Pagoda Latiaxis   (1″) 2.5 cm
Latiaxis pagodus (A. Adams, 1852). Japan. Offshore. Common. Very variable.

Dall's Latiaxis   (1.5″) 3.5 cm
Latiaxis dalli Emerson & D'Attilio, 1963. Caribbean. Deep water; rare.

Mactan Latiaxis   (1.5″) 3.5 cm
Latiaxis macutanica Kosuge, 1979. Off Mactan Island, Philippines. 100 m; uncommon.

Rose Latiaxis   (1.5″) ″) 3.5 cm
Latiaxis sentix (F. M. Bayer, 1971). Caribbean. Deep water; rare.

Short Coral-shell   (1.5″) 3.5 cm
Coralliophila abbreviata (Lamarck, 1816). S.E. Florida to Brazil. Bases of sea fans and on corals. Common.

Wide-spined Latiaxis   (1.2″). 3 cm
Latiaxis latipinnatus Azuma, 1961. Japan to central Philippines. 150 to 225 m; uncommon. Umbilicate.

Caribbean Coral-shell   (1″) 2.5 cm
Coralliophila caribaea Abbott, 1958. S.E. United States to Brazil. In holdfasts of seafans; common. Syn.: *plicata* of authors.

Aberrant Coral-shell   (1″) 2.5 cm
Coralliophila aberrans (C. B. Adams, 1850). Eastern United States to Brazil. Deep water; uncommon.

Small Coral-shell   (1″) 2.5 cm
Coralliophila parva (E. A. Smith, 1877). Galapagos Islands; Gulf of California. Shallow water; uncommon.

Quoy's Coral-shell   (1″) 2.5 cm
Quoyula madreporarum (Sowerby, 1832). Indo-Pacific. On corals; common.

Burrowing Coral-shell   (6″) 15 cm
Magilus antiquatus Montfort, 1810. Indo-Pacific. Bores into brain coral. Early whorls filled in. Uncommon.

Rapa Snail (2.5") 6 cm
Rapa rapa (L., 1758). Southwestern Pacific. Buried inside soft, yellow coral. Locally common.

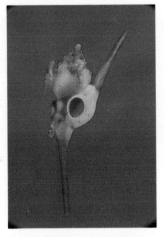

Genka Snail (1.5") 4 cm
Genkamurex varicosus (Kuroda, 1953). Genkai Sea, Japan. Offshore; uncommon.

Pavlova Typhis (1.5") 4 cm
Trubatsa pavlova (Iredale, 1936). Southeastern Australia. 100 to 220 m; uncommon.

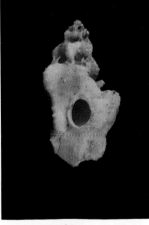

Longhorn Typhis (1") 2.5 cm
Trubatsa longicornis (Dall, 1888). Southern Florida and Cuba. Offshore to 600 m; rare.

Pinnate Typhis (0.8") 2 cm
Pterotyphis pinnatus (Broderip, 1833). Bahamas and Caribbean. Shallow water; uncommon.

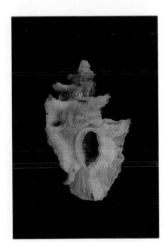

Triangular Typhis (1.5") 4 cm
Tripterotyphis triangularis (A. Adams, 1855). Bahamas and Caribbean. Shallow reefs; rare.

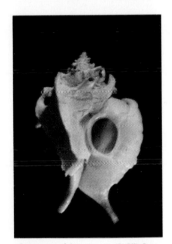

Clery's Typhis (0.8") 2 cm
Typhina cleryi (Petit, 1840). Brazil and Western Africa. Moderately deep water; uncommon.

Bullis's Typhis (1") 2.5 cm
Siphonochelus bullisi Gertman, 1969. Lower Caribbean. Deep water; rare. Holotype illustrated.

Cuming's Typhis (1.2") 3 cm
Haustellotyphis cumingii (Broderip, 1833). W. Mexico to Ecuador. Shallow water; fairly common.

Angas's Typhis (0.8") 2 cm
Prototyphis angasi (Crosse, 1863). S.E. Australia; New Zealand. Intertidal; locally common. Syn.: *eos* Hutton.

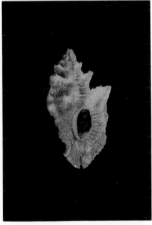

Fay's Typhis (1.2") 3 cm
Tripterotyphis fayae (Keen & Campbell, 1964). Western Mexico. Shallow water; uncommon.

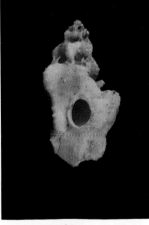

Coronate Typhis (1.2") 3 cm
Typhisopsis coronatus (Broderip, 1833). W. Mexico to Ecuador. Shallow water; uncommon; worn specimen here.

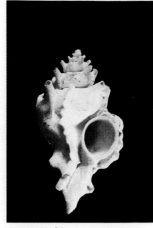

A small group of rare, deep-water species found throughout the world. The small shells have a very long siphonal canal. Spines occur on the shoulders of the whorls. The nuclear whorls are bulbous. Operculum chitinous. One genus, *Coluzea*, is limited to the region of New Zealand. The family has fewer than 30 living species.

Philippine Typhis   (0.8") 2 cm
Typhina philippensis (Watson, 1883). Southwestern Pacific; Australia. Offshore; uncommon. Syn.: *interpres* Iredale.

Yates's Typhis   (0.8") 2 cm
Typhina yatesi (Crosse & Fischer, 1865). Southern Australia; Victoria. Offshore; uncommon.

Grand Typhis   (1.3") 3.5 cm
Typhisala grandis (A. Adams, 1855). W. Mexico to Panama. Offshore; uncommon.

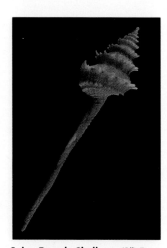

First Pagoda Shell   (2.5") 6 cm
Columbarium pagoda (Lesson, 1831). Japan. Offshore; common. Syn.: *costatum* Shikama; *stellatum* Habe.

False Pagoda Shell   (3") 7.5 cm
Columbarium pagodoides (Watson, 1882). Southeastern Australia. 1,200 m; rare. Paratype illustrated.

Spiny Pagoda Shell   (2") 5 cm
Columbarium spinicinctum (von Martens, 1881). Eastern Australia. Offshore, 50 to 130 m; uncommon.

Most Graceful Pagoda (2") 5 cm
Columbarium formosissimum Tomlin, 1928. Off South Africa in 200 m; uncommon.

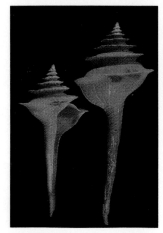

Bray's Pagoda Shell   (2.5") 6 cm
Columbarium brayi Clench, 1959. Southern Caribbean. 300 m; rare.

Atlantic Pagoda Shell(1") 2.5 cm
Columbarium atlantis Clench & Aguayo, 1938. Off northern Cuba. 500 to 700 m; rare. Holotype illus.

Bartlett's Pagoda Shell
     (1.5") 4 cm
Columbarium bartletti Clench & Aguayo, 1940. Caribbean. 300 to 600 m; rare. Holotype illus.

Bermudez's Pagoda Shell   (1")
2.5 cm *Columbarium bermudezi* Clench & Aguayo, 1938. Off Florida; Cuba. Deep water; rare. Holotype.

DOVE-SHELLS
FAMILY COLUMBELLIDAE

Large family of numerous genera and many species living in warm and tropical waters. Some dove-shells are tiny, few exceed an inch. Scavenging carnivores, they are especially active at night when they may be seen in sandy and muddy places at low tide. The family (which is also called Pyrenidae) is well represented in tropical waters.

Lance Strombina (1.2") 3 cm
Strombina lanceolata (Sowerby, 1832). Ecuador, Galapagos. Offshore; uncommon.

Recurved Strombina (1.2") 3 cm
Strombina recurva (Sowerby, 1832). Baja California to Peru. Offshore to 37 m; common. Syn.: *limonetta* Li.

Mrs. Deroy's Strombina (2") 5 cm
Strombina deroyae Emerson & D'Attilio, 1969. Galapagos Islands. 150 m; uncommon.

Blotchy Strombina (1") 2.5 cm
Strombina maculosa (Sowerby, 1832). Gulf of California to Panama. On offshore mud flats to 37 m; common.

Slender Strombina (2") 5 cm
Strombina fusinoidea Dall, 1916. Baja California to Panama. Offshore; uncommon. Syn.: *fusiformis* Hinds.

Slender Strombina (2") 5 cm
Strombina fusinoidea Dall, 1916. Resembles *S. recurva* but has more rounded shoulder and lacks shoulder tubercles.

Turret Strombina (1.4") 3.5 cm
Strombina turrita (Sowerby, 1832). Guatemala to Ecuador. Offshore at about 25 m; uncommon.

Humped Strombina (1") 2.5 cm
Strombina dorsata (Sowerby, 1832). Gulf of California to Ecuador. Offshore at 37 m; uncommon.

Peacock Strombina (0.8") 2 cm
Strombina pavonina (Hinds, 1844). W. Mexico to Panama. Offshore to about 37 m; uncommon.

Shouldered Strombina (1.2") 3 cm
Strombina angularis (Sowerby, 1832). W. Mexico to Panama. Offshore to 37 m; uncommon. Syn.: *subangularis* Lowe.

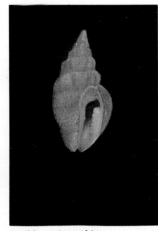

Caribbean Strombina (.7") 1.8 cm
Strombina pumilio (Reeve, 1859). Venezuela and Isla Margarita. Offshore; moderately common.

Stromboid Dove-shell (1.2") 3 cm
Columbella strombiformis Lamarck, 1822.
Gulf of California to Peru. Under intertidal
rocks; common. Syn.: *bridgesii* Reeve.

Blood-stained Dove-shell (1") 2.5 cm
Columbella haemastoma Sowerby, 1832.
Gulf of California to Ecuador, Galapagos.
Under intertidal rocks; moderately com-
mon.

Fat Dove-shell (1") 2.7 cm
Columbella major Sowerby, 1832. Gulf of
California to Peru. Under intertidal rocks;
moderately common.

Big-lip Dove-shell (0.9") 2.2 cm
Columbella labiosa Sowerby, 1822. Nicaragua to Ecuador. On exposed rocks; common. Syn.: *venilia* Duclos.

Rough Dove-shell (0.8") 2 cm
Anachis rugosa (Sowerby, 1832). Nicaragua
to Ecuador. Exposed rocks, mud flats; common. Syn.: *bicolor* Kiener.

Payta Dove-shell (1") 2.5 cm
Columbella paytensis Lesson, 1830. Ecuador to Peru, Galapagos. Intertidal; moderately common.

Burnt Dove-shell (0.8") 2 cm
Columbella fuscata Sowerby, 1832. Baja
California to Peru. Intertidal; moderately
common.

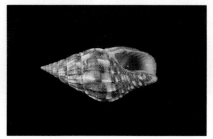

Varia Dove-shell (0.8") 2 cm
Anachis varia (Sowerby, 1832). W. Mexico
to Panama. Intertidal; common. Syn.:
veleda Duclos.

Zigzag Dove-shell (0.7") 1.8 cm
Anachis fluctuata (Sowerby, 1832). Nicaragua to Ecuador. Intertidal; common. Syn.:
costata Duclos.

Cone-shaped Dove-shell (1") 2.5 cm
Parametaria philippinarum (Reeve, 1843).
Philippines, Indonesia. Intertidal; uncom-
mon. Syn.: *coniformis* Sowerby.

Dupont's Dove-shell (1") 2.7 cm
Parametaria dupontii (Kiener, 1849). Gulf of
California, W. Mexico. Shallow water;
moderately common.

Common Dove-shell (0.8") 2 cm
Columbella mercatoria (L., 1758). Florida to
Brazil, Bermuda. Under rocks, shallow wa-
ter; common. Many synonyms.

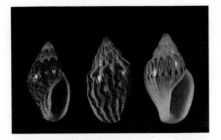

Smooth Dove-shell　　　(0.8″) 2 cm
Nitidella laevigata (L., 1758). Florida Keys, W. Indies, Bermuda. Shallow water; common. Outer lip smooth.

Rustic Dove-shell　　　(1.2″) 3 cm
Columbella rustica (L., 1758). Mediterranean to W. Africa. Shallow water; common. Many synonyms.

Rusty Dove-shell　　　(0.4″) 1 cm
Columbella rusticoides Heilprin, 1887. S. Florida; N.W. Cuba. Subtidal to 10 m; common.

Cone Dove-shell　　　(1″) 2.5 cm
Parametaria epamella (Duclos, 1846). Philippines. Intertidal; uncommon.

Yellow Dove-shell　　　(1″) 2.5 cm
Pyrene flava (Bruguière, 1789). Indo-Pacific. Subtidal; common. Very variable color and pattern.

Music Dove-shell　　　(0.6″) 1.5 cm
Mitrella scripta (L., 1758). Mediterranean. Offshore and beached; common. Syn.: *flaminea* Risso.

Lightning Dove-shell　　　(0.8″) 2 cm
Pyrene ocellata (Link, 1807). Indo-Pacific. Shallow water; common. Syn.: *fulgurans* Lamarck.

Telescoped Dove-shell　　　(1″) 2.5 cm
Pyrene punctata (Bruguière, 1789). Indo-Pacific. Offshore and beached; moderately common. Syn.: *torva* Dillwyn.

Bound Dove-shell　　　(0.5″) 1.2 cm
Dentimitrella vincta (Tate, 1893). Southern Australia, Tasmania. Offshore; common.

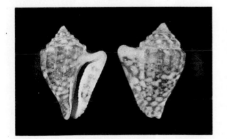

Harp Dove-shell　　　(0.5″) 1.2 cm
Microcithara harpiformis (Sowerby, 1832). W. Central America. Intertidal; uncommon.

San Felipe Dove-shell　　　(0.3″) 7 mm
Anachis sanfelipensis Lowe, 1935. North end of Gulf of California. Intertidal; uncommon.

Dotted Dove-shell　　　(0.7″) 1.8 cm
Pyrene versicolor (Sowerby, 1832). Indo-Pacific. Subtidal; common.

NEPTUNES, WHELKS AND ALLIES
FAMILY BUCCINIDAE

This is a very large and diverse family having many genera represented both in polar seas as well as the tropics. The fusiform shells may be drab in the cold seas and colorful in the tropics. Most have a large, horny, oval operculum. Hundreds of species are known.

Norwegian Volute Whelk
(5″) 12 cm
Volutopsius norvegicus (Gmelin, 1791). North Atlantic, North Sea. 90 to 250 m; common. Syn.: *norvegicus* Chemnitz.

Norwegian Volute Whelk
(5″) 12 cm
Volutopsius norvegicus (Gmelin, 1791). *V. largillierti* Petit is also a synonym.

Chestnut Volute Whelk
(3.5″) 9 cm
Volutopsius castaneus (Mörch, 1858). N. Japan to Alaska. Offshore; common.

Middendorff's Volute Whelk
(3.5″) 9 cm
Volutopsius middendorffi Dall, 1891. Arctic Seas, Bering Sea. Offshore; common.

Sinistral Arctic Whelk (3″)
7.5 cm *Pyrolofusus deformis* (Reeve, 1847). Bering Sea, Japan and Alaska. Offshore; common. Syn.: *harpa* Mörch.

Bering's Neptune (3″) 7.5 cm
Beringion behringii (Middendorff, 1848). Bering Sea. Uncommon. (*beringii* is misspelling.) Formerly in *Beringius*.

Kennicott's Neptune (3.5″) 9 cm
Beringion kennicottii (Dall, 1907). Alaska, Japan. Offshore; uncommon.

Marshall's Neptune (4″) 10 cm
Beringion marshalli (Dall, 1919). Japan; Bering Sea. Offshore; rare.

Turton's Neptune (3″) 7.5 cm
Neoberingius turtoni (Bean, 1834). Circum-arctic Seas. Offshore; uncommon.

Spitzbergen Colus (3″) 7.5 cm
Colus spitzbergeni (Reeve, 1855). Northern Norway, Siberia. Offshore; uncommon.

Herendeen Colus (2.5″) 6.5 cm
Colus herendeeni (Dall, 1902). Alaska. Offshore, 80 to 600 m; rare.

Near Colus (1.5") 3.5 cm
Colus howsei (Marshall, 1911). Western Europe. 35 to 170 m; common. Syn.: *propinquus* Adler, not Muenster.

Iceland Colus (3.5") 9 cm
Colus islandicus (Gmelin, 1791). Labrador to Norway. Offshore, 2 to 100 m; common.

Jeffreys's Colus (2.5") 6 cm
Colus jeffreysianus (Fischer, 1868). W. Europe. Offshore to 300 m; uncommon.

Stimpson's Colus (4") 10 cm
Colus stimpsoni (Mörch, 1867). Labrador to off North Carolina. Common. Syn.: *brevis* Verrill.

Twisted Colus (2.5") 6 cm
Colus tortuosus (Reeve, 1855). Arctic Europe. 27 to 500 m; uncommon.

Ventricose Colus (2") 5 cm
Colus ventricosus (Gray, 1839). Nova Scotia to off Maine. 10 to 100 m; uncommon.

Slender Colus (2.5") 6.5 cm
Colus gracilis (da Costa, 1778). W. Europe. Offshore to 800 m; common.

Turgid Colus (2.4") 6 cm
Colus turgidulus (Friele, 1877). W. Europe. Deep water; rare.

Fusiform Colus (1.6") 4.5 cm
Siphonorbis fenestratus (Turton, 1834). North Atlantic. 72 to 262 m; uncommon. Syn.: *fusiformis* Broderip, not Borson.

Ivory Colus (3") 7.5 cm
Siphonorbis ebur (Mörch, 1869). N.W. Europe. Cold seas, deep water; uncommon.

Destiny Colus (1.8") 4.5 cm
Turrisipho lachesis (Mörch, 1869). Northern Norway. Offshore; uncommon.

Plicate Colus (1.5") 4 cm
Plicifusus plicatus (A. Adams, 1863). Japan. Cold water. Offshore; common.

Kroyer's Colus   (3") 7.5 cm
Plicifusus kroyeri (Möller, 1842). Circumpolar seas; Greenland; Bering Sea. Common.

Grammatus Whelk   (4") 10 cm
Ancistrolepis grammatus (Dall, 1907). Off Yesso, Japan. Rare. Holotype illustrated.

Unicum Whelk   (3") 7.5 cm
Clinopegma unicum (Pilsbry, 1905). Japan. Form *polygramma* Dall, 1907, has spiral cords.

Magna Whelk   (3") 7.5 cm
Clinopegma magnum (Dall, 1895). Japan, cold water. 90 to 140 m. Uncommon.

Broad Japelion   (3.5") 9 cm
Japelion latus (Dall, 1918). Korean Straits; East China Sea. Uncommon.

Peri Japelion   (4") 10 cm
Japelion pericochlion (Schrenck, 1862). Off Hokkaido, Japan. Deep water. Common.

Adelphic Japelion   (3") 8 cm
Japelion adelphicus (Dall, 1907). Tosa Bay, Shikoku, Japan. Common.

Hirase's Japelion   (4") 10 cm
Japelion hirasei (Pilsbry, 1901). Hokkaido, Japan. Offshore; common.

Ovum Arctic Whelk (1.5") 4 cm
Liomesus dalei (Sowerby, 1825). N.W. Europe. Offshore, 72 to 180 m; common. Syn.: *ovum* Turton.

Ancient Neptune   (6") 15 cm
Neptunea antiqua (L., 1758). Western Europe to Scotland. Offshore to 1,000 m; common.

Fat Neptune   (4") 10 cm
Neptunea ventricosa form *behringiana* (Middendorff, 1848). Bering Sea. Offshore; common.

Rejected Neptune   (6") 15 cm
Neptunea despecta (L., 1758). Arctic Seas. Offshore; common.

Double Sculptured Neptune
(4″) 10 cm
Neptunea intersculpta (Sowerby, 1899). Arctic Seas; Japan. Offshore; uncommon.

Brother Neptune (4″) 10 cm
Neptunea intersculpta form *frater* Pilsbry, 1901. Japan. Offshore. One of several forms.

Pribiloff Neptune (4″) 10 cm
Neptunea intersculpta form *pribiloffensis* (Dall, 1919). One of several variations.

Clench's Neptune (4″) 10 cm
Neptunea despecta subspecies *clenchi* Clarke, 1956. N. Canada. Holotype illus.

Ithia Neptune (4″) 10 cm
Neptunea ithia (Dall, 1891). W. Canada to California. Offshore to 800 m; uncommon.

Smirna Neptune (3″) 7.5 cm
Neptunea smirnia (Dall, 1919). Alaska to Washington. 100 to 300 m; common. Syn.: *fukuae* Kira.

Arthritic Neptune (4″) 10 cm
Neptunea arthritica (Bernardi, 1857). N.E. China; Korea. 4 to 50 m; locally common.

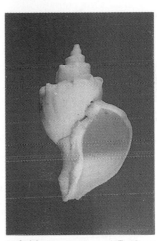

Arthritic Neptune (4″) 10 cm
Neptunea arthritica (Bernardi, 1857). A very variable species. Syn.: *cumingii* Crosse.

Fat Neptune (4″) 10 cm
Neptunea ventricosa (Gmelin, 1791). Arctic Seas; Bering Sea. Common. Syn.: *satura* Martyn.

Tabled Neptune (3″) 7.5 cm
Neptunea tabulata (Baird, 1863). W. Canada to California. Offshore, 40 to 400 m; fairly common.

Heros Neptune (4″) 10 cm
Neptunea heros (Gray, 1850). Arctic Seas; Japan. Uncommon. Syn.: *bulbacea* (Bernardi, 1808).

New England Neptune (3″)
7.5 cm *Neptunea lyrata* (Gmelin, 1791). Subspecies *decemcostata* (Say, 1826). New England. Offshore; common.

Left-handed Neptune
(3.5") 9 cm
Neptunea contraria L., 1771. Mediterranean; Eastern Atlantic. Offshore to deep water; moderately uncommon.

Phoenician Whelk (4") 11 cm
Neptunea lyrata form *phoenicea* (Dall, 1891). Off W. Canada. Deep water; common.

Kinoshita's Whelk (2") 5 cm
Parancistrolepis kinoshitai (Kuroda, 1931). Japan. Offshore to 100 m; uncommon.

Fusiform Whelk (2.3") 6 cm
Siphonalia fusoides (Reeve, 1846). Japan. Moderately deep water; common. Sometimes has pale brown spots.

Knobbed Whelk (2") 5 cm
Austrofusus glans (Röding, 1798). New Zealand. On sand at low-tide level and below; common.

Waller's Whelk (3") 7.5 cm
Siphonofusus walleri (Ladd, 1976). Philippines; S.W. Pacific. Offshore to 100 m; rare.

Hooped Whelk (1.8") 4.5 cm
Siphonalia trochulus (Reeve, 1843). Japan. Common. May have tubercles on shoulders. Syn.: *tokaiensis* Kira, 1959.

Bonnet Whelk (1.5") 4 cm
Siphonalia cassidariaeformis (Reeve, 1843). Japan. Offshore; common. Extremely variable in form and color.

Funereal Whelk (1.5") 4 cm
Siphonalia cassidariaeformis form *funerea* Pilsbry, 1895. Japan. Offshore; common. Color variation only.

Pfeffer's Whelk (2") 5 cm
Siphonalia pfefferi Sowerby, 1900. Southern Japan. Dredged 10 - 60 m; common. *S. pfeifferi* is misspelling.

Pretty-zoned Whelk (2") 5 cm
Siphonalia callizona Kuroda & Habe, 1961. Japan. Offshore; 100 to 200 m; uncommon.

Kellet's Whelk (5") 12 cm
Kelletia kelleti (Forbes, 1850). California to Baja California; Japan. 2 to 80 m; common.

Delightful Phos (1") 2.5 cm
Phos gaudens Hinds, 1844. Gulf of California to Ecuador. Offshore to 50 m; uncommon.

Grateloup's Phos (1") 2.5 cm
Phos grateloupianus Petit, 1853. West Africa, moderately common. Syn.: *ligatus* A. Adams.

Blue-mouth Phos (0.8") 2 cm
Phos cyanostoma A. Adams, 1850. Indian Ocean; S.E. Asia. Locally uncommon.

Articulate Phos (1.5") 4 cm
Phos articulatus Hinds, 1844. Gulf of California to Peru. Offshore to 100 m; moderately common.

Magnificent Phos (2") 5 cm
Nassaria magnifica (Lischke, 1871). Southern Japan. Dredged 20 - 255 m; uncommon.

Solid Phos (1.5") 4 cm
Nassaria solida Kuroda & Habe, 1961. Japan to N.E. Australia. Dredged 100 to 600 m; rare. Paratype illustrated.

Indian Phos (1") 2.5 cm
Nassaria coromandelica E. A. Smith, 1894. Bay of Bengal. Deep water; rare.

Acuminate Phos (1") 2.5 cm
Nassaria acuminata (Reeve, 1844). Tropical Indo-W. Pacific. Subtidal; uncommon. Syn.: *bitubercularis* A. Adams.

White Phos (1") 2.5 cm
Nassaria pusilla (Röding, 1798). Southern and S.E. Asia. 1 to 20 m; uncommon. Syn.: *nivea* Gmelin.

Acapulco Trajana (1") 2.5 cm
Trajana acapulcana Pilsbry & Lowe, 1932. Gulf of Tehuantepec; W. Mexico. Taken by shrimpers; uncommon.

Round-mouth Trajana
(1") 2.5 cm
Trajana perideris (Dall, 1910). W. Mexico. 37 to 55 m; uncommon.

Beau's Phos (1.5") 4 cm
Antillophos beaui (Fischer & Bernardi, 1860). Yucatan; Cuba; Lesser Antilles. Dredged 10 - 185 m; moderately rare.

Flaring Penion (5″) 13 cm
Penion cuvierianus (Powell, 1927). New Zealand. Deep water; common. Formerly *dilatatus* of authors. Syn.: *dispar* Powell; *rex* Finlay.

Waite's Penion (6″) 15 cm
Berylsma waitei (Hedley, 1903). Southeastern Australia; Tasmania. Trawled in moderate depths; uncommon.

Mandarin Penion (5″) 13 cm
Penion mandarina (Duclos, 1831). Southern Australia; Tasmania. Trawled or in crayfish pots; moderately common.

Ormes's Penion (7″) 18 cm
Penion ormesi Powell, 1927. Central New Zealand. Dredged in deep water; uncommon.

Ornamented Penion (2.5″) 6 cm
Aeneator comptus (Finlay, 1924). Northern New Zealand. Offshore; uncommon.

Common Pacific Phos (1.5″) 4 cm *Phos senticosus* (L., 1758). Indo-Pacific. Tidal sand and mud flats to 10 m; moderately common.

Woven Pacific Phos (1.2″) 3 cm *Phos textum* (Gmelin, 1791). Indo-W. Pacific. Shallow water in weedy coral-sand; moderately common.

Sharp-ribbed Phos (1.5″) 3.5 cm *Phos muriculatus* "Gould" Sowerby, 1859. Indo-W. Pacific; uncommon. Less sculptured than *P. senticosus*.

Basket Phos (1.4″) 3.5 cm
Phos virgatus Hinds, 1844. Indian Ocean; Sri Lanka; shallow water in sand; rare.

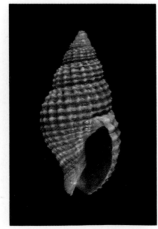

Veragua Phos (1″) 2.5 cm
Phos veraguensis Hinds, 1843. Gulf of California to Colombia. Offshore to considerable depths; moderately common.

Rosy Phos (1.5″) 4 cm
Phos roseatus Hinds, 1844. Indo-W. Pacific. Moderately deep water in mud and coral debris; uncommon.

Hirase's Phos (1″) 2.5 cm
Phos hirasei Sowerby, 1904. Southern Japan. Shallow water, subtidal in sand. Uncommon.

Checkerboard Engina
(0.8") 2 cm
Engina alveolata (Kiener, 1836). Indo-Pacific. Shallow water; common. Syn.: *lauta* Reeve.

Curious Engina (1") 2.5 cm
Engina epidromidea Melvill, 1894. Bombay. Shallow water; uncommon.

Striped Engina (0.8") 2 cm
Engina mendicaria (L., 1758). Indo-Pacific. Under rocks in shallow water; common.

Mauritian Engina (0.6") 1.5 cm
Engina bonasia von Martens, 1880. Indian Ocean. Shallow water; uncommon.

Lovely Engina (0.8") 2 cm
Engina pulchra (Reeve, 1846). Panama to Ecuador. Under intertidal stones; uncommon.

Crested Engina (1") 2.5 cm
Engina jugosa (C. B. Adams, 1852). Gulf of California to Ecuador; Galapagos. Offshore to 37 m; uncommon.

Banded Engina (0.6") 1.5 cm
Engina zonalis (Lamarck, 1822). Tropical Indo-Pacific. Shallow water; common. Syn.: *zonata* Reeve.

North's Long Whelk (2") 5 cm
Northia pristis (Deshayes, in Lamarck, 1844). West Mexico to Ecuador. Shallow water; moderately common.

Dire Whelk (1.5") 3.5 cm
Searlesia dira (Reeve, 1846). Alaska to Monterey, California. On rocks at low tide; common.

Clarke's False Cominella (0.8") 2 cm *Tasmeuthria clarkei* (Tenison-Woods, 1875). Australia; Tasmania. Shallow water; moderately common.

Speckled Whelk (2") 5 cm
Cominella adspersa (Bruguière, 1789). New Zealand. Sand flats and rocky ground. Solid shell.

Quoy's Whelk (0.8") 2 cm
Cominella quoyana (A. Adams, 1854). New Zealand. Rocky or sandy ground offshore; uncommon.

Basket Whelk   (1.5″) 4 cm
Cominella virgata H. & A. Adams, 1853. Northern New Zealand. On rocks in sheltered places; common.

Striped Burnupena   (1.5″) 4 cm
Burnupena papyracea form *tigrina* (Kiener, 1834). Cape Agulhas to East London, S. Africa. Rocky shores; common.

Girdled Burnupena   (2″) 5 cm
Burnupena papyracea form *cincta* (Röding, 1798). South Africa; Angola. Intertidal pools in crevices; common.

Spindle Euthria   (2.3″) 6 cm
Buccinulum corneum (L., 1758). Mediterranean. Offshore to 30 m; uncommon. A thick solid shell.

Large Lined Whelk   (1.5″) 4 cm
Buccinulum lineum (Martyn, 1784). Northern New Zealand. Intertidal stones; common. Variable.

Powell's Lined Whelk   (2″) 5 cm
Buccinulum pallidum Finlay, 1928, form *powelli* Ponder, 1971. New Zealand. Intertidal rocks; uncommon.

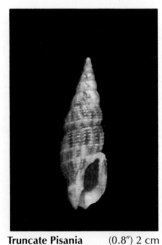

Truncate Pisania   (0.8″) 2 cm
Pisania truncata (Hinds, 1844). Japan; tropical Pacific. Shallow water; moderately common. Usually lacks early whorls.

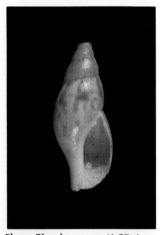

Flame Pisania   (1.5″) 4 cm
Pisania ignea (Gmelin, 1791). Tropical Indo-Pacific. Shallow water; common. Syn.: *flammulatum* Quoy & Gaimard.

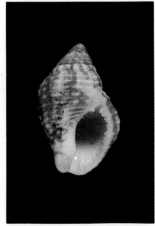

Tinted Pisania   (1″) 2.5 cm
Pisania tincta (Conrad, 1846). S.E. United States and West Indies. Intertidal and offshore; moderately common.

Miniature Triton Trumpet   (1.2″) 3 cm *Pisania pusio* (L., 1758). S.E. Florida, W. Indies; Brazil; Bermuda. Shallow water; moderately common.

Striate Pisania   (1.2″) 3 cm
Pisania striata (Gmelin, 1791). Mediterranean; Azores. Intertidal rocks; common. Syn.: *maculosa* Lamarck.

Brown-lined Truncaria
    (1.2″) 3 cm
Truncaria brunneocincta (Dall, 1896). Panama. Dredged at 100 m; rare. Holotype illustrated.

Cuming's Metula (1.5") 3.7 cm
Metula cumingii A. Adams, 1853. West Africa (Senegal). Shallow water; uncommon.

Pink Metula (1.5") 3.8 cm
Metula amosi Vanatta, 1913. Panama. Offshore in moderately deep water; uncommon.

Banded Pisania (1.1") 3 cm
Appisania fasciculata (Reeve, 1848). Philippines; S.W. Pacific. Shallow reefs; uncommon.

Hazel-brown Nassa (0.6")
1.5 cm *Gussonea compacta* (Nordsieck, 1968). Mediterranean. Shallow water; common. Family Nassariidae.

Tranquebar Goblet (1.5") 4 cm
Cantharus tranquebaricus (Gmelin, 1791). Southern Asia. Shallow water; common.

Ridged Goblet (1.5") 4 cm
Cantharus spiralis (Gray, 1839). Indian Ocean. Among intertidal rocks; common.

Waved Goblet (1.4") 3.5 cm
Cantharus undosus (L., 1758). Tropical Indo-Pacific. On muddy rocks and under dead coral; common.

Gray Goblet (0.7") 1.8 cm
Cantharus assimilis (Reeve, 1845). W. Africa; Cape Verde Is. Under stones in shallow water; common.

Elegant Goblet (1.8") 4.5 cm
Cantharus elegans (Griffith & Pidgeon, 1834). Baja California to Peru. On intertidal rocks; common.

Smoky Goblet (1") 2.5 cm
Cantharus fumosus (Dillwyn, 1817). Indo-Pacific. Shallow water; moderately uncommon. Syn.: *proteus* Reeve.

Wagner's Goblet (1") 2.5 cm
Cantharus wagneri (Anton, 1839). Tropical Pacific. Shallow water; moderately uncommon.

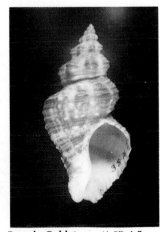

Pagoda Goblet (1.8") 4.5 cm
Cantharus pagodus (Reeve, 1846). W. Mexico to Panama. Shallow water; uncommon.

Strawberry Goblet (1") 2.5 cm
Pollia fragaria (Wood, 1828). Indian Ocean. Shallow water; uncommon. Syn.: *carolinae* Kiener; *bella* Reeve.

Beautiful Goblet (1") 2.5 cm
Pollia pulchra (Reeve, 1846). Indo-W. Pacific. Shallow water; uncommon.

Measle-mouth Cantharus (1") 2.5 cm
Cantharus sanguinolentus (Duclos, 1833). W. Mexico to Ecuador. Subtidal; common.

Ringed Cantharus (1") 2.5 cm
Cantharus ringens (Reeve, 1846). W. Mexico to Ecuador. Intertidal; common.

Pale Goblet (1.8") 4.5 cm
Solenosteira pallida (Broderip & Sowerby, 1829). Panama. Shallow water; moderately common.

Fusiform Goblet (2") 5 cm
Solenosteira fusiformis (Blainville, 1832). Panama to Peru. Intertidal rocks; common.

Canete's Whelk (2.5") 6 cm
Bartschia canetae (Clench & Aguayo, 1944). Off Cuba in 600 m; rare. Holotype illus.

Spout Goblet (1.5") 4 cm
Triumphis subrostrata (Wood, 1828). West Mexico to Colombia. Mud flats; locally common.

Ethiop Macron (2.5") 6.5 cm
Macron aethiops (Reeve, 1847). W. Mexico; common. Syn.: *kellettii* A. Adams.

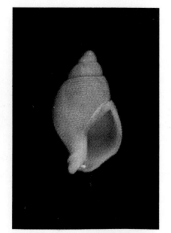

Swollen Florida Whelk (1") 2.5 cm
Ptychosalpinx globulus (Dall, 1889). Florida Straits and Bahamas. Deep water; rare.

Bartsch Whelk (1.5") 4 cm
Bartschia significans Rehder, 1943. Southern Florida. Deep water; uncommon.

Little Turnip Whelk (2") 5 cm
Tomlinia rapulum (Reeve, 1846). Malaya; Indonesia. Uncommon.

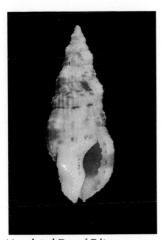

Maculated Dwarf Triton
(2.5") 6 cm
Colubraria muricata (Lightfoot, 1786). Indo-Pacific. Uncommon. Syn.: *maculosa* Gmelin.

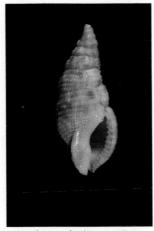

Twisted Dwarf Triton (2") 5 cm
Colubraria tortuosa (Reeve, 1844). Indo-W. Pacific. Reefs; uncommon. Syn.: *distorta* S. & W., not Lamarck.

Shiny Dwarf Triton (1.7") 4.5 cm
Colubraria nitidula (Sowerby, 1833) Tropical Indo-Pacific. Shallow water; uncommon.

Fantome's Dwarf Triton (1.5") 4 cm *Colubraria fantomei* Garrard, 1961. Japan to Australia; uncommon. Syn.: *castanea* Kuroda & Habe.

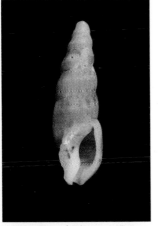

Narrow Dwarf Triton (1") 2 cm *Colubraria alfredensis* Bartsch, 1915. Port Alfred, S. Africa. Beached; uncommon. Holotype illustrated.

Obscure Dwarf Triton
(1.2") 3 cm
Colubraria obscura (Reeve, 1844). Florida to Brazil. Shallow reefs; uncommon.

Princely Dwarf Triton
(3") 7.5 cm
Colubraria procera (Sowerby, 1832). S.W. Mexico. Under rocks to 20 m; moderately rare.

Souverbie's Dwarf Triton (1.5") 3.5 cm *Colubraria souverbii* (Reeve, 1844). Philippines. 50 to 100 m; uncommon.

Spiral Babylon (2.5") 6.5 cm
Babylonia spirata (L., 1758). Indian Ocean. In mud to 60 m; common.

Japanese Babylon (3") 7.5 cm
Babylonia japonica (Reeve, 1842). Japan; Taiwan. Offshore 10-20 m; common. Has a dark brown periostracum.

Areola Babylon (2.5") 6.5 cm
Babylonia areolata (Link, 1807). S.E. Asia. On sand 10-20 m; common. Suture deep but not channeled.

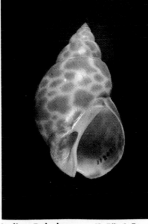

Indian Babylon (2.5") 6.5 cm
Babylonia zeylanica (Bruguière, 1789). Indian Ocean. Offshore; common. Siphonal canal tinged violet.

Pallid Babylon   (1.5″) 4 cm
Babylonia pallida (Perry, 1811). S.E. Asia; Indonesia. Offshore; common. Not *B. pallida* Kira.

Borneo Babylon   (1.5″) 4 cm
Babylonia borneensis (Sowerby, 1864). East Indies. Shallow water; uncommon.

Lutose Babylon   (2″) 5 cm
Babylonia lutosa (Lamarck, 1822). E. Asia. In mud; common.

Spotted Babylon   (1.5″) 4 cm
Babylonia papillaris (Sowerby, 1825). S. Africa. Offshore to 95 m; uncommon.

Bodalla Babylon   (1″) 2.5 cm
Zemira bodalla Garrard, 1966. Southern Queensland. On mud at 160 m; moderately common. In Olividae?

Common Northern Buccinum
                  (3″) 7.5 cm
Buccinum undatum L., 1758. Arctic Seas to New Jersey and to Portugal. 2-200 m; abundant.

Finely-striate Buccinum
                  (3.5″) 8 cm
Buccinum striatissimum Sowerby, 1899. Alaska to Japan. Deep water; uncommon.

Silky Buccinum   (2.5″) 6 cm
Buccinum scalariforme Möller, 1842. Arctic Seas to Wash. and Maine. Offshore; common. Syn.: *tenue* Gray, not Schröter.

Polar Buccinum   (2.5″) 6 cm
Buccinum polare Gray, 1839. Arctic Seas to Japan, to Alaska; N. Europe. Offshore; common.

Yellow-mouth Buccinum
                  (3″) 7.5 cm
Buccinum leucostoma Lischke, 1872. Japan. 50 to 60 m. Syn.: *chartium* Dall.

Flaky Buccinum   (3″) 7.5 cm
Buccinum hydrophanum Hancock, 1846. Canadian Arctic to Grand Banks. Offshore; common.

Angulate Buccinum   (2.5″) 6 cm
Buccinum angulosum Gray, 1839. Bering Sea; Alaska. Offshore; uncommon.

Zelotes Buccinum (2.5") 6 cm
Buccinum zelotes Dall, 1907. Sea of Japan. Deep water; uncommon. Holotype illustrated.

Isaotaki Buccinum (3") 7.5 cm
Buccinum isaotakii Kira, 1959 (1962). Sea of Japan. Deep water; uncommon.

Nippon Buccinum (2.5") 5 cm
Buccinum niponense Dall, 1907. Offshore, southern Japan. Uncommon.

Middendorff's Buccinum (4") 10 cm
Buccinum middendorffi Verkruzen, 1882. Arctic Seas; Japan; Siberia. Common.

Humphreys's Buccinum (3") 7 cm
Buccinum humphreysianum Bennett, 1825. Circumboreal; Japan; N. America. Common.

Torr's Whelk (2.5") 6 cm
Godfreyna torri Verco, 1909. Southern Australia. Offshore; common.

Ample Fragile Buccinum (1.5") 4 cm
Volutharpa ampullacea (Middendorff, 1848). Arctic Seas. Offshore; common.

SWAMP CONCHS, MELON CONCHS FAMILY MELONGENIDAE

Tropical in nature, this group of large, operculate conchs is usually found in brackish or muddy water near mangroves. They are carnivorous, feeding mostly on oysters and clams. There are about 30 species.

West Indian Crown Conch (5") 12 cm *Melongena melongena* (L., 1758). West Indies. Muddy, brackish water; intertidal; common.

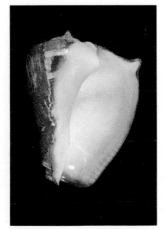

Pacific Crown Conch (6") 15 cm
Melongena patula (Broderip & Sowerby, 1829). W. Mexico to N. Ecuador. Intertidal mud creeks; common.

Common Crown Conch (3") 7.5 cm
Melongena corona (Gmelin, 1791). Florida to N.E. Mexico. Mangrove areas; abundant. Many variable forms.

Giant Hairy Melongena (6") 15 cm
Pugilina morio (L., 1758). Trinidad to Brazil; West Africa. Mangrove areas; common.

Spiral Melongena (6") 15 cm
Pugilina cochlidium (L., 1758).
Indian Ocean. Shallow, muddy
water. Syn.: *wardiana* Iredale.

Nutmeg Melongena (2.5") 7 cm
Volema myristica Röding, 1798.
S.W. Pacific. Shallow water,
sandy mud; common. Syn.: *ga-leodes* Lamarck.

Pear Melongena (2") 5 cm
Volema paradisiaca Röding,
1798. Indian Ocean. Intertidal
to 2 m; common. Syn.: *pyrum*
Gmelin, not Linnaeus.

(left) **Tuba False Fusus** (6") 14 cm
Hemifusus tuba (Gmelin, 1791).
Japan. (right) **Ternate False Fusus.** *H. ternatanus* (Gmelin).
S.E. Asia. Both common.

Thick-tail False Fusus (10")
25 cm *Hemifusus crassicaudus*
(Philippi, 1849). Indian Ocean
to Japan. Common. Syn.: *tuba*
of Kira.

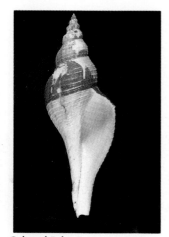

Colossal False Fusus (10") 25 cm
Hemifusus colosseus (La-marck, 1816). S.E. Asia; Taiwan.
Offshore; common.

Australian Trumpet (30") 80 cm
Syrinx aruanus (L., 1758). North
Australia. Intertidal to 10 m; lo-cally common. Periostracum
thick, gray.

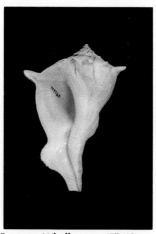

Perverse Whelk (7") 18 cm
Busycon perversum (L., 1758).
N.E. Mexico. Offshore to 20 m;
on sand bottom; uncommon.
Syn.: *kieneri* Philippi.

Lightning Whelk (to 16") 40 cm
Busycon contrarium (Conrad,
1840). S.E. United States. Subti-dal to 30 m; in sand. Large spec-imens white. Common.

Knobbed Whelk (8") 20 cm
Busycon carica (Gmelin, 1791).
Massachusetts to N.E. Florida.
Subtidal to 10 m; common.

Kiener's Whelk (7") 18 cm
Busycon carica subspecies *eli-ceans* (Montfort, 1810). North
Carolina to central east Florida.
Offshore; common.

Pear Conch (4") 10 cm
Busycon spiratum (Lamarck,
1816). S.E. United States and
N.E. Mexico. Shallow water;
common. Syn.: *pyrum* Dill.

Channeled Whelk (7") 18 cm
Busycon canaliculatum (L., 1758). Cape Cod, Massachusetts, to N.E. Florida. Common. Introduced to California 1948.

Turnip Whelk (5") 13 cm
Busycon coarctatum (Sowerby, 1825). Bay of Campeche, E. Mexico. Offshore; uncommon.

NASSA MUD SNAILS
FAMILY NASSARIIDAE

The mud snails, or basket shells, are shallow water, usually intertidal, mud dwellers. They occur in large colonies, and are scavengers. A few of the several hundred species live in deep water. The operculum is chitinous. The genus *Nassa* Lamarck is a synonym of *Nassarius*.

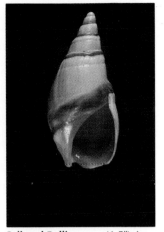

Callused Bullia (1.5") 4 cm
Bullia callosa (Wood, 1828). South Africa. Offshore to 30 m; common.

Annulate Bullia (2.5") 6 cm
Bullia annulata (Lamarck, 1816). False Bay to Port Alfred, S. Africa. Offshore to 100 m; common.

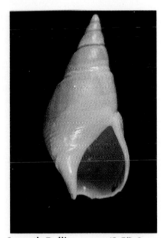

Smooth Bullia (2.5") 6 cm
Bullia tenuis (Reeve, 1846). False Bay to Natal, S. Africa. Offshore to 120 m; common. Syn.: *larva* Bartsch, 1915.

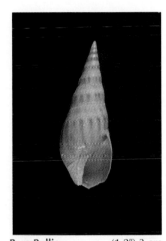

Pure Bullia (1.2") 3 cm
Bullia pura Melvill, 1885. South Africa. Subtidal; common. Syn.: *balteatus* Sowerby; *kraussi* Turton.

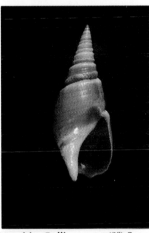

Mauritius Bullia (2") 5 cm
Bullia mauritiana (Gray, 1839). Indian Ocean. Subtidal; common. Syn.: *grayi* Reeve.

Ribbon Bullia (1.3") 3 cm
Bullia vittata (L., 1767). Indian Ocean. Intertidal, mud flats; common. Syn.: *buccinoidea* & *granulosa* Lamarck.

Gradated Bullia (2.5") 6 cm
Bullia gradata (Deshayes, 1844). E. South America. Subtidal; common. Syn.: *cochlidium* Kiener.

One-ridge Bullia (1.5") 4 cm
Bullia monilifera (Kiener, 1834). E. South America. Subtidal; common. Syn.: *armata* Gray.

Karachi Bullia (2") 5 cm
Bullia kurrachensis Angas, 1877. Karachi, Pakistan. Shallow water; locally common.

Globular Bullia   (1.5″) 4 cm
Bullia globulosa (Kiener, 1834).
S. Brazil to Argentina. Subtidal
on sand; common.

Myristic Nassa   (0.5″) 1.2 cm
Nassarius myristicatus (Hinds,
1844). W. Central America. Offshore; common.

Glossy Bullia   (1″) 2.5 cm
Cyllene glabrata A. Adams,
1851. Philippines. Offshore to
30 m; moderately common.

Eastern Mud Snail   (1″) 2.5 cm
Ilyanassa obsoleta (Say, 1822).
Nova Scotia to N. Florida. Mud
flats; abundant. Also California.

Pimpled Nassa   (1.5″) 4 cm
Nassarius papillosus (L., 1758).
Indo-Pacific. Intertidal to 10 m;
moderately common.

Glans Nassa   (1.5″) 4 cm
Nassarius glans (L., 1758). Indo-
Pacific. Intertidal; common.
Syn.: *particeps* Hedley; *li-
neatus* Röding.

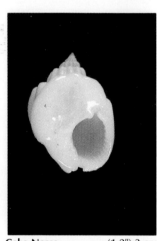

Cake Nassa   (1.2″) 3 cm
Nassarius arcularius (L., 1758).
Central and S.W. Pacific. Shal-
low sandy bays; abundant.
Syn.: *coronatus* Link; *plicata*
Röding.

Cone-shaped Nassa   (1″) 3 cm
Nassarius conoidalis (Deshayes, 1832). Indian Ocean.
Shallow water; common. Syn.:
clathrata Lamarck, not Born.

Triton Nassa   (1″) 2.5 cm
Nassarius tritoniformis (Kiener,
1841). Senegal, West Africa.
Offshore; common.

Torben Wolf Nassa   (1″) 2.5 cm
Nassarius wolffi Knudsen, 1956.
South West Africa. Offshore;
uncommon.

Clathrate Nassa   (0.5″) 1.2 cm
Nassarius clathratus (Born,
1778). Mediterranean and N.W.
Africa. Intertidal sand; common.

New Zealand Nassa   (0.8″) 2 cm
Nassarius aoteanus (Finlay,
1927). New Zealand. Shallow
water; common. Syn.: *coronatus* E. A. Smith.

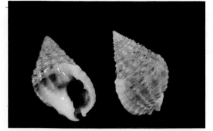

Common Eastern Nassa   (0.5") 1.2 cm
Nassarius vibex (Say, 1822). S.E. United States. Intertidal sand flats; abundant.

Latticed Nassa   (0.5") 1.2 cm
Nassarius cinisculus (Reeve, 1853). West Indies. Weedy shallows; common.

New England Nassa   (0.7") 1.8 cm
Nassarius trivittatus (Say, 1822). East United States. Offshore to 50 m; common.

Lovely Nassa   (0.7") 1.8 cm
Nassarius venustus (Dunker, 1847). Indo-Pacific Intertidal sand; uncommon.

Demoulia Nassa   (0.7") 1.8 cm
Nassarius desmoulioides (Sowerby, 1903). West and South Africa. 40 to 90 m; locally common.

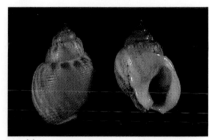

Mutable Nassa   (1.3") 3 cm
Nassarius mutabilis (L., 1758). Mediterranean; Black Sea; W. Africa. Offshore; common. Syn.: *inflata* Lamarck.

Netted Nassa   (1.4") 3 cm
Nassarius reticulatus (L., 1758). W. Europe; Mediterranean. Subtidal, mud and rocks; abundant.

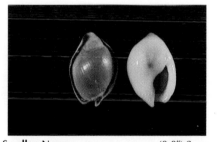

Swollen Nassa   (0.8") 2 cm
Nassarius gibbosulus (L., 1758). East Mediterranean. Intertidal, sand; common. Syn.: *circumcinctus* A. Adams.

Horn Nassa   (0.8") 2 cm
Nassarius cornicula (Olivi, 1792). Mediterranean and West Africa. Intertidal; common. Many synonyms; *olivacea* Risso; *politum* Bivona.

Gloomy Nassa   (0.4") 1 cm
Nassarius moestus (Hinds, 1844). W. Mexico. Intertidal; common. Syn.: *brunneostoma* Stearns, 1893.

Fat Nassa   (0.8") 2 cm
Nassarius corpulentus (C. B. Adams, 1852). W. Mexico to Ecuador. Subtidal, sand; common.

Western Mud Nassa   (0.8") 2 cm
Nassarius tiarula (Kiener, 1841). California to W. Mexico. Intertidal; common. Syn.: *tegula* Reeve; *major* Stearns.

Red-banded Nassa   (0.8") 2 cm
Nassarius pyrrhus (Menke, 1843). South Australia; Tasmania; New Zealand. Intertidal sands; common.

Splendid Nassa   (1.2") 3 cm
Nassarius speciosus (A. Adams, 1852). South Africa. Offshore to 90 m.

Pyramid Nassa   (0.8") 2 cm
Nassarius pyramidalis (A. Adams, 1852). South Africa. Subtidal to 200 m; common. Syn.: *filmerae* Sowerby; *rufanensis* Sowerby.

Distorted Nassa   (1") 2.5 cm
Nassarius distortus A. Adams, 1852. Indo-Pacific. Shallow water; common. Syn.: *monile* Kiener (not Linnaeus).

Bright Nassa   (0.7") 1.8 cm
Nassarius candens (Hinds, 1844). Marquesas Islands, Polynesia. Subtidal; locally uncommon.

Coronate Nassa   (1.3") 3 cm
Nassarius coronatus (Bruguière, 1789). Indo-Pacific. Intertidal, gray sands; common. Syn.: *bronni* Philippi.

Burned Nassa   (1") 2.5 cm
Nassarius crematus (Hinds, 1844). Japan— S.W. Pacific. Shallow water; uncommon. Syn.: *siquijorensis* A. Adams; *crenulatus* Lamarck.

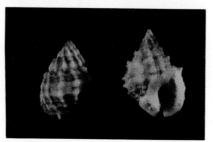

Horrid Nassa   (0.5") 1.2 cm
Nassarius horridus (Dunker, 1847). Indo-Pacific. Intertidal; common. Syn.: *muricatus* Quoy & Gaimard; *curtus* Gould.

Margarite Nassa   (1") 2.5 cm
Nassarius margaritiferus Dunker, 1847. Indo-Pacific. Intertidal; common. Syn.: *costellifera* A. Adams; *reticulatus* Quoy & Gaimard.

Olive Nassa   (1") 2.5 cm
Nassarius olivaceus (Bruguière, 1789). Indo-Pacific. Subtidal mud flats; common. Syn.: *badius* A. Adams.

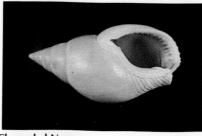

Channeled Nassa   (1.2") 3 cm
Nassarius dorsatus (Röding, 1798). Indo-Pacific. Intertidal flats; common. Syn.: *canaliculatus* Lamarck.

Gaudy Nassa   (1") 2.5 cm
Nassarius gaudiosus (Hinds, 1844). Indo-Pacific. Intertidal to 5 m; common. Syn.: *reeveanus* Dunker.

Rough Nassa (1.2") 3 cm
Nassarius hirtus (Kiener, 1834). Hawaii and Polynesia. Subtidal to 20 m; common. Syn.: *seminodosa* A. Adams.

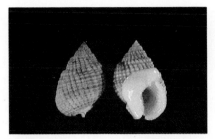

Whitish Nassa (0.7") 1.8 cm
Nassarius albescens (Dunker, 1846). Indo-Pacific. Shallow; coral sand; common. Syn.: *bicolor* Rousseau.

Distended Nassa (1") 2.5 cm
Nassarius sufflatus (Gould, 1860). Indian Ocean to Japan. Intertidal to 10 m; common. Syn.: *balteatus* Lischke; *kurodai* Tomlin.

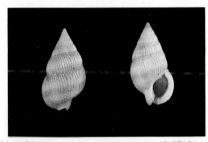

Neat Nassa (0.8") 2 cm
Nassarius concinnus (Powis, 1835). Indo-Pacific. Offshore; uncommon. Syn.: *abyssicola* A. Adams; *crebrilineata* Rousseau.

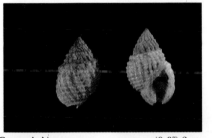

Gruner's Nassa (0.8") 2 cm
Nassarius gruneri (Dunker, 1846). S.W. Pacific. Intertidal; common. Syn.: *hispidus* Reeve.

Granulated Nassa (0.7") 1.8 cm
Nassarius graniferus (Kiener, 1834). S.W. Pacific. Intertidal to 6 m, coral sand; common. Syn.: *verrucosus* Bruguière.

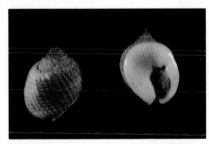

Globose Nassa (0.7") 1.8 cm
Nassarius globosus Quoy & Gaimard, 1833. S.W. Pacific. Intertidal flats; abundant. Syn.: *gibbosuloidea* Habe & Kosuge.

Black Nassa (1") 2.5 cm
Nassarius pullus (L., 1758). Indo-Pacific. Mud flats; common. Syn.: *thersites* Bruguière; *bimaculosus* A. Adams.

Loaded Nassa (0.7") 1.8 cm
Nassarius oneratus (Deshayes, 1863). Indo-Pacific. Intertidal; uncommon. Syn.: *obliqua* Rousseau.

Cyclops Nassa (0.3") 5 mm
Cyclope pellucida (Risso, 1826). Mediterranean. Subtidal, sand; common.

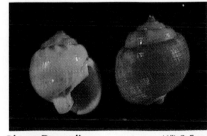

Obtuse Demoulia (1") 2.5 cm
Demoulia obtusata (Link, 1807). West Africa. Subtidal, sand; common. Syn.: *pinguis* A. Adams.

Blunted Demoulia (1") 2.5 cm
Demoulia retusa (Lamarck, 1816). South Africa. Offshore 10 to 110 m; common. Variable patterns.

One-banded Nassa (0.8") 2 cm
Nassarius cuvierii (Payraudeau, 1826). Mediterranean. Intertidal; common. Syn.: *unifasciatus* Kiener; and others.

Giant Western Nassa (2") 5 cm
Nassarius fossatus (Gould, 1849). British Columbia to W. Mexico. Intertidal, sandy mud; abundant.

TULIPS AND SPINDLES
FAMILY FASCIOLARIIDAE

The tulips and horse conchs are large carnivorous snails, without strong plicae or folds on the columella, usually with a good periostracum, and with a thick, horny, clawlike operculum. Mainly tropical shallow water.

Florida Horse Conch (2 ') 60 cm
Pleuroploca gigantea (Kiener, 1840). S.E. United States and N.E. Mexico. Subtidal to 30 m; common. Young are orange.

Panama Horse Conch
(1.5') 50 cm
Pleuroploca princeps (Sowerby, 1825). W. Mexico to Ecuador. Subtidal; common. Operculum ridged.

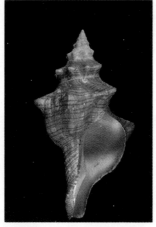

Trapezium Horse Conch
(6") 14 cm
Pleuroploca trapezium (L., 1758). Indo-Pacific. Shallow water; common.

Filamentous Horse Conch
(5") 12 cm
Pleuroploca filamentosa (Röding, 1798). Indo-Pacific. Common.

Smooth Horse Conch
(3") 7.5 cm
Pleuroploca glabra (Dunker, 1882). Japan. Intertidal rocks to 3 m; common.

Persian Horse Conch (5") 12 cm
Pleuroploca persica (Reeve, 1847). Indian Ocean. Offshore to 10 m; rare. Syn.: *ponderosa* Philippi.

South African Horse Conch
(6") 15 cm
Pleuroploca ocellifera (Lamarck, 1816). South Africa. 20 to 150 m; common. Syn.: *verruculatus* Lamarck.

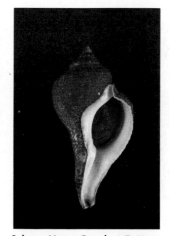

Salmon Horse Conch (4") 10 cm
Pleuroploca salmo (Wood, 1828). W. Mexico to Panama. Offshore; common. Syn.: *valenciennesi* Kiener.

Granose Horse Conch
(5") 12 cm
Pleuroploca granosa (Broderip, 1832). Gulf of California to N. Peru. Intertidal; common.

Heynemann's Horse Conch
(6") 15 cm
Pleuroploca heynemanni
(Dunker, 1876). South Africa.
Subtidal to 100 m; uncommon.
Syn.: *altredensis* Bartsch.

Drab Horse Conch (4") 10 cm
Pleuroploca lugubris (Reeve,
1847). South Africa. Intertidal
and offshore to 50 m; common.
Syn.: *badia* Krauss.

Box-tree Conch (3.5") 9 cm
Pleuroploca buxea (Reeve,
1847). W. Africa; Cape Verde Is.
Shallow water; locally common. Syn.: *fischeriana* Petit.

Box-tree Conch (3.5") 9 cm
Pleuroploca buxea (Reeve,
1847). The holotype of *Latirus
maximus* Sowerby, illustrated
here, is merely an old shell.

Banded Tulip (3.5") 9 cm
Fasciolaria lilium hunteria
(Perry, 1811). North Carolina to
Texas. Intertidal and down to 12
m; common. Neotype illus.

Branham's Tulip (4.5") 11.5 cm
Fasciolaria lilium branhamae
Rehder & Abbott, 1951. Gulf of
Campeche, Texas. Deep water;
uncommon. Holotype illus.

Bullis's Tulip (5") 12 cm
Fasciolaria lilium bullisi Lyons,
1972. Off N.W. Florida.
Dredged 73 - 119 m; uncommon. Holotype illustrated.

True Tulip (6") 15 cm
Fasciolaria tulipa (L., 1758).
Florida to Texas; W. Indies; Brazil. On sand in shallow water;
common.

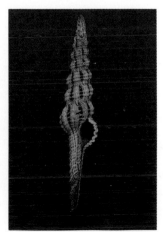

Precious Stone Shell (1.5") 4 cm
Latirolagena smaragdula (L.,
1758). Indo-Pacific. Intertidal
rocks; common. Syn.: *rustica*
Lamarck.

Thorn Latirus (1.5") 4 cm
Opeatostoma pseudodon (Burrow, 1815). W. Mexico to Peru.
Among rocks at low tide; common. Syn.: *cingulatum* Lamarck.

Spear Latirus (2") 5 cm
Dolicholatirus lancea (Gmelin,
1791). Tropical Indo-Pacific.
Coral reefs; uncommon. Syn.:
lanceola Reeve.

Cyrtulus Spindle (3") 7.5 cm
Cyrtulus serotinus Hinds, 1844.
Polynesia; rare. Only living
species in the genus *Cyrtulus*.

Barclay's Latirus   (2.3") 6 cm
Latirus polygonus (Gmelin, 1791). Indo-Pacific. Intertidal reefs; common. Form *barclayi* Reeve, 1847, on right.

Many-angled Latirus (3") 7.5 cm
Latirus polygonus (Gmelin, 1791). The black zones present in typical form.

Nodular Latirus   (3") 7.5 cm
Latirus nodatus (Gmelin, 1791). Tropical Indo-Pacific. Coral reef flats; uncommon. Syn.: *rigidus* Wood.

Gibbose Latirus   (2.7") 7 cm
Latirus gibbulus (Gmelin, 1791). Indo-W. Pacific. On reef flats in shallow water. Usually heavily encrusted.

Belcher's Latirus   (2") 5 cm
Latirus belcheri (Reeve, 1847). W. Pacific; moderately common.

Ornate Latirus   (2.5") 6 cm
Latirus amplustris (Dillwyn, 1817). Tropical Pacific. Coral areas; uncommon. Syn.: *aplustre* Sowerby.

Squamose Latirus   (1.4") 3.5 cm
Latirus squamosus Pease, 1863. Polynesia; uncommon. Indian Ocean records unconfirmed.

Bleeding Latirus   (2") 5 cm
Latirus sanguifluus (Reeve, 1847). Polynesia. Among corals in shallow water; uncommon.

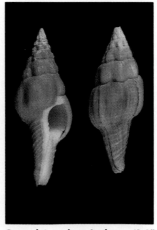

Prismatic Latirus   (2") 5 cm
Latirus iris (Lightfoot, 1786). Polynesia; uncommon. Periostracum iridescent when wet. Syn.: *prismaticus* Martyn.

Tower Latirus   (2") 5 cm
Latirus turritus (Gmelin, 1791). Indo-W. Pacific. Under dead coral or rocks in shallow water; moderately common.

Central American Latirus (2.2") 5.5 cm *Latirus mediamericanus* Hertlein & Strong, 1951. W. Mexico to Ecuador; uncommon. Syn.: *acuminatus* Wood.

Filose Latirus   (2") 5 cm
Latirus filosus (Schubert & Wagner, 1829). W. Africa. Offshore; uncommon.

Nagasaki Latirus (2″) 5 cm
Latirus nagasakiensis E. A. Smith, 1880. Southern Japan. Offshore; uncommon.

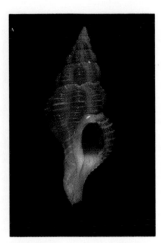

Kanda Latirus (1.5″) 4 cm
Latirus kanda Kuroda, 1950. Japan. Shallow water; uncommon.

Walker's Latirus (1″) 2.5 cm
Latirus walkeri Melvill, 1895. Western Australia. Among rocks in shallow water; moderately common.

Pagoda Latirus (1.2″) 3 cm
Latirus pagodaeformis Melvill, 1899. Northern Arabian Sea; Persian Gulf. Moderately deep water; rare.

Nassa-like Latirus (1.5″) 4 cm
Latirus nassoides (Reeve, 1847). Philippines. Shallow reefs; uncommon.

Paetel's Latirus (2″) 5 cm
Latirus paetelianus (Kobelt, 1874). Indo-W. Pacific. Among rocks; common. Solid brown or banded.

Strange Latirus (2.5″) 6.5 cm
Latirus abnormis (Sowerby, 1894). Pondoland; Natal; Zululand. Dredged down to 80 m; uncommon.

Gold-banded Latirus (1″) 2.5 cm
Latirus noumeensis (Crosse, 1870). Tropical Indo-Pacific. Intertidal and offshore; uncommon. Syn.: *aureocincta* Sby.

Armed Latirus (1.4″) 3.5 cm
Latirus armatus A. Adams, 1854. West Africa; Madeira; Canary Islands. Offshore; uncommon.

Brown-lined Latirus (3″) 7.5 cm
Latirus infundibulum (Gmelin, 1791). W. Indies to Brazil, S. Florida. Offshore to 60 m; uncommon.

Trochlear Latirus (2″) 5 cm
Latirus cariniferus (Lamarck, 1816). S.E. Florida; W. Indies. Rocky reefs; uncommon. Syn.: *macgintyi* Pilsbry.

Squat Latirus (2.5″) 6.5 cm
Latirus tumens Carpenter, 1856. West Mexico to Ecuador. On rocks 10 - 20 m; uncommon.

Hemphill's Latirus (2.2") 5.5 cm
Latirus hemphilli Hertlein &
Strong, 1951. Baja California to
Panama. Dredged to 27 m; un-
common.

Frilled Latirus (1.8") 4.5 cm
Latirus concentricus (Reeve,
1847). W. Mexico to Ecuador.
Offshore; uncommon. Syn.:
spadiceus Reeve.

Socorro Latirus (1.5") 4 cm
Latirus socorroensis Hertlein &
Strong, 1951. Off W. Mexico to
Clipperton Is. Dredged to 42
m; uncommon.

Vara's Latirus (3") 7 cm
Latirus varai Bullock, 1970. Off
east Cuba in 200 m. Rare. Holotype illus.

Waxy Latirus (2") 5 cm
Leucozonia cerata (Wood,
1828). Gulf of California to Panama; Galapagos. On rocks at
low tide; common.

White-spotted Latirus (.8") 2 cm
Leucozonia ocellata (Gmelin,
1791). S.E. Florida; W. Indies to
Brazil. Under intertidal rocks;
common.

Three-row Latirus (1.2") 3 cm
Latirus triserialis Lamarck, 1822.
West Africa. Uncommon.

Fleshy Peristernia (1") 2.5 cm
Peristernia incarnata (Kiener,
1840). Indo-Pacific. Under intertidal rocks and coral; moderately common.

Fine-net Peristernia
(1.4") 3.5 cm
Peristernia nassatula (Lamarck,
1822). Indo-Pacific. Reef flats;
common. Aperture rosy.

Sloping Peristernia (1.2") 3 cm
Peristernia fastigium (Reeve,
1847). Indo-Pacific. On dead
coral in shallow water; uncommon.

Australian Peristernia (1") 3 cm
Peristernia australiensis (Reeve,
1847). Queensland, Australia.
On intertidal reefs under dead
coral; common.

Philbert's Peristernia (1.2") 3 cm
Peristernia philberti (Récluz,
1844). South China Sea; uncommon. Aperture violet.

Singed Peristernia (1.2″) 3 cm
Peristernia ustulata (Reeve, 1847). Indo-Pacific. Coral areas; common. Syn.: *caledonica* Petit; *marquesana* Ad.

Beautiful Peristernia (1.2″) 3 cm
Peristernia pulchella (Reeve, 1847). Indian Ocean. Muddy sand in moderately deep water; uncommon.

Forskal's Peristernia (1″) 2.5 cm
Peristernia forskali (Tapparone-Canefri, 1879). Indian Ocean. Shallow water; uncommon.

Spiny Peristernia (1.4″) 3.5 cm
Peristernia columbarium (Gmelin, 1791). Central Pacific to Philippines; uncommon. Syn.: *spinosa* Deshayes.

Harford's Spindle (2″) 5 cm
Fusinus harfordii (Stearns, 1871). British Columbia to California. Moderately deep water; rare.

Distaff Spindle (6″) 15 cm
Fusinus colus (L., 1758). Tropical Indo-Pacific. Intertidal sands and offshore; common. Syn.: *tuberculata* Lamarck.

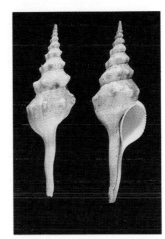

Wavy-edge Spindle (6″) 15 cm
Fusinus undatus (Gmelin, 1791). Tropical Pacific. Offshore; uncommon. All-white shell; brown periostracum.

Salisbury's Spindle (8″) 20 cm
Fusinus salisburyi Fulton, 1930. Japan; Queensland, Australia. Deep water; uncommon.

Giant Spindle (8″) 20 cm
Fusinus novaehollandiae (Reeve, 1848). New S. Wales to S. Australia. Deep water; moderately common.

Rusty Spindle (3.5″) 9 cm
Fusinus perplexus A. Adams, 1864. Form *ferrugineus* Kuroda & Habe. Japan. Offshore; locally common.

Legrand's Spindle (2″) 5 cm
Fusinus undulatus (Perry, 1811). Southern Australia. Common. Syn.: *legrandi* Tenison-Woods.

Granular Spindle (2.5″) 6.5 cm
Fusinus niponicus (E. A. Smith, 1879). Japan; Taiwan. Moderately deep water; uncommon.

Hayashi's Spindle (2") 5 cm
Fusinus hayashii (Habe, 1961). Southern Japan. Dredged at 100 m; rare. *F. niponicus* has longer siphonal canal.

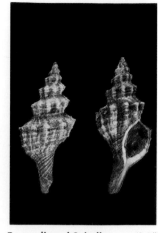

Brown-lipped Spindle (3.5") 9 cm *Fusinus tuberosus* (Reeve, 1847). South of Honshu, Japan. 20-40 m; uncommon. Syn.: *nigrirostratus* E. A. Smith.

Pitcairn Spindle (5") 12.5 cm *Fusinus galatheae bountyi* Rehder & Wilson, 1975. Off Pitcairn Is. Dredged 50-130 m; rare. Holotype illus.

Australian Spindle (4") 10 cm *Fusinus australis* (Quoy & Gaimard, 1833). Southern and western Australia. Shallow water; common.

Nicobar Spindle (4.5") 11.5 cm *Fusinus nicobaricus* (Röding, 1798). Indo-Pacific. Shallow water; common. Syn.: *laticostatus* Deshayes; *variegatus* Perry.

Boettger's Spindle (2") 5 cm *Fusinus boettgeri* (von Maltzan, 1884). West Africa. Offshore; uncommon.

Capart's Spindle (8") 20 cm *Fusinus caparti* Adam & Knudsen, 1969. Off Angola. Dredged at about 80 m; locally common.

White Spindle (3") 7.5 cm *Fusinus albinus* (A. Adams, 1855). Off Angola. Offshore; uncommon.

Kobelt's Spindle (2.5") 6.5 cm *Fusinus kobelti* (Dall, 1877). California. Shallow water to 70 m; moderately common. Holotype illus.

Du Petit's Spindle (8") 20 cm *Fusinus dupetitthouarsi* (Kiener, 1846). Baja California to Ecuador. Intertidal and offshore; moderately common.

Allyn Smith's Spindle (3.5") 9 cm *Fusinus allyni* McLean, 1970. Galapagos and Cocos Is. Dredged 128-146 m; uncommon.

Burnt Spindle (2") 5 cm *Fusinus ambustus* (Gould, 1853). Gulf of California. Mud flats and on rocks at low tide; common.

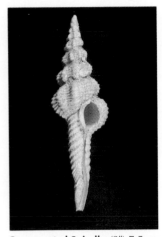

Panama Spindle   (5″) 12.5 cm
Fusinus panamensis Dall, 1908.
W. Mexico to Ecuador. Taken by
shrimp trawlers; common.

Sea Crown Spindle   (3″) 7.5 cm
Fusinus halistreptus (Dall,
1889). Florida Strait; Bahamas.
Deep water; rare. Holotype illus.

Ornamented Spindle (3″) 7.5 cm
Fusinus eucosmius (Dall, 1889).
Florida to Texas. Dredged 30-
100 m; uncommon. Holotype
illustrated.

Ceramic Spindle   (2″) 5 cm
Fusinus ceramidus (Dall, 1889).
Off Barbados. Dredged 140-210
m; rare. Holotype illustrated.

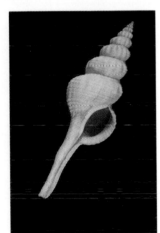

Turnip Spindle   (4″) 10 cm
Fusinus timessus (Dall, 1889).
Florida to Texas. Dredged 40-
120 m; uncommon. May be
white or orange.

Frenguell's Spindle   (4.5″)
11 cm *Fusinus frenguelli* (Carcelles, 1953). Southern Brazil;
Argentina. Dredged 30-160 m
on sand; uncommon.

Steger's Spindle   (5″) 12 cm
Fusinus stegeri Lyons, 1978.
Gulf of Mexico; off west Florida. 180 m. Holotype illustrated.

Coue's Spindle   (4″) 10 cm
Fusinus couei (Petit, 1853). Gulf
of Mexico; Texas. Taken by
shrimp trawlers; common.

Sicilian Spindle   (2.3″) 6 cm
Fusinus syracusanus (L., 1758).
Mediterranean; coast of N.W.
Africa; Canary Is. Offshore 4 to
40 m; common.

Flame Spindle   (3″) 7.5 cm
Propefusus pyrulatus (Reeve,
1847). Southern Australia; Tasmania. Shallow and deeper water; common.

Puzzling Spindle   (1″) 2.5 cm
Sinistralia maroccensis (Gmelin, 1791). W. Africa; Canary Is.
Shallow water, on rocks; uncommon.

OLIVE SHELLS
FAMILY OLIVIDAE

Small, glossy gastropods found
in all tropical and warm seas.
Columella with numerous fine
teeth. True olive shells *(Oliva)*
do not have an operculum.
Their shells are often extremely
variable in color pattern but are
consistent in shape within a
species.

Tent Olive   (3.5") 9 cm
Oliva porphyria (L., 1758). Gulf of California to Panama. Intertidal to 20 m; in sand; moderately common.

Veined Olive   (1.8") 4.5 cm
Oliva spicata (Röding, 1798). Gulf of California to Panama. Shallow water; common. Many synonyms.

Angled Olive   (2.2") 5.5 cm
Oliva incrassata (Lightfoot, 1786). West Mexico to Peru. Sandspits at low tide; common. Rarely golden.

Juliet's Olive   (1.8") 4.5 cm
Oliva julieta Duclos, 1833. Nicaragua to Peru. Offshore; rare living, uncommon dead.

Splendid Olive   (1.8") 4.5 cm
Oliva splendidula Sowerby, 1825. W. Mexico to Panama. Offshore; uncommon. Pattern constant.

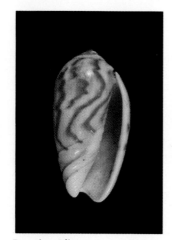

Peruvian Olive   (2") 5 cm
Oliva peruviana Lamarck, 1811. Peru and Chile. Extremely variable with several named color forms; common.

Fusiform Olive   (2") 5 cm
Oliva fulgurator (Röding, 1798). Lower Caribbean. Uncommon. Syn.: *fusiformis* Lamarck.

Lettered Olive   (2.2") 5.5 cm
Oliva sayana Ravenel, 1834. S.E. United States. Common. Syn.: *litterata* Lamarck. Yellow form is *citrina* Johnson.

Netted Olive   (1.5") 4 cm
Oliva reticularis Lamarck, 1810. S.E. Florida to Brazil; Bermuda. Shallow and deeper water; common. Variable pattern.

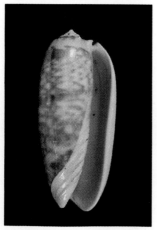

Red-mouth Olive   (2.5") 6.5 cm
Oliva miniacea (Röding, 1798). Tropical Indo-Pacific. Common. Orange aperture. Syn.: *erythrostoma* Lamarck.

Tessellate Olive   (1.2") 3 cm
Oliva tessellata Lamarck, 1811. Eastern Indian Ocean; Pacific. Moderately uncommon. Syn.: *tigrina* Marrat.

Oliva sericea (Röding, 1798). One of the few distinctive color forms of this lovely shell in which the aperture is white, not yellow.

Orange-mouth Olive (3″) 7.5 cm
Oliva sericea (Röding, 1798).
Tropical Indo-Pacific. Uncommon. Varies little in color pattern. Syn.: *textilina* Lam

Ornate Olive (2″) 5 cm
Oliva lignaria Marrat, 1868. Indian Ocean; India to West Australia. Common. Syn.: *ornata* Marrat, not Röding.

Pretty Olive (0.8″) 2 cm
Oliva sidelia Duclos, 1835. Tropical Indo-Pacific. Moderately uncommon. Sometimes all-white. Syn.: *lepida* Duclos.

Tricolor Olive (2.2″) 5.5 cm
Oliva tricolor Lamarck, 1811. Tropical Indo-Pacific. Common. Displays red, green and blue colors together.

Blood Olive (1.3″) 4.5 cm
Oliva reticulata (Röding, 1798). Indo-W. Pacific. Common. Columella bright red. Syn.: *sanguinolenta* Lamarck.

Purple-mouth Olive (2″) 5 cm
Oliva caerulea (Röding, 1798). Tropical Indo-Pacific. Uncommon. Aperture dark violet. Syn.: *episcopalis* Lamarck.

Inflated Olive (1.7″) 4.5 cm
Oliva bulbosa (Röding,1798). Indian Ocean to Indonesia. Common. Several named color forms. Syn.: *inflata* Lamarck.

Tiger Olive (2.2″) 5.5 cm
Oliva tigrina Lamarck, 1811. Tropical Indo-Pacific. Moderately common. Syn.: *glandiformis* Marrat; *fallax* Johnson.

Amethyst Olive (2″) 5 cm
Oliva annulata (Gmelin, 1791). Tropical Indo-Pacific. Common. Several striking color forms.

Amethyst Olive (2″) 5 cm
Oliva annulata (Gmelin, 1791). This common form is *amethystina* Röding, 1798.

Amethyst Olive (2″) 5 cm
Oliva annulata (Gmelin, 1791). Form *mantichora* Duclos, 1835. Upper part of body whorl is noticeably angled.

Hirase's Olive (1.7″) 4.5 cm
Oliva hirasei Kira, 1959. Southern Japan; Taiwan. Below low-tide level; uncommon.

Parkinson's Olive (0.5") 1.2 cm
Oliva parkinsoni Prior, 1975. New Guinea. Offshore; uncommon.

Bulow's Olive (1") 2.5 cm
Oliva buloui Sowerby, 1888. New Guinea; New Britain; Solomons. Uncommon. *O. bulowi* is misspelling.

Red-lip Olive (1.7") 4.5 cm
Oliva rubrolabiata H. Fischer, 1902. New Hebrides; New Caledonia. Moderately rare.

Rufula Olive (1.2") 3 cm
Oliva rufula Duclos, 1835. Philippines; Indonesia. Locally common. Distinctive color pattern consistent.

Lightning Olive (0.8") 2.2 cm
Oliva rufofulgurata Schepman, 1911. New Britain; Kei Island; Indonesia; Philippines. Moderately deep water; rare.

Peg Olive (1") 2.5 cm
Oliva paxillus Reeve, 1850. Indo-Pacific; Hawaii. Common. Syn.: *thomasi* Crosse; *sandwichensis* Pease.

Common Olive (1.2") 3 cm
Oliva oliva (L., 1758). Tropical Indo-Pacific. Shallow water; common. Syn.: *ispidula* of authors.

Oliva oliva (L., 1758). Until recently this was incorrectly referred to as *ispidula* Linné. Variable in somber colors.

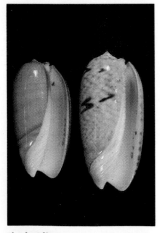

Black Olive (1.5") 4 cm
Oliva vidua (Röding, 1798). Tropical Indo-Pacific. Moderately common. Many named color forms, sometimes black.

Flame Olive (1.4") 3.5 cm
Oliva flammulata Lamarck, 1810. W. Africa; Cape Verde Islands. Shallow water; common. Syn.: *marmorea* Marrat.

Silk-clad Olive (0.8") 2 cm
Oliva panniculata Duclos, 1835. Indo-W. Pacific. Shallow water; moderately rare. Syn.: *williamsi* Melvill & Standen.

Carnelian Olive (0.9") 2.3 cm
Oliva carneola (Gmelin, 1791). Tropical Indo-Pacific. Common. Varies in shape and patterns.

Caldania Olive (0.8") 2 cm
Oliva caldania Duclos, 1835. W. and N. Australia; Indonesia. Moderately common. Syn.: *brettinghami* Bridgman.

Zelinda's Olive (1.5") 4 cm
Oliva zelindae Petuch, 1979. Islands off east Brazil, 2 to 10 m. Rare. Axial riblets.

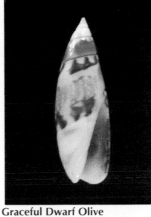

New Zealand Ancilla
(.5") 1.2 cm
Gracilispira novaezelandiae (Sowerby, 1859). Northern New Zealand. In sand offshore; common. Syn.: *firthi* Olsson.

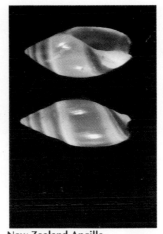

Graceful Dwarf Olive
(0.8") 2 cm
Olivella gracilis (Broderip & Sowerby, 1829). W. Mexico to Panama. Shallow water; common.

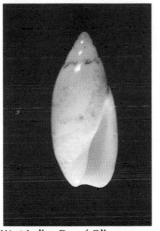

West Indian Dwarf Olive
(1.2") 3 cm
Olivella nivea (Gmelin, 1791). S.E. Florida to Brazil; Bermuda. Intertidal to 50 m; common.

Arrow Dwarf Olive
(0.7") 1.8 cm
Olivella petiolita (Duclos, 1835). West Indies; Caribbean. Uncommon. Syn.: *esther* Dall & Simpson.

Variable Dwarf Olive
(0.4") 1 cm
Olivella mutica (Say, 1822). North Carolina to Florida; Bahamas. Common. Sometimes brightly banded.

Dama Dwarf Olive (0.8") 2 cm
Olivella dama (Wood, 1828). Gulf of California to Acapulco. On sandspits, low tide; common. Spire apex violet.

Purple Dwarf Olive (1") 2.5 cm
Olivella biplicata (Sowerby, 1825). Vancouver Island (British Columbia) to Baja California. On sand to 50 m; common.

Twisted-plait Olive (1.2") 3 cm
Olivancillaria contortuplicata (Reeve, 1850). Uruguay to Brazil. Shallow water; common.

Ureta's Olive (1.4") 3.5 cm
Olivancillaria uretai Klappenbach, 1965. Argentina to Uruguay. On muddy sand; uncommon.

Gibbous Olive (2") 5 cm
Olivancillaria gibbosa (Born, 1778). Southern India; Sri Lanka. Common.

Sparkling Dwarf Olive   (0.8") 2 cm
Olivella nana (Lamarck, 1811). West Africa. Common. Syn.: *micans* Dillwyn; *minor* Dunker.

Argentine Dwarf Olive   (0.5") 1.2 cm
Olivella tehuelcha (Duclos, 1835). Argentina to Brazil. Intertidal on sand; common. Syn.: *tehuelchana* Orbigny.

Cingulate Ancilla   (2.3") 6 cm
Ancillista cingulata (Sowerby, 1830). Northern half of Australia. Sand flats. Common. Syn.: *inornata* E. A. Smith.

Ear Ancilla   (1.5") 4 cm
Olivancillaria vesica auricularia (Lamarck, 1810). Argentina; Brazil. Subtidal in sand. Common.

Mamillate Ancilla   (1.5") 3.7 cm
Amalda mamillata (Hinds, 1843). S.W. Pacific. Offshore to deep water; uncommon.

Spear-head Ancilla   (2") 5 cm
Amalda contusa (Reeve, 1864). S. Africa. Offshore to 100 m; uncommon. Syn.: *decipiens* Sowerby.

Golden-brown Ancilla   (2.5") 6 cm
Ancillista velesiana Iredale, 1936. S. Queensland and New South Wales. Trawled; moderately common.

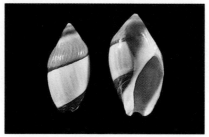

Aristocratic Ancilla   (2.2") 5.5 cm
Amalda optima (Sowerby, 1897). S. Africa; Mozambique. Offshore to deep water; moderately rare.

Margined Ancilla   (1.5") 4 cm
Amalda marginata (Lamarck, 1811). New South Wales; southern Australia; Tasmania. Shallow water; uncommon.

Montrouzier's Ancilla   (1.5") 4 cm
Amalda montrouzieri (Souverbie, 1860). New Caledonia; Fiji. Rare.

Edith's Ancilla   (0.6") 1.5 cm
Amalda edithae (Pritchard & Gatliff, 1899). Southern Australia. On submerged sandbanks; uncommon.

Blunt Ancilla   (1.5") 4 cm
Amalda obtusa (Swainson, 1825). South Africa. Offshore to 180 m; uncommon.

Ruddy Ancilla   (1″) 2.5 cm
Amalda rosea (Macpherson, 1951). New South Wales; Australia. Uncommon.

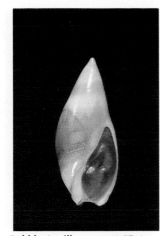

Bubble Ancilla   (1.5″) 4 cm
Amalda bullioides (Reeve, 1864). South Africa. Offshore, deep water; uncommon. Syn.: *dimidiata* von Martens.

Hinomoto Ancilla   (1.7″) 4.5 cm
Baryspira hinomotoensis (Yokoyama, 1922). Southern Japan. 50 to 200 m; uncommon.

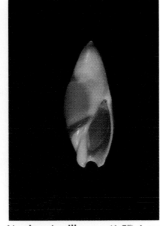

Urasima Ancilla   (1.5″) 4 cm
Baryspira hinomotoensis form *urasima* (Kira, 1955). Japan. Offshore; uncommon. More slender.

Tindall's Ancilla   (0.7″) 1.8 cm
Amalda tindalli (Melvill, 1898). Off western coast of India. Moderately deep water; uncommon.

Petterd's Ancilla   (0.9″) 2.2 cm
Amalda petterdi (Tate, 1893). Victoria (South Australia); Tasmania. Shallow water; uncommon.

Tankerville's Ancilla   (2″) 5 cm
Amalda tankervillii (Swainson, 1825). Northern coast of South America. In sand, 6 - 13 m; locally common.

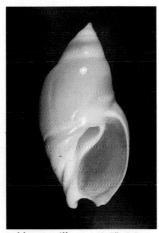

Golden Ancilla   (2.5″) 6.5 cm
Ancilla glabrata (L., 1758). Lower Caribbean. Offshore, in sand; uncommon. Syn.: *flavida* Lamarck.

Acuminate Ancilla   (1.2″) 3 cm
Ancilla acuminata (Sowerby, 1859). Red Sea; North Arabian Sea. Common. Syn.: *lineolata* A. Adams, *oryza* Reeve.

Delightful Ancilla   (1.5′) 4 cm
Ancilla suavis Yokoyama, 1922. Japan. Offshore, 160 - 200 m; uncommon.

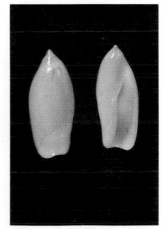

Wide-mouth Ancilla   (1.2″) 3 cm
Amalda ampla (Gmelin, 1791). Indian Ocean. Offshore to about 20 m; uncommon. Syn.: *candida* Lamarck.

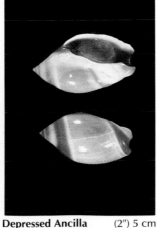

Depressed Ancilla   (2″) 5 cm
Amalda depressa (Sowerby, 1859). New Zealand. Intertidal sand flats. Moderately common.

Chinese Ancilla (2") 5 cm
Ancilla rubiginosa Swainson, 1823. China Sea. Shallow water; uncommon.

Brown-tipped Ancilla (2") 5 cm
Amalda muscae (Pilsbry, 1926). Northern half of Australia. Intertidal sand flats; common. Syn.: *elongata* Gray.

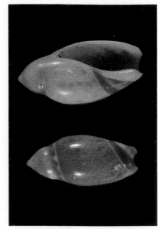

Reeve's Ancilla (0.8") 2 cm
Ancilla reevei E. A. Smith, 1904. South Africa. Moderately common. Syn.: *bipartita* Turton; *major* Turton.

White-banded Ancilla
(0.8") 2.1 cm
Ancilla fasciata (Reeve, 1864). South Africa. Offshore; common. Syn.: *ordinaria* E. A. Smith.

Necklace Ancilla (1") 2.5 cm
Ancilla monilifera (Reeve, 1864). Western Australia. Moderately common. Syn.: *lineata* Kiener, not Perry.

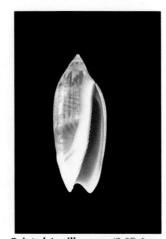

Pointed Ancilla (2.3") 6 cm
Agaronia acuminata (Lamarck, 1811). West Africa. Shallow water; common. Syn.: *annotata* Marrat.

Panama False Olive (2") 5 cm
Agaronia testacea (Lamarck, 1811). Gulf of California to Peru. Intertidal; common. Syn.: *reevei* Mörch.

Blotchy Ancilla (2") 5 cm
Agaronia nebulosa (Lamarck, 1811). Indian Ocean. Shallow water; common. Syn.: *intricata* Marrat.

Blotchy Ancilla (1.5") 4 cm
Agaronia nebulosa (Lamarck, 1811). Indian Ocean. Moderately common. Syn.: *labuanensis* Marrat (syntypes).

Open-mouth Ancilla (1.5") 4 cm
Agaronia propatula (Conrad, 1849). S.W. Mexico to Ecuador. Common. Syn.: *hiatula* of authors.

Travassos's Ancilla (2.5") 6.5 cm
Agaronia travassosi Morretes, 1938. Brazil. Offshore, 40 - 140 m; uncommon. Syn.: *lanei* Morretes; *langei* Zanardini.

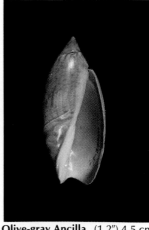

Olive-gray Ancilla (1.2") 4.5 cm
Agaronia hiatula (Gmelin, 1791). West Africa; Cape Verde Islands. Shallow water; common. Syn.: *cincta* Reeve.

MITERS
FAMILY MITRIDAE

This family contains several hundred species most of which are colorful and live in warm shallow seas. The shells are usually elongate to fusiform, and the columella bears several small plicae, or teeth. Recently the family Costellariidae (i.e. Vexillidae) has been separated off to contain *Vexillum, Pusia* and *Thala.*

Episcopal Miter (4") 10 cm
Mitra mitra (L., 1758). Indo-Pacific; Galapagos. In sand, shallow water; common. Syn.: *episcopalis* Linné.

Papal Miter (2") 5 cm
Mitra papalis (L., 1758). Entire Indo-Pacific. Coral rubble, 1 to 30 m; uncommon.

Pontifical Miter (2.5") 6.5 cm
Mitra stictica (Link, 1807). Indo-Pacific. Coral reefs, under rocks; common. Syn.: *pontificalis* Lamarck.

Bové's Miter (2.5") 6 cm
Mitra bovei Kiener, 1838. Red Sea and Persian Gulf. Subtidal, 1 to 30 m; uncommon. Syn.: *abacophora* Melvill.

Cardinal Miter (3") 7 cm
Mitra cardinalis (Gmelin, 1791). Indo-Pacific. In sand, shallow water; common. Syn.: *monachialis* Röding.

Particolored Miter (2") 5 cm
Mitra nubila nubila (Gmelin, 1791). Indo-Pacific. Coral sand; moderately rare. Syn.: *versicolor* Martyn; *lamarcki* Deshayes.

Ambiguous Miter (2.5") 6 cm
Mitra ambigua Swainson, 1829. Indo-Pacific. Coral reef flats; moderately common. Syn.: *limosa* Martyn.

Coffee Miter (2") 5 cm
Mitra coffea Schubert & Wagner, 1829. Entire Indo-Pacific. Syn.: *thaanumiana* Pilsbry from Hawaii. Holotype.

Coffee Miter (2") 5 cm
Mitra coffea Schubert & Wagner, 1829. Entire Indo-Pacific. Reef flats to 28 m; moderately common.

Imperial Miter (2") 5 cm
Mitra imperialis Röding, 1798. Entire Indo-Pacific. Coral areas; uncommon. Syn.: *digitalis* Link; *millepora* Lamarck.

Tessellate Miter (4") 10 cm
Mitra incompta (Lightfoot, 1786). Indo-Pacific. Reef flats to 40 m; rare. Syn.: *tessellata* Martyn; *reevei* Philippi.

Adusta Miter (2.5″) 6 cm
Mitra eremitarum Röding, 1798. S.W. Pacific. Intertidal reef flats; abundant. Syn.: *adusta* Lamarck; *flavofusca* Lamarck.

Speckled Miter (2.5″) 6 cm
Mitra guttata Swainson, 1824. Indian Ocean. Shallow water; rare. Syn.: *boswellae* J. Cate.

Stained Miter (3″) 7.5 cm
Mitra inquinata Reeve, 1844. Japan to Taiwan. Offshore, 20 to 110 m; uncommon. Syn.: *hanleyana* Dunker; *wrighti* Crosse.

Triplicate Miter (2.5″) 6 cm
Mitra triplicata von Martens, 1904. East Africa to Indonesia. Deep water to 1,400 m; uncommon.

Scorched Miter (2″) 5 cm
Mitra ustulata Reeve, 1844. Entire Indo-Pacific. Shallow reefs; uncommon. Variable. Syn.: *ignobilis* Reeve.

Pyramis Miter (2″) 5 cm
Mitra pyramis (Wood, 1828). Indo-Pacific. Shallow water to 50 m; uncommon.

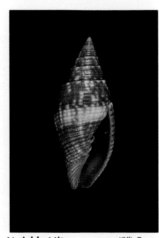

Variable Miter (2″) 5 cm
Mitra variabilis Reeve, 1844. Northern Australia. Intertidal to 100 m; common. Syn.: *polymorpha* Tomlin.

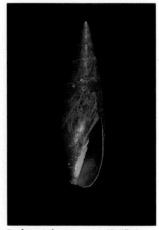

Carbon Miter (2.5″) 6 cm
Mitra carbonaria Swainson, 1822. Australia; New Zealand. Shallow water; common. Syn.: *badia, nigra, rhodia* Reeve.

Deynzer's Miter (1.2″) 3 cm
Mitra deynzeri Cernohorsky, 1980. Panglao Is., Philippines. Offshore; rare. Paratype illus.

Bald Miter (3.5″) 9 cm
Mitra glabra Swainson, 1821. South Australia; Tasmania. Intertidal pools to offshore; common. Spire high.

Troubled Miter (1.2″) 3 cm
Mitra aerumnosa Melvill, 1888. South Africa. Rare. Syn.: *simplex* Dunker.

Lightning Miter (2″) 5 cm
Mitra fulgurita Reeve, 1844. East Indies. Shallow water; rare. Syn.: *yaekoae* Habe & Kosuge.

Oriental Miter (2.5") 6 cm
Mitra orientalis Griffith & Pidgeon, 1834. W. Colombia to Chile. Offshore to 150 m; uncommon. Syn.: *maura* Brod.

Zoned Miter (3") 8 cm
Mitra fusiformis subspecies *zonata* Marryat, 1818. Mediterranean to West Africa. Subtidal to 130 m; uncommon. *M. fusiformis* Brocchi is a fossil.

Helen's Miter (4") 10 cm
Mitra helenae Radwin & Bibbey, 1972. Atlantic coast of Central America. Offshore in 10 to 30 m; rare.

Swainson's Miter (5") 13 cm
Mitra swainsoni Broderip, 1836. West Mexico to Ecuador. Subtidal, 15 to 150 m; moderately common. Syn.: *zaca* Strong.

Antillean Miter (5") 13 cm
Mitra swainsoni subspecies *antillensis* Dall, 1889. S.E. U. S. to Caribbean. Offshore; uncommon. Holotype.

Rusty Miter (2") 5 cm
Mitra ferruginea Lamarck, 1811. Entire Indo-Pacific. Intertidal reefs; common. Syn.: *vitulina* Dillwyn.

Red-painted Miter (1.5") 3.5 cm
Mitra rubritincta Reeve, 1844. Entire Indo-Pacific. Intertidal to 20 m; moderately common.

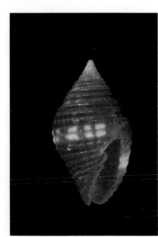

Kettle Miter (1.5") 3.5 cm
Mitra cucumerina Lamarck, 1811. Indo-Pacific. Shallow coral waters; common. Syn.: *ferrugata* Dillwyn.

Chrysalis Miter (1") 2.5 cm
Mitra chrysalis Reeve, 1844. Indo-Pacific. Intertidal to 3 m; common. Spiral grooves are punctate. Syn.: *buryi* M. & S.

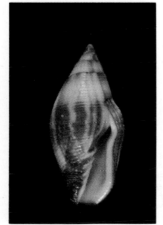

Colombella Miter (1.5") 4 cm
Mitra colombelliformis Kiener, 1838. Indo-Pacific. Shallow water, intertidal; common.

Strawberry Miter (2") 5 cm
Mitra fraga Quoy and Gaimard, 1833. Indo-Pacific. Intertidal coral reefs to 30 m; common. Syn.: *rubiginea* A. Adams.

Orange Miter (1.2") 3 cm
Mitra aurantia (Gmelin, 1791). Indo-Pacific. Shallow water; common. Syn.: *aurantiaca* Lamarck; *crassa* Swainson.

Gold-mouth Miter (1.2″) 3 cm
Mitra chrysostoma Broderip, 1836. Entire Indo-Pacific. Shallow reefs; common. Coarse spiral cords. Spire blunt.

Contracted Miter (1.5″) 3.5 cm
Mitra contracta Swainson, 1820. Indo-Pacific. Intertidal reef flats to 30 m; common. Apex pointed.

Tawny Miter (1.8″) 4.5 cm
Mitra fulvescens Broderip, 1836. Indo-Pacific. Subtidal; uncommon. Syn.: *ostergaardi* Pilsbry (holotype illus).

Vexillate Miter (1″) 2.5 cm
Mitra vexillum Reeve, 1844. S.W. Pacific. Reefs; uncommon.

Coronate Miter (1.2″) 3 cm
Mitra coronata Lamarck, 1811. Entire Indo-Pacific. Intertidal to offshore; common. Syn.: *tiarella* A. Adams.

Punctured Miter (2″) 5 cm
Mitra puncticulata Lamarck, 1811. S.W. Pacific; S. Japan. Intertidal coral reefs; uncommon. Syn.: *diadema* Swainson.

Flowery Miter (1.5″) 3.5 cm
Mitra aurora subspecies *floridula* Sowerby, 1874. Indo-Pacific. Shallow reefs to 24 m; common. Holotype illus.

Sophie's Miter (1.5″) 3.5 cm
Mitra sophiae Crosse, 1862. Australia to E. Polynesia. Intertidal to 60 m; uncommon.

Lens Miter (3″) 7 cm
Mitra lens Wood, 1828. West Mexico to Ecuador. Intertidal gravel to 28 m; common. Syn.: *dupontiae* Kiener.

Belcher's Miter (5″) 12 cm
Mitra belcheri Hinds, 1844. Gulf of California to Panama. Offshore to 100 m; uncommon.

Barbados Miter (1″) 2.5 cm
Mitra barbadensis (Gmelin, 1791). S. Florida to Brazil; Bermuda. Subtidal in rubble to 10 m; common.

Nodulose Miter (1.2″) 3 cm
Mitra nodulosa (Gmelin, 1791). S. Florida to Brazil; Bermuda. Intertidal to 20 m; common. Syn.: *brasiliensis* Oliveira.

Toothless Miter (1.5″) 3.5 cm
Dibaphus edentula (Sowerby, 1823). Entire Indo-Pacific. Intertidal reef flats; uncommon. Syn.: *philippi* Crosse.

Florida Miter (2.5″) 6 cm
Mitra florida Gould, 1856. Florida and the Caribbean. Sand bottom, 2 to 30 m; uncommon.

Poverty Miter (1″) 2.5 cm
Mitra paupercula (L., 1758). Entire Indo-Pacific. Intertidal flats among rubble; locally abundant. Syn.: *zebra* Lamarck.

Magpie Miter (1.3″) 3 cm
Mitra pica (Dillwyn, 1817). Indian Ocean and S.W. Pacific. Intertidal; uncommon. Syn.: *lineata* Swainson.

Blunted Miter (1″) 2.5 cm
Mitra retusa Lamarck, 1811. Indo-Pacific. Intertidal reefs; uncommon. Aperture mauve. Syn.: *virgata* Reeve.

Lettered Miter (1″) 2.5 cm
Mitra litterata Lamarck, 1811. Entire Indo-Pacific. Intertidal coral reef flats; common. Syn.: *maculosa* Reeve.

Shortened Miter (1.3″) 3 cm
Mitra decurtata Reeve, 1844. S.W. Pacific. Intertidal reef flats; uncommon. Outer lip very thick.

Acuminate Miter (1.5″) 3.5 cm
Mitra acuminata Swainson, 1824. Indo-Pacific. Intertidal coral reefs; moderately common.

Snake-tongue Miter (1″) 2.5 cm
Mitra pellisserpentis Reeve, 1844. Mauritius to E. Polynesia. Intertidal to 2 m; common. Smooth or granulose.

Snake-tongue Miter (1″) 2.5 cm
Mitra pellisserpentis subspecies *astricta* Reeve, 1844. Endemic to the Hawaiian Chain. Brown spiral lines.

Rehder's Miter (2.5″) 6 cm
Mitra rehderi Webb, 1958. Off Tosa, Japan. 180 m; rare. Holotype illustrated.

Taiwan Miter (3.5″) 9 cm
Mitra morchii A. Adams subspecies *taiwanica* Shikama & Chiang, 1977. Philippines to Taiwan; uncommon.

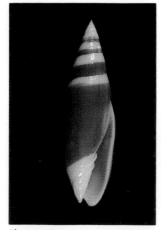

Chaste Miter   (2″) 5 cm
Scabricola casta (Gmelin, 1791).
Indo-Pacific. In sand. Uncommon. Cleaning removes brown
band. Syn.: *matronalis* Schum.

Eyed Miter   (1″) 2.5 cm
Scabricola ocellata (Swainson,
1831). Indo-Pacific. In sand.
Uncommon. Syn.: *incisa* A. Adams; *mariei* A. Adams.

Newcomb's Miter   (1.5″) 4 cm
Scabricola newcombii (Pease,
1869). Hawaiian and Midway Is.
(endemic). Subtidal, in sand.
Uncommon.

Reticulate Miter   (2″) 5 cm
Scabricola fissurata (Lamarck,
1811). Indian Ocean. In coral
sand and coral rubble. Uncommon. Reticulate pattern.

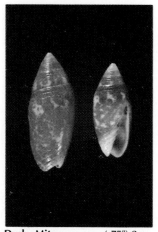

Dusky Miter   (.75″) 2 cm
Scabricola fusca (Swainson,
1824). Indo-Pacific. Uncommon in Indian Ocean, rare in
western Pacific. Syn.: *limata*
Reeve; *formosa* Reeve.

Snake Miter   (2″) 5 cm
Scabricola variegata (Gmelin,
1791). Philippines to Marquesas. In sand, shallow water.
Rare. Syn.: *serpentina* Lam.

Desetangs's Miter   (1″) 2.5 cm
Scabricola desetangsii Kiener,
1838. Philippine Islands. Subtidal in sand; uncommon.

File Miter   (1″) 2.5 cm
Cancilla filaris (L., 1771). Indo-
Pacific. Shallow water in sand;
common. Syn.: *filosa* Born;
nexilis Lamarck, 1811.

Most Superior Miter (1.2″) 3 cm
Cancilla praestantissima (Röding, 1798). Indo-Pacific. Shallow water in coral sand; uncommon.

Horn-colored Miter   (1.3″) 3 cm
Cancilla carnicolor (Reeve,
1844). Indo-Pacific. Shallow water; uncommon. Syn.: *millepunctata* Sowerby; *pura* Ad.

Pease's Miter   (1.5″) 3.8 cm
Cancilla peasei (Dohrn, 1860).
S.W. Pacific. Shallow flats; uncommon. Syn.: *langfordi*
Pilsbry.

Philippine Miter   (1.5″) 3.8 cm
Cancilla bacillum (Lamarck,
1811). S.W. Pacific. Shallow reef
flats; common. Syn.: *astyagis*
Dohrn.

Flecked Miter (2″) 5 cm
Neocancilla granatina (Lamarck, 1811). Tropical Indo-Pacific. In sand, shallow water. Uncommon.

Gloriola Miter (1.5″) 4 cm
Cancilla gloriola Cernohorsky, 1970. Philippines. Shallow water; uncommon. Syn.: *gracilis* Reeve, not Lea.

Butterfly Miter (2″) 5 cm
Neocancilla papilio (Link, 1807). Indo-Pacific. In sand. Uncommon. Syn : *sphaerulata* Martyn; *leucostoma* Gmelin.

Isao Taki Miter (2.5″) 6 cm
Neocancilla takiisaoi Kuroda & Sakurai, 1959. Japan and Pitcairn Is. Shallow water; rare.

Orange Miter (1.5″) 4 cm
Neoncancilla arenacea (Dunker, 1852). Marquesas (endemic). Coral sand and rubble offshore. Rare.

Clathrus Miter (1.5″) 4 cm
Neocancilla clathrus (Gmelin, 1791). Indo-Pacific. Shallow flats; uncommon. Syn.: *crenifera* Lamarck; *emersoni* Pilsbry.

Senegal Miter (1.2″) 3 cm
Cancilla carinata Swainson, 1824. West Africa. Shallow water; uncommon. Syn.: *senegalensis* Reeve.

Cernohorsky's Miter (1.2″) 3 cm
Cancilla cernohorskyi (Rehder & Wilson, 1975). Off Pitcairn Island; E. Polynesia. Rare. Holotype illustrated.

Hinds's Miter (1.2″) 3.5 cm
Subcancilla hindsii (Reeve, 1844). West Mexico to Ecuador. Offshore to 51 m; uncommon.

Bright-spotted Miter (1″) 2.5 cm
Subcancilla calodinota (S.S. Berry, 1960). West Mexico to Costa Rica. Offshore to 46 m; uncommon.

Red-lettered Miter (1″) 2.5 cm
Subcancilla erythrogramma (Tomlin, 1931). West Mexico to Colombia. 18 to 37 m; uncommon. Syn.: *lineata* Broderip.

Isabelle's Miter (4″) 10 cm
Cancilla isabella (Swainson, 1831). Western Pacific; Japan. Offshore to 50 m; uncommon.

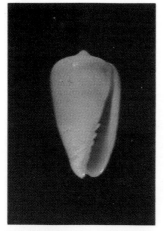

Bonelike Miter (1") 2.5 cm
Imbricaria punctata (Swainson, 1821). Indo-Pacific. In sand, offshore; uncommon. Syn.: *truncata* Kiener; *ossea* Reeve.

Olive-shaped Imbricaria
(0.3") 7 mm
Imbricaria olivaeformis (Swainson, 1821). Tropical Pacific. Intertidal sand; locally common.

Conus Miter (1.3") 3.5 cm
Pterygia conus (Gmelin, 1791). S.W. Pacific. Subtidal, shallow, sand; locally common. Syn.: *conulus* Röding.

Carbon Imbricaria (0.7") 1.8 cm
Imbricaria carbonacea (Hinds, 1844). West and S.W. Africa. Subtidal sands; moderately common.

Finger Miter (1.6") 4.5 cm
Pterygia dactylus (L., 1767). Indo-Pacific. In sand. Uncommon. Syn.: *nucella* Röding; *obesa* Reeve.

Finger Miter (1.6") 4.5 cm
Pterygia dactylus (L., 1767). Smooth form without spiral cut lines.

Nut Miter (2") 5 cm
Pterygia nucea (Gmelin, 1791). Indo-Pacific. In sand. Uncommon. Syn.: *spuria* Gmelin; *olivaria* Lamarck.

Fenestrate Miter (1.5") 4 cm
Pterygia fenestrata (Lamarck, 1811). Indo-Pacific. Shallow water, sand; uncommon. Syn.: *radula* Sowerby.

Crenulate Miter (1.3") 3 cm
Pterygia crenulata (Gmelin, 1791). Indo-Pacific. In sand. Uncommon. Syn.: *toleranda* Iredale; *fastidiosa* Iredale.

Crenulate Miter (1.3") 3.5 cm
Pterygia crenulata (Gmelin, 1791). Indo-Pacific; uncommon. Form *undulosa* Reeve, 1844, shown here.

Chinese Miter (1.5") 4 cm
Pterygia sinensis Reeve, 1844. East Asia. Offshore to 30 m; moderately common.

Modest Miter (0.75") 1.9 cm
Pterygia pudica (Pease, 1860). Central Pacific. Moderately rare. Syn.: *lifouana* Crosse; *subtexturata* Garrett.

Rough Miter (2″) 5 cm
Pterygia scabricula (L., 1758). Indo-Pacific. Shallow coral waters; rare. Syn.: *texturata* Lamarck.

RIBBED MITERS
FAMILY COSTELLARIIDAE
(VEXILLIDAE)

These miters have been placed in a separate family on the basis of major soft part, anatomical differences. The interior of the aperture of the shell is always lirate, while in the Mitridae it is smooth. The Vexillidae have strong, sharp axial ribs, and sometimes strong spiral threads, or striae.

Plaited Miter (1.5″) 4 cm
Vexillum plicarium (L., 1758). Indo-Pacific. In sand. Uncommon. Syn.: *plicatum* Röding; *lividum* Röding.

Rugose Miter (2″) 5 cm
Vexillum rugosum (Gmelin, 1791). Indo-Pacific. In sand. Uncommon. Syn.: *corrugata* Lamarck; *hybrida* Kiener.

Little Fox Miter (2″) 5 cm
Vexillum vulpecula (L., 1758). Indo-Pacific. In sand; common. Very variable. Syn.: *variabilis* Link; *caffrum* Linné.

Blood-striped Miter (1.5″) 4 cm
Vexillum transpositum (Dautzenberg & Bouge, 1923). Indo-Pacific. Moderately rare. Syn.: *strigosa* Gmelin.

Jukes's Miter (1.3″) 3.5 cm
Vexillum jukesii (A. Adams, 1853). Western Australia. Uncommon. Syn.: *interrupta* A. Adams; *superbiens* Melvill.

Queen Miter (2.3″) 6 cm
Vexillum regina (Sowerby, 1828). West Pacific. Uncommon. Syn.: *citrina* Gmelin; *compressa* Sowerby.

Colorful Queen Miter
(2.3″) 6 cm
Vexillum regina form *filiareginae* J. Cate, 1961. Philippines. Shallow water; uncommon.

Ribboned Miter (2″) 5 cm
Vexillum taeniatum (Lamarck, 1811). Indo-Pacific. Shallow water. Moderately rare. Syn.: *vittata* Swainson.

Formosan Miter (1.5″) 4 cm
Vexillum formosense (Sowerby, 1890). Indonesia to Fiji; Taiwan. Offshore to 20 m; uncommon. Syn.: *utravis* Melvill.

Scarlet Miter (3″) 7.5 cm
Vexillum coccineum (Reeve, 1844). China and Taiwan. Offshore from 3 to 30 m; locally common.

Costate Miter (2.5″) 6 cm
Vexillum subdivisum (Gmelin, 1791). Indo-Pacific. Subtidal, in sand; common. Variable. Syn.: *lyratum* and *nigrina* Lamarck.

Costellate Miter (2.5″) 6 cm
Vexillum subdivisum form *costellaris* (Lamarck, 1811). West Pacific. Uncommon.

Gruner's Miter (2.5″) 6 cm
Vexillum gruneri (Reeve, 1844). S.W. Pacific. Shallow water; common. Syn.: *modesta* Reeve.

Stainforth's Miter (1.5″) 4 cm
Vexillum stainforthi (Reeve, 1841). S.W. Pacific. Shallow water. Uncommon.

Taylor's Miter (2″) 5 cm
Vexillum taylorianum (Sowerby, 1874). Philippines; Melanesia. Offshore; common.

Blood-stained Miter
(0.7″) 1.8 cm
Vexillum cruentatum (Gmelin, 1791). Red Sea to Samoa. Shallow water; uncommon. Syn.: *harpifera* Lamarck.

Dennison's Miter (2″) 5 cm
Vexillum dennisoni (Reeve, 1844). Philippines and Indonesia. Shallow water; uncommon.

Granular Miter (2″) 5 cm
Vexillum granosum (Gmelin, 1791). Indo-Pacific. Shallow water; moderately common. Syn.: *cancellata* Röding.

Bloodsucker Miter (2″) 5 cm
Vexillum sanguisugum (L., 1758). Indo-Pacific. Shallow reefs; common. Syn.: *stigmataria* Lamarck.

Basket Miter (0.7″) 1.8 cm
Vexillum lubens (Reeve, 1845). Indo-Pacific. In sand. Moderately rare. Syn.: *corbicula* Sowerby; *diamesa* Hervier.

Decorated Miter (1.5″) 4 cm
Vexillum unifasciatum (Wood, 1828). Indo-Pacific. Subtidal; uncommon. Syn.: *clathrata* and *decora* Reeve.

Pinpricked Miter (1″) 2.5 cm
Vexillum acupictum (Reeve, 1844). Entire Indo-Pacific. Shallow water; uncommon.

Miraculous Miter   (2") 5 cm
Vexillum mirabile (A. Adams, 1853). S.W. Pacific. Shallow water, sand, to 53 m; uncommon. Syn.: *angulosa* Reeve.

Half-banded Miter   (1") 2.5 cm
Vexillum semifasciatum (Lamarck, 1811). Red Sea to Samoa. Shallow water, sand; common.

Spiny Miter   (1") 2.5 cm
Vexillum echinatum (A. Adams, 1853). Tropical Indo-Pacific. In sand. Uncommon. Syn.: *mucronata* Broderip.

Crowned Miter   (1.2") 3 cm
Vexillum stephanucha (Melvill, 1897). Persian Gulf. Offshore; rare.

Saffron Miter   (.75") 1.9 cm
Vexillum crocatum (Lamarck, 1811). Indo-Pacific. Sand and coral rubble. Uncommon. Syn.: *aurantia* Broderip.

Beautiful Florida Miter   (0.5") 1.2 cm *Vexillum pulchellum* (Reeve, 1843). S.E. Florida and West Indies. Subtidal to 30 m; uncommon.

Half-brown Miter   (0.7") 1.8 cm
Vexillum epiphanea Rehder, 1943. S.E. Florida; Bahamas; Bermuda. Subtidal to 3 m; uncommon.

Bernhard's Miter   (0.7") 1.8 cm
Vexillum bernhardiana (Röding, 1798). Indo-Pacific. Shallow water reefs; uncommon. Syn.: *muriculata* Lamarck.

Thousand-rib Miter   (1.2") 3 cm
Vexillum millecostatum (Broderip, 1836). Melanesia. Shallow water; uncommon. Syn.: *evelynae* Melvill.

Turban Miter   (0.7") 1.8 cm
Vexillum turben (Reeve, 1844). Western Pacific to Polynesia. Subtidal to 20 m; uncommon. Syn.: *kanaka* Pilsbry.

Cancellaria Miter   (1") 2.5 cm
Vexillum cancellarioides (Anton, 1839). Indo-Pacific. Reef flats; uncommon. Syn.: *tuberculata* Kiener; *nodosa* Swain.

Ebony Miter   (0.8") 2 cm
Vexillum ebenus (Lamarck, 1811). Mediterranean; W. Europe. Shallow water; common. Syn.: *defranceii* Payraudeau.

Roughened Miter   (1") 2.5 cm
Vexillum exasperatum (Gmelin, 1791). Entire Indo-Pacific area. Shallow reef flats; common. Syn.: *torulosa* Lamarck.

Patriarchal Miter   (1.3") 3 cm
Vexillum patriarchalis (Gmelin, 1791). Entire Indo-Pacific area. Shallow reef flats to 4 m; uncommon.

Reeve's Bloodied Miter   (0.7") 1.8 cm
Vexillum consanguineum (Reeve, 1845). Tropical West Pacific. Coral reef sand flats; uncommon. Syn.: *russa* Gould.

Specious Miter   (0.7") 1.8 cm
Vexillum speciosum (Reeve, 1844). Indo-Pacific. Shallow water to 5 m; uncommon. Syn.: *trizonalis* Dautzenberg.

Fiery Miter   (0.7") 1.8 cm
Vexillum moelleri (Küster, 1840). Hawaiian Islands to Polynesia and New Caledonia. Moderately rare. Syn.: *flammulata* Pease; *zebrina* Garrett; *baldwinii* Melvill.

Black-banded Miter   (0.6") 1.5 cm
Vexillum luculentum (Reeve, 1845). Philippines to Samoa. Under coral. Uncommon. Syn.: *diachroa* A. Adams & Reeve; *graeffei* Crosse.

Amanda Miter   (0.7") 1.8 cm
Vexillum amanda (Reeve, 1845). Tropical Pacific. Shallow reef flats; uncommon.

Golden Miter   (0.5") 1.2 cm
Vexillum aureolatum (Reeve, 1844). Tropical Indo-Pacific. In sand under coral. Uncommon. Syn.: *pilsbryi* Hedley; *bizonalis* Dautzenberg & Bouge.

Woldemar's Miter   (1") 2.5 cm
Zierliana woldemarii (Kiener, 1838). Tropical Pacific. Moderately common. Very variable. Syn.: *solidula* Reeve; *creniplicata* A. Adams.

**CHANK SHELLS
FAMILY TURBINELLIDAE
(XANCIDAE)**

The heavy chank and vase shells have 3 to 5 strong, squarish, spiral teeth on the columella. Most species feed on worms and clams in the shallow waters of tropical shores. The operculum is chitinous and clawlike. Eggs are laid in horny, circular capsules. There are about two dozen species.

Ceramic Vase   (4") 10 cm
Vasum ceramicum (L., 1758). Entire Indo-Pacific, except Red Sea. 1 to 4 m; moderately common. 3 columellar folds.

Armed Vase   (2") 5 cm
Vasum armatum (Broderip, 1833). Eastern Polynesia. Lower columella white; two rows of equal-size knobs. Locally common.

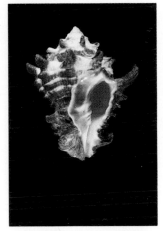

Common Pacific Vase (2.5″) 6 cm *Vasum turbinellus* (L., 1758). Entire Indo-Pacific. Intertidal to 2 m; abundant. Syn.: *cornigera* Lamarck.

Common Pacific Vase (2.5″) 6 cm *Vasum turbinellus* form *cornigerum* (Lamarck, 1822). Spines extra long. Philippines. Common.

Imperial Vase (3″) 7.5 cm *Vasum tubiferum* (Anton, 1839). Central Philippines only. Shallow water. Locally common. Syn.: *imperialis* Reeve.

Rhinoceros Vase (3″) 7.5 cm *Vasum rhinoceros* (Gmelin, 1791). Central East Africa. Intertidal; locally common. Yellow color form rare.

Crosse's Vase (3.5″) 9 cm *Vasum crosseanum* (Souverbie, 1875). Seychelles islands. Offshore, shallow water; rare.

Truncate Vase (3″) 7 cm *Vasum truncatum* (Sowerby, 1892). South Africa. Offshore; rare. Periostracum is thick and with bristles.

Truncate Vase (2″) 5 cm *Vasum truncatum* (Sowerby, 1892). Young specimen has low nodules and is slightly umbilicate.

Helmet Vase (2.5″) 6 cm *Vasum cassiforme* (Kiener, 1841). Brazil. Shallow water to 2 m; locally uncommon. Syn.: *cassidiformis* Kiener.

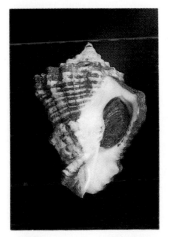

Caribbean Vase (3″) 7.5 cm *Vasum muricatum* (Born, 1778). Florida and Caribbean. Subtidal to 2 m; common.

Latirus-shaped Vase (3″) 7.5 cm *Siphovasum latiriforme* (Rehder & Abbott, 1951). Gulf of Campeche, Mexico. Offshore to 50 m; rare. Holotype illus.

Latirus-shaped Vase (3″) 7.5 cm *Siphovasum latiriforme* (Rehder & Abbott, 1951). Orange color form, very rare. Sometimes yellow.

Globe Vase (1″) 2.5 cm *Vasum globulus* subspecies *nuttingi* (Henderson, 1919). Lesser Antilles. Shallow water; locally common.

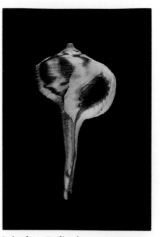

Spiny Caribbean Vase
(2.5") 6 cm
Vasum capitellum (L., 1758). Caribbean. Offshore reefs; uncommon.

Armored Tudicula   (2.5") 6 cm
Tudicula armigera (A. Adams, 1855). Western Australia. Offshore to 30 m; locally common.

Kurtz's Tudicula   (3") 7 cm
Tudicula armigera subspecies *kurtzi* Macpherson, 1963. Western Australia. Offshore; Uncommon.

Spineless Tudicula   (1.7") 4 cm
Tudicula inermis Angas, 1878. Western and N. Australia. Offshore 10 to 30 m; rare.

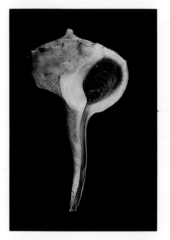

Spiral Tudicla   (3") 7 cm
Tudicla (not *Tudicula*) *spirillus* (L., 1767). S.E. India. Offshore to 20 m; locally common.

Zanzibar Tudicula   (1.5") 4 cm
Tudicula zanzibarica Abbott, 1958. Zanzibar. Offshore, sand, 6 m; rare. Holotype illustrated.

True Afer   (2") 5 cm
Afer afer (Gmelin, 1791). West Africa. Offshore, 1 to 5 m; uncommon.

Cuming's Afer   (3") 7 cm
Afer cumingii (Reeve, 1844). Japan to Taiwan. Offshore to 50 m; common. Syn.: *couderti* Petit.

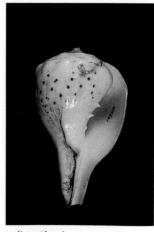

Purple-mouth Afer   (1") 2.5 cm
Afer porphyrostoma (Adams & Reeve, 1847). West Africa. Offshore to 40 m; rare.

Flinder's Vase   (6") 15 cm
Altivasum flindersi (Verco, 1914). S. and W. Australia. Offshore, deep water; uncommon. Syn.: *aurantiacus* Verco.

West Indian Chank   (8") 20 cm
Turbinella angulata (Lightfoot, 1786). Bahamas, N. Cuba, E. Mexico to Panama. Common.

Indian Chank   (4") 10 cm
Turbinella pyrum (L., 1758) S.E. India and Ceylon. Abundant offshore. Left-handed rare (Sacred Chank of India).

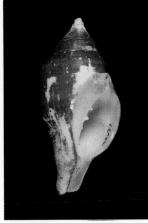

**HARP SHELLS
FAMILY HARPIDAE**

There are fewer than two dozen species in this colorful family. The strong axial ribs and wide aperture and smooth columella are characteristic. Most are tropical shallow-water dwellers. There is no operculum. Eggs are laid in soft capsules. Australia has a few deep-water rare species.

Great Indian Chank (6") 15 cm
Turbinella pyrum form *napus* Lamarck, 1822. As individual becomes older, the shell becomes swollen, smoother.

Andaman Chank (6") 15 cm
Turbinella pyrum subspecies *fusus* Sowerby, 1825. Andaman Sea. Offshore to 15 m; locally common.

Brazilian Chank (5") 13 cm
Turbinella laevigata Anton, 1839. N.E. Brazil. Subtidal to 4 m; locally common. Syn.: *ovoidea* Kiener.

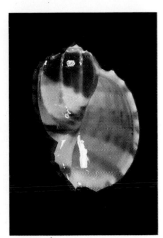

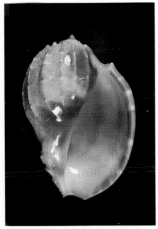

Minor Harp (2") 5 cm
Harpa amouretta Röding, 1798. Entire Indo-Pacific. Intertidal to 3 m on sand; common. Syn.: *minor* Lamarck; *crassa* Krauss.

Imperial Harp (3") 8 cm
Harpa costata (L., 1758). Islands of S.W. Indian Ocean (Mauritius). Shallow water; rare. Syn.: *imperialis* Lamarck.

Ventral Harp (4") 10 cm
Harpa ventricosa Lamarck, 1816. Red Sea to S. Africa. Subtidal; common. Spire low, shoulder spines strong.

David Harp (3") 8 cm
Harpa davidis Röding, 1798. Andaman Sea; Maldives. Uncommon. Few ribs, brown blotch with white triangle.

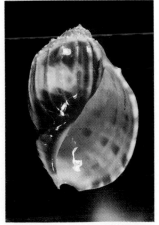

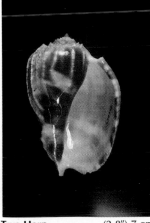

Major Harp (3.5") 9 cm
Harpa major Röding, 1798. Entire Indo-Pacific. Common. Shell heavy, oval; narrow white band between brown blotches.

Polynesian Harp (1") 2.6 cm
Harpa gracilis Broderip & Sowerby, 1829. Polynesia; Clipperton Island. Coral sand dweller; uncommon.

Articulate Harp (3.5") 9 cm
Harpa articularis Lamarck, 1822. S.W. Pacific. Common. Narrow, brown-lined ribs; large weak brown spot.

True Harp (2.8") 7 cm
Harpa harpa (L., 1758). Entire Indo-Pacific; common. Shell stout, shouldered, ribs flat; blotches of orangish between.

Panama Harp   (3″) 8 cm
Harpa crenata Swainson, 1822. W. Mexico to W. Colombia. Offshore to 30 m; uncommon.

Doris Harp   (2.5″) 6 cm
Harpa doris Röding, 1798. Cape Verde Islands to Angola; Ascension Island. Rare. Syn.: *rosea* Lamarck.

Punctate Harp   (1.3″) 3.5 cm
Austroharpa punctata (Verco, 1896). South Australia. Offshore, 30 to 40 m; very rare.

Exquisite Harp   (1″) 2.4 cm
Austroharpa exquisita (Iredale, 1931). S.E. and South Australia. Offshore from 50 to 160 m; uncommon.

Wilson's Harp   (1″) 2.5 cm
Austroharpa wilsoni Rehder, 1973. Western Australia. Offshore, 120 to 240 m; rare.

VOLUTES
FAMILY VOLUTIDAE

The large colorful volutes are among the most popular collector's items. Many live in deep water and are difficult to obtain. Only a few genera, such as *Voluta* and *Neptuneopsis*, have an operculum. The columella may have strong, slanting ridges, or plicae, or be very weak. All are carnivorous, and most are tropical.

Hebrew Volute   (6″) 15 cm
Voluta ebraea L., 1758. N. and N.E. Brazil. On coral, rock or sand, 10-20 fathoms. Common. Syn.: *chorosina* Lamarck.

Common Music Volute   (3″)
7.5 cm *Voluta musica* L., 1758. Caribbean. On sand to 5 fathoms. Locally common. Syn.: *lineata* Röding; *guinaica* Lamarck.

De Marco's Music Volute   (3.2″) 8 cm (lower): *demarcoi* Olsson, 1965. (upper): form *morrisoni* Petuch, 1980. W. Caribbean. Offshore; uncommon.

Green Music Volute   (2″) 5 cm
Voluta virescens Lightfoot, 1786. S.W. Caribbean. Offshore; rare. Variable.

Deepsea Volute   (3.5″) 9 cm
Volutocorbis abyssicola (Adams & Reeve, 1850). South Africa. Deep water to 550 m; uncommon.

Boswell's Volute   (2″) 5 cm
Volutocorbis boswellae Rehder, 1969. S. Africa. Dredged, 80 to 300 m. Rare. Holotype illus.

Corroded Volute (1") 2.5 cm
Volutocorbis gilchristi (Sowerby, 1902). South Africa. Trawled, 150-200 fathoms. Rare.

Grimy Volute (2.5") 6 cm
Volutocorbis lutosa Koch, 1948. South Africa to Senegal. 40 to 100 fathoms. Locally common. Syn.: *nicklesi* Rosso, 1976.

Kilburn's Volute (1.5") 4 cm
Volutocorbis kilburni Rehder, 1974. South Africa. Deep water; 400 m; rare. Holotype illustrated.

Minute Volute (1") 2.5 cm
Volutocorbis nana Rehder & Weaver, 1974. Off Natal, South Africa. 400 m; rare. Holotype illus.

Studer's Volute (2") 5 cm
Ternivoluta studeri (von Martens, 1897). New South Wales; Australia. Offshore; uncommon.

Beau's Lyria (2.5") 6.5 cm
Lyria beauii (Fischer & Bernardi, 1857). Lesser Antilles; W. Indies. Moderately deep water. Rare.

Archer's Lyria (2.5") 5 cm
Lyria archeri (Angas, 1865). Lesser Antilles. Offshore in sand; rare.

Delessert's Lyria (2") 5 cm
Lyria delessertiana (Petit, 1842). Madagascar to Comoro Island; Seychelles. Uncommon.

Quekett's Lyria (2") 5 cm
Lyria quekettii (E.A. Smith, 1901.) South Africa; Mozambique. 320 to 360 m; and from fish stomachs. Rare.

Delightful Lyria (1.2") 3 cm
Lyria deliciosa (Montrouzier, 1859). New Caledonia. On algae in coral-sand pockets, shallow water. Rare.

Lyre-formed Lyria (4") 10 cm
Lyria lyraeformis (Swainson, 1821). E. Africa. Offshore, moderately deep water. Uncommon.

Miter-shaped Lyria (2") 5 cm
Lyria mitraeformis (Lamarck, 1811). South Australia. Offshore; moderately common. Syn.: *grangeri* Sowerby.

Anna Lyria   (2") 5 cm
Lyria anna (Lesson, 1835). Indonesia. Rare. No reliable records available. Syn.: *costata* Swainson; *harpa* Swainson.

Kuroda's Lyria   (3.5") 9 cm
Lyria kurodai (Kawamura, 1964). Taiwan. Trawled in 44 m; rare.

Flat-ribbed Volute   (3") 7.5 cm
Lyria planicostata (Sowerby, 1903). Taiwan to Philippines. Offshore; uncommon. Syn.: *santoensis* Ladd.

Taiwan Lyria   (3") 7.5 cm
Lyria taiwanica Lan, 1975. Taiwan, central Philippines. Offshore to 100 m. Rare. Syn.: *kawamurai* Habe.

Heart Lyria   (1.5") 4 cm
Lyria cordis Bayer, 1971. Greater Antilles. Deep water, 174 m; rare. Holotype illustrated.

Vega's Lyria   (2.3") 6 cm
Lyria vegai Clench & Turner, 1967. Dominican Republic; W. Indies. Offshore. Rare. Ribbed on first 2 whorls only. Holotype.

Barnes's Lyria   (1.2") 3 cm
Lyria barnesii (Gray, 1825). Lower California to Peru. Sand and mud, 40 - 80 m; uncommon. Syn.: *harpa* Barnes.

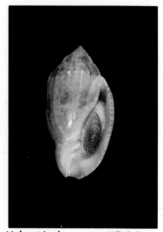

Helmet Lyria   (1") 2.5 cm
Lyria cassidula (Reeve, 1849). Japan. Offshore, 20 to 40 m; common.

Guilding's Lyria   (1") 2.5 cm
Enaeta cylleniformis (Sowerby, 1844). S.E. Florida to Brazil. Shallow water, coral sand, 1 to 10 m; locally common.

Cuming's Lyria   (1.2") 3 cm
Enaeta cumingii (Broderip, 1832). W. Mexico to Peru. Intertidal to 2 m, sandy mud; common. Syn.:*pedersenii* Verrill.

Silklike Volute   (4") 10 cm
Ericusa sericata Thornley, 1951. New South Wales to Queensland, Australia. 80 to 300 m; moderately common.

Lightning Volute   (4") 10 cm
Ericusa fulgetra (Sowerby, 1825). South Australia. Sand bars at low tide to 250 m. Uncommon.

Sowerby's Volute   (5.5") 14 cm
Ericusa sowerbyi (Kiener, 1839).
S. Australia; Tasmania. 10 - 200
m. Moderately common. Syn.:
fusiformis Swainson.

Festive Volute   (4.5") 11 cm
Festilyria festiva (Lamarck,
1811). E. Africa; southern Arabia. Offshore; rare.

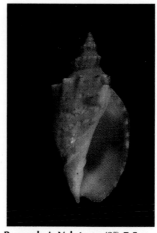

Ponsonby's Volute   (3") 7.5 cm
Festilyria ponsonbyi (E. A.
Smith, 1901). Natal, South Africa. Offshore, 40 to 100 m;
rare.

Roadnight's Volute   (8") 20 cm
Livonia roadnightae (McCoy,
1881). Southern Australia. Offshore, 50 to 200 m; uncommon.
Syn.: *quisqualis* Iredale.

Soulie's Volute   (4") 10 cm
Cymbium souliei Marche-
Marchad, 1974. Ghana, W. Africa. Offshore; uncommon.

Cucumber Volute   (5") 12.5 cm
Cymbium cucumis Röding,
1798. Senegal, West Africa. Offshore, 10 to 50 m; uncommon.
Syn.: *rubiginosa* Swainson.

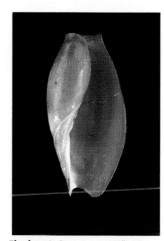

Elephant's Snout   (10") 27 cm
Cymbium glans (Gmelin, 1791).
Senegal to Gulf of Guinea. Littoral to 12 m; moderately common. Syn.: *proboscidalis* Lam.

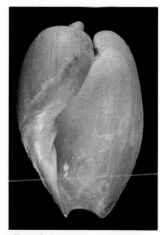

Olla Volute   (4") 10 cm
Cymbium olla (L., 1758). Southern Spain to Oran; Algeria and
Morocco. Dredged, 50 to 100
m; uncommon.

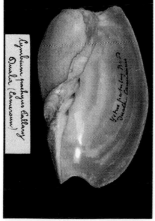

Dilated Baler   (4") 10 cm
Cymbium pachyus (Pallary,
1930). West Africa. Littoral to 10
m; uncommon. Similar *C. olla*
has lower spire. Holotype illus.

African Neptune Volute
         (8") 20 cm
Cymbium pepo (Lightfoot,
1786). West Africa. Uncommon. Syn.: *neptuni* Gmelin.

Indian Volute   (9") 23 cm
Melo melo (Lightfoot, 1786).
Malaysia; South China Sea. On
mud to 10 m; uncommon.
Syn.: *indica* Gmelin.

Crowned Baler   (8") 20 cm
Melo aethiopica (L., 1758). Indonesia. Offshore; uncommon. Syn.: *tessellata* Lamarck;
nautica Lamarck.

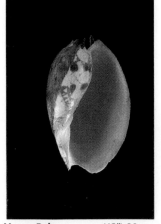

Heavy Baler   (12") 30 cm
Melo umbilicatus Sowerby, 1826. Australia to New Guinea. Shallow water; uncommon. Spines hide protoconch.

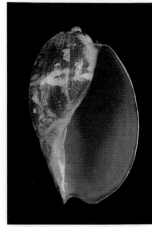

Milton Baler   (12") 30 cm
Melo miltonis (Griffith & Pidgeon, 1834). S.W. Australia. Shallow water; common. Shoulder spines curve inwards.

Crown Volute   (2.5") 6 cm
Cymbiola cymbiola (Gmelin, 1791). Indonesia. Offshore; uncommon. Syn.: *corona* Dillwyn; *flammula* Wood.

Banded Crown Volute
    (2.5") 6 cm
Cymbiola cymbiola (Gmelin, 1791). Indonesia. Offshore; uncommon. Banded color form.

Princely Volute   (4") 10 cm
Cymbiola aulica (Sowerby, 1825). Southern Philippines. On sand, 4 to 50 m; uncommon. May be yellow or orange.

Cathcart's Volute   (4") 10 cm
Cymbiola aulica form *cathcartiae* Reeve, 1856. Variation with reduced spines and lacking red color.

Golden-mouth Volute   (2") 5 cm
Cymbiola chrysostoma (Swainson, 1824). Indonesia. Rare. No reliable records available. Syn.: *luteostoma* Deshayes.

Yellow Volute   (3") 7.5 cm
Cymbiola flavicans (Gmelin, 1791). Northern Australia; New Guinea. Shallow water; moderately common.

Imperial Volute   (8") 20 cm
Aulica imperialis (Lightfoot, 1786). Southern Philippines. On sand, shallow water; common. Syn.: *robinsona* Burch.

Robinson's Volute   (8") 20 cm
Aulica imperialis form *robinsona* J. Q. Burch, 1954. Southern Philippines; uncommon.

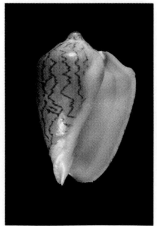

Noble Volute   (5.5") 14 cm
Cymbiola nobilis (Lightfoot, 1786). Taiwan to Singapore. Littoral to 100 m; common. Syn.: *scapha* Gmelin.

Bullate Volute   (2.5") 6 cm
Callipara bullatiana Weaver & Dupont, 1967. South Africa. Offshore and beached; moderately common. Syn.: *bullata* Swainson.

Magnificent Volute (10″) 25 cm
Cymbiola magnifica (Gebauer, 1802). East Australia. On sand to 120 m; moderately common. Syn.: *altispira* Mayblom.

Rossini's Volute (8″) 18 cm
Cymbiola rossiniana (Bernardi, 1859). New Caledonia area only. Offshore in 3 to 10 m; uncommon.

Thatcher's Volute (3.5″) 9 cm
Cymbiolacca thatcheri (McCoy, 1868). Chesterfield Island, north of New Caledonia. Rare.

Wiseman's Volute (3″) 7.5 cm
Cymbiolacca wisemani (Brazier, 1870). Queensland. Offshore reefs, 1 to 30 m; uncommon. Syn.: *randalli* Stokes.

Graceful Volute (3.2″) 8 cm
Cymbiolacca cracenta McMichael, 1963. Queensland, Australia. 20 to 50 m; uncommon.

Deshayes's Volute (3.5″) 9 cm
Cymbiola deshayesi (Reeve, 1855). New Caledonia. Shallow water; moderately common.

Blood-red Volute (4″) 10 cm
Cymbiola rutila (Broderip, 1826). N.E. Australia; New Guinea. On sand, shallow water; moderately common.

Beautiful Volute (3″) 7.5 cm
Cymbiolacca pulchra (Sowerby, 1825). North Queensland. Sand, down to 60 m; common. Syn.: *woolacottae* McMichael.

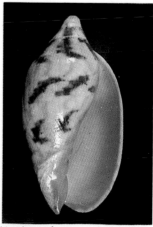

Neilsen's Volute (3″) 7.5 cm
Cymbiolacca pulchra color form *neilseni* McMichael, 1963. Australia. Uncommon.

Perry's Volute (3″) 7.5 cm
Cymbiolacca pulchra color form *perryae* Ostergaard & Summers, 1957. Lacks dark spots. Holotype illustrated.

Dotted Volute (2.7″) 7 cm
Cymbiolacca peristicta McMichael, 1963. N. Queensland, Australia. On sand, shallow water; uncommon.

Norris's Volute (3″) 7.5 cm
Cymbiola rutila norrisi (Gray, 1838). Papua to Solomons. Shallow water; moderately common. Syn.: *ruckeri* Crosse.

Entangled Volute (3″) 7.5 cm
Cymbiolacca perplicata (Hedley, 1902). Coral Sea; N.E. Australia. Offshore; rare.

Sophia's Volute (2.5″) 6.5 cm
Cymbiola sophia (Gray, 1846). Northern Australia; Arafura Sea. On mud to 40 m; moderately common.

Irvin's Volute (4″) 10 cm
Cymbiola irvinae (E. A. Smith, 1909). Western Australia. On sand and shells, 50 to 150 m; moderately rare.

Snowy Volute (2.5″) 6.5 cm
Cymbiola nivosa (Lamarck, 1804). Western Australia. On sand to 40 m; common. Spines solid.

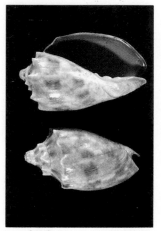

Erased Volute (2.5″) 6.5 cm
Cymbiola nivosa form *oblita* (E. A. Smith, 1909). Western Australia. Spines on shoulder. Uncommon.

Bat Volute (3″) 8 cm
Cymbiola vespertilio (L., 1758). Philippines to N. Australia. On mud to 20 m; common. Syn.: *mitis* and *serpentina* Lamarck.

Angular Volute (6″) 15 cm
Zidona dufresnei (Donovan, 1823). Rio de Janeiro to central Argentina. 40 to 80 m; common. Syn.: *angulata* Swainson.

Maidservant Volute (6″) 15 cm
Adelomelon ancilla (Lightfoot, 1786). Uruguay and Argentina. Offshore; uncommon. Syn.: *barattinii* Klap. & Ureta.

Beck's Volute (14″) 35 cm
Adelomelon beckii (Broderip, 1836). Brazil; Argentina. Sand and mud to 64 m; uncommon. Syn.: *fusiformis* Kiener.

Rios's Volute (8″) 20 cm
Adelomelon riosi Clench & Turner, 1964. Argentina. Dredged, 50 to 200 m; rare. Holotype illus.

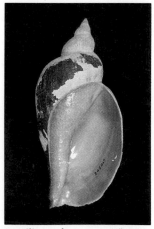

Brazilian Volute (6″) 15 cm
Adelomelon brasiliana (Lamarck, 1811). Southern Brazil; Argentina. Sand or mud to 70 m; common.

Paradox Volute (10″) 25 cm
Adelomelon paradoxa (Lahille, 1895). Argentina; Falkland Is. Offshore; uncommon.

Cotton's Volute (12″) 30 cm
Cottonia nodiplicata (Cox, 1910). W. and S. Australia. Offshore in 4 to 210 m; uncommon. Syn.: *dannevigi* Verco.

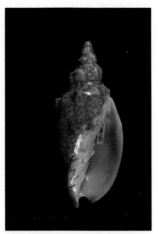

American Volute (2″) 5 cm
Odontocymbiola americana (Reeve, 1856). Central Brazil. Offshore in 10 to 80 m; uncommon. Syn.: *cleryana* Petit.

Magellanic Volute (7″) 19 cm
Odontocymbiola magellanica (Gmelin, 1791). Argentina; Chile. Offshore; locally common. Many synonyms.

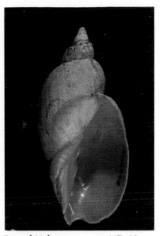

Pescal Volute (4″) 10 cm
Odontocymbiola pescalia Clench and Turner, 1964. Argentina. Offshore, deep water; rare. Holotype illustrated.

Alarcon Volute (2.5″) 6 cm
Miomelon alarconi Stuardo & Villas, 1974. Chile. Offshore in deep water; rare. Holotype illustrated.

Spartan Volute (3″) 8 cm
Tractolira sparta Dall, 1896. Gulf of Panama to West Mexico. Abyssal; rare. Holotype illustrated.

Bednall's Volute (4″) 10 cm
Volutoconus bednalli (Brazier, 1878). Northern Territory, Australia. On sand, 10 to 40 m; moderately rare.

Cone-shaped Volute (2.7″) 7 cm
Volutoconus coniformis (Cox, 1871). Northwestern Australia. Littoral to 20 m; rare.

Gross's Volute (4″) 10 cm
Volutoconus grossi (Iredale, 1927). New South Wales and Queensland. 50 to 100 m; moderately rare.

Hargreaves's Volute
(3.5″) 10 cm
Volutoconus hargreavesi (Angas, 1872). Western Australia. 40 to 240 m; rare. Syn.: *daisyae* Weaver.

Kreusler's Volute (3.2″) 8 cm
Notovoluta kreuslerae (Angas, 1865). South Australia. Sand and rubble, 14 to 160 m; moderately rare.

Hunter's Volute (5.5″) 14 cm
Cymbiolista hunteri Iredale, 1931. East Australia. 10 to 150 m; common. Syn.: *marmorata* Swainson.

Arab Volute (6″) 15 cm
Alcithoe arabica (Gmelin, 1791). New Zealand. Offshore; moderately common. Syn.: *jaculoides* Powell.

Swainson's Volute (8″) 20 cm
Alcithoe swainsoni Marwick, 1926. New Zealand. 8 to 100 m; common. Syn.: *elongata* Swainson; *ostenfeldi* Iredale.

Calva Volute (8″) 20 cm
Alcithoe swainsoni form *calva* Powell, 1928. New Zealand. Offshore; deep water. A smooth form.

Fusus Volute (3″) 8 cm
Alcithoe fusus (Quoy & Gaimard, 1833). New Zealand. Offshore; 6 to 120 m; uncommon. Syn.: *gracilis* Swainson.

Laroche's Volute (4″) 10 cm
Alcithoe larochei Marwick, 1926. North Island; New Zealand. 60 to 700 m; uncommon.

Pratas Volute (3″) 7.5 cm
Sigaluta pratasensis Rehder, 1967. Off Pratas Island, China Sea. 600 m; rare. Holotype illustrated.

Cukri Volute (3″) 7.5 cm
Sigaluta cukri Rokop, 1972. Off Baja California; Mexico. Deep water, very rare. Holotype illustrated.

Knox's Volute (3″) 7.5 cm
Teremelon knoxi Dell, 1956. South Island, New Zealand. 400 to 700 m; rare.

Vexillate Volute (3″) 7.5 cm
Harpulina arausiaca (Lightfoot, 1786). Ceylon and South India. Offshore to 10 m; uncommon. Syn.: *vexillum* Gmelin.

Brown-lined Volute (3″) 7.5 cm
Harpulina lapponica (L., 1767). Sri Lanka; southern India. Offshore; common. Syn.: *interpuncta* Reeve.

Astonishing Volute (4.5″) 11 cm
Iredalina mirabilis Finlay, 1926. New Zealand. 300 to 800 m; rare. Syn.: *aurantia* Powell.

Cordero's Volute (2″) 5 cm
Provocator corderoi Carcelles, 1947. S. Uruguay to Patagonia. 2 to 250 m; rare.

Polished Volute (3″) 7.5 cm
Fulgoraria leviuscula Rehder, 1969. Off Pratas Island, China Sea. 310 m; rare. Holotype illustrated.

Davies's Volute (5″) 13 cm
Fulgoraria daviesi (Fulton, 1938). Shikoku Island, Japan. 150 to 250 m; common.

Kaneko Volute (5″) 13 cm
Fulgoraria kaneko Y. Hirase, 1922. Japan to Chekiang Province, China. 150 to 300 m; rare. Syn.: *hayashii* Habe & Ito.

Humerose Volute (4″) 10 cm
Fulgoraria humerosa Rehder, 1969. South China Sea. 300 m; rare. Holotype illus.

Cancellate Volute (4″) 10 cm
Fulgoraria cancellata Kuroda & Habe, 1950. Off central Japan in 200 m; moderately common.

Clara Volute (4″) 10 cm
Fulgoraria clara (Sowerby, 1914). Off Honshu Island, Japan in 10 to 400 m; moderately common.

Hamille's Volute (5″) 13 cm
Fulgoraria hamillei (Crosse, 1869). Taiwan; Japan. Sand or sandy clay, offshore. Uncommon.

Delicate Volute (2″) 5 cm
Fulgoraria delicata (Fulton, 1940). Japan. 150 to 400 m; common. Paratype illustrated.

Hirase's Volute (6″) 15 cm
Fulgoraria hirasei (Sowerby, 1912). Japan. Offshore. Common. Sold in Honshu fish markets.

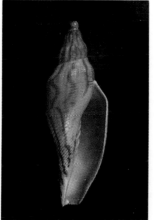

Asian Flame Volute (4″) 10 cm
Fulgoraria rupestris (Gmelin, 1791). Taiwan; China. Uncommon. Syn.: *fulminata* Lamarck; *aurantia* Shikama & Kosuge.

Stearns's Volute (5″) 13 cm
Arctomelon stearnsii Dall, 1872. Alaska. Offshore in 50 to 200 m; locally common.

Gunther's Volute (1.5″) 4 cm
Paramoria guntheri (E. A. Smith, 1886). Southern Australia. 40-80 m; moderately rare. Syn.: *adcocki* Tate.

Dampier's Volute   (1.2″) 3 cm
Amoria dampieria Weaver, 1960. Western Australia. Offshore; uncommon.

Pretext Volute   (2.5″) 6 cm
Amoria praetexta (Reeve, 1849). Western Australia. Subtidal to 50 m on sand; uncommon.

Channeled Volute   (2.5″) 6 cm
Amoria canaliculata (McCoy, 1869). Queensland. On coral and sand, to 150 m; uncommon. Syn.: *harfordi* Cox.

Damon's Volute   (4″) 10 cm
Amoria damonii Gray, 1864. Northern Australia. Littoral to 10 m; common. Syn.: *reevei* Sowerby; *keatsiana* Ludbrook.

Elliot's Volute   (3.5″) 8.5 cm
Amoria ellioti (Sowerby, 1864). Western Australia. In sand, low-tide level. Moderately common.

Gray's Volute   (3″) 7.5 cm
Amoria grayi Ludbrook, 1953. Northern Territory to Western Australia. Offshore to 50 m; moderately common.

Carol's Volute   (2.5″) 6.5 cm
Amoria maculata (Swainson, 1822). Queensland, Australia. Littoral to 80 m; common. Syn.: *caroli* Iredale.

Turner's Volute   (2″) 5 cm
Amoria turneri (Griffith & Pidgeon, 1834). Northern Australia. 10 to 40 m; common. Syn.: *normaniae* Cotton.

MacAndrew's Volute (3″) 7.5 cm
Amoria macandrewi (Sowerby, 1887). Barrow Island, Australia. Shallow water. Uncommon. Holotype illus.

Desirable Volute   (3.5″) 9 cm
Amoria exoptanda (Reeve, 1849). South Australia. On gravel, 12 to 20 m; rare.

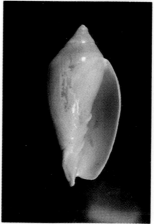

Sclater's Volute   (4″) 10 cm
Amoria sclateri (Cox, 1869). Bass Straits, Tasmania. Offshore, 40 to 60 m; uncommon. Syn.: *kingi* Cox.

Wavy Volute   (3.5″) 9 cm
Amoria undulata (Lamarck, 1804). S. Australia; Tasmania. On sand to 50 m; common. Syn.: *angasi* Sowerby.

Lorois's Volute   (3″) 8 cm
Harpulina loroisi Valenciennes, 1863. Ceylon and southern India. Offshore. Uncommon.

Fire-mouth Volute   (3″) 8 cm
Fusivoluta pyrrhostoma (Watson, 1882). South Africa. Offshore from 80 to 400 m; uncommon.

Barnard's Volute   (4″) 10 cm
Fusivoluta barnardi Rehder, 1969. Natal to Mozambique. Offshore, 40 to 700 m; uncommon. Paratype illus.

Barry Clarke's Volute (4″) 10 cm
Fusivoluta clarkei Rehder, 1969. Off Mozambique in 480 to 600 m; uncommon. Paratype illustrated.

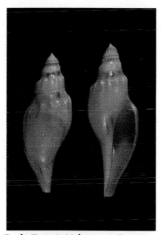

De la Torre's Volute   (4″) 10 cm
Volutifusus torrei (Pilsbry, 1937). Cuba. Offshore, 20 to 400 m; rare. Paratypes.

Aguayo's Volute   (4.5″) 11.3 cm
Volutifusus aguayoi (Clench, 1940). Off east coast of Florida. Deep water. Rare. Holotype illus.

The Junonia   (4″) 10 cm
Scaphella junonia (Lamarck, 1804). S.E. United States. Offshore. Uncommon. Syn.: *johnstoneae* Clench (darker form).

Butler's Junonia   (4.5″) 11 cm
Scaphella junonia subspecies *butleri* Clench, 1953. Gulf of Campeche, Mexico. Locally uncommon offshore.

Dubious Volute   (6″) 15 cm
Scaphella dubia (Broderip, 1827). S.E. United States. 50 to 300 m; uncommon. Syn.: *schmitti* Bartsch.

Kiener's Volute   (8″) 20 cm
Scaphella dubia subspecies *kieneri* Clench, 1946. Northern areas of the Gulf of Mexico in 100 to 200 m; locally common.

Neptune Volute   (2″) 5 cm
Scaphella neptunia (Clench & Aguayo, 1940). South of Jamaica. 600 m; rare. Illustrated holotype is immature.

Evelyn's Volute   (7″) 18 cm
Scaphella evelina Bayer, 1971. Lower Caribbean. Deep water to 641 m; rare. Holotype (9 cm) illustrated.

Gould's Volute   (4″) 10 cm
Scaphella gouldiana (Dall, 1887). Off south Florida. Banded form rare. Variable.

Atlantis Volute   (3″) 7.5 cm
Scaphella gouldiana form *atlantis* Clench, 1946. Off Cuba, deep water; rare.

Cuban Volute   (2.5″) 6 cm
Scaphella gouldiana form *cuba* Clench, 1946. Off Cuba, deep water. Holotype illustrated.

Dohrn's Volute   (4″) 10 cm
Scaphella gouldiana form *dohrni* (Sowerby, 1903). S.E. United States, offshore, 80 to 1,000 m; uncommon.

Gilchrist's Volute   (7″) 18 cm
Neptuneopsis gilchristi (Sowerby, 1898). South Africa. 33 to 250 m; moderately common.

Spotted Flask   (2.5″) 6.5 cm
Ampulla priamus (Gmelin, 1791). Portugal to N.W. Africa. 50 to 300 m; uncommon. Syn.: *stercuspulicum* Gmelin.

Tibia Volute   (2.4″) 6 cm
Teramachia tibiaeformis Kuroda, 1931. Southern Japan. Offshore to 300 m; uncommon. Genus in Turbinellidae.

The Williams's Volute (5″) 13 cm
Teramachia johnsoni form *williamsorum* Rehder, 1972. (holotype) S.W. Pacific. Deep water.

Dall's Volute   (8″) 20 cm
Teramachia dalli (Bartsch, 1942). Central Philippines. Deep water to 800 m; rare. Holotype illus.

Smith's Volute   (6″) 15 cm
Teramachia smithi (Bartsch, 1942). Central Philippines. Deep water in 500 to 860 m; very rare. Holotype illus.

Chestnut Volute   (2″) 4.8 cm
Calliotectum vernicosum Dall, 1890. Ecuador and Galapagos Islands. Deep water. Rare.

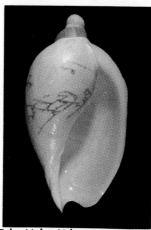

False Melon Volute (10″) 26 cm
Livonia mammilla (Sowerby, 1844). S.E. Australia. Dredged, to 200 m; uncommon. Syn.: *leucostoma* Mayblom.

Slim Benthovolute (3″) 7.5 cm
Benthovoluta gracilior Rehder,
1967. Philippine Islands. Deep
water in 1,000 m; rare. Holotype illustrated.

Cortez's Volute (3″) 7.5 cm
Surculina cortezi (Dall, 1908).
Off southern California. Deep
water in 1,900 m; rare. Holotype illus. Family Turbinellidae.

Alaska Miter-volute (2″) 5 cm
Volutomitra alaskana Dall, 1902.
Alaska to California. Offshore
to 160 m; rare. Holotype illus.
Family Volutomitridae.

Erebus Miter-volute (2″) 5 cm
Volutomitra erebus Bayer, 1971.
Off East Colombia. Deep wa-
ter; rare. Holotype illustrated.

Persephone Miter-volute
(2″) 5 cm
Volutomitra persephone Bayer,
1971. Gulf of Panama. Deep water; rare. Holotype illustrated.

THE NUTMEGS
FAMILY CANCELLARIIDAE

The cancellarias are mainly
tropical in distribution with
many interesting variations in
shape. The columella bears
several strong, slanting plicae.
There is no operculum. Most
specimens illustrated here are
from the collection of Richard
E. Petit.

Common Nutmeg (1.5″) 3 cm
Cancellaria reticulata (L., 1767).
S.E. United States to Brazil.
Subtidal to 30 m; common.
Rarely albino.

Adele's Nutmeg (1.5″) 3 cm
Cancellaria reticulata subspecies *adelae* Pilsbry, 1940.
Florida Keys. Shallow water;
uncommon. Paratype illus.

Scaled Nutmeg (0.6″) 1.5 cm
Scalptia scalata (Sowerby,
1833). Indian Ocean. Offshore,
shallow water; common.

Elegant Nutmeg (1.5″) 4 cm
Cancellaria elegans Sowerby,
1821. Australia to Philippines.
Shallow water; uncommon.

Oblong Nutmeg (1.2″) 3 cm
Cancellaria oblonga Sowerby,
1825. Indo-Pacific. Offshore;
uncommon. Syn.: *bifasciata*
Deshayes.

Reeve's Nutmeg (1.5″) 4 cm
Cancellaria reeveana Crosse,
1861. Japan to Philippines. Offshore to 10 m; common.

Chinese Nutmeg　(1.5″) 4 cm
Cancellaria sinensis Reeve, 1856. East Asia. Offshore to 30 m; common.

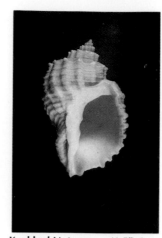

Knobbed Nutmeg　(1.5″) 4 cm
Cancellaria nodulifera Sowerby, 1825. Japan. Offshore, shallow water; uncommon.

Spengler's Nutmeg　(2″) 5 cm
Cancellaria spengleriana Deshayes, 1830. Japan. Offshore to 20 m; common.

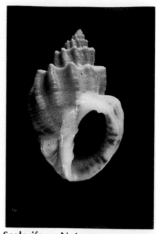

Scalariform Nutmeg
(0.7″) 1.8 cm
Scalptia scalariformis (Lamarck, 1822). Australia. Shallow water; locally common.

Granular Nutmeg　(1″) 2.5 cm
Cancellaria granosa Sowerby, 1832. South Australia and Tasmania. Shallow water; common.

Western Nutmeg　(1″) 2.5 cm
Cancellaria westralis Garrard, 1975. Australia. Shallow water; locally common.

Spiral Nutmeg　(1.3″) 3 cm
Cancellaria spirata Lamarck, 1822. Australia. Shallow water; locally common.

Amasia Nutmeg　(0.7″) 1.8 cm
Scalptia amasia (Iredale, 1930). Australia. Offshore; locally common.

Fearful Nutmeg　(1″) 2.5 cm
Cancellaria anxifer Iredale, 1925. East Australia. Offshore to 60 m; locally common.

Milky Nutmeg　(1.5″) 4 cm
Cancellaria lactea Deshayes, 1830. South Australia; Tasmania. Offshore; nutmegs.

Similar Nutmeg　(1″) 2.5 cm
Cancellaria similis Sowerby, 1833. Mediterranean and West Africa. Common.

Cancellate Nutmeg　(1.2″) 3 cm
Cancellaria cancellata (L., 1767). West Africa. Shallow water to 10 m; common.

Funnel Nutmeg (0.8") 2 cm
Olssonella funiculata (Hinds, 1843). West Mexico to Panama. Offshore; uncommon.

Fisherman's Nutmeg (1") 2.5 cm
Cancellaria piscatoria (Gmelin, 1791). West Africa. Subtidal to 5 m; locally common.

Dim Nutmeg (1") 2.5 cm
Cancellaria urceolata Hinds, 1843. West Mexico to Ecuador. Offshore to 73 m; common.

White Nutmeg (1") 2.5 cm
Cancellaria albida Hinds, 1843. West Mexico to Ecuador. Offshore to 128 m; moderately common.

Obese Nutmeg (2") 5 cm
Cancellaria obesa Sowerby, 1832. West Mexico to Ecuador. Intertidal to 90 m; common. Syn.: *acuminata* Sowerby.

Helmet Nutmeg (1.2") 4 cm
Cancellaria cassidiformis Sowerby, 1832. Gulf of California to Peru. Intertidal to 37 m; common.

Solid Nutmeg (1") 2.5 cm
Cancellaria solida Sowerby, 1832. West Mexico to Peru. Offshore to 37 m; common.

Cuming's Nutmeg (1.7") 4.5 cm
Cancellaria cumingiana Petit, 1844. West Mexico. Offshore; rare.

Toothed Nutmeg (1") 2.5 cm
Cancellaria indentata Sowerby, 1832. West Mexico to Ecuador. Offshore to 110 m; common.

Jewel Nutmeg (0.6") 1.5 cm
Cancellaria gemmulata Sowerby, 1832. West Mexico to Panama; Galapagos. Offshore to 73 m; uncommon.

Blood-mouthed Nutmeg (1") 2.5 cm
Cancellaria haemastoma Sowerby, 1832. Galapagos Islands; uncommon.

Balboa Nutmeg (1.5") 4 cm
Cancellaria balboae Pilsbry, 1931. West Mexico to Panama. 18 to 53 m; uncommon.

Jay's Nutmeg   (0.7") 1.8 cm
Cancellaria jayana Keen, 1958. West Mexico to Panama. Off-shore to 75 m; common.

Cooper's Nutmeg   (3") 7 cm
Cancellaria cooperi Gabb, 1865. California to West Mexico. Off-shore to 600 m; uncommon.

Crawford's Nutmeg   (2") 5 cm
Cancellaria crawfordiana (Dall, 1891). California. 30 to 400 m; uncommon.

Crawford's Nutmeg   (2") 5 cm
Cancellaria crawfordiana (Dall, 1891). Holotype specimen from off Drake's Bay, California, 48 m.

Io Nutmeg   (1.5") 4 cm
Cancellaria io Dall, 1896. Gulf of California. 600 m; rare. Holo-type illustrated.

Club Nutmeg   (1") 2.5 cm
Cancellaria clavatula Sowerby, 1832. West Mexico to Peru. Off-shore to 110 m; common. Syn.: *elata* Hinds, 1843.

Habe's Nutmeg   (0.7") 1.8 cm
Nipponaphera habei Petit, 1972. Japan to Taiwan. Off-shore; uncommon.

Half-clear Nutmeg (0.5") 1.2 cm
Nipponaphera semipellucida (Adams and Reeve, 1850). Ja-pan. Offshore; uncommon.

Bayer's Nutmeg   (0.8") 2 cm
Admetula bayeri Petit, 1976. Off Yucatan, Mexico. Deep water; rare. Holotype illustrated.

Campbell's Nutmeg
         (0.7") 1.8 cm
Olssonella campbelli Shasky, 1961. West Mexico. 18 to 91 m; uncommon.

Oblique Nutmeg   (1") 2.5 cm
Scalptia obliquata (Lamarck, 1822). Indo-Pacific. Subtidal; common. A very variable spe-cies. See variation.

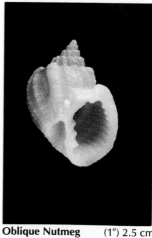

Oblique Nutmeg   (1") 2.5 cm
Scalptia obliquata (Lamarck, 1822). Indo-Pacific. Few-ribbed variety; moderately common.

Two-color Nutmeg (0.7") 1.8 cm
Scalptia bicolor (Hinds, 1843).
Indo-Pacific. Subtidal; common.

Lamellose Nutmeg (0.5") 1.2 cm
Scalptia lamellosa (Hinds, 1843). Indo-Pacific. Offshore; uncommon.

Textured Nutmeg (1") 2.5 cm
Scalptia textilis (Kiener, 1841). Indo-Pacific. Shallow water; uncommon.

Crosse's Nutmeg (0.8") 2.1 cm
Scalptia crossei (Semper, 1861). S.W. Pacific. Shallow water; locally common. Syn.: *serrata* Reeve.

Scaled Nutmeg (0.7") 1.8 cm
Scalptia scalarina (Lamarck, 1822). Indo-Pacific. Shallow water; common.

Hollow Nutmeg (1") 2.5 cm
Scalptia foveolata (Sowerby, 1848). South Africa. Offshore; common.

Disjunct Nutmeg (1") 2.5 cm
Trigonostoma semidisjuncta (Sowerby, 1848). South Africa. Offshore; common.

Strong's Nutmeg (0.5") 1.2 cm
Agatrix strongi (Shasky, 1961). Gulf of California. Offshore, deep water; rare.

Triangular Nutmeg (1") 2.5 cm
Trigonostoma pellucida (Perry, 1811). S.W. Pacific. Offshore, shallow water; rare. Syn.: *trigonostoma* Lamarck.

Antique Nutmeg (0.7") 1.8 cm
Trigonostoma antiquata (Hinds, 1843). Australia to Japan. Offshore; rare.

Laseron's Nutmeg (0.5") 1.2 cm
Trigonostoma laseroni (Iredale, 1936). Australia. Shallow water; locally common.

Philippi's Nutmeg (1") 2.5 cm
Trigonostoma tenerum (Philippi, 1848). S. Florida. Offshore, shallow water; uncommon. Syn.: *stimpsoni* Calkins.

Amakusa Nutmeg (0.7") 1.8 cm
Scalptia amakusana (Petit, 1974). Japan. Shallow water; locally common.

Withrow's Nutmeg (1") 2.5 cm
Scalptia withrowi (Petit, 1976). West Africa. Shallow water; locally common.

Angle-mouth Nutmeg
(1") 2.5 cm
Trigonostoma goniostoma (Sowerby, 1832). W. Mexico to Panama. Intertidal to 5 m; common.

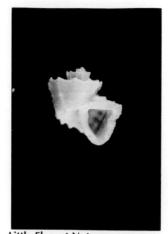

Little Elegant Nutmeg
(0.4") 1 cm
Trigonostoma elegantulum M. Smith, 1947. West Mexico to Ecuador. Offshore; uncommon.

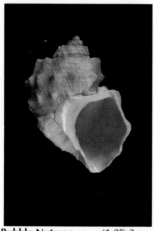

Bubble Nutmeg (1.2") 3 cm
Trigonostoma bullatum (Sowerby, 1832). West Mexico to Panama. Offshore to 82 m; common.

Miller's Nutmeg (1") 2.5 cm
Trigonostoma milleri Burch, 1949. Costa Rica; Galapagos. Offshore to 30 m; uncommon. Holotype illus.

Miller's Nutmeg (1") 2.5 cm
Trigonostoma milleri Burch, 1949. Variation in shape in a specimen from the Galapagos.

Mercado's Nutmeg (1.3") 3 cm
Scalptia mercadoi (Old, 1968). Philippines. Offshore; uncommon to rare.

Tessellate Nutmeg (1") 2.5 cm
Aphera tessellata (Sowerby, 1832). West Mexico to Peru. Offshore; uncommon. Type of subgenus *Aphera*.

Miter-shaped Nutmeg
(1") 2.5 cm
Narona mitriformis (Sowerby, 1832). Panama to Peru. Subtidal to 37 m; uncommon.

Basket Nutmeg (1") 2.5 cm
Cancellaria corbicula Dall, 1908. California. Deep water; rare. Holotype illustrated.

Big-spired Nutmeg (0.7") 1.8 cm
Fusiaphera macrospira (Adams & Reeve, 1850). S.W. Pacific to Japan. Offshore; uncommon.

Corrugated Nutmeg
(0.7″) 1.8 cm
Cancellaria corrugata Hinds, 1843. West Mexico to Ecuador. Offshore to 31 m; rare.

Banded Nutmeg   (2″) 5 cm
Gerdiella cingulata Olsson & Bayer, 1972. Caribbean. Deep water; rare. Holotype illus.

Santa Nutmeg   (1.5″) 4 cm
Gerdiella santa Olsson & Bayer, 1972. Florida Straits. Deep water; rare. Holotype illustrated.

Clark's Slim Nutmeg (1″) 2.5 cm
Perplicaria clarki M. Smith, 1947. W. Mexico to Panama. Intertidal; rare.

Spiny Nutmeg   (1″) 2.5 cm
Cancellaria centrota Dall, 1896. W. Mexico to Panama. Offshore in 120 m; rare.

Lyrate Nutmeg   (1″) 2.5 cm
Cancellaria lyrata (Brocchi, 1814). West Africa. Subtidal; uncommon.

Gladiator Nutmeg   (1.5″) 4 cm
Cancellaria gladiator Petit, 1976. Galapagos Islands. 200 m; rare. Paratype illustrated.

MARGINELLAS
FAMILY MARGINELLIDAE

One of the most beautiful families of the marine gastropods. Usually less than an inch in size, always highly polished, and with several strong teeth on the columella. Most of the 650 species live in sand in the tropics. West Africa has the most species. *Prunum, Glabella,* etc., are subgenera.

Pringle's Marginella (3″) 7.5 cm
Afrivoluta pringlei Tomlin, 1947. South Africa. 100 to 300 m; uncommon. Originally considered a volute.

Desjardin's Marginella (2″) 5 cm
Marginella desjardini Marche-Marchad, 1957. Ivory Coast, West Africa. Offshore to 100 m; uncommon.

Belcher's Marginella   (1″)
2.5 cm *Marginella belcheri* Hinds, 1844. Mauritania; West Africa. Moderately deep water; uncommon.

Adanson's Marginella   (1″)
2.5 cm *Marginella adansoni* Kiener, 1834. West Africa. Shallow water; uncommon. Syn.: *bifasciata* Sowerby.

Clery's Marginella (0.8") 2 cm
Marginella cleryi Petit, 1836. Mauritania to Gambia. Dredged in sand or mud, 20 m; uncommon.

Golden Marginella (1") 2.5 cm
Marginella aurantia Lamarck, 1822. West Africa. Under rocks, in sand, shallow water; moderately uncommon.

Goodall's Marginella (1") 2.5 cm
Marginella goodalli Sowerby, 1825. West Africa. Offshore; moderately common.

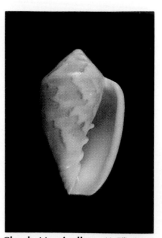

Cloudy Marginella (1.5") 4 cm
Marginella nebulosa (Röding, 1798). South Africa. Offshore to 75 m and beached; uncommon. Syn.: *nubeculata* Lam.

Fringed Marginella (0.8") 2 cm
Marginella limbata Lamarck, 1822. Canary Is., West Africa. Uncommon.

Spotted Marginella (0.8") 2 cm
Marginella persicula (L., 1758). West Africa; Cape Verde Islands. Moderately common. Syn.: *guttata* Link.

Plain Marginella (1") 2.5 cm
Marginella cornea Lamarck, 1822. Mauritania to Dahomey. Shallow water; moderately common.

Girdled Marginella (1") 2.5 cm
Marginella cingulata (Dillwyn, 1817). West Africa. In sand or mud; common. Syn.: *lineata* Lamarck.

Almond Marginella (0.6") 1.5 cm
Marginella amygdala Kiener, 1841. Mauritania to Rio Muni; common. Syn.: *gambiensis* Redfield.

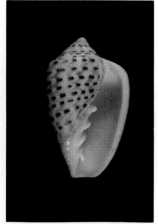

Mosaic Marginella (1") 2.5 cm
Marginella mosaica Sowerby, 1846. South Africa. Offshore, but usually found beached; moderately uncommon.

Bland Marginella (1") 2.5 cm
Marginella blanda Hinds, 1844. Senegal, West Africa. Offshore; uncommon.

Striped Marginella (1.5") 4 cm
Marginella strigata (Dillwyn, 1817). S.E. Asia. Shallow water; uncommon. Syn.: *praecalłosa* Higgins.

Petit's Marginella (1.4") 3.5 cm
Marginella petitii Duval, 1841. West Africa. Moderately deep water; uncommon.

Sebastian's Marginella (1.5") 4 cm
Marginella sebastiani Marche & Rosso, 1979. Senegal. Offshore; moderately common. See also *desjardini*.

Glistening Marginella (1") 2.5 cm
Marginella irrorata Menke, 1828. West Africa. Offshore; moderately common. Like a small *M. glabella*.

Ermine Marginella (1.2") 3 cm
Marginella faba (L., 1758). West Africa; uncommon. Once a great rarity among collectors. Syn.: *erminea* Röding.

Toothed Marginella (1") 2.5 cm
Marginella denticulata (Link, 1807). West Africa. Moderately uncommon. Syn.: *bifasciata* Lamarck (a banded form).

Shiny Marginella (1.2") 3 cm
Marginella glabella (L., 1758). N.W. Africa; Cape Verde Islands. Offshore to 80 m; moderately common.

Queen Marginella (1.3") 3.5 cm
Marginella pseudofaba Sowerby, 1846. West Africa. Moderately deep water; rare. Syn.: *imperatrix* Sykes.

Cuming's Marginella (1") 2.5 cm
Marginella helmatina Rang, 1832. Gambia to Angola. Shallow water; uncommon. Syn.: *cumingiana* Petit.

Olivelike Marginella (0.7") 1.8 cm
Marginella olivaeformis Kiener, 1834. Senegal to Gold Coast. Moderately common. Syn.: *hindsiana* Petit.

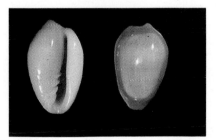

Encircled Marginella (0.8") 2 cm
Marginella cincta Kiener, 1834. West Africa. Offshore at about 40 m; moderately uncommon.

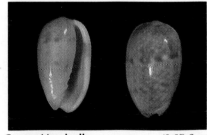

Canary Marginella (0.8") 2 cm
Marginella canaryensis Clover, 1972. Off Canary Islands and Morocco. Trawled, 60-120 m; rare.

Harplike Marginella (1") 2.5 cm
Marginella harpaeformis Sowerby, 1846. West Africa; moderately uncommon. Similar to *M. faba* but smaller and spotted.

Music Marginella   (0.7") 1.8 cm
Marginella musica Hinds, 1844. West Africa. Moderately deep water; rare. Close to *M. diadochus* but smaller.

Carmine Marginella   (0.3") 7 mm
Marginella hematita Kiener, 1841. S.E. United States to Brazil. Uncommon; offshore. Syn.: *philtata* M. Smith.

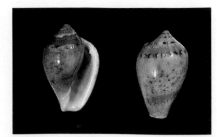

Hubert's Marginella   (0.7") 1.8 cm
Marginella huberti Clover, 1972. Angola. In coral rubble at 30 m and beached; uncommon.

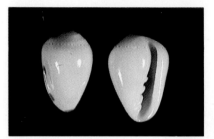

Atlantic Marginella   (0.5") 1.2 cm
Marginella apicina Menke, 1828. S.E. United States and West Indies. Shallow water; common. About 1 in 5,000 sinistral.

Obese Marginella   (0.7") 1.8 cm
Marginella obesa Redfield, 1846. Lower Caribbean; Brazil. Shallow water under rocks; uncommon. Syn.: *similis* Sowerby.

Storer's Marginella   (0.6") 1.5 cm
Marginella storeria Couthouy, 1837. Gulf of Mexico. Moderately deep water; uncommon.

Largillier's Marginella   (1") 2.5 cm
Marginella largillieri Kiener, 1841. Eastern Brazil. Offshore on sand, rocks or coral; rare.

Lilac Marginella   (1") 2.5 cm
Marginella lilacina Sowerby, 1846. Northeastern Brazil. Offshore on sand and broken shells; uncommon.

Martin's Marginella   (1.2") 3 cm
Marginella martini Petit, 1853. Off Rio de Janeiro, Brazil. Offshore on sand, 10 - 55 m; uncommon.

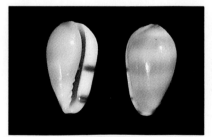

Roosevelt's Marginella   (1") 2.5 cm
Marginella roosevelti Bartsch & Rehder, 1940. Caribbean; Bahamas. Deep water; rare. Large form of *M. carnea*?

Short-spired Marginella   (0.8") 2 cm
Marginella curta Sowerby, 1832. Ecuador to Chile. In sand, 2 - 20 m; uncommon.

Stout Marginella   (0.8") 2 cm
Marginella robusta Sowerby, 1904. Southern Atlantic; Ascension Island. Uncommon.

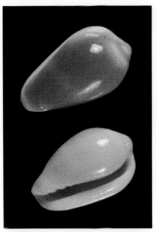

Orange Marginella (0.8″) 2 cm
Marginella carnea Storer, 1837.
S.E. Florida, West Indies. Offshore in grass to 20 m; moderately common.

Royal Marginella (1.2″) 3 cm
Marginella labiata Kiener, 1841.
Yucatan to Central America;
West Indies. In sand at low
tide; moderately common.

White-spotted Marginella
(0.8″) 2 cm
Marginella guttata (Dillwyn,
1817). S.E. Florida; West Indies
Under rocks, shallow water.

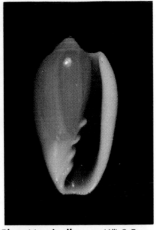

Plum Marginella (1″) 2.5 cm
Marginella prunum (Gmelin,
1791). Lower Caribbean to Brazil. Common. Syn.: *caerules-
cens* Lamarck.

Matthews's Marginella (2″) 5 cm
Marginella matthewsi Van Mol
& Tursch, 1967. N.E. Brazil. Offshore at about 25 m; moderately rare.

Thick Marginella (1″) 2.5 cm
Marginella marginata (Born,
1778). West Indies. In sand and
eel grass; common. Many synonyms.

Orange-banded Marginella
(0.5″) 1.2 cm
Marginella avena Kiener, 1834.
S.E. United States to Brazil.
Shallow water; common.

Delicate Marginella (1.2″) 3 cm
Marginella sapotilla Hinds,
1844. Panama to Ecuador. In
sand or mud at low tide; common. Syn.: *burchardi* Dunker.

Maclean's Marginella
(1.8″) 4.5 cm
Marginella macleani (Roth,
1978). Ecuador; rare. Holotype
illustrated.

Twinned Marginella
(0.5″) 1.2 cm
Marginella accola (Roth &
Coan, 1968). Panama. Interti-
dal; rare. Type *M. porcellana*
(Gmelin) analog in Caribbean.

Anson's Marginella
(0.5″) 1.2 cm
Marginella ansonae Clover,
1976. Madagascar. Shallow water; uncommon.

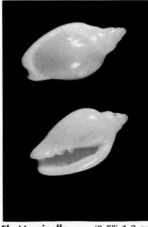

Fly Marginella (0.5″) 1.2 cm
Marginella muscaria Lamarck,
1822. Southern Australia; Tasmania. Low tide to 10 m; common. Syn.: *lactea* Hutton.

Narrow Marginella   (1") 2.5 cm
Marginella angustata Sowerby, 1846. Sri Lanka. Offshore to deep water; common.

Fischer's Marginella   (0.4") 1 cm
Marginella fischeri Bavay, 1902. Philippines. Offshore; uncommon.

Red Sea Marginella   (1") 2.5 cm
Marginella obtusa Sowerby, 1846. Red Sea; north Arabian Sea. In sand and mud 20 - 80 m; uncommon. Syn.: *mirabilis* H. Adams.

Peppered Marginella   (1") 2.5 cm
Marginella piperata Hinds, 1844. South Africa. Usually found beached; common. Syn.: *strigata* Sowerby.

Bairstow's Marginella   (0.6") 1.6 cm
Marginella bairstowi Sowerby, 1886. South Africa. Usually found beached; moderately common. Like a small *M. mosaica*.

Woolly Marginella   (1.2") 3 cm
Marginella floccata Sowerby, 1889. South Africa. On beaches; uncommon.

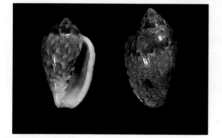

Rosy Marginella   (1") 2.5 cm
Marginella rosea Lamarck, 1822. South Africa. On beaches; moderately common.

Wavy-line Marginella   (1.2") 3 cm
Marginella lineolata Sowerby, 1886. South Africa. Offshore to 90 m; uncommon.

Brown-line Marginella   (1") 2.5 cm
Marginella diadochus A. Adams & Reeve, 1848. South Africa. Dredged in deep water; rare.

Fettered Marginella   (1") 2.5 cm
Marginella nodata Hinds, 1844. West Africa. Offshore; rare. Very few specimens in private collections.

Pink Marginella   (0.8") 2 cm
Marginella pergrandis (Clover, 1974). South Arabian coast; Masirah Island; Gulf of Oman. On beaches; rare.

Elegant Marginella   (1.8") 4.5 cm
Marginella elegans (Gmelin, 1791). Burma to S.W. Thailand. In sand 4 to 6 m; uncommon.

Ornate Marginella (1") 2.5 cm
Marginella ornata Redfield, 1870. South Africa. Usually found beached; moderately common. Syn.: *vittata* Reeve.

Broad Marginella (1") 2.5 cm
Marginella ventricosa G. Fischer, 1807. S.E. Asia; Indonesia. Shallow water, in mud; moderately common. Syn.: *quinqueplicata* Lamarck.

Four-lined Marginella (0.8") 2 cm
Marginella quadrilineata Gaskoin, 1849. Philippines; Northern Borneo. In sand and mud; uncommon.

Three-plaited Marginella (1") 2.5 cm
Marginella tricincta Hinds, 1844. Singapore to Taiwan. Offshore to 40 m; uncommon.

Broken-line Marginella (0.3") 7 mm
Marginella interruptolineata Mühlfeld, 1816. Lower Caribbean. Shallow water; common.

Sarda Marginella (1") 2.5 cm
Marginella sarda Kiener, 1834. Indian Ocean. Uncommon.

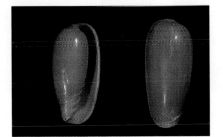

Finger Marginella (1") 2.5 cm
Marginella dactylus Lamarck, 1822. S.E. Asia; Indonesia. Uncommon.

Philippine Marginella (0.6") 1.5 cm
Marginella philippinarum Redfield, 1848. Philippines. Shallow water; common.

TURRIDS
FAMILY TURRIDAE

Turrids form the largest of all molluscan families in number of species. Hallmark is a notch or sinus in upper part of outer lip. Found in all seas from shallow water to abyssal depths turrids have a well-developed poison gland associated with radula. Some harpoon prey in the manner of cone shells. Operculum sometimes present.

Wavy-line Turrid (1") 2.5 cm
Perrona lineata (Lamarck, 1816). West Africa to Cape of Good Hope. Offshore; uncommon. Wavy lines follow lines of growth.

Nifat Turrid (2") 5 cm
Perrona nifat (Bruguière, 1789). West Africa. Offshore; moderately common. A solid and heavy shell.

Obese Turrid (1.4") 3.5 cm
Perrona obesa (Reeve, 1842). Angola. Offshore; uncommon. Whorls markedly stepped.

Deshayes's Turrid (2.5") 6.5 cm
Gemmula deshayesii (Doumet, 1839). Japan; China; Hong Kong. Offshore; moderately common.

Melvill's Turrid (2.3") 6 cm
Gemmula congener cosmoi (Sykes, 1930). Japan. Dredged 100 - 200 m; uncommon.

Splendid Turrid (2.5") 6.5 cm
Gemmula speciosa (Reeve, 1843). Philippines; China Sea; Arabian Sea. Deep water; uncommon.

Kiener's Turrid (2.5") 6.5 cm
Gemmula kieneri (Doumet, 1840). Japan; China Sea; Philippines. Deep water; uncommon.

Atlantic Gem Turrid (2") 5 cm
Gemmula periscelida (Dall, 1889). West Indies; S.E. United States. From 200 m; rare. Holotype illus.

Albatross Turrid (3") 7.5 cm
Gemmula diomedea Powell, 1964. Philippines. Dredged 200 - 700 m; rare. Holotype illus.

Graeffe's Turrid (1") 2.5 cm
Gemmula graeffei (Weinkauff, 1875). Fiji; Queensland; Philippines. Offshore; moderately common.

Luzon Turrid (2") 5 cm
Pinguigemmula philippinensis Powell, 1964. Philippines. Deep water; rare. Holotype illus.

Tesch's Turrid (2") 5 cm
Ptychosyrinx timorensis teschi Powell, 1964. Indonesia. Deep water; rare. Holotype illus.

Indian Turrid (3.5") 9 cm
Lophiotoma indica (Röding, 1798). Sri Lanka to Australia; Fiji. Moderately deep water; uncommon.

Marbled Turrid (1.8") 4.5 cm
Lophiotoma acuta (Perry, 1811). Indo-Pacific. Shallow to deep water; common. Most widespread living turrid.

Light-wine Turrid (2.2") 5.5 cm
Lophiotoma leucotropis (Adams & Reeve, 1850). Japan; Taiwan to Philippines. Offshore; uncommon.

Unedo Turrid (3.5″) 9 cm
Gemmula unedo (Kiener, 1839). Japan; Indonesia; Persian Gulf. Deep water; uncommon. Syn.: *invicta* Melvill.

Keeled Turrid (1.3″) 4.5 cm
Lophiotoma polytropa (Helbling, 1779). Philippines; Moluccas; New Caledonia. Offshore; uncommon.

White Giant Turrid (3.5″) 9 cm
Polystira albida (Perry, 1811). South Florida to Texas; West Indies. 50 - 250 m; common. Syn.: *virgo* Lamarck.

Delicate Giant Turrid (3″) 7.5 cm
Polystira tellea (Dall, 1889). Florida to Louisiana. Moderately deep water; moderately common.

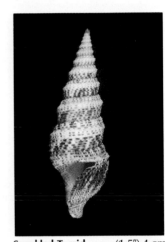

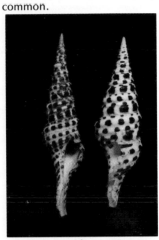

Noble Giant Turrid (3.5″) 9 cm
Polystira nobilis (Hinds, 1843). Gulf of California to Panama. Offshore to 165 m; uncommon.

Necklace Turrid (2″) 5 cm
Xenoturris cingulifera (Lamarck, 1822). Tropical Indo-Pacific. Shallow and deeper water; common.

Speckled Turrid (1.5″) 4 cm
Xenoturris millepunctata (Sowerby, 1908). South Pacific; Japan. Tidal flats and offshore; uncommon.

Babylonia Turrid (3″) 7.5 cm
Turris babylonia (L., 1758). Tropical Pacific (not Australia). Shallow and deeper water; uncommon.

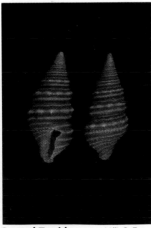

Supreme Turrid (6″) 15 cm
Turris crispa crispa (Lamarck, 1816). Indo-Pacific. Offshore; uncommon. Largest of living turrids.

Intricate Turrid (1.8″) 4.5 cm
Turris crispa intricata Powell, 1964. Hawaiian Islands. 8 - 60 m; rare. Holotype illus.

Large Perverse Turrid (2″) 5 cm *Antiplanes major* Bartsch, 1944. California. 80 - 600 m; common. Always sinistral. Holotype illus.

Crested Turrid (1″) 2.5 cm
Turridrupa bijubata (Reeve, 1843). Tropical Indo-Pacific. Intertidal; moderately common.

Kaderly's Turrid   (3") 7.5 cm
Comitas kaderlyi (Lischke, 1872). Japan to Philippines. Dredged 140 to 1600 m; uncommon.

Miter-shaped Turrid (1.5") 3 cm
Genota mitriformis (Wood, 1828). West Africa. Offshore; uncommon. Syn.: *mitraeformis* Kiener.

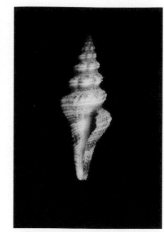

Surinam Turrid   (1.3") 3.5 cm
Fusiturricula jaquensis (Sowerby, 1850). Surinam; Brazil. Moderately deep water; rare.

Fenimore's Turrid   (2") 5 cm
Fusiturricula fenimorei Bartsch, 1934. Puerto Rico. Deep water; rare.

Wax-beaded Turrid (2.5") 6.5 cm
Leucosyrinx tenoceras Dall, 1889. S.E. United States; Lesser Antilles. 1000 to 1500 m; rare. Holotype illus.

Olivaceous Knefastia
             (1.8") 4.5 cm
Knefastia olivacea (Sowerby, 1833). Gulf of California to Ecuador. Offshore; common.

Elegant Star Turrid (1.8") 4.5 cm
Cochlespira elegans (Dall, 1881). Cuba; Florida. Dredged 60-400 m; rare. Formerly *Ancistosyrinx*.

Dull Star Turrid   (2") 5 cm
Cochlespira pulchella semipolita Powell, 1969. Philippines. Deep water; rare. Holotype illus.

Goode's Turrid   (3.5") 9 cm
Aforia goodei (Dall, 1890). Western Americas. Deep water; uncommon. Syn.: *persimilis* Dall (holotype illus.).

Ridged Turrid   (3") 7.5 cm
Aforia circinata (Dall, 1873). Bering Sea; Alaska to Japan. Deep water; uncommon. Syn.: *diomedea* Bartsch.

Ringed Turrid   (2.9") 7.5 cm
Phymorhynchus cingulatus (Dall, 1890). Galapagos. Dredged at about 2,400 m; rare. Holotype illustrated.

Cadenas's Turrid   (1.5") 4 cm
Clavus cadenasi (Clench & Aguayo, 1939). Off Cuba. Deep water; rare. Holotype illus. Is *johnsoni*?

Johnson's Turrid   (1.5") 4 cm
Clavus johnsoni (Bartsch, 1934). Puerto Rico. Deep water; rare. Holotype illustrated.

Baird's Turrid   (1.4") 3.5 cm
Pleurotomella bairdii Verrill & Smith, 1884. Off Delaware and Chesapeake Bays. Dredged about 3,250 m; rare.

Hadria Turrid   (1.2") 3 cm
Pleurotomella hadria Dall, 1889. Off North Carolina. 800 to 1500 m; rare. Holotype illus.

Graceful Atlantic Turrid
            (1") 2.5 cm
Pleurotomella chariessa Watson, 1881. North Atlantic to off North Carolina. 1,000 m; rare.

Carpenter's Turrid   (2.5") 6.5 cm
Megasurcula carpenteriana (Gabb, 1865). California to Baja California. Offshore to 480 m on mud; common.

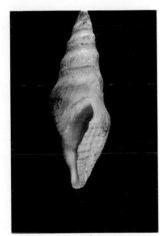

Carpenter's Turrid   (2.5") 6.5 cm
Megasurcula carpenteriana (Gabb, 1865). Described under other names, including *tremperiana* Dall (holotype illus.).

Pink Turrid   (1.2") 3 cm
Phenatoma novaezelandiae (Reeve, 1843). New Zealand. Shallow to deep water on sand; uncommon.

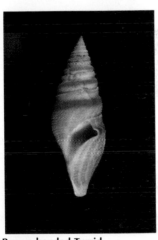

Brown-banded Turrid
            (1.5") 4 cm
Bathytoma viabrunnea (Dall, 1889). S.E. Florida; West Indies. 200 to 700 m; rare.

Two-edged Turrid   (1.5") 3 cm
Clavatula bimarginata (Lamarck, 1822). West Africa. Offshore; uncommon.

Ima's Turrid   (2") 5 cm
Imaclava ima (Bartsch, 1944). Gulf of California. Offshore; rare. Holotype illustrated.

Lean Turrid   (1.5") 4 cm
Hindsiclava alesidota (Dall, 1889). North Carolina to Florida; Barbados. 50 to 150 m; uncommon. Syn.: *macilenta* Dall.

Jeffreys's Turrid   (1.2") 3 cm
Clathrodrillia jeffreysii (E. A. Smith, 1875). Japan. Offshore; uncommon.

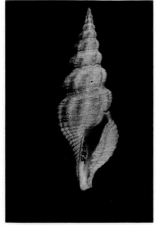

Lavinia Turrid (2") 5 cm
Ptychobela lavinia (Dall, 1919). West Mexico to Peru. Habitat unknown; rare. Holotype illus.

Saddened Turrid (1") 2.5 cm
Compsodrillia tristicha (Dall, 1889). Gulf of Mexico. Deep water; rare. Holotype illus.

Muricate Turrid (1") 2.5 cm
Clavatula muricata (Lamarck, 1822). West Africa. Offshore; locally uncommon.

Gaboon Turrid (1.4") 3.5 cm
Clavatula gabonensis Melvill, 1923. Senegal. Offshore; uncommon.

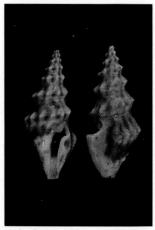

Little-dog Turrid (1") 2.5 cm
Clavus canicularis (Röding, 1798). Western Pacific. Shallow water; uncommon. Syn.: *auriculifera* Lamarck.

Brown-spot Turrid (2") 4.7 cm
Imaclava unimaculata (Sowerby, 1834). West Mexico to Colombia. 20 to 70 m; uncommon.

Diadem Turrid (1.2") 3 cm
Clavatula diadema (Kiener, 1840). West Africa. Offshore; uncommon.

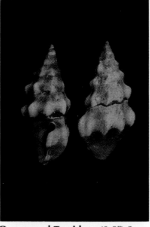

One-zoned Turrid (0.8") 2 cm
Clavus unizonalis (Lamarck, 1822). Western Pacific. Shallow water; common.

Enna Turrid (1") 2.5 cm
Clavus enna Dall, 1918. Philippines; S.W. Pacific. Uncommon. Syn.: *unifasciata* E. A. Smith, not Deshayes.

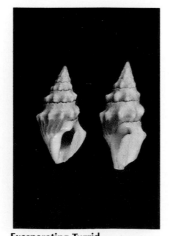

Exasperating Turrid
(0.6") 1.5 cm
Austroclavus exasperatus (Reeve, 1843). Indian Ocean. 1 to 30 m; uncommon.

Rose-tinted Turrid (1.5") 4 cm
Clavus rosalinus Marrat, 1877. West Africa. Offshore; uncommon.

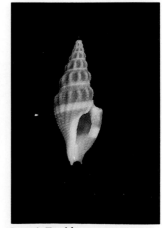

Bayer's Turrid (1") 2.5 cm
Glyphostoma bayeri Olsson, 1971. Gulf of Panama. Deep water; rare. Holotype illustrated.

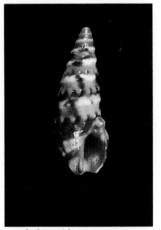

Mottled Turrid (1") 2.5 cm
Pilsbryspira amathea (Dall, 1919). West Mexico. Among rocks at low tide; common. Holotype illus.

Janet's Turrid (1") 2.5 cm
Splendrillia janetae Bartsch, 1934. Gulf of Mexico; West Indies. Deep water; rare. Holotype illus.

Two-toned Turrid (1") 2.5 cm
Carinodrillia dichroa Pilsbry & Lowe, 1932. Gulf of California to Ecuador. On gravel 10 to 40 m; uncommon.

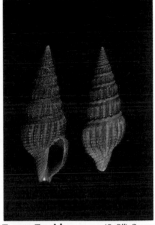

Tampa Turrid (0.8") 2 cm
Crassispira tampaensis Bartsch & Rehder, 1939. S.W. Florida. Offshore; uncommon. Paratype illus.

Sanibel Turrid (1") 2.5 cm
Crassispira sanibelensis Bartsch & Rehder, 1939. West Florida; Bahamas. Offshore; uncommon. Holotype illus.

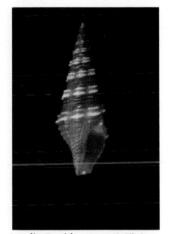

Javelin Turrid (0.8") 2 cm
Compsodrillia jaculum (Pilsbry & Lowe, 1932). West Mexico to Panama. Offshore 10 to 40 m; uncommon.

Turned Turrid (3") 7.5 cm
Turricula tornata (Dillwyn, 1817). India to Thailand. Offshore to 35 m on mud; uncommon. Syn.: *flammea* Schum.

Java Turrid (2.5") 6.5 cm
Turricula javana (L., 1758). Indo-W. Pacific; Japan. Shallow and deeper water on mud; common.

Kamakura Turrid (2") 5 cm
Comitas kamakurana (Pilsbry, 1895). Japan. Offshore; uncommon. Syn.: *laysanica* Dall.

Wrinkled Turrid (1.8") 4.5 cm
Fusiturris undatiruga (Bivona, 1832). Mediterranean. Moderately deep water; uncommon.

Remarkable Turrid (3.5") 9 cm
Nihonia mirabilis (Sowerby, 1914). Japan. Moderately deep water; rare.

Japanese Wonder Shell (3.5") 9 cm
Thatcheria mirabilis Angas, 1877. Japan to Philippines. Deep water; common. In family Thatcheriidae.

CONES
FAMILY CONIDAE

Primarily inhabitants of warm, shallow water, cones are most numerous in the tropical Indo-Pacific. The poison of some cones may be lethal to humans. A diminutive operculum is usually present. Eggs are deposited in purse-shaped capsules. More than 300 cone species are recognized, but many synonyms have been created.

INDO-PACIFIC and
JAPANESE CONES

The richest area in species of cones is the tropical Western Pacific and Indian Oceans. Many deep-water species are yet to be discovered. Japan has a unique cool-water fauna with many cones, as well as many Indo-Pacific species in the south.

Marble Cone (4") 10 cm
Conus marmoreus L., 1758. Indo-Pacific. On sand, shallow water; common. Typical form illus. Rarely all-white.

Vidua Cone (3") 7 cm
Conus marmoreus L., 1758, form *vidua* Reeve, 1843, has pattern in two broad bands. Alias *bandanus* of authors.

Conus marmoreus L., 1758. The form *nigrescens* Sowerby, 1859, is usually under 7.5 cm (3") and black in color. Samoa to New Caledonia.

Conus marmoreus L., 1758. This is the white form *suffusa* Sowerby (holotype illus.), restricted to New Caledonia; moderately common.

Imperial Cone (3") 7.5 cm
Conus imperialis L., 1758. Indo-Pacific. On intertidal reefs; common.

Western Imperial Cone
(3") 7.5 cm
Conus imperialis subspecies *fuscata* Born, 1778. East Africa. Common. Syn.: *viridula* Lam.

Nicobar Cone (2.5") 6.5 cm
Conus araneosus nicobaricus Hwass, 1792. N.E. Indian Ocean to Philippines. Shallow water; common.

Zoned Cone (2.5") 6.5 cm
Conus zonatus Hwass, 1792. Seychelles to India and Sumatra. Shallow reefs; uncommon. Syn.: *edwardi* Preston.

Textile Cone (3") 7.5 cm
Conus textile L., 1758. Indo-Pacific. Shallow water; common.

Queen Victoria Cone (2") 5 cm
Conus victoriae Reeve, 1843. Northern Territory and Western Australia. Shallow water; moderately common.

Ambassador Cone (1.2") 3 cm
Conus legatus Lamarck, 1810.
Pacific (not Hawaii). Shallow
water; uncommon. *C. canonicus* lacks pink background.

Philippine Cone (2") 5 cm
Conus telatus Reeve, 1848.
Southern Philippines. Moderately deep water; moderately
common.

Paulucci's Cone (2.2") 5.5 cm
Conus paulucciae Sowerby,
1877. Southern Indian Ocean
Offshore; moderately rare.
May be a form of C. *aureus*.

Abbas Cone (2.4") 6 cm
Conus abbas Hwass, 1792.
Indo-Pacific. On reefs; uncommon. Syn.: *corbula* Sowerby;
cuctrios Sowerby.

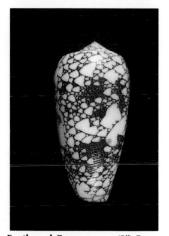

Feathered Cone (2") 5 cm
Conus pennaceus Born, 1778.
Indo-Pacific. Offshore to moderate depths; common. Varies
considerably in shape.

Conus pennaceus Born, 1778.
One of many names given to
this cone is *praelatus* Hwass. It
represents an uncommon form
of the species.

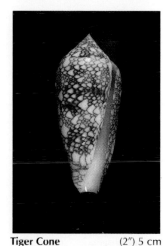

Tiger Cone (2") 5 cm
Conus canonicus Hwass, 1792.
Indo-Pacific. Under rocks on
reefs; moderately common.
Syn.: *tigrinus* Sowerby.

Princely Cone (4") 10 cm
Conus aulicus L., 1758. Indo-
Pacific. On intertidal reefs; uncommon. Lacks vertical black
lines of C. *textile*.

Conus pennaceus Born, 1778.
The name *episcopus* Hwass has
been applied to shells with a
broad body whorl and narrowly
angled shoulder.

Gilded Cone (3.2") 8 cm
Conus auratus Hwass, 1792. Society Islands and Tuamotu Islands. On intertidal reefs; rare.
May be a form of C. *aulicus*.

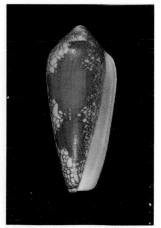

Dignified Cone (2.4") 6 cm
Conus magnificus Reeve, 1843.
Indo-Pacific. Shallow water;
common. Long known to collectors (erroneously) as C. *episcopus*.

Aureus Cone (2") 5 cm
Conus aureus Hwass, 1792.
Indo-W. Pacific. Under rocks,
on reefs; rare. C. *textile* is more
ventricose.

Gold-leaf Cone   (1.5″) 3.5 cm
Conus auricomus Hwass, 1792.
Indo-Pacific. On intertidal
reefs; uncommon. Syn.: *dacty-
losus* Kiener.

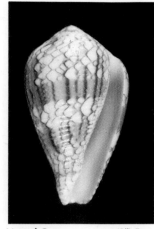

Netted Cone   (2″) 5 cm
Conus retifer Menke, 1829.
Indo-Pacific. Shallow water;
uncommon. Syn.: *sulcata* Sowerby; *solidus* Sowerby.

Natal Cone   (1.5″) 4 cm
Conus natalis Sowerby, 1857.
South Africa. Offshore; common (as a beached shell). Syn.:
gilchristi Sowerby.

Glory-of-the-Sea   (4″) 10 cm
Conus gloriamaris Chemnitz,
1777. Western Pacific. Shallow
and deep water; moderately
rare.

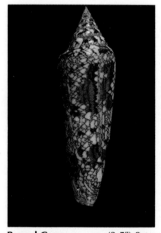

Bengal Cone   (3.5″) 9 cm
Conus bengalensis (Okutani,
1968). Bay of Bengal. Moderately deep water; moderately
rare.

Glory-of-India   (5″) 12.5 cm
Conus milneedwardsi Jous-
seaume, 1894. Indian Ocean;
China Sea. Offshore; rather
rare. Syn.: *clytospira*
M. & S.

Vice Admiral Cone   (1.5″) 4 cm
Conus locumtenens Blumen-
bach, 1791. Red Sea; N.W. Indian Ocean. Common. Syn.:
acuminatus Hwass.

Saffron Cone   (3″) 7.5 cm
Conus colubrinus Lamarck,
1810. Western Pacific; Samoa;
Sri Lanka. Moderately deep water; rare. Alias *C. crocatus* Lam.

Crocatus Cone   (3″) 7.5 cm
Conus colubrinus form *crocatus* Lamarck, 1810. S.W. Pacific.
5 to 20 m; uncommon in Solomons.

Thailand Cone   (3″) 7.5 cm
Conus colubrinus form *thailan-
dis* da Motta, 1978. Andaman
Sea; Thailand. 10-30 m; locally
common.

Admiral Cone   (2.5″) 6 cm
Conus ammiralis L., 1758. Indo-
W. Pacific. In sand or coral; uncommon. Amount of white
background varies.

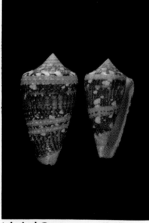

Admiral Cone   (2.5″) 6 cm
Conus ammiralis L., 1758. The
coronate, granulose form at
left is Indian Ocean subspecies
archithalassus Hwass.

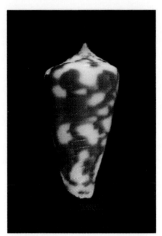

Keatlike Cone (1″) 2.5 cm
Conus keatiformis Shikama & Oishi, 1977. S.E. Asia. Offshore; rare.

Amadis Cone (2.5″) 6.5 cm
Conus amadis Gmelin, 1791. Indian Ocean; Indonesia. Offshore; moderately common. Syn.: *C. lozeti* Richard (freak).

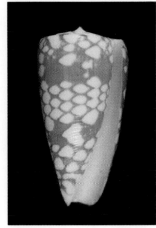

Noble Cone (2″) 5 cm
Conus nobilis nobilis L., 1758. Eastern Indian Ocean; Indonesia. Offshore; moderately rare. Syn.: *cordigera* Sowerby.

Victor Cone (2″) 5 cm
Conus nobilis subspecies *victor* Broderip, 1842. Islands of Bali-Flores Strait area. Offshore; rare.

Marquesas Cone (1.5″) 4 cm
Conus nobilis subspecies *marchionatus* Hinds, 1843. Marquesas Islands. Offshore; uncommon.

Geography Cone (4″) 10 cm
Conus geographus L., 1758. Indo-Pacific. Shallow water; common. Like *C. tulipa* but has less convex sides.

Tulip Cone (2.5″) 6 cm
Conus tulipa L., 1758. Indo-Pacific. Shallow water; common. Has killed humans with its venom.

Fragile Geography Cone 3 cm
Conus geographus subspecies *fragillissimus* Petuch, 1979. Ethiopia; Red Sea. 1 to 3 m; uncommon. Holotype illus.

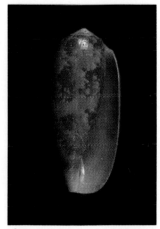

Obscure Cone (1.2″) 3 cm
Conus obscurus Sowerby, 1833. Indo-Pacific. Offshore; moderately common. Lacks coronations of *C. geographus*.

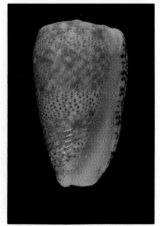

Rhododendron Cone (2″) 5 cm
Conus adamsonii Broderip, 1836. Central and S.W. Pacific. Subtidal; rare. Syn.: *rhododendron* Jay.

Rhododendron Cone (2″) 5 cm
Conus adamsonii Broderip, 1836. Live-collected specimens have yellow aperture. Not uncommon in Phoenix Is.

Mascarene Cone (2″) 5 cm
Conus julii Lienard, 1870. Mauritius and Reunion Island. Moderately deep water; rare. Varies little.

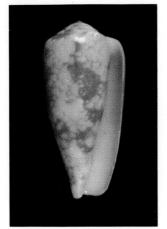

Ruddy Cone   (2.5") 6 cm
Conus rubiginosus Hwass, 1792. Indonesia; Philippines. Shallow water; rare.

Circumcision Cone   (2.5") 6 cm
Conus circumcisus Born, 1778. Western Pacific. Offshore to moderate depths; uncommon. Syn.: *brazieri* Sowerby.

Aurisiacus Cone   (2") 5 cm
Conus aurisiacus L., 1758. Indonesia; Australia. Offshore; rare. Pink color suggests fading.

Sazanka's Cone   (1.2") 3 cm
Conus sazanka Shikama, 1970. Western Pacific. Offshore; uncommon. Syn.: *kurzi* Petuch.

Terebra Cone   (2.5") 6 cm
Conus terebra Born, 1778. Indo-Pacific. Under rocks on intertidal reefs; moderately common. Syn.: *thomasi* Sby.

Miterlike Cone   (1") 2.5 cm
Conus mitratus Hwass, 1792. Indo-Pacific. Intertidal and offshore; uncommon. Apex often eroded.

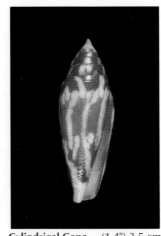

Cylindrical Cone   (1.4") 3.5 cm
Conus cylindraceus Broderip & Sowerby, 1830. Indo-Pacific. Offshore; uncommon. Always very glossy.

Acorn Cone   (1.2") 3 cm
Conus glans Hwass, 1792. Indo-Pacific. Shallow water; moderately common. May be confused with *C. tenuistriatus.*

Leaden Cone   (1.2") 3 cm
Conus scabriusculus Dillwyn, 1817. Western Pacific. Shallow water; common. Syn.: *fabula* Sowerby; *plumbeus* Reeve.

Scarlet Cone   (1.5") 4 cm
Conus coccineus Gmelin, 1791. South Pacific. Shallow water; moderately common. Syn.: *solandri* Broderip & Sowerby.

Thin-line Cone   (1.4") 3.5 cm
Conus tenuistriatus Sowerby, 1857. Indo-Pacific. Shallow water; common. Sometimes purplish. Apex bright pink.

Tender Cone   (1.5") 4 cm
Conus artoptus Sowerby, 1833. Australia to Philippines. In sand offshore; uncommon. Wrongly known as *tenellus.*

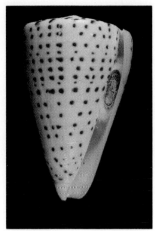

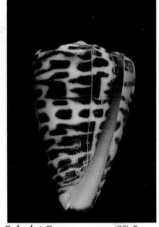

Lettered Cone (4″) 10 cm
Conus litteratus L., 1758. Indo-Pacific. Intertidal and subtidal; common. Very thick and heavy. Base pointed, stained purplish.

Leopard Cone (5.5″) 14 cm
Conus leopardus (Röding, 1798). Indo-Pacific. Shallow water; common. Heaviest of all cones. Base blunt, white.

Ivory Cone (2″) 5 cm
Conus eburneus Hwass, 1792. Indo-Pacific. On sand and reefs; common. Very variable in pattern and shape.

Polyglot Cone (2″) 5 cm
C. eburneus Hwass, 1792. Among several attractive varieties is *polyglotta* Weinkauff, 1874, commonly found in the

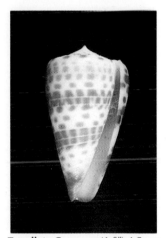

Jickeli's Cone (1.4″) 3.5 cm
Conus jickelii Weinkauff, 1873. Western Indian Ocean. Deep water; rare. A lightweight shell.

Tessellate Cone (1.8″) 4.5 cm
Conus tessulatus Born, 1778. Indo-Pacific. Shallow water; common. *C. tessellatus* is misspelling.

Violet-base Cone (1.5″) 4 cm
Conus suturatus suturatus Reeve, 1844. Eastern Indian Ocean; western Pacific. Offshore; moderately common.

Hawaiian Cone (0.8″) 2 cm
Conus suturatus sandwichensis Walls, 1978. Hawaiian Islands (endemic). Offshore; uncommon. Holotype illustrated.

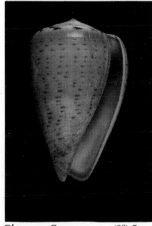

Subulate Cone (1.4″) 3.5 cm
Conus subulatus subulatus Kiener, 1845. Southern India; Sri Lanka to Solomons. Offshore; uncommon. Syn.: *colli-*

Sharp-angled Cone (1″) 2.5 cm
Conus acutangulus Lamarck, 1810. Indo-Pacific. Offshore; uncommon.

Oak Cone (3″) 7.5 cm
Conus quercinus Lightfoot, 1786. Indo-Pacific. Offshore; common. This heavy shell varies little.

Glaucous Cone (2″) 5 cm
Conus glaucus L., 1758. Western Pacific. Offshore; uncommon. Syn.: *fraxinus* Röding.

Beech Cone   (4") 10 cm
Conus betulinus L., 1758. Indo-Pacific. Shallow water; common. Spots vary in shape and size.

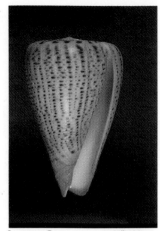

Fig Cone   (3") 7.5 cm
Conus figulinus L., 1758. Indo-Pacific. Shallow water; common. Syn.: *loroisii* Kiener.

Suratan Cone   (4") 10 cm
Conus suratensis Hwass, 1792. Indian Ocean and S.W. Pacific. Uncommon. Syn.: *agrestis* Mörch.

Flag Cone   (3.2") 8 cm
Conus vexillum Gmelin, 1791. Indo-Pacific. Offshore; common. Syn.: *sumatrensis* Hwass; *robillardi* Bernardi.

Namocanus Cone   (3") 7.5 cm
Conus namocanus Hwass, 1792. Indian Ocean. Shallow water; common. May have spiral stripes. Syn.: *badius* Kiener.

Weasel Cone   (2.5") 6 cm
Conus mustelinus Hwass, 1792. Indo-W. Pacific. Shallow water; uncommon. May be confused with *C. capitaneus*.

Captain Cone   (2.5") 6 cm
Conus capitaneus L., 1758. Indo-Pacific. Intertidal; common. Syn.: *classiarius* Hwass; *ceciliae* Crosse.

Little Captain Cone   (1.2") 3 cm
Conus capitanellus Fulton, 1938. Southern Japan; Taiwan. Deep water; moderately rare.

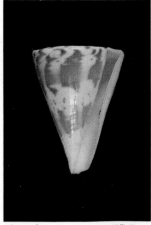

Trigonal Cone   (2") 5 cm
Conus trigonus Reeve, 1848. Northern and western Australia. Intertidal mud flats; uncommon. Not *badius* Kiener.

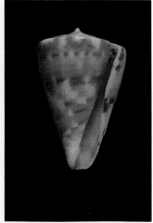

Reference Cone   (1.5") 3.7 cm
Conus advertex Garrard, 1961. Off southern Queensland and New South Wales. Moderately deep water; uncommon.

Voluminous Cone   (1.5") 4 cm
Conus voluminalis Reeve, 1843. Eastern Indian Ocean; western Pacific. Deep water; uncommon. Syn.: *macarae* Bernardi.

General Cone   (2.5") 6.5 cm
Conus generalis generalis L., 1767. Pacific. Intertidal; common. Very variable.

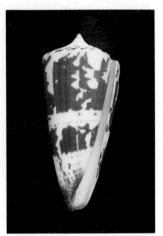

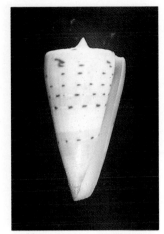

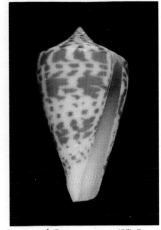

Maldive Cone (2.5″) 6.5 cm
Conus generalis subspecies *maldivus* Hwass, 1792. Indian Ocean. Common.

Bough Cone (3″) 7.5 cm
Conus thalassiarchus Sowerby, 1834. S. Philippines. Intertidal to 2 m; common. Spire height varies.

Necklace Cone (2.2″) 5.5 cm
Conus monile Hwass, 1792. Eastern Indian Ocean. Moderately deep water; uncommon. Syn.: *anadema* Tomlin.

Engraved Cone (2″) 5 cm
Conus inscriptus Reeve, 1843. Indian Ocean. Offshore; common. Syn.: *keati* Sowerby; *planiliratus* Sowerby.

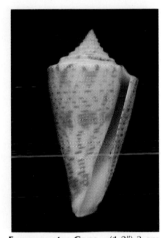

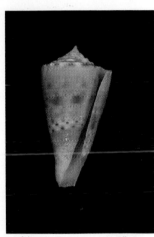

Kimio's Cone (0.8″) 2 cm
Conus kimioi (Habe, 1965). Japan; Taiwan; Philippines. Deep water; rare.

Scullett's Cone (1.8″) 4.5 cm
Conus sculletti Marsh, 1962. Southern Queensland and northern New South Wales. Deep water; uncommon.

Eugrammatus Cone (1.2″) 3 cm
Conus eugrammatus Bartsch & Rehder, 1943. S.W. Pacific; Hawaii. Offshore; rare. Syn.: *wakayamaensis* Kuroda.

Otohime's Cone (1.2″) 3 cm
Conus otohimeae Kuroda & Ito, 1961. Southern Japan to Philippines. Deep water; rare. Syn.: *aphrodite* Petuch, 1979.

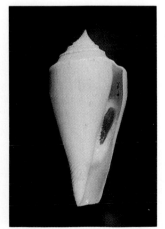

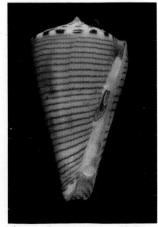

Siebold's Cone (3″) 7.5 cm
Conus sieboldii Reeve, 1848. Japan; Taiwan. Deep water; common. Syn.: *rarimaculata* Sowerby.

Ione Cone (2.2″) 5.5 cm
Conus ione Fulton, 1938. Southern Japan. Deep water; uncommon. *C. sieboldii* similar but lacks violet color.

Teramachi's Cone (3″) 7.5 cm
Conus teramachii (Kuroda, 1956). S. Japan to South Africa. Deep water; moderately rare. Syn.: *torquatus* von Martens.

Hirase's Cone (2″) 5 cm
Conus hirasei (Kira, 1956). Southern Japan to Taiwan. Deep water; rare.

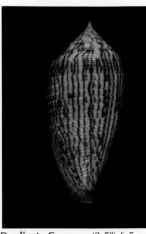

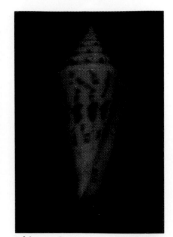

Austral Cone   (2.5″) 6 cm
Conus australis Holten, 1802. Southern Japan; China Sea. Dredged, about 40 m; common. Syn.: *alabasteroides* Shikama.

Duplicate Cone   (2.5″) 6.5 cm
Conus duplicatus Sowerby, 1823. Southern Japan; Taiwan; Solomons. Deep water; rare.

Kurohara's Cone   (2.5″) 6.5 cm
Conus duplicatus Sowerby, 1823. Described recently as *armadillo* Shikama (extreme variant) and *kuroharai* Habe (illus.).

Ichinose Cone   (2.5″) 6 cm
Conus ichinoseana (Kuroda, 1956). Southern Japan to Taiwan; Philippines. Deep water; uncommon. Syn.: *prioris* Kuroda.

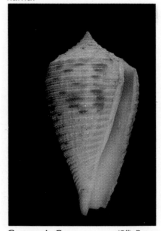

Granger's Cone   (2″) 5 cm
Conus grangeri Sowerby, 1900. Taiwan; Philippines. Deep water; uncommon. *C. sulcatus* similar but sides straighter.

Flat-ridge Cone   (1.5″) 4 cm
Conus eucoronatus Sowerby, 1903. Natal, South Africa; southern Mozambique. Deep water; rare.

Pagoda Cone   (1.5″) 4 cm
Conus pagodus Kiener, 1846. Japan; Taiwan; Philippines. Deep water; common. Formerly *cancellatus* Hwass.

Orbigny's Cone   (2.2″) 5.5 cm
Conus orbignyi Audouin, 1831. Indo-Pacific. In deep water; locally common. Syn.: *planicostatus* Sowerby.

Comatose Cone   (1.8″) 4.5 cm
Conus comatosa Pilsbry, 1904. Southern Japan to Taiwan; moderately rare. Sculptured form. Syn.: *dormitor* Pilsbry.

Hypo Cone   (1.2″) 3 cm
Conus hypochlorus Tomlin, 1937. Central Philippines. Deep water; uncommon. Syn.: *croceus* E. A. Smith (not Sowerby).

Wickerwork Cone   (1.5″) 4 cm
Conus vimineus Reeve, 1849. Philippines. Moderately deep water; moderately common. Light and fragile shell.

Spindle Cone   (1.4″) 3.5 cm
Conus aculeiformis Reeve, 1844. Indo-Pacific. Offshore, to 300 m; uncommon. Syn.: *longurionis* Kiener.

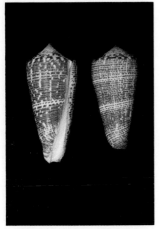

St. Thomas Cone (3") 7.5 cm
Conus thomae Gmelin, 1791. Indonesia Offshore; formerly rare. Syn.: *omaicus* Hwass; *jousseaumei* Couturier.

Virgin Cone (3") 7.5 cm
Conus virgo L., 1758. Indo-Pacific. Shallow water; common. Large purple blotch at base.

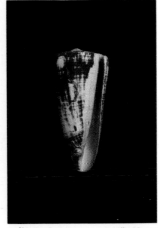

False Virgin Cone (1.5") 4 cm
Conus emaciatus Reeve, 1849. Indo-Pacific. Shallow water; common. Sculpture of fine spiral threads.

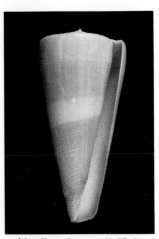

Celine's Cone (4") 10 cm
Conus coelinae Crosse, 1858. Hawaii to New Caledonia; Philippines. Offshore; rare. Holotype illus.

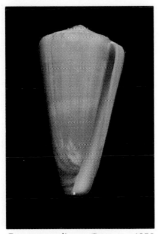

Conus coelinae Crosse, 1858. Very similar to *C. virgo* but more slender and lacks purple or violet base. This specimen without periostracum.

Conus coelinae Crosse, 1858. Shells from Midway and Hawaiian Islands are form *spiceri* Rehder & Bartsch (paratype).

Conus coelinae Crosse, 1858. An elongated, brighter colored form, described as *berdulinus* Veillard, 1972. Syn.: "kintoki."

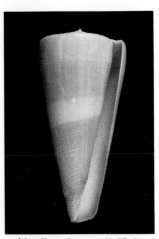

Kashiwajima Cone (2.5") 6 cm
Conus kashiwajimensis Shikama, 1971. S. Japan to Taiwan; Sri Lanka. Deep water; rare. Probably is *coelinae*.

Augur Cone (2.5") 6 cm
Conus augur Lightfoot, 1786. Indian Ocean; S.W. Pacific. Shallow reef areas; moderately common.

Tribble's Cone (3.4") 8.5 cm
Conus tribblei Walls, 1977. Taiwan; Philippines; Solomons. Deep water; moderately common. Holotype illustrated.

Conus tribblei Walls, 1977. Distinguishable from *C. recluzianus* by its lack of undulate shoulders. Named after a pet cat.

Bayan's Cone (2.5") 6 cm
Conus bayani Jousseaume, 1872. Indian Ocean. Moderately deep water; uncommon.

Urashima Cone   (2.5") 6 cm
Conus urashimanus Kuroda & Ito, 1961. Southern Japan; Philippines. Deep water; moderately common.

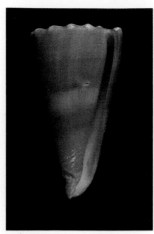

Récluz's Cone   (2.5") 6.5 cm
Conus recluzianus Bernardi, 1853. S.W. Pacific. Deep water; moderately common. Syn.: *gloriakiiensis* K. & I.

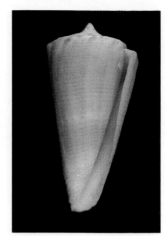

Nielsen's Cone   (2") 5 cm
Conus nielsenae Marsh, 1962. Northern Australia; Kermadec Islands. Offshore; moderately uncommon.

Nielsen's Cone   (1.2") 3 cm
Conus nielsenae Marsh, 1962. Western Australia. Locally common. Form *reductaspiralis* Walls, 1979 (holotype illus.).

Nada Cone   (1") 2.5 cm
Conus nadaensis (Azuma & Toki, 1970). Off Nada, Wakayama, Japan. Uncommon.

Calf Cone   (2") 5 cm
Conus vitulinus Hwass, 1792. Indo-Pacific. On reefs, under coral; common. Syn.: *praeclarus* Fenaux.

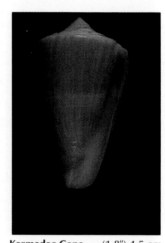

Kermadec Cone   (1.8") 4.5 cm
Conus kermadecensis Iredale, 1913. China Sea; Australia to E. Africa. Moderate depths; uncommon.

Striatellus Cone   (1.8") 4.5 cm
Conus striatellus Link, 1807. Indo-Pacific. Shallow water; moderately common. Syn.: *pulchrelineatus* Hopwood.

Comma Cone   (1.8") 4.5 cm
Conus connectens A. Adams, 1855. Western Pacific. Subtidal; moderately rare. Syn.: *pulchellus* Swainson.

Singed Cone   (2.8") 7 cm
Conus consors Sowerby, 1833. Indo-Pacific. Offshore; uncommon. Syn.: *anceps* A. Adams; *daullei* Crosse.

Magus Cone   (2.5") 6 cm
Conus magus L., 1758. Indo-Pacific. Shallow water; common. Syn.: *carinatus* Swainson.

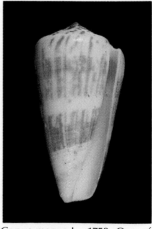

Conus magus L., 1758. One of the most variable of all cones with a seemingly endless range of color patterns.

Multilinear Cone (1.2″) 3 cm
Conus polygrammus Tomlin, 1937. Western Pacific. Uncommon. Syn.: *multilineatus* Sowerby (holotype illus.).

Bubble Cone (2.5″) 6 cm
Conus bullatus L., 1758. Indo-Pacific. Offshore; uncommon. Syn.: *pongo* Shikama & Oishi, 1977.

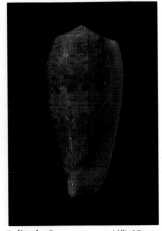

Bubble Cone (2.5″) 6 cm
Conus bullatus L., 1758. Variety *articulata* Dautzenberg is much appreciated by collectors.

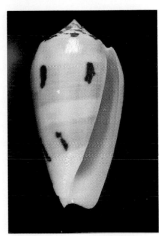

Palisade Cone (4″) 10 cm
Conus cervus Lamarck, 1822. Philippines. Offshore; rare. Recently rediscovered. A classic rarity among cones.

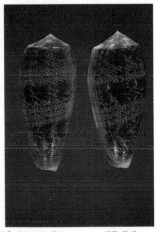

Vic Wee's Cone (3″) 7.5 cm
Conus vicweei Old, 1973. Sumatra to Thailand. Deep water; moderately rare. Paratypes illus.

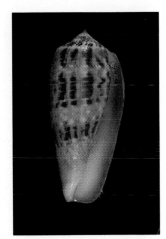

Du Savel's Cone (2″) 5 cm
Conus dusaveli (H. Adams, 1872). Ryukyu Islands; Philippines. Deep water; moderately rare.

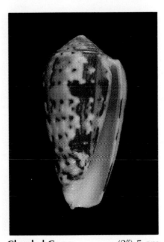

Clouded Cone (2″) 5 cm
Conus floccatus Sowerby, 1839. Pacific. Offshore reefs in deep water; moderately rare.

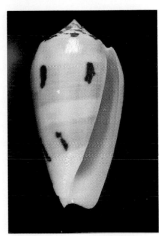

Floridus Cone (2.5″) 6 cm
Conus floridus Sowerby, 1858. N.E. Indian Ocean; W. Thailand. Offshore; uncommon. Syn.: *chusaki* da Motta.

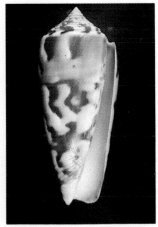

Governor Cone (2.5″) 6 cm
Conus gubernator Hwass, 1792. Indian Ocean. Shallow water; common.

Barthelemy's Cone (2.5″) 6 cm
Conus barthelemyi Bernardi, 1861. Indian Ocean. Offshore; moderately rare. Syn.: *gaugini* Richard & Salvat.

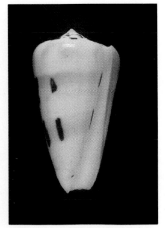

Prampart's Cone (2.5″) 6 cm
Conus barthelemyi form *leehmani* da Motta & Rockel, 1979. Uncommon. Indian Ocean.

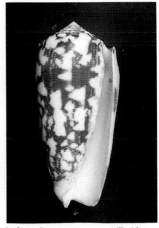

Striate Cone (4″) 10 cm
Conus striatus L., 1758. Indo-Pacific. Shallow water; common. *C. terminus* similar but lacks hairlines.

Planorbis Cone   (1.8″) 4.5 cm
Conus planorbis Born, 1778. Indo-Pacific. Offshore; common. Syn.: *chenui* Crosse.

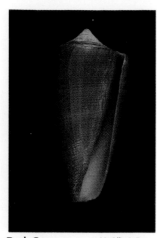

Dark Cone   (1.8″) 4.5 cm
Conus furvus Reeve, 1843. S.W. Pacific. Offshore to moderate depths; common. Numerous synonyms.

Black-spot Cone   (1.2″) 3 cm
Conus nigropunctatus Sowerby, 1857. Indo-Pacific. Shallow water; moderately common.

Monastic Cone   (2″) 5 cm
Conus monachus L., 1758. Indo-Pacific. Shallow water; common. Syn.: *achatinus* Gmelin; *vinctus* A. Adams.

Parian Cone   (1.2″) 3 cm
Conus parius Reeve, 1844. Philippines to New Hebrides. On reefs, under coral; common.

Rayed Cone   (2.5″) 6 cm
Conus radiatus Gmelin, 1791. Fiji to Philippines. Moderate depths; common. Spiral ridges on spire whorls.

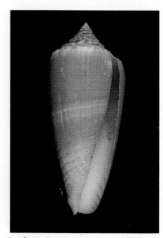

Prefect Cone   (2″) 5 cm
Conus ochroleucus Gmelin, 1791. Philippines; New Guinea. Moderately deep water; common. Syn.: *praefectus* Hwass.

Pilkey's Cone   (2.5″) 6 cm
Conus pilkeyi Petuch, 1974. Fiji to Philippines. Offshore; uncommon. Close to *C. ochroleucus* but spire lower.

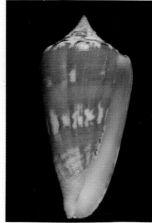

Janus Cone   (2.5″) 6 cm
Conus janus Hwass, 1792. East coast of central Africa and the Mascarene Islands. Offshore; uncommon.

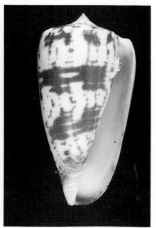

Specter Cone   (1.5″) 4 cm
Conus spectrum L., 1758. Western Pacific. Offshore; moderately common.

Stillate Cone   (1.5″) 4 cm
Conus spectrum form *stillatus* Reeve, 1849, comes from Australia. Common.

Sprinkled Cone   (1.4″) 3.5 cm
Conus conspersus Reeve, 1844. Philippines; Indonesia. Moderately deep water; uncommon. (Form *daphne* Boivin, 1864.)

Wittig's Cone (1.4") 3.5 cm
Conus wittigi Walls, 1977. Sunda Island (Indonesia). Shallow water; rare. Has tented pattern of a "textile" cone.

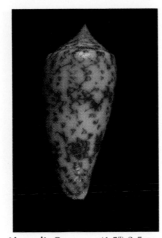

Lienard's Cone (1.5") 3.5 cm
Conus lienardi Bernardi & Crosse, 1861. Melanesia (New Caledonia). Locally common. Variable patterns.

Lienard's Cone (1.4") 3.5 cm
Conus lienardi Bernardi & Crosse, 1861. Melanesia (New Caledonia). Shallow water; uncommon. Close to *C. cinereus*.

Lynceus Cone (2.5") 6.5 cm
Conus lynceus Sowerby, 1857. Indo-Pacific. Offshore; moderately uncommon. Aperture pink.

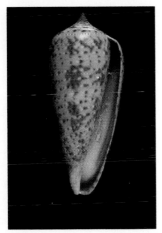

Sunburnt Cone (2") 5 cm
Conus cinereus Hwass, 1792. Western Pacific; Indonesia. Offshore; common. Form *gubba* Kiener is almost black.

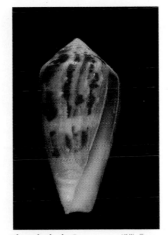

Thunderbolt Cone (2") 5 cm
Conus fulmen Reeve, 1843. Southern Japan to Ryukyus. Deep water; locally common. Syn.: *kirai* Kuroda.

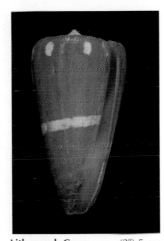

Lithograph Cone (2") 5 cm
Conus litoglyphus Hwass, 1792. Indo-Pacific. Shallow water; common. *C. lithoglyphus* is misspelling.

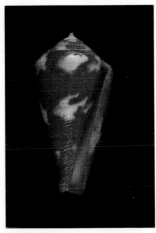

Pertusus Cone (1.2") 3 cm
Conus pertusus Hwass, 1792. Indo-Pacific. Offshore to moderate depths; uncommon.

Back-end Cone (1") 2.5 cm
Conus aplustre Reeve, 1843. Australia. Intertidal; common. Syn.: *lugubris* Reeve.

Back-end Cone (1") 2.5 cm
Conus aplustre Reeve, 1843. A young specimen showing special color patterns.

Angas's Cone (1.4") 3.5 cm
Conus angasi Tryon, 1883. E. Australia. Moderately deep water; uncommon. Syn.: *metcalfei* Angas.

Papilla Cone (1.4") 3.5 cm
Conus papilliferus Sowerby, 1834. Eastern Australia. Shallow water; common.

Anemone Cone   (2") 5 cm
Conus anemone Lamarck, 1810. Southern Australia. Offshore; common.

Anemone Cone   (2") 5 cm
Conus anemone Lamarck, 1810. One of numerous forms, this has been called *peronianus* Iredale.

Hyena Cone   (2") 5 cm
Conus hyaena Hwass, 1792. India, Bay of Bengal. Tide pools and offshore; common. Syn.: *mutabilis* Reeve.

Cuming's Cone   (1") 2.5 cm
Conus cumingii Reeve, 1848. Philippines to Solomons and Queensland. Moderate to shallow water; uncommon.

Cabrit's Cone   (1") 2.5 cm
Conus cabritii Bernardi, 1858. New Caledonia (endemic). Shallow water; uncommon. Syn.: *vayssetianus* Crosse.

Admirable Cone   (1.5") 4 cm
Conus praecellens A. Adams, 1854. Western Pacific. Deep water; moderately common. Syn.: *sowerbyi* Sowerby.

Rat Cone   (1.8") 4.5 cm
Conus rattus Hwass, 1792. Indo-Pacific. Shallow water; common. Syn.: *taitensis* Hwass; *viridis* Sowerby.

Smoky Cone   (1") 2.5 cm
Conus fumigatus Hwass, 1792. Red Sea area. Shallow water; moderately common. Syn.: *pazii* Bernardi; *adustus* Sowerby.

Klem's Cone   (2") 5 cm
Conus klemae (Cotton, 1953). Southern Australia. Offshore to moderate depths; uncommon. Syn.: *coralinus* Habe & Kosuge.

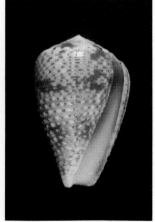

Cat Cone   (1.5") 4 cm
Conus catus Hwass, 1792. Indo-Pacific. Intertidal, on reefs; common. Syn.: *discrepans* Sowerby; *purus* Pease.

Soldier Cone   (3") 7.5 cm
Conus miles L., 1758. Indo-Pacific. Offshore to moderate depths; common. Periostracum thick.

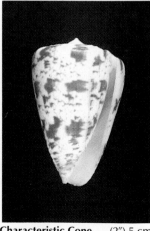

Characteristic Cone   (2") 5 cm
Conus caracteristicus G. Fischer, 1807. Indo-W. Pacific. Shallow water; moderately common.

Yellow Pacific Cone (1.5″) 4 cm
Conus flavidus Lamarck, 1810. Indo-Pacific. Shallow water; common. Lacks coronations on spire whorls.

Frigid Cone (1.5″) 4 cm
Conus frigidus Reeve, 1848. Pacific. Shallow water; locally common. Has 3 spiral ridges on each spire whorl.

Livid Cone (2″) 5 cm
Conus lividus Hwass, 1792. Indo-Pacific. Shallow water, common. Has prominent rounded coronations.

Bloodstained Cone (1.4″) 3.5 cm
Conus sanguinolentus Quoy & Galmard, 1834. Indo-Pacific. Shallow water; common.

Little Cone (1.2″) 3 cm
Conus parvulus Link, 1807. Western Pacific. Shallow water; moderately common.

Morelet's Cone (1.5″) 4 cm
Conus moreleti Crosse, 1858. Indo-Pacific. On reefs, under coral; locally common.

Ringed Cone (1.5″) 4 cm
Conus balteatus Sowerby, 1833. Indo-Pacific. On intertidal reefs; uncommon.

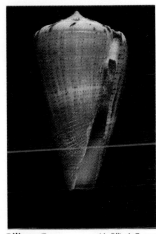

Bilious Cone (1.8″) 4.5 cm
Conus biliosus (Röding, 1798). Indian Ocean. Shallow water; common. Syn.: *piperatus* Dillwyn.

Meyer's Bilious Cone (1.8″) 4.5 cm
Conus biliosus subspecies *meyeri* Walls, 1979. South Africa. Holotype illus.

Burnt Cone (1.2″) 3 cm
Conus encaustus Kiener, 1845. Marquesas Islands. Shallow water; common. Thick and heavy. Syn.: *praetextus* Reeve.

Muricate Cone (1.4″) 3.5 cm
Conus muriculatus Sowerby, 1833. S.W. Pacific. Offshore; uncommon. Smooth and granulose forms occur.

Coffee Cone (1.8″) 4.5 cm
Conus excavatus Sowerby, 1866. Red Sea; western Indian Ocean. Offshore; common. Syn.: *coffeae* of authors.

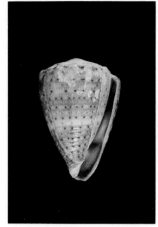

Abbreviated Cone   (1.6") 4 cm
Conus abbreviatus Reeve, 1843. Hawaiian Islands (endemic). Reefs; common.

Ringed Cone   (1.4") 3.5 cm
Conus taeniatus Hwass, 1792. Red Sea; northwestern Indian Ocean. Offshore; common.

Red Sea Cone   (1") 2.5 cm
Conus erythraeensis Reeve, 1843. Red Sea and adjacent areas. Shallow water; common. Thick and heavy for its size.

Thousand-spot Cone (1") 2.5 cm
Conus miliaris Hwass, 1792. Indo-Pacific. Shallow water; common. Syn.: *barbadensis* Hwass.

Crowned Cone   (1.2") 3 cm
Conus coronatus Gmelin, 1791. Indo-Pacific. Intertidal reefs; common.

Lightning Cone   (1") 2.5 cm
Conus fulgetrum Sowerby, 1834. Indo-Pacific. Shallow water; moderately common. Syn.: *scaber* Kiener.

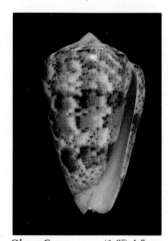

Obese Cone   (1.8") 4.5 cm
Conus zeylanicus Gmelin, 1791. Indian Ocean. Shallow water; moderately uncommon. Note hairlines in the pattern.

Fly-specked Cone   (2") 5 cm
Conus stercusmuscarum L., 1758. Western Pacific. Shallow water; common. Spots may fuse into blotches.

Sand-dusted Cone   (1.5") 4 cm
Conus arenatus Hwass, 1792. Indo-Pacific. Shallow water; common. Granulose specimens are known.

Flea-bite Cone   (2.5") 6 cm
Conus pulicarius Hwass, 1792. Indo-Pacific. Intertidal, in sand; common.

Hebrew Cone   (1.5") 4 cm
Conus ebraeus L., 1758. Indo-Pacific (including coast of Central America). Shallow water; common. Rarely pinkish.

Vermiculate Cone   (1.2") 3 cm
Conus chaldeus (Röding, 1798). Indo-Pacific (including coast of Central America). In sand, shallow water; common.

Stupella Cone   (2.8") 7 cm
Conus stupella (Kuroda, 1956).
Southern Japan and Taiwan.
Deep water; moderately rare.
Fresh shells violet.

Grand Cone   (5") 12.5 cm
Conus pergrandis (Iredale,
1937). Western Pacific. Deep
water; rare. Syn.: *fletcheri* Petuch & Mendenhall.

Smirna Cone   (3") 7.5 cm
Conus smirna Bartsch & Rehder, 1943. Southern Japan; Hawaii. Deep water; rare. Syn.:
profundorum Kuroda.

Glossy Cone   (1") 2.5 cm
Conus clarus E. A. Smith, 1881.
Southern and Western Austra-
lia. Offshore; uncommon.
Syn.: *segravei* Gatliff.

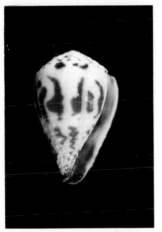

Marriage Cone   (1") 2.5 cm
Conus sponsalis sponsalis
Hwass, 1792. Indo-Pacific. Shallow water; common. Syn.:
nanus Sowerby.

Music Cone   (0.8") 2 cm
Conus musicus Hwass, 1792.
Indo-W. Pacific. Shallow water;
locally common. *C. sponsalis*
more convex.

South African Music Cone 2 cm
Conus musicus subspecies *par-
vatus* Walls, 1979. South Africa.
Reef beaches; common. Holotype illus.

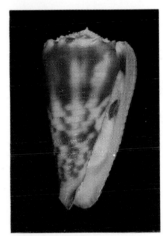

Molucca Cone   (1.5") 4 cm
Conus moluccensis Küster,
1838. Western Pacific. Offshore; rare. Outer lip concave.
Syn.: *stainforthii* Reeve.

Proximus Cone   (1.4") 3.5 cm
Conus proximus Sowerby,
1859. Western Pacific. Moderately deep water; moderately
rare. Outer lip straight.

Proximus Cone   (1.4") 3.5 cm
Conus proximus Sowerby,
1859. A New Guinea color form
without large blotches. Uncommon.

Mariel's Cone   (1.4") 3.5 cm
Conus marielae Rehder &
Wilson, 1975. Marquesas Islands. Moderately deep water;
rare. Holotype illustrated.

Stormy Cone   (1.8") 4.5 cm
Conus nimbosus Hwass, 1792.
Indo-W. Pacific. Moderately
deep water; uncommon. Spire
whorls have strong spiral.

Red-stained Cone   (1.5″) 4 cm
Conus rufimaculosus Macpherson, 1959. East Australia. Deep water; moderately common.

Cocceus Cone   (1.5″) 4 cm
Conus cocceus Reeve, 1844. Western Australia. Shallow water; locally common. Syn.: *kieneri* Crosse.

Memi's Cone   (1.2″) 3 cm
Conus memiae (Habe & Kosuge, 1960). Western Pacific. Deep water; rare. Syn.: *adonis* Shikama.

Violet-mouth Cone (1.4″) 3.5 cm
Conus iodostoma Reeve, 1843. Western Indian Ocean. Offshore; uncommon.

Timor Cone   (1.5″) 4 cm
Conus timorensis Hwass, 1792. Mauritius to New Guinea. Moderately deep water; rare. Syn.: *traversianus* Smith.

Nisus Cone   (2″) 5 cm
Conus stramineus Lamarck, 1810. Indo-W. Pacific. Offshore; common. Syn.: *alveolus* Sowerby; *nisus* Kiener.

Minnamurra Cone   (1″) 2.5 cm
Conus minnamurra (Garrard, 1961). S.E. Australia. Deep water; uncommon.

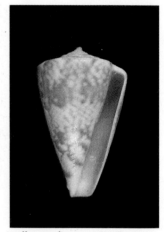

Wallangra Cone   (1.4″) 3.5 cm
Conus wallangra (Garrard, 1961). Southern Queensland; northern New South Wales. Deep water; uncommon.

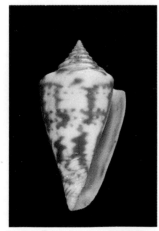

Brown-flame Cone   (1.2″) 3 cm
Conus lentiginosus Reeve, 1844. Northern Indian Ocean. Shallow water; moderately common.

Clay Cone   (2″) 5 cm
Conus argillaceus Perry, 1811. N.W. Indian Ocean. Coral reefs; uncommon. Syn.: *splendidulus* Sowerby.

Luteus Cone   (1.2″) 3 cm
Conus luteus Sowerby, 1833. Indo-Pacific. Dredged or beach; moderately rare. Usually rather worn.

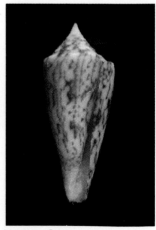

Neptune Cone   (1.5″) 4 cm
Conus neptunus Reeve, 1843. S.W. Pacific. Deep water; rare. Pattern constant. Syn.: *neptunoides* E. A. Smith.

Sulcate Cone (2.8″) 7 cm
Conus sulcatus Hwass, 1792. Japan; Taiwan; Bay of Bengal to Solomons. Offshore; common. Syn.: *bocki* Sowerby.

Deep-grooved Cone (1.5″) 4 cm
Conus mucronatus Reeve, 1843. China Sea; Philippines. Offshore; common. Syn.: *alabaster* Reeve.

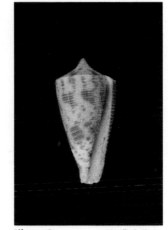

Siboga Cone (1.4″) 3.5 cm
Conus sibogae Schepman, 1913. Indonesia to Queensland. Moderately deep water; uncommon. Holotype illus.

Thin-line Cone (1.1″) 2.7 cm
Conus filicinctus Schepman, 1913. Java. Deep water; rare. Holotype illustrated.

Distant Cone (3.5″) 9 cm
Conus distans Hwass, 1792. Indo-Pacific. Shallow reefs; common. Syn.: *waterhousei* Brazier.

Stigmatic Cone (1.5″) 4 cm
Conus stigmaticus A. Adams, 1853. S.W. Pacific. Reefs; uncommon. May be form of *cinereus*.

Ribbon Cone (1.4″) 3.5 cm
Conus lemniscatus Reeve, 1849. Northern Indian Ocean. Offshore; uncommon. Syn.: *sagittatus* Sowerby.

Varius Cone (1.5″) 4 cm
Conus varius L., 1758. East Africa to Fiji. Shallow sands; common. Syn.: *hevassii* A. Adams.

Axelrod's Cone (0.6″) 1.6 cm
Conus axelrodi Walls, 1978. Taiwan to New Guinea. Offshore; moderately common. Holotype illustrated.

Boeticus Cone (1.2″) 3 cm
Conus boeticus Reeve, 1844. Indo-Pacific. On sand, shallow water; common. Very variable pattern.

Kinoshita's Cone (2.8″) 7 cm
Conus kinoshitai (Kuroda, 1956). China Sea; Philippines; Solomons. Moderately deep water; uncommon.

Chiang's Cone (0.8″) 2 cm
Conus chiangi (Azuma, 1972). Taiwan; southern Japan. Offshore coral banks; uncommon. Possibly a turrid.

Pöhl's Cone (2.5") 6 cm
Conus poehlianus Sowerby, 1887. S.W. Pacific. Shallow sands; uncommon.

Mauritian Cone (1.2") 3 cm
Conus cernicus H. Adams, 1869. Western Indian Ocean. Offshore; uncommon. Syn.: *propinquus* E. A. Smith.

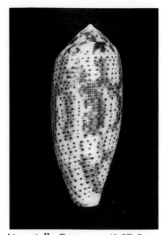

Nussatella Cone (1.2") 3 cm
Conus nussatella L., 1758. Indo-Pacific. Shallow water; common.

Tendineus Cone (2") 5 cm
Conus violaceus Gmelin, 1791. Indian Ocean. Fairly common on reefs. Syn.: *tendineus* Hwass.

Illustrious Cone (3.4") 8.5 cm
Conus excelsus Sowerby, 1908. Western Pacific. Offshore; rare. Syn.: *tannaensis* Cotton; *nakayasui* Shikama & Habe.

Exceptional Cone (1.5") 4 cm
Conus eximius Reeve, 1849. S.E. Asia; Philippines. Shallow water; uncommon.

Schepman's Cone (1") 2.5 cm
Conus schepmani Fulton, 1936. S.W. Pacific. Deep water; rare. Syn.: *elegans* Schepman not Sowerby.

Typhon Cone (1.5") 4 cm
Conus typhon Kilburn, 1975. Off Natal and Mozambique. Deep water; uncommon.

Cuvier's Cone (1.5") 4 cm
Conus cuvieri Crosse, 1858. Red Sea. Shallow water; uncommon. Very thin and light.

Burnished Cone (0.5") 1.2 cm
Conus rutilus Menke, 1843. Southern half of Australia; Tasmania. Shallow water; moderately common. Usually eroded.

Pontifical Cone (1.2") 3 cm
Conus dorreensis Peron, 1807. Western Australia. Shallow water; common. Syn.: *pontificalis* Lamarck.

MEDITERRANEAN CONES

Only one living cone is found in the Mediterranean, although it is very variable and has received over 80 names. Rarely, sinistral specimens are found. Forms or subspecies of *C. ventricosus* occur in N.W. Africa and the Canary Islands.

WEST AFRICAN and SOUTH AFRICAN CONES

The West African cones are so variable that their speciation is not clear. Some are variants of the Mediterranean Cone. Others are distinct. South Africa has a mixture of endemics, Indian Ocean and West African species.

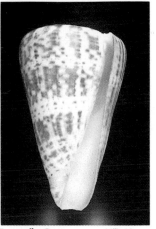

Mediterranean Cone (1.5") 4 cm
Conus ventricosus Gmelin, 1791. Mediterranean; West Africa. Shallow water; common. Syn.: *mediterraneus* Hwass.

Mediterranean Cone (1.5") 4 cm
Conus ventricosus Gmelin, 1791. Forms such as *aemulus* Reeve and *hybridus* Kiener are very closely related.

Butterfly Cone (4") 10 cm
Conus pulcher Lightfoot, 1786. S.W. Africa. Shallow water; common. Syn.: *prometheus* Hwass; *papilionaceus* Hwass.

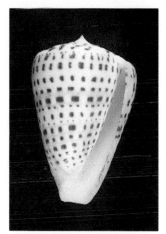

Lesser Butterfly Cone (2") 5 cm
Conus byssinus (Röding, 1798). West Africa. Shallow water; moderately common. Has been confused with *C. pulcher*.

Variable Cone (1.2") 3 cm
Conus variegatus Kiener, 1845. Southern West Africa. Shallow water; moderately common. Syn.: *chytreus* Tryon.

Variable Cone (1.2") 3 cm
Conus variegatus Kiener, 1845. There are many banded varieties of this cone, some very striking.

Onion Cone (1.2") 3 cm
Conus bulbus Reeve, 1843. Southern West Africa. Intertidal and offshore; common. Syn.: *zebroides* Kiener.

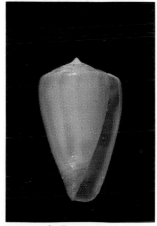

Clover's Cone (1") 2.5 cm
Conus soaresi Trovao, 1978. Senegal; West Africa. Shallow water; uncommon. Syn.: *cloveri* Walls, 1978. Type illus.

Clover's Cone (1") 2.5 cm
Conus soaresi Trovao, 1978. Uncommon and slightly variable cone. Given two names within days of each other.

Cape Verde Cone (1.4") 3.5 cm
Conus venulatus Hwass, 1792. Cape Verde Islands. Shallow water; uncommon. Syn.: *nivosus* Lamarck; *trochulus* Reeve.

Cape Verde Cone (1.4") 3.5 cm
Conus venulatus Hwass, 1792. This species also occurs along the West African coast. Shells are often eroded.

Girdled Cone (1.2") 3 cm
Conus balteus Wood, 1828.
Cape Verde Islands (endemic).
Shallow water; uncommon.
Very variable in pattern.

Conus balteus Wood, 1828.
One of the synonyms of this
cone is *cuneolus* Reeve. The
name was based on a dark-col-
ored shell.

Trader Cone (1.2") 3 cm
Conus mercator L., 1758. West
Africa; Cape Verde Islands.
Shallow water; locally com-
mon. Syn.: *lamarckii* Kiener.

Ambiguous Cone (1.5") 4 cm
Conus ambiguus Reeve, 1844.
West Africa. 1 to 30 m; moder-
ately common. Syn.: *gernanti*
Petuch.

Turtle Cone (2") 5 cm
Conus ermineus Born, 1778.
West Africa; West Indies. Off-
shore; moderately common.
Syn.: *ranunculus* Hwass.

Ruddy Cone (1.5") 4 cm
Conus tinianus Hwass, 1792.
South Africa. Shallow water;
common, as beach shells. Perfect shells rare.

Tasle's Cone (1.5") 4 cm
Conus taslei Kiener, 1845. S.W.
Africa. Shallow to moderately
deep water; uncommon. Syn.:
desidiosus A. Adams.

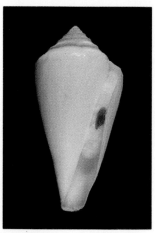

Turret Cone (3") 7.5 cm
Conus altispiratus Sowerby,
1873. South Africa. Offshore,
60-700 m; uncommon. Syn.:
turritus Sowerby.

Algoa Cone (1.5") 4 cm
Conus algoensis Sowerby,
1834. South Africa. Offshore;
common as a beach shell. On
left is form *simplex* Sowerby.

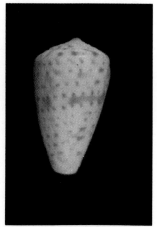

Jeffreys Bay Cone (1.5") 4 cm
Conus infrenatus Reeve, 1848.
South Africa. Offshore; common as a beach shell. *C. visa-
genus* Kilburn may be this.

Bairstow's Cone (1.5") 4 cm
Conus bairstowi Sowerby,
1889. Cape Province, South Africa. Beach shells only known;
uncommon.

Guinea Cone (2") 5 cm
Conus guineensis Gmelin,
1791. South Africa. Offshore;
common as a beach shell. Syn.:
informis Hwass.

FLORIDA and
CARIBBEAN CONES

From Bermuda to northern Brazil the Western Atlantic supports fewer than four dozen species of cones. Recent scuba diving has been bringing up new varieties in the West Indies.

Hybrid Cone (1.2") 3 cm
Conus aemulus Reeve, 1844, form *hybridus* Kiener, 1845. West Africa. Common. C. *aemulus* has dotted white lines.

Hybrid Cone (1.2") 3 cm
Conus aemulus form *hybridus* Kiener, 1845. West Africa. Variation in pattern.

Garter Cone (2") 5 cm
Conus genuanus L., 1758. West Africa. Shallow water. Fairly common. Syn.: *sphinx* Röding.

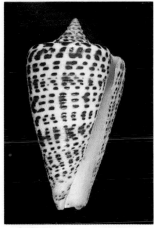

Alphabet Cone (2") 5 cm
Conus spurius Gmelin, 1791. S.E. United States and West Indies. Common. Syn.: *proteus* Hwass.

Gold-banded Cone (2.5") 6 cm
Conus spurius form *aureofasciatus* Rehder & Abbott, 1951. A freak color form from the Gulf of Mexico. Rare.

Lorenz's Cone (2.5") 6 cm
Conus spurius subspecies *lorenzianus* Dillwyn, 1817. Many races exist to the south of Florida.

Lorenz's Cone (2.5") 6 cm
This form is from Honduras in deep water. Some forms have large brown blotches.

Lorenz's Cone (2.5") 6 cm
Conus spurius subspecies *lorenzianus* Dillwyn, 1817. This is the typical form found in Colombia and Venezuela.

Sennott's Cone (1.2") 3 cm
Conus sennottorum Rehder & Abbott, 1951. Off Yucatan; rare. Most specimens are more pear-shaped.

Crown Cone (2") 5 cm
Cone regius Gmelin, 1791. Georgia; South Florida; West Indies; Brazil. Moderately deep water; common.

Yellow Crown Cone (2") 5 cm
Conus regius Gmelin, 1791. This striking color form is called *citrinus* Gmelin, 1791.

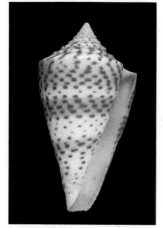

Sozon's Cone (3″) 7.5 cm
Conus delessertii Récluz, 1843. S.E. United States. Offshore reefs; uncommon. Syn.: *sozoni* Bartsch.

Centurion Cone (2″) 5 cm
Conus centurio Born, 1778. Caribbean. Moderate depths, or beached; uncommon. Syn.: *woolseyi* M. Smith.

Amphiurgus Cone (1.5″) 4 cm
Conus amphiurgus Dall, 1889. S.E. United States; Puerto Rico; Yucatan. Offshore; uncommon. Holotype illus.

Julia Clench's Cone (1.5″) 4 cm
Conus amphiurgus form *juliae* Clench, 1942. S.E. United States. 2 to 50 m; uncommon.

Carrot Cone (1.5″) 4 cm
Conus daucus Hwass, 1792. N.E. Brazil and Caribbean. Offshore; uncommon. Syn.: *pastinaca* Lamarck.

Jucunda Cone (1.2″) 3 cm
Conus jucundus Sowerby, 1887. Caribbean. Like *cardinalis* but aperture white, not pink.

Abbott's Cone (1.3″) 3 cm
Conus abbotti Clench, 1946. Bahamas. Rare. Holotype illus.

Thin Cone (1″) 2.5 cm
Conus attenuatus Reeve, 1844. Caribbean. Shallow water; moderately rare. Often more slender than this specimen.

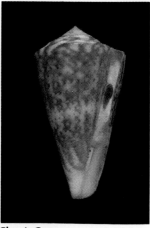

Florida Cone (1.5″) 4 cm
Conus floridana Gabb, 1868. S.E. United States. Common. Top: holotype, form *burryae* Clench, 1942.

Mouse Cone (1.2″) 3 cm
Conus mus Hwass, 1792. S.E. Florida; West Indies; Bermuda. Rocky shore beaches; locally common.

Turtle Cone (2.5″) 6 cm
Conus ermineus Born, 1778. Gulf of Mexico to Brazil; West Africa. Offshore; common. Syn.: *testudinarius* Hwass.

Clery's Cone (1.5″) 4 cm
Conus clerii Reeve, 1844. Brazil to N. Argentina. Offshore; uncommon. Syn.: *clenchi* Martins.

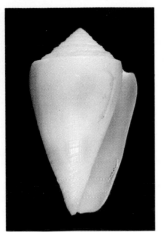

Bermuda Cone (1.5″) 4 cm
Conus mindanus Hwass, 1792.
Bermuda to Brazil. Offshore;
locally common. Syn.: *bermu-
densis* Clench.

Conus mindanus Hwass, 1792.
A confusing species with numerous forms, including this
pustulose one. Sometimes
darkly colored.

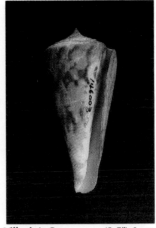

Villepin's Cone (2.5″) 6 cm
Conus villepinii Fischer &
Bernardi, 1857. Florida to Brazil. Deep water; rare. Syn.: *fos-
teri* Cl. & Ag. (holotype).

Glory-of-the-Atlantic (2″) 5 cm
Conus granulatus L., 1758. S.E.
Florida and West Indies. Offshore rock slabs. 5 to 70 m; uncommon.

Cardinal Cone (1.4″) 3.5 cm
Conus cardinalis Hwass, 1792.
Caribbean. Shallow reefs; lo-
cally common. Aperture rose.

Pat's Cone (1″) 2.5 cm
Conus patae Abbott, 1971.
South Florida; Jamaica; Bahamas. Dredged; rare. Has axial
plications.

Kulkulcan Cone (0.7″) 1.8 cm
Conus kulkulcan Petuch, 1980.
Caribbean. Shallow reefs; uncommon. May be a dark form
of *cardinalis*.

Hieroglyphic Cone (0.8″) 2 cm
Conus hieroglyphus Duclos,
1833. Netherlands Antilles; Jamaica. Shallow water; moderately rare. Syn.: *armillatus* Ad.

Pinpoint Cone (0.8″) 2 cm
Conus puncticulatus Hwass,
1792. Caribbean to northern
Brazil. Offshore; common.
Syn.: *columba* Hwass.

Brazil Cone (1″) 2.5 cm
Conus beddomei Sowerby,
1901. Central Brazil. Shallow
water; uncommon. Syn.: *brasiliensis* Clench.

Maze's Cone (1.8″) 4.5 cm
Conus mazei Deshayes, 1874.
South Florida to Brazil. Offshore to deep water; moderately rare.

Raines's Cone (0.8″) 2 cm
Conus mazei Deshayes, 1874.
Young form with carinate margins. Form *rainesae* McGinty,
1953. Gulf of Mexico.

Coudert's Cone (1″) 2.5 cm
Conus couderti Bernardi, 1860. Lesser Antilles. Near reefs. 1 to 10 m; rare to uncommon.

Golden Cone (1.8″) 4.5 cm
Conus aurantius Hwass, 1792. Southern Caribbean. Uncommon.

Matchless Cone (2″) 5 cm
Conus cedonulli L., 1767. West Indies. Moderately deep water; rare.

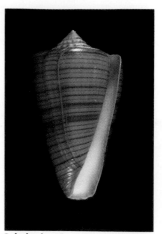

Caledonica Cone (2″) 5 cm
Conus cedonulli form *caledonicus* Hwass, 1792. Lesser Antilles. Rare.

Austin's Cone (2″) 5 cm
Conus cancellatus Hwass, 1792. Gulf of Mexico to Brazil. Offshore; uncommon. Syn.: *austini* Rehder & Abbott.

Stimpson's Cone (1.5″) 4 cm
Conus stimpsoni Dall, 1902. S.E. United States to Yucatan. Deep water; uncommon. Holotype illus.

Armored Cone (1.4″) 3.5 cm
Conus armiger Crosse, 1858, form *frisbeyae* Clench & Pulley, 1952 (holotype illus.). Syn.: *bajanensis* Usticke; *clarki* R. & A.

Jasper Cone (1″) 2.5 cm
Conus jaspideus Gmelin, 1791. Gulf of Mexico to central Brazil. Offshore to moderate depths; common. Highly variable.

Stearns's Cone (0.8″) 2 cm
Conus jaspideus Gmelin, 1791. The relatively narrow and elongate variety, known as *stearnsii* Conrad, occurs in Florida.

Verrucose Cone (1″) 2.5 cm
Conus jaspideus Gmelin, 1791. This pustuled form is common in Caribbean. Form *verrucosus* Hwass.

PANAMIC CONES (EASTERN PACIFIC)

A rich cone fauna exists from the Gulf of California to northern Ecuador. Many species are endemic, but some are closely related to Caribbean cones. A few are Indo-Pacific escapees.

Kerstitch's Cone (1.5″) 4 cm
Conus kerstitchi Walls, 1978. West Mexico and Baja California. Offshore; rare. Holotype illustrated.

Tiara Cone (1") 2.5 cm
Conus tiaratus Sowerby, 1833. West Mexico to Ecuador; Galapagos. Shallow water; common. Syn.: *roosevelti* B. & R.

Magistrate Cone (2.5") 6.5 cm
Conus archon Broderip, 1833. Gulf of California to Panama. Offshore to 100 m; uncommon. Syn.: *sanguineus* Kiener.

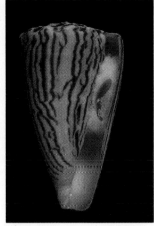

Prince Cone (3.6") 9 cm
Conus princeps L., 1758. Gulf of California to Ecuador. Shallow water; uncommon.

Orange Prince Cone (2.5") 6 cm
Conus princeps L., 1758. Rare form *apogrammatus* Dall, 1910, having fine axial streaks.

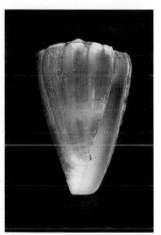

Gladiator Cone (1.2") 3 cm
Conus gladiator Broderip, 1833. Gulf of California to Peru. Shallow water; common.

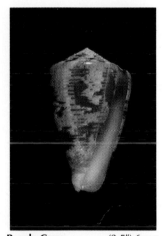

Purple Cone (2.5") 6 cm
Conus purpurascens Sowerby, 1833. Gulf of California to Peru. Intertidal rock ledges; moderately common.

Spiderweb Cone (1.8") 4.5 cm
Conus lucidus Wood, 1828. Baja California to Ecuador; Galapagos. Offshore; locally common.

Bosch's Cone (1") 2.5 cm
Conus boschi Clover, 1972. Oman coast and N.W. Indian Ocean. Offshore; uncommon.

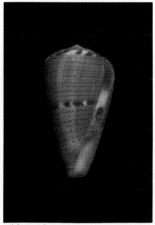

Ribboned Cone (1.2") 3 cm
Conus vittatus Hwass, 1792. Gulf of California to Ecuador. Offshore; uncommon. Color pattern variable.

Pear-shaped Cone (4") 10 cm
Conus patricius Hinds, 1843. Gulf of California to Ecuador. Offshore; common. Syn.: *pyriformis* Reeve.

Ferguson's Cone (4") 10 cm
Conus fergusoni Sowerby, 1873. Gulf of California to Ecuador. Offshore to moderate depths; common.

Orion Cone (1.2") 3 cm
Conus orion Broderip, 1833. West Mexico to Colombia. Shallow water; rare. Syn.: *drangai* Schwengel.

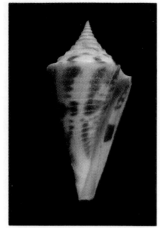

Arched Cone (1.5″) 4 cm
Conus arcuatus Broderip &
Sowerby, 1829. Gulf of California to Colombia. Moderately
deep water; common.

Recurved Cone (2.5″) 6 cm
Conus recurvus Broderip, 1833.
W. Mexico to Ecuador. Offshore; common. Name con-
served. Syn.: *incurvus* Brod.

Poorman's Cone (2″) 5 cm
Conus poormani Berry, 1968.
Gulf of California to Gulf of
Panama. Offshore; uncom-
mon.

Virgate Panama Cone (2″) 5 cm
Conus virgatus Reeve, 1849.
West Mexico to Ecuador. Shallow water; moderately common. Syn.: *signae* Bartsch.

Dall's Cone (1.5″) 4 cm
Conus dalli Stearns, 1873. West
Mexico to Panama. Uncom-
mon. Holotype illustrated.

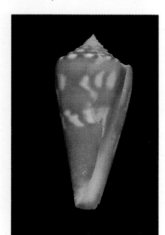

Guaymas Cone (2″) 5 cm
Conus xanthicus Dall, 1910.
Gulf of California. Deep water;
rare. Syn.: *chrysocestus* Berry.

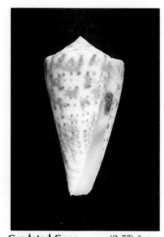

Gradated Cone (2.5″) 6 cm
Conus gradatus Wood, 1828.
Gulf of California to Peru. Off-
shore; common.

Grooved Cone (1.4″) 3.5 cm
Conus tornatus Sowerby, 1833.
Gulf of California to Ecuador.
Offshore; moderately com-
mon.

Interrupted Cone (1.5″) 4 cm
Conus ximenes Gray, 1839.
Gulf of California to Peru. Intertidal; common. Syn.: *inter-
ruptus* Wood.

Wood's Brown Cone (2″) 5 cm
Conus brunneus Wood, 1828.
Gulf of California; Baja California to Ecuador. Intertidal to
moderate depths; common.

Diadem Cone (1.5″) 4 cm
Conus diadema Sowerby, 1834..
Gulf of California to Panama;
Galapagos. Intertidal rocky
ledges; moderately common.

Bartsch's Cone (1.5″) 4 cm
Conus bartschi Hanna &
Strong, 1949. Gulf of California
to Costa Rica. Offshore, 10-50
m; moderately rare.

AUGER SHELLS
FAMILY TEREBRIDAE

Large family of long, slender shells with many whorls. Smooth or ornamented, often highly colored, they differ from turret-shells by having short anterior canal and narrow aperture. Thin operculum is placed on small foot. Radula with one or two teeth. Sand-dwelling carnivores of warm waters.

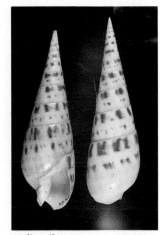

Marlinspike (6") 15 cm
Terebra maculata (L., 1758). Indo-Pacific. In sand, shallow water; common. Thick and heavy. Syn.: *maculosa* Pfeiffer.

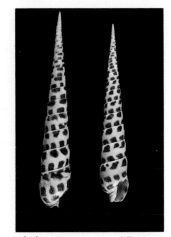

Subulate Auger (5") 13 cm
Terebra subulata (L., 1767). Indo-Pacific. In sand, shallow water; moderately common. Syn.: *tigreum* Montfort.

Agate Auger (2.5") 6 cm
Terebra achates Weaver, 1960. Hawaii. 3 to 100 m; uncommon. Punctate spiral striae.

Spotted Auger (5") 13 cm
Terebra guttata (Röding, 1798). Indo-Pacific. Shallow water, sand; uncommon. Syn.: *oculatum* Dillwyn; *loroisi* Deshayes.

Fly-spotted Auger (5") 13 cm
Terebra areolata (Link, 1807). Indo-Pacific. In sand, shallow water; moderately common. Syn.: *muscaria* Lamarck.

Faval Auger (2.7") 7 cm
Terebra senegalensis Lamarck, 1822. West Africa. In sand; moderately common. Syn.: *faval* Orbigny.

Dimidiate Auger (5") 13 cm
Terebra dimidiata (L., 1758). Indo-Pacific. In sand, shallow water; common. Syn.: *carnea* Perry; *splendens* Deshayes.

Sandbeach Auger (2.5") 6 cm
Impages hectica (L., 1758). Entire Indo-Pacific. Intertidal sand beaches; locally common.

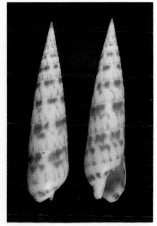

Short Auger (2.5") 6 cm
Terebra chlorata Lamarck, 1822. Indo-Pacific. Shallow water to 10 m, in sand; moderately common.

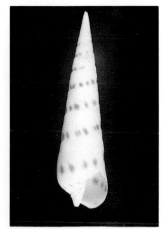

Tiger Auger (2.7") 7 cm
Terebra felina (Dillwyn, 1817). Indo-Pacific. In sand; moderately common. Syn.: *tigrinum* Gmelin; *suffusa* Pease.

Argus Auger (2.7") 7 cm
Terebra argus Hinds, 1844. Pacific. In sand; moderately rare. Syn.: *brachygyra* Pilsbry.

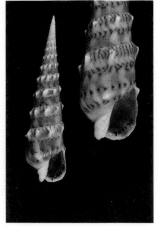

Crenulate Auger (4″) 10 cm
Terebra crenulata (L., 1758). Indo-Pacific. In sand, shallow water; moderately common. Syn.: *varicosum* Gmelin.

Finely Crenulate Auger (4″) 10 cm
Terebra crenulata form *interlineata* Deshayes, 1859. Indian Ocean; uncommon.

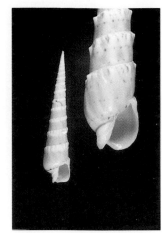

Fimbriate Auger (4″) 10 cm
Terebra crenulata form *fimbriata* Deshayes, 1857. Knobs usually finer. Intergrades exist. Common.

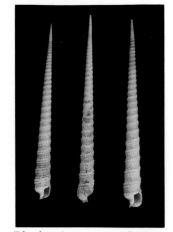

Triseriate Auger (4″) 10 cm
Terebra triseriata Gray, 1834. S.W. Pacific. Shallow water; uncommon. Syn.: *cancellata* Röding.

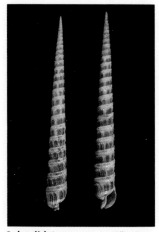

Splendid Auger (5″) 13 cm
Terebra pretiosa Reeve, 1842. Eastern Asia. Moderately rare, especially full grown and perfect.

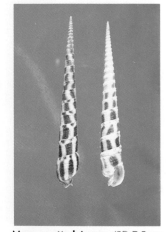

Many-spotted Auger (3″) 7.5 cm
Terebra commaculata (Gmelin, 1791). Indo-Pacific. On sand, shallow water; uncommon. Syn.: *myuros* Lamarck.

Pencil Auger (1.2″) 3 cm
Hastula penicillata (Hinds, 1844). Indo-Pacific. Shallow water; locally common. Syn.: *betsyae* R. D. Burch.

Lance Auger (2.5″) 6.5 cm
Hastula lanceata (L., 1767). Indo-Pacific. On sand, shallow water; common. Syn.: *oahuensis* Pilsbry.

Wide-mouth Auger (1.7″) 4.5 cm
Hastula stylata (Hinds, 1844). Indo-Pacific. On sand, shallow water; uncommon. Aperture conspicuously dilated.

Duplicate Auger (2″) 5 cm
Duplicaria duplicata (L., 1758). Indo-W. Pacific. In sand, shallow water; common. Syn.: *lamarckii* Kiener; *reevei* Desh.

Unrolled Auger (2.5″) 6 cm
Duplicaria evoluta (Deshayes, 1859). West Pacific; North Australia. On sand, shallow water; moderately common.

Cerithlike Auger (2″) 5 cm
Terebra cerithina Lamarck, 1822. Indo-Pacific. In sand; moderately common. Syn.: *pulchra* Hinds.

Funnel Auger (1.3″) 3 cm
Terebra funiculata Hinds, 1844.
Tropical western Pacific. Subtidal to 20 m; uncommon.

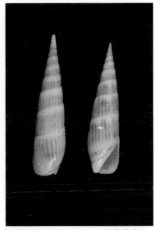

Inconstant Auger (1″) 2.5 cm
Hastula inconstans (Hinds, 1844). Hawaiian Islands. Steep sand beaches; locally common.

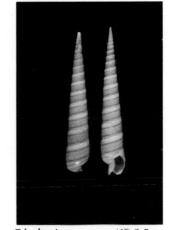

Tricolor Auger (1″) 2.5 cm
Terebra tricolor Sowerby, 1825. Hawaiian Islands. Offshore to 10 m; uncommon.

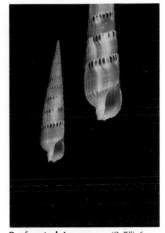

Perforated Auger (2.5″) 6 cm
Terebra pertusa Born, 1778. Bay of Bengal to Hawaii. Offshore to 20 m; uncommon. Syn.: *undata* Blainville.

Babylonian Auger (3″) 8 cm
Terebra babylonia Lamarck, 1822. Indo-Pacific. Shallow water to 5 m; common.

Similar Auger (2″) 5 cm
Terebra affinis Gray, 1834. Indo-Pacific. Shallow water to 10 m; common. Syn.: *striata* Quoy & Gaimard.

Thaanum's Auger (2″) 5 cm
Terebra thaanumi Pilsbry, 1921. Hawaiian Islands. Offshore, 40-80 m; uncommon.

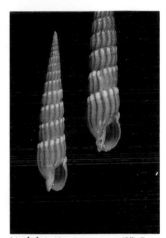

Undulate Auger (2″) 5 cm
Terebra undulata Gray, 1834. S.W. Pacific. Shallow water; uncommon. Syn.: *approximata* Deshayes.

Column Auger (1.6″) 4 cm
Terebra columellaris Hinds, 1844. S.W. Pacific. Shallow water; uncommon. Syn.: *propinqua* Pease.

Red-cloud Auger (2″) 5 cm
Terebra nebulosa Sowerby, 1825. Tropical Indo-Pacific. Offshore; uncommon.

Dussumier's Auger (2″) 5 cm
Terebra dussumieri Kiener, 1839. Korea to China. Shallow water; locally common.

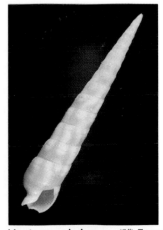

Montgomery's Auger (3″) 7 cm
Terebra montgomeryi R. Burch, 1965. Marianas Is. Reefs; rare. Holotype illus.

Shiny Pacific Auger   (1″) 2.5 cm
Hastula nitida (Hinds, 1844).
S.W. Pacific. Subtidal to 160 m;
common. Syn.: *plicatella*
Deshayes; *cernica* Sowerby.

Hollowed Auger   (2″) 5 cm
Terebra alveolata Hinds, 1844.
Indo-Pacific. In sand; moder-
ately common.

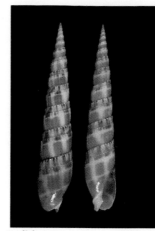

Radish Auger   (2″) 5 cm
Duplicaria raphanula (Lamarck,
1822). Indo-Pacific; South Africa. In sand; uncommon.
Syn.: *caledonica* Sowerby.

Gould's Auger   (2.3″) 5.5 cm
Terebra gouldi Deshayes, 1859.
Hawaiian Chain. Subtidal from
1 to 100 m; locally common.

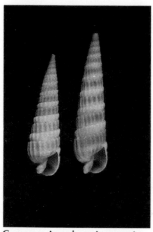

Common American Auger 4 cm
Terebra dislocata (Say, 1822).
S.E. United States to Brazil; California to Panama. Intertidal to
30 m; common.

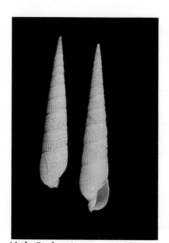

Little Basket Auger (1.2″) 3 cm
Terebra nassula Dall, 1889. West
Indies. Offshore to 1,200 m.
Types illustrated.

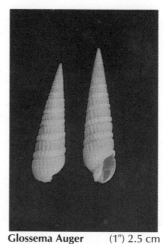

Glossema Auger   (1″) 2.5 cm
Terebra glossema Schwengel,
1940. S.E. Florida; Cuba; Bahamas. Offshore to 8 fathoms;
moderately common. Para-
type.

Shiny Atlantic Auger (1.5″) 4 cm
Hastula hastata (Gmelin, 1791).
S.E. Florida to Brazil; Bermuda.
Intertidal to 10 m; common.

Evelyn's Auger   (1.5″) 4 cm
Terebra evelynae Clench &
Aguayo, 1939. Northern Cuba.
Deep water; rare. Holotype il-
lustrated.

Gray Atlantic Auger (1.5″) 4 cm
Hastula cinerea (Born, 1778).
Florida to Brazil; West Mexico
to Ecuador. Sand beaches;
common. Syn.: *livida* Dill.

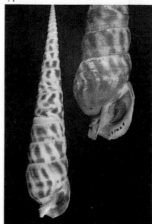

Flame Auger   (4.3″) 11 cm
Terebra taurina (Lightfoot,
1786). Florida; Texas to Brazil.
On sand offshore; uncommon.
Syn.: *flammea* Lamarck.

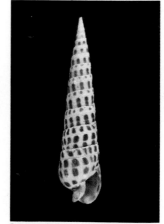

Ornate Auger   (3.3″) 8.5 cm
Terebra ornata Gray, 1834. Gulf
of California to Ecuador; Galapagos. Intertidal and offshore;
moderately common.

Zebra Auger (4") 10 cm
Terebra strigata Sowerby, 1825. Gulf of California to Galapagos. Shallow water; moderately common. Syn.: *zebra* Kiener.

Robust Auger (4.7") 12 cm
Terebra robusta Hinds, 1844. Baja California to Galapagos. Shallow water; common. Syn.: *lingualis* Hinds.

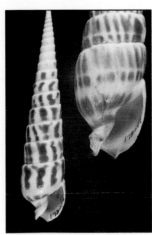

Variegate Auger (3") 7.5 cm
Terebra variegata Gray, 1834. Baja California to Ecuador. In sand, intertidal and offshore; moderately common.

Ecuadorian Auger (4") 10 cm
Terebra argosysia Olsson, 1971. Off Ecuador in moderately deep water. Holotype illustrated.

Tuberculate Auger (2.4") 6 cm
Terebra tuberculosa Hinds, 1844. West Mexico to Guatemala. Intertidal to 45 m; common.

Roosevelt's Auger (2") 5 cm
Terebra roosevelti Bartsch & Rehder, 1939. Baja California. Offshore shallow water; rare. Holotype illus.

Hancock's Auger (3") 7.5 cm
Terebra hancocki Bratcher & Burch, 1970. Dredged off west Panama; rare.

SUBCLASS OPISTHOBRANCHIA

Marine snails with both sexes in each individual (hermaphrodite). Gills behind heart. Rarely with shell or operculum. Includes bubble shells (Bullidae), sea hares (Aplysiidae), nudibranchs. Family Pyramidellidae has augerlike shells. Many are parasitic.

Dolabrate Pyram (1.2") 3 cm
Pyramidella dolabrata (L., 1758). Both Indo-Pacific and Caribbean. Shallow sand bays; common. Syn.: *terebelloides* Ad.

Terebra Pyram (1.2") 3 cm
Pyramidella dolabrata color form *terebellum* (Müller, 1774). Indo-Pacific; uncommon.

Needle Pyram (2") 5 cm
Pyramidella acus (Gmelin, 1791). Indo-Pacific. Shallow water, sand; common. Syn.: *guttata* Link; *maculosa* Lamarck.

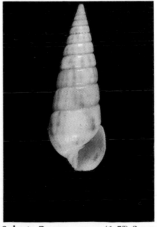

Sulcate Pyram (1.5") 3 cm
Pyramidella sulcata (A. Adams, 1854). Indo-Pacific. Shallow water to 10 m; moderately common.

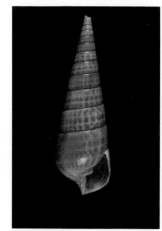

Tessellate Pyram   (1.3″) 3 cm
Pyramidella sulcata form *tessellata* (A. Adams, 1854). Indo-Pacific. Shallow water in sand; common.

Marmorate Niso   (1″) 2.5 cm
Niso marmorata (Sowerby, 1834). Cape Verde Islands; N.W. Africa. Shallow water; uncommon.

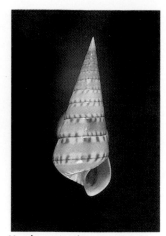

Henderson's Niso   (1″) 2.5 cm
Niso hendersoni Bartsch, 1953. North Carolina to both sides of Florida. 30 to 220 m; rare.

Girdled Niso   (0.8″) 2 cm
Niso balteata Sowerby, 1900. South Africa. Shallow water. Moderately common. *Niso* is in prosobranch family Melanellidae.

Conrad's Turbonille (0.3″) 7 mm
Turbonilla conradi Bush, 1899. West coast of Florida. Shallow water. Locally common. Many species in this genus.

Giant Leucotina   (1.5″) 3.5 cm
Leucotina gigantea (Dunker, 1877). Japan. Sandy mud, 10 to 50 m; uncommon.

Ventricose Milda   (1.3″) 3 cm
Milda ventricosa (Guérin, 1830). S.W. Pacific. Shallow water; uncommon.

Cat's Ear Otopleura (0.8″) 2 cm
Otopleura auriscati (Holten, 1802). S.W. Pacific. Shallow, sandy areas. Uncommon.

Lathe Acteon   (1″) 2.5 cm
Acteon tornatilis (L., 1767). West Europe and Mediterranean. Shallow water; common.

Striped Acteon   (1″) 2.5 cm
Acteon virgatus (Reeve, 1842). S.W. Pacific. Shallow water. Rare.

Eloise's Acteon   (1″) 2.5 cm
Acteon eloisae Abbott, 1973. S.E. Arabia. Shallow water; locally uncommon.

Solid Pupa   (1″) 2.5 cm
Pupa solidula (L., 1758). Indo-Pacific. Shallow water in sand; common. Syn.: *roseomaculata* Iredale.

Lined Bubble (1″) 2.5 cm
Bullina lineata (Gray, 1825).
Indo-Pacific. 1 to 30 m; common. Syn.: *nobilis* Habe; *errans* Iredale.

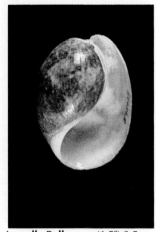

Ampulle Bulla (1.5″) 3.5 cm
Bulla ampulla L., 1758. Indo-Pacific. Shallow grass beds; abundant. Family Bullidae.

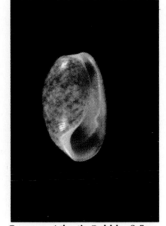

Common Atlantic Bubble 2.5 cm
Bulla striata Bruguière, 1792. Florida to Brazil; Mediterranean. Intertidal; locally abundant. Syn.: *occidentalis* A. Ad.

Australian Bubble (2″) 5 cm
Bulla botanica Hedley, 1918. Australia. Warm shallows; common. Syn.: *australis* Gray, not Ferussac.

White Pacific Atys (1.5″) 3.5 cm
Atys naucum (L., 1758). Indo-Pacific. Common. Rarely red-streaked, form *strigata* Pilsbry, 1917. Family Atyidae.

Cylindrical Atys (1″) 2.5 cm
Atys cylindricus (Helbling, 1779). Indo-Pacific. Common. Sometimes more slender.

Royal Paper-bubble (1″) 2.5 cm
Aplustrum amplustre (L., 1758). Indo-Pacific. Moderately common. Syn.: *fasciatum* Schumacher.

Zoned Paper-bubble (1.5″) 4 cm
Hydatina zonata (Lightfoot, 1786). Indo-Pacific. 10 to 50 m; locally uncommon. Syn.: *velum* Gmelin. In Hydatinidae.

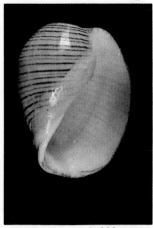

Green-lined Paper-bubble 5 cm
Hydatina physis (L., 1758). Indo-Pacific. Common. Similar *H. vesicaria* (Lightfoot, 1786) from Caribbean.

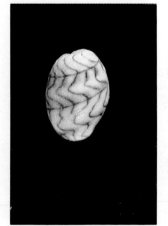

Miniature Melo (0.5″) 1.2 cm
Micromelo undatus (Bruguière, 1792). Florida to Brazil. Intertidal, green algae; uncommon.

Say's Paper-bubble (0.5″) 1.2 cm
Haminoea solitaria (Say, 1822). Massachusetts to Carolinas. Intertidal grass; abundant.

Woody Canoe-bubble
(2.5″) 6 cm
Scaphander lignaria (L., 1758). Western Europe. Offshore in sand; locally common.

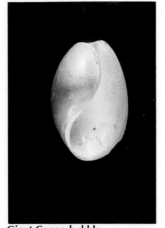

Giant Canoe-bubble
(1.5") 3.5 cm
Scaphander punctostriatus
Mighels, 1841. Arctic Seas to
N.W. Europe; to West Indies.
Offshore; uncommon.

Solute Akera   (1.5") 3.5 cm
Akera soluta (Gmelin, 1791).
Indo-Pacific. Shallow grass
beds; locally common.

Shoulderblade Sea Cat (2") 5 cm
Dolabella auricularia (Lightfoot, 1786). Indo-Pacific and
tropical Eastern Pacific. Shell
buried in 5 inch (12 cm) animal.

Emerald Bubble   (0.3") 7 mm
Smaragdinella calyculata (Broderip & Sowerby, 1829). Tropical
West Pacific; intertidal algae;
common. Syn.: *viridis* Rang.

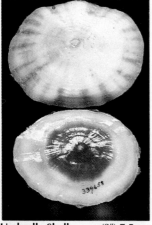

Umbrella Shell   (3") 7.5 cm
Umbraculum umbraculum
(Lightfoot, 1786). Indo-Pacific;
Caribbean. Rare. Animal (4") 10
cm.

SEA BUTTERFLIES
PTEROPODA

Small, pelagic gastropods with
fleshy wings for swimming.
Abundant in all major seas. A
major source of food for some
whales. There are 15 genera
and about a hundred species,
some lacking shells. Shells
found at great depths on ocean
floor.

Three-toothed Cavoline
(0.6") 1.5 cm
Cavolinia tridentata (Niebuhr,
1775). Worldwide; open seas.
Abundant.

Uncinate Cavoline (0.6") 1.5 cm
Cavolinia uncinata (Rang,
1829). Worldwide, open seas.
More abundant in warm wa-
ters.

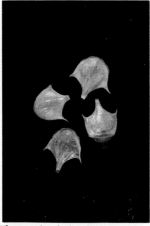

Three-spined Cavoline
(0.4") 1 cm
Diacria trispinosa (Blainville,
1821). Worldwide, open seas.
Locally abundant.

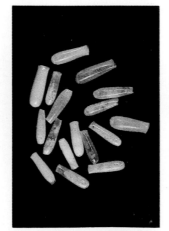

Cigar Pteropod   (0.2") 5 mm
Cuvierina columnella (Rang,
1827). Worldwide, open seas.
Common in the Atlantic.

Pyramid Clio   (0.9") 2.2 cm
Clio pyramidata L., 1767.
Worldwide, open seas. Many
forms, including three from
Antarctica.

Cuspidate Clio   (0.9") 2.2 cm
Clio cuspidata (Bosc, 1802).
Worldwide, pelagic. Abundant.

LAND SNAILS
SUBCLASS PULMONATA

Although most members of this subclass are typical garden and woodland snails that have lungs for breathing air, a number of families are associated with marine and brackish conditions. A few of the better-known species are included here.

New Zealand Titiko   (1") 2.5 cm
Amphibola crenata (Gmelin, 1791). New Zealand. Estuarine muds; common. Syn.: *avellana* Bruguière. Operculum present.

Say's False Limpet   (0.7") 1.8 cm
Siphonaria alternata Say, 1826. S.E. United States; Bahamas. Intertidal rock shore; common.

Striped False Limpet   (1") 2.5 cm
Siphonaria pectinata (L., 1758). Florida to Texas; Caribbean. Intertidal rocks; locally common.

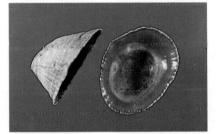

Lesson's False Limpet   (1") 2.5 cm
Siphonaria lessoni (Blainville, 1824). Peru; Chile to Brazil. Intertidal rocks; common.

Giant False Limpet   (2") 5 cm
Siphonaria gigas Sowerby, 1825. West Mexico to North Peru. Intertidal rocks; common.

White False Limpet   (1") 2.5 cm
Trimusculus reticulatus (Sowerby, 1835). Central California to West Mexico. Intertidal rocks; uncommon.

Eastern Melampus   (0.6") 1.5 cm
Melampus bidentatus Say, 1822. Quebec to Texas; West Indies. Marsh grasses; abundant.

Banded Melampus   (0.4") 1 cm
Melampus fasciatus Deshayes, 1830. Central Pacific. Shady, wooded shores; common.

Yellow Melampus   (0.5") 1.2 cm
Melampus luteus Quoy & Gaimard, 1832. Indo-Pacific; estuarine; common.

Bat Cassidula   (0.4") 1 cm
Cassidula vespertilionis (Lesson, 1831). Philippine Islands. Mangroves; locally common.

Rugose Cassidula   (1") 2.5 cm
Cassidula rugata Menke, 1853. South Australia. Mud shores; locally common.

Midas Ear Cassidula (3″) 7.5 cm
Ellobium aurismidae (L., 1758).
S.W. Pacific. Near mangroves;
locally abundant.

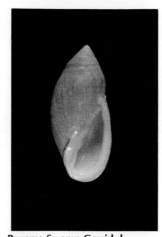

Panama Swamp Cassidula
(1″) 2.5 cm
Ellobium stagnalis (Orbigny,
1835). El Salvador to Ecuador.
Mangrove swamps; common.

Judas Ear Cassidula (2″) 5 cm
Ellobium aurisjudae (L., 1758).
S.W. Pacific. Mangrove
swamps; common.

Cat's Ear Cassidula (1″) 2.5 cm
Cassidula aurisfelis Bruguière,
1789. West Australia. Mangroves; common.

Nucleus Cassidula (0.6″) 1.5 cm
Cassidula nucleus (Gmelin,
1791). Indo-Pacific. Mangrove
areas. Common. Syn.: *muste-
lina* Deshayes.

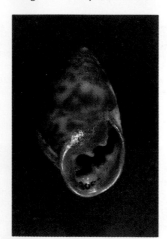

Common Pythia (1.2″) 3 cm
Pythia scarabaeus (L., 1758).
S.W. Pacific. Woodland snail;
common. Many forms.

Reeve's Pythia (1.2″) 3 cm
Pythia reeveana Pfeiffer, 1853.
Philippine Islands; locally com-
mon.

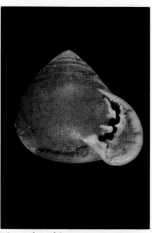

Trigonal Pythia (0.8″) 2 cm
Pythia trigonus Troschel, 1840.
Philippine Islands. Locally un-
common.

TUSK SHELLS
CLASS SCAPHOPODA

Worldwide in shallow and deep
waters, these small shells are
open at each end. Water is
pumped in and out of the small
end which protrudes above the
sand. About 1,000 species,
many requiring a hand lens to
identify. Small slit at narrow
end distinguishes some species.

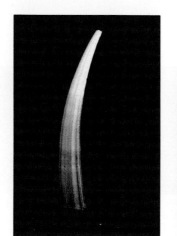

Elephant Tusk (3″) 7.5 cm
Dentalium elephantinum (L.,
1758). Southern Philippines to
Japan. 2 to 40 m; common.

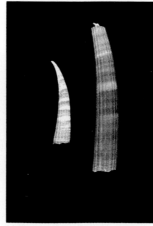

Formosan Tusk (2″) 5 cm
Dentalium formosum Adams &
Reeve, 1850. Eastern Asia. 1 to
20 m; uncommon. Syn.: *hirasei*
Kira; *festivum* Sowerby.

Vernede's Tusk (6″) 15 cm
Dentalium vernedei Sowerby,
1860. East Asia. 20 to 100 m;
common.

Boar's Tusk (2″) 5 cm
Dentalium aprinum L., 1766. Indo-Pacific. 2 to 40 m; common. Syn.: *taiwanum* Kuroda.

Senegal Tusk (1.5″) 3.5 cm
Dentalium senegalense Dautzenberg, 1891. West Africa. Uncommon. 11 to 13 ribs.

New Zealand Tusk (2.5″) 6 cm
Dentalium zelandicum Sowerby, 1860. New Zealand. Widespread in subtidal waters; common.

Octagonal Tusk (2″) 5 cm
Dentalium octangulatum Donovan, 1804. Indo-Pacific. Offshore to 100 m; common. 8 rounded ribs.

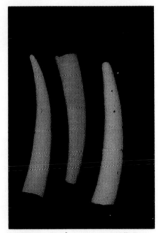
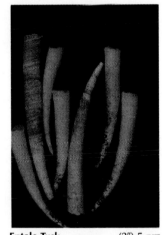

European Tusk (1″) 2.5 cm
Dentalium dentale L., 1766. Mediterranean and Adriatic. Shallow to deep water; common. 18 - 20 ribs.

Common Tusk (2″) 5 cm
Dentalium vulgare da Costa, 1778. British Isles to Mediterranean. Intertidal to 1,000 m; common. No apical notch.

Entale Tusk (2″) 5 cm
Dentalium entale L., 1758. N.W. Europe. Offshore; common. Subspecies *stimpsoni* Henderson, 1920, from New England.

Indian-money Tusk (2″) 5 cm
Dentalium pretiosum Sowerby, 1860. Alaska to Baja California. 1 to 150 m; locally abundant. Formerly used as money.

Half-scratched Tusk (1″) 2.5 cm
Dentalium semistriolatum Guilding, 1834. South Florida and West Indies. 1 to 200 m; common.

Ivory Tusk (2″) 5 cm
Dentalium eboreum Conrad, 1846. S.E. United States and West Indies. 1 to 20 m; common.

Elongate Tusk (3.5″) 9 cm
Dentalium longitrorsum Reeve, 1842. Indo-Pacific; common. Smooth; rarely pinkish.

Elephant Cadulus (1″) 2.5 cm
Cadulus elephas Henderson, 1920. West Indies. Deep water; uncommon. End narrows.

CHITONS
CLASS POLYPLACOPHORA

Known also as the Coat-of-Mail shells and Amphineura, these mollusks have 8 shelly plates bound at their margins by a girdle which may have scales or bristles. The foot is broad. Identification may depend on removing valves. About 600 living species.

Rugata Chiton (0.6") 1.5 cm
Lepidopleurus rugatus Pilsbry, 1892. Monterey to Baja California. Sublittoral rocks; common.

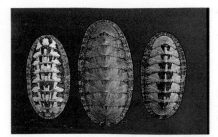

Many-colored Chiton (1.5") 4 cm
Ischnochiton versicolor (Sowerby, 1840). Australia. Sublittoral. Common. Girdle scales with striae.

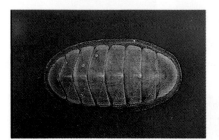

Contracted Chiton (2") 5 cm
Ischnochiton contractus (Reeve, 1874). South Australia. On pen shells; abundant. Multicolored.

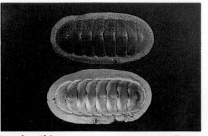

Regular Chiton (1.5") 4 cm
Ischnochiton regularis (Carpenter, 1855). Southern California. Intertidal; common. Girdle scales minute, rounded.

Elongate Chiton (1.5") 4 cm
Ischnochiton elongatus (Blainville, 1825). South Australia; Tasmania. Under rocks; common.

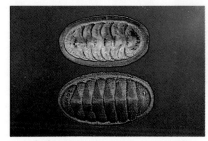

Austral Chiton (2") 5 cm
Ischnochiton australis (Sowerby, 1840). South and eastern Australia. Under littoral rocks; common. Syn.: *lugubris* Gould.

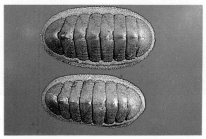

Evanida Chiton (3") 8 cm
Ischnochiton evanida (Sowerby, 1840). Southern Australia; Tasmania. Very common.

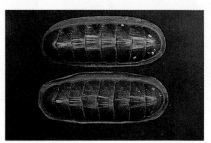

Torre's Chiton (1.5") 4 cm
Ischnochiton torrei Iredale & May, 1916. South and West Australia. Common. Girdle orange.

Lineolate Chiton (2") 5 cm
Ischnochiton lineolatus (Blainville, 1825). South and West Australia. Abundant. Syn.: *iredalei* Dupuis.

Merten's Chiton (1.5") 4 cm
Lepidozona mertensii (Middendorff, 1847). Alaska to Baja California. Subtidal; common. Color variable.

Florida Slender Chiton (1") 2.5 cm
Stenoplax floridana (Pilsbry, 1892). Lower Florida Keys. Intertidal to 1 m; common.

Conspicuous Chiton (5") 12 cm
Stenoplax conspicua (Dall, 1879). California to West Mexico. Intertidal; common.

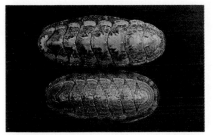

Magdalena Chiton (3") 7.5 cm
Stenoplax magdalenensis (Hinds, 1845). West Mexico. Variations.

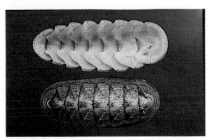

Magdalena Chiton (3") 7.5 cm
Stenoplax magdalenensis (Hinds, 1845). West Mexico. Intertidal; common.

Elevated Chiton (3") 7.5 cm
Stenoplax alata (Sowerby, 1840). S.W. Pacific; Philippines. Intertidal; common.

Veiled Pacific Chiton (1.5") 4 cm
Placiphorella velata Dall, 1879. California to W. Mexico. Intertidal; common.

Lined Red Chiton (1.5") 4 cm
Tonicella lineata (Wood, 1815). Japan to Alaska to California. Subtidal to 90 m; common.

Northern Red Chiton (1") 2.5 cm
Tonicella rubra (L., 1767). Arctic Seas to Europe; California and New York. 1 to 200 m; common.

Hidden Chiton (1.2") 3 cm
Tonicella insignis (Reeve, 1847). Alaska to Washington. Common. Syn.: *submarmoreus* Middendorff.

Mottled Red Chiton (1") 2.5 cm
Tonicella marmorea (Fabricius, 1780). Arctic Seas to New England; Europe and Western Canada. Common. Girdle smooth.

Elegant Chiton (2") 5 cm
Tonicia elegans (Frembley, 1827). Chile and Peru. Littoral to 5 m; common.

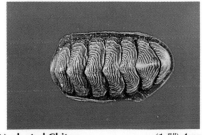

Neglected Chiton (1.5") 4 cm
Onisthochiton neglectus (Rochebrune, 1881). New Zealand. Littoral rocks. Common. Syn.: *opinionosus* Iredale and Hull.

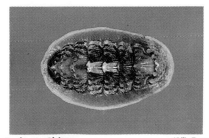

Forbes's Chiton (2") 5 cm
Tonicia forbesii Carpenter, 1857. West Mexico to Panama. Sublittoral rocks; common. Girdle naked.

Hartweg's Chiton   (1.5″) 3.5 cm
Cyanoplax hartwegii (Carpenter, 1855). Washington to Baja California. Intertidal; common.

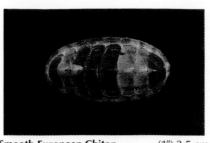

Smooth European Chiton   (1″) 2.5 cm
Callochiton achatinus (Brown, 1827). N.W. Europe and Mediterranean. Common. Syn.: *laevis* Montagu, not Osbeck.

Eastern American Chiton   (0.8″) 2 cm
Chaetopleura apiculata (Say, 1830). Massachusetts to Florida. 1 to 20 m; common; on shells and rocks.

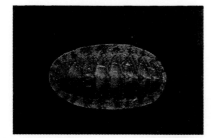

Decorated Chiton   (1″) 2.5 cm
Callistochiton decoratus Pilsbry, 1893. Central California to West Mexico. Littoral rocks; uncommon.

Albida Chiton   (3″) 7.5 cm
Plaxiphora albida (Blainville, 1825). Southern Australia. Littoral; common. Girdle hairs broad.

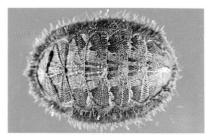

Mossy Mopalia   (1.5″) 3.5 cm
Mopalia muscosa (Gould, 1846). Alaska to Baja California. Intertidal; common. Syn.: *lignosa* Gould.

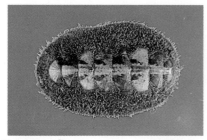

Hairy Mopalia   (1.5″) 3.5 cm
Mopalia ciliata (Sowerby, 1840). Alaska to California. Intertidal; common. Variable colors.

Hairy Mopalia   (1.5″) 3.5 cm
Mopalia ciliata (Sowerby, 1840). Alaska to California. Variations in color patterns.

Laevior Chiton   (1.5″) 3.5 cm
Mopalia laevior Pilsbry, 1918. Washington to Baja California. Intertidal. Moderately common.

Laevior Chiton   (1.5″) 3.5 cm
Mopalia laevior Pilsbry, 1918. Shows variation in sculpture and colors.

Acute Chiton   (1.5″) 3.5 cm
Mopalia acuta Carpenter, 1855. California to Baja California. Intertidal; common. Syn.: *chloris* Dall.

Hinds's Mopalia   (3.5″) 9 cm
Mopalia hindsii (Reeve, 1847). Alaska to West Mexico. Under intertidal rock ledges; common.

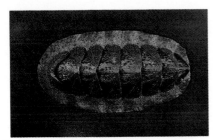

Volvox Chiton (3") 7.5 cm
Lorica volvox (Reeve, 1847). South Australia; New South Wales. Under stones at low tide; uncommon.

Hauraki Chiton (2.5") 6 cm
Lorica haurakiensis Mestayer, 1921. New Zealand. Intertidal rocks; common.

Angas's Chiton (2") 5 cm
Loricella angasi (H. Adams, in Adams & Angas, 1864). East Australia. Intertidal; uncommon.

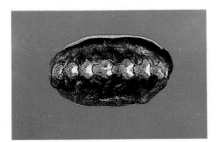

Black Katy Chiton (2.5") 6 cm
Katharina tunicata (Wood, 1815). Alaska to S. California. Intertidal; very common.

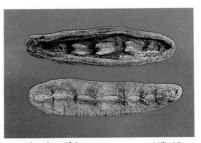

Striate Slender Chiton (4") 10 cm
Cryptoplax striata (Lamarck, 1819). Southern Australia; Tasmania. Subtidal rocks; common.

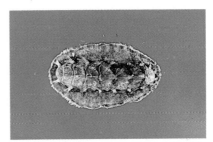

Hemphill's Chiton (1") 2.5 cm
Craspedochiton hemphilli (Pilsbry, 1893). Live specimen. Florida Keys. See dried specimen below.

Fuzzy West Indian Chiton (3") 7 cm
Acanthopleura granulata (Gmelin, 1791). South Florida and West Indies. Intertidal rocks; common. Live.

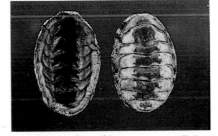

Fuzzy West Indian Chiton (3") 7 cm
Acanthopleura granulata (Gmelin, 1791). Dried specimens.

Hemphill's Chiton (1") 2.5 cm
Craspedochiton hemphilli (Pilsbry, 1893). Florida Keys and West Indies. Sublittoral on dead coral; common.

Exquisite Chiton (1.5") 3.5 cm
Acanthochitona exquisita (Pilsbry, 1893). Gulf of California. Uncommon; intertidal.

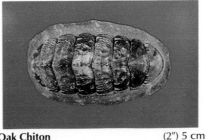

Oak Chiton (2") 5 cm
Chiton quercinus Gould, 1846. Eastern Australia. Intertidal; common.

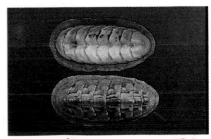

Translucent Chiton (2") 5 cm
Chiton translucens Hedley & Hull, 1909. Eastern Australia. Intertidal; common.

West Indian Chiton   (2.5″) 6 cm
Chiton tuberculatus L., 1758. S.E. Florida and West Indies. Intertidal; common.

Green Chiton   (2″) 5 cm
Chiton viridis Spengler, 1797. West Indies. Intertidal; common.

Marbled Chiton   (2.5″) 6 cm
Chiton marmoratus Gmelin, 1791. S.E. Florida and the West Indies. Littoral rocks; common.

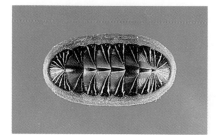

White-striped Chiton   (1.5″) 3.6 cm
Chiton albolineatus Broderip & Sowerby, 1829. West Mexico. Under intertidal rock ledges; uncommon.

Articulate Chiton   (3″) 7.5 cm
Chiton articulatus Sowerby 1832. West Mexico. Intertidal rocks; moderately common.

Stokes's Chiton   (3″) 7.5 cm
Chiton stokesii Broderip, 1832. West Mexico to Chile. Intertidal rocks; common.

Magnificent Chiton   (4″) 10 cm
Chiton magnificus Deshayes, 1844. Chile. Intertidal rocks; locally common.

Squamose Chiton   (3″) 7.5 cm
Chiton squamosus L., 1764. West Indies. Intertidal; common.

Serpent-skin Chiton   (2″) 5 cm
Chiton pelliserpentis Quoy & Gaimard, 1835. New Zealand; South Australia; Tasmania. Rocks; common.

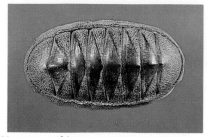

Marquesas Chiton   (3″) 7.5 cm
Chiton marquesanus Pilsbry, 1893. Marquesas Islands; Polynesia. Uncommon.

Sulcate Chiton   (4″) 10 cm
Chiton sulcatus Wood, 1815. Galapagos Islands. Locally common.

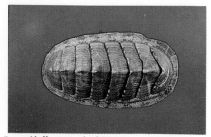

Beautifully-zoned Chiton   (3″) 7.5 cm
Chiton calliozonus Pilsbry, 1893. Southern Australia; Tasmania. Rocks in sandy pools; common.

CLASS BIVALVIA

Also known as the pelecypods, this class includes the clams, oysters, scallops and other bivalves having two shelly valves hinged at the top. There is no head or radular teeth, and feeding is done by the gills. There are about 10,000 living species, some in rivers and lakes.

AWNING CLAMS
FAMILY SOLEMYIDAE

A primitive group of cigar-shaped clams having a glossy periostracum extending beyond the thin shelly valves. The hinge has no true teeth. These clams live in burrows in mud. Some live in shallow water, but others are deep-sea dwellers.

Atlantic Awning Clam   (1″) 2.5 cm
Solemya velum Say, 1823. Nova Scotia to northern Florida. Shallow water 1 to 12 m in mud; locally common.

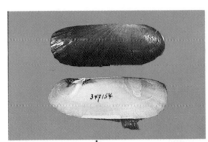

Australian Awning Clam   (2″) 5 cm
Solemya australis Lamarck, 1818. South Australia, Tasmania. Subtidal to 10 m; common.

SUPERFAMILY
NUCULACEA

Includes the Nut Clams which have pearly interiors and numerous, fine teeth in the hinge (taxodonts). Includes families Nuculidae, Nuculanidae and Malletiidae. Most of the several hundred species live in very deep water. Some shallow-water species are very common and serve as food for ducks and fish.

Atlantic Nut Clam   (0.3″) 7 mm
Nucula proxima Say, 1822. Nova Scotia to Texas; Bermuda. Subtidal in sandy mud; abundant.

Sulcate Nut Clam   (0.7″) 1.8 cm
Nucula sulcata (Bronn, 1831). Norway to Mediterranean. 5 to 2,250 m; common. Syn.: *decussata* Sowerby.

Superb Nut Clam   (0.8″) 2 cm
Nucula superba Hedley, 1902. N.E. Australia and S.W. Pacific. Subtidal in sand; moderately common.

Rugose Nut Clam   (0.3″) 7 mm
Nucula rugosa Odhner, 1918. Indian Ocean. In sand, 30 to 40 m; uncommon.

Miraculous Nut Clam   (1″) 2.5 cm
Nucula mirifica Dall, 1907. Off Japan. 600 m; uncommon.

Divaricate Nut Clam   (1″) 2.5 cm
Acila divaricata (Hinds, 1843). China and Japan. Offshore; uncommon.

Castrensis Nut Clam   (0.5″) 1.2 cm
Acila castrensis (Hinds, 1843). Bering Sea to Baja California. 8 to 200 m; common.

Wondrous Nut Clam   (1.5″) 3.5 cm
Acila mirabilis (Adams and Reeve, 1850). Korea and Japan. Offshore in deep water; uncommon.

Fulton's Nut Clam   (1″) 2.5 cm
Acila fultoni (E. A. Smith, 1892). Bay of Bengal, India. Deep water; rare.

Coarse Nut Clam   (1″) 2.5 cm
Scaeoleda illepida Iredale, 1929. South Australia. Subtidal from 5 to 100 m; locally common.

Polished Nut Clam   (1″) 2.5 cm
Nuculana polita (Sowerby, 1833). West Panama. 13 to 73 m; uncommon.

Müller's Nut Clam   (1″) 2.5 cm
Nuculana pernula (Müller, 1771). Arctic Seas around N. America, Europe. Offshore common.

File Yoldia   (2″) 5 cm
Yoldia limatula (Say, 1831). Nova Scotia to North Carolina. Subtidal, 1 to 10 m; locally common.

Arctic Yoldia   (1.2″) 3 cm
Yoldia hyperborea Lovén, 1859. Arctic Seas, Alaska to Norway. Deep water; moderately common.

Broad Yoldia   (2″) 5 cm
Yoldia thraciaeformis Storer, 1838. Arctic North America to N. Carolina and Puget Sound. Offshore; common.

Cooper's Yoldia   (1.2″) 3 cm
Yoldia cooperi Gabb, 1865. Southern California. Offshore; uncommon.

Scissors Yoldia   (1″) 2.5 cm
Yoldia scissurata Dall, 1897. Arctic Seas to California. 16 to 150 m; common. Syn.: *ensifera* Dall.

Scissors Yoldia   (1″) 2.5 cm
Yoldia scissurata (Dall, 1897). This is the holotype of the synonym *Y. ensifera* Dall.

Japanese Yoldia   (0.7″) 1.8 cm
Portlandia japonica (Adams and Reeve, 1850). Japan. 10 to 250 m on sandy mud; common.

Pointed Nut Clam (0.3") 7 mm
Nuculana acuta (Conrad, 1831). Eastern U.S. to Brazil. Shallow water; abundant.

Pacific Malletia (1") 2.5 cm
Malletia pacifica Dall, 1897. Alaska to California. Offshore, 300 to 650 m; uncommon.

Chilean Malletia (1.5") 3.5 cm
Malletia chilensis Des Moulins, 1832. Chile and Peru. Offshore in moderately deep water; uncommon.

ARK CLAMS
FAMILY ARCIDAE

Heavy, squarish, porcelaneous shells living in warm seas. A few live in very deep water. Some spin a byssus which serves as an anchor. The hinge bears numerous taxodont teeth which may vary in number, even within a species. The blackish, horny ligament is helpful in identification. There are about 200 species in the family.

Noah's Ark (2.5") 6 cm
Arca noae L., 1758. Mediterranean; N.W. Africa. Subtidal to 119 m on rocks; common. Variable in shape.

Atlantic Turkey Wing (3") 7 cm
Arca zebra (Swainson, 1833). S.E. United States to Brazil; Bermuda. Shallow rock reefs; common. Syn.: *occidentalis* Philippi.

Panamic Turkey Wing (3") 7 cm
Arca pacifica (Sowerby, 1833). W. Mexico to Peru. Under rocks, subtidal to 137 m; common.

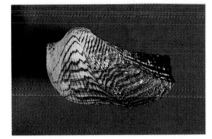

Ventricose Ark (3") 7 cm
Arca ventricosa Lamarck, 1819. S.W. Pacific; Polynesia. Shallow reefs; common.

Mossy Ark (2") 5 cm
Arca imbricata Bruguière, 1789. S.E. United States to Brazil. Shallow reefs, under rocks; common. Syn.: *umbonata* Lamarck.

Indo-Pacific Ark (2.5") 6 cm
Arca navicularis Bruguière, 1789. Indo-Pacific; Japan. Shallow water on rocks; common.

Indo-Pacific Ark (1.5") 3.5 cm
Arca navicularis Bruguière, 1789. Young specimens have more distinct ribs and squarish outline.

Changeable Ark (1.5") 3 cm
Arca mutabilis (Sowerby, 1833). W. Mexico to Ecuador. Subtidal among rocks to 82 m; common.

Four-sided Ark   (1.5") 3 cm
Arca tetragona Poli, 1795. Norway to Cape Verde Islands. Subtidal to deep water, on rocks; common.

Hazelnut Ark   (1") 2.5 cm
Arca avellana Lamarck, 1819. Indo-Pacific. Shallow reefs; common.

Kobelt's Ark   (0.7") 1.8 cm
Arca boucardi Jousseaume, 1894. Japan and Korea. Among rocks, 9 to 80 m. Syn.: *kobeltiana* Pilsbry; common.

Senile Ark   (2.5") 6 cm
Senilia senilis (L., 1758). West Africa. Estuarine sands; common. Shell heavy.

Blood Ark   (2") 5 cm
Anadara ovalis (Bruguière, 1789). Cape Cod to Texas; to Brazil. Shallow water; common. Syn.: *campechiensis* Gmelin.

Eared Ark   (3") 7.5 cm
Anadara notabilis (Röding, 1798). S.E. United States to Brazil. Shallow water; common. Syn.: *deshayesi* Hanley.

Transverse Ark   (1.5") 3.5 cm
Anadara transversa (Say, 1822). Cape Cod to Texas. Intertidal to 10 m; common. Syn.: *sulcosa* van Hyning.

Cut-ribbed Ark   (5") 12 cm
Anadara floridana (Conrad, 1869). S.E. United States and Greater Antilles. Shallow water; uncommon.

Grand Ark   (4") 10 cm
Anadara grandis (Broderip & Sowerby, 1829). W. Mexico to Peru. Near mangroves in black mud; common.

Burnt-end Ark   (2") 5 cm
Anadara uropygimelana (Bory St. Vincent, 1824). Indo-Pacific. Shallow sand to 4 m; locally common.

Scapha Ark   (2.5") 6 cm
Anadara scapha (L., 1758). Indo-Pacific. Shallow waters; common.

Antique Ark   (2.5") 6 cm
Anadara antiquata (L., 1758). Indo-Pacific. Shallow waters. Common.

Granular Ark (2.5″) 6 cm
Anadara granosa (L., 1758). S.W. Pacific.
Muddy sand, shallow; abundant.

Half-crenate Ark (2.5″) 6 cm
Anadara subcrenata (Lischke, 1869). China
coast, Korea and Japan. Shallow water;
common.

Hairy Rib Ark (2.5″) 6 cm
Anadara setigericosta (Nyst, 1848). Indian
Ocean; S.E. Asia. Shallow water; uncom-
mon.

Incongruous Ark (2″) 5 cm
Anadara brasiliana (Lamarck, 1819). S.E.
United States to Brazil. Shallow water,
sand; common. Syn.: *incongrua* Say.

Ponderous Ark (2.5″) 6 cm
Noetia ponderosa (Say, 1822). Virginia to
Texas. Shallow water; common. Umbones
point backwards.

European Bearded Ark (2″) 5 cm
Barbatia barbata (L., 1758). Mediterranean
to N.W. Africa. Subtidal under stones to 280
m; common.

White Bearded Ark (2″) 5 cm
Barbatia candida (Helbling, 1779). S.E.
United States to Brazil. Shallow reefs, on
rocks; common.

Decussate Ark (2″) 5 cm
Barbatia velata (Sowerby, 1843). Indo-Paci-
fic. Shallow reefs, on rocks; common.
Syn.: *decussata* Sowerby; *lima* Sowerby.

Reeve's Ark (3″) 7.5 cm
Barbatia reeveana (Orbigny, 1846). W. Mex-
ico to Peru. Intertidal to 100 m; abundant.
Syn.: *nova* Mabille.

Almond Ark (1.5″) 3.5 cm
Barbatia amygdalumtostum (Röding, 1798).
Indo-Pacific. Coral reefs; under rocks;
abundant. Syn.: *fusca* Bruguière.

Red-brown Ark (1.5″) 3 cm
Barbatia cancellaria (Lamarck, 1819). S. Florida to Brazil. Intertidal to 4 m among coral
boulders; common.

Oblique Ark (1.5″) 3 cm
Barbatia obliquata (Wood, 1828). Philippines. Shallow reefs; locally common.

Stone-boring Ark   (3″) 7.5 cm
Litharca lithodomus (Sowerby, 1833). Nicaragua to Peru. Bores in subtidal rock; locally uncommon.

Hooded Ark   (3″) 7.5 cm
Cucullaea labiata (Lightfoot, 1786). S.W. Pacific. Offshore to 100 m; locally common. Syn.: *auriculifera* Lamarck.

Hooded Ark   (3″) 7.5 cm
Cucullaea labiata (Lightfoot, 1786). S.W. Pacific. Interior coloration is variable, sometimes white, purple or brown.

Half-propellor Ark   (3″) 7.5 cm
Trisidos semitorta (Lamarck, 1819). S.E. Asia; Japan. Shallow water; moderately common.

Propellor Ark   (3″) 7.5 cm
Trisidos tortuosa (L., 1758). Japan to East Indies. Shallow water; locally common.

Twisted Ark   (2″) 5 cm
Trisidos torta (Mörch, 1850). China coast. Shallow water; uncommon.

Shaggy Bathyark   (1″) 2.5 cm
Bathyarca ectocomata (Dall, 1886). Lesser Antilles, West Indies. Deep water, 164 to 320 m; uncommon. Paratype illus.

Bubble Bathyark   (1″) 2.5 cm
Bathyarca pompholax (Dall, 1908). Off California in deep water; rare.

ALMOND ARKS
FAMILY LIMOPSIDAE

Related to the ark shells, these small, thin, obliquely oval clams are usually covered with a velvety, brown periostracum. The teeth are numerous and about the same size. The ligament is external, small and in the center of the hinge. Most species live in deep water.

Scratched Limopsis   (1″) 2.5 cm
Limopsis multistriata (Förskal, 1775). Red Sea and Indian Ocean. Offshore; common.

Vagina Limopsis   (1.5″) 3 cm
Limopsis vaginata Dall, 1891. Bering Sea and Alaska. Offshore; uncommon.

Tajima's Limopsis   (1.5″) 3 cm
Limopsis tajimae Sowerby, 1914. Off Japan in deep water. Uncommon.

Banded Limopsis (1″) 2.5 cm
Limopsis zonalis Dall, 1904. Gulf of Panama. Dredged in 1,000 m; uncommon. Paratype illustrated.

Marion Limopsis (1.5″) 3 cm
Limopsis marionensis E. A. Smith, 1885. Antarctic. Dredged offshore; rare.

Ruiz Limopsis (1″) 2.5 cm
Limopsis ruizana Rehder, 1971. Off Chile in deep water; rare. Holotype illustrated here.

BITTERSWEET CLAMS
FAMILY
GLYCYMERIDIDAE

Like the ark clams these bivalves have taxodont teeth in the hinge. The shells are heavy, compressed and oval. There are about 150 known species, most living in the Indo-Pacific. They prefer shallow water and sand bottoms. They are used for food in Europe and Asia.

Comb Bittersweet (2″) 5 cm
Glycymeris pectunculus (L., 1758). Tropical Indo-Pacific. Shallow water; common.

Gold-flowing Bittersweet (2″) 5 cm
Glycymeris auriflua (Reeve, 1843). S.W. Pacific. Shallow water; uncommon.

Comb Bittersweet (1″) 2.5 cm
Glycymeris pectinata (Gmelin, 1791). S.E. United States to Brazil. Shallow water; common. 20 to 40 fine small ribs.

Silky Bittersweet (1.5″) 4 cm
Glycymeris sericata (Reeve, 1843). West Indies. Shallow water, sand. Uncommon.

Unequal Bittersweet (1.5″) 3.7 cm
Glycymeris inaequalis (Sowerby, 1833). Gulf of California to Peru. Offshore, 4 to 24 m; common. Syn.: *assimilis* Sowerby.

Muscat Bittersweet (1.5″) 3.5 cm
Glycymeris muskatensis Melvill, 1897. N.W. Indian Ocean. Offshore in 5 to 30 m; locally common.

Flat-ribbed Bittersweet (3″) 7 cm
Glycymeris laticostata (Quoy & Gaimard, 1835). New Zealand. Shallow water; common.

Clark's Bittersweet (2″) 5 cm
Glycymeris clarki (Nicol, 1951). Philippines. Deep water; uncommon. Holotype illustrated.

White-lined Bittersweet (3") 7.5 cm
Glycymeris albolineata (Lischke, 1872). Japan. Offshore from 5 to 20 m; common.

Reeve's Bittersweet (3") 7.5 cm
Glycymeris reevei (Mayer, 1868). S.W. Pacific. Shallow water to 50 m; locally common.

Rayed Bittersweet (2") 5 cm
Glycymeris radians (Lamarck, 1819). South Australia and Tasmania. Subtidal to 300 m; common.

Atlantic Bittersweet (2") 5 cm
Glycymeris undata (L., 1758). S.E. United States to Brazil. Offshore from 2 to 56 m; common.

Violet Bittersweet (2.5") 6 cm
Glycymeris violacescens (Lamarck, 1819). Mediterranean. Shallow water, sand. Common.

Clothed Bittersweet (3") 7.5 cm
Glycymeris vestita (Dunker, 1877). Japan and S.W. Pacific. Shallow water; common.

European Bittersweet (3") 7.5 cm
Glycymeris glycymeris (L., 1758). Norway to the Mediterranean. Offshore; common. Syn.: *orbiculata* Pennant.

Pilose Bittersweet (2.5") 6 cm
Glycymeris pilosa (L., 1767). Mediterranean and Canary Islands. Offshore to 150 m; uncommon.

Decussate Bittersweet (2") 5 cm
Glycymeris decussata (L., 1758). S.E. Florida to Brazil. Shallow water; moderately common.

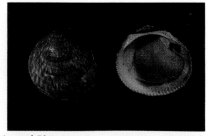

Pennaceus Bittersweet (2.5") 6 cm
Glycymeris pennacea (Lamarck, 1819). West Indies. Uncommon. Shallow water.

Oblique Bittersweet (2") 5 cm
Glycymeris obliqua (Reeve, 1843). W. Australia. Shallow water; uncommon.

Austral Bittersweet (2") 5 cm
Glycymeris australis (Quoy & Gaimard, 1832). Australia. Shallow water; uncommon.

Giant Bittersweet (4") 10 cm
Glycymeris gigantea (Reeve, 1843). Gulf of California. Offshore from 7 to 13 m; locally common.

American Bittersweet (4.5") 11 cm
Glycymeris americana (De France, 1829).. S.E. United States to Brazil. Offshore to 40 m; moderately common.

SEA MUSSELS
FAMILY MYTILIDAE

The true mussels are abundant throughout the world, mainly in intertidal and shallow water. The darkly colored, thin, but strong shells have a weak hinge with a few small teeth. Most attach themselves to rocks, but several genera burrow in peat, rocks and corals. The Blue Mussel is a favorite seafood in Europe.

Common Blue Mussel (3") 7.5 cm
Mytilus edulis L., 1758. Worldwide subarctic seas; United States. Intertidal to 10 m; abundant. Rarely rayed.

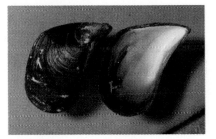

Mediterranean Blue Mussel (4") 10 cm
Mytilus galloprovincialis Lamarck, 1819. Western Europe; Mediterranean. Intertidal to 4 m; abundant. Many synonyms.

Green Mussel (2") 5 cm
Perna viridis (L., 1758). Indian Ocean to S.W. Pacific. Shallow water; common. Syn.: *smaragdinus* Gmelin. Single tooth in right valve.

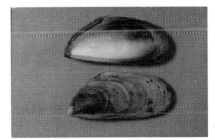

Chorus Mussel (4") 10 cm
Choromytilus chorus (Molina, 1782). Peru to Tierra del Fuego. Intertidal to 3 m on rocks; common. One central tooth.

Perna Mussel (3") 7 cm
Perna perna (L., 1758). West Africa; lower Caribbean. Mangrove roots; locally common. *Chloromya* is a synonym of *Perna*.

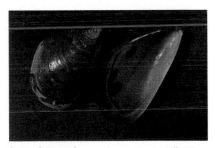

Channel Mussel (6") 15 cm
Perna canaliculus (Gmelin, 1791). New Zealand. On subtidal rocks; common.

Black-ribbed Mussel (6") 15 cm
Aulacomya ater (Molina, 1782). Brazil to Chile and Peru. Intertidal to 30 m; common. Syn.: *magellanicus* Gmelin.

Crenate Mussel (2") 5 cm
Aulacomya ater form *crenata* (Lamarck, 1819). A young form of *ater*. Syn.: *americanus* Orbigny.

Maori Mussel (3") 7 cm
Aulacomya ater maoriana (Iredale, 1915). New Zealand. Rocky subtidal; common.

Californian Mussel   (8″) 20 cm
Mytilus californianus Conrad, 1837. Intertidal to 50 m on rocks; abundant. Ribbed. Syn.: *californicus* Clessin.

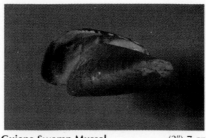

Guiana Swamp Mussel   (3″) 7 cm
Mytella guyanensis (Lamarck, 1819). W. Mexico to Ecuador; Venezuela to Brazil. On stones in muddy intertidal zone; common.

Falcate Swamp Mussel   (3″) 7 cm
Mytella falcata (Orbigny, 1846). W. Mexico to Ecuador; Venezuela to Uruguay. Mud near mangroves; common.

Box Mussel   (1″) 2.5 cm
Septifer bilocularis (L., 1758). Indo-Pacific. Intertidal rocks in mud; common. Internal deck at end.

Bifurcate Mussel   (1″) 2.5 cm
Septifer bifurcatus (Conrad, 1837). California to W. Mexico. Intertidal on rocks; common.

Hooked Mussel   (2″) 5 cm
Ischadium recurvum (Rafinesque, 1820). Cape Cod to West Indies. Estuarine; intertidal; common. Syn.: *hamatus* Say.

Atlantic Ribbed Mussel   (3″) 7.5 cm
Geukensia demissa (Dillwyn, 1817). East Canada to Florida; introduced to Calif. Peat marshes; common. Syn.: *plicatulus* Lamarck.

Scorched Mussel   (0.7″) 1.8 cm
Brachidontes exustus (L., 1758). S.E. United States to Uruguay. Estuarine, intertidal; common.

Impact Mussel   (1.5″) 4 cm
Modiolarca impacta (Hermann, 1782). New Zealand. In nests under rocks, intertidal; common.

Senhouse's Mussel   (1″) 2.5 cm
Musculus senhousia (Benson, 1842). East Asia. In eelgrass beds from 1 to 20 m; common.

California Date Mussel   (1″) 2.5 cm
Adula californiensis (Philippi, 1847). West Canada to southern California. In rocks, shallow water; common.

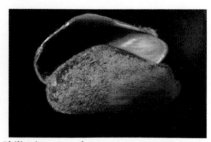

Philippine Mussel   (3″) 7.5 cm
Modiolus philippinarum Hanley, 1843. Indo-Pacific. Shallow water flats; abundant.

Northern Horse Mussel   (5") 13 cm
Modiolus modiolus (L., 1758). Arctic Seas to New Jersey; to Spain; to California; Japan. Low-tide mark to 10 m; abundant.

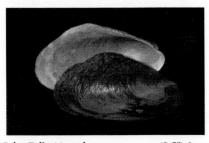

False Tulip Mussel   (2.5") 6 cm
Modiolus modiolus subspecies *squamosus* Beauperthuy, 1967. S.E United States and Caribbean. Umbones not swollen. No rose colors. Common.

Tulip Mussel   (3") 7.5 cm
Modiolus americanus (Leach, 1815). S.E. United States; W. Mexico to Peru. Shallow water; abundant. Syn.: *tulipa* Lamarck; *pseudotulipus* Olsson.

European Date Mussel   (3.5") 9 cm
Lithophaga lithophaga (L., 1758). France to Mediterranean; Red Sea. Subtidal to 60 m; bores in rock; common.

Antillean Date Mussel   (4") 10 cm
Lithophaga antillarum (Orbigny, 1842). S.E. Florida to Brazil. Subtidal, soft coral rocks; common. Syn.: *corrugata* Philippi.

Scissor Date Mussel   (2") 5 cm
Lithophaga aristata (Dillwyn, 1817). S.E. United States to Brazil; S. Calif. to Peru; Mediterranean. Subtidal in soft rocks; common.

Cylinder Date Mussel   (3") 7.5 cm
Lithophaga teres (Philippi, 1846). Indo-Pacific. Shallow water, in soft rocks; common.

Black Date Mussel   (2") 5 cm
Lithophaga nigra (Orbigny, 1842). S.E. Florida to Brazil. Shallow water, in coral rocks; common. Syn.: *caribaea* Philippi.

Mahogany Date Mussel   (1.5") 3.5 cm
Lithophaga bisulcata (Orbigny, 1842). S.E. United States to Brazil; Bermuda. Common rock-borer. Syn.: *appendiculata* Philippi.

Plume Date Mussel   (2") 5 cm
Lithophaga plumula (Hanley, 1844). California to Peru. In rocks and *Spondylus* shells; common. Syn.: *kelseyi* Hertlein & Strong.

PEN SHELLS
FAMILY PINNIDAE

Large, thin, but strong, shells, fan-shaped and living buried in sand and gravel. Attached to submerged rocks and shells by a thick, silky byssus. About 25 known species, mostly tropical. *Pinna* with a weak groove in middle of each valve. Absent in *Atrina*.

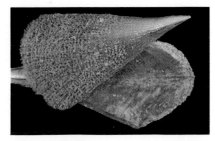

Noble Pen Shell   (24") 60 cm
Pinna nobilis L., 1758. Mediterranean. Offshore to 20 m; common. Variable sculpture. Syn.: *gigas* Chemnitz.

Prickly Pen Shell (6")15 cm
Pinna muricata L., 1758. East Africa to Polynesia. Subtidal to 60 m, silty sand, grass; common. Many synonyms; *philippinensis* Reeve.

Bicolor Pen Shell (16") 40 cm
Pinna bicolor Gmelin, 1791. East Africa to Hawaii and Japan. Subtidal to 4 m in sand. Syn.: *atropurpurea* Sowerby. Sometimes rayed.

Rugose Pen Shell (16") 40 cm
Pinna rugosa Sowerby, 1835. W. Mexico to Panama. In mud, intertidal; common.

Rude Pen Shell (20") 50 cm
Pinna rudis L., 1758. Mediterranean to Angola; Caribbean. Offshore in rock crevices; uncommon. Syn.: *pernula* Chemnitz (and Röding).

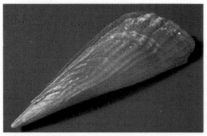

Amber Pen Shell (10") 26 cm
Pinna carnea Gmelin, 1791. S.E. United States to Brazil. Intertidal to 3 m in sand; common. Syn.: *flabellum* Lamarck.

Saw-toothed Pen Shell (10") 26 cm
Atrina serrata (Sowerby, 1825). S.E. United States and West Indies. Shallow water in sand; common.

Stiff Pen Shell (10") 26 cm
Atrina rigida (Lightfoot, 1786). S.E. United States and Caribbean. Shallow water in sandy mud; common. Syn.: *rigida* Dillwyn.

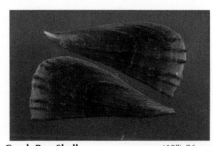

Comb Pen Shell (10") 26 cm
Atrina pectinata (L., 1767). India, Japan to Fiji. Subspecies *zelandica* (Gray, 1835) from New Zealand. Common. Syn.: *japonica* Reeve, and others.

Tuberculose Pen Shell (8") 20 cm
Atrina tuberculosa (Sowerby, 1835). W. Mexico to Panama. Shallow water; sandy mud; locally common.

Half-Naked Pen Shell (8") 20 cm
Atrina seminuda (Lamarck, 1819). S.E. United States to Argentina. Offshore; common. Syn.: *patagonica* Orbigny.

Indo-Pacific Pen Shell (16") 40 cm
Atrina vexillum (Born, 1778). East Africa to Polynesia. Subtidal from 1 to 60 m; common. Syn.: *nigra* Dillwyn; *tenuis* Habe.

Baggy Pen Shell (8") 20 cm
Streptopinna saccata (L., 1758). Entire Indo-Pacific. Among rocks and crevices on reefs; uncommon. Syn.: *inusitata* Iredale.

WINGED OYSTERS
PEARL OYSTERS
FAMILY PTERIIDAE

A large family of tropical oysters having mother-of-pearl interiors. A strong byssus spun by the foot attaches the oysters to rocks, gorgonian stems and wharf pilings. Pearls from the genus *Pinctada* are of gem quality. Family Isognomonidae has many teeth in the hinge.

Penguin Wing Oyster (3") 7 cm
Pteria penguin (Röding, 1798). Indo-Pacific. Shallow water; common. Syn.: *macroptera* Lamarck.

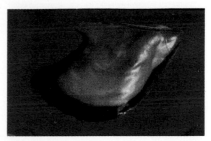

Penguin Wing Oyster (10") 25 cm
Pteria penguin form *lotorium* (Lamarck, 1819). Larger specimens lack long wings. Common.

Golden Wing Oyster (3") 7.5 cm
Pteria crocea (Lamarck, 1819). Central Pacific; Philippines. Shallow water; uncommon.

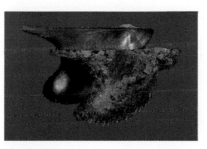

Atlantic Wing Oyster (3") 7.5 cm
Pteria colymbus (Röding, 1798). S.E. United States to Brazil. Attaches to alcyonarians, 1 to 5 m; common. Syn.: *atlantica* Lamarck.

European Wing Oyster (3") 7.5 cm
Pteria hirundo (L., 1758). W. Europe; Mediterranean. Offshore in 1 to 290 m; common. Syn.: *tarentina* Lamarck.

Loven's Wing Oyster (1.5") 4 cm
Pteria loveni (Dunker, 1872). Japan; Western Pacific. Attached to seawhips 3 to 80 m; common.

Western Wing Oyster (3") 7.5 cm
Pteria sterna (Gould, 1851). S. California to Peru. Subtidal to 30 m; common. Syn.: *peruviana* Reeve.

Black Wing Oyster (3") 7.5 cm
Pteria avicula (Holten, 1802). S.W. Pacific. Shallow water; common. Syn.: *peasei* Dunker.

Cape Wing Oyster (2.5") 6 cm
Pteria capensis (Sowerby, 1892). S.E. Africa; South Africa. Shallow water to offshore; common.

Bearded Wing Oyster (2") 5 cm
Pteria longisquamosa (Dunker, 1852). West Indies. Offshore in shallow water; uncommon. Syn.: *viridizona* Dall.

Pearl Oyster (8") 20 cm
Pinctada margaritifera (L., 1758). Indo-Pacific. Offshore 5 to 30 m; locally common. Source of pearls.

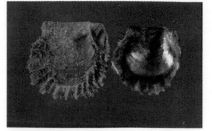

Atlantic Pearl Oyster (3″) 7.5 cm
Pinctada imbricata Röding, 1798. S.E. United States to Brazil. Shallow water; common. Syn.: *radiata* Leach.

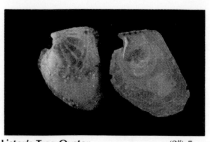

Lister's Tree Oyster (2″) 5 cm
Isognomon radiatus (Anton, 1839). S. Florida, Texas, West Indies to Brazil. Intertidal rock flats; common. Syn.: *listeri* Hanley.

Saddle Tree Oyster (4″) 10 cm
Isognomon ephippium (L., 1758). Indo-Pacific. Muddy estuaries; common on rocks intertidally.

Flat Tree Oyster (3″) 7.5 cm
Isognomon alatus (Gmelin, 1791). Florida to Brazil; Bermuda. Near mangroves, on rocks; common.

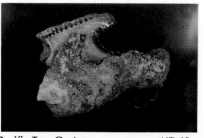

Pacific Tree Oyster (4″) 10 cm
Isognomon isognomum (L., 1758). Indo-Pacific. Intertidal to 2 m; common. Genus is in family Isognomonidae.

Rayed Tree Oyster (3″) 7.5 cm
Isognomon perna (L., 1767). Indo-Pacific. Shallow reefs; common. Syn.: *costellata* Conrad.

Two-toned Tree Oyster (1.5″) 4 cm
Isognomon bicolor (C. B. Adams, 1845). Shallow water, in rock crevices; common. Syn.: *chemnitzianus* Orbigny.

HAMMER OYSTERS
FAMILY MALLEIDAE

Unlike the Isognomonidae which have numerous alternating teeth and ligamental blocks, this family has a large, oblique ligament at the center of the hinge. The hinge is often produced at each side, thus giving some species a "hammer" shape. The interior is semi-nacreous. Most live in tropical waters, on reef flats or in crevices of coral rocks.

Sponge Finger Oyster (2.5″) 6 cm
Vulsella vulsella (L., 1758). Indo-Pacific. Shallow water in sponges; uncommon. Syn.: *lingulata* Lamarck.

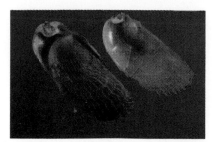

Sponge Finger Oyster (2.5″) 6 cm
Vulsella vulsella form *lingulata* Lamarck, 1801. More elongate and rayed than the typical form. Rare.

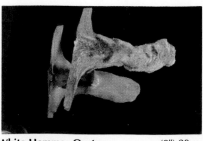

White Hammer Oyster (8″) 20 cm
Malleus albus Lamarck, 1819. Indo-Pacific. Shallow water on grass and rock flats; common.

Common Hammer Oyster (8″) 20 cm
Malleus malleus (L., 1758). Indo-Pacific. Shallow water; common. Syn.: *vulgaris* Lamarck.

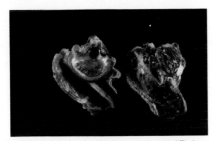

American Hammer Oyster (1.5") 4 cm
Malvimalleus candeanus (Orbigny, 1842). S.E. United States; West Indies. Coral rock crevices; locally common.

SCALLOPS
FAMILY PECTINIDAE

A large and popular family, both as collectors' items and as food. The genera are very complex and the divisions are arbitrary. Amateur collectors may call them all *Pecten*. Many species are capable of swimming by snapping their valves. Most species are tropical, but a few live in polar waters. Sculpture differs on opposite valves.

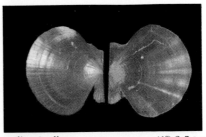

Hyaline Scallop (1") 2.5 cm
Lissopecten hyalinus (Poli, 1795). W. Europe; Mediterranean. Shallow water; common.

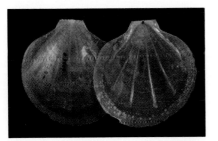

Siboga Glass Scallop (2") 5 cm
Propeamussium sibogai Dautzenberg & Bavay, 1912. Japan; deep water; common.

Watson's Glass Scallop (2.5") 6 cm
Propeamussium watsoni (E. A. Smith, 1885). East Indies. Deep water; rare.

Alcock's Glass Scallop (2") 5 cm
Propeamussium alcocki (E. A. Smith, 1885). Bay of Bengal, India. 1400 m; rare.

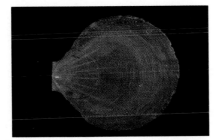

Dall's Glass Scallop (2") 5 cm
Propeamussium dalli (E. A. Smith, 1886). Gulf of Mexico and West Indies. Deep water; uncommon in collections.

Colbeck's Scallop (3") 7.5 cm
Adamussium colbecki (E. A. Smith, 1902). Antarctic waters. Dredged in 200 m; locally common.

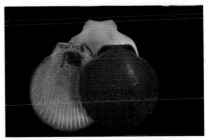

Asian Moon Scallop (3") 7.5 cm
Amusium pleuronectes (L., 1758). S.W. Pacific, India, Japan. Offshore to 30 m; abundant.

Australian Moon Scallop (3") 7.5 cm
Amusium pleuronectes subspecies *australiae* Habe, 1964. N. Australia; offshore; common.

Japanese Moon Scallop (4") 10 cm
Amusium japonicum (Gmelin, 1791). Japan. Offshore in 10 to 100 m; common.

Ballot's Moon Scallop (4") 10 cm
Amusium japonicum subspecies *balloti* (Bernardi, 1861). New Caledonia and N. Australia. Common.

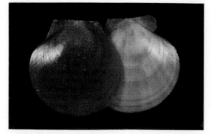

Smudged Moon Scallop   (1.5″) 4 cm
Amusium obliteratum (L., 1758). South China Sea. Offshore; rare.

Laurent's Moon Scallop   (3″) 7.5 cm
Amusium laurenti (Gmelin, 1791). Caribbean. Offshore in 50 to 200 m; uncommon.

Paper Moon Scallop   (2″) 5 cm
Amusium papyraceum (Gabb, 1873). Gulf of Mexico to Brazil. Offshore in 50 to 120 m; locally common.

Kelp Scallop   (1″) 2.5 cm
Leptopecten latiauratus (Conrad, 1837). California to W. Mexico. On kelp weeds; common. Syn.: *monotimeris* Conrad.

Bald Scallop   (2.5″) 6 cm
Proteopecten glaber (L., 1758). Portugal to the Adriatic. Offshore, 6 to 900 m; common. Syn.: *distans* Lamarck.

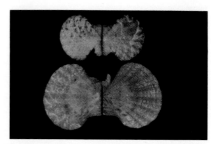

Club Scallop   (1″) 2.5 cm
Peplum clavatum (Poli, 1795). W. Europe to Mediterranean. Offshore, 5 to 1,000 m; common. Syn.: *inflexum* Poli.

Great Scallop   (5″) 12 cm
Pecten maximus (L., 1758). N.W. Europe to Madeira. Offshore, 3 to 1,000 m; common edible scallop. Syn.: *vulgaris* da Costa.

St. James's Scallop   (5″) 12 cm
Pecten maximus subspecies *jacobaeus* (L., 1758). Mediterranean; Canary Is. Offshore, 5 to 100 m; common, edible.

Keppel's Scallop   (4″) 10 cm
Pecten keppelianus Sowerby, 1905. Cape Verde Islands. Shallow water; uncommon.

Triple-ridged Scallop   (1.5″) 4 cm
Serratovola tricarinata (Anton, 1839). Philippines, East Indies. Offshore to 50 m; uncommon. Syn.: *passerina* Hinds.

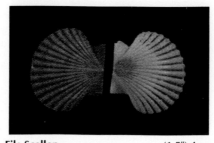

File Scallop   (1.5″) 4 cm
Pecten aspera Sowerby, 1842. Melanesia. Shallow water; uncommon.

Box Scallop   (2″) 5 cm
Pecten pyxidata Born, 1780. Indo-Pacific. Shallow water; common.

Chinese Scallop (1.5") 3.5 cm
Pecten sinensis Sowerby, 1842. China and Japan. Shallow water; common. Syn.: *puncticulatus* Dunker.

Japanese Baking Scallop (3") 8 cm
Pecten albicans Schröter, 1802. China and Japan. Offshore, 10 to 80 m; abundant. Syn.: *laqueatus* Sowerby.

Tasmanian Scallop (3") 8 cm
Pecten meridionalis Tate, 1887. Tasmania; S. Australia. Offshore; common.

New Zealand Scallop (4") 10 cm
Pecten novaezelandiae Reeve, 1853. New Zealand. Intertidal to offshore; common.

Zigzag Scallop (3") 7.5 cm
Pecten ziczac (L., 1758). S.E. United States to Brazil; Bermuda. 1 to 40 m; locally common. Rarely albino.

Ravenel's Scallop (2") 5 cm
Pecten raveneli Dall, 1898. S.E. United States and West Indies. Offshore; locally common. Many colors.

Chazalie's Scallop (1") 2.5 cm
Pecten chazaliei Dautzenberg, 1900. S. Florida to Brazil. Offshore from 20 to 150 m; uncommon. Syn.: *tereinus* Dall.

Tumbez Scallop (2") 5 cm
Pacipecten tumbezensis (Orbigny, 1846). W. Mexico; Offshore to 90 m; uncommon.

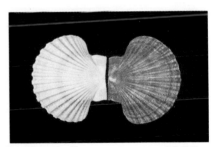

San Diego Scallop (3") 7.5 cm
Pecten diegensis Dall, 1898. California and W. Mexico. Offshore to 150 m; uncommon.

Vogdes's Scallop (4") 10 cm
Pecten vogdesi Arnold, 1906. W. Mexico to Panama. Offshore to 155 m; common.

Silken Scallop (2.5") 6 cm
Pecten sericeus Hinds, 1845. W. Mexico to Peru; Galapagos. 13 to 155 m; uncommon.

Lunar Mexican Scallop (3") 7.5 cm
Pecten lunaris S. S. Berry, 1963. W. Mexico. 55 to 82 m; uncommon. Paratype illustrated.

Sunburst Scallop   (1.5″) 4 cm
Aequipecten heliacus (Dall, 1925). S. Florida and West Indies; rare. Holotype illustrated.

Giant Pacific Scallop   (8″) 25 cm
Patinopecten caurinus (Gould, 1850). Alaska to California. Offshore; locally abundant. Commercially fished.

Atlantic Deepsea Scallop   (8″) 25 cm
Placopecten magellanicus (Gmelin, 1791). Labrador to N. Carolina. Offshore; commercially fished.

Yesso Scallop   (7″) 22 cm
Patinopecten yessoensis Jay, 1857. N. Japan. Offshore; common.

Leopard Scallop   (2.5″) 6 cm
Annachlamys leoparda (Reeve, 1853). Northern Australia. Offshore in shallow water; uncommon.

Convex Scallop   (2″) 5 cm
Mesopeplum convexum (Quoy & Gaimard, 1835). New Zealand. Offshore; uncommon.

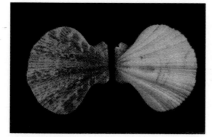

Tasman Scallop   (2.5″) 6 cm
Notochlamys tasmanica (Adams & Angas, 1863). Tasmania and South Australia. 20 to 80 m; uncommon.

Carol's Scallop   (2″) 5 cm
Mesopeplum caroli Iredale, 1929. Eastern Australia. Offshore to 160 m; locally common.

Reeve's Scallop   (2″) 5 cm
Annachlamys reevei (Adams and Reeve, 1850). S.W. Pacific. Offshore to 30 m; locally common.

Macassar Scallop   (3″) 7 cm
Annachlamys macassarensis Chenu, 1845. S.W. Pacific. Offshore to 30 m; uncommon.

Queen Scallop   (3″) 7 cm
Aequipecten opercularis (L., 1758). N.W. Europe to Azores and Mediterranean. Common; edible.

Swift's Scallop   (3.5″) 8 cm
Swiftopecten swiftii (Bernardi, 1858). Japan. Offshore to 50 m; locally common.

Spathate Scallop (1″) 2.5 cm
Aequipecten phrygium (Dall, 1886). S.E. United States and the West Indies. Offshore, deep water; uncommon.

Wavy-lined Scallop (2″) 5 cm
Aequipecten lineolaris (Lamarck, 1819). S.E. Florida and Caribbean. Offshore, 14 to 100 m; uncommon.

European Calico Scallop (1.2″) 3 cm
Argopecten solidulus (Reeve, 1853). Mediterranean and West Africa. Offshore; common. Syn.: *commutatus* Monterosato.

European Calico Scallop (1.2″) 3 cm
Argopecten solidulus (Reeve, 1853). Coloration variable. Lower valve usually lighter in color. Mediterranean specimen.

Distant Scallop (1.5″) 4 cm
Comptopallium vexillum (Reeve, 1853). Indo-Pacific. Shallow water; uncommon. Syn.: *digitatus* Hinds; *zeteki* Hertlein; *evecta* Iredale.

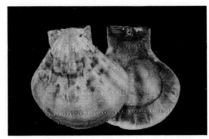

Strange's Scallop (1.5″) 4 cm
Comptopallium strangei (Reeve, 1852). N.E. Australia. Shallow water; uncommon.

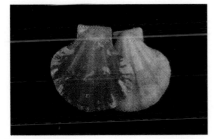

Plicate Scallop (1.5″) 4 cm
Decatopecten plicus (L., 1758). Western Pacific; S. Japan. Offshore; common.

Cloak Scallop (2″) 5 cm
Decatopecten amiculum (Philippi, 1835). Indo-Pacific. Shallow water; uncommon.

Nodular Scallop (2″) 5 cm
Decatopecten nodiferus (Sowerby, 1842). Indo-Pacific. Offshore to 100 m; uncommon. Syn.: *langfordi* D., B. & R.

Nodular Scallop (2″) 5 cm
Decatopecten nodiferus (Sowerby, 1842). This is the holotype of *langfordi* Dall, Bartsch and Rehder, 1938, from Hawaii.

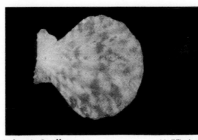

Spicer's Scallop (1.5″) 4 cm
Comptopallium spiceri Rehder, 1944. Line Islands (south of Hawaii). Rare. Holotype illustrated.

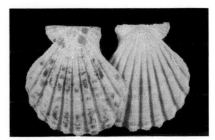

Radula Scallop (3″) 7.5 cm
Comptopallium radula (L., 1758). Indo-Pacific. Shallow reefs; common.

Patagonian Scallop　　　(3") 7 cm
Chlamys lischkei (Dunker, 1850). Argentina and Chile. Offshore; abundant. Syn.: *patagonica* King.

Histrionic Scallop　　　(1.5") 4 cm
Excellichlamys histrionica (Gmelin, 1791). Western Tropical Pacific. Shallow water; uncommon.

Blood-stained Scallop　　　(1") 2.5 cm
Excellichlamys sanguinolenta (Gmelin, 1791). Red Sea and N.W. Indian Ocean. Shallow water; uncommon.

Spectacular Scallop　　　(1") 2.5 cm
Excellichlamys spectabilis (Reeve, 1853). S.W. Pacific; Japan. Offshore to 10 m; uncommon.

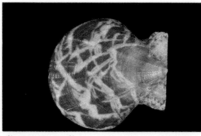

Felippone's Scallop　　　(2.5") 6 cm
Aequipecten felipponei (Dall, 1922). Uruguay and Argentina. Offshore; common.

Gardner's Scallop　　　(1.5") 3.5 cm
Serratovola gardneri (E. A. Smith, 1903). Indo-Pacific. Shallow water; uncommon. Syn.: *dayriti* Grau.

Link's Scallop　　　(1.5") 3.5 cm
Pacipecten leucophaeus (Reeve, 1852). Lower Caribbean. Dredged offshore; locally common. Syn.: *linki* Dall, 1926.

All's Scallop　　　(1") 2.5 cm
Cryptopecten alli Dall, Bartsch & Rehder, 1938. Hawaiian Islands. Deep water; rare. Holotype illustrated.

Singapore Scallop　　　(1.5") 3.5 cm
Volachlamys singaporina (Sowerby, 1842). S.E. Asia. Shallow water; uncommon.

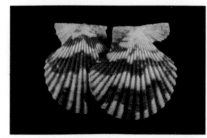

Tranquebar Scallop　　　(1.5") 3.5 cm
Volachlamys tranquebarica (Gmelin, 1791). Indian Ocean. Shallow flats to 6 m; common.

Tiger Scallop　　　(2") 5 cm
Semipallium tigris (Lamarck, 1819). Western Pacific; S. Japan. Shallow water; common.

Mel Ward's Scallop　　　(2.5") 6 cm
Semipallium wardiana Iredale, 1939. North and Western Australia. Under rocks on reefs. Uncommon.

Rough American Scallop (1.2") 3 cm
Aequipecten muscosus (Wood, 1828). S.E. United States to Brazil. Common. Rarely lemon-yellow. Syn.: *exasperatus* Sowerby.

Thistle Scallop (1") 2.5 cm
Aequipecten acanthodes (Dall, 1925). S.E. Florida and Caribbean. Grass flats; uncommon. Holotype illus.

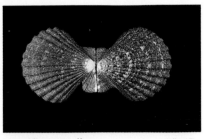

Magnificent Scallop (7") 17 cm
Lyropecten magnificus (Sowerby, 1835). Galapagos Islands. Offshore, 3 to 50 m; uncommon.

Specious Scallop (1.5") 4 cm
Cryptopecten speciosum (Reeve, 1853). Western Pacific; S. Japan. Shallow water; uncommon. Syn.: *Gloriopallium*.

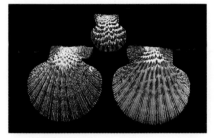

Royal Cloak Scallop (2") 5 cm
Cryptopecten pallium (L., 1758). Indo-Pacific. Shallow water on reefs; common.

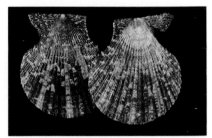

Senatorial Scallop (3") 7.5 cm
Chlamys senatoria (Gmelin, 1791). S.E. Asia and Indian Ocean. Offshore; common.

Noble Scallop (3") 7.5 cm
Chlamys senatoria subspecies *nobilis* (Reeve, 1852). Japan. Offshore to 20 m; locally abundant. Many colors.

Glorious Scallop (3") 7.5 cm
Chlamys gloriosa (Reeve, 1852). Japan and S. Korea. Offshore; uncommon.

Townsend's Scallop (6") 15 cm
Chlamys townsendi (Sowerby, 1895). N.W. Indian Ocean. Offshore to 20 m; common.

Lion's Paw (4.5") 11 cm
Lyropecten nodosa (L., 1758). S.E. United States to Brazil; Ascension Is. Offshore to 30 m; locally common.

Austral Scallop (2.5") 6 cm
Chlamys australis (Sowerby, 1847). Western and S. Australia. Offshore; common.

Prickly Scallop (3") 7 cm
Chlamys asperrima (Lamarck, 1819). S. Australia; Tasmania. Subtidal to 100 m; abundant.

Atlantic Bay Scallop   (2.5") 6 cm
Argopecten irradians irradians (Lamarck, 1819). Massachusetts to New Jersey. Shallow grass areas; abundant.

Carolina Bay Scallop   (2.5") 6 cm
Argopecten irradians subspecies *concentricus* (Say, 1822). Maryland to Louisiana. Abundant. Lower valve white, fatter.

Texas Bay Scallop   (2.5") 6 cm
Argopecten irradians subspecies *amplicostatus* (Dall, 1898). Texas to Colombia. Common. 15 ribs.

Nucleus Scallop   (1.2") 3 cm
Argopecten nucleus (Born, 1778). S.E. Florida and Caribbean. Shallow water; common. Ears with 5 riblets.

Calico Scallop   (2.5") 6 cm
Argopecten gibbus (L., 1758). S.E. United States to Brazil. Shallow water to 30 m; abundant. Syn.: *dislocatus* Say.

Purplish Scallop   (5") 13 cm
Argopecten purpuratus (Lamarck, 1819). Peru to Chile. Sandy bottom, to 30 m; abundant. Commercially fished.

Circular Scallop   (4") 10 cm
Argopecten circularis (Sowerby, 1835). W. Mexico to Peru. Subtidal to 100 m; abundant. Food species.

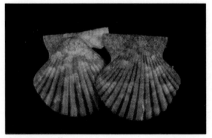

Hirasé's Scallop   (2.5") 6 cm
Argopecten hirasei (Bavay, 1904). Japan. Shallow water; common. Syn.: *awajiensis* Pilsbry.

Unequal Scallop   (1") 2.5 cm
Argopecten inaequivalvis (Sowerby, 1842). Western Pacific; Japan. Offshore, 10 to 50 m; uncommon.

African Fan Scallop   (2") 5 cm
Chlamys flabellum (Gmelin, 1791). West Africa from Mauritania to Angola. Shallow water; moderately common.

St. Helena Scallop   (1") 2.5 cm
Aequipecten atlanticus (E.A. Smith, 1890). St. Helena Is., Atlantic. Offshore; rare. Holotype illustrated.

Tryon's Scallop   (2") 5 cm
Aequipecten glyptus (Verrill, 1882). S.E. United States. Dredged by shrimpers in the Gulf of Mexico; uncommon.

Dr. Ruschenberger's Scallop (3") 7.5 cm
Chlamys ruschenbergerii (Tryon, 1869). N.W. Indian Ocean. Offshore, moderately common. Syn.: *decoriata* Lamy.

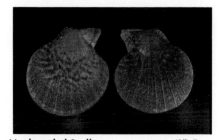

Much-scaled Scallop (2") 5 cm
Chlamys multisquamata (Dunker, 1864). S.E. Florida, Bahamas and Cuba. Rock crevices, 10 to 50 m; rare.

Dieffenbach's Scallop (2.5") 6 cm
Chlamys dieffenbachi (Reeve, 1853). New Zealand. Offshore; common. Syn.: *celator* Finlay.

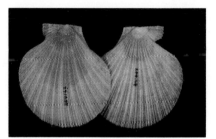

Iceland Scallop (3.5") 8 cm
Chlamys islandica (Müller, 1776). Arctic Seas to Massachusetts; to Washington State; to N. Europe. Abundant.

Wainwright Scallop (3") 7.5 cm
Chlamys wainwrightensis MacNeil, 1967. Alaska. Offshore. Holotype illus. May be form of *islandica*.

Kitten Scallop (1") 2.5 cm
Camptonectes tigrinus (Müller, 1776). W. Europe; cold waters; common. Syn.: *triradiatus* Müller; *laevis* Pennant.

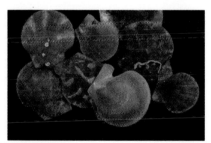

Striate Scallop (0.6") 1.5 cm
Camptonectes striatus (Müller, 1776). Arctic Seas; W. Europe, cold water, 7 to 80 m; common. Syn.: *rimulosa* Philippi.

Seven-rayed Scallop (1.5") 3.5 cm
Pseudamussium septemradiatum (Müller). Arctic European seas to W. Europe. Cold waters, 11 to 180 m; common.

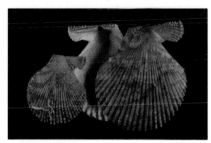

Variable Scallop (2.5") 6 cm
Chlamys varia (L., 1758). Norway to Mediterranean. Offshore, 1 to 1000 m; common. Syn.: *monotis* da Costa.

Snow Scallop (2.5") 6 cm
Chlamys nivea (Mac Gillivray, 1825). N. Great Britain. Offshore; locally common. About 45 riblets.

Sulcate Scallop (1.7") 4 cm
Chlamys sulcata (Müller, 1776). Arctic Seas; N.W. Europe. Offshore to 850 m; common.

Cat's Paw Scallop (2.5") 6 cm
Manupecten pesfelis (L., 1758). Mediterranean and N.W. Africa. Offshore, 10 to 225 m; common. Syn.: *corallinus* Poli.

Palmer's Scallop   (1.5") 4 cm
Aequipecten palmeri (Dall, 1897). Gulf of California. Intertidal to 90 m; uncommon.

Superb Scallop   (2.5") 6 cm
Anguipecten superbus (Sowerby, 1842). S.W. Pacific and Japan. 10 to 80 m; uncommon.

Lambert's Scallop   (2.5") 6 cm
Anguipecten lamberti (Souverbie, 1874). S.W. Pacific to Hawaii. Shallow water to 600 m; uncommon. Syn.: *gregoryi* D., B. & R.

Buried Scallop   (2") 5 cm
Chlamys funebris (Reeve, 1853). Australia. Shallow water. Uncommon.

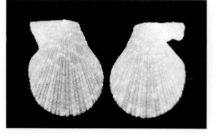

Tinted Scallop   (1.3") 3 cm
Chlamys tincta (Reeve, 1853). Table Bay to Natal, South Africa. Also red, violet and mottled.

Tinted Scallop   (1.3") 3 cm
Chlamys tincta (Reeve, 1853). Variations in color in this common South African scallop.

Beribboned Scallop   (2") 5 cm
Chlamys lemniscata (Reeve, 1853). S. Japan and S.W. Pacific. Offshore, 30 to 300 m; uncommon.

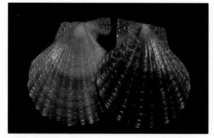

Squamose Scallop   (2.5") 6 cm
Chlamys squamosa (Gmelin, 1791). S.W. Pacific. Shallow water; common.

Scaly Pacific Scallop   (3") 7.5 cm
Chlamys squamata (Gmelin, 1791). Japan and W. Pacific. Offshore from 1 to 50 m; uncommon.

Ghostly Scallop   (1.5") 4 cm
Chlamys larvata (Reeve, 1853). Japan. Offshore; common. Syn.: *ootanii* Azuma.

Darwin's Scallop   (2") 5 cm
Chlamys tehuelchus (Orbigny, 1846). Brazil to Argentina. Offshore, 10 to 120 m; common. Syn.: *darwini* Reeve.

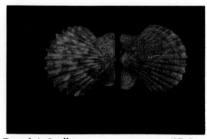

Darwin's Scallop   (2") 5 cm
Chlamys tehuelchus (Orbigny, 1846). Ribbing and coloring can vary depending on depth of water.

Farrer's Scallop (1.5") 4 cm
Chlamys farreri (Jones and Preston, 1904). N. China, Korea and Japan. 15 to 60 m; common. Syn.: *nipponensis* Kuroda.

Scaly-ribbed Scallop (2.5") 6 cm
Chlamys scabricostata (Sowerby, 1915). Western Australia. Offshore; uncommon.

Jousseaume's Scallop (1.5") 4 cm
Chlamys jousseaumei (Bavay, 1904). Japan. Shallow water; uncommon.

Fine-grained Scallop (1") 2.5 cm
Chlamys asperulata (Adams & Reeve, 1850). Japan and Korea. 1 to 20 m; uncommon. Syn.: *pelseneeri* Dautzenberg & Bavay.

Golden Scallop (2") 5 cm
Bractechlamys aurantiaca (Adams & Reeve, 1850). Western Pacific; Japan. Offshore to 20 m; uncommon.

Zealandic Scallop (1.2") 3 cm
Chlamys zelandiae (Gray, 1843). New Zealand. Subtidal to 30 m; under rocks, common.

Bifrons Scallop (3") 7.5 cm
Equichlamys bifrons (Lamarck, 1819). South Australia and Tasmania. Low-tide mark to 40 m; common.

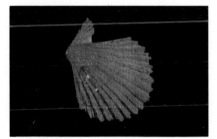

Forked Scallop (1") 2.5 cm
Chlamys dichroa (Suter, 1909). New Zealand. Offshore to 100 m; uncommon.

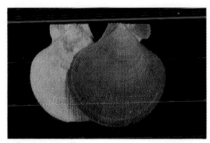

Little Gem Scallop (1.5") 3 cm
Chlamys gemmulata (Reeve, 1853). New Zealand. Subtidal to 30 m; common. Syn.: *radiatus* Hutton.

Delicate Scallop (3") 7.5 cm
Chlamys delicatula (Hutton, 1873). New Zealand; Antarctic. Shallow water to 30 m; common. Syn.: *subantarctica* Hedley.

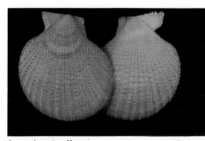

Charming Scallop (2.5") 6 cm
Chlamys incantata Hertlein, 1972. Off Santa Cruz Is., Galapagos, in 200 m; rare.

Amand Scallop (1.5") 4 cm
Chlamys amandi Hertlein, 1935. Off Chile. Deep water. Syn.: *australis* Philippi; *phalara* Roth.

Irregular Scallop   (1.5") 4 cm
Chlamys irregularis (Sowerby, 1842). Japan to Hawaii. Offshore 3 to 150 m; uncommon. Syn.: *cookei* D., B. & R.; *midwayensis* Habe & Okutani.

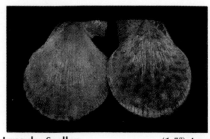

Irregular Scallop   (1.5") 4 cm
Chlamys irregularis (Sowerby, 1842). This is the Hawaiian holotype of *cookei* Dall, Bartsch & Rehder, 1938.

Judd's Scallop   (1") 2.5 cm
Haumea juddi Dall, Bartsch & Rehder, 1938. Hawaiian Islands. 8 to 100 m; abundant.

White-spotted Scallop   (1.5") 4 cm
Chlamys luculenta (Reeve, 1853). N. Australia. Offshore; uncommon.

White-lined Scallop   (1") 2.5 cm
Chlamys albolineata (Sowerby, 1887). Japan and Ryukyu Islands. Shallow water; uncommon.

Pacific Pink Scallop   (2.5") 6.5 cm
Chlamys hastata hericia (Gould, 1850). Alaska to California. Offshore, 1 to 40 m; common.

Pacific Pink Scallop   (2.5") 6.5 cm
Chlamys hastata hericia (Gould, 1850). Holotype specimen (7.5 cm). Rarely white (*albida* Dall).

Pacific Spear Scallop   (2.5") 6 cm
Chlamys hastata hastata (Sowerby, 1843). Monterey to Newport Bay, California. Offshore; uncommon.

Freckled Scallop   (1.5") 4 cm
Chlamys lentiginosa (Reeve, 1853). South Japan to S.W. Pacific. Shallow reefs; common.

Sentis Scallop   (1.5") 4 cm
Chlamys sentis (Reeve, 1853). S.E. United States to Brazil. Subtidal to 4 m; common under rocks.

Ornate Scallop   (1.5") 4 cm
Chlamys ornata (Lamarck, 1819). S.E. Florida to Brazil. Subtidal to 4 m; uncommon, under rocks.

Mildred's Scallop   (1.5") 4 cm
Chlamys mildredae (Bayer, 1943). Believed to be a hybrid between *sentis* and *ornata*. Holotype illus.

Blistered Scallop (1.5") 4 cm
Cryptopecten vesiculosus (Dunker, 1877). Japan. Offshore, 50 to 600 m; uncommon.

Antillean Scallop (1") 2.5 cm
Lyropecten antillarum (Récluz, 1853). S.E. Florida and the West Indies. Subtidal, 2 to 30 m; uncommon.

Coral Scallop (1") 2.5 cm
Lyropecten corallinoides (Orbigny, 1834). Azores; Canary Islands and Cape Verde. Offshore from 12 to 36 m; rare.

Miraculous Scallop (1.5") 4 cm
Mirapecten mirificus (Reeve, 1853). Philippines to Hawaii. Offshore to 200 m; uncommon. Syn.: *thaanumi* D., B. & Rehder.

Pacific Lion's Paw (5") 12.5 cm
Lyropecten subnodosus (Sowerby, 1835). Gulf of California to Peru. Offshore; locally common.

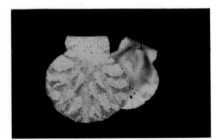

Maldive Scallop (1.8") 4.5 cm
Juxtamusium maldivense (E. A. Smith, 1903). Central Indian Ocean to the Marshall Islands. 60 to 70 m; common.

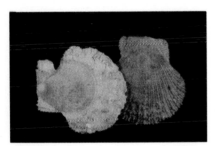

Little Boy Scallop (1.2") 3 cm
Chlamys multistriata (Poli, 1795). Norway to the Azores and Mediterranean. 2 to 2,000 m; common. Older shells distorted. Syn.: "*pusio* L."

Giant Rock Scallop (6") 15 cm
Hinnites giganteus (Gray, 1825). W. Canada to W. Mexico. Young resemble *Chlamys*. Common on subtidal rocks. Syn.: *multirugosus* Gale.

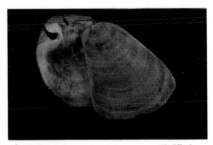

Pedum Oyster (2.5") 6 cm
Pedum spondyloideum (Gmelin, 1791). Indo-Pacific. Embedded in brain corals; uncommon. Syn.: *pedum* Röding; *spondyloides* Lamarck. Subfamily Peduminae.

KITTEN PAWS
FAMILY PLICATULIDAE

This is a small family of oysterlike bivalves having a deeply sunk resilium in the hinge with a long tooth on each side. Ribs usually large and few. Only a few species are living today.

Atlantic Kitten's Paw (1") 2.5 cm
Plicatula gibbosa Lamarck, 1801. S.E. United States to Brazil. Subtidal to 20 m; abundant. Syn.: *ramosus* Lamarck.

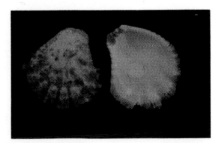

Pacific Kitten's Paw (1") 2.5 cm
Plicatula plicata (L., 1758). Indo-Pacific. Offshore on gravel bottom, 1 to 50 m; common. Syn.: *imbricata* Menke.

THORNY OYSTERS
FAMILY SPONDYLIDAE

Although resembling oysters, the Thorny Oysters or Chrysanthemum Shells are more closely related to the scallops. The "ball-and-socket" hinge is characteristic. Marine growths on the long spines offer camouflage. Great variation in shape, colors and spines makes identification of the two dozen or more species difficult.

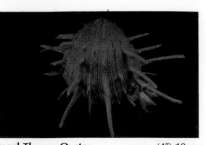

Regal Thorny Oyster   (4") 10 cm
Spondylus regius (L., 1758). Western Pacific. On rocks, 5 to 50 m; common. Syn.: *cumingii* Sowerby.

Imperial Thorny Oyster   (3") 7.5 cm
Spondylus imperialis Chenu, 1843. Japan. Offshore; 5 to 50 m; common.

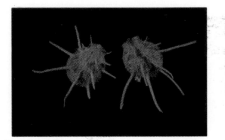

Wright's Thorny Oyster   (3") 7.5 cm
Spondylus wrightianus Crosse, 1872. Western Australia. Offshore to 50 m; locally common.

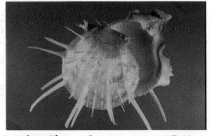

American Thorny Oyster   (4") 10 cm
Spondylus americanus Hermann, 1781. S.E. United States to Brazil. Offshore on cliffs and wrecks from 10 to 50 m; locally common.

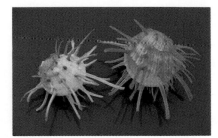

American Thorny Oyster   (4") 10 cm
Spondylus americanus Hermann, 1781. These are cleaned specimens. In life, they are covered with sponges and algae. Syn.: *echinatus* Martyn.

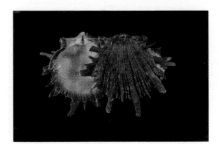

Pacific Thorny Oyster   (5") 13 cm
Spondylus princeps Broderip, 1833. Gulf of California to Panama. Offshore; locally common. Good specimens uncommon.

Nude Thorny Oyster   (2.5") 6 cm
Spondylus anacanthus Mawe, 1823. Japan. 30 to 200 m; uncommon. Syn.: *lima* Chenu; *nudus* Sowerby.

Cat's Tongue Oyster   (3.5") 9 cm
Spondylus linguaefelis Sowerby, 1847. Hawaiian Is. Offshore; uncommon. Syn.: *gloriosus, mimus, kauiensis* Dall, Bartsch, and Rehder.

Many-spined Thorny Oyster   (3") 7 cm
Spondylus multimuricatus Reeve, 1856. Philippines; W. Pacific. Common. In sheltered waters.

Golden Thorny Oyster   (4") 10 cm
Spondylus versicolor Schreibers, 1793. W. Pacific; Japan to Philippines. Common. Syn.: *aurantius* Lamarck.

Chinese Thorny Oyster   (3") 7 cm
Spondylus sinensis Schreibers, 1793. Japan to East Indies; common. Syn.: *digitatus* Perry; *petroselinus* Röding; *multilamellatus* Lamarck.

Ducal Thorny Oyster   (4″) 10 cm
Spondylus squamosus Schreibers, 1793. Indo-Pacific. Common. Syn.: *ducalis* Röding; *spathuliferus* Lamarck; *lamarcki* Chenu.

European Thorny Oyster   (3″) 7.5 cm
Spondylus gaederopus L., 1758. Mediterranean; N.W. Africa. Intertidal to 20 m; common.

JINGLE SHELLS
FAMILY ANOMIIDAE

A curious group of thin, semi-translucent shells that attach to rocks, other shells and wood. The lower valve has a large, circular indentation through which protrudes the foot and byssus. The flesh has a very distasteful alumlike flavor. Most species are abundant in shallow water, a few are found in mangroves. Small windowpanes are made from *Placuna*.

American Jingle Shell   (1.5″) 3.5 cm
Anomia simplex (Orbigny, 1842). Eastern United States to Brazil. Shallow water; common. Black if buried in mud.

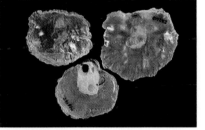

European Jingle Shell   (2″) 6 cm
Anomia ephippium (L., 1758). Norway to the Mediterranean and Black Sea. Intertidal to 30 m; abundant.

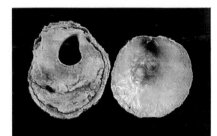

False Pacific Jingle   (3″) 7.5 cm
Monia macroschisma (Deshayes, 1839). Alaska to California; Japan. Intertidal to 70 m; common on rocks and wharf pilings.

False Zealandic Jingle   (3.5″) 9 cm
Monia zelandica (Gray, 1843). New Zealand. Subtidal; uncommon.

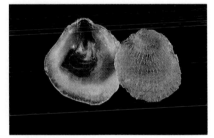

False Atlantic Jingle   (1″) 2.5 cm
Pododesmus rudis (Broderip, 1834). S.E. United States to Brazil. Subtidal to 10 m on rocks and wrecks. Syn.: *decipiens* Philippi.

Mangrove Jingle Shell   (1″) 2.5 cm
Enigmonia aenigmatica (Holten, 1803). East Indies; Philippines. On mangrove roots; common. Syn.: *rosea* Gray.

Saddle Oyster   (7″) 17 cm
Placuna sella (Gmelin, 1791). S.W. Pacific; S.E. Asia. Subtidal; common.

Windowpane Oyster   (4″) 10 cm
Placuna placenta (L., 1758). Philippines; S.E. Asia. Lagoons; abundant. Used in shellcraft.

TRUE OYSTERS
FAMILY OSTREIDAE

The edible oysters are well known in most parts of the world and are a major source of seafood. The shell material is porcelaneous, not nacreous; the pearls from edible oysters have little value. The genus *Crassostrea* has a purple muscle scar and one deep valve. *Ostrea* is white and both valves about the same. All shells are variable in shape.

  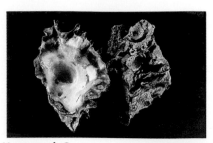

Cock's-comb Oyster (3.5") 9 cm
Lopha cristagalli (L., 1758). Indo-Pacific. Subtidal to 6 m; locally common.

Frons Oyster (2") 5 cm
Lopha frons (L., 1758). S.E. United States to Brazil. Variable in shape. On rocks or on seawhip stems; common.

Honeycomb Oyster (3") 7.5 cm
Hyotissa hyotis (L., 1758). Caribbean and Indo-Pacific. Shallow water to 30 m; uncommon.

  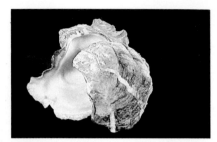

Eastern American Oyster (3.5") 8.5 cm
Crassostrea virginica (Gmelin, 1791). Nova Scotia to Gulf of Mexico. Intertidal to 10 m; abundant. Introduced to Hawaii.

Caribbean Edible Oyster (3") 7.5 cm
Crassostrea rhizophorae (Guilding, 1828). West Indies to Brazil. Inner margin of lower valve is purplish. Abundant.

Auckland Rock Oyster (3.5") 9 cm
Crassostrea glomerata (Gould, 1850). New Zealand. Common, shallow water, edible species. Holotype illustrated.

  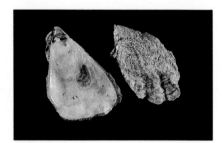

Giant Pacific Oyster (6") 15 cm
Crassostrea gigas (Thunberg, 1793). Japan; W. Canada to California, Hawaii. Round or elongate. Common edible species.

Common European Oyster (3") 8 cm
Ostrea edulis L., 1758. W. Europe; Mediterranean. Common, commercial species.

Native Pacific Oyster (2.5") 6 cm
Ostrea lurida Carpenter, 1864. Alaska to Baja California. Alias the Olympic Oyster. Intertidal; common.

 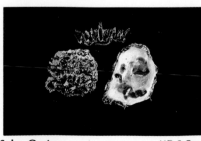

Hooded Oyster (2.5") 6 cm
Saccostrea cucullata (Born, 1778). S.W. Pacific. Shallow water; common. Syn: *Saxostrea.*

Spiny Oyster (1") 2.5 cm
Saccostrea kegaki Torigoe and Imaba, 1981. Japan. Shallow water; common. Syn.: *spinosa* Deshayes; *echinata* of Japanese authors.

FILE CLAMS
FAMILY LIMIDAE

The surface of these clams has many small prickles resembling a file. These unique bivalves have long, sticky tentacles which aid them in swimming. Most species are tropical and build nests spun from the byssus exuded by the foot. There are about 100 species, some large and living in deep water.

Spiny Lima (1.5″) 4 cm
Lima lima (L., 1758). S.E. Florida to Brazil.
Under stones, 1 to 150 m; common. Syn.:
squamosa Lamarck.

Caribbean Spiny Lima (1.5″) 4 cm
Lima lima form *caribaea* Orbigny, 1842.
West Indies. Spines finer. Shallow reefs;
common.

Panamanian Lima (1.3″) 3 cm
Lima lima subspecies *tetrica* Gould, 1851.
W. Mexico to Ecuador. 10 to 120 m; uncom-
mon. Holotype illustrated.

Indo-Pacific Spiny Lima (2″) 5 cm
Lima vulgaris Link, 1807. Indo-Pacific. 1 to
20 m; common. Syn.: *sowerbyi* Deshayes;
nipponica Oyama.

Few-ribbed Lima (2″) 5 cm
Lima paucicostata Sowerby, 1843. Red Sea;
N.W. Indian Ocean. 1 to 20 m; uncommon.

Rough Lima (2″) 5 cm
Lima scabra (Born, 1778). S.E. United States
to Brazil. Subtidal to 30 m, under rocks;
common.

Rough Lima (2″) 5 cm
Lima scabra, smoothish form with very fine
ribs, *glacialis* Gmelin, 1791. Syn.: *tenera*
Sowerby (not Turton).

Basilan Lima (1.5″) 3.5 cm
Limaria basilanica (Adams & Reeve, 1850).
Indo-Pacific. Shallow reefs to 20 m; com-
mon. Syn.: *orientalis* Adams & Reeve.

Fragile Lima (1″) 2.5 cm
Limaria fragilis (Gmelin, 1791). Indo-Paci-
fic; Japan. Subtidal to 20 m; common.
Syn.: *kiiensis* Oyama; *auaua* D., B. & R.

Inflated Lima (1.5″) 3.5 cm
Limaria inflata (Gmelin, 1791). W. Europe.
Subtidal; common. Syn.: *tuberculata* Olivi.

Hians Lima (1.5″) 3.5 cm
Limaria hians (Gmelin, 1791). Norway to
Mediterranean. Subtidal to 28 m; common.
Syn.: *linguata* Lamarck.

Philippine Giant Lima (8″) 20 cm
Acesta philippinensis (Bartsch, 1913). Off
Luzon, Philippines, in 600 m; uncommon.
Holotype illustrated.

Rathbun's Giant Lima (6") 15 cm
Acesta rathbuni (Bartsch, 1913). Philippines; deep water; uncommon. Holotype illus. Syn.: *dalli* Bartsch, nude name.

Colombian Giant Lima (5") 12 cm
Acesta colombiana H. Vokes, 1970. S.W. Caribbean; deep water; rare. Holotype illustrated.

Diomedea Giant Lima (1.6") 4 cm
Acesta diomedae (Dall, 1908). Off Galapagos Is. In 1,400 m; rare. Holotype illustrated.

European Giant Lima (5") 10 cm
Acesta excavata (Fabricius, 1779). Norway to Azores. Offshore, 190 to 2,635 m; uncommon.

BROOCH CLAMS
FAMILY TRIGONIIDAE

These deep-water, iridescent clams were widely spread in Europe and Asia during early geologic times, but are now limited to a few species found in southern Australia. It is believed that they gave rise to the freshwater unionid mussel family. They are dredged offshore in S.E. Australia and used in jewelry.

Australian Brooch Clam (2") 5 cm
Neotrigonia margaritacea (Lamarck, 1804). Offshore to 50 m; common. Syn.: *pectinata* Lamarck; *antarctica* Péron.

LUCINA CLAMS
FAMILY LUCINIDAE

A large, well-known family of usually white, hard-shelled clams in which the cardinal teeth are small, and the anterior muscle scar is narrow and long. There are no long siphons, so the clams make a tube to the surface with their foot. Many genera and species, worldwide, shallow to deep water.

Thick American Lucina (2") 5 cm
Lucina pectinata (Gmelin, 1791). S.E. United States to Brazil. Shallow water to 10 m; common. Syn.: *jamaicensis* Chemnitz.

Corrugate Lucina (2") 5 cm
Eamesiella corrugata (Deshayes, 1843). Japan to East Indies. Intertidal to 10 m; locally common.

Northeast American Lucina (2.5") 6 cm
Lucinoma filosa (Stimpson, 1851). Eastern Canada to the Gulf of Mexico. Offshore to 50 m; common. Anterior lateral tooth absent.

Heroic Lucina (3.5") 9 cm
Lucinoma heroica (Dall, 1901). Gulf of California. Very deep water; rare. Lectotype illustrated.

Pennsylvanian Lucina (2") 5 cm
Linga pensylvanica (L., 1758). S.E. United States and the West Indies. Shallow water to 2 m; common.

Florida Lucina (1.5″) 4 cm
Pseudomiltha floridana (Conrad, 1833). Gulf of Mexico. Shallow water, to 20 m; common. Small deep pit in front of umbo.

Californian Lucina (1″) 2.5 cm
Codakia californica (Conrad, 1837). California and Baja California. Intertidal to 100 m; common.

American Tiger Lucina (3″) 7.5 cm
Codakia orbicularis (L., 1758). S.E. United States to Brazil. Subtidal to 5 m in coral sand; common.

Dwarf American Lucina (1″) 2.5 cm
Ctena orbiculata (Montagu, 1808). S.E. United States to Brazil. Shell obese. Shallow water to 200 m; common.

Bella Lucina (1″) 2.5 cm
Ctena bella (Conrad, 1837). Indo-Pacific; Hawaii. Intertidal to 3 m; abundant.

Interrupted Lucina (2.5″) 6 cm
Codakia paytenorum (Iredale, 1937). Indo-Pacific. Intertidal to 10 m; common. Syn.: *interrupta* Reeve, not Lamarck.

Punctate Lucina (4″) 10 cm
Codakia punctata (L., 1758). Indo-Pacific. Shallow sands; common. Interior pitted. Syn.: *thaanumi* Pilsbry.

Distinguished Lucina (5.5″) 14 cm
Codakia distinguenda (Tryon, 1872). W. Mexico to Panama. Intertidal to 2 m; uncommon. Syn.: *colpoica* Dall; *pinchoti* Pilsbry & Lowe.

Pacific Tiger Lucina (4″) 10 cm
Codakia tigerina (L., 1758). Indo-Pacific. Subtidal to 20 m; common. Syn.: *exasperata* Reeve.

Buttercup Lucina (2″) 5 cm
Anodontia alba Link, 1807. S.E. United States and the West Indies. Subtidal to 1 m, near mangroves; common. Syn.: *chrysostoma* Philippi, 1847.

Chalky Buttercup Lucina (3.5″) 9 cm
Anodontia philippina (Reeve, 1850). S.E. United States; Cuba; Bermuda. Uncommon. Syn.: *schrammi* Crosse.

Toothless Lucina (1.5″) 3.5 cm
Anodontia edentula (L., 1758). Red Sea to Hawaii. Subtidal to 50 m; common. Syn.: *globosum* Förskal; *hawaiiensis* D., B. & Rehder.

American Cross-hatched Lucina (0.8") 2 cm
Divaricella quadrisulcata (Orbigny, 1842). S.E. United States to Brazil. Shallow water to 100 m; abundant.

Toothed Cross-hatched Lucina (1") 2.5 cm
Divaricella dentata (Wood, 1815). S.E. Florida and West Indies. Shallow water; moderately common.

Fat Cross-hatched Lucina (1") 2.5 cm
Divaricella gibba (Gray, 1825). West Africa. Offshore to 10 m; locally common.

Dall's Cross-hatched Lucina (1.5") 3.5 cm
Divaricella dalliana (Vanatta, 1901). South Africa. Shallow water; moderately common.

Cuming's Cross-hatched Lucina (1") 2.5 cm
Divaricella cumingi (Adams & Angas, 1863). South Australia. Just offshore to 400 m; common.

Children's Lucina (3") 7.5 cm
Miltha childreni (Sowerby, 1826). Eastern South America. Shallow water to 20 m; uncommon.

Common Basket Lucina (3.5") 9 cm
Fimbria fimbriata (L., 1758). Indo-Pacific. Shallow water; common. In family Fimbriidae.

Sowerby's Basket Lucina (3") 7.5 cm
Fimbria soverbii (Reeve, 1841). S.W. Pacific. 5 to 20 m; uncommon to rare.

DIPLODON CLAMS
FAMILY UNGULINIDAE

A relatively obscure group of small white clams. Some build nests. Worldwide cool waters and mostly in deep water. Valves are usually globular and fat. Hinge with 2 main teeth, one of which is split. Lateral teeth absent. No pallial sinus.

Rosy Diplodon (1") 2.5 cm
Ungulina cuneata (Spengler, 1782). West Africa. In muddy sand near shore; common. Syn.: *rubra* Roissy; *oblonga* Daudin.

Rotund Diplodon (1") 2.5 cm
Diplodonta rotundata (Montagu, 1803). England to Mediterranean. Offshore, deep water; common.

Verrill's Diplodon (1") 2.5 cm
Diplodonta verrilli Dall, 1900. Off Cape Cod to North Carolina. In 30 to 140 m; uncommon. Syn.: *turgida* Verrill & Smith.

JEWEL BOXES
FAMILY CHAMIDAE

These are neither oysters nor *Spondylus* Thorny Oysters, but a family of rock clams with crude teeth in the hinge. Usually one valve is solidly attached to the rock surface. Some species have numerous, colorful frills and spines. Most species are tropical and live in shallow water.

Zelandic Diplodon (0.8") 2 cm
Felaniella zelandica (Gray, 1835). New Zealand. Offshore 1 to 40 m; common.

Lazarus Jewel Box (3") 7.5 cm
Chama lazarus L., 1758. Indo-Pacific. Rock bottoms from 1 to 20 m; moderately common.

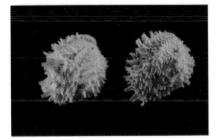

Reflexed Jewel Box (2.5") 6 cm
Chama reflexa Reeve, 1846. Indo-Pacific. Offshore on rocks; moderately common.

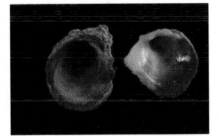

Purple-edged Jewel Box (3") 7.5 cm
Chama iostoma Conrad, 1837. Indo-Pacific. Intertidal rocks to 100 m; common.

Leafy Jewel Box (2.5") 6 cm
Chama macerophylla (Gmelin, 1791). S.E. United States to Brazil. Shallow water on rocks and in clumps; common.

Corrugated Jewel Box (1") 2.5 cm
Chama congregata Conrad, 1833. S.E. United States to Brazil. Shallow water. On rocks; common.

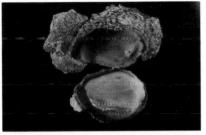

Cherry Jewel Box (1") 2.5 cm
Chama sarda Reeve, 1847. South Florida and the Caribbean; Brazil. Offshore, 3 to 50 m; uncommon.

Smoothed-edged Jewel Box (2.5") 6 cm
Chama sinuosa Broderip, 1835. S. Florida to Brazil. Uncommon. Syn.: *firma* Pilsbry & McGinty (paratype illus.).

Clear Jewel Box (2") 5 cm
Chama arcana Bernard, 1976. Oregon to California. Intertidal to offshore; common. *C. pellucida* Broderip is from Chile.

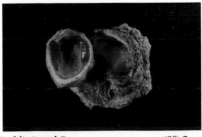

Budd's Jewel Box (2") 5 cm
Chama buddiana C. B. Adams, 1852. Panama to Ecuador; Galapagos Is. Subtidal on rocks; common. Syn.: *rubropicta* Bartsch & Rehder.

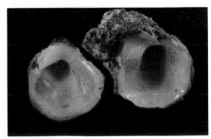

Gryphin Jewel Box (3") 7.5 cm
Pseudochama gryphina (Lamarck, 1819). N.W. Africa; Senegal. Subtidal, shallow water; moderately common.

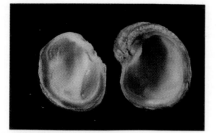

Left-handed Jewel Box (3″) 7.5 cm
Pseudochama radians (Lamarck, 1819). S.E.
United States to Brazil. 1 to 80 m; common.
Syn.: *ferruginea* Reeve.

Exogyra Jewel Box (3″) 7.5 cm
Pseudochama exogyra (Conrad, 1837). Oregon to Panama. Intertidal; on rocks, common.

Florida Spiny Jewel Box (1.5″) 4 cm
Arcinella cornuta Conrad, 1866. S.E. United
States. Subtidal, 6 to 80 m; common.

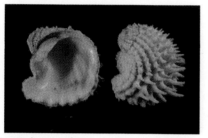

True Spiny Jewel Box (2″) 5 cm
Arcinella arcinella (L., 1767). West Indies to
Brazil. Offshore to 80 m; locally common.

PARASITIC CLAMS
SUPERFAMILY LEPTONACEA

Several hundred very small, white clams
live in association with other marine organisms. The main families are the Leptonidae, Galeommatidae, and Lasaeidae. Some
brood their young. Identifications are very
difficult and require examination of the
hinge teeth under a microscope. Two unusual examples are included here.

Deshayes's Myllita Clam (0.5″) 1.2 cm
Myllita deshayesi Orbigny & Récluz, 1850.
South and western Australia. Commonly
washed ashore on beaches.

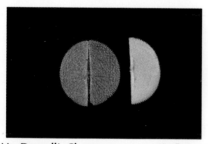

MacDougall's Clam (0.4″) 1 cm
Ephippodonta macdougalli Tate, 1888.
South Australia. Lives in mud burrows of
the shrimp *Axius*. Uncommon.

CARDITA CLAMS
FAMILY CARDITIDAE

The shells are heavy, with radial ribs and
crenulate margins. No pallial sinus. Lunule
small. Hinge with two unequal teeth in the
left valve. In some, a small byssus is
present. In most, the young are brooded in
the mantle cavity. Many are tropical and
live in shallow water.

Half-round Cardita (3″) 7.5 cm
Beguina semiorbiculata (L., 1758). Tropical
S.W. Pacific. Shallow reefs among rocks;
locally common.

Senegal Cardita (1.5″) 4 cm
Cardita senegalensis Reeve, 1843. West Africa. Intertidal to 3 m; common.

Variegate Cardita (1″) 2.5 cm
Cardita variegata Bruguière, 1792. Indo-Pacific. Shallow reefs, under stones; locally
common.

Similar Cardita (2″) 5 cm
Carditamera affinis (Sowerby, 1833). W.
Mexico to Peru. Shallow water; common.
Syn.: *californica* Deshayes.

Broad-ribbed Cardita (1.2") 3 cm
Carditamera floridana Conrad, 1838. South Florida and east Mexico. Shallow water; locally abundant.

Australian Cardita (2") 5 cm
Cardita crassicosta (Lamarck, 1819). Western and South Australia. Shallow water to 100 m; common.

Thick-ribbed Cardita (2") 5 cm
Cardita crassicostata (Sowerby, 1825). W. Mexico to Peru. Intertidal to 110 m; common. Syn.: *cuvieri* Broderip.

Wide-ribbed Cardita (1.5") 4 cm
Cardita laticostata Sowerby, 1833. Gulf of California to N. Peru. Low-tide line to 55 m; common. Syn.: *tricolor* Sowerby.

Varia Cardita (2") 5 cm
Cardita varia (Broderip, 1832). Galapagos Islands. Shallow water; rare.

Ajar Cardita (1.5") 4 cm
Cardita ajar Bruguière, 1792. West Africa. Shallow water. Moderately common.

Tankerville's Cardita (2") 5 cm
Cardita tankervillei (Wood, 1828). West Africa. Offshore to 10 m; common.

Northern Cardita (1.5") 4 cm
Cyclocardia borealis (Conrad, 1831). Labrador to off North Carolina. A food for fish on the Grand Banks; abundant.

Fine-ribbed Cardita (1.5") 4 cm
Cyclocardia crebricostata (Krause, 1885). Alaska to California. Offshore, 20 to 80 m; common in Alaska. Syn.: *alaskana* Dall (holotype illus.).

ASTARTE CLAMS
SUPERFAMILY CRASSATELLACEA

Consists of the families Astartidae and Crassatellidae, the former having a dark periostracum and living in cold waters. The latter family is mostly tropical and with larger, more elongate shells. The strong hinge has 2 cardinal teeth in the left valve, 3 in the right.

Waved Astarte (1.2") 3 cm
Astarte undata Gould, 1841. Labrador to off New Jersey. 10 to 208 m; common.

Lentil Astarte (1.5") 4 cm
Astarte crenata (Gray, 1824), subspecies *subequilatera* Sowerby, 1854. Arctic Seas to N.E. Florida. Deep water; common.

Sulcate Astarte (1") 2.5 cm
Astarte sulcata (da Costa, 1778). Arctic Seas (shallow water) to the Mediterranean (deep water). Common.

Chestnut Astarte (1") 2.5 cm
Astarte castanea (Say, 1822). Nova Scotia to off New Jersey. Offshore from 2 to 50 m; common.

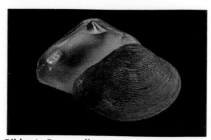

Gibbes's Crassatella (2.5") 6 cm
Eucrassatella speciosa (A. Adams, 1852). S.E. United States and the West Indies. Shallow water; common. Syn.: *gibbesi* Tuomey & Holmes.

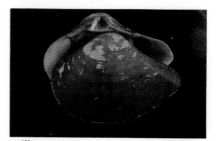

Antillean Crassatella (3") 7.5 cm
Eucrassatella antillarum (Reeve, 1842). Caribbean. Offshore; rare.

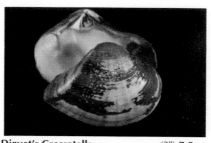

Diguet's Crassatella (3") 7.5 cm
Eucrassatella digueti Lamy, 1917. W. Mexico to Colombia. Subtidal to 128 m; common.

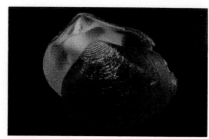

King Crassatella (3") 7.5 cm
Eucrassatella kingicola (Lamarck, 1805). S.E. and S. Australia. Offshore to 50 m; common.

Deceptive Crassatella (3") 7.5 cm
Eucrassatella decipiens (Reeve, 1842). S.W and S. Australia. Uncommon. May be a rugose form of *kingicola*.

THE COCKLES
FAMILY CARDIIDAE

The cockle family is one of the largest and best-known of the bivalves. There are several hundred species, ranging from the Great Ribbed Cockle of West Africa to the Heart Cockle of the Philippines. Hinge with 2 cardinal teeth in each valve; one anterior and posterior lateral tooth in the left valve.

Great Ribbed Cockle (4") 10 cm
Cardium costatum L., 1758. West Africa as far south as Angola. 1 to 30 m; common.

Hians Cockle (3") 7.5 cm
Ringicardium hians (Brocchi, 1814). Mediterranean. Intertidal to 30 m; common.

Ringens Cockle (3") 7.5 cm
Ringicardium ringens (Bruguière, 1789). West Africa. Offshore; common.

European Spiny Cockle (3") 7.5 cm
Acanthocardia aculeata (L., 1767). Europe and West Africa. Subtidal to 30 m; moderately common.

Poorly-ribbed Cockle (2") 5 cm
Acanthocardia paucicostata (Sowerby, 1839). Mediterranean and West Africa; Black Sea. Intertidal to 290 m; common.

European Prickly Cockle (2") 5 cm
Acanthocardia echinata (L., 1758). W. Europe, N.W. Africa and Mediterranean. Shallow water; common.

Tuberculate Cockle (2.5") 6 cm
Acanthocardia tuberculata (L., 1758). England to Mediterranean; Canary Is. 15 to 100 m; common.

Sand Cockle (2.5") 6 cm
Acanthocardia spinosa (Lightfoot, 1786). Mediterranean. Subtidal to 4 m; common. Syn.: *erinaceus* Lamarck.

Magnum Cockle (3.5") 9 cm
Trachycardium magnum (L., 1758). Florida Keys to Brazil. 32 to 35 ribs. Shallow water; uncommon. Syn.: *marmoreum* Lamarck.

Yellow American Cockle (2") 5 cm
Trachycardium muricatum (L., 1758). S.E. United States to Brazil. Shallow water; common.

American Prickly Cockle (2") 5 cm
Trachycardium egmontianum (Shuttleworth, 1856). S.E. United States to east Mexico. 27 to 31 ribs. Abundant. Rarely albino.

Even Cockle (2.5") 6 cm
Trachycardium isocardia (L., 1758). West Indies; Venezuela and off east Florida. Offshore, 1 to 20 m; moderately common.

Giant Pacific Cockle (6") 15 cm
Trachycardium quadragenarium (Conrad, 1837). California to W. Mexico. Subtidal to 150 m; common.

Slender Cockle (2") 5 cm
Trachycardium procerum (Sowerby, 1833). S.W. Mexico to Chile. Shallow water. Syn.: *laticostatum* Sowerby.

Partner Cockle (2.5") 6 cm
Trachycardium consors (Sowerby, 1833). W. Mexico to Ecuador. Shallow water; common. Syn.: *hornelli* Tomlin.

Panama Thorny Cockle (1.5") 4 cm
Trachycardium senticosum (Sowerby, 1833). Gulf of California to Peru. Offshore to 80 m; common.

Reddish Cockle   (2.5") 6 cm
Trachycardium rubicundum (Reeve, 1844). Indian Ocean. Shallow water. Uncommon.

Elongate Cockle   (3") 7 cm
Trachycardium elongatum (Bruguière, 1789). Indian Ocean and S.W. Pacific. Shallow waters; uncommon.

Enode Cockle   (2.5") 6 cm
Trachycardium enode (Sowerby, 1841). Japan; Indo-Pacific. Shallow waters. Common.

Orbit Cockle   (2.5") 6 cm
Trachycardium orbita (Sowerby, 1833). S.W. Pacific; Hawaiian Islands. Shallow reef waters; moderately common.

Orbit Cockle   (2.5") 6 cm
Trachycardium orbita (Sowerby, 1833). S.W. Pacific; Hawaii. Syn.: *hawaiiensis* D., B. & Rehder (holotype illus).

Many-spined Cockle   (2.5") 6 cm
Trachycardium multispinosum (Sowerby, 1841). Indo-Pacific; uncommon. Syn.: *pulchricostatum* Iredale.

Angulate Cockle   (2.5") 6 cm
Trachycardium angulatum (Lamarck, 1822). Indo-Pacific. Shallow sand areas to 20 m; moderately common.

Reeve's Cockle   (2.5") 6 cm
Trachycardium reeveanum (Dunker, 1852). Australia. Shallow water; uncommon.

Pacific Yellow Cockle   (2.5") 6 cm
Trachycardium flavum (L., 1758). Widespread in the Indo-Pacific. Shallow water; common.

Saw-ribbed Cockle   (2.5") 6 cm
Trachycardium serricostatum (Melvill & Standen, 1899). Arabia to Ceylon. Shallow water; common.

Subrugose Cockle   (2.5") 6 cm
Trachycardium subrugosum (Sowerby, 1840). Indo-Pacific. Shallow water; moderately common.

Fan-shaped Cockle   (2.5") 6 cm
Trachycardium pectiniforme (Born, 1778). Indian Ocean. Shallow water; common.

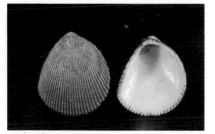

Burchard's Cockle (2.5") 6 cm
Trachycardium burchardi (Dunker, 1877). Japan. Low-tide zone to 20 m; common.

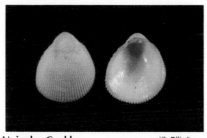

Unicolor Cockle (2.5") 6 cm
Trachycardium unicolor (Sowerby, 1840). Indo-Pacific. Shallow water. Common.

Spiny Paper Cockle (1.5") 4 cm
Papyridea soleniformis (Bruguière,1789). S.E. United States to Brazil. Low tide to 30 m; common.

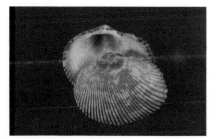

Panama Paper Cockle (1.5") 4 cm
Papyridea aspersa (Sowerby, 1833). W. Mexico to N. Peru. Shallow water; moderately common.

Atlantic Strawberry Cockle (1.2") 3 cm
Americardia media (L., 1758). S.E. United States to Brazil. 1 to 30 m; moderately common.

St. Helena Cockle (1") 2.5 cm
Trigoniocardia speciosa (Adams & Reeve, 1850). St. Helena Is., South Atlantic. Shallow water; rare.

Western Strawberry Cockle (1.5") 4 cm
Americardia biangulata (Broderip & Sowerby, 1829). S. California to Ecuador. Intertidal to 170 m.

Victor Cockle (1") 2.5 cm
Ctenocardia victor (Angas, 1872). W. Pacific. Offshore to 100 m; uncommon.

Pacific Strawberry Cockle (1.2") 3 cm
Fragum fragum (L., 1758). Indo-Pacific. Shallow water; abundant.

Unedo Cockle (1.5") 4 cm
Fragum unedo (L., 1758). Indo-Pacific. Shallow water to 50 m; common.

Arching Strawberry Cockle (1") 2.5 cm
Fragum fornicatum (Sowerby, 1840). S.W. Pacific; Philippines. Offshore to 30 m; uncommon.

Pacific Half Cockle (1.2") 3 cm
Lunulicardia hemicardia (L., 1758). S.W. Pacific to N. Australia. Shallow water; uncommon.

Tumor Cockle   (1.5″) 3.5 cm
Lunulicardia tumorifera (Lamarck, 1819). Western Australia. Offshore in shallow water; uncommon.

Guichard's Cockle   (1.5″) 3.5 cm
Lunulicardia guichardi (Bernardi, 1857). New Caledonia. Shallow water; rare.

Blunted Cockle   (1.5″) 4 cm
Lunulicardia retusa (L., 1758). Indo-Pacific. Shallow water to 50 m; uncommon.

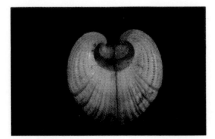

Partly-blunted Cockle   (1.5″) 4 cm
Lunulicardia subretusa (Sowerby, 1841). Indo-Pacific. Shallow water to 20 m; uncommon.

True Heart Cockle   (2″) 5 cm
Corculum cardissa (L., 1758). Indo-Pacific. Intertidal on reefs. Locally abundant. Many colors and shapes.

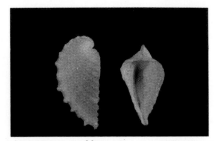

Dione Heart Cockle   (0.5″) 1.2 cm
Corculum dionaeum (Broderip & Sowerby, 1829). Central Pacific Islands. Shallow water; locally common.

Asiatic Cockle   (2″) 5 cm
Trachycardium asiaticum (Bruguière, 1792). Indo-Pacific. Shallow water; common in S.W. Pacific.

Exasperating Cockle   (2″) 5 cm
Nemocardium exasperatum (Sowerby, 1841). Western Australia. Shallow water; uncommon.

De la Beche's Cockle   (2.5″) 6 cm
Nemocardium bechei (Reeve, 1847). Japan to Australia. Offshore from 10 to 70 m; common. Syn.: *probatum* Iredale.

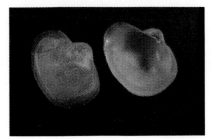

Cuming's Cockle   (1″) 2.5 cm
Lophocardium cumingii (Broderip, 1833). W. Mexico to Colombia. Offshore from 22 to 26 m; rare.

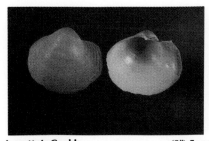

Annette's Cockle   (2″) 5 cm
Lophocardium annettae (Dall, 1889). Gulf of California to Costa Rica. Subtidal to 40 m; uncommon.

Lyrate Cockle   (2″) 5 cm
Lyrocardium lyratum (Sowerby, 1841). Japan to N. Australia. 10 to 100 m; moderately common.

Aeolian Cockle (2″) 5 cm
Lyrocardium aeolicum (Born, 1778). West
Africa; Cape Verde Islands. Shallow water;
rare. *Cardium pectinatum* L. is a dubious
name.

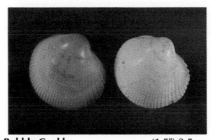

Bubble Cockle (1.5″) 3.5 cm
Fulvia aperta (Bruguière,1789). Japan to the
East Indies. 10 to 30 m; common. *Cardium
bullatum* L. is a dubious name.

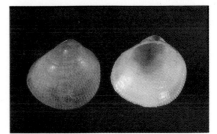

Austral Cockle (1.5″) 3.5 cm
Fulvia australis (Sowerby, 1841). Japan to
East Indies. 10 to 30 m; moderately com-
mon.

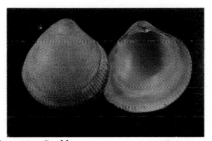

Japanese Cockle (1.5″) 3.5 cm
Fulvia mutica (Reeve, 1844). China; Korea;
Japan. 10 to 60 m; common. Syn.: *japoni-
cum* Dunker; *annae* Pilsbry.

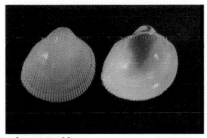

Rackett's Cockle (1.5″) 4 cm
Laevicardium racketti (Donovan, 1825). S.E.
to S.W. Australia. Shallow water; abundant.

Vanhyning's Cockle (4″) 10 cm
Dinocardium robustum subspecies *vanhy-
ningi* Clench & Smith, 1944. West Florida.
Shallow water; abundant.

Giant Atlantic Cockle (4″) 10 cm
Dinocardium robustum (Lightfoot, 1786).
Virginia to north Florida to N.E. Mexico.
Shallow water; common.

Giant Pacific Cockle (7″) 17 cm
Laevicardium elatum (Sowerby, 1833). S.
California to Panama. Subtidal mud flats to
4 m; common.

Oblong Cockle (3″) 7.5 cm
Laevicardium oblongum (Gmelin, 1791).
Mediterranean to the Canary Is. 4 to 200 m;
common.

Common Egg Cockle (2″) 5 cm
Laevicardium laevigatum (L., 1758). S.E.
United States to Brazil. Shallow water; lo-
cally common. Syn.: *vitellinum* Reeve.

Morton's Egg Cockle (1″) 2.5 cm
Laevicardium mortoni (Conrad, 1830). Massachusetts to Texas. Intertidal to 4 m; common.

Ravenel's Egg Cockle (1″) 2.5 cm
Laevicardium pictum (Ravenel, 1861). S.E.
United States to Brazil. Offshore from 10 to
150 m; common.

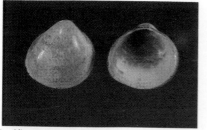

Pacific Coast Egg Cockle   (1") 2.5 cm
Laevicardium substriatum (Conrad, 1837).
California to Gulf of California. Intertidal to
10 m; common.

Attenuated Cockle   (2") 5 cm
Laevicardium attenuatum (Sowerby, 1841).
Japan to East Indies. Shallow water; un-
common.

Two-rayed Cockle   (2") 5 cm
Laevicardium biradiatum (Bruguière, 1789).
Japan to East Indies; Indian Ocean. 1-20 m,
common.

Many-dotted Cockle   (2") 5 cm
Discors multipunctatum (Sowerby, 1841).
S.W. Pacific and East Indies. Shallow water;
uncommon.

Giant Philippine Cockle   (6") 15 cm
Plagiocardium pseudolima (Lamarck,
1819). Philippines, East Indies. Subtidal;
common. Rarely albino.

Hairy Cockle   (2") 5 cm
Plagiocardium setosum (Redfield, 1846).
S.W. Pacific; N.W. Australia. Shallow wa-
ter; common.

Common European Cockle   (2") 5 cm
Cerastoderma edule (L., 1758). Norway to
N.W. Africa. Shallow water; abundant.
Many synonyms.

Exigua Cockle   (1") 2.5 cm
Parvicardium exiguum (Gmelin, 1791). W.
Europe. Subtidal to 5 m; common.

Iceland Cockle   (2.5") 6 cm
Clinocardium ciliatum (Fabricius, 1780).
Arctic Seas in Europe, Asia and North
America. Offshore; common.

Nuttall's Cockle   (5") 12 cm
Clinocardium nuttalli (Conrad, 1837).
Bering Sea to S. California. Offshore to 30
m; common.

Bering Sea Cockle   (3") 7.5 cm
Clinocardium californiense (Deshayes,
1839). Northern Japan to Alaska (not California). 10 to 100 m; common. Syn.: *uchi-
dai* Habe.

Greenland Cockle   (3.5") 9 cm
Serripes groenlandicus (Bruguière,1789).
Acrtic Seas in Europe, Asia, North America.
Offshore to 50 m; common.

La Perouse's Cockle (4") 10 cm
Serripes laperousii (Deshayes, 1839). Northern Japan to Alaska in 50 to 100 m; common. Syn.: *fujinensis* Yokoyama.

GIANT CLAMS
FAMILY TRIDACNIDAE

Limited to the tropical waters of the Indo-Pacific, these large clams rest on the bottom with the hinge down and the gaping edge up, so that sunlight may reach the huge rolled edges of the mantle. Algal food is grown in the fleshy mantle. There are fewer than a dozen species of these giant clams, the largest reaching a weight of 500 pounds.

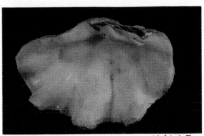

Giant Clam (4 ft) 1.7 m
Tridacna gigas (L., 1758). S.W. Pacific. Offshore, near reefs 2 to 20 m; locally common.

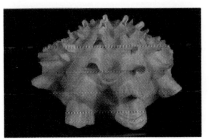

Fluted Giant Clam (12") 30 cm
Tridacna squamosa Lamarck, 1819. Indo-Pacific, except Hawaii. Shallow reefs to 10 m; locally common.

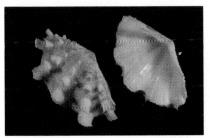

Fluted Giant Clam (12") 30 cm
Tridacna squamosa Lamarck, 1819. Indo-Pacific. These are young specimens which may be orange, pink, yellow or white. Syn.: *imbricata* Röding.

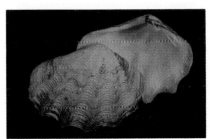

Crocus Giant Clam (4") 10 cm
Tridacna crocea Lamarck, 1819. S.W. Pacific; S. Japan. Lives in pockets in reef flats. Common.

Elongate Giant Clam (10") 24 cm
Tridacna maxima (Röding, 1798). Entire Indo-Pacific. Shallow coral reefs; common. Syn.: *elongata* Lamarck.

Bear Paw Clam (8") 20 cm
Hippopus hippopus (L., 1758). S.W. Pacific. Shallow water coral reefs; common.

China Clam (8") 20 cm
Hippopus porcellanus Rosewater, 1982. A smooth and yellowish species found in the Sulu Sea area of the Philippines. Common.

MACTRA CLAMS
FAMILY MACTRIDAE

Sometimes called the Trough or Surf Clams, this worldwide family is characterized by a strong, toothed hinge bearing a large, spoon-shaped depression, the chondrophore, into which fits a horny pad. Some species are a major source of food. There are about 100 species, most living in shallow water.

Violet Mactra (2.5") 6 cm
Mactra violacea Gmelin, 1791. Indian Ocean to Philippines. Shallow water; common.

Wedge Mactra (1.5") 4 cm
Mactra cuneata Gmelin, 1791. Indo-Pacific. Shallow water to 20 m; common.

Radiate Mactra (3") 7.5 cm
Mactra grandis Gmelin, 1791. East Indies. Shallow water; common. Syn.: *radiata* Spengler.

Agate Mactra (3") 7.5 cm
Mactra achatina Holten, 1802. Indo-Pacific. Shallow water to 50 m; common. Syn.: *ornata* Gray; *maculosa* Lamarck.

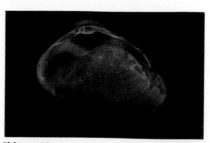

Chinese Mactra (4") 10 cm
Mactra chinensis Philippi, 1846. China; Korea; Japan. Intertidal to 20 m; common. Syn.: *sulcataria* Reeve.

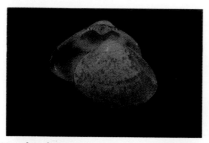

Maculated Mactra (3") 7.5 cm
Mactra maculata Gmelin, 1791. Indo-Pacific. Shallow water. 1 to 30 m; common.

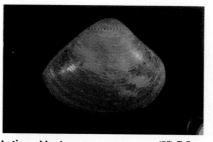

Antique Mactra (3") 7.5 cm
Mactra antiquata (Spengler, 1802). Indo-Pacific. Shallow water to 50 m; common. Syn.: *cornea* Reeve; *spectabilis* Lischke.

Turgid Mactra (3.5") 9 cm
Mactra turgida Gmelin, 1791. Indian Ocean. Intertidal to 10 m; common.

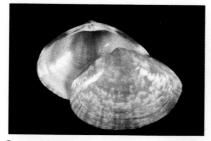

Ornate Mactra (2.5") 6 cm
Mactra ornata Gray, 1836. East Asia; Japan. Sand, 10 to 60 m. Common.

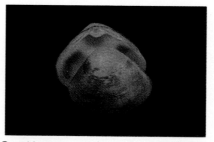

Pure Mactra (2") 5 cm
Mactra pura Deshayes, 1853. South Australia and Tasmania. Intertidal to 5 m; common.

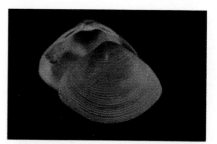

Reddish Mactra (2") 5 cm
Mactra rufescens Lamarck, 1818. Western Australia and Tasmania. Low-tide area; abundant.

Discors Mactra (3.5") 9 cm
Mactra discors Gray, 1837. New Zealand. Shallow water, sand areas. Common.

Rayed Mactra (1.5") 4 cm
Mactra corallina (L., 1758). British Isles to Mediterranean. Shallow water; common. Form *stultorum* L. is rayed.

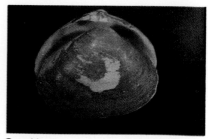

Gray Mactra (4") 10 cm
Mactra glauca Born, 1778. British Isles (rare) to Mediterranean (common). In shallow water. Syn.: *helvacea* Lamarck.

Glossy Mactra (3") 7.5 cm
Mactra glabrata L., 1767. West Africa and South Africa. Shallow water; common.

Hooked Mactra (3") 7.5 cm
Spisula falcata (Gould, 1850). Washington to California. Shallow water; moderately common.

Fragile Atlantic Mactra (2.5") 6 cm
Mactra fragilis Gmelin, 1791. S.E. United States to Brazil. Shallow water to 10 m; common.

Caribbean Winged Mactra (3.5") 9 cm
Mactrellona alata (Spengler, 1802). Caribbean to Brazil. Offshore. 1 to 20 m; locally common.

Plicate Mactra (2") 5 cm
Harvella plicataria (L., 1767). Indian Ocean. Shallow water. Rare.

Elegant Mactra (2") 5 cm
Harvella elegans (Sowerby, 1825). Gulf of California to Peru. Offshore. 28 to 80 m; moderately common.

Ripe Mactra (4") 10 cm
Mactrellona exoleta (Gray, 1837). Gulf of California to Peru. Offshore to 24 m; moderately common.

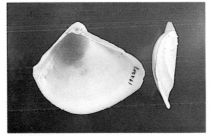

Sloping Mactra (3.5") 9 cm
Mactrellona clisia (Dall, 1915). Gulf of California to Ecuador. Offshore; uncommon.

Pallid Dwarf Mactra (2") 5 cm
Mulinia pallida (Broderip & Sowerby, 1829). W. Mexico to northern Peru. Intertidal to 25 m; common.

Atlantic Surf Clam (5") 13 cm
Spisula solidissima (Dillwyn, 1817). Nova Scotia to South Carolina. Surf line to 50 m; locally abundant. Major food. Smaller subsp. *similis* (Say, 1822), Florida to Texas.

Stimpson's Mactra (4.5") 11 cm
Spisula polynyma (Stimpson, 1860). Arctic Seas to off Rhode Island and to Puget Sound; Japan. Common.

Hemphill's Mactra (6") 15 cm
Spisula hemphilli (Dall, 1894). Central California to Baja California. Just offshore; common.

Catilliform Mactra   (5″) 13 cm
Spisula catilliformis (Conrad, 1867). Puget Sound to California. Offshore to 30 m; uncommon.

Spengler's Mactra   (4″) 10 cm
Scissodesma spengleri (L., 1767). South Africa. Common on beaches of False Bay. Syn.: *Schizodesma*.

Equal-sized Mactra   (2.5″) 6 cm
Spisula aequilateralis (Deshayes, 1854). New Zealand. Ocean beaches; common.

Solid Mactra   (1.5″) 3.5 cm
Spisula solida (L., 1758). Finland to Spain. Intertidal to 100 m; common.

Subtruncate Mactra   (1″) 2.5 cm
Spisula subtruncata (da Costa, 1778). Finland to the Canary Islands, Mediterranean. Common.

Rostrate Mactra   (2.5″) 6 cm
Mactra rostrata (Spengler, 1802). Tropical West Africa. Shallow water; common. Syn.: *cumingiana* Petit.

Glassy Mactra   (2″) 5 cm
Mactra nitida Gmelin, 1791. West Africa. Shallow water; common.

Snowy Mactra   (4″) 10 cm
Spisula nivea (Gmelin, 1791). West Africa. Shallow water; common.

Common Rangia   (2″) 5 cm
Rangia cuneata (Sowerby, 1831). Maryland to Texas. Estuarine bays. Low tide to 20 m; common.

Nicobar Mactra   (2″) 5 cm
Meropesta nicobarica (Gmelin, 1791). Indian Ocean and East Indies. Shallow water; uncommon.

Rugose Mactra   (3″) 7.5 cm
Eastonia rugosa (Helbling, 1779). Mediterranean to West Africa. Shallow water; common.

Snout Otter Clam   (3″) 7.5 cm
Lutraria rhynchaena Jonas, 1844. Western and South Australia. Shallow water; common. Syn.: *philippinarum* Reeve.

European Otter Clam (6″) 15 cm
Lutraria lutraria (L., 1758). N.W. Europe to West Africa. Intertidal to 55 m; common.

Oblong Otter Clam (6″) 15 cm
Lutraria magna (da Costa, 1778). Western Europe. Shallow water; common. Syn.: *oblonga* Gmelin.

Lance Mactra (4″) 10 cm
Resania lanceolata Gray, 1852. New Zealand. Ocean beaches; uncommon.

Scimitar Mactra (3.5″) 9 cm
Zenatia acinaces (Quoy & Gaimard, 1835). New Zealand. Ocean beaches; uncommon.

Pacific Coast Gaper (8″) 20 cm
Tresus nuttalli (Conrad, 1837). Puget Sound to Baja California. Offshore to 20 m; common.

Channeled Duck Clam (2.5″) 6 cm
Raeta plicatella (Lamarck, 1818). S.E. United States to Argentina. Shallow water to 6 m; common. Syn.: *canaliculata* Say.

Smooth Duck Clam (2″) 5 cm
Anatina anatina (Spengler, 1802). S.E. United States to Brazil. Intertidal to 20 m; uncommon. Syn.: *lineata* Say.

Arctic Wedge Clam (1.5″) 4 cm
Mesodesma arctatum (Conrad, 1830). Greenland to Maryland. Intertidal to 100 m; cold water; common. Member of the Mesodesmatidae.

Marisco Wedge Clam (3″) 7.5 cm
Mesodesma mactroides Deshayes, 1854. S. Brazil to Argentina. Shallow water; common food clam.

Giant Wedge Clam (3.5″) 9 cm
Mesodesma donacium (Lamarck, 1818). Peru and Chile. Intertidal sand flats; common food clam.

Subtriangular Wedge Clam (3″) 7.5 cm
Paphies subtriangulata (Wood, 1828). New Zealand. Intertidal beaches; common. This genus in family Mesodesmatidae.

Pipi Wedge Clam (2.5″) 6 cm
Paphies australis (Gmelin, 1791). New Zealand. Mud and sand beaches; common.

Brief Jackknife Clam   (3.5") 9 cm
Solen brevis Gray, in Hanley, 1842. South
Asia, Indian Ocean. Mud flats; locally common.

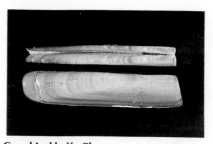

Grand Jackknife Clam   (5") 13 cm
Solen grandis Dunker, 1862. Korea to East
Indies. Intertidal to 20 m; common.

Truncate Jackknife Clam   (7") 17 cm
Solen truncata Wood, 1815. Indian Ocean.
Sandy mud flats; common.

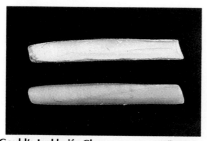

Gould's Jackknife Clam   (4") 10 cm
Solen strictus Gould, 1861. China and Japan. Sandy mud flats; common. Syn.:
gouldi Conrad; *corneus* Sowerby.

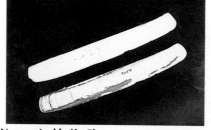

Narrow Jackknife Clam   (4.3") 11 cm
Ensis ensis (L., 1758). Norway to Mediterranean. Subtidal to 80 m; common. Family
Cultellidae.

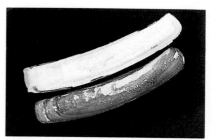

Atlantic Jackknife Clam   (8") 20 cm
Ensis directus Conrad, 1843. East Canada to
Carolinas. Intertidal sand flats; common.

Macha Jackknife Clam   (7") 17 cm
Ensis macha (Molina, 1782). S. Chile and
Argentina. Sandy mud, 2 to 25 m; common.

Cultellus Clam   (3") 7.5 cm
Ensiculus cultellus (L., 1758). S. Japan to the
East Indies. Shallow water to 50 m; common. (Family Cultellidae).

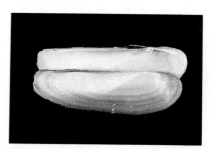

Attenuated Phaxas   (3") 7.5 cm
Phaxas attenuatus (Dunker, 1862). Japan.
Offshore from 10 to 50 m; common. Syn.:
albidus Adams & Reeve.

Sunset Siliqua   (3") 7.5 cm
Siliqua radiata (L., 1758). Indian Ocean.
Shallow mud areas; common. (Family
Cultellidae).

Atlantic Razor Clam   (2") 5 cm
Siliqua costata Say, 1822. East Canada to
North Carolina. Sandy beaches, 1 to 20 m;
common.

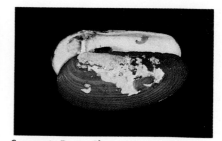

Squamate Razor Clam   (3") 7.5 cm
Siliqua squama Blainville, 1824. Newfoundland to Cape Cod, Mass. Offshore;
uncommon.

Toheroa Clam (3.5") 9 cm
Paphies ventricosa (Gray, 1843). New Zealand. Ocean beaches; locally common, edible clam.

Fat Anapella Clam (1.2") 3 cm
Anapella pinguis Crosse & Fischer, 1864. Western and South Australia; Tasmania. On sand beaches; common.

Chinese Anapella Clam (1") 2.5 cm
Caecella chinensis Deshayes, 1855. S.W. Pacific; Japan. Shallow water; common. Syn.: *zebuensis* Deshayes.

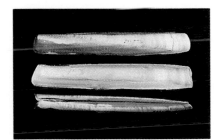

Striate Beach Clam (1") 2.5 cm
Atactodea striata (Gmelin, 1791). S.W. Pacific. Intertidal sand beaches; abundant. In family Mesodesmatidae.

Smooth Beach Clam (1") 2.5 cm
Atactodea striata (Gmelin, 1791) form *glabrata* (Gmelin, 1791). Intertidal with *A. striata*.

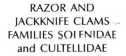

RAZOR AND JACKKNIFE CLAMS FAMILIES SOLENIDAE and CULTELLIDAE

A large family of burrowing, shallow-water, elongate clams with a worldwide distribution. Many are edible. The long, slender *Solen* and *Ensis* clams live in burrows in the sand of intertidal flats. The Butter Clams, *Siliqua*, are a favorite source of tender clams. Delicate shells have an internal reinforcing rib. The hinge teeth are very small cardinals.

European Razor Clam (5") 12 cm
Solen vagina L., 1758. Western Europe, Mediterranean; W. Africa. Intertidal; common. Syn.: *marginatus* Pennant (and Pulteney).

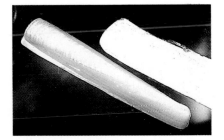

Giant Razor Clam (8") 20 cm
Ensis siliqua (L., 1758). Norway to Portugal. Intertidal; to 20 m; common. Family Cultellidae.

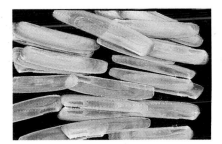

Green Jackknife Clam (2") 5 cm
Solen viridis Say, 1821. Rhode Island to Texas. Intertidal flats; uncommon. Single tooth at end of valve.

Oblique Jackknife Clam (6") 15 cm
Solen obliquus Spengler, 1794. West Indies to Brazil. Muddy sand; common.

Blunt Jackknife Clam (4") 10 cm
Solen sicarius Gould, 1850. W. Canada to Baja California. Intertidal flats to 50 m; common.

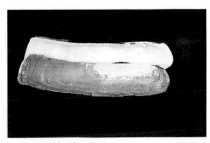

Rough Jackknife Clam (6") 15 cm
Solen rudis (C. B. Adams, 1852). Costa Rica to N. Peru. Intertidal; common.

Pacific Razor Clam   (5") 13 cm
Siliqua patula (Dixon, 1788). Alaska to California. Ocean beach flats; common edible species.

Winter's Siliqua   (3") 7.5 cm
Siliqua winteriana Dunker, 1852. East Indies. Shallow muddy areas; uncommon.

TELLINS
FAMILY TELLINIDAE

This is one of the colorful, popular families of thin, oval clams common in most parts of the world. The brightly colored species are mostly found in shallow tropical seas. There are many small white species very difficult to identify. The shells are usually compressed, the pallial sinus large and the cardinal teeth small.

Sunrise Tellin   (3") 7.5 cm
Tellina radiata L., 1758. S.E. United States to the Caribbean. Shallow coral sand areas; common. *T. unimaculata* Lamarck is unrayed form of this species.

Elegant Tellin   (4") 10 cm
Tellina chariessa Salisbury, 1934. Indo-Pacific. Shallow reef waters; rare. Syn.: *elegans* Wood.

Tonga Tellin   (3") 7.5 cm
Tellina tongana Quoy & Gaimard, 1835. S.W. Pacific; S. Japan. Shallow water; uncommon.

Great Caribbean Tellin   (4.5") 11 cm
Tellina magna Spengler, 1798. S.E. United States and West Indies; Bermuda. Shallow water; uncommon.

Perna Tellin   (3") 7.5 cm
Tellina perna Spengler, 1798. East Africa to Hawaii. Shallow water to 20 m; uncommon.

Rostrate Tellin   (3") 7.5 cm
Tellina rostrata L., 1758. S.W. Pacific. Shallow water to 20 m; uncommon. Syn.: *vulsella* Hanley, 1844.

Squalid Tellin   (1.5") 4 cm
Tellina squalida Pulteney, 1799. Norway to Portugal. Sandy shores; rare.

Foliated Tellin   (3") 7.5 cm
Phylloda foliacea (L., 1758). S.W. Pacific. Offshore from 5 to 20 m; locally common.

Spengler's Tellin   (2") 5 cm
Tellina spengleri Gmelin, 1791. S.W. Pacific. Shallow water to 20 m; uncommon. Syn.: *rostrata* Hanley.

Smooth Tellin (3″) 7.5 cm
Tellina laevigata L., 1758. S.E. United States and Caribbean. 1 to 16 m; locally common.

Speckled Tellin (2.5″) 6 cm
Tellina listeri Röding, 1798. S.E. United States to Brazil; Bermuda. 1 to 100 m; common. Syn.: *interrupta* Wood.

Cuming's Tellin (2″) 5 cm
Tellina cumingii Hanley, 1844. W. Mexico to Colombia. 18 to 150 m; common.

Purple Tellin (2″) 5 cm
Tellina purpurea Broderip & Sowerby, 1829. Gulf of California to Colombia. Shallow water; common.

West African Tellin (3″) 7.5 cm
Tellina madagascariensis Gmelin, 1791. West Africa. Shallow water; common.

Little White Tellin (2.5″) 6 cm
Tellina albinella Lamarck, 1818. Southern coasts of Australia. Common.

Cross Tellin (2″) 5 cm
Tellina staurella Lamarck, 1818. Indo-Pacific. Shallow water to 30 m; moderately common.

Virgate Tellin (3″) 7.5 cm
Tellina virgata L., 1758. Indo-Pacific. 1 to 30 m; common. Syn.: *jubar* Hanley; *lata* Quoy and Gaimard.

Alternate Tellin (2.5″) 6 cm
Tellina alternata Say, 1822. S.E. United States. Shallow water to 150 m; common.

Angulate Tellin (2″) 5 cm
Tellina angulosa Gmelin, 1791. S. Florida to Uruguay. Subtidal to 8 m; fairly common.

Watermelon Tellin (2″) 5 cm
Tellina punicea Born, 1778. Lower Caribbean to Brazil. Shallow water; locally common.

Rose Petal Tellin (1.5″) 3.5 cm
Tellina lineata Turton, 1819. Florida to Texas to Brazil. Low-tide line to 30 m; common. Syn.: *brasiliana* Lamarck.

Bodegas Tellin (2") 5 cm
Tellina bodegensis Hinds, 1845. W. Canada to the Gulf of California. Subtidal to 30 m; common.

Great Alaskan Tellin (3") 7.5 cm
Tellina lutea Wood, 1828. Japan to Alaska. 15 to 50 m; common. Syn.: *alternidentata* Broderip and Sowerby.

Flat Tellin (2.5") 6 cm
Tellina planata L., 1758. Mediterranean and West Africa. Intertidal; common.

Story Tellin (0.8") 2 cm
Tellina fabula Gmelin, 1791. Norway to the Black Sea. Intertidal to 14 m; common. Syn.: "*fabula* Gronovius".

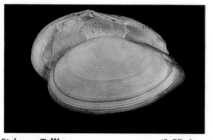

Strigose Tellin (2.5") 6 cm
Tellina strigosa Gmelin, 1791. West Africa. Shallow water to 10 m; common.

Boxlike Tellin (2") 5 cm
Tellina capsoides Lamarck, 1818. Indo-Pacific. Shallow water; moderately common.

Faust Tellin (3") 7.5 cm
Tellina fausta Pulteney, 1799. S.E. United States and the Caribbean. 1 to 30 m; common.

Remies Tellin (3") 7.5 cm
Tellina remies L., 1758. Indo-Pacific. Shallow water; common.

Thick Tellin (2.5") 6 cm
Tellina crassa Pennant, 1777. Norway to Senegal, West Africa. Offshore to 150 m, common.

Donax Tellin (1") 2.5 cm
Tellina donacina L., 1758. British Isles to Mediterranean. 1 to 50 m; common.

Inflated Tellin (2.5") 6 cm
Tellina inflata Gmelin, 1791. S.W. Pacific. 1 to 10 m; common. Syn.: *striatula* Hanley.

Disk Tellin (1.5") 4 cm
Tellina disculus Deshayes, 1855. New Zealand. Subtidal beaches; common.

Palate Tellin   (2″) 5 cm
Tellina palatam (Iredale, 1929). Indo-Pacific. Subtidal to 20 m; common. Syn.: *rugosa* Born, not Pennant.

Rasp Tellin   (2.5″) 6 cm
Tellina scobinata L., 1758. Indo-Pacific. Shallow water; common. Syn.: *elizabethae* Pilsbry.

Cat's Tongue Tellin   (2.5″) 6 cm
Tellina linguafelis L., 1758. S.W. Pacific. Shallow water to 30 m; uncommon.

Gargadia Tellin   (1″) 2.5 cm
Tellina gargadia L., 1758. S.W. and Central Pacific. Shallow water; uncommon.

Fragile Tellin   (1.5″) 4 cm
Gastrana fragilis (L., 1758). N.W. Europe; Mediterranean; Black Sea. Intertidal flats; common.

Abildgaard's Tellin   (1.2″) 3 cm
Gastrana abildgaardiana (Spengler, 1798). South Africa to Mozambique. Near beaches; uncommon.

Thin Tellin   (0.7″) 1.8 cm
Tellina tenuis da Costa, 1778. Norway to N.W. Africa. Scarce in Mediterranean. Intertidal to 10 m; abundant.

Tampa Tellin   (0.7″) 1.8 cm
Tellina tampaensis Conrad, 1866. South half of Florida to Texas; West Indies. Shallow water; common.

Victoria Tellin   (2″) 5 cm
Tellina victoriae Gatliff & Gabriel, 1914. Southern Australia; Tasmania. Near shore; uncommon.

Large Strigilla   (1″) 2.5 cm
Strigilla carnaria (L., 1758). South half of Florida to Argentina. Shallow waters; locally common.

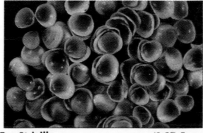

Pea Strigilla   (0.2″) 5 mm
Strigilla pisiformis (L., 1758). Bahamas to Brazil. Just offshore; abundant in sand.

False Red Strigilla   (0.7″) 1.8 cm
Strigilla pseudocarnaria Boss, 1969. Caribbean. Uncommon. Pallial sinus reaches front muscle scar.

White Crested Tellin　　　(1.5″) 4 cm
Tellidora cristata (Récluz, 1842). S.E. United States. Intertidal to 10 m; uncommon.

Atlantic Grooved Macoma　　(2.5″) 6 cm
Psammotreta intastriata (Say, 1827). S.E. United States and Caribbean. Shallow water to 5 m; common.

Paper Grooved Macoma　　　(3″) 7.5 cm
Psammotreta papyracea (Gmelin, 1791). Mauritania to Angola, West Africa. Intertidal; common. Syn.: *lacunosa* Schroter.

Saddle Grooved Macoma　　(3″) 7.5 cm
Psammotreta ephippium (Spengler, 1798). S.E. Asia. Shallow water; uncommon.

Plicate Grooved Macoma　　(3″) 7.5 cm
Psammotreta plicata (Valenciennes, 1846). Indian Ocean. Shallow water; rare.

Pacific Grooved Macoma　　(3″) 7.5 cm
Psammotreta obesa (Deshayes, 1855). California to W. Mexico. Low-tide mark to 50 m; common.

Balthic Macoma　　　　　(1.2″) 3 cm
Macoma balthica (L., 1758). Arctic Seas; W. Europe; N.E. United States. Shallow water; common. White or pinkish. No lateral teeth in this genus.

Chalky Macoma　　　　　(2″) 5 cm
Macoma calcarea (Gmelin, 1791). Arctic Seas; W. Europe; North American cold waters. Offshore; common.

Constricted Macoma　　　(2″) 5 cm
Macoma constricta (Bruguière, 1792). Florida and Texas to Brazil. Offshore to 4 m; common.

Tageluslike Macoma　　　(2″) 5 cm
Macoma tageliformis Dall, 1900. Gulf of Mexico to Brazil. Offshore to 100 m; locally common.

White Sand Macoma　　　(4″) 10 cm
Macoma secta (Conrad, 1837). W. Canada to Gulf of California. Intertidal to 50 m; common.

Bent-nose Macoma　　　(3″) 7.5 cm
Macoma nasuta (Conrad, 1837). Alaska to Baja California. Intertidal mud flats to 50 m; common.

Lily Tellin (3") 7.5 cm
Tellina liliana Iredale, 1915. New Zealand. Sand beaches to offshore; common.

DONAX and BEAN CLAMS
FAMILY DONACIDAE

These small, wedge-shaped clams are found in large numbers on warm-water beaches in most parts of the world. When waves are washing the beach, the clams feed for a few seconds, and then burrow back under the sand. There are almost 60 worldwide species, many being brightly colored. A broth is made from some species.

Coquina Donax (0.6") 1.5 cm
Donax variabilis Say, 1822. New York to Texas. Sand beaches; locally and seasonally common. Syn.: *fossor* Say (New York to Virginia).

Toothed Donax (1") 2.5 cm
Donax denticulatus L., 1758. S.W. Caribbean to Brazil. Sloping beaches; locally abundant. Pinpoints on sides.

Striate Donax (1") 2.5 cm
Donax striatus L., 1767. Lower Caribbean to Brazil. Common. Posterior concave, with fine threads.

Rugose Donax (2") 5 cm
Donax rugosus L., 1758. West Africa. Abundant on beaches. Posterior with concentric rows of granulations.

Truncate Donax (1.2") 3 cm
Donax trunculus L., 1758. Portugal; Mediterranean; Black Sea. Intertidal sand beaches; common.

Banded Donax (1.2") 3 cm
Donax vittatus (da Costa, 1778)'. Norway to N.W. Africa; Mediterranean. Sandy bays; common.

California Donax (1") 2.5 cm
Donax californicus Conrad, 1837. California to Panama. Sandy bays; common.

Panama Donax (1.2") 3 cm
Donax panamensis Philippi, 1849. W. Mexico to Ecuador. Sand beaches; common. Syn.: *assimilis* of authors.

Carinate Donax (1.2") 3 cm
Donax carinatus Hanley, 1843. W. Mexico to Colombia. Shallow water to 24 m; common. Syn.: *rostratus* C. B. Adams.

Townsend's Donax (1.2") 3 cm
Donax townsendi Sowerby, 1894. Persian Gulf and N.W. Indian Ocean. Sandy bays; common.

Pacific Bean Donax (0.7") 1.8 cm
Donax faba Gmelin, 1791. Indo-Pacific.
Beach slopes; locally abundant.

Cuneate Donax (1.5") 4 cm
Donax cuneatus L., 1758. Indo-Pacific.
Beach slopes; locally common.

Saw Donax (2") 5 cm
Donax serra Röding, 1798. South Africa.
Beaches; common. Syn.: *aurantiaca*
Krauss.

Goolwa Donax (2") 5 cm
Plebidonax deltoides (Lamarck, 1818).
South Australia. Sandy shores; abundant.

Leather Donax (2") 5 cm
Hecuba scortum (L., 1758). East Indies; Indian Ocean. Mud bays; common. Syn.: *pubescens* L.

Giant False Donax (2.5") 6 cm
Iphigenia brasiliana (Lamarck, 1818). South
half of Florida to Brazil. Shallow water to 4
m; common.

Galatea Clam (3.5") 9 cm
Galatea paradoxa (Born, 1778). Liberia to
Congo, Africa. Estuaries of rivers; common.

SANGUIN and GARI CLAMS FAMILY PSAMMOBIIDAE

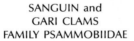

Known also as sunset clams this group is
almost entirely associated with the warm,
black muds of bays of continents and large
islands. The shells are usually purple in
color, with some degree of red, and the
periostracum is usually dark. The pallial sinus is large. The hinge has two small cardinals but no lateral teeth.

Faeroe Gari (2.3") 6.5 cm
Gari fervensis (Gmelin, 1791). W. Europe to
West Africa. Shallow water; common.
Syn.: *bornii* Gmelin; *faerveensis* Chemnitz.

Depressed Gari (2") 5 cm
Gari depressa (Pennant, 1777). Norway to
Mediterranean; N.W. Africa. Offshore to
50 m. Common.

Tripartite Gari (2.5") 6 cm
Gari tripartita (Deshayes, 1854). Indian
Ocean to Philippines. Shallow water; uncommon.

Stanger's Gari (3") 7.5 cm
Gari stangeri (Gray, 1843). New Zealand.
Sandy beaches; common.

Spotted Gari (2") 5 cm
Gari maculosa (Lamarck, 1818). Japan and China. Shallow water to 30 m; common.

Gaudy Asaphis (2.5") 6 cm
Asaphis deflorata (L., 1758). S.E. Florida to Brazil. Intertidal, near mangroves; common. Also purple.

Pacific Asaphis (2.5") 6 cm
Asaphis violascens (Förskal, 1775). Indo-Pacific; common. Syn.: *dichotoma* Anton. Coarsely ribbed.

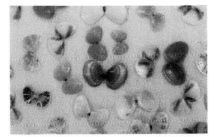

Small False Donax (0.7") 1.8 cm
Heterodonax bimaculatus (L., 1758). Southern Florida and West Indies. Many colors. Beach slopes; locally common.

Pacific False Donax (0.8") 2 cm
Heterodonax pacificus (Conrad, 1837). Southern California to Panama. Sand beaches; common.

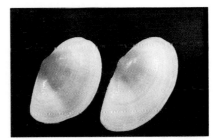

Atlantic Sanguin (2") 5 cm
Sanguinolaria sanguinolenta (Gmelin, 1791). Southern Florida; Texas to Brazil. Shallow water; uncommon.

Operculate Sanguin (3") 7.5 cm
Sanguinolaria cruenta (Lightfoot, 1786). Caribbean to Brazil. Shallow water; uncommon. Syn.: *operculata* Gmelin.

Tellinlike Sanguin (3") 7.5 cm
Sanguinolaria tellinoides A. Adams, 1850. Gulf of California to Ecuador. Shallow water; uncommon.

Bertin's Sanguin (3") 7.5 cm
Sanguinolaria bertini Pilsbry & Lowe, 1932. Baja California to Peru. Intertidal flats; common.

Elongate Gari (2.5") 6 cm
Psammotaea elongata (Lamarck, 1818). Indo-Pacific. Intertidal sandy mud; common. Syn.: *violacea* Lamarck.

Solid Sanguin (2.5") 6 cm
Hiatula solida (Reeve, 1857). Indian Ocean. Shallow water; uncommon. Syn.: *Soletellina.*

Diphos Sanguin (5") 12 cm
Hiatula diphos (L., 1771). Indo-Pacific. Low tide to 30 m; common. Syn.: *Soletellina violacea* Lamarck; *adamsi* Reeve.

Plane Sanguin   (5") 12 cm
Hiatula planulata (Reeve, 1857). Southeast Asia. Intertidal; common.

Chinese Sanguin   (5") 12 cm
Hiatula chinensis (Mörch, 1854). Color variation showing white rays. Used as food.

Boeddinghaus Sanguin   (3") 7 cm
Hiatula boeddinghausi (Lischke, 1870). Japan. Intertidal flats to 50 m; common.

Glassy Sanguin   (2") 5 cm
Hiatula nitida (Gray, 1843). New Zealand. Intertidal sand flats; common.

Two-rayed Sanguin   (2.5") 6 cm
Hiatula biradiata (Wood, 1815). Southern Australia; Tasmania. Intertidal; common. Syn.: *nymphalis* Reeve.

California Sunset Clam   (4") 10 cm
Gari californica (Conrad, 1849). Alaska to W. Mexico. Offshore to 50 m; common.

Nuttall's Mahogany Clam   (5") 12 cm
Sanguinolaria nuttallii (Conrad, 1837). California to Baja California. Near estuaries in mud; common.

SOLECURTUS CLAMS
FAMILY SOLECURTIDAE

Gaping at both ends, these short tubular clams are characterized by curious cross-hatch scratches on the surface. Some, like *Tagelus,* are smooth outside. Right valve with two jutting cardinal teeth; only one in left valve. Shallow water; burrow in mud. Mostly tropical.

Scraper Solecurtus   (3") 7.5 cm
Solecurtus strigilatus (L., 1758). Mediterranean to western Africa. Intertidal flats; common. *S. strigillatus* is misspelling.

Pacific Solecurtus   (2") 5 cm
Solecurtus pacificus Pease, 1870. Central Pacific; rare. Syn.: *S. albus* Blainville?

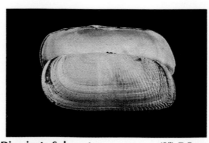

Divaricate Solecurtus   (3") 7.5 cm
Solecurtus divaricatus (Lischke, 1869). Japan; Korea to Taiwan. Intertidal to 10 m; common.

Similar Japanese Solecurtus   (2.5") 6 cm
Solecurtus consimilis Kuroda & Habe, 1961. Southern half of Japan. 10 to 50 m on sand; uncommon.

Sharp Azor Clam   (2") 5 cm
Azorinus acutidens (Broderip & Sowerby, 1829). East Indies; Philippines. Shallow muddy areas; common.

Bean Solen   (3") 7.5 cm
Pharus legumen (L., 1758). Norway to Senegal and Mediterranean. Sandy bays to 80 m; common.

Purplish American Tagelus   (1.5") 3.5 cm
Tagelus divisus (Spengler, 1794). Eastern United States to Brazil. Shallow sandy mud areas, 1 to 20 m; common.

Stout American Tagelus   (3") 7.5 cm
Tagelus plebeius (Lightfoot, 1786). Eastern United States to Brazil. Intertidal to 5 m; common. Syn.: *gibbus* Spengler.

Californian Tagelus   (3.5") 9 cm
Tagelus californianus (Conrad, 1837). Monterey, California, to W. Mexico. Intertidal sand flats; common.

Affinis Tagelus   (2") 5 cm
Tagelus affinis (C. B. Adams, 1852). Southern California to Ecuador. Sand flats; common in Panama.

Dombey's Tagelus   (3.5") 9 cm
Tagelus dombeii (Lamarck, 1818). W. Mexico to Peru. Subtidal to 5 m; common.

Adanson's Tagelus   (2.6") 7 cm
Tagelus adansonii (Bosc, 1801). Mauritania to Angola. Estuaries; abundant. Syn.: *angulatus* Sowerby.

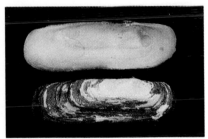

Constricted Tagelus   (2") 5 cm
Sinovacula constricta (Lamarck, 1818). Southeastern Asia. Estuaries, mud; common.

Rugose Tagelus   (2") 5 cm
Sinovacula rugosa (L., 1767). East Indies; southeastern Asia. Shallow muddy bays; common.

Greenish Tagelus   (2") 5 cm
Sinovacula virens (L., 1767). Southeastern Asia; East Indies. Shallow bays in mud; common.

SEMELE CLAMS
FAMILY SEMELIDAE

The colorful Semele clams are found in shallow, warm waters around the world. In addition to an external ligament, there is a chitinous resilium embedded in a diagonal groove in the hinge. Some species have a barklike periostracum, others have colorful exteriors. There are about 70 species.

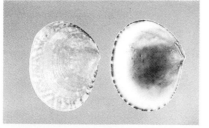

Purplish American Semele   (1.4") 3 cm
Semele purpurascens (Gmelin, 1791). S.E. United States to Brazil. 1 to 20 m, in sand; common. Red or purple.

Cancellate Semele   (0.7") 1.8 cm
Semele bellastriata (Conrad, 1837). S.E. United States to Brazil. Shallow sandy areas; common. Syn.: *donovani* McGinty.

White Atlantic Semele   (1.5") 4 cm
Semele proficua (Pulteney, 1799). S.E. United States to Brazil. Shallow sandy areas to 10 m; common. Rarely pink-rayed.

Heart-shaped Semele   (2") 5 cm
Semele cordiformis (Holten, 1803). Japan to S.E. Asia. Shallow water; moderately common. Syn.: *sinensis* Reeve.

Rough Semele   (2.5") 6 cm
Semele crenulata (Sowerby, 1853). Southwestern Pacific. Shallow sandy bays; uncommon. Syn.: *scabra* Hanley, 1856.

Beautiful Semele   (2") 5 cm
Semele formosa (Sowerby, 1833). Gulf of California to Ecuador. Shallow water; uncommon.

Rose Petal Semele   (1.7") 4.5 cm
Semele rubropicta Dall, 1871. Alaska to Mexico. 40 to 100 m; uncommon.

Bark Semele   (3") 7 cm
Semele decisa (Conrad, 1837). San Pedro, California, to W. Mexico. Pebbles and sand, 1 to 20 m; common.

Solid Semele   (3.5") 8 cm
Semele solida Gray, 1828. Peru and Chile. Lower intertidal, sand. Common.

Corrugate Semele   (4") 9 cm
Semele corrugata (Sowerby, 1833). Ecuador to Chile. Intertidal; abundant. Common food.

California Cumingia   (1") 2.5 cm
Cumingia californica Conrad, 1837. Intertidal rock crevices, wharf pilings to 50 m; common.

Flat Furrow Clam   (2.5") 6 cm
Scrobicularia plana (da Costa, 1778). Norway to Senegal. Intertidal to 2 m; common. Family Scrobiculariidae.

FALSE MUSSELS
FAMILY DREISSENIDAE

This is a strange group of bivalves related to the venerid and tellinid clam, but which have invaded freshwater and resemble the *Mytilus* blue mussels. They live attached to pilings and clog waterpipes. The narrow end of the valve has a septum or ledge.

Zebra Mussel   (2″) 5 cm
Dreissena polymorpha (Pallas, 1771). Europe and Asia Minor. Freshwater lakes, streams; abundant.

ARCTICA CLAMS
SUPERFAMILY ARCTICACEA

Shells resembling the venerid clams but having 2 or 3 cardinal teeth and well-developed lateral teeth. There is no pallial sinus. The genus *Arctica* is cold water, while *Trapezium* is limited to tropical waters.

Ocean Quahog   (4″) 10 cm
Arctica islandica (L., 1767). Newfoundland to off North Carolina. Dredged from 10 to 160 m; abundant. Commercial food clam.

Carinate Trapezium Clam   (2″) 5 cm
Trapezium bicarinatum (Schumacher, 1817). Indo-Pacific. Shallow reef sands; common. Syn.: *angulatum* Lamarck.

Oblong Trapezium Clam   (2.5″) 6 cm
Trapezium oblongum (L., 1758). Indo-Pacific. Shallow water reefs; common. Family Trapeziidae.

HEART CLAMS
FAMILY GLOSSIDAE

This curious family of bivalves has a coiled umbo which gives the clam a swollen heart shape. It is an ancient group which is survived by only a few species including the well-known Oxheart Clam of Europe. A few species are found in the tropics. Formerly known as the Isocardiidae.

Oxheart Clam   (3.5″) 9 cm
Glossus humanus (L., 1758). Norway to the Mediterranean. Offshore 8 to 3,000 m; common. Syn.: *Isocardia cor* L.

Oxheart Clam   (3.5″) 9 cm
Glossus humanus (L., 1758). European Seas. A popular shell that is also used as food. Another view.

Moltke's Heart Clam   (1.5″) 3.5 cm
Meiocardia moltkiana (Spengler, 1783). East Indies; Philippines. Shallow water; uncommon. Syn.: *moltkiana* Gmelin.

CALYPTO CLAMS
FAMILY VESICOMYIDAE

This is an obscure, mainly deepsea, family of clams. They are seldom seen in amateur collections. There are only three living genera, the largest being the Calypto Clams. One giant species has been recently found in deepsea rifts off the Galapagos Islands.

Magnificent Calypto Clam   (7″) 18 cm
Calyptogena magnifica Boss & Turner, 1980. Off Galapagos, near deepsea hot springs; locally common. Holotype illustrated.

CORBICULA CLAMS
FAMILY CORBICULIDAE

This small family of clams lives in freshwater and estuaries. Most have a purplish shell and a thick glossy or hairy periostracum. The Asian Clam was introduced to United States rivers in 1938 and has become a nuisance throughout the country.

Asian Clam (1.3") 3 cm
Corbicula fluminea (Müller, 1774). Asia; East Indies; United States. Rivers and lakes; abundant. Syn.: *manilensis* Philippi.

Violet Batissa Clam (3") 7.5 cm
Batissa violacea (Lamarck, 1806). Philippines and Indonesia. Freshwater ponds; common.

Strong Batissa Clam (3") 7.5 cm
Batissa fortis Prime, 1860. New Guinea and Solomon Islands. Rivers; locally common.

Common Geloina (2.5") 6 cm
Geloina coaxans (Gmelin, 1791). Japan to the East Indies. Estuaries and ponds; common.

Florida Marsh Clam (1") 2.5 cm
Polymesoda maritima (Orbigny, 1842). Florida to Texas. Brackish warm water. Syn.: *floridana* Conrad.

Carolina March Clam (1.5") 4 cm
Polymesoda caroliniana (Bosc, 1801). Virginia to Texas. Tidal estuaries in freshwater. In sand; common.

Agreeable Marsh Clam (1.5") 4 cm
Polymesoda placans (Hanley, 1845). Central America. Freshwater rivers near the sea; locally abundant.

VENUS CLAMS
FAMILY VENERIDAE

A large and well-known family of hard-shelled clams found in most parts of the world. In cold seas many species, such as the Quahog or hard-shell clam, are used for food. In warmer waters the species are more colorful. There are numerous genera and hundreds of species.

Warty Venus (2.5") 6 cm
Venus verrucosa (L., 1758). Southern British Isles to Mediterranean. Intertidal to 12 m. Common edible species.

Chamber Venus (1.5") 3.5 cm
Circomphalus casinus (L., 1758). Norway to Senegal; Mediterranean. Intertidal sand; common. Syn.: *discinus* Lamarck.

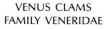

Chicken Venus (1.5") 4 cm
Chamelea gallina (L., 1758). Mediterranean. Intertidal sand flats; common.

Embossed Venus (2.5″) 6 cm
Venus toreuma Gould, 1851. Indo-Pacific. Shallow sandy areas; uncommon.

Lamellate Venus (2″) 5 cm
Antigona lamellaris Schumacher, 1817. Indo-Pacific. Coral sand, shore to 20 m; uncommon. Syn.: *lamarckii* Gray.

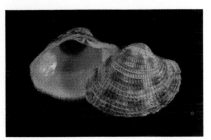

Lamellate Venus (2″) 5 cm
Antigona lamellaris Schumacher, 1817. Some specimens have a rosy interior and a more colorful exterior.

Ford's Venus (2″) 5 cm
Circomphalus fordi (Yates, 1890). Southern California. Shallow water; uncommon.

Empress Venus (1.5″) 3.5 cm
Circomphalus strigillinus (Dall, 1902). Southeastern United States. Offshore to 200 m; uncommon.

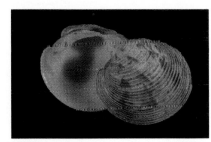

Rigid Venus (3″) 7 cm
Ventricolaria rigida (Dillwyn, 1817). Florida Keys (rare) to West Indies (common) and Brazil.

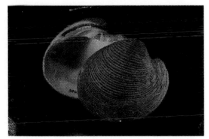

Even-heart Venus (2.5″) 6 cm
Ventricolaria rigida subspecies *isocardia* (Verrill, 1870). W. Mexico to Ecuador. Common.

Youthful Venus (3.5″) 9 cm
Periglypta puerpera (L., 1771). Indo-Pacific. Shallow water to 20 m; locally common.

Reticulate Venus (3.5″) 9 cm
Periglypta reticulata (L., 1758). Indo-Pacific. Shallow water to 20 m; locally common. Syn.: *edmondsoni* D., B. & R.

Crispate Venus (3″) 7.5 cm
Periglypta crispata (Deshayes, 1854). Indo-Pacific. Shallow water; uncommon.

Clathrate Venus (3″) 7.5 cm
Periglypta clathrata (Deshayes, 1853). Indo-Pacific. Shallow water; uncommon.

Chemnitz's Venus (3.5″) 9 cm
Periglypta chemnitzi (Hanley, 1844). Southwestern Pacific. 1 to 20 m; common. Syn.: *fischeri* Récluz.

Scaly-ridged Venus (4″) 10 cm
Circomphalus foliaceolamellosus (Dillwyn, 1817). Western Africa. Shallow water; common.

Script Venus (1.5″) 4 cm
Circe scripta (L., 1758). Indo-Pacific. 1 to 20 m; locally common. Syn.: *personata* Deshayes.

Rivula Venus (1.5″) 4 cm
Circe rivularis (Born, 1778). Western Australia. Shallow water; common.

Freckled Venus (1.5″) 4 cm
Circe lentiginosa (Mörch, 1853). Indian Ocean. Shallow water; uncommon.

Corrugate Venus (1.5″) 4 cm
Circe corrugata (Deshayes, 1853). Red Sea. Shallow water; moderately common.

Crocus Venus (2″) 5 cm
Circe crocea (Hanley, 1843). Red Sea. Sandy bays; locally common.

Pretty-backed Venus (2″) 5 cm
Circe callipyga (Born, 1778). Indian Ocean. Sandy bays; locally common.

Forked Venus (1.5″) 3.5 cm
Gafrarium divaricatum (Gmelin, 1791). Indo-Pacific. Shallow sandy areas; common. Syn.: *aequivoca* Sowerby.

Tumid Venus (1.5″) 3.5 cm
Gafrarium tumidum Röding, 1798. Indo-Pacific. Shallow water to 20 m; common. Syn.: *gibbia* Lamarck.

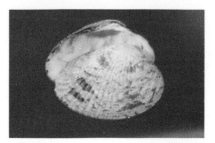

Pectinate Venus (1.5″) 3.5 cm
Gafrarium pectinatum (L., 1758). Indo-Pacific. Shallow sandy areas to 20 m; common.

Mauve Sunetta (2″) 5 cm
Sunetta menstrualis (Menke, 1843). Eastern Asia; Australia. Uncommon. Syn.: *excavata* Hanley; *magnifica* Reeve.

Fossate Sunetta (1.5″) 4 cm
Sunetta effossa (Reeve, 1843). Northwestern Indian Ocean. Shallow water; locally common.

Pure Sunetta   (3") 7 cm
Sunetta meroe (L., 1758). Southeastern Asia and Indian Ocean. Shallow water; common.

Truncate Sunetta   (1.5") 4 cm
Sunetta truncata (Deshayes, 1853). Indian Ocean and southeastern Asia. Shallow water; common.

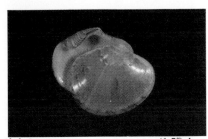

Cleft Sunetta   (1.5") 4 cm
Sunetta vaginalis (Menke, 1843). Western Australia. Shallow water; uncommon.

Solander's Sunetta   (1.5") 4 cm
Sunettina solanderii (Gray, 1825). Indian Ocean and southeastern Asia; Japan. 10 to 50 m; uncommon.

Karachi Sunetta   (2") 5 cm
Sunetta kurachensis Sowerby, 1895. Northwestern Indian Ocean. Shallow water. Locally common.

Poker-chip Venus   (3") 7 cm
Meretrix lusoria (Röding, 1798). Eastern Asia. Shallow water to 20 m; abundant.

Triple Tivela   (1.5") 4 cm
Tivela tripla (L., 1777). Western Africa. Shallow water; moderately common.

Ponderous Tivela   (3") 7.5 cm
Tivela ponderosa (Philippi, 1844). Northwestern Indian Ocean. Shallow water; locally common. Non Schumacher, 1817.

Flattened Tivela   (2") 5 cm
Tivela planulata (Broderip & Sowerby, 1830). W. Mexico to Ecuador. Shallow sandy areas; common.

Byron Tivela   (2") 5 cm
Tivela byronensis (Gray, 1838). W. Mexico to Ecuador. Intertidal beaches to 73 m; common. Syn.: *radiata* Sowerby.

Trigonal Tivela   (1.2") 3 cm
Tivela mactroides (Born, 1778). West Indies to Brazil. Shallow water; common.

Ventricose Tivela   (3") 7.5 cm
Tivela ventricosa (Gray, 1838). Brazil and Uruguay. Shallow sandy areas; common.

Pismo Clam   (5″) 12 cm
Tivela stultorum (Mawe, 1823). California and Baja California. Sandy intertidal flats; common edible species.

Tumid Pitar Venus   (1.5″) 4 cm
Pitar tumens (Gmelin, 1791). Canaries; western Africa. Intertidal sands; locally common.

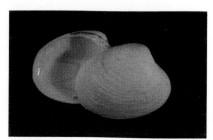

White Pitar Venus   (1.5″) 4 cm
Pitar albidus (Gmelin, 1791). West Indies to Brazil. Shallow water; common.

Prow Pitar Venus   (1.5″) 4 cm
Pitar prora (Conrad, 1837). Southwestern Pacific. Shallow water; common.

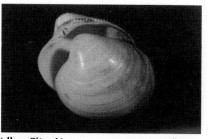

Yellow Pitar Venus   (2″) 5 cm
Pitar citrinus (Lamarck, 1818). Indo-Pacific. Shallow water; common.

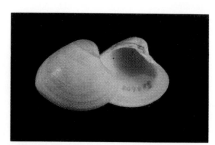

Japanese Pitar Venus   (1.5″) 4 cm
Pitar japonicus Kuroda & Kawamoto, 1956. Offshore, 10 to 50 m; uncommon.

Concise Pitar Venus   (2″) 5 cm
Pitar concinnus (Sowerby, 1835). W. Mexico to Peru. Intertidal to 73 m; common.

Lightning Venus   (1.5″) 4 cm
Pitar fulminatus (Menke, 1828). S.E. United States to Brazil. Shallow water; common.

Schwengel's Venus   (1.5″) 4 cm
Pitar cordatus (Schwengel, 1951). Gulf of Mexico to Brazil. Offshore, 60 to 100 m; locally common.

Simpson's Venus   (0.7″) 1.8 cm
Pitar simpsoni (Dall, 1889). Southern half of Florida and the West Indies. 1 to 40 m; locally common.

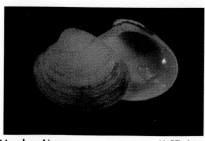

Morrhua Venus   (1.5″) 4 cm
Pitar morrhuanus (Linsley, 1848). Eastern Canada to off North Carolina. 1 to 50 m; common.

Rough Pitar Venus   (1″) 2.5 cm
Pitar rudis (Poli, 1795). Mediterranean to Senegal. Shallow water to 500 m; common.

Wounded Pitar Venus (1.7") 4.5 cm
Pitar vulneratus (Broderip, 1835). W. Mexico to Panama. Intertidal to 15 m; common.

Unicolor Pitar Venus (1.7") 4.5 cm
Pitar unicolor (Sowerby, 1835). W. Mexico to Ecuador. Offshore to 11 m; common.

Curled Pitar Venus (2") 5 cm ·
Pitar circinatus (Born, 1778). West Indies to Brazil. Shallow water; common. Subspecies *alternatus* (Broderip, 1835) from Panama is similar.

Rosy Pitar Venus (1.5") 3.5 cm
Pitar roseus (Broderip & Sowerby, 1829). W. Mexico to Panama. Shallow water to 73 m; common.

Royal Comb Venus (1.5") 4 cm
Pitar dione (L., 1758). West Indies. Subtidal beaches; locally common.

Prostitute Venus (2") 5 cm
Pitar lupanaria (Lesson, 1830). W. Mexico to Peru. Intertidal beaches to 3 m; common.

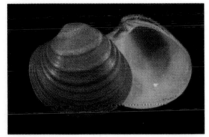

Purple Amiantis (3.2") 8 cm
Amiantis purpurata (Lamarck, 1818). Brazil to Argentina. Intertidal to 2 m; common.

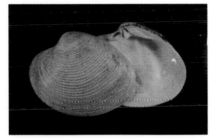

Beauty Amiantis (4") 10 cm
Amiantis callosa (Conrad, 1837). California to W. Mexico. Subtidal to 4 m; common.

Reddish Callista (3") 7.5 cm
Callista erycina (L., 1758). Southwestern Pacific to Japan. 1 to 20 m; moderately common. Syn.: *spuma* Röding.

Lilac Callista (4") 10 cm
Callista erycina form *lilacina* (Lamarck, 1818). Western Australia. Shallow water; common.

Bardwell's Callista (3") 7.5 cm
Callista bardwelli Clench & McLean, 1936. Western Australia. Shallow water; uncommon. Holotype illus.

Planatella Callista (3") 7.5 cm
Paradione planatella (Lamarck, 1818). Indian Ocean. Uncommon. Syn.: *costata* Chemnitz; *nioba* Clench & McLean (holotype illus.).

Grata Callista (3″) 7.5 cm
Callista grata (Deshayes, 1853). East Indies; northern Australia. Shallow sands; uncommon. Syn.: *pectoralis* Sowerby (not Lamarck).

King's Callista (2″) 5 cm
Paradione kingi (Gray, 1827). Eastern and southern Australia. Intertidal to 5 m; common.

Unequal Callista (2″) 5 cm
Callista impar (Lamarck, 1818). Indian Ocean and southwestern Pacific. Shallow, sand areas; common.

Flower Callista (2″) 5 cm
Callista florida (Lamarck, 1818). Indian Ocean. Shallow sandy bays; locally common.

China Callista (2.5″) 6 cm
Callista chinensis (Holten, 1803). Southwestern Pacific. 2 to 50 m; common. Syn.: *sinensis* Sowerby.

Festive Callista (2.5″) 6 cm
Callista chinensis form *festiva* Reeve, 1864. Southwestern Pacific. Smoother form. Common.

Short-snouted Callista (3″) 7.5 cm
Callista brevisiphonata (Carpenter, 1865). Japan. 1 to 30 m; locally common. Syn.: *chishimana* Pilsbry.

Umbo Callista (3″) 7.5 cm
Callista umbonella (Lamarck, 1818). Red Sea and Persian Gulf. Shallow water; common.

Snowy Callista (2.5″) 6 cm
Callista umbonella form *nivea* (Hanley, 1843). Persian Gulf. A white form. Locally common.

Smooth Callista (3″) 7.5 cm
Callista chione (L., 1758). English Channel to Mediterranean. 8 to 100 m; common.

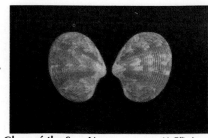

Glory-of-the-Seas Venus (1.5″) 4 cm
Callista eucymata (Dall, 1890). S.E. Florida to Brazil. Offshore 30 to 200 m; uncommon.

Many-rayed Callista (3″) 7.5 cm
Callista multiradiata (Sowerby, 1851). Western Indian Ocean. Shallow water; uncommon.

Sunray Venus   (5″) 12 cm
Macrocallista nimbosa (Lightfoot, 1786).
S.E. United States to Texas. 1 to 30 m; locally abundant.

Calico Clam   (2″) 5 cm
Macrocallista maculata (L., 1758). S.E.
United States to Brazil. 1 to 20 m; locally abundant. Rarely albino.

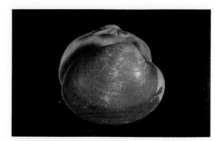

Golden Callista   (4″) 10 cm
Megapitaria aurantiaca (Sowerby, 1831). W.
Mexico to Ecuador. Tidal flats to 10 m; common. Syn.: *aurantia* Sowerby.

Squalid Callista   (4″) 10 cm
Megapitaria squalida (Sowerby, 1835). W.
Mexico to Peru. Sandy mud flats; abundant.

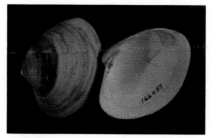

Texas Venus   (3″) 7.5 cm
Agriopoma texasiana (Dall, 1892). N.W.
Florida to northeastern Mexico. 8 to 25 m; moderately common.

Camp Pitar Venus   (1.5″) 3.5 cm
Lioconcha castrensis (L., 1758). Indo-Pacific. Shallow sand flats; common.

Hieroglyphic Venus   (1.5″) 3.5 cm
Lioconcha hieroglyphica (Conrad, 1837).
S.W. and central Pacific. Coral sands; common.

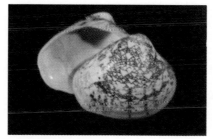

Ornate Pitar Venus   (1″) 2.5 cm
Lioconcha ornata (Lamarck, 1817). Indo-Pacific. Sandy coral areas; common. Syn.:
picta Lamarck.

Lorenz's Pitar Venus   (2″) 5 cm
Lioconcha lorenziana (Dillwyn, 1817). S.W.
Pacific. Muddy sand flats to 20 m; uncommon. Syn.: *hebraea* Sowerby; *sowerbyi*
Deshayes.

Smooth Washington Clam   (4″) 10 cm
Saxidomus gigantea (Deshayes, 1839).
Alaska to California. Common, edible Alaskan seafood.

Common Washington Clam   (4″) 10 cm
Saxidomus nuttalli (Conrad, 1837). California to Baja California. "Butter Clam" is common, edible, intertidal species.

Purple Washington Clam   (4″) 10 cm
Saxidomus nuttalli subspecies *purpuratus*
(Sowerby, 1852). Japan. Intertidal to 20 m;
common.

Tierra del Fuego Venus   (3.5″) 9 cm
Humilaria exalbida (Dillwyn, 1817). Brazil to Argentina. 25 to 70 m; uncommon.

Kennerley's Venus   (3.5″) 9 cm
Humilaria kennerleyi (Reeve, 1863). Alaska to California. 6 to 40 m; locally common.

Samarangia Clam   (2″) 5 cm
Samarangia quadrangularis (Adams & Reeve, 1850). Western Pacific. 10 to 30 m; rare. Shell yellow, smooth under sand coating.

Disk Dosinia   (3″) 7.5 cm
Dosinia discus (Reeve, 1850). S.E. United States and Bahamas. Shallow sand bars; common. 50 ridges per inch.

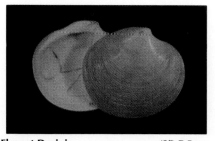

Elegant Dosinia   (3″) 7.5 cm
Dosinia elegans Conrad, 1846. S.E. United States; Caribbean. Shallow water; common. 22 ridges per inch.

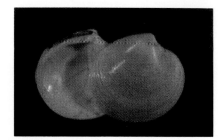

Concentric Dosinia   (3″) 7.5 cm
Dosinia concentrica (Born,1778). Cuba and Mexico to Brazil. Shallow water; common. Syn.: *dosin* Adanson.

Mature Dosinia   (2″) 5 cm
Dosinia exoleta (L., 1758). Norway to western Africa; Mediterranean. Intertidal to 20 m; common. Syn.: *radiata* Reeve.

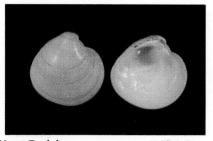

Heart Dosinia   (1.5″) 3.5 cm
Dosinia isocardia (Dunker, 1843). Western Africa. Shallow water; common.

Chinese Dosinia   (3″) 7.5 cm
Dosinia sinensis (Gmelin, 1791). China; southwestern Pacific. Shallow sandy areas to 10 m; common.

Histrio Dosinia   (2.5″) 6 cm
Dosinia histrio (Gmelin, 1791). Southwestern Pacific to Japan. Shallow water to 30 m; common.

Red Sea Dosinia   (2.5″) 6 cm
Dosinia erythraea Romer, 1860. Northwestern Indian Ocean. Shallow water; common.

Lunate Dosinia   (3.5″) 9 cm
Dosinia bilunulata (Gray, 1838). Japan. Subtidal to 50 m; locally common.

Japanese Dosinia (2.5″) 6 cm
Dosinia japonica (Reeve, 1850). Japan. Shallow water to 50 m; common.

Troschel's Dosinia (3″) 7.5 cm
Dosinia troscheli (Lischke, 1873). Japan. 10 to 30 m; common.

Scaled Dosinia (2.5″) 6 cm
Dosinia scalaris (Menke, 1843). Western and southern Australia. Shallow water; common.

Juvenile Dosinia (2″) 5 cm
Dosinia juvenilis (Gmelin, 1791). Philippines and southwestern Pacific. Shallow water; common. Syn.: *juvenis* Dillwyn.

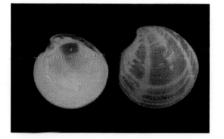

Variegated Dosinia (2″) 5 cm
Dosinia variegata (Gray, 1838). Indian Ocean. Shallow water; uncommon.

Bluish Dosinia (2.5″) 6 cm
Dosinia caerulea (Reeve, 1850). Japan. 10 to 30 m; common.

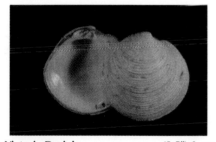

Victoria Dosinia (2.5″) 6 cm
Dosinia victoriae Gatliff & Gabriel, 1914. Victoria and South Australia. Beaches to 80 m; common.

Maori Dosinia (2″) 5 cm
Dosinia maoriana Oliver, 1923. New Zealand. Shallow water; uncommon.

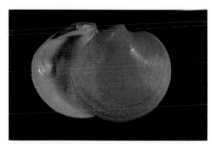

Subrosa Dosinia (2″) 5 cm
Dosinia subrosea (Gray, 1835). New Zealand. Common on beaches to 3 m.

Subrosa Dosinia (2″) 5 cm
Dosinia subrosea (Gray, 1835). New Zealand. Some specimens are white, others pinkish rose. Common.

Old Woman Dosinia (3″) 7 cm
Dosinia anus (Philippi, 1848). New Zealand. Intertidal sand flats to 3 m; common.

Anna's Dosinia (2″) 5 cm
Dosinia semiobliterata Deshayes, 1853. Gulf of California to Panama. Syn.: *annae* Carpenter.

Ponderous Dosinia (6") 15 cm
Dosinia ponderosa (Gray, 1838). W. Mexico to northern Peru. 3 to 60 m; moderately common.

Dunker's Dosinia (2") 5 cm
Dosinia dunkeri (Philippi, 1844). W. Mexico to northern Peru. Intertidal to 55 m; common.

Zealandic Dosinula (2.5") 6 cm
Dosina zelandica Gray, 1835. New Zealand. Mud flats and rubble; common. (Not a *Dosinia*.)

Atlantic Cyclinella (1") 2.5 cm
Cyclinella tenuis (Récluz, 1852). Virginia to Texas to Brazil. 1 to 100 m; common.

Singley's Cyclinella (1.5") 3.5 cm
Cyclinella singleyi Dall, 1902. W. Mexico to Panama. Subtidal in estuaries; common.

Amethyst Gem Clam (0.2") 5 mm
Gemma gemma (Totten, 1834). Eastern Canada to Texas; introduced to Puget Sound, Washington. Common.

Brown Gem Clam (0.2") 5 mm
Parastarte triquetra (Conrad, 1846). Florida to Texas. Intertidal sand bars; common.

Milky Pacific Venus (2") 5 cm
Compsomyax subdiaphana (Carpenter, 1864). Alaska to Gulf of California. In mud, 10 to 50 m; common.

Lettered Venus (3.5") 9 cm
Tapes literatus (L., 1758). Indo-Pacific. Shallow water; locally common. Syn.: *radiata* Gmelin; *punctata* Gmelin. *T. litterata* is misspelling.

Spotted Venus (3.5") 9 cm
Tapes literatus form *guttulatus* Röding, 1798. Indo-Pacific; common. Syn.: *adspersa* Lamarck, 1818.

Turgid Venus (3") 7.5 cm
Tapes dorsatus (Lamarck, 1818). Southwestern Pacific. Shallow water; common. Syn.: *turgida* and *ovulaea* Lamarck.

Arakan Venus (1") 2.5 cm
Timoclea arakana (G. & H. Nevill, 1871). South Africa to Ceylon. Uncommon. Syn.: *arakensis* E. A. Smith; *malonei* Vanatta.

European Aurora Venus (1.5″) 4 cm
Venerupis aurea (Gmelin, 1791). Norway to Mediterranean and Black Sea. Intertidal; abundant. Syn.: *texturata* Lamarck.

Variegate Venus (1.5″) 4 cm
Ruditapes variegatus (Sowerby, 1852). Indo-Pacific. Intertidal; abundant. Syn.: *punicea* and *cinerea* Deshayes.

Rooster Venus (2.5″) 6 cm
Paphia gallus (Gmelin, 1791). Indian Ocean to Australia. Intertidal; common. Syn.: *malabarica* "Chemnitz"; *sinuosa* Lamarck.

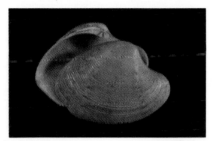

Rooster Venus (2.5″) 6 cm
Paphia gallus form *lentiginosa* (Reeve, 1864). Indian Ocean. Some specimens are spotted.

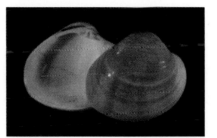

Fertile Venus (2.5″) 6.5 cm
Marcia opima (Gmelin, 1791). Eastern Africa to the East Indies. Intertidal; common. Syn.: *triradiata* Gmelin; *pinguis* Hanley.

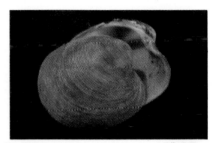

Cor Venus (3″) 7.5 cm
Paphia cor (Sowerby, 1853). Northern Indian Ocean; Persian Gulf. Shallow water; locally common.

Japan Venus (2.5″) 6 cm
Marcia japonica (Gmelin, 1791). Indo-Pacific. Common. Syn.: *striata* Gmelin; *tristis* and *elegantina* Lamarck; *aurisiaca* Wood.

Hiant Venus (2.5″) 6 cm
Marcia hiantina (Lamarck, 1818). Eastern Africa to Australia. Common. Syn.: *rimularis* and *flammiculata* Lamarck; *luzonica* Sowerby.

Scalarina Venus (1.5″) 4 cm
Katelysia scalarina (Lamarck, 1818). Southern Australia and Tasmania. Intertidal; common food. Syn.: *polita* Nielsen, 1964.

Aphrodina Venus (1.5″) 4 cm
Katelysia scalarina form *aphrodina* (Lamarck, 1818). Southern Australia. Sculpture is very variable in this species.

Strigose Venus (1.5″) 4 cm
Katelysia scalarina form *strigosa* (Lamarck, 1818). Some specimens are more elongate than others. Southern Australia

Smoky Venus (1.5″) 4 cm
Eumarcia fumigata (Sowerby, 1853). Southern Australia; Tasmania. Intertidal mud flats; abundant.

Butterfly Venus (3") 7.5 cm
Paphia alapapilionis Röding, 1798. Indian Ocean. Common. Syn.: *papilionacea* Lamarck; *rotundata* Gmelin (not Linné).

Lovely Venus (3") 7.5 cm
Paphia amabilis (Philippi, 1847). Japan and China. 10 to 70 m; uncommon.

Lovely Venus (3") 7.5 cm
Paphia amabilis (Philippi, 1847). Japan and China. Some specimens lack the spottings.

Sulcose Venus (3") 7.5 cm
Paphia crassisulca (Lamarck, 1818). Indian Ocean. Shallow water; uncommon. Syn.: *sulcosa* Philippi; *meroaeformis* Sowerby.

Varnished Venus (3") 7.5 cm
Paphia vernicosa (Gould, 1861). Japan and China. Offshore to 50 m; uncommon. Syn.: *graeffei* Dunker.

Equilateral Venus (3") 7.5 cm
Gomphina aequilatera (Sowerby, 1825). Eastern Asia; Japan. Common. Syn.: *melanaegis* Romer; *veneriformis* Lamarck of authors.

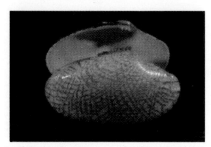

Undulating Venus (3") 7.5 cm
Paphia undulata (Born, 1778). Red Sea to Australia and Japan. Common. Syn.: *scordalus* Iredale.

Textile Venus (3") 7.5 cm
Paphia textile (Gmelin, 1791). Eastern Africa to S.W. Pacific; Japan. Shallow mudflats. Syn.: *textrix* Chemnitz.

Well-carved Venus (3") 7.5 cm
Paphia euglypta (Philippi, 1847). Japan. 10 to 40 m; common. Syn.: *lischkei* Fischer & Metivier, 1971?

Dura Venus (2.5") 6 cm
Venerupis dura (Gmelin, 1791). Morocco to Angola. Intertidal; common. Syn.: *rariflamma* Lamarck.

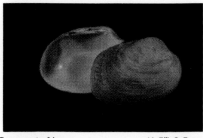

Corrugate Venus (1.5") 3.5 cm
Venerupis corrugata (Gmelin, 1791). Western Africa to Natal, South Africa. Intertidal; common. Syn.: *dactyloides* Sowerby.

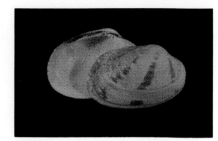

Pullet Venus (1.5") 3.5 cm
Venerupis corrugata subspecies *pullastra* (Montagu, 1803). Norway to N.W. Africa. Intertidal; common. Syn.: *senegalensis* Gmelin.

Decussate Venus (2″) 5 cm
Venerupis decussata (L., 1758). British Isles to Mediterranean. Intertidal; common. Syn.: *reticulata* da Costa.

Filipino Venus (2″) 5 cm
Ruditapes philippinarum (Adams & Reeve, 1850). S.E. Asia; introduced to Hawaii and Pacific United States. Intertidal; abundant.

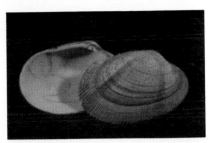

Filipino Venus (2″) 5 cm
Ruditapes philippinarum (Adams & Reeve, 1850). Many color variations. Syn.: *indica* Sowerby; *violascens* Deshayes; *semidecussata* Reeve.

Milky Venus (1.5″) 4 cm
Venerupis galactites (Lamarck, 1818). Southern half of Australia. Intertidal; common.

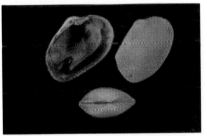

Gray Venus (1.5″) 4 cm
Irus griseus (Lamarck, 1818). Southern Australia and Tasmania. Offshore; uncommon. Syn.: *diemenensis* Quoy & Gaimard.

Reflexed Venus (1″) 2.5 cm
Irus reflexus (Gray, 1843). New Zealand. Rock crevices at low-tide zone; common. Syn.: *siliqua* Deshayes.

Elegant Venus (1.5″) 3.5 cm
Irus elegans (Deshayes, 1853). New Zealand. In soft rocks at low-tide zone; common.

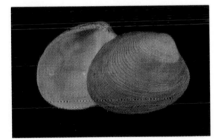

Largilliert's Venus (3″) 7.5 cm
Ruditapes largillierti (Philippi, 1847). New Zealand and Tasmania. Common. Syn.: *intermedia* Quoy & Gaimard.

Californian Irus Venus (1″) 2.5 cm
Irus lamellifera (Conrad, 1837). Monterey to San Diego, California. In soft shale, subtidal; common.

Stutchbury's Venus (2.5″) 6.5 cm
Chione stutchburyi (Wood, 1828). New Zealand. Intertidal mud flats; common.

Cross-barred Venus (1.3″) 3 cm
Chione cancellata (L., 1758). S.E. United States to Brazil. Intertidal to 20 m; abundant. Rarely rose inside.

Cross-barred Venus (1.3″) 3 cm
Chione cancellata (L., 1758). This West Indian form is larger and more colorful. Syn.: *subrostrata* Lamarck.

Crass Venus (1") 2.5 cm
Chione crassa (Quoy & Gaimard, 1835).
New Zealand. Offshore, 2 to 36 m; uncommon.

Smooth Pacific Venus (2.5") 6.5 cm
Chione fluctifraga (Sowerby, 1853). San Pedro, California, to W. Mexico. Intertidal; common.

Frilled California Venus (2.5") 6.5 cm
Chione undatella (Sowerby, 1835). San Pedro, California, to Peru. Shallow sand flats; common.

Common Californian Venus (2.5") 6.5 cm
Chione californiensis (Broderip, 1853). Southern California to Panama. Intertidal sands; common. Syn.: *succinctus* Valenciennes.

Kellett's Panama Venus (1.5") 3.5 cm
Chione kellettii (Hinds, 1845). W. Mexico to northern Peru. Offshore, 46 to 73 m; moderately common.

Gnidia Venus (3.5") 9 cm
Chione gnidia (Broderip & Sowerby, 1829). W. Mexico to Peru. Intertidal to 33 m; common.

Partially-rough Venus (1.7") 4.5 cm
Anomalocardia subrugosa (Wood, 1828). West Mexico to Peru. Intertidal mud flats; abundant food clam.

Imperial Venus (1") 2.5 cm
Chione latilirata (Conrad, 1841). S.E. United States to Brazil. Offshore to 40 m; common.

King Venus (1.5") 3.5 cm
Chione paphia (L., 1767). West Indies to Brazil. Shallow water; moderately common.

Clench's Venus (1") 2.5 cm
Chione clenchi Pulley, 1952. Texas to northeastern Mexico. Offshore to 60 m; uncommon.

Australian Chicken Venus (1.5") 3.5 cm
Tawera gallinula (Lamarck, 1818). South Australia. Intertidal to 40 m; common. Sometimes all white.

Squamose Venus (1") 2.5 cm
Anomalocardia squamosa (L., 1758). Indo-Pacific. Muddy sand flats; common.

Half-imbricate Venus (1.5″) 3.5 cm
Chione subimbricata (Sowerby, 1835). W. Mexico to northern Peru. Intertidal sand flats; common.

Projecting Venus (1″) 2.5 cm
Anomalocardia producta Kuroda & Habe, 1951. Japan to southeastern Asia. Intertidal; common. Syn.: *impressa* Anton.

West Indian Pointed Venus (1″) 2.5 cm
Anomalocardia brasiliana (Gmelin, 1791). West Indies to Brazil. Shallow water; common.

Wedding Cake Venus (2.5″) 6 cm
Callanaitis disjecta (Perry, 1811). South Australia; Tasmania. Subtidal to 48 m; moderately common. Syn.: *lamellata* Lamarck.

Wooden Venus (1.3″) 3 cm
Bassina calophylla (Philippi, 1836). Northern Australia; East Indies. Offshore to 20 m; uncommon.

Yate's Venus (2″) 5 cm
Bassina yatei (Gray, 1835). New Zealand. Sandy beach flats; common.

Tiara Venus (1.5″) 3.5 cm
Placamen tiara (Dillwyn, 1817). Indo-Pacific. Subtidal to 50 m; moderately common. Syn.: *foliacea* Philippi.

Flowery Venus (1.5″) 3.5 cm
Clausinella chlorotica (Philippi, 1849). Philippines and Indonesia. Shallow bays; uncommon.

Isabelle's Gray Venus (1.5″) 3.5 cm
Clausinella isabellina (Philippi, 1849). Southwestern Pacific. Shallow sand flats; uncommon.

Heavy Venus (1.5″) 3.5 cm
Clausinella gravescens (Menke, 1843). East Indies and Philippines. Shallow bays; uncommon.

Striated Venus (1.5″) 3.5 cm
Chamelea striatula (da Costa, 1778). Norway to northwestern Africa. Intertidal to offshore; common.

Thaca Venus (3″) 7 cm
Protothaca thaca (Molina, 1782). Peru to Chile. Lower intertidal flats; common. Syn.: *dombeii* Lamarck.

Northern Quahog (3.5") 9 cm
Mercenaria mercenaria (L., 1758). Eastern Canada to Georgia. Lagoons; common. Small ones called "cherrystones." Sides smooth.

Southern Quahog (4") 10 cm
Mercenaria campechiensis (Gmelin, 1791). Georgia, Florida, northwestern Cuba. Common, inshore waters. Sides rough.

Texas Quahog (3.5") 9 cm
Mercenaria mercenaria subspecies *texana* (Dall, 1902). Northern Gulf of Mexico. Shallow lagoons; common.

Brazilian Comb Venus (1.5") 4 cm
Protothaca pectorina (Lamarck, 1818). Lower Caribbean to Brazil. Intertidal; common.

Heavy-ribbed Venus (2") 5 cm
Protothaca crassicosta (Deshayes, 1835). New Zealand. Intertidal sand flats; common.

Thin-shelled Littleneck (3") 7.5 cm
Protothaca tenerrima (Carpenter, 1856). Western Canada to W. Mexico. Intertidal to 3 m; common.

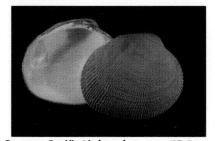

Common Pacific Littleneck (2") 5 cm
Protothaca staminea (Conrad, 1837). Alaska to Baja California. Beach flats; abundant. Rarely mottled.

Jedo Venus (2.5") 6 cm
Protothaca jedoensis (Lischke, 1874). Japan; Korea; northwestern China. Intertidal to 20 m; common. Syn.: *hirasei* Pilsbry.

Beaded Venus (1.3") 3 cm
Protothaca granulata (Gmelin, 1791). West Indies. Muddy sand flats; common.

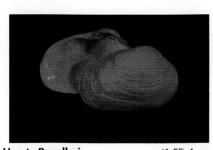

Monstrous Petricola (1") 2.5 cm
Petricola monstrosa (Gmelin, 1791). South Africa. Boring in shale; uncommon. Rare in collections.

Hearty Rupellaria (1.5") 4 cm
Rupellaria carditoides (Conrad, 1837). Western Canada to Baja California. Bores in hard rock; common.

False Angel Wing (2") 5 cm
Petricola pholadiformis (Lamarck, 1818). Eastern Canada to Uruguay; Norway to Black Sea. Bores in intertidal peat; common.

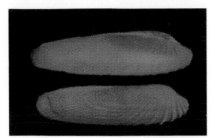

Parallel Petricola   (2.5") 6 cm
Petricola parallela Pilsbry & Lowe, 1932. W. Mexico to Nicaragua. Intertidal to 15 m; common.

Atlantic Rupellaria   (1") 2.5 cm
Rupellaria typica (Jonas, 1844). Southeastern United States to Brazil. Bores in coral; common.

Conrad's False Mussel   (0.7") 1.8 cm
Mytilopsis leucophaeata (Conrad, 1831). New York to eastern Mexico. Brackish water; common. Family Dreissenidae.

SOFT-SHELL CLAMS
FAMILY MYIDAE

This family includes the popular American soft-shell or "steamer" clam which has a thin, brittle shell. The two siphons are welded into one thick tube. The hinge has a spoon-shaped shelf in the left valve. The clams live in mud several centimeters below the surface.

Soft-shell Clam   (3.5") 9 cm
Mya arenaria L., 1758. Eastern Canada to North Carolina; N.W. United States. Mud flats, intertidal; common. Popular seafood.

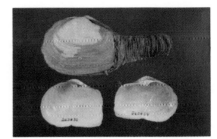

Truncate Soft-shell Clam   (2.5") 6 cm
Mya truncata L., 1758. Arctic seas to western Europe; N.E. United States; Alaska to Washington. 1 to 10 m; common.

California Glass Mya   (1") 2.5 cm
Cryptomya californica (Conrad, 1837). Alaska to northern Peru. Live next to worm and crab burrows. Common.

Chubby Mya   (2.5") 6 cm
Platyodon cancellatus (Conrad, 1837). Western Canada to California. Burrows in hard-packed clays in shallow water; moderately common.

African Duck Clam   (1.5") 3.5 cm
Tugonia anatina (Gmelin, 1791). Western Africa. Shallow water in mud; uncommon in collections.

CORBULA CLAMS
FAMILY CORBULIDAE

These small, thick-shelled clams usually have a smaller and flatter left valve which fits snugly into the larger right valve. The resilium and ligament are set in a spoon-shaped pocket. There are many species, most found offshore in sandy bottoms.

Sulcate Corbula   (0.5") 1.2 cm
Corbula sulcata Lamarck, 1801. Western Africa. Offshore to 20 m; locally common.

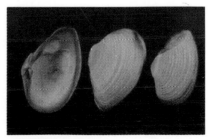

Red-toothed Corbula   (0.5") 1.2 cm
Corbula erythrodon Lamarck, 1818. Northeastern Asia; Japan. Offshore to 20 m; common.

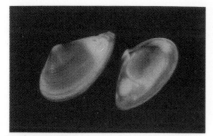

Ovulate Corbula   (1") 2.5 cm
Corbula ovulata Sowerby, 1833. W. Mexico to Peru. Sand areas, 2 to 55 m; common.

Dietz's Corbula   (0.5") 1.2 cm
Corbula dietziana C. B. Adams, 1852. S.E. United States to Brazil. Offshore from 2 to 50 m; common.

Swift's Corbula   (0.3") 7 mm
Corbula swiftiana C. B. Adams, 1852. Northeastern United States to Texas and West Indies. Offshore; common.

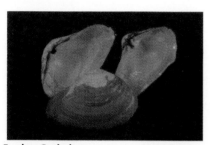

Erodon Corbula   (1") 2.5 cm
Erodona mactroides (Bosc, 1802). Brazil to Argentina. Muddy bottoms in brackish water; common.

ROCK-BORER CLAMS
FAMILY GASTROCHAENIDAE

This is a small family of rock- and coral-boring clams, lacking hinge teeth, and having a large foot that makes the valves widely gape. The siphons produce calcareous tubes that protrude from the substrate.

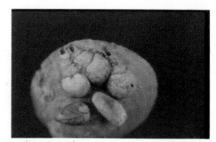

Bowl-Boring Clam   (0.5") 1.2 cm
Gastrochaena cymbium Spengler, 1783. Indo-Pacific. Bores into shells and makes surface tubes. Rare. Syn.: *lagenula* Lamarck.

Cuneiform Clam   (1") 2.5 cm
Gastrochaena cuneiformis Spengler, 1783. Indo-Pacific. Bores into Porites corals; common. Syn.: *gigantea* Deshayes; *hawaiiensis* D., B. & R.

Atlantic Rocellaria   (0.7") 1.8 cm
Rocellaria hians (Gmelin, 1791). S.E. United States to Brazil. Bores into corals; common.

Atlantic Spengler Clam   (1") 2.5 cm
Spengleria rostrata (Spengler, 1783). S.E. Florida to Brazil. Bores in soft coral rock; uncommon.

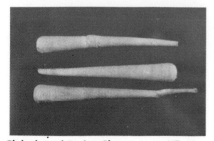

Club-shaped Boring Clam   (4") 10 cm
Eufistulana mumia (Spengler, 1783). East Indies and Philippines. Rare. Valves inside tube. Syn.: *clava* Gmelin.

SAXICAVE and
PANOPE CLAMS
FAMILY HIATELLIDAE

Shells small to very large, white, with weak hinge, and with long siphons. Brown ligament external. Usually cold-water and deep mud inhabitants. Famous Geoduck Clam of America is favorite food.

Arctic Saxicave   (1") 2.5 cm
Hiatella arctica (L., 1767). Arctic seas to deep, cold water in Caribbean and to off Panama. Variable shapes; common.

Atlantic Geoduck (5") 12.5 cm
Panopea bitruncata Conrad, 1872. (Pronounced "goo-ee-duk.") S.E. United States. Intertidal to 50 m; locally uncommon, deep in mud.

Pacific Geoduck (9") 23 cm
Panopea generosa (Gould, 1850). Alaska to Gulf of California. Intertidal to 10 m, in deep mud; locally common. *Panope* is misspelling.

European Panopea (9") 23 cm
Panopea glycymeris (Born, 1778). Mediterranean; N.W. Africa. 10 to 100 m; uncommon in collections. Syn.: *aldrovandi* Menard.

South American Panopea (4") 10 cm
Panopea abbreviata Valenciennes, 1839. Brazil to Antarctic. 25 to 75 m; Syn.: *antarctica* Gould.

Mrs. Smith's Panopea (4") 10 cm
Panopea smithae Powell, 1950. New Zealand. Offshore to 150 m; uncommon.

New Zealand Panopea (3") 7.5 cm
Panopea zelandica (Quoy & Gaimard, 1835). Intertidal sand flats to 20 m; uncommon.

Priapus Panopea (4") 10 cm
Panomya priapus (Tilesius, 1822). Arctic seas; Alaska. Deep water. Syn.: *beringiana* Dall (holotype illustrated).

PHOLADS and PIDDOCKS
FAMILY PHOLADIDAE

A worldwide, abundant group of clams that burrow into mud, clay, wood and hard rock. Pholad clams have external accessory plates. Under the beaks of the valves is a pair of shelly projections, or apophyses. The Angel Wing of Florida may live as deep as 3 feet in the mud. *Martesia* is found in floating wood.

European Piddock (4") 10 cm
Pholas dactylus L., 1758. Western Europe; Mediterranean. Bores in sandstone; common.

Campeche Angel Wing (3.5") 9 cm
Pholas campechiensis Gmelin, 1791. S.E. United States to Texas and to Brazil. Subtidal in mud or rotten wood; uncommon.

Fallen Angel Wing (2") 5 cm
Barnea truncata (Say, 1822). Eastern United States to Brazil; Senegal to Gold Coast. In peat and clay, intertidal; common.

White Piddock (2.5") 6 cm
Barnèa candida (L., 1758). Norway to Mediterranean; Black Sea. In peat and clay; common.

Angel Wing (6") 15 cm
Cyrtopleura costata (L., 1758). Eastern U.S. to Brazil. In mud, as deep as two feet; locally common. Rarely pink-stained.

Wart-necked Piddock (3") 7.5 cm
Chaceia ovoidea (Gould, 1851). Central California to W. Mexico. In soft shale, 20 inches deep; common. Siphon has orange warts.

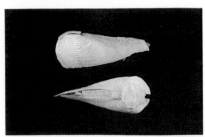

Striate Martesia (1") 2.5 cm
Martesia striata (L., 1758). S.E. United States to Brazil; W. Mexico to Peru. In floating wood; common.

PANDORA CLAMS
FAMILY PANDORIDAE

Very compressed, flat clams with a pearly interior. The hinge has one or two internal ribs, rather than teeth. Top edge of one valve overlaps the other. Several dozen species, mostly cold-water dwellers.

Say's Pandora (1") 2.5 cm
Pandora trilineata Say, 1822. North Carolina to Texas. Subtidal to 120 m; moderately common.

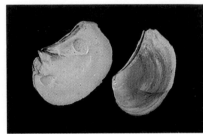

Gould's Pandora (1.5") 4 cm
Pandora gouldiana Dall, 1886. Eastern Canada to off North Carolina. Intertidal to 200 m; common.

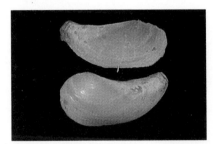

Unequal Pandora (1") 2.5 cm
Pandora inaequivalvis (L., 1758). England to Mediterranean. Intertidal to 5 m; common. Syn.: *margaritacea* Lamarck.

Punctate Pandora (1.5") 4 cm
Pandora punctata Conrad, 1837. Western Canada to Baja California. Intertidal to 40 m; common.

Grand Pandora (2") 5 cm
Pandora grandis Dall, 1877. Alaska to Oregon. Offshore, 100 m; uncommon. Holotype illustrated.

LANTERN CLAMS
FAMILY LATERNULIDAE

These mud-dwellers have very delicate, pearly shells, usually fat and elongate. Most of the dozen-or-so species live in tropical seas in shallow water. The shells gape at the hind end, and the umbones have an external slit. There are no teeth in the hinge.

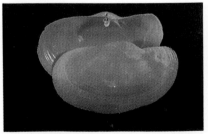

Truncate Lantern Clam (3.5") 9 cm
Laternula truncata (Lamarck, 1818). Indian Ocean and southwestern Pacific. Common. Syn.: *rostrata* Lamarck.

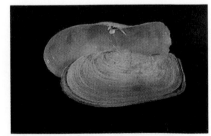

Duck Lantern Clam (3") 7.5 cm
Laternula anatina (L., 1758). Indian Ocean. Shallow mud areas; common.

LYONSIA CLAMS
FAMILY LYONSIIDAE

These strange little clams have weakly pearlized shells with no hinge teeth. Under the hinge is a loose, shelly plate, or tooth, called a lithodesma. *Lyonsia* live in mud, while *Entodesma* may spin a nest or live within sponges and tunicates (sea squirts).

Pearly Lyonsia (1") 2.5 cm
Entodesma beana (Orbigny, 1842). S.E. United States to Brazil. Lives within sponges in shallow water. Uncommon.

Northwest Ugly Clam (4") 10 cm
Entodesma saxicolum Baird, 1863. Alaska to California. Found in rock crevices and holes; common.

FALSE CHAMAS
FAMILY MYOCHAMIDAE

These odd clams are mostly limited to the Australasian area. They are very compressed, somewhat pearly, usually triangular in shape, without hinge teeth, but have a free, stony lithodesma. Some species have the right valve cemented to other shells or to rocks.

Striate Myadora (1.5") 3.5 cm
Myadora striata (Quoy & Gaimard, 1835). New Zealand. Intertidal sand flats to 20 m; common.

FALSE OYSTERS
FAMILY CLEIDOTHAERIDAE

Members of this unique group of clams superficially look like oysters. They are pearly inside and the irregular right valve is cemented to rocks. There is a single, large tooth in the left valve. A lithodesma is present. The siphons are very short and separate. Limited to the Australian region.

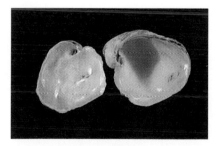

White False Oyster (2.5") 6 cm
Cleidothaerus albidus (Lamarck, 1819). Tasmania; southern Australia. Subtidal on rocks to 45 m; locally common.

SPOON CLAMS
FAMILY PERIPLOMATIDAE

Widely distributed in many parts of the world in shallow seas, the *Periploma* clams are slightly pearly, fragile, with one convex and one flat valve, and without hinge teeth. A resilium rests in two spoon-shaped chondrophores.

Unequal Spoon Clam (0.8") 2 cm
Periploma margaritaceum (Lamarck, 1801). South Carolina to Texas. Intertidal sand flats; common. Syn.: *inequale* C. B. Adams.

Lea's Spoon Clam (1") 2.5 cm
Periploma leanum (Conrad, 1831). Nova Scotia to North Carolina. Offshore to 50 m; common.

Round Spoon Clam (1.5") 3.5 cm
Periploma discus Stearns, 1890. Southern California and W. Mexico. Offshore in mud bottoms; uncommon.

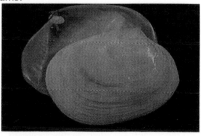

Western Spoon Clam (1.5") 3.5 cm
Periploma planiusculum (Sowerby, 1834). California to Peru. Subtidal to 20 m; common.

THRACIA CLAMS
FAMILY THRACIIDAE

Most of these cold-water clams are porcelaneous, white, smoothish, or with a chalky granular surface. There are no teeth in the hinge, but there is a spoon-shaped chondrophore pointing obliquely towards the back. Fewer than 50 known living species.

Angas's Spoon Clam   (3") 7.5 cm
Periploma angasi Crosse & Fischer, 1864. Southern half of Australia. Shallow water; uncommon.

Conrad's Thracia   (3") 7.5 cm
Thracia conradi Couthouy, 1838. Eastern Canada to New York. Subtidal to 300 m, 6 inches in mud; locally common.

Corbuloid Thracia   (2") 5 cm
Thracia corbuloides Blainville, 1825. Mediterranean. 4 to 8 m, in sand; common.

Pubescent Thracia   (2.3") 6 cm
Thracia pubescens (Pulteney, 1799). N.W. Europe to western Africa; Mediterranean. Intertidal to offshore; common.

Wavy Pacific Thracia   (1.5") 3.5 cm
Cyathodonta undulata Conrad, 1849. California to Baja California. Shallow water; uncommon.

CUSPIDARIA CLAMS
FAMILY CUSPIDARIIDAE

Small deep-water clams having a long extension of the back end to accommodate the siphons. External ligament elongated. Resilium in a small, spoon-shaped fossette. Numerous species.

Glacial Cuspidaria   (1.3") 3 cm
Cuspidaria glacialis (G. O. Sars, 1878). Arctic seas to northern North America and northern Europe. 70 to 2,000 m; common.

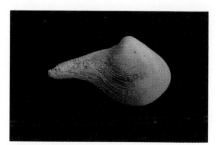

Rostrate Cuspidaria   (1") 2.5 cm
Cuspidaria rostrata (Spengler, 1793). Arctic seas to the West Indies. Offshore from 100 to 2,000 m; uncommon.

Noble Cuspidaria   (1.5") 4 cm
Cuspidaria nobilis (A. Adams, 1864). Offshore from 50 to 200 m; moderately common.

Panama Cuspidaria   (1") 2.5 cm
Cuspidaria panamensis Dall, 1908. Gulf of Panama. 1,100 m; rare in collections. Holotype illustrated.

VERTICORD CLAMS
FAMILY VERTICORDIIDAE

A curious group of deep-water clams having a pearly interior, usually finely ribbed, with the beaks rolled forward above a deep lunular indentation. Ligament internal, supported by a lithodesma. Numerous species.

Sharp-ribbed Verticord   (0.5″) 1.2 cm
Verticordia acuticostata (Philippi, 1884). Off southern Florida and the West Indies. Deep water; uncommon.

Most Elegant Euciroa   (1.5″) 4 cm
Euciroa elegantissima (Dall, 1881). Off S.E. United States and Cuba in 300 to 1,500 m; rare.

Galathea Euciroa   (1.5″) 4 cm
Euciroa galatheae Dell, 1956. New Zealand. Deep water; rare.

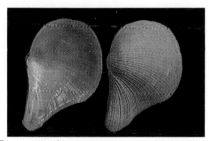

Rostrate Euciroa   (1.5″) 4 cm
Acreuciroa rostrata (Thiele & Jaekel, 1931). Japan. Deep water. Syn.: *teramachii* Kuroda.

Gould's Halicardia   (1.3″) 3 cm
Halicardia gouldi Dall, Bartsch & Rehder, 1938. Hawaii. Deep water; rare. Holotype illustrated.

WATERING POT CLAMS
FAMILY CLAVAGELLIDAE

Resembling shelly worm tubes with a watering pot spout, these strange bivalves begin life as normally shaped clams, but soon grow long tubes as they grow deeper into the sandy bottom. Some grow in small heaps.

Austral Clavagella   (1.5″) 4 cm
Clavagella australis Sowerby, 1829. East Indies; Indian Ocean. Uncommon.

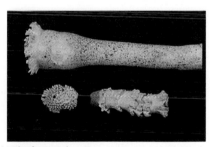

Vaginal Watering Pot   (8″) 20 cm
Brechites attrahens (Lightfoot, 1786). Indian Ocean; East Indies. Syn.: *Aspergillum* and *Penicillus vaginiferus* Lamarck. Common in muddy sand.

Giant Watering Pot   (12″) 30 cm
Brechites giganteus (Sowerby, 1888). Southern Japan. Buried in sand, 40 to 50 m; locally common.

Ramose Watering Pot   (4″) 10 cm
Brechites ramosus (Dunker, 1882). Eastern Asia. Offshore, 10 to 155 m; uncommon.

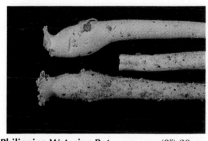

Philippine Watering Pot   (8″) 20 cm
Brechites strangulatus Chenu, 1843. Japan to Australia. Common. Syn.: *clavatus* and *zebuensis* Chenu.

Common Watering Pot   (5″) 12 cm
Brechites penis (L., 1758). Indian Ocean to East Indies. Common. Syn.: *javanus* Bruguière; *aquaria* Burrow; *annulosus* Reeve.

CLASS CEPHALOPODA

Includes the octopuses, squids, as well as the forms with shells, such as the Nautilus, *Spirula* and *Sepia* squids. There are about 650 living species, most being oceanic squids, many of which are used for bait and food. All have a parrotlike beak and radular teeth. Only shelled forms are mentioned here.

PAPER NAUTILUS
FAMILY ARGONAUTIDAE

The thin, parchmentlike, white shell of this relative of the octopus is actually a cradle secreted by two of the animal's arms for the purpose of protecting its tiny eggs. Argonauts live in the open warm seas of the world. There are fewer than a dozen species.

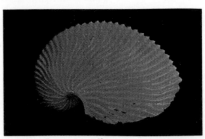

Common Paper Nautilus   (8") 20 cm
Argonauta argo L., 1758. Warm worldwide seas; pelagic. Common seasonally. Males have no shell.

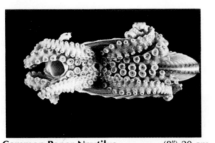

Common Paper Nautilus   (8") 20 cm
Argonauta argo L., 1758. Under view showing 8 tentacles. After eggs hatch, female dies and sheds "cradle."

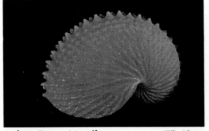

Nodose Paper Nautilus   (5") 13 cm
Argonauta nodosa Lightfoot, 1786. Indo-Pacific. Cool oceanic seas. Locally common.

Brown Paper Nautilus   (1.5") 4 cm
Argonauta hians Lightfoot, 1786. Warm Pacific and Atlantic oceanic seas. Uncommon.

Brown Paper Nautilus   (1.5") 4 cm
Argonauta hians Lightfoot, 1786. Some specimens have smaller and more numerous nodules. Rare.

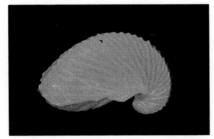

Noury's Paper Nautilus   (1.5") 4 cm
Argonauta nouryi Lorois, 1852. Baja California to Peru; uncommonly washed ashore.

Gruner's Paper Nautilus   (1.5") 4 cm
Argonauta gruneri Dunker, 1852. Southwestern Pacific. May be extreme form of *nouryi*.

SEPIA SQUIDS
FAMILY SEPIIDAE

Also known as cuttlefish and well known in Europe and the Orient as a popular seafood, the internal chalky pens of these squids are found in shell collections and are used in domestic birdcages as a source of lime. Squids give off a brown sepia ink. Our measurements refer to the interior cuttlebone.

Common Cuttlefish   (5") 12 cm
Sepia officinalis L., 1758. Mediterranean; western Europe. Inshore oceanic waters; abundant.

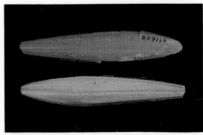

Common Cuttlefish   (2") 60 cm
Sepia officinalis L., 1758. Head bears 8 arms and 2 tentacles. Can change colors. In order Sepioidea. Photo by Raymon Hixon.

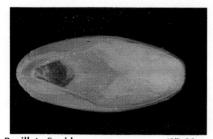

Papillate Squid   (8") 20 cm
Sepia papillata Quoy & Gaimard, 1832. Indian Ocean; South Africa. Open pelagic conditions; common.

SPIRULAS
FAMILY SPIRULIDAE

The small, attractive coiled white shells, resembling rams' horns, found on many tropical beaches, are the internal brace for a small deepsea squid, the *Spirula*. Each of its tiny, pearly chambers contains gas. When the squid dies and its flesh rots, the shell floats to the surface of the ocean and is washed ashore.

Common Spirula   (1") 2.5 cm
Spirula spirula (L., 1758). Worldwide, warm seas, living at depths of 1,000 m; dead shells on beaches. Common.

CHAMBERED NAUTILUS
FAMILY NAUTILIDAE

Once dominating the ancient seas of the world, the genus *Nautilus* is now limited to fewer than a half dozen living species, all found in the southwestern Pacific. Dead shells float as far away as East Africa and Japan. The animal has about 90 tentacles. The chambers are filled with gas and keep the creature balanced in midwater.

Chambered Nautilus   (6") 15 cm
Nautilus pompilius L., 1758. Philippines and Palau Islands, living colonies. Floating dead shells elsewhere. Syn.: *repertus* Iredale.

Chambered Nautilus   (6") 15 cm
Nautilus pompilius L., 1758. A sectioned shell showing the internal chambers.

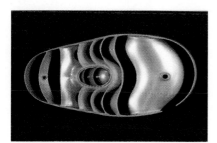

Chambered Nautilus   (6") 15 cm
Nautilus pompilius L., 1758. A specimen sectioned in another plane, showing the hole through which a blood tube runs.

New Caledonia Nautilus   (7") 18 cm
Nautilus macromphalus Sowerby, 1849. New Caledonia. Locally common in offshore waters.

Umbilicate Nautilus   (7") 18 cm
Nautilus scrobiculatus Lightfoot, 1786. New Guinea and Solomon Islands. Uncommon. Syn.: *umbilicata* Sowerby.

Doubtful Squid   (6") 15 cm
Sepia incerta E. A. Smith, 1916. South Africa. Inshore water; uncommon.

Plee's Arrow Squid   (8") 20 cm
Doryteuthis pleii (Blainville, 1823). S.E. United States to Brazil; Bermuda. Lives near surface of open ocean; common. In order Teuthoidea. Photo by Roger T. Hanlon.

Briar Octopus   (12") 30 cm
Octopus briareus Robson, 1929. S.E. United States and West Indies. Intertidal under rocks; common. In order Octopoda. Photo by Roger T. Hanlon.

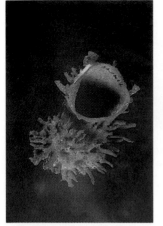

Turbo-shaped Hydroid (3") 7 cm *Hydactinia echinata* (Fleming, 1828). Arctic and Boreal seas. A colony of hydroid animals. A hermit crab lives inside.

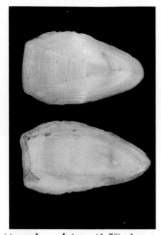

Mesoplax plates, (1.5") 4 cm long, of the boring bivalve, *Pholas orientalis* Gmelin, 1791.

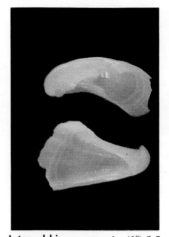

Internal hinge supports, (1") 2.5 cm, of the Florida Angel Wings, *Cyrtopleura costata* (L., 1758). Once described as a *Crepidula.*

An immature **"bulla"** stage of the cowrie, *Cypraea tigris* L., 1758. (1") 2.5 cm. When mature, the lip thickens with teeth.

An immature stage of the **Bullmouth Helmet,** *Cypraecassis rufa* (L., 1758). (2") 5 cm. Adults, 3 times as large, have thick lips.

Young stage of the **Common Spider Conch,** *Lambis lambis* (L., 1758). (2") 5 cm. Adults have large projections on the outer lip.

Young stage of the **Pelican's Foot,** *Aporrhais pespelecani* (L., 1758) from Europe. (1") 2.5 cm. Adults have flaring lip with spines.

Worm tube of cemented sand grains produced by the polychaete worm, *Pectinaria.* (2") 5 cm. Tropical shallow water in sand.

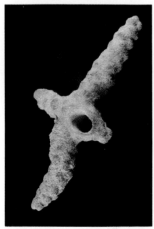

Texas Longhorn, a colony of the bryozoan *Hippoporidra edax* (Busk). (3") 7 cm. Gulf of Mexico. Starts on tiny dead gastropod shell; inhabited by hermit crab.

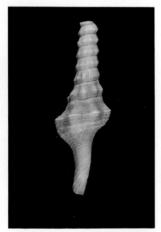

Young stage of **Australian Trumpet,** *Syrinx aruanus* (L., 1758). (1.5") 4 cm. Early whorls developed in egg capsule. Adult shell up to (30") 80 cm.

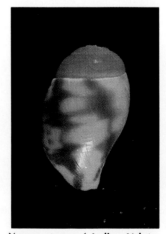

Young stage of **Indian Volute,** *Melo melo* (Lightfoot, 1786), recently hatched. (1.3") 3 cm. Southwestern Pacific. Adults reach (10") 25 cm.

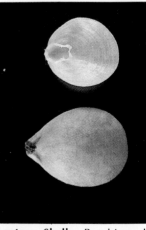

Lantern Shells. Brachiopod, *Terebratulina species.* Hole accommodates wormlike stalk. Live in sand offshore; world seas. (1.5") 4 cm. Many species.

TAXONOMIC CLASSIFICATION OF MOLLUSCA WITH MAJOR BIBLIOGRAPHIC REFERENCES

This is an outline classification of the Mollusca down to the family level with the major genera included. At various levels we have cited current works that are useful for further information on various groups. From the references given here the reader may acquire all information relating to dates, authors, generic and subgeneric groups, and geographical data of species not included in this book. Groups with an asterisk (*) are not included in this edition.

MAJOR BIBLIOGRAPHIC SOURCES

Paetel, Fr. 1887-1891. *Catalog der Conchylien—Sammlung von Fr. Paetel.* Berlin. 2 vols., 1,476 pp. Species arranged phylogenetically. No dates.

Ruhoff, Florence A. 1980. *Index to the Species of Mollusca Introduced from 1850 to 1870.* Smithsonian Contributions to Zoology, no. 294, 640 pp. Washington, D.C.

Sherborn, C. D. 1902, 1922. *Index Animalium.* Cambridge, and British Museum, London. Alphabetical list of all animals described from 1758 to 1800 (First Section) and 1801 to 1850 (Second Section). Gives authors, dates, and references.

Wagner, R. J. L. and R. T. Abbott. 1978. *Standard Catalog of Shells.* 400 pp. (with supplements). American Malacologists, Inc., Box 2255, Melbourne, Florida 32901. Gives species, authors, dates, ranges of many major groups of marine mollusks.

The Zoological Record. Section 9 on *Mollusca.* Zoological Society of London, Regent's Park, London NW1 4RY. Published annually, 1864 to date. Lists works published each year with subject cross-references.

CURRENT JOURNALS ON MOLLUSCA

Archiv für Molluskenkunde. (vol. 112, 1981). c/o Natur-Museum, Senckenberg-Anlage 25, 6000 Frankfurt am Main 1, W. Germany.

Basteria. Tijdschrift van de Nederlandse Malacologische Vereniging. (vol. 45, 1981). c/o Zoological Museum, Plantage Middenlaan 53, Amsterdam-C, Netherlands.

Bulletin of the American Malacological Union (1932 to date). c/o Secretary, 3706 Rice Boulevard, Houston, Texas 77005.

Bulletin of the Institute of Malacology. (vol. 2, 1981). Institute of Malacology, 6-36 Midoricho 3 Chome, Tanashi City, Tokyo 188, Japan.

Bulletin of Malacology Republic of China. (vol. 8, 1981). Taiwan Museum, No. 2 Siang-Yang Rd., Taipei, Taiwan.

(La) *Conchiglia* (English edition: The Shell). La Conchiglia, Via Tomacelli, 146 (I. V. piano), 00186 Rome, Italy. Non-technical, popular monthly.

Conchiglie. Notiziario mensile della Unione Malacologica Italiana vols. 1-14. Unione Malac. Italiana, Via de Sanctis 73, 20141 Milan, Italy. Continued as *Bollettino Malacologico.*

Hawaiian Shell News. (vol. 29, new series, 1981). Hawaiian Malacological Society, P. O. Box 10391, Honolulu, Hawaii 96816. Non-technical, popular monthly.

Johnsonia. (vol. 5, 1974). Monographs of the Marine Mollusca of the Western Atlantic. Museum Comparative Zoology, Cambridge, MA 02138.

Journal of Conchology (vol. 31, 1981). Conchological Society of Great Britain and Ireland, c/o Dept. Geology, Liverpool University, England L69 3BX.

Journal of the Malacological Society of Australia. (vol. 5, 1981). c/o Western Australian Museum, Francis St., Perth, Western Australia 6000, Australia.

Journal of Molluscan Studies (formerly *Proceedings of the Malacological Society of London*). (vol. 47, 1981). Mal. Soc. London, c/o Dept. of Zoology, Bedford College, Regent's Park, London, England NW1 4NS.

Malacologia (vol. 20, 1981). c/o Dept. Malacology, Academy of Natural Sciences of Philadelphia, 19th and The Parkway, Philadelphia, PA 19103.

Malakologische Abhandlungen. (vol. 8, 1981). Staatlichen Museum für Tierkunde in Dresden. Augustusstrasse 2, 801 Dresden, E. Germany.

Monographs of Marine Mollusca (no. 1, 1978). American Malacologists, Inc., P. O. Box 2255, Melbourne, Florida 32901.

Nautilus (The). (vol. 95, 1981). Quarterly. American Malacologists, Inc. P. O. Box 2255, Melbourne, Florida 32901.

Occasional Papers on Mollusks (no. 59, 1981). Dept. of Mollusks, Museum of Comparative Zoology, Cambridge, Mass. 02138.

Of Sea and Shore. (vol. 11, 1981). P. O. Box 33, Port Gamble, Washington 98364. Popular quarterly on conchology.

Pariah (The). (no. 7, 1980). Jerry G. Walls, P. O. Box 42, Hightstown, New Jersey 08520. Published irregularly. Mainly scientific notes on cones, cowries, etc.

Proceedings of the Malacological Society of London, now called *Journal of Molluscan Studies* (see above).

Texas Conchologist. (vol. 17, 1981). c/o Constance Boone, editor, 3706 Rice Boulevard, Houston, Texas 77005.

Veliger (The). (vol. 24, 1981). Malacozoological Society of California, 1584 Milvia St., Berkeley, Calif. 94709.

Venus, Japanese Journal of Malacology. (vol. 23, 1981). c/o National Science Museum, 23-1, Hyakunincho-3, Shinjuku-ku, Tokyo 160, Japan.

Phylum Mollusca

Abbott, R. Tucker. 1972. *Kingdom of the Seashell.* 256 pp. Color illus. Crown Publications, N.Y. Popular introduction to Mollusca.

Cooke, A. H. 1895. *Mollusca.* Cambridge Natural History Series, vol. 3, 535 pp. Macmillan & Co., London.

Dance, S. Peter. 1974. *The Collector's Encyclopedia of Shells.* 288 pp. McGraw-Hill, N. Y. German edition, 1977, *Das grosse Buch der Meeres Muscheln,* ed. R. von Cosel, has extensive bibliography.

Götting, K.-J. 1974. *Malakozoologie.* Grundriss der Weichtierkunde. 320 pp. Gustav Fischer Verlag, Stuttgart.

Grassé, P. P. (editor). (1960). *Traité de Zoologie:* Franc, A.: *Bivalvia* (vol. 5, pt. 2); Fischer and Franc: *Polyplacophora et Aplacophora* (vol. 5, pt. 2); Franc, A.: *Gastropoda et Scaphopoda* (vol. 5, pt. 3). Masson & Cie, Paris.

Hyman, Libbie H. 1967. *The Invertebrates,* vol. 6: *Mollusca:* Aplacophora, Polyplacophora, Monoplacophora, Gastropoda. 792 pp. McGraw-Hill Book Co., N.Y. Extensive bibliography.

Moore, R. C. (editor). *Treatise on Invertebrate Paleontology. Mollusca:* Parts J-N. Geological Society of America, P. O. Box 1719, Boulder, Colorado 80302.

Morton, J. E. 1967. *Molluscs.* An Introduction to their Form and Functions. Hutchinson Univ. Library, London; Harper Torchbooks, N.Y.

Salvini-Plawen, L. and R. Tucker Abbott. 1974. *The Mollusks,* in Grzimek's *Animal Life Encyclopedia,* vol. 3, pp. 19-225. Van Nostrand-Reinhold Co., N.Y.

Solem, Alan. 1974. *The Shell Makers. Introducing Mollusks.* 1974. 289 pp. John Wiley & Sons, N.Y.

Thiele, J. 1931-35. *Handbuch der systematischen Weichtierkunde.* vols. 1 and 2, 1,154 pp. Gustav Fischer Verlag, Jena. Reprint, 1967. A. Asher, Amsterdam.

Yonge, C. M. and T. E. Thompson. 1976. *Living Marine Molluscs.* 288 pp. Collins and Sons, London.

Class Monoplacophora

Knight, J. Brookes and E. L. Yochelson. 1960. *Monoplacophora.* In R. C. Moore's *Treatise on Invertebrate Paleontology,* vol. I (eye), pt. 1, pp. 77-84.

Salvini-Plawen, L. V. and R. Tucker Abbott. 1974. *Monoplacophora.* In Grzimek's *Animal Life Encyclopedia.* Chapter 4, pp. 47-49.

Wagner, R. J. L. and R. Tucker Abbott. 1978. *Standard Catalog of Shells.* p. 00-001. List of living species.

Class Gastropoda

Fretter, V. and A. Graham. 1962. *British Prosobranch Molluscs.* 755 pp. The Ray Society, London.

Kaicher, Sally D. 1973 to date. *Card Catalogue of World-wide Shells.* 3121 A 61st Terrace South, St. Petersburg, Florida 33716. Several popular families completed.

Moore, R. C. (editor). 1960. *Treatise on Invertebrate Paleontology.* Part I (eye), Mollusca 1. *Gastropoda,* pp. 84-351 (Archaeogastropoda). By Knight, Cox, Keen, et al.

Tryon, G. W. Jr. 1880-1898. *Manual of Conchology,* vols. 2-17. Academy of Natural Sciences, Philadelphia. (continued by Henry A. Pilsbry, vols. 10-17). Out of print. Monographs of most marine gastropods.

Wenz, W. 1938-60. *Gastropoda (Prosobranchia)* in: Schindewolf's *Handbuch der Palaozoologie,* vol. 6, 1,639 pp. Wenz, W. and A. Zilch: *Gastropoda (Euthyneura),* 834 pp. (1960). Verlag Gebr. Borntraeger, Berlin. Recent and fossil classification.

Subclass Prosobranchia
(Streptoneura)

Order Archaeogastropoda
(Diotocardia)

Superfamily Pleurotomariacea
(Slit Shells)

Family Pleurotomariidae. Genera: *Entemnotrochus* Fischer, 1885; *Mikadotrochus* Lindholm, 1927; *Perotrochus* Fischer, 1885; *Pleurotomaria* Defrance, 1826.

Bayer, F. M. 1965. New Pleurotomarid Gastropods from the Western Atlantic, with a summary of the recent species. *Bull. Marine Sciences,* vol. 15, pp. 737-796, 35 figs.

Kosuge, S. 1972. Slit shells of the world. *Natural Science Mus.,* Tokyo, vol. 39, pp. 1-20, 23 figs.

Kuroda, T. 1955. A new Pleurotomaria from Japan, with a note on a specimen of *P. rumphii* Schepman collected from Taiwan. *Venus,* vol. 18, pp. 211-221, 2 pls.

Wagner, R. J. L. and R. T. Abbott. 1978. List of Living Pleurotomariidae. *Standard Catalog of Shells,* 3rd ed., p. 00-151.

Family Scissurellidae (Scissurelles)* Genera: *Scissurella* Orbigny, 1824; *Incisura* Hedley, 1904; *Sinezona* Finlay, 1927.

McLean, J. H. 1967. West American Scissurellidae. *Veliger*, vol. 9, pp. 404-410.

Family Haliotidae (Abalones; Ormers). Genus *Haliotis* Linné, 1758 (numerous subgenera).

Foster, R. W. 1946. The family Haliotidae in the western Atlantic. *Johnsonia*, vol. 2, no. 21, pp. 37-40.

Howorth, Peter C. 1978. *The Abalone Book*. 80 pp. Naturegraph Publ., California.

Owen, B., McLean J. and M. Meyer. 1971. Hybridization in the Eastern Pacific Abalones (Haliotis). *Bull.* no. 9, *Los Angeles Co. Museum Nat. Hist.*, California. 37 pp.

Pilsbry, H. A. 1890. Family Haliotidae. In Tryon's *Manual of Conchology*, Philadelphia, vol. 12, pp. 72-126, 24 color pls.

Superfamily Fissurellacea
(Keyhole Limpets)

Family Fissurellidae. About 30 genera, including *Fissurella* Bruguière, 1789; *Lucapina* Sowerby, 1835; *Lucapinella* Pilsbry, 1890; *Macroschisma* Sowerby, 1839; *Megatebennus* Pilsbry, 1890; *Diodora* Gray, 1821; *Megathura* Pilsbry, 1890; *Emarginula* Lamarck, 1801; *Clypidina* Gray, 1847; *Hemitoma* Swainson, 1840; *Puncturella* Lowe, 1827; *Rimula* Defrance, 1827; *Tugali* Gray, 1843, and *Zeidora* A. Adams, 1860.

McLean, J. H. 1967. West American Species of Lucapinella. *Veliger*, vol. 9, pp. 349-352.

Metivier, B. 1972. Sur quelques Fissurellidae du nord, nord-est du Brésil. *Bull. Mus. Hist. Nat. Paris* (Zool.), no. 32, pp. 405-420, 2 pls.

Nordsieck, F. 1974. Genus Emarginula in the European seas. *La Conchiglia*, vol. 6, no. 4, pp. 5-7.

Perez Farfante, I. 1943. The genera *Fissurella, Lucapina* and *Lucapinella* in the western Atlantic. *Johnsonia*, vol. 1, no. 10, 20 pp., illus.

Perez Farfante, I. 1943. The genus *Diodora* in the western Atlantic. *Johnsonia*, vol. 1, no. 11, 20 pp., illus.

Perez Farfante, I. 1947. The genera *Zeidora, Nesta, Emarginula, Rimula* and *Puncturella* in the western Atlantic. *Johnsonia*, vol. 2, no. 24, pp. 93-148, illus.

Pilsbry, H. A. 1890. Family Fissurellidae. In Tryon's *Manual of Conchology*, Philadelphia, vol. 12, pp. 140-323, 64 pls.

Turner, R. D. 1959. The genera *Hemitoma* and *Diodora* in the western Atlantic. *Johnsonia*, vol. 3, no. 39, pp. 334-344, illus.

Superfamily Patellacea
(True Limpets)
(formerly Docoglossa)

Family Patellidae (Limpets). Genera: *Patella* Linné, 1758; *Helcion* Montfort, 1810; *Nacella* Schumacher, 1817; *Cellana* H. Adams, 1869.

Powell, A. W. B. 1973. The patellid limpets of the world (Patellidae). *Indo-Pacific Mollusca*, vol. 3, no. 15, pp. 75-205.

Family Acmaeidae (Limpets). Genera: *Acmaea* Eschscholtz, 1833; *Lottia* Gray, 1833; *Scurria* Gray, 1847; *Colisella* Dall, 1871; *Notoacmaea* Iredale, 1915, and others.

Ponder, W. F. and R. G. Creese. 1980. A revision of the Australian species of *Notoacmaea, Collisella* and *Patelloida* (Acmaeidae). *Jour. Mal. Soc. Australia*, vol. 4, pp. 167-208.

Family Lepetidae (Deep-water Limpets)* Genera: *Lepeta* Gray, 1847; *Iothia* Gray, 1850 (syn: *Pilidium*); *Propilidium* Forbes, 1849.

Superfamily Cocculinacea*
(Deep-water Limpets)

Family Cocculinidae* Genus: *Cocculina* Dall, 1882.

Family Lepetellidae* Genera: *Lepetella* Verrill, 1880; *Addisonia* Dall, 1882, and others.

Superfamily Trochacea
(Top-Shells)

Family Trochidae (Top-Shells). Numerous genera, including in **Subfamily Trochinae:** *Trochus* Linné, 1758; *Tectus* Montfort, 1810; *Clanculus* Montfort, 1810. In **Subfamily Umboniinae:** *Umbonium* Link, 1807; *Isanda* H. and A. Adams, 1854; *Monilea* Swainson, 1840. In **Subfamily Solariellinae:** *Solariella* Wood, 1842; *Cidarina* Dall, 1909; *Minolia* A. Adams, 1860. In **Halistylinae:** *Halistylus* Dall, 1890. In **Calliostomatinae:** *Calliostoma* Swainson, 1840; *Astele* Swainson, 1855; *Photinula* H. and A. Adams, 1854. In **Subfamily Gibbulinae:** *Gibbula* Risso, 1829; *Cittarium* Philippi, 1847; *Gaza* Watson, 1879; *Norrisia* Bayle, 1880. In **Subfamily Monodontinae:** *Monodonta* Lamarck, 1799; *Bankivia* Krauss, 1848; *Diloma* Philippi, 1845; *Tegula* Lesson, 1835, and others. In **Subfamily Angariinae:** *Angaria* Röding, 1798 (syn: *Delphinula*). In **Subfamily Margaritinae:** *Margarites* Gray, 1847; *Euchelus* Philippi, 1847; *Lischkeia* Fischer, 1879, and others.

Clench, W. J. & R. T. Abbott. 1943. The genera *Gaza* and *Livona* in the western Atlantic. *Johnsonia*, vol. 1, no. 12, 9 pp., illus.

Clench, W. J. & R. D. Turner. 1960. The genus *Calliostoma* in the western Atlantic. *Johnsonia*, vol. 4, no. 40, pp. 1-80, illus.

Noda, H. 1975. Turriculid Gastropods of Japan. *Science Rep. Tohoku Univ.* (Geol.), vol. 45, pp. 51-82, illus.

Nordsieck, F. 1975. The genus *Osilinus* Philippi, 1847, in the European Seas. *La Conchiglia*, vol. 6, pp. 21-23.

Perron, F. E. 1975. Carnivorous *Calliostoma* (Prosobranchia: Trochidae) from the Northeastern Pacific. *Veliger*, vol. 18, pp. 52-54.

Pilsbry, H. A. 1889. Trochidae, Stomatiidae, Pleurotomariidae, Haliotidae. In Tryon's *Manual of Conchology*, Philadelphia, vol. 11, 519 pp.

Quinn, James F. 1979. Systematics and Zoogeography . . . Trochidae . . . Straits of Florida . . . *Malacologia*, vol. 19, pp 1-62.

Rehder, H. A. 1955. The genus *Turricula* Dall. *Proc. Mal. Soc. London*, vol. 31, pp. 222-226.

Family Stomatellidae. Genera: *Stomatella* Lamarck, 1816; *Gena* Gray, 1850; *Broderipia* Gray, 1847; *Synaptocochlea* Pilsbry, 1890, and others.

Family Turbinidae. Numerous genera, including in **Subfamily Astraeinae:** *Astraea* Röding, 1798; *Bolma* Risso, 1826; *Cookia* Lesson, 1832; *Guildfordia* Gray, 1850. In **Subfamily Turbininae:** *Turbo* Linné, 1758. In **Subfamily Homalopomatinae:** *Homalopoma* Carpenter, 1864; *Leptothyra* Pease, 1859, and others.

Beu, A. G. and W. F. Ponder. 1979. A revision of the species of *Bolma* Risso. *Rec. Australian Mus.*, vol. 32, pp. 1-68, 19 figs.

Family Cyclostrematidae (syn: Liotiidae). Genera: *Cyclostrema* Marryat, 1818; *Liotia* Gray, 1847; *Arene* H. and A. Adams, 1854; *Liotina* Fischer, 1885; *Coronadoa* Bartsch, 1946. In **Subfamily Skeneinae:** *Skenea* Fleming, 1825; *Ganesa* Jeffreys, 1883; *Parviturbo* Pilsbry & McGinty, 1945, and others.

Abbott, R. Tucker. 1950. The Genus *Cyclostrema* in the Western Atlantic. *Johnsonia*, vol. 2, no. 27, pp. 193-200.

McLean, J. H. 1969. The Families Liotiidae and Skeneidae in the Eastern Pacific. *Echo*, no. 2, p. 18.

Family Phasianellidae. Genera: *Phasianella* Lamarck, 1804; *Tricolia* Risso, 1826; *Gabrielona* Iredale, 1917.

Robertson, R. 1958. The family Phasianellidae in the western Atlantic. *Johnsonia*, vol. 3, no. 37, pp. 245-283, illus.

Robertson, R. 1973. The genus *Gabrielona* (Phasianellidae) in the Indo-Pacific and West Indies. *Indo-Pacific Mollusca*, vol. 3, no. 14, pp. 41-61, illus.

Superfamily Neritacea
(Nerites)

Family Neritopsidae. Genus: *Neritopsis* Grateloup, 1832.

Family Neritidae. Genera: *Nerita* Linné, 1758; *Puperita* Gray, 1857; *Neritina* Lamarck, 1816; *Neritodryas* von Martens, 1869; *Septaria* Férussac, 1807; *Theodoxus* Montfort, 1810; *Neritilia* von Martens, 1879; *Smaragdia* Issel, 1869.

Russell, H. D. 1941. The Recent mollusks of the family Neritidae of the Western Atlantic. *Bull. Mus. Comp. Zoology* (Harvard), vol. 88, pp. 345-404, 7 pls.

Family Helicinidae* Terrestrial, such as *Helicina* and *Eutrochatella*.

Family Phenacolepadidae* Genera: *Phenacolepas* Pilsbry, 1891; *Plesiothyreus* Cossmann, 1888.

Family Hydrocenidae* Terrestrial genus *Hydrocena* Pfeiffer, 1847.

Family Titiscaniidae* Shell-less Indo-Pacific snails.

Order Caenogastropoda

Superfamily Cyclophoracea* Terrestrial families such as Cyclophoridae (*Cyclophorus* Montfort, 1810), Poteriidae (*Poteria* Gray, 1850), Pupinidae, and others.

Superfamily Viviparacea* Freshwater Apple Snails. Such genera as *Viviparus, Campeloma, Pila, Pomacea*, etc.

Superfamily Valvatacea* Freshwater genus *Valvata* Müller, 1774.

Superfamily Littorinacea
(Periwinkles)

Family Pomatiasidae* Terrestrial, operculate snails.

Family Chondropomidae* Terrestrial, operculate snails.

Family Lacunidae. Genus: *Lacuna* Turton, 1827. May be a subfamily of Littorinidae.

Family Littorinidae. Genera: *Littorina* Férussac, 1821; *Haloconcha* Dall, 1886; *Cremnoconchus* Blanford, 1869; *Peasiella* Nevill, 1884; *Tectarius* Valenciennes, 1833; *Nodilittorina* von Martens, 1897; *Echininus* Clench & Abbott, 1942, and others.

Barkman, J. J. 1955. On the distribution and ecology of *Littorina obtusata* (L.) and its subspecific units. *Arch Neerl. Zool.*, vol. 11, pp. 22-86.

Clench, W. J. & R. T. Abbott. 1942. The genera *Tectarius* and *Echininus* in the western Atlantic. *Johnsonia*, vol. 1, no. 4, 4 pp., illus.

Rosewater, J. R. 1970. The family Littorinidae in the Indo-Pacific. Part I. The subfamily Littorininae. *Indo Pacific Mollusca*, vol. 2, no. 11, pp. 417-506, illus.

Rosewater, J. R. 1972. The family Littorinidae in the Indo-Pacific. Part II. The subfamilies Tectariinae and Echininae. *Indo-Pacific Mollusca*, vol. 2, no. 12, pp. 507-528, illus.

Superfamily Rissoacea

Family Hydrobiidae* Freshwater operculate snails.

Family Truncatellidae* Semi-terrestrial snails.

Families Stenothyridae;* **Hydrococcidae; Bithyniidae; Iravadiidae; Micromelaniidae; Assimineidae; Aciculidae,** all freshwater or semi-terrestrial snails.

Family Vitrinellidae. Genera: *Vitrinella* C. B. Adams, 1850; *Pseudomalaxis* Fischer, 1885; *Cochliolepis* Stimpson, 1858; *Teinostoma* H. & A. Adams, 1854, and others.

Moore, D. R. 1965. New species of Vitrinellidae from Gulf of Mexico and Adjacent Waters. *Nautilus*, vol. 78, pp. 73-79.

Pilsbry, H. A. & A. A. Olsson. 1945 and 1952. Vitrinellidae of the Panamic Province. *Proc. Acad. Nat. Sci. Phila.*, vol. 97, pp. 249-278, pls. 22-30; vol. 104, pp. 35-88, pls. 2-13.

Pilsbry, H. A. & T. L. McGinty. 1945. Cyclostrematidae and Vitrinellidae of Florida. *Nautilus*, vol. 59, nos. 1-3, pp. 1-83, 4 pls.; ibid., vol. 60, pp. 12-18; ibid., vol. 63, pp. 85-87.

Family Caecidae. Genera: *Caecum* Fleming, 1813; *Meioceras* Carpenter, 1858, and others.

Moore, D. R. 1962. The systematic position of the family Caecidae. *Bull. Marine Sci.*, vol. 12, pp. 695-701.

Moore, D. R. 1972. Ecological and Systematic Notes on Caecidae from St. Croix, U.S. Virgin Islands. *Bull. Marine Sci.*, vol. 22, pp. 881-899.

Family Rissoidae* Genera: *Rissoa* Fréminville, 1814; *Alvania* Risso, 1826; *Cingula* Fleming, 1828, and others.

Bartsch, P. 1911. The Recent and fossil mollusks of the genus Alvania. *Proc. U.S. Nat. Mus.*, vol. 41, pp. 333-362, pls. 29-32.

Coan, Eugene. 1964. A proposed revision of the Rissoacean families . . . *Veliger*, vol. 6, pp. 164-171.

Family Rissoinidae. Genera: *Rissoina* Orbigny, 1840; *Zebina* H. & A. Adams, 1854, and others.

Bartsch, P. 1915. Recent and fossil mollusks of the genus Rissoina from the West Coast of America. *Proc. U.S. Nat. Mus.*, vol. 49, pp. 33-63, pls. 28-33.

Laseron, C. F. 1956. The Families Rissoinidae and Rissoidae from the Solanderian . . . *Australian Jour. Marine and Freshwater Res.*, vol. 7, pp. 384-484.

Superfamily Rissoellacea*

Families Rissoellidae, Skeneopsidae, Omalogyridae, Cyclostremellidae and **Cingulopsidae.** All minute marine snails.

Robertson, R. 1961. A second Western Atlantic Rissoella and a list of the species in the Rissoellidae. *Nautilus*, vol. 75, pp. 21-26.

Superfamily Tornacea*

Family Tornidae. Genera: *Tornus* Turton & Kingston, 1830; *Macromphalina* Cossmann, 1888.

For families **Architectonicidae, Epitoniidae, Janthinidae, Triphoridae,** see the Order Heteropoda at the end of the Prosobranchs (after Turridae).

Superfamily Cerithiacea

Family Turritellidae (Turret-shells and Worm-shells). Genera: *Turritella* Lamarck, 1799: *Haustator* Montfort, 1810; *Mesalia* Gray, 1847; *Vermicularia* Lamarck, 1799.

Garrard, T. A. 1972. A revision of Australian Recent and Tertiary Turritellidae. *Jour. Mal. Soc. Australia*, vol. 2, pp. 267-337.

Marwick, J. 1957. Generic revision of the Turritellidae. *Proc. Mal. Soc. London*, vol. 32, pp. 144-166.

Family Siliquariidae (Slit Worm-shells). Genus: *Siliquaria* Bruguière, 1789.

Family Vermetidae (Worm-shells). Genera: *Vermetus* Daudin, 1800; *Bivonia* Gray, 1842; *Petaloconchus* Lea, 1843; *Serpulorbis* Sassi, 1827; *Tripsycha* Keen, 1961.

Hadfield, M. G., Kay, E. A. et al. 1972. The Vermetidae of the Hawaiian Islands. *Marine Biol.*, vol. 12, pp. 81-98.

Keen, A. Myra. 1961. A Proposed Reclassification of the Gastropod family Vermetidae. *Bull. British Museum (Nat. Hist.)*, Zoology, vol. 7, pp. 181-213.

Families Syrnolopsidae,* Thiaridae,* Pleuroceridae* and **Melanopsidae.*** Freshwater operculate snails.

Family Abyssochrysidae. Genus *Abyssochrysos* Tomlin, 1927.

Houbrick, R. S. 1979. Classification and systematic relationships of the Abyssochrysidae, a relict family of bathyal snails (Prosobranchia: Gastropoda). *Smithsonian Contr. Zool.* No. 290, 21 pp., illus.

Family Potamididae (Horn Shells). Genera: *Cerithidea* Swainson, 1840; *Pirenella* Gray, 1847; *Pyrazus* Montfort, 1810; *Telescopium* Montfort, 1810; *Terebralia* Swainson, 1840; *Batillaria* Benson, 1840; *Rhinocoryne* von Martens, 1900.

Bequaert, J. C. 1942. *Cerithidea* and *Batillaria* in the western Atlantic. *Johnsonia*, vol. 1, no. 5, 11 pp., illus.

Family Cerithiidae. Genera: *Cerithium* Bruguière, 1789; *Gourmya* Bayle, 1884; *Clypeomorus* Jousseaume, 1888; *Rhinoclavis* Swainson, 1840; *Campanile* Bayle, 1884; and others.

Houbrick, R. S. 1974. The genus *Cerithium* in the western Atlantic. *Johnsonia*, vol. 5, no. 50, pp. 33-84.

Houbrick, R. S. 1978. The family Cerithiidae in the Indo-Pacific. Part I: The genera *Rhinoclavis, Pseudovertagus* and *Clavocerithium*. *Monographs of Marine Mollusca*, no. 1, 130 pp., illus.

Jousseaume, F. P. 1931. Cerithiidae de la Mer Rouge. *Jour. de Conchyliologie*, vol. 74, pp. 270-296.

Family Cerithiopsidae.* Genera: *Cerithiopsis* Forbes & Hanley, 1849; *Seila* A. Adams, 1841, and others.

Laseron, C. F. 1955. The Family Cerithiopsidae from the Solanderian and Dampierian Zoogeographical Provinces. *Australian Jour. Marine and Freshwater Res.*, vol. 7, pp. 151-182.

Family Diastomidae.* Genera: *Diastoma* Deshayes, 1850; *Alaba* H. & A. Adams, 1853, and others.

Family Planaxidae. Genera: *Planaxis* Lamarck, 1822; *Hinea* Gray, 1847.

> Smith, E. A. 1872. A List of the Genus *Planaxis*, with Descriptions of Eleven New Species. *Ann. Mag. Natural History* (series 4), vol. 9, pp. 37-47.

Family Modulidae. Genus *Modulus* Gray, 1842.

> Abbott, R. T. 1944. The genus *Modulus in the western Atlantic. Johnsonia*, vol. 1, no. 14, 6 pp., illus.

Superfamily Eulimacea
(Aglossa)

Family Eulimidae. Genera: *Eulima* Risso, 1826; *Balcis* Leach, 1847, and others.

Family Stiliferidae.* Genera: *Stilifera* Broderip, 1832; *Mucronalia* A. Adams, 1860, and others.

Families Paedophoropodidae* and **Entoconchidae.*** Snails parasitic in other invertebrates.

Superfamily Hipponicacea
(Hoof-Shells)

Family Hipponicidae (Hoof-Shells). Genera: *Hipponix* Defrance, 1819; *Malluvium* Melvill, 1906.

> Morrison, J. P. E. 1965. Notes on the genera of Hipponicidae. *Bull. Amer. Malacol. Union,* vol. 32, pp. 33-34.

Family Fossariidae. Genera: *Fossarus* Philippi, 1840; *Iselica* Dall, 1918.

Family Vanikoroidae. Genus *Vanikoro* Quoy & Gaimard, 1832.

> Smith, E. A. 1908. On the Known Recent Species of the Genus *Vanikoro. Proc. Mal. Soc. London,* vol. 8, pp. 104-117.

Superfamily Crepidulacea
(syn: Calyptraeacea)
(Slipper Shells)

Family Trichotropidae. Genera: *Trichotropis* Broderip & Sowerby, 1829; *Iphinoe* H. & A. Adams, 1854, and others.

Family Capulidae (Cap Shells). Genus: *Capulus* Montfort, 1810.

Family Crepidulidae (syn: Calyptraeidae). (Slipper Shells). Genera: *Calyptraea* Lamarck, 1799; *Cheilea* Modeer, 1793; *Crepidula* Lamarck, 1799; *Crucibulum* Schumacher, 1817; *Crepipatella* Lesson, 1830.

> Hoagland, K. E. 1977. Systematic review of fossil and Recent *Crepidula* and discussion of evolution of the Calyptraeidae. *Malacologia,* vol. 16, pp. 353-420.

Family Xenophoridae (Carrier-Shells). Genera: *Xenophora* G. Fischer, 1807; *Stellaria* Schmidt, 1832.

> Beu, A. G. 1977. New Zealand Cenozoic Gastropods of the genus *Xenophora* Fischer, 1807. *Jour. Royal Soc. N. Z.,* vol. 7, pp. 229-241, 27 figs.
>
> Clench, W. J. & C. G. Aguayo. 1943. The genera *Xenophora* and *Tugurium* in the western Atlantic. *Johnsonia,* vol. 1, no. 8, 6 pp., illus.
>
> Travis, Byron W. 1974. A particular study of some *Xenophora. Of Sea and Shore,* Winter, 1973-74, pp. 187-188; Fall, 1974, pp. 141-143.

Superfamily Strombacea

Family Strombidae (True conchs). Genera: *Strombus* Linné, 1758; *Lambis* Röding, 1798; *Terebellum* Röding, 1798; *Rimella* Agassiz, 1840.

> Abbott, R. T. 1960. The genus *Strombus* in the Indo-Pacific. *Indo-Pacific Mollusca,* vol. 1, no. 2. pp. 33-146, illus.
>
> Abbott, R. T. 1961. The genus *Lambis* in the Indo-Pacific. *Indo-Pacific Mollusca,* vol. 1, no. 3, pp. 147-174, illus.
>
> Jung, P., & Abbott, R. T. 1967. The genus *Terebellum* (Gastropoda: Strombidae). *Indo-Pacific Mollusca,* vol. 1, no. 7, pp. 445-454, illus.
>
> Clench, W. J. & Abbott, R. T. 1941. The genus *Strombus* in the western Atlantic. *Johnsonia,* vol. 1, no. 1, 15 pp., illus.
>
> Walls, Jerry G. 1980. *Conchs, Tibias, and Harps.* 191 pp., color illus. T. F. H. Publications, New Jersey.

Family Aporrhaidae (Pelican's-foot). Genus: *Aporrhais* da Costa, 1778.

Family Struthiolariidae (Ostrich-foot). Genera: *Struthiolaria* Lamarck, 1816; *Perissodonta* von Martens, 1883.

Superfamily Atlantacea
(Heteropoda)

> Van der Spoel. 1976. Pseudothecosomata, Gymnosomata and Heteropoda. 484 pp., illus., maps. Bohn, Scheltema and Holkema, Holland.

Family Atlantidae. Genus: *Atlanta* Lesueur, 1817. Pelagic.

Family Carinariidae. Genus: *Carinaria* Lamarck, 1801. Pelagic.

Family Pterotracheidae. Naked, pelagic snails.

Superfamily Lamellariacea

Family Lamellariidae. Genera: *Lamellaria* Montagu, 1815; *Velutina* Fleming, 1821, and others.

Family Eratoidae. Genera: *Trivia* Broderip, 1837; *Erato* Risso, 1826, and others.

Families Pseudosacculidae; Asterophilidae. Parasitic snails.

Superfamily Cypraeacea

Family Cypraeidae (Cowries). Genera: *Cypraea* Linné, 1758 (numerous subgenera, such as *Mauritia, Zoila,* etc.).

> Allan, Joyce. 1960. *Cowry Shells of World Seas.* 170 pp. Georgian House, Melbourne, Australia. Now out-dated.
>
> Burgess, C. M. 1970. *The Living Cowries.* 389 pp., 44 color pls. A. S. Barnes & Co., Cranbury, New Jersey.
>
> Schilder, F. A. & M. Schilder. 1939. Prodrome of a monograph on living Cypraeidae. *Proc. Malac. Soc. London,* vol. 23, pp. 119-231.
>
> Taylor, J., Walls, J. G. 1975. *Cowries.* 288 pp., color. illus. Neptune City, New Jersey.
>
> Wilson, B. R. & McComb, J. A. 1967. The genus *Cypraea* (subgenus *Zoila* Jousseaume). *Indo-Pacific Mollusca,* vol. 1, no. 8, pp. 457-484, color illus.

Family Ovulidae (Egg shells). Genera: *Ovula* Bruguière, 1789; *Calpurnus* Montfort, 1810; *Primovula* Thiele, 1925; *Simnia* Risso, 1829; *Cyphoma* Röding, 1798; *Volva* Röding, 1798, and others.

> Cate, C. N. 1973. A systematic revision of the Recent Cypraeid family Ovulidae (Mollusca: Gastropoda). *Veliger,* vol. 15 (Supplement), 116 pp., illus.

Family Pediculariidae. Genus *Pedicularia* Swainson, 1840.

Superfamily Naticacea

Family Naticidae (Moon Shells). Genera: *Natica* Scopoli, 1777; *Globularia* Swainson, 1840; *Policines* Montfort, 1810; *Lunatia* Gray, 1847; *Sinum* Röding, 1798, and others.

> Cernohorsky, W. O. 1971. The Family Naticidae in the Fiji Islands. *Records Auckland Inst. and Mus.,* vol. 8, pp. 169-208.
>
> Kilburn, R. N. 1976. A revision of the Naticidae of Southern Africa and Mozambique (Mollusca). *Annals Natal Mus.,* vol. 22, pp. 829-884.
>
> Marincovich, Louie, Jr. 1977. Cenozoic Naticidae of the Northeastern Pacific. *Bull. Amer. Paleontology,* vol. 70, no. 294, pp. 169-494.

Superfamily Tonnacea

Family Tonnidae (Tun Shells). Genera: *Tonna* Brünnich, 1772; *Malea* Valenciennes, 1833; *Eudolium* Dall, 1889; In **Subfamily Oocorythinae:** *Oocorys* Fischer, 1883; *Dalium* Dall, 1889.

> Kilias, R. Tonnidae. 1962. Tonnacea Teil 4. *Das Tierreich,* Lief 77, illus. Berlin.
>
> Turner, R. D. 1948. The family Tonnidae in the western Atlantic. *Johnsonia,* vol. 2, no. 26, pp. 165-192, illus.

Family Ficidae (Fig shells). Genus: *Ficus* Röding, 1798.

> Smith, E. A. 1894. A list of the Recent species of the genus *Pirula* Lamarck, with notes respecting the synonymy. *Jour. Malac.,* vol. 3, pp. 64-69.

Family Cassidae (Helmet shells). Genera: *Cassis* Scopoli, 1777; *Cypraecassis* Stutchbury, 1837; *Casmaria* H. & A. Adams, 1853; *Phalium* Link, 1807; *Sconsia* Gray, 1847; *Galeodea* Link, 1807 (syn: *Cassidaria); Morum* Röding, 1798.

Abbott, R. T. 1968. The Helmet Shells of the World (Cassidae). Part 1. *Indo-Pacific Mollusca,* vol. 2, no. 9, pp. 15-201, illus.

Clench, W. J. 1944. The genera *Casmaria, Galeodea, Phalium* and *Cassis* in the western Atlantic. *Johnsonia,* vol. 1, no. 16, 16 pp., illus.

Clench, W. J., & Abbott, R. T. 1943. The genera *Cypraecassis, Morum, Sconsia* and *Dalium* in the western Atlantic. *Johnsonia,* vol. 1, no. 9, 8 pp., illus.

Dance, S. P., & Emerson, W. K. 1967. Notes on *Morum dennisoni* (Reeve) and related species (Gastropoda: Tonnacea). *Veliger,* vol. 10, pp. 91-98, 1 pl. (Lists all recent species described up to 1967).

Superfamily Cymatiacea (Lindner, 1975)

Family Cymatiidae (Tritons). Genera: *Cymatium* Röding, 1798; *Argobuccinum* Herrmannsen, 1846; *Gyrineum* Link, 1807; *Charonia* Gistel, 1848; *Distorsio* Röding, 1798, and others.

Bayer, Ch. 1933. Catalogue of the Cymatiidae in Rijksmuseum Nat. Hist. *Zoolog. Mededeel.,* Leiden, vol. 16, pp. 33-59.

Beu, A. G. 1970. The mollusca of the genus *Charonia. Trans. Royal Soc. New Zealand,* vol. 11, pp. 203-223, 5 pls.

Beu, A. G. 1978. The marine fauna of New Zealand: The molluscan genera *Cymatona* and *Fusitriton. New Zealand Oceanogr. Inst.,* Memoir 65, 44 pp., 12 figs.

Clench, W. J., & Turner, R. D. 1957. The Family Cymatiidae in the western Atlantic. *Johnsonia,* vol. 3, no 36, pp. 189-244, illus.

Dell, R. K. & Dance, S. P. 1963. The molluscan genus *Ranella* and the distribution of *Ranella olearium* (Linnaeus). *Proc. Malac. Soc. London,* vol. 35, pp. 159-166, illus.

Emerson, W. K., & Puffer, E. L. 1953. A catalogue of the Molluscan Genus *Distorsio* (Gastropoda, Cymatiidae). *Proc. Biol. Soc. Washington,* vol. 66, pp. 93-108.

Kilias, R. 1973. Cymatiidae. Tonnacea Teil 2. *Das Tierreich,* Lief 92, illus. Berlin.

Lewis, Hal. 1972. Notes on the Genus *Distorsio* with Descriptions of New Species. *The Nautilus,* vol. 86, pp. 27-50.

Family Bursidae (Frog shells). Genus: *Bursa* Röding, 1798.

Beu, A. G. 1977. A new species of *Bufonaria* (Bursidae) from Mozambique. *Annals Natal Mus.,* vol. 23, pp. 87-91.

Morrison, J. P. E. 1949. Notes on Florida species of Bursa. *Annual Report, 1949,* Amer. Mal. Union, p. 10.

Oyama, K. 1964. On the confused usage of the genus Ranella and its allies. *Venus,* vol. 22, pp. 317-336.

Superfamily Muricacea

Family Columbariidae (Pagoda shells). Genera: *Columbarium* von Martens, 1881; *Coluzea* Allan, 1926.

Clench, W. J. 1944. The genus *Columbarium* in the western Atlantic. *Johnsonia,* vol. 1, no. 15, 4 pp., illus.

Darragh, Thos. A. 1969. A Revision of the family Columbariidae. *Proc. Royal Soc. Victoria,* vol. 83, pp. 63-119.

Family Muricidae (Murex and Rock shells). Numerous genera and subgenera. In **Subfamily Muricinae:** *Murex* Linné, 1758; *Chicoreus* Montfort, 1810; *Siratus* Jousseaume, 1880; *Homalocantha* Mörch, 1852; *Phyllonotus* Swainson, 1833, and others. In **Subfamily Ocenebrinae:** *Ocenebra* Gray, 1847; *Eupleura* H. & A. Adams, 1853; *Ceratostoma* Herrmannsen, 1846, and others. In **Subfamily Trophoninae:** *Trophon* Montfort, 1810; *Boreotrophon* Fischer, 1884, and others. In **Subfamily Typhinae:** *Typhis* Montfort, 1810; *Pterotyphis* Jousseaume, 1880, and others. In **Subfamily Thaidinae:** *Purpura* Bruguière, 1789; *Thais* Röding, 1798; *Drupa* Röding, 1798, and others. In **Subfamily Rapaninae:** *Rapana* Schumacher, 1817; *Chorus* Gray, 1847; *Forreria* Jousseaume, 1880.

Beu, A. G. 1970. New Zealand gastropod molluscs of the genus *Pteropurpura* Jousseaume. *Trans. Royal Soc. New Zealand,* Biol. Sci., vol. 12, pp. 133-143.

Clench, W. J. 1947. The genera *Purpura* and *Thais* in the western Atlantic. *Johnsonia,* vol. 2, no. 23, pp. 61-91, illus.

Clench, W. J., & Perez Farfante, I. 1945. The genus *Murex* in the western Atlantic. *Johnsonia,* vol. 1, no. 17, 58 pp., illus.

Emerson, W. K. 1973. The genus *Drupa* in the Indo-Pacific. *Indo-Pacific Mollusca,* vol. 3, no. 13, pp. 1-40, illus.

Fair, Ruth H. 1976. *The Murex Book:* An illustrated Catalogue of Recent Muricidae. 138 pp. Obtainable from Seashell Treasures, P. O. Box 730, Oakhurst, California 93644. Useful.

Gertman, R. L. Cenozoic Typhinae of the Western Atlantic Region. *Tulane Studies Geol.,* vol. 7, pp. 143-191, 8 pls.

Harasewych, M. G. & R. H. Jensen. 1979. Review of the subgenus *Pterynotus* (Gastropoda: Muricidae) in the Western Atlantic. *Nemouria* (Delaware Mus. Nat. Hist.), no. 22, pp. 1-16.

Keen, A. Myra. 1944. Catalogue and revision of the gastropod subfamily Typhinae. *Jour. Paleont.,* vol. 18, pp. 50-72, 20 figs.

Pain, T. 1976. The Muricinae of the West African Marine Province. *Brit. Shell Coll. Club.* Newsletter No. 24, 7 pp., illus.

Radwin, G. E., & D'Attilio, A. 1976. *Murex Shells of the World.* An illustrated guide to the Muricidae. Stanford Univ. Press, 284 pp., illus.

Vokes, E. H. 1964. Supraspecific groups in the subfamilies Muricinae and Tritonaliinae. *Malacologia,* vol. 2, pp. 1-41.

Vokes, E. H. 1968. Cenozoic Muricidae of the Western Atlantic Region. Pt. IV-Hexaplex and Murexiella. *Tulane Studies Geol.,* vol. 6, pt. 2-3, pp. 85-126, 8 pls.

Vokes, E. H. 1971. Catalogue of the genus *Murex* Linné (Mollusca: Gastropoda); Muricinae, Ocenebrinae. *Bull. Amer. Paleont.* vol. 61, no. 268, 141 pp.

Family Coralliophilidae (Syn: Magilidae). Coral-shells. Genera: *Coralliophila* H. & A. Adams, 1853; *Latiaxis* Swainson, 1840; *Lataxiena* Jousseaume, 1888; *Magilus* Montfort, 1810; *Rapa* Bruguière, 1792, and others.

D'Attilio, A. 1978. A catalog of Coralliophilidae *Festivus* (San Diego Shell Club), vol. 10, no. 10, pp. 69-96.

Superfamily Buccinacea

Family Buccinidae (Whelks). Numerous genera, including *Buccinum* Linné, 1758; *Cantharus* Röding, 1798; *Cominella* Gray, 1850; *Engina* Gray, 1839; *Neptunea* Röding, 1798; *Phos* Montfort, 1810; *Colus* Röding, 1798; *Volutopsius* Mörch, 1857; and others.

Campbell, G. B. 1961. Colubrariidae (Gastropoda) of tropical West America, with a new species. *Nautilus,* vol. 74, pp. 136-142.

Cernohorsky, W. O. 1971. Indo-Pacific Pisaniinae and Related Buccinid Genera. *Records Auckland Inst. and Mus.,* vol. 8, pp. 137-167.

Habe, T. 1965. Notes on the ivory shell genus *Babylonia* Schlüter. *Bull. Nat. Sci. Mus.,* Tokyo, vol. 8, pp. 115-124, 1 pl.

Orr, V. 1956. The South African genus *Burnupena* (Buccinidae). *Proc. Acad. Nat. Sci. Philadelphia,* vol. 108, pp. 249-263, 2 pls.

Ponder, W. F. 1972. Notes on Some Australian Species and Genera of the Family Buccinidae. *Jour. Mal. Soc. Australia,* vol. 2, pp. 249-265.

Family Columbellidae (Dove-shells). Genera: *Columbella* Lamarck, 1799; *Pyrene* Röding, 1798; *Strombina* Mörch, 1852, and others.

Pace, S. 1902. Contributions to the Study of the Columbellidae. *Proc. Mal. Soc. London,* vol. 5, no. 1, pp. 36-154.

Radwin, G. E. 1968. New Taxa of Western Atlantic Columbellidae (Gastropoda, Prosobranchia). *Proc. Biol. Soc. Washington,* vol. 81, p. 143-150.

Wagner, R. J. L., & Abbott, R. T. 1978. List of Columbellidae. *Standard Catalog of Shells,* 3rd ed. pp. 15-503–15-522.

Family Fasciolariidae (Tulip and Spindle shells). Numerous genera, such as: *Fasciolaria* Lamarck, 1799; *Pleuroploca* Fischer, 1884; *Latirus* Montfort, 1810; *Peristernia* Mörch, 1852; *Fusinus* Rafinesque, 1815.

Bullock, R. C. 1974. A contribution to the systematics of some West Indian *Latirus. Nautilus,* vol. 88, pp. 69-79.

Hollister, S. C. 1956. On the status of *Fasciolaria distans* Lamarck. *Nautilus,* vol. 70, pp. 73-84.

Melvill, J. C. 1891. An historical account of the genus *Latirus* (Montfort) and its dependencies, with description of eleven new species, and a catalogue of *Latirus* and *Peristernia.* Mem. Lit. Phil. Soc. Manchester, vol. 34, pp. 365-411, 1 pl.

Melvill, J. C. 1911. An enumeration of the additions made to the genus Latirus Montfort. *Jour. Conch.,* vol. 13, pp. 164-178.

Family Melongenidae (Crown Conchs). Genera: *Busycon* Röding, 1798; *Melongena* Schumacher, 1817; *Syrinx* Röding, 1798; *Pugilina* Schumacher, 1817, and others.

Bayer, Ch. 1952. Catalogue of the genera *Melongena* and *Semifusus. Zoolog. Mededeel., Rijksmus.* Leiden, vol. 31, pp. 265-299.

Clench, W. J., & Turner, R. D. 1956. The family Melongenidae in the western Atlantic. *Johnsonia*, vol. 3, no. 35, pp. 161-187, illus.

Hollister, S. C. 1958. A Review of the Genus *Busycon* and its Allies-Part 1. *Palaeontographica Americana*, vol. 4, no. 28, 124 pp.

Family Nassariidae (Nassa Mud Shells). Many genera, such as: *Nassarius* Duméril, 1806; *Ilyanassa* Stimpson, 1865; *Cyllene* Gray, 1838; *Demoulia* Gray, 1838.

Addicott, W. O. 1965. Some Western American Cenozoic gastropods of the genus *Nassarius*. *U. S. Geol. Surv. Prof. Paper, 503-B*, 60 pp.

Cernohorsky, W. O. 1972, Indo-Pacific Nassariidae. *Record Auckland Inst. and Mus.*, vol. 9, pp. 125-194.

Demond, Joan. 1951. Key to the Nassariidae of the west coast of North America. *Nautilus*, vol. 65, pp. 15-17.

Superfamily Volutacea

Family Olividae. (Olive Shells). Genera: *Oliva* Bruguière, 1789; *Agaronia* Gray, 1839; *Ancilla* Lamarck, 1799; *Olivella* Swainson, 1831; *Melapium* H. & A. Adams, 1853; *Zemira* H. & A. Adams, 1853.

Burch, J. Q., & R. L. 1963. Genus *Olivella* in eastern Pacific. *Nautilus*, vol. 77, pp. 1-8.

Chavan, A. 1965. Essai de reclassification des Olividae: Ancillinae (Gastropoda). *Bull. Soc. Geol. de France*, vol. 7, pp. 102-109.

Kilburn, R. N. 1981. Revision of the Genus *Ancilla* Lamarck, 1799. *Annals Natal Mus.*, vol. 24, pp. 349-463.

Klappenbach, M. 1965. Consideraciones sobre el genero *Olivancillaria* y descripcion de dos nuevas species argentinas y uruguayas. *Com. Zool. Mus. Hist. Nat. Montev.*, vol. 8, 10 pp., 2 pls.

Olsson, A. A. 1956. Studies on the Genus *Olivella*. *Proc. Acad. Nat. Sci. Philadelphia*, vol. 108, pp. 155-225.

Olsson, A. A., & S. P. Dance. 1966. The Linnaean Olives. *Bull. Amer. Paleont.*, vol. 50, pp. 215-224.

Ponder, W. F. & T. A. Darragh. 1975. The genus *Zemira* H. & A. Adams. *Jour. Mal. Soc. Australia*, vol. 3, pp. 89-105, illus.

Wagner, R. J. L., & Abbott, R. T. 1978. List of Olividae. *Standard Catalog of Shells*, Greenville, Delaware. pp. 18-801-18-813.

Zeigler, R. F., & Porreca, H. C. 1969. *Olive Shells of the World*. 96 pp., 13 color pls. Obtainable from Shell Cabinet, Box 29, Falls Church, Virginia 22046.

Family Turbinellidae (Syn: Vasidae). Vase shells and Chanks. Genera: *Turbinella* Lamarck, 1799 (syn: *Xancus* Röding); *Vasum* Röding, 1798; *Tudicula* H. & A. Adams, 1863; *Tudicla* Röding, 1798; *Afer* Conrad, 1858, and others.

Abbott, R. T. 1950. The genera *Xancus* and *Vasum* in the western Atlantic. *Johnsonia*, vol. 2, no. 28, pp. 201-219, illus.

Abbott, R. T. 1959. The family Vasidae in the Indo-Pacific. *Indo-Pacific Mollusca*, vol. 1, no. 1, pp. 15-32, illus.

Vokes, E. H. 1964. The genus *Turbinella* in the New World. *Tulane Studies Geol.*, vol. 2, pp. 39-68, 3 pls.

Vokes, E. H. 1966. The genus *Vasum* in the New World. *Tulane Studies Geol.*, vol. 5, pp. 1-36, 6 pls.

Family Volutomitridae. Genera: *Volutomitra* H. & A. Adams, 1853; *Microvoluta* Angas, 1877, and others.

Cernohorsky, W. O. 1970. Systematics of the families Mitridae & Volutomitridae. *Bull. Auckland Inst. and Mus.* no. 8, 190 pp., 18 pls.

Family Mitridae (Miter shells). Genera: *Mitra* Lamarck, 1798; *Pterygia* Röding, 1798; *Imbricaria* Schumacher, 1817, and others.

Cernohorsky, W. O. 1976. The Mitridae of the World. Part I. The subfamily Mitrinae. *Indo-Pacific Mollusca*, vol. 3, no. 17, pp. 273-528, illus.

Family Costellariidae (Syn.: Vexillidae) (Miter shells). Genera: *Vexillum* Röding, 1798; *Pusia* Swainson, 1840, and others.

Pechar, Peter., Prior, Chris., & Parkinson, B. 1980. *Mitre Shells from the Pacific and Indian Oceans*. 56 pls. Robert Brown & Assoc. Bathurst, Australia.

Family Harpidae (Harp shells). Genera: *Harpa* Röding, 1798; *Austroharpa* Finlay, 1931.

Rehder, H. A. 1973. The family Harpidae of the world. *Indo-Pacific Mollusca*, vol. 3, no. 16, pp. 207-274, illus.

Family Marginellidae (Margin shells). Many genera, such as *Marginella* Lamarck, 1799; *Hyalina* Schumacher, 1817; *Cystiscus* Stimpson, 1865, and others.

Coan, E., & Roth, B. 1966. The West American Marginellidae. *Veliger*, vol. 8, pp. 276-299.

Laseron, C. F. 1957. A New Classification of the Australian Marginellidae. *Australian Jour. Marine and Freshwater Res.*, vol. 8, pp. 274-311.

Tomlin, J. R. le B. 1917. A systematic list of the Marginellidae. *Proc. Malac. Soc. London*, vol. 12, pp. 242-306. (A list of names with authors and dates of worldwide species.)

Wagner, R. J. L., & Abbott, R. T. 1978. List of Marginellidae. *Standard Catalog of Shells*, Greenville, Delaware, pp. 22-001–22-015.

Family Cancellariidae (Nutmegs). Several genera (and many subgenera): *Cancellaria* Lamarck, 1799; *Admete* Kröyer, 1842; *Trigonostoma* Blainville, 1827; *Scalptia* Jousseaume, 1887, and others.

Family Volutidae (Volutes). Many genera, including: *Voluta* Linné, 1758; *Volutocorbis* Dall, 1890; *Neptuneopsis* Sowerby, 1898; *Cymbium* Röding, 1798; *Cymbiola* Swainson, 1831; *Fulgoraria* Schumacher, 1817; *Lyria* Gray, 1847; *Scaphella* Swainson, 1832; *Amoria* Gray, 1855; *Zidona* H. & A. Adams, 1853, and others.

Clench, W. J. 1946. The genera *Bathyaurinia, Rehderia* and *Scaphella* in the western Atlantic. *Johnsonia*, vol. 2, no. 22, pp. 41-60, illus.

Clench, W. J., & Turner, R. D. 1964. The Subfamilies Volutinae, Zidoninae, Odontocymbiolinae and Calliotectinae in the western Atlantic. *Johnsonia*, vol. 4, no. 43, pp. 129-180, illus.

Weaver, C. S., & duPont, J. E. 1970. *The Living Volutes*. 375 pp., 79 color pls. Delaware Museum of Natural History, Greenville, Delaware. Useful but out-of-date.

Superfamily Conacea

Family Conidae (Cone shells). Genus: *Conus* Linné, 1758 (many subgenera).

Clench, W. J. 1942. The genus *Conus* in the western Atlantic. *Johnsonia*, vol. 1, no. 6, 40 pp., illus.

Dautzenberg, Ph. 1937. Famille Conidae. *Resultats Scientifique du Voyage aux Indes Orientales Neerlandaises*, vol. 2, fascicule 18, 284 pp. Bruxelles.

Kilburn, R. N. 1971. A Revision of the Littoral Conidae of the Cape Province South Africa. *Annals Natal Mus.*, vol. 21, pp. 37-54.

Marsh, J. A. & Rippingale, O. H. 1974. *Cone Shells of the World*. 180 pp., illus. Jacaranda Press. 3rd ed. Out-of-date.

Tomlin, J. R. le B. 1937. Catalogue of Recent and fossil cones. *Proc. Malac. Soc. London*, vol. 22, pp. 205-330, 333.

Walls, Jerry G. 1978. *Cone Shells*: A Synopsis of the Living Conidae. 1011 pp. T. F. H. Publications, Neptune City, New Jersey. Very useful.

Family Terebridae (Auger shells). Genus: *Terebra* Bruguière, 1789 (and many subgenera).

Burch, R. D. 1965. New Terebrid Species from the Indo-Pacific. *Veliger*, vol. 7, pp. 241-253.

Dautzenberg, Ph. 1935. Famille Terebridae (et Mitridae). *Resultats Scientifiques du Voyage aux Indes Orientales Neerlandaises*, vol. 2, fascicule 17, 208 pp. Bruxelles.

Salisbury, R. 1978. Hawaii's Fifty-odd Terebra. *Hawaiian Shell News*, vol. 26, no. 8, pp. 7-10.

Family Turridae (Turrids). Numerous genera and subgenera, including: *Turris* Röding, 1798; *Gemmula* Weinkauff, 1875; *Polystira* Woodring, 1928; *Clavatula* Lamarck, 1801; *Clavus* Montfort, 1810; *Drillia* Gray, 1838; *Mangelia* Risso, 1826; *Thatcheria* Angas, 1877, and others.

Hedley, C. A. 1922. A Revision of the Australian Turridae. *Records Australian Mus.*, vol. 13, pp. 213-259.

McLean, J. H. 1971. A Revised Classification of the Family Turridae from the Eastern Pacific. *Veliger*, vol. 14, pp. 114-130.

Powell, A. W. B. 1964. The family Turridae in the Indo-Pacific. Part I. The subfamily Turrinae. *Indo-Pacific Mollusca*, vol. 1, no. 5, pp. 227-345, illus.

Powell, A. W. B. 1966. The Molluscan Families Speightiidae and Turridae. *Bull. 5, Auckland Institute and Museum*, 184 pp.

Powell, A. W. B. 1967. The famiy Turridae in the Indo-Pacific. Part 1a. The subfamily Turrinae concluded. *Indo-Pacific Mollusca*, vol. 1, no. 7, pp. 409-431, illus.

Powell, A. W. B. 1969. The family Turridae in the Indo-Pacific. Part 2. The subfamily Turriculinae. *Indo-Pacific Mollusca*, vol. 2, no. 10, pp. 207-415, illus.

Order Heterogastropoda
Superfamily Architectonicacea

Family Architectonicidae (Sundials). Genera: *Architectonica* Röding, 1798; *Heliacus* Orbigny, 1842; *Philippia* Gray, 1847.

Bayer, Charles. 1948. Catalogue of the Solariidae in the Rijksmuseum van Natuurlijke Hist. *Zool. Verhandel.* no. 4, 44 pp.

Marche-Marchad, J. 1969. Les Architectonicidae de la Cote Occidentale d'Afrique. *Bull. Inst. Fondament. d'Afr. Noire*, ser. A, vol. 31, pp. 461-486, 10 figs.

Robertson, R. 1970. Systematics of Indo-Pacific *Philippia* (Psilaxis), Architectonicid gastropods with eggs. *Pacific Science*, vol. 24, pp. 66-83.

Robertson, R. 1973. On the fossil history and intrageneric relationships of *Philippia* (Architectonicidae). *Proc. Acad. Nat. Sci., Phila.*, vol. 125, pp. 37-46.

Family Epitoniidae (Wentletraps). Many genera, including: *Epitonium* Röding, 1798 (syn: *Scalaria* Lamarck); *Amaea* H. & A. Adams, 1853; *Sthenorytis* Conrad, 1862; *Cirsotrema* Mörch, 1852; *Opalia* H. & A. Adams, 1853.

Clench, W. J., & Turner, R. D. 1950. The genera *Sthenorytis, Cirsotrema, Acirsa, Opalia* and *Amaea* in the western Atlantic. *Johnsonia*, vol. 2, no. 29, pp. 221-246, illus.

Clench, W. J., & Turner, R. D. 1951. The genus *Epitonium* in the western Atlantic. Part I. *Johnsonia*, vol. 2, no. 30, pp. 249-288, illus.

Clench, W. J., & Turner, R. D. 1952. The genera *Epitonium* (Part II), *Depressiscala, Cylindriscala, Nystiella* and *Solutiscala* in the western Atlantic. *Johnsonia*, vol. 2, no. 31, pp. 289-356, illus.

Family Janthinidae (Purple Sea Snails). Genera: *Janthina* Röding, 1798; *Recluzia* Petit, 1853.

Laursen, Dan. 1953. The genus *Ianthina* [Janthina]. Monograph. *Dana-Reports*, vol. 6, pp. 1-40.

Families Aclididae,* Mathildidae,* Toriniidae* and **Triphoridae.*** Small marine snails.

Kosuge, S. 1966. The family Triphoridae and its Systematic Position. *Malacologia*, vol. 4, pp. 297-324.

Marshall, B. A. 1977. The Dextral Triforid Genus *Metaxia* in the South-west Pacific. *New Zealand Jour. Zool.*, vol. 4, pp. 111-117.

Subclass Opisthobranchia
(Bubble shells and Sea Hares)
(Arrangement after T. E. Thompson, Ph.D.)

Marcus, Ernest & Evelyn, 1967. *Tropical American Opisthobranchs. Studies Tropical Oceanography*, Miami, vol. 6, pp. 3-137.

Pilsbry, H. A. 1843-1896. Order Opisthobranchiata. In Tryon's *Manual of Conchology*, Philadelphia. vols. 15 (436 pp., 61 pls.) and 16 (262 pp., 74 pls.).

Thompson, T. E. 1976. *Biology of Opisthobranch Molluscs*. vol. 1, 207 pp. Ray Society, London.

Family Acteonidae (Acteons). Genera: *Acteon* Montfort, 1810; *Pupa* Röding, 1798 (syn: *Solidula*), and others.

Rudman, W. B. 1971. The family Acteonidae in New Zealand. *Jour. Mal. Soc. Australia*, vol. 2, pp. 205-214.

Family Bullinidae. Genus: *Bullina* Férussac, 1822.

Rudman, W. B. 1971. The genus *Bullina* in New Zealand. *Jour. Mal. Soc. Australia*, vol. 2, pp. 195-203.

Family Hydatinidae. Genera: *Hydatina* Schumacher, 1817; *Micromelo* Pilsbry, 1895.

Suborder Diaphanacea*

Family Diaphanidae. Genera: *Diaphana* Brown, 1827, and others.

Family Notodiaphanidae. Genus: *Notodiaphana* Thiele, 1917.

Suborder Retusacea*

Family Retusidae. Genera: *Retusa* Brown, 1827; *Rhizorus* Montfort, 1810.

Suborder Ringiculacea*

Family Ringiculidae. Genus: *Ringicula* Deshayes, 1838.

Suborder Bullacea

Family Bullidae (Bubble Shells). Genus: *Bulla* Linné, 1758.

Willan, R. C. 1978. The nomenclature of three Pacific *Bulla* species. *Jour. Mal. Soc. Australia*, vol. 4, pp. 57-68.

Suborder Atyacea

Family Atyidae. Genera: *Atys* Montfort, 1810; *Haminoea* Turton & Kingston, 1830, and others.

Suborder Philinacea

Families Scaphandridae (*Scaphander* Montfort, 1810); **Gastropteridae;* Aglajidae;* Philinidae;* Philinoglossidae.***

Bullis, H. 1956. The genus *Scaphander* in the Gulf of Mexico and notes on the western Atlantic species. *Bull. Marine Science*, vol. 6, pp. 1-17.

Suborder Runcinacea*

Family Runcinidae. Genus: *Runcina* Forbes & Hanley, 1853.

Order Pyramidellomorpha

Family Pyramidellidae. Numerous genera: *Pyramidella* Lamarck, 1799; *Odostomia* Fleming, 1813, and others.

Dall, W. H., & Bartsch, Paul. 1909. Monograph of West American Pyramidellid Mollusks. *Bull. 68, U. S. Nat. Mus.*, 258 pp.

Laseron, C. F. 1959. The Family Pyramidellidae from North Australia. *Australian Jour. Marine and Freshwater Res.*, vol. 10, pp. 177-267.

Melvill, J. C. 1910. A revision of the species of Pyramidellidae occurring in the Persian Gulf, Gulf of Oman and North Arabian Sea. *Proc. Mal. Soc. London*, vol. 9, pp. 171-206.

Order Thecosomata
(Pteropods)

Families Limacinidae and **Cavoliniidae.** Genera: *Limacina* Bosc, 1817; *Cavolinia* Abildgaard, 1791; *Clio* Linné, 1767.

van der Spoel, S. 1976. Pseudothecosomata, Gymnosomata and Heteropoda (Gastropoda), 484 pp., 246 figs. Bohn, Scheltema & Holkema, Utrecht, Holland.

Families Peraclidae,* Cymbuliidae,* Desmopteridae.*

Order Gymnosomata*
(Naked Pteropods, several families)

Order Aplysiomorpha*
(Aplysia Sea Hares and Akeridae)

Order Pleurobranchomorpha*
(Sea Slugs)

Order Acochlidiacea*
(Sand Nudibranchs)

Order Sacoglossa*
(Sea Slugs)

Order Nudibranchia*
(Sea Slugs)

Subclass Pulmonata*
(Air-breathing land snails)

Order Basommatophora

Superfamily Siphonariacea

Family Siphonariidae (False limpets). Genus: *Siphonaria* Sowerby, 1823.

Hubendick, B. 1946. Systematic monograph of the Patelliformia. *Kungl. Svenska Vetensk. Handl.*, ser. 3, vol. 23, no. 5, pp. 1-93, 6 pls.

Family Trimusculidae. Genus: *Trimusculus* Schmidt, 1818.

Family Amphibolidae. Genus: *Amphibola* Schumacher, 1817.

Superfamily Melampiacea

Family Melampidae. Genera: *Melampus* Montfort, 1810; *Ellobium* Röding, 1798; *Pedipes* Bruguière, 1792, and others.

Clench, W. J. 1964. The genera *Pedipes* and *Laemodonta* in the Western Atlantic. *Johnsonia*, vol. 4, no. 42, pp. 117-127.

Hubendick, B. 1956. A Conchological Survey of the Genus *Plecotrema* (Ellobiidae). *Proc. Mal. Soc. London*, vol. 32, pp. 110-126.

Morrison, J. P. E. 1964. Notes on American Melampidae. *Nautilus*, vol. 77, pp. 119-121.

Family Otinidae. Genus: *Otina* Gray, 1847

Class Polyplacophora
(Chitons)

Burghardt, G. E., & L. E. 1969. *A collector's guide to West Coast chitons.* San Francisco Aquarium Soc. Special Pub. no. 4, 45 pp., 4 pls.

Haddon, A. 1886. Report on the Polyplacophora. *Report Scientific Results Voyage Challenger. Zoology*, vol. 15.

Iredale, T., & Hull, A. 1923-1925. Monograph of the Australian loricates. *Australian Zoologist*, vol. 3.

Kaas, P. 1972. Polyplacophora of the Caribbean Region. *Uitgaven Natuurw. Stud Kring Suriname*, no. 71, pp. 1-162, 9 pls.

Kaas, P., & van Belle, R. A. 1980. *Catalogue of Living Chitons.* 144 pp. W. Backhuys, Publ., Rotterdam.

Yakovleva, A. M. 1965. Shell bearing mollusks (Loricata) of the USSR. Israel Program Sci. translations, Jerusalem, 127 pp. (*Zool. Inst. Akad. Nauk USSR*, no. 45).

Order Paleoloricata*
(Ancient Chitons)

Families Lepidopleuridae, Hanleyidae,* Choriplacidae.*

Order Neoloricata
(Modern Chitons)

Suborder Ischnochitonina

Families Ischnochitonidae; Schizoplacidae; Chitonidae; Callochitonidae; Mopaliidae; Chaetopleuridae.

Suborder Acanthochitonina

Family Acanthochitonidae. Genus: *Acanthochitona* Gray, 1821.

Class Scaphopoda
(Tusk-shells)

Emerson, W. K. 1962. A classification of the scaphopod mollusks. *Jour. Paleo.*, vol. 36, pp. 461-482.

Habe, T. 1964. Scaphopoda of Japan. Fauna Japonica. *Biogeographical Society of Japan*, Tokyo, 59 pp.

Henderson, J. B. 1920. A monograph of the East American Scaphopod Mollusks. *Bull. 111, U.S. Nat. Mus.*, 177 pp., 20 pls.

Palmer, C. P. 1974. A Supraspecific Classification of the Scaphopod Mollusca. *Veliger*, vol. 17, pp. 115-123.

Pilsbry, H. A., & Sharp, B. 1897-98. Class Scaphopoda. In Tryon's *Manual of Conchology*, Philadelphia, vol. 17, 280 pp.

Family Dentaliidae. Genus: *Dentalium* Linné, 1758.

Family Siphonodentaliidae. Genera: *Siphonodentalium* Sars, 1859; *Cadulus* Philippi, 1884, and others.

Class Bivalvia
(Pelecypoda; Clams)

Moore, R. C. 1969. Bivalvia. *Treatise on Invertebrate Paleontology*, part IV, vols. 1-3. Geol. Soc. Amer. Best reference.

Vokes, H. E. 1967. Genera of the Bivalvia: a systematic and bibliographic catalog. *Bull. Amer. Paleont.*, vol. 51, no. 232.

Order Nuculoida

Family Nuculidae (Nut clams). Genera: *Nucula* Lamarck, 1799; *Acila* H. & A. Adams, 1858, and others.

Schenck, H. G. 1934. Classification of Nuculid Pelecypods. *Bull. Mus. Roy. Hist. Nat. Belg.*, vol. 10, no. 20, 77 pp.

Family Nuculanidae. Genera: *Nuculana* Link, 1807; *Adrana* H. & A. Adams, 1858; *Yoldia* Möller, 1842, and others.

Family Malletiidae. Genera: *Malletia* Des Moulins, 1832; *Tindaria* Bellardi, 1875, and others.

Order Solemyoida
(Awning clams)

Family Solemyidae. Genus: *Solemya* Lamarck, 1818.

Subclass Pteriomorpha

Order Arcoida

Family Arcidae (Ark shells). Genera: *Arca* Linné, 1758; *Barbatia* Gray, 1842; *Trisidos* Röding, 1798; *Anadara* Gray, 1847; *Scapharca* Gray, 1847; *Senilia* Gray, 1842.

Habe, T. 1965. The Arcid subfamily Anadarinae in Japan and its adjacent areas. *Bull. Nat. Sci. Mus., Tokyo*, vol. 8, pp. 71-85, 2 pls.

Lamy, A. 1907. Revision des *Arca* Vivants du Museum d'Histoire Naturelle de Paris. *Jour. de Conchyl.*, vol. 55, pp. 199-307.

Rost, Helen. 1955. A Report on the Family Arcidae. *Allan Hancock Pacific Expeditions*, vol. 20, pp. 177-249.

Tevesz, M. J. S., & Carter, J. G. 1979. Form and function in *Trisidos* (Bivalvia) and a comparison with other burrowing arcoids. *Malacologia*, vol. 19, pp. 77-85.

Family Noetiidae. Genus: *Noetia* Gray, 1857, and others.

Family Cucullaeidae. Genus: *Cucullaea* Lamarck, 1801.

Superfamily Limopsacea

Family Limopsidae. Genera: *Limopsis* Sassi, 1827, and others.

Family Glycymerididae (Bittersweet clams). Genera: *Glycymeris* da Costa, 1778; *Axinactis* Mörch, 1861, and others. (Glycymeridae is incorrect.)

Nicol, D. 1945. Genera and Subgenera of the Pelecypod Family Glycymeridae. *Jour. Paleont.*, vol. 19, pp. 616-621.

Families Manzanellidae* and Philobryidae.* Minute deep-water clams.

Order Mytiloida

Superfamily Mytilacea

Family Mytilidae (Marine mussels). Many genera. In **Subfamily Mytilinae:** *Mytilus* Linné, 1758; *Aulacomya* Mörch, 1853; *Brachidontes* Swainson, 1840; *Geukensia* Poel, 1959; *Perna* Retzius, 1788; *Septifer* Récluz, 1848. In **Subfamily Crenellinae:** *Crenella* Brown, 1827; *Musculus* Röding, 1798; *Adula* H. & A. Adams, 1857. In **Subfamily Modiolinae:** *Modiolus* Lamarck, 1799; *Amygdalum* Mühlfeld, 1811, and others.

Lamy, E. 1936. Revision des Mytilidae Vivants. *Jour. de Conchyl.*, vol. 80. pp. 66-102, 107-198, 229-295, 307-363.

Soot-Ryen, T. 1955. A Report on the Family Mytilidae. *Allan Hancock Pacific Expeditions*, vol. 20, pp. 1-175.

Turner, R. D., & Boss, K. J. 1962. The genus *Lithophaga* in the western Atlantic. *Johnsonia*, vol. 4, no. 41, pp. 81-116, illus.

Superfamily Pinnacea

Family Pinnidae (Pen shells). Genera: *Pinna* Linné, 1758; *Atrina* Gray, 1842; *Streptopinna* von Martens, 1880.

Rosewater, J. R. 1961. The family Pinnidae in the Indo-Pacific. *Indo-Pacific Mollusca*, vol. 1, no. 4, pp. 175-226, illus.

Turner, R. D., & Rosewater, J. R. 1958. The family Pinnidae in the western Atlantic. *Johnsonia*, vol. 3, no. 38, pp. 285-326, illus.

Order Pterioida

Superfamily Pteriacea

Family Pteriidae (Pearl oysters). Genera: *Pteria* Scopoli, 1777; *Pinctada* Röding, 1798, and others.

Family Isognomonidae (Mangrove oysters). Genera: *Isognomon* Lightfoot, 1786; *Crenatula* Lamarck, 1803.

Fischer-Piette, E. 1976. Revision des Aviculidées 1. *Crenatula, Pedalion, Foramelina. Jour. de Conchyl.*, vol. 113, pp. 3-42.

Family Malleidae (Hammer oysters). Genera: *Malleus* Lamarck, 1799; *Vulsella* Röding, 1798.

Boss, K. J., & Moore, D. R. 1967. Notes on *Malleus (Parimalleus) candeanus* (Orbigny). *Bull. Marine Science*, vol. 17, pp. 85-94.

Superfamily Pectinacea

Family Pectinidae (Scallops). Numerous genera and subgenera: *Pecten* Müller, 1776; *Amusium* Röding, 1798; *Chlamys* Röding, 1798; *Argopecten* Monterosato, 1899; *Nodipecten* Dall, 1898; *Placopecten* Verrill, 1897; *Hinnites* Defrance, 1821; *Pedum* Lamarck, 1799, and others.

Bavay, A. 1936. In Lamy's Catalogue des Pectinidae Vivants du Mus. National d'Hist. Natur. Paris. *Jour. de Conchyl.*, vol. 79, pp. 306-321.

Fleming, C. A. 1950. The genus *Pecten* in the West Pacific. *Jour. de Conchyl.*, vol. 90, pp. 276-282.

Grau, Gilbert. 1959. Pectinidae of the eastern Pacific. Univ. So. Calif. Publ., *Allan Hancock Pacific Exped.*, vol. 23, 308 pp., 57 pls.

Oyama, K. 1944. Classification of the genus *Propeamussium. Venus*, vol. 13, pp. 240-254.

Roth, Barry. 1975. Description of a new species of pectinid bivalve from the Juan Fernandez Islands, Chile. *Jour. Mal. Soc. Australia*, vol. 3, no. 2, pp. 81-87.

Waller, Thomas R. 1972. The Pectinidae of Eniwetok Atoll, Marshall Islands. *Veliger*, vol. 14, no. 3, pp. 221-264.

Suborder Ostreina

Superfamily Ostreacea
(Oysters)

Galtsoff, Paul S. 1964. *The American Oyster.* 480 pp. Bulletin 64, U. S. Fish and Wildlife Service, Wash., D. C.

Joyce, E. A., Jr. 1972. A partial bibliography of oysters, with annotations. *Special Sci. Report* No. 34, 846 pp., *Florida Dept. Natural Resources.* Abstracts of 4,117 research papers.

Stenzel, H. B. 1971. Oysters. In Bivalvia, Part IV, vol. 3 of *Treatise on Invertebrate Paleontology. Geol. Soc. Amer.*, pp. 953-1224.

Family Gryphaeidae. Genera: *Hyotissa* Stenzel, 1971; *Neopycnodonte* Stenzel, 1971.

Family Ostreidae. Genera: *Ostrea* Linné, 1758; *Crassostrea* Sacco, 1897; *Lopha* Röding,1798; *Saccostrea* Dollfus & Dautzenberg, 1920.

Family Plicatulidae (Kitten paws). Genus: *Plicatula* Lamarck, 1801.

Yonge, C. M. 1975. The status of the Plicatulidae and the Dimyidae in relation to the superfamily Pectinacea. *Jour. Zool. London*, vol. 176, pp. 545-553.

Family Spondylidae (Thorny oysters). Genus: *Spondylus* Linné, 1758.

Fulton, Hugh C. 1915. A list of the Recent Species of *Spondylus* Linné, with some Notes and Descriptions of Six New Forms. *Jour. of Conchology*, vol. 14, nos. 11 & 12.

Family Dimyidae. Genus: *Dimya* Rouault, 1850.

Superfamily Anomiacea

Family Anomiidae (Jingle shells). Genera: *Anomia* Linné, 1758; *Placuna* Lightfoot, 1786; *Enigmonia* Iredale, 1918; *Pododesmus* Philippi, 1837, and others.

Superfamily Limacea

Family Limidae (File clams). Genera: *Lima* Bruguière, 1797; *Acesta* H. & A. Adams, 1858; *Limea* Brown, 1831, and others.

Lamy, E. 1930-31. Revision des Limidae Vivants. *Jour. de Conchyl.*, vol. 74, nos. 2, 3 & 4.

Subclass Palaeoheterodonta
Order Trigoniidea

Family Trigoniidae. Genus: *Neotrigonia* Cossmann, 1912.

Subclass Heterodonta
Order Veneroida

Superfamily Lucinacea

Family Lucinidae (Lucine clams). Numerous genera: *Lucina* Bruguière, 1797; *Phacoides* Agassiz, 1845; *Codakia* Scopoli, 1777; *Miltha* H. & A. Adams, 1857; *Anodontia* Link, 1807; *Divaricella* von Martens, 1880, and others.

Chavan, A. 1937-38. Essai Critique de Classification des Lucines. *Jour. de Conchyl.*, vol. 81, pp. 133-153; 198-216; 237-282; 59-97; 105-130; 215-243.

Chavan, A. 1951. Essai Critique de Classification des Divaricella. *Bull. Inst. Royal Sci. Nat. Belgique*, vol. 27, pp. 1-27.

Family Fimbriidae (Fimbria clams). Genus: *Fimbria* Mühlfeld, 1811.

Nicol, David. 1950. Recent species of the lucinoid pelecypod Fimbria. *Jour. Wash. Acad. Sci.*, vol. 40, pp. 82-87.

Family Thyasiridae (Thyasira clams). Genus: *Thyasira* Leach, 1818.

Family Ungulinidae (Diplodon clams). Genera: *Ungulina* Roissy, 1805; *Diplodonta* Brown, 1831, and others.

Chavan, A. 1962. Essai critique de classification des Ungulinidae [Diplodontidae]. *Bull. Inst. Royal Sci. Nat. Belgique*, vol. 38, pp. 1-23.

Superfamily Chamacea

Family Chamidae (Jewel Boxes). Genera: *Chama* Linné, 1758; *Arcinella* Schumacher, 1817; *Pseudochama* Odhner, 1917.

Bayer, F. M. 1943. The Florida species of the family Chamidae. *Nautilus*, vol. 56, pp. 116-124.

Nicol, D. 1952. Nomenclatorial review of genera and subgenera of Chamidae. *Jour. Wash. Acad. Sci.*, vol. 52, pp. 154-156.

Nicol, D. 1952. Revision of the pelecypod genus *Echinochama. Jour. Paleont.*, vol. 26, pp. 803-817, 2 pls.

Superfamily Galeommatacea*
(small Lepton clams)

Families Galeommatidae,* Erycinidae,* Kelliidae,* Leptonidae,* Montacutidae,* Chlamydoconchidae,* and others.

Superfamily Carditacea

Family Carditidae (Carditid clams). Genera: *Cardita* Bruguière, 1792; *Beguina* Röding, 1798; *Venericardia* Lamarck, 1801, and others.

Lamy, E. 1922. Revision des Carditacea Vivants du Museum National d'Histoire Naturelle de Paris. *Jour. de Conchyl.*, vol. 66, pp. 218-368.

Family Condylocardiidae* Genera: *Condylocardia* Bernardi, 1896; *Cuna* Hedley, 1902, and others.

Superfamily Crassatellacea

Family Astartidae. Genus: *Astarte* Sowerby, 1816, and others.

Family Crassatellidae. Genera: *Crassinella* Guppy, 1874; *Eucrassatella* Iredale, 1924, and others.

Darragh, T. A. 1964. A preliminary revision of the living species of Eucrassatella. *Jour. Mal. Soc. Australia,* no. 8, pp. 3-9.

Harry, Harold W. 1966. Studies on bivalve molluscs of the genus Crassinella in the Northwestern Gulf of Mexico: anatomy, ecology and systematics. *Publ. Inst. Marine Science, Texas,* vol. 11, pp. 65-89.

Lamy, E. 1917. Revision des Crassatellidae vivants du Museum d'histoire naturelle de Paris. *Jour. de Conchyl.,* vol. 62, pp. 197-270.

Superfamily Cardiacea
(Cockles)

Family Cardiidae (Cockles). Numerous genera: *Cardium* Linné, 1758; *Trachycardium* Mörch, 1853; *Fragum* Röding, 1798; *Corculum* Röding, 1798; *Nemocardium* Meek, 1876; *Laevicardium* Swainson, 1840; *Clinocardium* Keen, 1936; *Serripes* Gould, 1841, and others.

Clench, W. J., & Smith, L. C. 1944. The family Cardiidae in the western Atlantic. *Johnsonia,* vol. 1, no. 13, 32 pp., illus.

Kafanov, A. I. 1980. Systematics of the subfamily Clinocardiinae Kafanov, 1975. *Malacologia,* vol. 19, pp. 297-328.

McLean, R. A. 1956. The Cardiidae of the western Atlantic. *Mem. Soc. Cub. Hist. Nat.,* vol. 13, pp. 157-173.

Superfamily Tridacnacea
(Giant Clams)

Family Tridacnidae. Genera: *Tridacna* Bruguière, 1797; *Hippopus* Lamarck, 1799.

Rosewater, J. R. 1965. The family Tridacnidae in the Indo-Pacific. *Indo-Pacific Mollusca,* vol. 1, no. 6, pp. 347-396, illus.

Superfamily Mactracea

Family Mactridae (Surf or Trough clams). Numerous genera: *Mactra* Linné, 1767; *Rangia* Des Moulins, 1832; *Spisula* Gray, 1837; *Lutraria* Lamarck, 1799; *Tresus* Gray, 1853; *Anatina* Schumacher, 1817; *Raeta* Gray, 1853, and others.

Lamy, Ed. 1916. Revision des Mactridae vivants. *Jour. de Conchyl.,* vol. 61, pp. 173-291.

Family Mesodesmatidae (Giant Wedge clams). Genera: *Mesodesma* Deshayes, 1832; *Atactodea* Dall, 1898; *Davila* Gray, 1853; *Ervilia* Turton, 1822, and others.

Lamy, Ed. 1915. Revision des Mesodesmatidae vivants du Museum d'Hist. Nat. Paris. *Jour. de Conchyl.,* vol. 62, pp. 1-50.

Sakurai, K., & Habe, T. 1973. Family Mesodesmatidae of Japan and Adjacent Areas with the Description of a New Species. *Venus,* vol. 32, pp. 4-8.

Superfamily Solenacea

Family Solenidae (Razor and Jackknife clams). Genus: *Solen* Linné, 1758.

Habe, T. 1965. Family Solenidae in Japan and its adjacent areas. *Venus,* vol. 23, pp. 188-197, 1 pl.

Family Cultellidae. Genera: *Ensis* Schumacher, 1817; *Cultellus* Schumacher, 1817; *Pharella* Gray, 1854; *Siliqua* Mühlfeld, 1811.

Van Urk, R. M. 1964. The genus *Ensis* in Europe. *Basteria,* vol. 28, pp. 13-44.

Superfamily Tellinacea

Family Tellinidae (Tellin clams). Numerous genera: *Tellina* Linné, 1758; *Strigilla* Turton, 1822; *Macoma* Leach, 1819; *Apolymetis* Salisbury, 1929; *Gastrana* Schumacher, 1817; *Psammotreta* Dall, 1900, and others.

Boss, K. J. 1966. The subfamily Tellininae in the western Atlantic. The genus *Tellina* (Part I). *Johnsonia,* vol. 4, no. 45, pp. 217-272, illus.

Boss, K. J. 1968. The subfamily Tellininae in the western Atlantic. The genera *Tellina* (Part II) and *Tellidora. Johnsonia,* vol. 4, no. 46, pp. 273-344, illus.

Boss, K. J. 1969. The subfamily Tellininae in the western Atlantic. The genus *Strigilla. Johnsonia,* vol. 4, no. 47, pp. 345-366, illus.

Boss, K. J. 1969. The Subfamily Tellininae in South African Waters. *Bull. Mus. Comparative Zoology,* vol. 138, no. 4, pp. 81-162.

Coan, E. V. 1971. The Northwest American Tellinidae. *Veliger,* suppl. to vol. 14, 63 pp., 12 pls.

Family Donacidae (Wedge or Bean clams). Genera: *Donax* Linné, 1758; *Hemidonax* Mörch, 1870; *Iphigenia* Schumacher, 1817, and others.

Family Psammobiidae (Garidae) (Sunset clams). Genera: *Gari* Schumacher, 1817; *Asaphis* Modeer, 1793; *Heterodonax* Mörch, 1853; *Sanguinolaria* Lamarck, 1799; *Soletellina* Blainville, 1824.

Family Scrobiculariidae. Genus: *Scrobicularia* Schumacher, 1815.

Lamy, E. 1914. Revision des Scrobiculariidae Vivants. *Jour. de Conchyl.,* vol. 61, pp. 243-268.

Family Semelidae (Semele clams). Genera: *Semele* Schumacher, 1817; *Abra* Lamarck, 1818; *Cumingia* Sowerby, 1883; *Theora* H. & A. Adams, 1856, and others.

Boss, K. J. 1972. The genus *Semele* in the western Atlantic. *Johnsonia,* vol. 5, no. 49, pp. 1-32, 12 pls.

Family Solecurtidae (False Razor clams). Genera: *Solecurtus* Blainville, 1824; *Azorinus* Récluz, 1869; *Pharus* Brown, 1844; *Tagelus* Gray, 1847, and others.

Superfamily Gaimardiacea*

Family Gaimardiidae.* Genus: *Gaimardia* Gould, 1852.

Superfamily Arcticacea

Family Arcticidae. Genus: *Arctica* Schumacher, 1817.
Family Bernardinidae.* Genus: *Bernardina* Dall, 1910.
Family Trapeziidae. Genera: *Trapezium* Mühlfeld, 1811; *Coralliophaga* Blainville, 1824.

Solem, G. A. 1954. Living Species of the Pelecypod Family Trapeziidae. *Proc. Mal. Soc. London,* vol. 31, pp. 64-84.

Superfamily Glossacea

Family Glossidae (formerly Isocardiidae) (Oxheart clams). Genera: *Glossus* Poli, 1795; *Meiocardia* H. & A. Adams, 1857.
Family Vesicomyidae. Genus: *Vesicomya* Dall, 1886.

Superfamily Veneracea

Family Veneridae (Venus clams). Many genera and subgenera. Genera: *Venus* Linné, 1758; *Periglypta* Jukes-Browne, 1914; *Gafrarium* Röding, 1798; *Sunetta* Link, 1807; *Tivela* Link, 1807; *Pitar* Römer, 1857; *Saxidomus* Conrad, 1837; *Dosinia* Scopoli, 1777; *Tapes* Mühlfeld, 1811; *Paphia* Röding, 1798; *Venerupis* Lamarck, 1818; *Chione* Mühlfeld, 1811; *Mercenaria* Schumacher, 1817; *Protothaca* Dall, 1902, and others.

Clench, W. J. 1942. The genera Dosinia, Macrocallista and Amiantis in the western Atlantic. *Johnsonia,* vol. 1, no. 3, 8 pp., illus.

Dall, W. H. 1902. Synopsis of the family Veneridae and of the North American Recent species. *Proc. U. S. Nat. Mus.,* vol. 26, pp. 335-412.

Fischer-Piette, E., & Delmas, D. 1967. Révision des mollusques Lamellibranches du genre Dosinia Scopoli. *Mem. Mus. Nat. Hist. Nat. Paris* (N.S.), vol. 47A, pp. 1-91, 16 pls.

Fischer-Piette, E., & Metivier, B. 1971. Revision des Tapetinae, *Memoires de Museum Nat. d'Histoire Naturelle* (N.S.), Ser. A, Zool., vol. 71, pp. 1-106, 15 pls.

Frizzell, D. L. 1936. Preliminary reclassification of veneracean pelecypods. *Mus. Royal Hist. Nat. Belgique,* Bull. 5, no. 34. 84 pp.

Nielsen, B. J. 1964. Studies of the genus Katelysia Römer, 1857. *Mem. National Mus.,* Melbourne, Australia, no. 26, pp. 219-257.

Palmer, K. V. W. 1927. The Veneridae of eastern America, Cenozoic and Recent. *Palaeontol. Americana,* vol. 1, pp. 209-522, 45 pls.

Family Petricolidae. Genus: *Petricola* Lamarck, 1801.
Family Cooperellidae. Genus: *Cooperella* Carpenter, 1864.

Order Myoida
Superfamily Myacea

Family Myidae (Soft-shell clams). Genera: *Mya* Linné, 1758; *Cryptomya* Conrad, 1848; *Platyodon* Conrad, 1837, and others.

Foster, R. W. 1946. The genus *Mya* in the western Atlantic. *Johnsonia*, vol. 2, no. 20, pp. 29-35, illus.

Family Corbulidae (Corbula clams). Genus: *Corbula* Bruguière, 1797.

Vokes, H. E. 1945. Supraspecific groups of the pelecypod family Corbulidae. *Bull. 5, Amer. Mus. Nat. Hist.*, New York, pp. 1-32, 4 pls.

Superfamily Gastrochaenacea

Family Gastrochaenidae (Rock-borers). Genus: *Gastrochaena* Spengler, 1783.

Superfamily Hiatellacea

Family Hiatellidae (Saxicave clams). Genera: *Hiatella* Bosc, 1801; *Cyrtodaria* Reuss, 1801; *Panomya* Gray, 1857; *Panopea* Menard, 1807.

Lamy, E. 1924. Revision des Saxicavidae vivants du Museum National d'Histoire Naturelle de Paris. *Jour. de Conchyl.*, vol. 68, pp. 218-248.

Nesis, K. N. 1965. Ecology of *Cyrtodaria siliqua* and history of the genus *Cyrtodaria* (Bivalvia: Hiatellidae). *Malacologia*, vol. 3, pp. 197-210.

Robertson, R. 1963. Bathymetric and geographic distribution of *Panopea bitruncata*. *Nautilus*, vol. 76, pp. 75-82.

Superfamily Pholadacea

Family Pholadidae (Angel Wings; Piddocks). Genera: *Pholas* Linné, 1758; *Barnea* Leach, 1826; *Cyrtopleura* Tryon, 1862; *Martesia* Sowerby, 1824; *Zirfaea* Leach, 1842.

Turner, R. D. 1954. The family Pholadidae in the western Atlantic and the eastern Pacific Part I—Pholadinae. *Johnsonia*, vol. 3, no. 33, pp. 1-63, illus. Part II, vol. 3, no. 34 (1955).

Family Teredinidae (Shipworms). Genera: *Teredo* Linné, 1758; *Bankia* Gray, 1842.

Clench, W. J., & Turner, R. D. 1946. The genus *Bankia* in the western Atlantic. *Johnsonia*, vol. 2, no. 19, pp. 1-28, illus.

Turner, R. D. 1966. A survey and illustrated catalogue of the Teredinidae. *Mus. Comp. Zool. Harvard*, 265 pp., 64 pls.

Subclass Anomalodesmata
Order Pholadomyoida

Family Pholadomyidae. Genus: *Pholadomya* Sowerby, 1823.

Superfamily Pandoracea

Family Pandoridae (Pandora clams). Genus: *Pandora* Bruguière, 1797.

Boss, K. J., & Merrill, A. S. 1955. The family Pandoridae in the western Atlantic. *Johnsonia*, vol. 4, No. 44, pp. 181-215, illus.

Families Cleidothaeridae,* Laternulidae (*Laternula* Röding, 1798); **Lyonsiidae** (*Lyonsia* Turton, 1822); **Myochamidae** (*Myochama* Stutchbury, 1830); **Periplomatidae** (Genus *Periploma* Schumacher, 1817); **Thraciidae** (*Thracia* Sowerby, 1823).

Lamy, Ed. 1925. Revision des Lyonsiidae vivants. *Jour. de Conchyl.*, vol. 72, pp. 237-313.

Lamy, Ed. 1932. Revision des Thraciidae vivants. *Jour. de Conchyl.*, vol. 75, pp. 213 and 285.

Lamy, Ed. 1932. Revisions des Periplomatidae vivants. *Jour. de Conchyl.*, vol. 75, p. 303.

Superfamily Poromyacea
(Septibranch clams)

Families Poromyidae (*Poromya* Forbes, 1844); **Cuspidariidae** (Dipper clams, *Cuspidaria* Nardo, 1840); **Verticordiidae** (*Verticordia* Sowerby, 1844).

Bernard, F. R. 1974. Septibranchs of the eastern Pacific (Bivalvia: Anomalodesmata). *Allan Hancock Monogr. Marine Biol.*, No. 8, pp. 1-279.

Superfamily Clavagellacea
(Watering Pot clams)

Family Clavagellidae. Genera: *Clavagella* Lamarck, 1818; *Brechites* Guettard, 1770; *Penicillus* Bruguière, 1789.

Smith, Brian J. 1971. A revision of the family Clavagellidae from Australia, with descriptions of two new species. *Jour. Mal. Soc. Australia*, vol. 2, pp. 135-161.

Class Cephalopoda
(Squid, Octopus, Nautilus)

Donovan, D. T. 1964. Cephalopod Phylogeny and classification. *Biol. Revues*, vol. 39, pp. 259-287.

Lane, Frank W. 1960. *Kingdom of the Octopus.* Sheridan House, N.Y.

Subclass Tetrabranchiata
(Chambered Nautilus)

Family Nautilidae. Genus: *Nautilus* Linné, 1758.

Hamada, T., et al. 1980. *Nautilus macromphalus* in captivity. *Tokai Univ. Press*, Japan. 80 pp., color illus.

Stenzel, H. B. 1964. Living Nautilus. In: R. C. Moore's *Treatise on Invertebrate Paleontology*, Part K, Mollusca 3, pp. 59-93.

Subclass Dibranchiata
(Squid and Octopus)

Voss, G. L. 1956. A review of the cephalopods of the Gulf of Mexico. *Bull. Mar. Sci.*, vol. 6, pp. 85-178.

Order Teuthoidea

Family Loliginidae (Arrow Squids). Genera: *Loligo* Schneider, 1784; *Doryteuthis* Naef, 1912; *Architeuthis* Steenstrup, 1857, and others.

Order Sepioidea

Family Spirulidae (Ram's Horn shell). *Spirula* Lamarck, 1801.
Family Sepiidae (Cuttlefish Bones). Genus: *Sepia* Linné, 1758, and other families.

Order Octopoda

Superfamily Argonautoidea

Family Argonautidae (Paper Nautilus). Genus: *Argonauta* Linné, 1758.

Young, J. Z. 1960. Observations on *Argonauta* and especially its method of feeding. *Proc. Zool. Soc. London*, vol. 133, pp. 471-479, 2 figs., 2 pls.

Superfamily Octopodoidea

Family Octopodidae (Octopus). Genus: *Octopus* Lamarck, 1799, and other families.

Regional Books

We are listing here the major semi-popular and scientific faunal works on the mollusks of various major regions. We recommend them for your library shelf, since they usually give detailed descriptions, synonymies and biological information about local species, particularly the smaller ones. Many thousands of smaller faunal papers are listed in the *Zoological Record* (London).

Western Atlantic (East Canada to Caribbean to east South America; Bermuda).

Abbott, R. T. 1974. *American Seashells*, Marine Mollusks of the Atlantic and Pacific Coasts of North America. 2nd ed. 663 pp., 6,500 species, about 3,000 illustrated.

Abbott, R. T. 1958. *The Marine Mollusks of Grand Cayman Island,* British West Indies. Monograph II, Acad. Nat. Sci., Philadelphia, 138 pp.

Abbott, R. T. 1968. *Sea Shells of North America.* 280 pp., 850 species in color, with biology. Golden Press, New York.

Altena, C. O. Van R. 1969-75. *The Marine Mollusca of Surinam (Dutch Guiana)* Parts 1 to 3, Rijksmus. Nat. Hist. Leiden.

Andrews, Jean. 1977. *Shells and Shores of Texas.* 365 pp. Univ. of Texas Press, Austin.

Bousefield, E. L. 1960. *Canadian Atlantic Shells.* 72 pp. National Museum of Canada, Ottawa. Also a French edition.

Perry, Louise M., & Schwengel, Jeanne S. 1955. *Marine Shells of the Western Coast of Florida.* 318 pp., 55 pls. and frontispiece. Paleontological Research Institution, Ithaca, New York.

Rios, E. C. 1975. *Brazilian Marine Mollusks Iconography.* 331 pp., 91 pls. Museu Oceanografico do Rio Grande, Rio Grande, Brazil.

Warmke, G. L., & Abbott, R. T. 1961. *Caribbean Seashells.* 348 pp. Livingston Press, Narberth, Pennsylvania, also Dover Publications, New York.

Eastern Atlantic (Western Europe; Mediterranean; West Africa).

Arrecgros, J. 1971. *Coquillages Marins.* 64 pp., many illustrations in color. Editions Payot. Lausanne. Mediterranean and N.E. Atlantic shells.

Bouchet, Ph., Danrigal F., & Huyghens, C. 1979. *Sea Shells of Western Europe.* 144 pp., color illus. American Malacologists, Inc., Melbourne, Florida. (Coquillages des Cotes Atlantique et de la Manche).

Burnay, Luis Pisani, & Monteiro, Antonio Antunes. 1977. *Seashells from Cape Verde Islands* (1). 88 pp., monochrome photos. Privately published. Lisbon. Partial survey of gastropods of Cape Verdes.

McMillan, Nora F. 1968. *British Shells.* 12 + 196 pp., 80 pls. (32 in color). Warne. London, New York.

Möller Christensen, J., & Dance, S. Peter. 1980. *Seashells. Bivalves of the British and Northern European Seas.* 124 pp., color illus. Penguin Books. Harmondsworth.

Nicklés, Maurice. 1950. *Mollusques Testacés Marins de la Côte Occidentale d'Afrique.* 269 pp., text illustrations. Lechevalier. Paris.

Nordsieck, Fritz. 1968. *Die europäischen Meeres-Gehauseschnecken (Prosobranchia).* 8 + 273 pp., 35 pls. (4 in color). Fischer. Stuttgart. First of 3 volumes on molluscs of European waters.

Nordsieck, Fritz. 1969. *Die europäischen Meeresmuscheln (Bivalvia).* 8 + 256 pp., 27 pls. (2 in color). Fischer. Stuttgart. Includes species from Black Sea.

Nordsieck, Fritz. 1972. *Die europäischen Meeresschnecken (Opisthobranchia mit Pyramidellidae; Rissoacea).* 13 + 327 pp., 41 pls. (4 in color). Fischer, Stuttgart. Includes numerous new species.

Parenzan, Pietro. 1970-76. *Carta d'Identita delle Conchiglie del Mediterraneo.* 3 vols. (Vol. 1 Gasteropodi, 283 pp., 53 pls., vol. 2 (in 2 parts) Bivalvi, 546 pp., 79 pls.) Bios Taras. Taranto. Particularly good line illustrations.

Tebble, Norman. 1966. *British Bivalve Seashells.* 212 pp., text illustrations and 12 pls., mostly in color. British Museum (Natural History). London. Very detailed descriptions and good figures.

Indo-Pacific (Hawaii, South Seas, Indian Ocean, Japan).

Brost, F. B., & Coale, R. D. 1971. *A Guide to Shell Collecting in the Kwajalein Atoll.* 12 + 157 pp., 28 pls. Tuttle, Rutland. Ecological and descriptive account of about 200 species.

Cernohorsky, Walter O. 1971. *Marine Shells of the Pacific.* 248 pp., text illustrations, 60 pls. Pacific Publications. Sydney. Revised edition of the first of 3 volumes published to date.

Cernohorsky, Walter O. 1972. *Marine Shells of the Pacific.* Volume 2. 411 pp., text illustrations, 68 pls. (4 in color). Pacific Publications. Sydney.

Cernohorsky, Walter O. 1978. *Tropical Pacific Marine Shells.* 352 pp., text illustrations, 68 pls. (4 in color). Pacific Publications, Sydney, Australia. Virtually a continuation of the above title.

Habe, T. 1971. *Shells of Japan.* 139 pp., text illustrations and colored pls. Hoikusha. Osaka. Attractively illustrated pocket guide.

Habe, T., & Ito, K. 1965. *Shells of the World in Colour.* Vol. 1, The Northern Pacific. 9 + 176 pp., 56 pls., mostly in color. Hoikusha. Osaka. Text in Japanese, names in scientific Latin or English.

Habe, T., & Kosuge, S. 1966. *Shells of the World in Colour.* Vol. 2, The Tropical Pacific. 9 + 193 pp., 68 color pls. Hoikusha. Osaka. Text in Japanese, names in scientific Latin or English.

Hinton, A. G. 1972. *Shells of New Guinea and the Central Indo-Pacific.* 18 + 94 pp., 44 color pls. Jacaranda Press & Robert Brown & Associates Pty Ltd., Port Moresby, Melbourne. Particularly useful for Papua New Guinea.

Hornell, James. 1951. *Indian Molluscs.* 96 pp., text illustrations and a color pl. Bombay Natural History Society. Bombay. A popular handbook.

Iredale, T., & McMichael, D. F. 1962. *A Reference List of the Marine Mollusca of New South Wales.* Memoir 11, Australian Mus., pp. 1-109.

Kay, E. Alison. 1979. *Hawaiian Marine Shells.* 653 pp., B. P. Bishop Museum Special Publication 64 (4). Major treatment.

Kira, Tetsuaki, & Habe, Tasashige. 1962-64. *Shells of the Western Pacific in Color.* Vol 1 (by Kira), 224 pp., 72 color pls., vol 2 (by Habe), 233 pp., 66 color pls. Hoikusha. Osaka.

Kuroda, T., & Habe, T. 1952. *Checklist and Bibliography of the Recent Mollusca of Japan.* 210 pp. Tokyo.

Kuroda, T., Habe, T., & Oyama, K. 1971. *The Sea Shells of Sagami Bay.* 489 + 51 pp., illus. Maruzen Co., Tokyo.

Salvat, Bernard, & Rives, Claude. 1975. *Coquillages de Polynesie.* 391 pp., illustrated throughout in color. Les Editions du Pacifique. Papeete.

Spry, J. F. 1964. The Sea Shells of Dar es Salaam. Part 1—Pelecypoda (Bivalves). 41 pp., 8 pls. (4 in color). Part 2—Gastropods (1968). Tanzania Society. Dar es Salaam.

South Africa.

Barnard, K. H. 1958, 1959, 1963. Contributions to the knowledge of South African Marine Mollusca. Parts 2 and 3. *Annals South African Museum,* vols. 44, 45 and 47. Technical coverage of prosobranch gastropods.

Kennelly, D. H. 1969. *Marine Shells of Southern Africa.* 5 + 123 pp., 46 monochrome pls. and 2 color pls. Books of Africa (Pty) Ltd. Cape Town. Has useful locality information.

Kensley, Brian. 1973. *Sea-shells of Southern Africa. Gastropods.* 236 pp., text illustrations, some in color. Maskew Miller. Cape Town. A useful if rather uncritical survey.

Australasia (Australia, New Zealand).

Allan, Joyce. 1959. *Australian Shells.* 21 + 487 pp., text illustrations and 44 pls., some in color. Georgian House, Melbourne. Revised edition of an excellent popular book.

Coleman, Neville. 1975. *What Shell is That?* 308 pp., illustrated throughout in color. Hamlyn, Sydney, London, etc. Beautifully illustrated survey emphasizing interest of living mollusks in natural habitats.

Cotton, Bernard C. 1959. *South Australian Mollusca. Archaeogastropoda.* 449 pp., text illustrations and color frontispiece. Handbooks of the Flora and Fauna of South Australia. Adelaide. No further volumes on the gastropods have been published.

Cotton, Bernard C. 1961. *South Australian Mollusca. Pelecypoda.* 363 pp., text illustrations. Handbooks of the Flora and Fauna of South Australia. Adelaide. A revision of a work first published in 1938.

Cotton, Bernard C. 1964. *South Australian Mollusca. Chitons.* 151 pp., text illustrations and color frontispiece. Handbooks of the Flora and Fauna of South Australia. Adelaide. Authoritative.

Macpherson, J. Hope, & Gabriel, C. J. 1962. *Marine Molluscs of Victoria.* 15 + 475 pp., text illustrations. Melbourne University Press. A well-documented survey for beginners and advanced students alike.

May, W. L., & Macpherson, J. Hope. 1958. *An Illustrated Index of Tasmanian Shells.* Tasmanian Government, Hobart. A collection of reduced but adequate figures of all Tasmanian species.

Powell, A. W. B. 1979. *New Zealand Mollusca, Marine, Land and Freshwater Shells.* 500 pp., 82 pls. Wm Collins, Ltd.

Wilson, B. R., & Gillett, Keith. 1971. *Australian Shells.* 168 pp., text illustrations and 106 color pls. Tuttle, Rutland & Tokyo. Exquisite photos, marine gastropods only.

Eastern Pacific.

Abbott, R. Tucker. 1974. *American Seashells.* 2nd ed., 663 pp., 6,500 species, about 3,000 illustrated.

Keen, A. Myra. 1971. *Sea Shells of Tropical West America.* 14 + 1,064 pp., fully illustrated in monochrome and color. Stanford University Press, Stanford. A mammoth regional fauna unique in molluscan literature.

McLean, James H. 1969. *Marine Shells of Southern California.* 104 pp., illustrated. Los Angeles County Museum of Natural History, Science Series 24, Zoology No. 11. Excellent for the serious collector.

Olsson, Axel A. 1961. *Mollusks of the Tropical Eastern Pacific.* Panamic-Pacific Pelecypoda. 574 pp., 86 pls. Paleontological Research Inst., Ithaca, N. Y. Well illustrated and with many new species described.

INDEX TO POPULAR NAMES

INDEX TO SCIENTIFIC NAMES

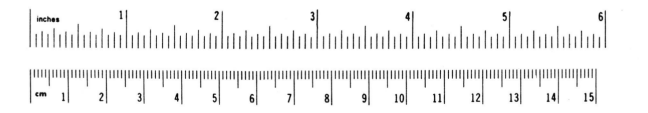

About the Authors

R. TUCKER ABBOTT is one of the leading conchologists of the world, having served as a research scientist and field collector for forty years at Harvard University, the Smithsonian Institution and the Academy of Natural Sciences of Philadelphia. Dr. Abbott has led numerous expeditions for mollusks to China, the Philippines, Africa, Cuba and other out-of-the-way collecting grounds. He is Editor in Chief of *The Nautilus*, one of the oldest and most influential scientific periodicals concerned with malacology, and also the author of numerous popular books including *American Seashells* and *Kingdom of the Seashell*.

Florida Conservation News observed, "R. Tucker Abbott is to seashell collectors what John J. Audubon was to birdwatchers, and his books on seashell identification form the backbone of most shell collectors' libraries."

S. PETER DANCE is a conchologist, natural historian and writer. Formerly with The British Museum (Natural History), the Manchester Museum and the National Museum of Wales, he is a frequent visitor to the United States where he is well known for his lectures. Both marine and land mollusks have been the subject of his many scientific articles. His books include *Shell Collecting: An Illustrated History*, *The Collector's Encyclopedia of Shells* and the *Art of Natural History*.